346.052
PLA

W9-BSQ-828

Contents

Preface

*S*ince the first edition of this book, which was written in 1995, there have been substantial and dramatic changes in both the federal and state transfer tax (estate/gift) systems. The modifications to these parts of the Internal Revenue Code have created increasing interest on the part of family members to reduce the anticipated transfer taxes impact.

The second edition of this book in 1999 included an overview of the transfer tax provisions in the Taxpayer Relief Act of 1997; the third edition detailed the important provisions of the Estate, Gift, and Generation-Skipping Transfer Tax Act, signed into law on June 5, 2001. In addition, the highlights of the Regulations Covering Required Minimum Distributions established by the Internal Revenue Service on January 11, 2000, are set forth. This fourth edition includes a detailed discussion of the new law that took effect on January 1, 2011, and, for two years at least, avoided having the estate tax revert to what it had been in 2001.

This book, more than any of the prior editions, provides new information regarding the most current planning techniques. Through numerous private letter and revenue rulings of the Internal Revenue Service, a large number of choices are available to reduce a potential transfer tax impact.

It is again significant to be aware of, that estate planning does not end at one's passing, as postmortem planning in many areas can create substantial transfer tax savings by the survivor spouse.

This edition includes the most recent estate, gift tax, and generation-skipping tax laws that were signed into law by the president of the United States on January 2, 2013 pursuant to the American Taxpayer Relief Act of 2012.

Acknowledgments

My thanks to a superb editor, Claire Abramowitz, and my assistant Patricia Wagner, who both helped me put this book together. I am also forever indebted to my clients for their support and inspiration.

What This Book Means and Why You Should Read It

*E*state planning is a complex, ongoing process. One must put together and assemble various available devices, techniques, and strategies to accomplish two main objectives: an effective, orderly continuity of your affairs after your death, and the maximum sheltering of your property against transfer taxes.

Good estate planning is complicated. Every person, as well as every family, has his own special needs. Estate planning, generally speaking, is divided into two separate and distinct phases. The first phase takes place during your lifetime, when you do the actual planning and creation. During this period, you will set up the wealth protection and transfer cost-reduction devices that are available and applicable to your circumstances. This phase includes the ongoing need to make revisions as dictated by life's changes.

The second phase occurs after your death. During this very important period, action needs to be taken in the following areas: (1) postmortem transfer tax planning elections that can reduce taxation; (2) the administration and settlement of your affairs; and (3) the eventual transfer of your assets to your beneficiaries.

In many states, the legal procedure implemented to effectuate the settlement of an estate is the probate process. This proceeding is administered by the courts, which both validates the will of the estate owner and supervises the transactions that take place during the administration of the estate. Whenever possible, the probate process should be avoided. The probating of a will gives rise to unnecessary and often excessive expenses and delays that are both frustrating and time consuming. Fortunately, in the vast majority of situations, probate is not inevitable, and alternatives can be adopted.

In selecting the format for passing your property to your heirs, you basically have two choices: the use of a trust or the use of a will. The theme of this book focuses on the benefits of selecting a living trust to achieve this goal. The concept of the living trust is to provide you and your heirs with continuity in the ownership and management of your property, along with the traditional estate tax deferrals and avoidances. If it is important to you that your property is transferred to your heirs without the interruption and involvement of third parties and the unnecessary costs incident thereto, the living trust is for you.

Thanks to recent media attention and publicity, people have become much more aware of the existence of the living trust and its benefits. There is, however, a dearth of professionals possessing the expertise to both advise and prepare one. The living trust itself must be extensive! If it is not, it cannot cover all the contingencies that could arise during your lifetime and those of your survivors. Even though most of these contingencies will never occur, they need to be addressed for the trust agreement to be effective.

In order for you to fully understand and appreciate what a living trust is and what it can do for you, you must have an awareness of the basics of the estate planning process and an overall understanding of its fundamental elements. This book will take you step by step, using clear and concise language, through the gamut of options available and help you find the solutions to the puzzles that are inherent in the estate planning process. You will be presented with every important detail of creating what should be the basic document of every estate plan, the living trust. The reasons why you should avoid probate and the important instances in which you should avoid the joint ownership of property are discussed as well.

This book is designed for individuals with estates of all sizes. When estates are large, there are various methods available to save, reduce, avoid, and defer potential transfer and income taxes. These are usually found in the form of different types of trusts. This book explains, in simple and plain language, how these strategies can be implemented. The benefits of the many available estate planning methods are described; their downsides are explained as well. It is important to note and stress that during periods of low interest rates and/or down economies, value reduction techniques benefit. During such period, assets can be sold to family members at not only a reduced value but on a lesser return to the seller.

In gift transactions, fair market values are less, which means you can give more for less transfer (gift) tax impact.

The use of the living trust, no matter the amount or kind of property involved, eliminates the need and expense of probate and does not require the blessings of the courts for the transfer of your property. There is no downside to it. Everyone should have a living trust no matter the size of his or her estate.

This book is not a do-it-yourself kit. It is not intended to be a substitute for competent advisors. However, after reading it, you should be able to understand the options that are open to you and intelligently work with your professional advisor in the creation of your specific plan.

Included also are important subjects that are not traditionally covered in books of this kind. These include retirement benefits, Medicaid, asset protection, planning for children with special needs, and estate planning for persons who are at the risk of AIDS, family-limited partnerships, the probate process, the living trust, GRITS, GRATS and GRUTS.

This book is the product of more than fifty years of experience in this field. After you have read it and familiarized yourself with its contents, I honestly believe it will give you the impetus to think about your own circumstances and proceed with the formulation of your own plan. Of course, you should seek the advice of an expert familiar with estate planning.

I know of no greater emotional and material benefit than having your heirs avoid the annoyance, nuisance, and unnecessary costs of probate. Creating a plan that gives your heirs maximum wealth protection, avoidance of unnecessary capital gains taxation, and the sheltering of assets from potential transfer taxes to the highest amount possible are probably the greatest material gifts any person can bestow. The living trust can do all of this for you and your family.

❖

CHAPTER 1

The Development of an Estate Plan

*T*his chapter provides an overview of the entire process of the planning of an estate. In other words, what are the things that must be considered and prioritized, e.g., where and what are my assets; what form should my estate plan take (living trust or will); who will inherit my estate; how much will he or she receive and in what manner (outright or in trust); who should assist in the development of my plan; what steps should I consider to reduce the eventual taxes both during my lifetime and upon my death; who shall be the managers of my estate; who will take care of my minor children; have I forgotten anything or overlooked anyone; have I balanced the inheritances depending on the needs of my survivors; have I created potential litigation among my survivors; and have I coordinated all strategies and devices?

The answers to these questions will form the foundation for the plan itself.

What Is an Estate?

An estate includes all property owned by you less all of your liabilities. To plan an estate, its values and components must be first determined. Therefore, a critical and important step in the process of estate planning is the creation of a written inventory. Not only is the identity of assets important, but where they are located can be just as significant. Assets that are held in a safe deposit box or property not readily identifiable, such as foreign bank accounts or real property, may never be found.

The inventory should contain the following information: (1) the description and location of the property; (2) the ownership (individual, tenancy-in-common, joint or shared) and the percentage owned; (3) the cost and fair market value of each of the assets; (4) liabilities and debts; (5) beneficiary designations (who is to receive retirement benefits, life insurance proceeds, annuities, and similar benefits); (6) whether any assets are subject to any agreements (corporate or partnership interests); and (7) whether it is community or separate property.

A complete inventory of your property will not only avoid the headaches that can be created in locating the property after your death, but also minimize the costs that are incident to such a process. At the end of this book, there is a suggested inventory form to aid in the preparation of this information.

The Probate Estate

This is the portion of the estate that must go through the probate process before it can be transferred. Property left by a will is normally subject to this procedure. All property that is inherited at death by various probate-avoidance methods, such as the living trust, joint tenancy, insurance, and beneficiary designations, is not included in the probate estate. Property that is held in the living trust is not subject to probate because it is not owned by you. The optimum estate plan should be totally free of probate assets.

The Taxable Estate

This is the property that's currently subject to potential transfer tax, when you die. It is the gross value of all property owned by you less all administration and funeral expenses, claims against the estate, debts, marital and charitable deductions, and casualty and theft losses.

The Beneficiaries

The selection of the beneficiaries is a basic element of the estate plan. The choice of who will inherit what depends upon many factors, i.e., personal, need, tax considerations, age, and competence. Questions have to be posed and resolved: Can my survivors manage their affairs? What will be required for their support and maintenance? What is best for their comfort and welfare?

Special Assets

Certain assets may require special consideration, such as an asset that will have to be sold after your death, like a business interest. Thought has to be given as to its valuation and the method of its liquidation. If similar types of interests are to be retained by your survivors, you should determine who will manage such interests and the liquidity needs of assets of this nature.

Participants in the Process

Those participants who are necessary to create and implement your plan and assume the final responsibility for the achievement of the desired results must be included in the planning process. The attorney is usually responsible for the overall creation of the plan. An accountant may be called upon to provide financial information required to properly identify and define your assets and liabilities. Other individuals, such as life insurance agents, financial consultants, and financial planners, may help to provide a view as to other aspects of the financial plan such as benefit recommendations, tax information, budgets, and investment management.

Liquidity Needs

The liquidity needs of an estate must be considered and defined. This would include deciding whether the size of the estate should be increased. Steps can be put into place, for both short- and long-term planning, to achieve these results, such as (1) an increase in life insurance coverage; (2) gifts of income-producing property to lower-tax-bracket family members; (3) an increase in employee benefit programs; (4) changes in existing portfolio investments; and (5) consideration of the asset appreciation potential of tax shelter annuities.

Reduction of Transfer Tax Costs

In addition, you must consider in this process the various ways to reduce costs that will arise at death. These will include (1) making lifetime gifts and sales; (2) maximizing the use of the deductions, tax deferrals, avoidances, and credits that are available; (3) the use of life insurance trusts; (4) providing instructions for the management and assistance in the distribution of certain assets that require special expertise; (5) creating a structure for the valuation of assets that do not have a readily ascertainable fair market value, such as shares of stock of a closely held corporation, real estate, or certain tangible personal property; (6) contemplation of making the estate eligible for the use of any relief payment section under any transfer tax code in effect at such time; (7) avoiding probate through the use of trusts and survivor property arrangements; and

(8) consideration of the state of your domicile when you die. Each state maintains its own laws controlling property located in it, in addition to potentially imposing transfer taxes.

Fiduciaries

The selection of fiduciaries (executors or personal representatives, trustees, or guardians) is probably one of the most difficult tasks in formulating an estate plan. Consideration in this regard must be given, where applicable, to corporate representatives, such as banks and trust companies, in the appropriate situations.

Coordination of All Plans

The increased use of probate-avoidance devices makes estate planning even more complicated. As such, consideration must be given to the coordination of the disposition of probate and nonprobate assets. You should consider nonprobate assets as property that you have transferred during your lifetime except that you have retained the total right during your lifetime to alter the distribution upon your death. This would include life insurance, Totten trusts, joint bank accounts, and plans with beneficiary designations. Your living trust, will, and any other documents providing death payment instructions must be reviewed to be sure there are no ambiguities among all of these devices.

Personal Concerns

In the planning process, an order of priorities must be observed. For example, if your assets are insufficient to provide financial security for your surviving spouse and children, your spouse is usually given the larger share of your estate and your children are provided solely for their educational needs. This is a personal decision that you must make. Consideration must be given to the short- and long-term needs of the beneficiaries—their competency, ability to be self-supporting, and ability to manage money and property. Their ages and health must be weighed in this process as well. You may wish to favor a handicapped beneficiary. On the other hand, irresponsible beneficiaries may be given a larger share than their siblings, on the theory that their needs or their families' needs may be greater than those of beneficiaries who are committed to a work ethic.

The Human Element

The success of any estate plan depends on the human element. An estate plan that is balanced should not cause litigation or dissension among family members or hatred of you. Money, it has been said, "is the root of all evil." Weaknesses, such as greed, dishonesty, and divisiveness, often surface when money is involved. Measures should be taken to deflect conflicts of this kind, such as (1) the equalization of bequests to children both in amounts and in the manner of the distribution (outright or in trust); (2) careful selection of the guardian for a minor child, since the guardian must supervise the management of the minor's property; and (3) the proper balance if you have had multiple marriages and you have multiple sets of children. Other considerations include children who have special needs that require planning by special experts in order to coordinate the programs available to them. Unmarried couples who have no statutory rights to inherit the other's property must create special methods for transferring their property to the survivor in order, in many cases, to avoid litigation with a hostile family. Finally, it is worth noting that, just as we have the right to leave our property to whomever we want (subject to statutory restrictions), we have the right to disinherit anyone (subject to the same restrictions).

Preventing a Challenge to the Estate

An excellent method of preventing a challenge to your estate is an "in terrorem" provision in your living trust or will that provides for the revocation or forfeiture of a legacy if a beneficiary contests the validity of the document or its distribution of property.

Funeral and Burial Plans

Your estate plan should consider funeral and burial plans as well, which may include cremation arrangements and the donation of body parts to organ banks for medical transplants and/or research. The use of a will or a living trust as a device for an anatomical gift is usually not a good idea. The effectiveness of any organ for transplant depends upon immediate removal. Usually this can be best planned by creating an instrument in the form of a card (which should be witnessed by at least two witnesses) or other documents to provide for the anatomical gift, which can be carried by you.

❖

CHAPTER 2

Selecting Who Receives the Benefits of Your Estate

*T*his chapter describes the process of designating those who will receive your property: who they are, how much you should leave them, and in what form (outright or in trust). You will also find out whether you can disinherit anyone (which in many cases depends upon the laws of the state where you live); what happens if you fail to provide for alternatives in case a beneficiary should predecease you, and what can be done with pets.

A beneficiary is the recipient of all or a portion of your estate. Beneficiaries can be members of your immediate family, charities, trusts, relatives, friends, and other organizations.

The selection process requires consideration of (1) the laws of the state that controls the distributions; (2) the potential transfer tax, consequences, if any; and (3) the needs of the particular individuals involved. Your beneficiaries can receive their inheritances either outright or in trust. If a beneficiary is a child, his or her share will be held by a custodian until he or she attains majority (usually eighteen years of age). Bequests can be made in a dollar amount or of a percent of the estate.

Alternates

Alternate beneficiaries should be selected in the event the primary beneficiaries predecease the estate owner. If a primary beneficiary dies before the estate owner, the inheritance might lapse. Bequests that lapse will either pass through a residuary disposition or by intestacy, if none exists. A residuary disposition can be effectuated by including a provision in your living trust or will that sets forth who is to receive all of your remaining property not specifically given to the named beneficiaries. Certain inheritances, however, are prevented from lapsing by state law, as the result of the blood relationship of the parties. In New York State, for example, a bequest to a child who predeceases a parent will not lapse, but will pass down to the children of the predeceased child.

Intestacy

Passing assets by intestacy means that, if one dies owning assets in his or her name and has not created a distribution instrument (living trust or will), the property will pass to the closest blood heirs of that person under the laws of the state where he or she maintained permanent residence (domicile) at the time of death. In such event, it is the state that provides the terms of the stream of distribution. This would not apply, however, if the asset itself has a distribution beneficiary, such as the designation of a beneficiary of an insurance policy, a retirement plan, or a jointly held asset.

Surviving Spouse

In most states, a surviving spouse is protected by law and must receive part of the estate. Therefore, appropriate provisions must be made for the spouse in order for that person to receive no less than his or her legal share and is the form prescribed by state law (outright or in trust). An example of the protection afforded spouses by law is illustrated in community property states. In this case, a surviving spouse has no legal claim to the other spouse's property. This is because community property states automatically divide property between the spouses as they acquire it during their marriage. Each spouse has the right to dispose of his or her one-half of the community property as he or she sees fit. Unmarried couples living together, however, have no such rights of inheritance unless a binding agreement, giving the other person specific rights of inheritance, has been entered into during their lifetimes.

Minors

When minors are named as beneficiaries, they can receive their share outright or it can be placed in a trust. Most states prevent a minor (someone under eighteen years of age) from owning property outright. A guardian of the property can be designated to be responsible for managing the bequest until the minor attains majority. The guardian's management is subject to whatever restrictions are placed on the gift. (For a more detailed description of minors as beneficiaries, see chapter 18.)

Common Disaster

The laws of most states provide that, in the event of a common disaster, each of the people involved is presumed to have survived the other. That means if you and your spouse die in a common accident and it cannot be ascertained who died first, each of you will be deemed to have survived the other and your estates will be distributed accordingly. This means that each of your respective estates would pass as if the other person had died first. States that follow the Uniform Probate Code require a beneficiary to survive the estate owner by 120 hours. A clause can be inserted in a living trust or will that not only creates a different presumption, but provides that a beneficiary must survive by a certain amount of time to be considered to have survived the other person. However, for a spouse, potential transfer tax law limits the period to six (6) months for the unlimited marital deduction to be available.

Pets

Pets are an estate planning challenge. In most jurisdictions, pets are considered just another piece of property. However, for many, a pet is extremely important and considered a person and not just property.

Certain states, like California, allow people to leave part of their estate to an animal in "honorary trust" (which is not a legal trust).

Many states have legislation similar to that passed in New York in 1996, which allows a pet owner to create a trust, either inter vivos (during lifetime) or testamentary (by living trust or will) to provide for the care of a pet. Before this law was passed, a trust could not be established for a pet nor could a pet be the beneficiary of a trust or receive an outright gift.

The use of the principal and income of the trust may be enforced by a person designated for that purpose, or if no one is appointed, the court may appoint an enforcer. The trust must terminate upon the death of all the animals covered by the trust or the expiration of twenty-one years, whichever comes first. The court has the right to reduce a fund that appears to be too large for the care of a pet. Any overage would be paid to the estate owner's estate.

The Residuary Beneficiary

Your living trust or will should name a residuary beneficiary or beneficiaries and alternates as well. These are the persons or organizations that will receive the balance of your property not specifically given and will also work to pass those gifts that may have lapsed.

Personal Expressions

In recent years, explanations or personal commentaries have been omitted in many living trusts and wills. There are instances, however, when reasons for particular gifts or disinheritances are meaningful and may even discourage legal challenges.

For example, a parent may leave unequal shares to two children and give a reason, i.e., one child is wealthy and the other is not. Given such an explanation, the advantaged child might not seek to challenge the legacy; or if one child may be disadvantaged, physically or mentally, and therefore will have special needs, an expression of this fact may have the same dissuasive effect.

Disinheritance

The laws of most states do not protect children from disinheritance. The best formula for disinheriting a child is to leave the child a token amount that effectively serves as a disinheritance. This can include a provision of explanation. Alternatively, you can expressly disinherit a child by a specific clause, which could also include a statement as to why.

Forgiving Debts

Any debt, whether written or oral, can be forgiven. This works to release the person who is responsible for the debt and has no income tax impact.

Unmarried Partners

Unmarried couples or partners living together have no rights of inheritance. They are free to deal with their property as they see fit. If they have entered into an agreement that provides for specific rights of inheritance, an agreement of this nature will usually be enforceable.

Abatement

If your estate does not have sufficient assets to satisfy all of your bequests and debts, then your bequests will be proportionately reduced. Specific bequests, which are those that give a beneficiary a specific article (for example, a car or certain shares of stock), are usually the last items that are reduced, with residuary and cash bequests being reduced first.

In creating a selection of beneficiaries, you should set down all of the potential persons, their order of priority, any special needs they might have, and what your legal obligations are, if any, to any of them. Once this and your assets, liabilities, and the tax consequences are determined, you can then determine who is to get what and how.

❖

CHAPTER 3

Wills

When you think of estate planning, your thoughts usually focus on a will. The most common questions asked are: What is a will? Must you have a will? What happens if you die without one? This chapter answers these questions and describes this form of passing your property. At the end of this chapter is a list of the important elements that must be provided in a will.

Since people differ, their wills differ. There is no single prototype of a will. However, the basic goals are all the same. This chapter tells you when a will is necessary, who can execute a will, when a will is a legal document, the different kinds of wills, what are the common and uncommon elements of a will, and what can be incorporated into a will by reference. Understanding the role of a will in the overall estate planning process is very important. A will is nothing more than a simple statement of what you want to happen with your property after you die.

It has been estimated that one out of every three wills is contested. This is an unbelievably high statistic. Because of the history of fraud and undue influence, the laws of our states are very strict insofar as wills are concerned.

What Is a Will?

A will is usually the first thing you contemplate when planning your estate. It is the written document that provides for the distribution of your property when you die. Every will must go through probate. Because of this, in most instances, a will is not the best way to pass your property to your survivors. Other devices, such as a living trust, are generally preferable. However, a will is still a useful document that should be created as a stopgap to any other probate avoidance devices used and for certain other purposes. There are certain limitations on what you can do under a will, however, and they must always be considered.

These are:
- What are the rights of my surviving spouse? (Most states afford the spouse a right to inherit.)
- What are the rights of my children? (Most states do not require you to leave anything to your children.)
- If I create a trust, how long can it last, and can the income from it be accumulated? (All states limit how long a noncharitable trust can last and some limit how long income can be accumulated and not distributed.)
- Can I give an unlimited amount to a charity? (Many states limit the amount that can be given to charity if there are surviving family members.)

When Is a Will Necessary?

A will is necessary to designate guardians for the person and property of minor children (under eighteen years of age). In the vast majority of jurisdictions in our country, a living trust cannot designate a guardian to both care for the child and manage the child's property. It must be done in a will.

A will is also necessary to transfer property to your living trust that was not transferred before your death. This is known as a pour-over will. A will is also necessary in most jurisdictions to disinherit someone.

In order for a will to be a legal document, most states require the following:
- You must be a legal adult (at least eighteen years old).
- You must have testamentary capacity.
- The will must comply with the technical will-drafting requirements of the state.
- The will should be typewritten or printed.
- The will must have at least one provision setting forth the plan of distribution of your property.
- You must appoint at least one executor or personal representative.
- You must date the will.
- You must sign the will in the presence of witnesses (usually not less than two).

Since laws vary from state to state, it is always advisable to verify the legal status of your will if you move.

Testamentary Capacity

In order to create a legally valid will, the law requires that you possess "testamentary capacity," meaning, (1) you must know the nature and extent of your property; (2) you must know who the people are who would inherit your estate, if there was no will; and (3) you must understand the distribution plan you have created under your will. Once you have created a legally valid will, you are called the "testator" (male) or "testatrix" (female) of that will.

Witnesses

A will must be signed and witnessed in accordance with the technical requirements of each state. Most states have similar rules for the execution of wills. A will need not be notarized, recorded, or filed in the court.

Witnesses are usually persons who do not inherit under the will. These people witness your signature and then sign the will themselves as witnesses. You must tell the witnesses that the instrument they are witnessing is your will, but the witnesses do not have to read it or be told what it contains.

Like the testator, the witnesses must be competent. This generally means that, at the time the will is executed, the witnesses must be mature enough and of sufficient mental capacity to understand and appreciate the nature of the act they are witnessing and be able to testify in court, should it be necessary.

Formalities of Execution

The appropriate formality of execution is to have the testator and the witnesses in the same room. All should sign the document, using the same pen, with the testator signing or initialing each page. After a will has been executed, it should never be taken apart once it has been stapled together.

Self-Proving Wills

The great majority of states have adopted a self-proving will procedure. After executing the will, the testator and the witnesses, in the presence of a notary public, sign an affidavit stating that all of the requisites for due execution have been complied with. If this is done, certain formalities later on required by the courts in the proving of the will can be dispensed with.

Safeguarding a Will

Once a will has been executed, it is important to safeguard it. It is best if the will is safeguarded by the lawyer who prepared it. A will placed in a safe deposit box may not be conveniently available to the heirs, since safe deposit boxes may, under local law, be sealed for a period of time after the death of the box holder. Most states that had statutes restricting the probate of lost wills have repealed them. If a will is lost or destroyed without the consent of the testator, in many states this does not prevent its probate, provided its contents are proved. In a proceeding in the state of New York, in re Juriga's Will, 1955 140 N.Y.S. 2d §56, a carbon copy was produced and it was deemed sufficient proof of the contents of the original will.

Statutory Wills

In response to a public demand for a legally valid will that can be written on an easily available printed form, several states have authorized simple "statutory wills." Presently, California, Maine, Michigan, and Wisconsin have approved statutory wills. In a statutory will, spaces are provided where the testator simply writes in the names of the beneficiaries. However, these instruments have been highly criticized in the legal profession because they can create a great deal of problems. Individuals should not try to write their own wills, as they may do more harm than good. Trying to cut corners in the making of a will could create great problems for the testator's estate.

Holographic Wills

A holographic will is one written entirely in the testator's hand and signed by the testator. Generally, in states that recognize holographic wills, attesting witnesses are not required. The rationale is that it is difficult to forge a person's handwriting. However, because of the possibility of forgery, these documents are viewed very strictly by the courts.

About half of the states permit holographic wills. In those states, a holographic will supersedes a prior formally executed will. Under the Uniform Probate Code, a holographic will is valid, whether or not it has been witnessed, if the signature and the material provisions are in the handwriting of the testator. If any printed-material provisions are eliminated, the handwritten portion must show the testator's intentions, and the key distribution provisions must be in the testator's handwriting. The state attorney's office of each state should be checked to verify if holographic wills are valid in that state.

Divorce

The effect of a divorce upon the validity of certain provisions of a will varies from state to state. In New York State, for example, if a marriage is ended by divorce, then all provisions to a spouse in a will are void. In some states, the law treats the former spouse as if he or she predeceased the decedent, so as to protect the children in the estate plan. In other states, the transfer to the former spouse is simply "null and void." However, in a life insurance policy, the former spouse named as the beneficiary will be held as the beneficiary by contract law, if there was no legal change made by the policyholder during his or her lifetime.

Marriage

What happens if you execute a will and subsequently marry? A large majority of our states have laws that award the spouse an intestate share, unless it appears from the will that the omission was intentional. If the spouse is provided for in the will or by certain will substitutes, which meet the statutory requirement as to amount, then he or she will not be awarded an intestate share. An example of this is a trust annuity created during the life of the testator that will pay income for the life of the surviving spouse.

A Residuary Clause

A will should include a residuary clause. This clause in a will is usually the most important. It provides for a distribution of the remainder of the estate after all of the other specific and cash bequests have been made. The residuary bequest can be made to a single beneficiary, either outright or in trust, to two or more beneficiaries in stated proportions, or to a class of beneficiaries such as "children." The residuary clause can function as a blanket contingency clause should any bequest or contingent bequest made under the will fail. A bequest that fails, for whatever reason, would turn over to and be added into the residue of the estate. As previously mentioned, this residue also includes any assets not specifically accounted for in the will. Therefore, it is important that you select a residuary beneficiary or beneficiaries.

It is always a good idea to incorporate a residuary clause into the will even if you have selected contingent beneficiaries for all bequests. There is always the possibility that a contingent beneficiary might die before you. Furthermore, even if all beneficiaries do survive the testator, there may still be estate assets remaining that were not disposed of and, therefore, could be subject to intestacy, which means that since you have died without a will, your property would be distributed to your nearest blood heirs in accordance with the order of distribution as set forth under the laws of your state. Your property escheats (that is, goes to the state government) after passing through intestacy, if no blood heirs can be found. A residuary clause is a good way to avoid the undesirable prospect of estate assets falling into the coffers of the state government.

Oral Wills

Oral wills (also called "nuncupative" wills) are only valid in a minority of states and, even where valid, are acceptable only if made under special circumstances, such as the will-maker's perception of imminent death. Some states impose far more restrictive limits. In some states, an oral will can be made only by someone serving in the armed forces, just before death being certain, and only for a limited amount of personal property.

Video or Film Wills

At present, no video or film wills are recognized by state law. In 2002, Indiana was the only state with legislation specifically addressing the use of videotape in the probate process.

The Indiana statute permitted the use of a videotape as proof of the testator's intentions, mental state and capacity, the authenticity of the will, and any other matter the court determines relevant to the probate of the will.

A videotape of the will-execution ceremony can have potential advantages. Unlike witnesses, whose memories may fade as time passes, a videotape is highly accurate. It allows the court to better evaluate the testator's condition by preserving evidence, such as demeanor, voice tone and inflection, facial expressions, and gestures. A videotape may also have psychological benefits for both the testator and the survivors. The testator may feel more confident that his intended plan will take effect, and the survivors may be comforted by viewing the testator delivering a final message.

Although videotaping a will-execution ceremony may have significant benefits, there are potential problems. In some cases, steps can be taken to reduce or eliminate these problems; in others, it might be better to forego taping the ceremony.

If the testator's physical appearance or demeanor is poor, it may be advisable not to videotape the ceremony. Although a situation may otherwise seem appropriate for videotaping, a video should not be used if the testator's outward appearance, age, disability, or other habits may prejudice a judge or jury, or lead them to conclude that the testator was incompetent or unduly influenced.

Another potential problem is the possibility that someone might alter the videotape. The alteration could be accidental, although careful storage procedures should reduce the risk. A videotape could also be intentionally altered; however, it is more difficult to alter a videotape than a written document.

Joint Wills

A joint will is a will made by two people, usually a married couple. When the first spouse dies, the will leaves everything to the survivor and designates how the estate will pass on when he or she dies. A joint will is, in effect, a contract and does not allow changes to the final disposition of the estate. There is no guarantee, however, that the final beneficiaries will receive anything, since there is nothing to prevent the survivor from consuming all the property. If you wish to control the ultimate distribution of your estate after your spouse dies, you are better off selecting a legal device known as a QTIP trust (see chapter 9). This type of trust will also insure the benefit of a marital deduction under any transfer tax in effect at such time, which might not be available in the estate of the first spouse who dies under a joint will.

Challenges to a Will

Challenges to a will are common. A will can be contested on grounds of mental incompetency (lack of testamentary capacity) or by proving that the will was procured by fraud, duress, or undue influence. For this to be successful, it must be shown that a third party was able to manipulate the testator in creating a document that was not his or her will, but that of another person.

After-Born Children

If children are born after you make a will, it is wise to revise it to reflect your new situation. Most states, however, have specific statutes providing for "after-born children," treating them as if they were alive at the time of the making of the original will.

Incorporation by Reference

In a majority of states, memos or other writings can become part of a will by incorporation by reference thereto, provided that the writing is identifiable with reasonable certainty and that the writing is in existence at the time the will is created. However, this view is not universally accepted.

Under the majority view, a person may provide in his or her will that tangible personal property is to be divided among individuals who are named in a memo located in a safe deposit box. In addition, the Uniform Probate Code and the State of Florida permit incorporation by reference provided that the list is signed and describes with "reasonable certainty" the items and the beneficiaries. The list may be prepared either before or after the execution of the will and may be changed after its initial preparation. It is not necessary to physically attach the list to the will.

In a minority of states, including New York, however, such memos or lists are not secure estate planning devices. These jurisdictions feel that incorporation by reference should not be permitted out of concern that such an unattested document could invite fraud. In a classic New York case in which incorporation by reference was denied, the decedent's will directed that a parcel of real estate be divided into four parcels among each of decedent's four sons. The will included a legal description of the property. A diagram of the property was physically attached to the will following the signatures of the decedent and the witnesses; one paragraph of the will referred to the diagram and stated "I do hereby incorporate the same herein." Even so, the Surrogate's Court held that the diagram violated the New York rule against incorporation by reference and thus had no legal significance.

Even in states where incorporation by reference is not allowed, there are exceptions to the rule. A New York court has held that a reference in the testator's will that half of his residuary estate was to be distributed to individuals named in his wife's will was valid. The testator and his wife both died when the Lusitania was torpedoed at the beginning of World War I. Of course it can be argued that this is not a true exception to the incorporation by reference doctrine because the wife's will had been executed in accordance with statutory requirements.

The New York Estates, Powers, and Trust Law allows a person to distribute all or part of his estate to an inter vivos trust (a "pour-over") if the trust was executed before or concurrently with his or her will and was executed in the manner required by state law for recording the conveyance of real property.

Another exception to the doctrine of incorporation by reference in states such as New York is the doctrine of "facts of independent significance." If a testator leaves a cash bequest to each person "who is an employee of mine at the time of my death," or leaves "all my tangible property located in my apartment at the time of my death" to a beneficiary, the bequest, although the exact details of it are not set forth in the will, is not necessarily invalid. As long as the facts can be readily ascertained, for example, what tangible property is actually located in the apartment at such time, the bequest can be valid under the doctrine of independent significance. A New York surrogate court has applied this doctrine to hold that a testator's direction to pay the claims of those persons taking care of him during his last illness created valid claims by those persons.

Lastly, on the subject of incorporation by reference, an interesting variation to that means of including other memos or writings in a will is where a will refers to a list of personal property that is itself attached to the will as the last page. In another New York case, the three-page will was signed on the third page. The will referred to an attached list of personal property and the list was attached as page 4. The court found that the attached schedule was "constructively inserted" at the point referred to in the will.

Even though a will that refers to an outside list may not be valid to dispose of such property, the will may, nevertheless, be admitted to probate and the other portions of the will given effect.

Codicils

A codicil is a supplement to an existing will. It has to be executed with the same formality as the will. Because both the will and any codicil to it have to be offered for probate, it is often better to create a new will. There are certain circumstances though when the use of a codicil is preferable to a new will. For example, when a testator whose competency may be questioned wishes to change his or her will. In such a case the use of a codicil would be a better choice than creating a new will, because if a new will was signed and denied probate, former wills would have to be located, which might have been destroyed or lost. If a codicil were used, then even if it were not admitted to probate, at least the prior will could be.

Forms of Wills and Provisions

There is no set standard form for a will. However, the underlying purpose of the will is basic: to transfer property from the estate owner to the beneficiaries.

The following is a list of the elements, both common and less common, that should be included in a will:

a. The identity of the person who created the will by name and family relationships.
b. The declaration by the testator of his or her residence. A statement to this effect, even though not legally binding, is at least some indication of the testator's thinking.
c. The revocation of all prior wills and codicils.
d. Burial, funeral directives, donation of body parts, and perpetual care directions. As a result of the delay between death and probate, anatomical gifts should be covered by arrangements made during your lifetime.
e. Payment of debts and administration expenses.
f. Distribution of tangible personal property.
g. Distribution of real estate to include specific gifts ("devises") and "legal life estates." A legal life estate is the same as a bequest in trust, wherein a person is given the life use of certain real property and no trustee is required. A legal life estate will qualify for a potential transfer tax marital deduction as QTIP property.
h. Legacies that fall into the following four categories:
   • Specific bequests
   • General cash bequests
   • Cash bequests payable out of certain property
   • Residuary bequests
   If, at the time of death, the testator no longer owns an asset specifically given, that particular legacy will not be effective. As such, alternate provisions for such an event should be provided, such as a cash bequest.
i. Trusts can be created out of the property of the testator for spouses, children, or others; however, consideration has to be given to the

extent to which trust principal may be withdrawn by or on behalf of trust beneficiaries.

j. Legacies that terminate. If a beneficiary dies prior to the testator, the legacy lapses and, as a general rule, would pass down to the residuary beneficiary. Anti-lapse statutes in most states prevent the lapsing of a bequest to a child who predeceases his or her parent by in turn passing down the legacy to the children of such predeceased child. Will provisions can direct what happens if a beneficiary should die before the testator by making alternate directives.

k. Where appropriate, disinheritance may be provided for.

l. Allocation of the payment of death taxes.

m. Appointment of fiduciaries: executors, personal representatives, trustees, custodians of gifts to minors, and guardians of the person and property.

n. Survivorship. In certain situations, it is important to set forth in what order individuals have died in order for their respective estates to be distributed to designated beneficiaries in the event of a common disaster.

o. Investment and other powers of the fiduciary should be expressed, including those concerning a business owned by the testator. The will should expressly set forth whether the business is to continue or be sold or liquidated.

p. If the testator holds any powers to withdraw the principal of a trust or to direct its eventual distribution or its termination, the exercise or nonexercise of these rights should be considered. As a general rule, the testator is deemed to have exercised them under a residuary clause contained in a will.

q. Precatory provisions. These are expressions of wishes that are not binding, as they are intended as something the testator would like to see happen but does not direct them to take place.

r. Explanations that offer personal touches to a will have generally been abandoned today. This may be because lawyers do not want to be burdened with this type of preparation. A statement by the testator can, however, make a gift more meaningful and perhaps even discourage contests. For example, the wish of Benjamin Franklin in his will dated July 17, 1788, provides an insight as to his taste regarding jewelry:

"The king of France's picture, set with 408 diamonds, I give to my daughter Sarah, requesting that she not form any of those diamonds into ornaments . . . and thereby introduce or countenance the expensive, vain and useless fashion of wearing jewels in this country."

The will of Doris Duke, who left no part of her estate ($1.2 billion) to the companion she adopted at age thirty-five, sets forth her state of mind regarding this person:

"I am convinced that I should not have adopted Chawdi Heffner—I have come to the realization that her primary motive was financial gain. I believe that, like me, my father would not have wanted her to have benefitted under the trusts which he created, and similarly, I do not wish her to benefit from my estate."

(Miss Heffner later commenced litigation challenging the will.)

s. Gifts may be made to a class of persons such as children, issue, grandchildren, nieces, and nephews.

t. Charitable bequests, which can be outright or in trust.

u. Certain limitations, such as the following, have to be considered as well:
   • Rights of a surviving spouse
   • Rights, if any, of children
   • The rule against perpetuities limiting the time property can be held in trust

v. As discussed in chapter 9, disclaimers are very significant postmortem planning tools. The use of a disclaimer permits the shifting of property from the intended person to other individuals without the imposition of gift or transfer taxes to anyone. As such, a provision providing for such an event should be included if it is a part of the overall plan.

Trusts

In addition to a will, a living trust should be created. The size of the estate will determine the type of living trust that should be employed and the kind of sub-trusts that will come into existence after your death. Most of the states in this country require a formal probate proceeding if the estate owners' assets exceed ten thousand dollars.

A "testamentary trust" is created under a will and takes effect only after death, which means after the assets have been subject to the probate process.

If you die owning property in your name, your will has to be probated. What the probate process is about and its impact is set forth in detail in the next chapter of this book.

Ethical Wills

Many people today create ethical wills. The purposes of which are to leave messages for posterity. Certain persons are interested in recording their values in case they are not around to pass them on. Ethical wills, which are not legal wills, are often created by persons who are close to dying. There is no traditional form for an ethical will. It can be typed or handwritten and usually sets forth the emotions of the maker of the will. A popular form of an ethical will is a letter to the children of the family expressing a list of items that are important, such as education, love, family, etc. On the other side, an ethical will can be used to chastise a person who may not have a chance to respond.

Drafting the Will, i.e., the planning process: Questions that need to be answered

- Are there a sufficient amount of assets to provide for the support and maintenance of the family?
- Are there any special funeral or burial instructions?
- Who is to receive the tangible personal property?
- Are there any cash gifts to be given?
- Are there any specific gifts to be made?
- How is real property to be distributed?
- What provisions are to be made for children?
- Are there any trusts to be created?
- How is the potential transfer tax, if any, to be paid?
- Who should serve as Executor, Trustee and Guardian?
- How often should my Will be reviewed (at least every five years or whenever there is a change in family circumstances (birth, funeral, divorce, etc.)?
- Should my Will contain an in-terrorem clause?
- A non-U.S. citizen who may own property situated both in the United States and elsewhere should consider a special will covering the property situated in the United States in addition to a will disposing of foreign-sited property.

The In-Terrorem Clause

Based upon the changes that have taken place in the traditional family setting (assets placed in trusts, the disinheritance in toto or in part of children), this type of clause must be seriously considered in the creation of a will or a trust.

The use of an in-terrorem or chill clause will act to discourage a challenge to the document that is making the disposition or to any provision set forth therein because if the beneficiary is unsuccessful in the change, he or she will normally receive nothing under the dispositive document. A standard clause of this kind usually simply provides, "if any beneficiary hereunder should directly or indirectly contest the will or trust, such beneficiary will inherit nothing hereunder."

Ethical Wills

An ethical will is not a legally binding document. It can be in any form chosen by the author. The purpose of an ethical will is to express to the next generation personal values and does not deal with the passing of assets. In others, the contents are usually the lasting and permanent messages we wish to pass on to our children. The contents of such a treatise can be a significant preparation for the next generation on how to manage a deal with the wealth of the family.

In addition, there are usually contained in the personal expressions of love and guidance in the further conduct and affairs of the family.

The ethical will is an important opportunity to not only express financial family matters but the parents' intentions as to how and under what circumstance the family should ethically evolve.

CHAPTER 4

Understanding the Probate Process and the Administration of an Estate

*M*ost people really do not understand what probate is. The probate process can be torturous and agonizing. It can be costly, frustrating, and time consuming. With proper estate planning, it can be avoided. The value of an estate will usually determine whether a formal probate proceeding is required. In most states, if the value of the assets in your name is less than ten thousand dollars, an informal proceeding—usually by affidavit—is permitted to pass title to property. In this chapter you will learn all about the legal procedures involved in the administration of an estate by the courts. It explains who participates in it, how compensation is fixed for the managers of an estate, where probate originated, and whether it's necessary.

What Is It?

Probate is one of the ways to pass absolute title to your property to your survivors. It is the legal process by which a court validates your will and supervises the administration of the estate thereafter. For some, the word "probate" has taken on a sinister meaning. This is because it is complex, tediously slow, costly (legal fees in many instances are determined by the size of the estate), and, in most instances, totally unnecessary. The complexity of the process includes the filing of the necessary court documents to institute the proceedings; notification to creditors and disposition of any claims; the gathering and valuation of the assets of the estate; the filing of the tax and accounting proceedings; and the eventual transfer of the assets to the heirs and closing of the estate. If, however, you create a living trust, your estate, exclusive of any required potential transfer tax proceedings, can be settled in a matter of hours as opposed to a matter of years. Avoiding the probate process is, in most instances, the most significant reason to establish a living trust.

If your will is not a valid legal document or if you die without a will, your property will pass to your closest blood relatives, who will be determined by the law of your home state. This is called dying "intestate," which means in Latin, "without a will." In either of these events, your estate is subject to the courts.

The Fiduciary

In your will, you designate an executor or personal representative. This person (the "fiduciary") is in charge of administering the affairs of the estate and of carrying out the terms of your will. The fiduciary marshals and takes possession of your assets, manages and invests them, settles the debts, completes unfinished business, settles any required potential transfer tax proceedings, and eventually transfers the assets to your beneficiaries in accordance with the terms of your will. It is therefore important that you select a fiduciary who is responsible and competent. The executor usually hires an attorney who is experienced in probate matters. The executor and attorney are usually compensated based upon the existing formats in the state where the services are performed. The commissions paid to executors or personal representatives are usually based upon a percentage of the value of the estate as determined by a set sliding scale rate under the law of the state; for example, under the New York law, the commissions are computed as follows (for receiving and paying out): 5 percent of the first $100,000 of the estate; 4 percent of the next $200,000; 3 percent of the next $700,000; 2½ percent on the next $4 million; and 2 percent on all sums exceeding $5 million. Attorneys can be compensated either by a percent of the gross value of the probate estate or on a fee fixed by the court. In addition, the estate is required to pay the court costs, which include filing fees and similar expenses. Many lawyers charge estates at an hourly rate for their services in matters of this kind. In some states the courts will set the fees solely on a "reasonable" basis. In addition, there are court-processing fees and other transaction costs that an estate incurs during the probate administration period. The varying range of probate costs will depend on the size and complexity of the estate as well as the state in which it is administered. These fees can range from 4.5 percent of the gross estate on large estates to 9 percent or more on small estates.

When Is Probate Necessary?

There are a few instances when probate is mandatory:
- To designate guardians (persons and property for minor children) that can only be designated in a will.
- To distribute property not transferred during one's lifetime to probate avoidance devices. This is usually accomplished by a simple pour-over will, which provides that any property not transferred during one's lifetime be transferred to a trust or other device to be held and distributed in accordance with its terms.
- If the decedent was involved in litigation.
- If the decedent was heavily in debt, the probate process is a good forum to settle those matters and cut off creditors' claims.

Probate's Origin

The history of probate is rooted in England, and our current formal proceedings were started after the American Revolution.

In England today, however, they have simplified their system to provide that the executor named in the will is only required to file an accounting of the assets and liabilities of the estate with the tax department, which values the property and assesses any potential transfer tax. The actual validating of the will, called a "Grant of Probate," is routinely performed on a very prompt basis. The executor administers the estate without the intervention of the courts, and only if a contest arises or any other kind of dispute evolves does the court get involved.

In most civil law countries, the probate system is even less complicated. In these jurisdictions, when you sign your will, it is notarized by a notary who has semi-judicial authority. After your death, the executor can perform all administration functions without the intervention of the court.

Disputes are taken care of in the same manner as any other legal dispute.

Length of Probate

Because of the court's requirements and office delays, the usual probate proceeding can last for years. This can result in an erosion of assets through the imposition of fees or a deterioration in property values through improper management and investment. By comparison, except for the filing and completion of tax proceedings, property placed in a living trust can be transferred shortly after the death of the estate owner.

Probate Avoidances

In response to the system of probate, and in order to avoid it, many methods have been developed. This means you can employ alternate techniques to pass property to your heirs when you die, without incurring the costs associated with probate. The major avoidance vehicles are the living trust, joint-tenancy ownership, life insurance, irrevocable trusts, and bank accounts. All of these methods are discussed at length in this book. The living trust is the most important means of avoiding probate and is really coming into its own. It is legal in every state, and attorneys have finally acknowledged its benefit and the fact that it has no downside. Even certified public accountants, who do not usually focus on estate planning for their clients, are confirming the advisability of using a living trust.

New Disclosure Requirements for Attorneys

In 1995, New York State enacted a statute (covering all wills and codicils executed after January 1, 1996) providing that attorneys who are named as executors in wills that they, or anyone affiliated with them, have prepared must disclose to the testator, prior to execution of the will, that (1) subject to limited statutory exceptions, any person, including an attorney, is eligible to serve as an executor; (2) absent an agreement to the contrary, such person, including an attorney, will receive a statutory commission for serving as executor; and (3) if an attorney serves as executor, such attorney is entitled to both executor's statutory commissions and reasonable compensation for legal services. Attorneys must also obtain a written acknowledgment of disclosure from the testator. Model disclosure forms that satisfy the disclosure requirements of the statute are provided in the statute.

Drafting a will naming oneself as an executor poses a unique conflict to the attorney/draftsperson. On the one hand, with few exceptions, the testator or testatrix has the right to name whomever he or she pleases to serve as executor. On the other hand, there is a confidential relationship between the attorney and his or her client. Under the Code of Professional Responsibility, the attorney/draftsperson is directed to avoid even the appearance of abuse of that relationship. Thus, he or she must avoid "consciously influencing a client to name the lawyer as executor."

The new statute is designed to address situations where the client may think or presume that naming his or her attorney as executor will reduce the commissions and/or legal fees charged to the estate.

The new law applies only to attorneys, not other professionals, and only if such attorney or an "affiliated" attorney drafts a will naming such attorney as an executor.

The failure to obtain a written acknowledgment of disclosure from the testator will result in the commissions of the attorney/executor being reduced by one-half. If the executor is serving as a co-executor, the reduction is based upon the statutory commission due that executor.

It is important to note that the law does not apply to trustees of inter vivos (revocable or irrevocable) or testamentary trusts. The statute may serve to encourage increased use of revocable inter vivos trusts.

Acknowledgment of Disclosure Forms

A. When the testator is informed prior to the execution of the will

   (i)   subject to limited statutory exceptions, any person, including the testator's spouse, child, friend or associate, or an attorney, is eligible to serve as an executor;

  (ii)   absent an agreement to the contrary, any person, including an attorney, who serves as and executor is entitled to receive an executor's statutory commissions;

 (iii)   absent execution of a disclosure acknowledgment, the attorney who prepared the will, a then affiliated attorney, or an employee of such attorney or a then affiliated attorney, who serves as an executor shall be entitled to one-half the commissions he or she would otherwise be entitled to receive; and

 (iv) if such or an affiliated attorney renders legal services in connection with the executor's official duties, such attorney or a then affiliated attorney is entitled to receive just and reasonable compensation for such legal services, in addition to the executor's statutory commissions.

Testator's written acknowledgment of disclosure. An acknowledgment by the testator of the disclosure required by subdivision one of this section must be set forth in a writing executed by the testator in the presence of at least one witness other than the executor-designee. Such writing, which must be separate from the will, but which may be annexed to the will, and which may be executed prior to, concurrently with or subsequently to a will in which an attorney, a then affiliated attorney, or an employee of such attorney or a then affiliated attorney is an executor-designee and must be filed in the proceeding for the issuance of letters testamentary to the executor-designee.

B. When set forth in a writing executed prior to or concurrently with a will: Prior to signing my will, I was informed that
  (i)   subject to limited statutory exceptions, any person, including my spouse, my child, a friend or associate, or an attorney, is eligible to serve as my executor;
  (ii) absent an agreement to the contrary, any person, including an attorney, who serves as an executor for me is entitled to receive statutory commissions for executorial services rendered to my estate;
  (iii) absent execution of this disclosure acknowledgment, the attorney who prepared the will, a then affiliated attorney, or an employee of such attorney or a then affiliated attorney, who serves as an executor shall be entitled to one-half the commissions he or she would otherwise be entitled to receive; and
  (iv) if such attorney serves as my executor, and he or she or another attorney affiliated with such attorney renders legal services in connection with the executor's official duties, he or she is entitled to receive just and reasonable compensation for those legal services, in addition to the commissions to which an executor is entitled.

_____   _____
(WITNESS)   (TESTATOR)

_____   _____
DATED   DATED

Estate Administration

The required steps the executor has to take:

Once the executor is officially appointed, there are a series of proceedings that must be observed, such as, the gathering of the assets of the deceased and awareness of the liabilities; the amount of liquidity that will be required and creating a reserve for same; which includes debts, administration expenses, and potential transfer tax, if any; the filing of the deceased's final income tax return; the filing of any transfer tax proceedings (if required); the filing of the estate's income tax return (if required); and the eventual distribution of the assets in accordance with the deceased's dispositive documents (will/trust).

One of the first transfer tax items the executor may need to entertain is whether to file for an extension to file any required returns.

Certain Forms and Dates of Final Filing

Form No.	Title	Due Date
SS-4	Application for Employer Identification Number	As soon as possible. Needed to collect assets, open accounts, and file tax returns.
709	United States Gift (and Generation-Skipping Transfer) Tax Return	Generally, April 15 following the calendar. Year when the gifts were made.
1040	U.S. Individual Income Tax Return	Generally, April 15 of the year after death.
1041	U.S. Income Tax Return for Estates and Trusts	Fifteenth day of 4th month after end of Estate's tax year.
1041-ES	Estimated Income Tax for Estates and Trusts	Generally, April 15, June 15 and Jan. 15 for calendar year filers.
4768	Application for Extension of Time to File a transfer tax Return and/or Pay transfer tax	See form instructions.
4810	Request for Prompt Assessment Under Internal Revenue Code Section 6501 (d)	Form 1040 or Form 1041.
4868	Application for Automatic Extension of Time to File U.S. Individual Income Tax Return	Generally, April 15 of the year after death. If return had not been filed for calendar year prior to decedent's death, and decedent dies before April 15, Form 4868 must be filed by April 15 of that year.

Ancillary Probate Proceeding

Where a non–New York State decedent owns real property located in New York, the decedent's will must be probated in the decedent's domicile state/county and the probated will (exemplified proceeding) is submitted to the surrogate's court of the county in which the real property is located.

The foregoing is a primary reason to hold title to foreign real estate in a revocable trust to avoid an ancillary probate proceeding.

Spouse's Right of Election Proceeding

Regardless of the provisions of each will under the laws of the State of New York, a surviving spouse can elect to take outright the greater of (x) $50,000 or (y) one-third (⅓) of the decedent's net estate (before any potential transfer tax) unless the spouse has waived his or her right in a premarital or postmarital agreement.

Miscellaneous Preliminary Letters Testamentary Probate Proceedings

An executor can usually be appointed within a matter of weeks from filing of the petition for probate. If an executor is needed to act sooner, the executor nominated in the will can obtain "preliminary letters testamentary."

Unusual reasons for obtaining preliminary letters testamentary:

a. Securities transactions that must be attended too.

b. Real estate closings (decedent's death shortly before scheduled closing).

c. Unusually large number of required parties to the probate of the will that may result in time delay in obtaining full letters testamentary.

d. Anticipation of a will contest.

Tax Filings

1. Final income tax return—IRS Form 1040 and NYS Form IT-201
   The final income tax return for a decedent is due on April 15 following the year of death, reporting only those items of income and deductions attributable to the pre-death period.

   Fiduciary income tax returns—IRS Form 1041 and NYS Form IT-205

After the decedent's death, the estate becomes its own taxpayer, with its own income tax return due by either:

In the case of calendar year estates, April 15 of the year following the year of death.

In the case of fiscal year estates, 15th day of the fourth month following the close of the estate's fiscal year, which fiscal year must be elected by the estate.

2. Estate Tax Returns—NYS Form ET-706 is required to be filed within 9 months from the date of the decedent's death.

Fiscal Year Election

An estate may elect to be treated, for income tax purposes, as a fiscal year, as opposed to a calendar year taxpayer.

Election to Treat a Revocable Trust as Part of an Estate for Income Tax Purposes

This election permits a revocable trust to be treated as part of the estate, for income tax purposes, which permits the revocable trust to take advantage of miscellaneous deductions and elections that are not available to trusts.

CHAPTER 5

Co-ownership of Property

$\mathcal{T}$his chapter gives you a broad overview of the various forms of co-ownership, what they mean, and how they work. Certain states have abolished joint tenancy in certain situations and these are described as well.

Ownership in a community property jurisdiction is described in detail and you will learn which states have it and what it's all about.

There are three basic types of co-ownership of property:

1. Joint ownership with a right of survivorship and tenancies by the entirety, which can only be created between individuals who are married

2. Tenancies-in-common, in which each co-owner owns an undivided fractional interest in the property, and which form of ownership subjects the property to probate

3. Community property, a special form of co-ownership between spouses that exists in nine states

Joint ownership of property should not be created or used as a substitute for a will or living trust. If the joint owners were to die simultaneously and there were no will or living trust in existence, the assets would pass to those perhaps not intended, which would be the nearest blood relatives of each joint owner (on a one-half-each basis).

Joint ownership of property, although it allows you to avoid probate, carries with it distinct downsides. For potential transfer tax purposes, these deal mainly in the loss of a "stepped-up value" of the property at the time of the death of the co-owner (not in community property states)(and not if no transfer tax is in effect at such time). The stepped-up value is the value property is increased to (fair market value) at the time of the owner's death, which is the income tax basis to the heirs. If the alternate valuation date is in effect under a potential transfer tax code at such time, the basis for income tax purposes can be the fair market value of the property on the alternate valuation date (six [6] months after the date of death). The increase in the basis value of estate assets that can reduce or eliminate capital gains taxes upon its eventual sale. The failure to obtain an increased value could result in adverse income tax consequences to the heirs of an estate.

Upon the death of the survivor of jointly owned property, his or her assets will be subject to probate, so that joint ownership does not fully eliminate the probate process. A joint owner could be subject to creditor's claims and the asset could be lost. A living trust offers the benefits of co-ownership without these risks. It provides for the survivorship aspect, avoidance of probate, and provides the survivors with assets needed immediately after the person's death.

Joint Tenancy

Joint tenancy is the simplest probate avoidance method. In this type of ownership, each person's interest can be disposed of without the consent of the other owner. It also can provide for the "right of survivorship," allowing the survivor to inherit the deceased owner's share without probate. In approximately thirty states, a similar form of ownership called a "tenancy-by-the-entirety" is allowable. This method, which can only be used by a married couple, offers the right of survivorship (like a joint tenancy) except that in the tenancy-by-the-entirety, each joint tenant is deemed to own the entire interest. This prevents the sale or transfer of property without the consent of the other joint owner.

The disadvantages of these forms of ownership are (1) joint ownership could cost the heirs a certain amount of their inheritance because a unified credit, which may be in effect at such time under a transfer tax code, may not be applicable in the estate of the first to die; (2) in certain instances, the creation of a joint interest may be subject to gift taxes; and (3) potentially a partial loss of increased tax basis as a result of the inability to step-up the value to the value at the date of death, if such a process is available at such time.

Tenancy-in-Common

A tenancy-in-common is another form of joint tenancy that permits each owner to dispose of his or her share independently. When one owner dies, his or her share will usually pass on to his or her heirs rather than to the joint owner. The advantage of this form of joint ownership is that the asset can be transferred to a living trust and thus avoid probate and provide a survivorship feature.

Bank Accounts

You can use joint tenancy bank accounts to avoid probate and provide funds to heirs. Most forms of bank accounts can be owned in joint tenancy, including checking, savings, and certificates of deposit. To open such an account, everyone involved signs as joint tenants with right of survivorship. When one joint tenant dies, the survivor(s) can have access to the account, with no need to go through probate.

Under the Uniform Probate Code, during the owner's lifetime, a joint account belongs proportionately to each contributor, thereby permitting each to revoke the joint ownership at any time. Under the laws of many states, including the State of New York, each joint owner has the right to an equal percentage of the joint account.

Under a joint tenancy arrangement, the property automatically is inherited by the surviving owner(s). Other forms of shared ownership such as tenancy-in-common and community property (see below) do not create a survivorship right. In those cases, how each share owner's interest will be disposed of is determined by a will or living trust.

Multiple individuals can own the same property as joint tenants provided they each have an equal interest. If they own different interests in the property, the form of ownership is a tenancy-in-common, which does not allow the right of survivorship.

While states have laws spelling out the legal consequences of joint accounts, most states leave it to the persons who create the account to define the rights of the joint holders of the account per an agreement signed when the account is opened. Joint bank accounts generally fall into one of the three following categories:

1. *Joint tenancy with immediate vesting:* Each joint owner, on the creation of the account, acquires an interest in one-half of the funds deposited, and neither can withdraw more than half without accounting to the other.
2. *Revocable account:* Each can withdraw the full amount on deposit without accounting to the other. Avoid using this type of account if there is any serious possibility that the would-be named joint tenant would "misappropriate" the funds.

3. *Convenience account:* One person deposits all the funds and has the sole right to the funds while both are alive. The other can make deposits and withdrawals only as "agent" for the owner.

All three types provide for survivorship. In the case of the convenience account, however, while it is clear that the individual supplying the funds receives the funds when he or she is the survivor, if the other person survives, whether he or she receives the funds depends on the deposit agreement and the local law.

In New York (effective January 10, 1991), the "convenience account," if funded with separate property, will remain the separate property of the depositor. No gift is inferred upon the opening of such an account and on the death of the depositor the other person does not have a right of survivorship.

You can create bank accounts that prevent a joint owner from withdrawing any funds before your death. During your lifetime, the beneficiary of such an account normally has no rights to the account and is entitled to such funds only after your death. If the beneficiary of such an account should predecease you, an account of this kind would pass under the residuary clause of your will. In the State of New York, these accounts are commonly called Totten trust accounts, and this form of nonprobate passing is limited only to bank accounts.

Safe Deposit Box

A joint tenancy safe deposit box can be a sensible place to keep important personal documents. Either joint tenant can obtain access to the documents when they are required.

In many states with state death taxes, safe deposit boxes are sealed by the bank as soon as it is notified of the death of an owner. The contents cannot be released until the box is inventoried by a government official or a waiver is obtained, which is usually a relatively simple procedure.

State Laws on Joint Tenancy

The following states have limited or abolished joint tenancy as described:
- *Alaska:* No joint tenancy in real estate except for husband and wife
- *North Carolina:* No joint tenancy for any property except joint bank accounts
- *Pennsylvania:* No joint tenancy in real estate (has been questioned in court decisions)

- *South Carolina:* Real estate joint tenancy must include words with right of survivorship
- *Tennessee:* No joint tenancy for any property except in the case of husband and wife
- *Texas:* No joint tenancy in any property unless there is an agreement in writing between joint owners

Joint Tenancy in Community Property States

Nine states—Arizona, California, Idaho, Louisiana, Nevada, New Mexico, Texas, Washington, and Wisconsin—have a form of co-ownership of property known as community property.

The community property systems may vary from state to state, but there are certain common concepts. All property acquired by a husband and wife during their marriage, while they reside in a community property state, is community property. It belongs to each of the marriage partners, share and share alike, each owning one-half thereof. They share not only in the physical property acquired, but also in the income from the property and their salaries, wages, and other compensation for services.

At the same time, each person may still own separate property. They may also hold property between them in joint tenancy. A married couple can convert community property to separate property or vice versa. A change in the form of ownership can be decided by the couple. Any such changes should be formalized by an agreement in order to have a clear, written record of the parties' desires should a future dispute arise as to ownership rights.

Spouses can agree prior to their marriage through a prenuptial agreement that they will not be bound by the community property laws of their state of residence.

In general, community property assets retain that character even after the parties have moved to a noncommunity property state, unless the parties themselves are able to adjust their rights between themselves. Thus, if you are living in a community property state, you and your spouse may have acquired a community property bank account. If you move into a noncommunity property state and take the proceeds of the account with you, the money still retains its community character. If you then invest it in real estate in your new home state, the real estate may still be viewed as community real estate.

If you are a couple who moves from a noncommunity property state to a community property state, the personal property you acquired in the former state, whether tangible or intangible (stocks and bonds and the like), retains its character as separate, joint, or whatever other form of ownership it originally had. Real estate will retain the form of ownership assigned to it. Real estate in a community property state acquired by either spouse while married may be treated as community property without regard to the domicile or residence of the spouses. It has been held that the law of the state where the real estate is situated determines whether the income therefrom is community property.

Basis of Decedent's and Survivor's Interest

The general rule is that the values for income tax purposes of property acquired from a decedent is the fair market value of the property on the date of his or her death or on the alternate valuation date if the executor so elects. Where property is held jointly by spouses in common law states, the surviving spouse could receive a stepped-up basis (if such is available under a transfer tax code in effect at such time) of only one-half of the value of the property. The survivor's half carries over his or her original basis.

Uniform Marital Property Act

The Uniform Marital Property Act (UMPA), adopted in Wisconsin and under consideration in a number of other states, is a form of "community property" law similar to the existing community property laws. Its principal effect is to institute a legal presumption, which may be rebutted by evidence, that all property owned by a married couple is presumed to be so-called marital property that is equally divisible between the spouses. It will apply in cases of property divisions upon divorce and at death.

Most states have adopted "equitable distribution" statutes that govern the dispositions of property upon divorce. UMPA represents a modification of equitable distribution policy in that the parties are presumed to own all property acquired after the marriage equally.

Like community property laws, UMPA provides a full step-up in the tax basis of property received by a surviving spouse. This has the effect of reducing post-death property capital gains on any appreciated property sold after the death of a spouse.

Third Parties

If a spouse considers placing property into joint tenancy with someone other than his or her spouse, and if the property is the separate property of the spouse, that's permissible. However, if the property is community property, the surviving spouse would have a claim against the estate of the deceased spouse and the surviving joint tenant for his or her one-half interest in the property. The surviving spouse could successfully contend that the deceased spouse had the authority only to transfer his or her half of the community property into joint tenancy with someone else.

Simultaneous Death

If joint tenants die simultaneously, their interest in the property will pass according to their wills. Usually the residuary clause in the will passes this on to the residuary beneficiaries of the estate. This cannot be done with a living trust since it only works to dispose of property transferred to it. A pour-over backup will would transfer the jointly owned property to the trust, which in turn would distribute it under the terms of the trust.

Tax Rules

The value of jointly owned property is included in your taxable estate. The amount is based on how much you contributed when the jointly owned property was created or bought. If you put up all the money to purchase a piece of joint property, the full market value of the property will be included in your taxable estate.

Joint Tenancy as a Taxable Gift

When a person purchases property in joint tenancy or holds property as a sole owner and creates a joint tenancy in the property, there probably will be a taxable gift unless each of the joint tenants makes the same amount of contribution. This impact is nothing more than the general rule that, where property is transferred for less than full and adequate consideration in money or money's worth, the amount by which the property exceeds the value of the consideration is a gift.

If the value of that gift exceeds the amount of the then Annual Gift Exclusions, the donor must file a gift tax return and gift taxes are assessed, subject to the availability of the applicable lifetime exemption of the donor, which presently is $1 million.

There are some limited exceptions to the rule that a gift is made whenever a sole owner places property in joint tenancy. If a joint bank account is created, with one person actually contributing all the funds, no taxable gift is created at that time. The same rule applies for buying United States savings bonds in joint tenancy. Only when the person who didn't contribute half the original deposit or cost takes possession of more than his original contribution (by withdrawing money from the bank account, or selling an interest in the bond) will there be a taxable gift.

No gift taxes are assessed against any gift made between husband and wife. Either spouse may transfer any separately owned property into joint tenancy with the other spouse without concern over gift taxes.

Taxation of Community Property

The creation of joint ownership can permit the splitting of income, with each joint owner paid up to his or her respective share. This may generate some savings. These benefits are not available with savings bonds and most bank savings accounts where one depositor creates the account. In addition, creation of an account with a child under eighteen years of age will not afford any savings since a child under eighteen (18) is taxed at his or her parent's tax rate on unearned income in excess of $1,000.

For community property held in joint tenancy, the tax basis rules are different for married couples. Both shares of community property held in joint tenancy are entitled to a stepped-up basis upon the death of a spouse, no matter what contributions were made to the initial purchase. Thus, if a husband and wife own community property real estate in joint tenancy worth $500,000 at the husband's death, the basis of both the husband's and wife's share of that real estate is stepped up to $500,000 (no matter who paid for what, originally).

To get the full stepped-up basis, however, you must prove that the joint tenancy property is community property. Otherwise, only the half belonging to the deceased spouse gets the stepped-up basis. Under the tax law, there is a presumption that joint tenancy property is not community property. In certain situations, a couple may hold title to community property solely as a probate avoidance device. Records should be kept to properly identify the property and its origin. One way to do this is to place a notation on the property ownership document itself.

The use of the living trust as a probate avoidance device, rather than joint tenancy, permits a married couple to avoid probate and qualify both halves of the property for the beneficial increase in the value of the entire property to its date-of-death value. No matter what the form of ownership, if the property is community property, it will be entitled to a stepped-up basis.

Termination

In most states, as long as joint tenants are alive, any of them can terminate the joint tenancy, without consent of the other.

Creditors

Creditors of a joint tenant can legally pursue that joint tenant's interest, but not the other joint tenants' interests. If there is an attachment, a court may order the whole property sold to reach the debtor's share.

As a general rule, upon the death of a joint owner, the survivor will take the property outside of the deceased tenant's obligations.

Deathbed Creations

If an owner of property is terminal, creating a joint tenancy of his or her property is a last-minute probate-avoidance device, if no previous estate planning has been done. Since the surviving joint tenant did not contribute toward the property, he or she (other than a spouse) will get a full stepped-up basis to market value on the death of the individual creating the joint tenancy.

Personal Property

Joint tenancies for personal property can be created without documents of title for all tangible personal property. To create a joint tenancy for personal property that doesn't have a formal document of title, all you have to do is declare in an acknowledged written document that you and the co-owners own the property "in joint tenancy" or "as joint tenants."

In spite of the pitfalls and disadvantages of spouses owning property jointly, there may be limited situations where it may be desirable. In addition to avoidance of probate, a bank account jointly owned will provide easy access for both spouses during their lifetimes and after the death of one for his or her survivor.

If a person owns a closely held business, placing other property in joint ownership with a spouse might qualify the business for certain transfer tax benefits. If property other than the business property (which could be fully included in the person's gross estate) was placed in joint ownership, half of the value would be removed from the person's estate, which could aid in achieving the percentage. Because of the unlimited marital deduction, this type of transfer can be accomplished without any gift tax imposition. See chapter 26 for a detailed explanation of these benefits.

Lastly, in many jurisdictions, a spouse who may be vulnerable to claims of third parties could protect a home or other real estate from such claims by owning such property with a spouse as tenants by the entirety.

❖

CHAPTER 6

Trusts

*T*his chapter discusses trusts, including their particular characteristics and components, such as the grantor, the beneficiary, the trustee, the written provisions, and property. Each one has a significant importance in the operation and workings of the device. Trusts are either irrevocable or revocable. They are either inter vivos (created during lifetime) or testamentary (created upon death). Since trusts are income-producing entities, they must respond to the tax code.

An important reason for creating a trust is to avoid putting substantial amounts of income-producing property in the hands of a child or an adult who is not financially mature.

By having a basic understanding of a trust and what it can be used for, you will have a better understanding of other chapters in this book, including the living trust and the various roles that a trust plays in the estate planning process.

The trust is an extremely flexible device that is free from the downsides of other estate planning devices.

What Is It?

A trust is a legal device that can satisfy a multitude of needs in personal financial planning. The written trust permits you to transfer the enjoyment of property to others, while leaving legal ownership out of their hands. Certain property interests created by trusts may be considered gifts and may be subject to gift tax.

Trusts may be created to avoid, defer, or decrease income and transfer taxes; or to provide steady and controlled support for minors, incompetents, and other dependents. Trusts may be used in the business place.

Employee benefit trusts and voting trusts are examples of this kind of use. To understand how a trust works, you must first become familiar with the basic terms and the necessary requirements for establishing a trust.

The Grantor

The individual who creates the trust is known as the "grantor." The grantor decides what property will be transferred into the trust, the purpose of the trust, who the trustee will be, whom the beneficiaries will be, the terms of the trust, and how the trust funds may be utilized.

The Trustee

The "trustee" is the owner of legal title to the property in the trust. The trust exists exclusively for the benefit of the beneficiary, with the trustee being responsible for the management of the trust assets, keeping them separate and accounted for. The trustee is entitled to a fee or commission for these services but receives no benefit from the trust, unless he or she is also a beneficiary. A trust may have more than one trustee. The trustee is designated by the grantor. However, if the grantor fails to designate a successor trustee, the court will name a successor.

The selection of the trustee can be in many instances the most difficult part of creating a trust. The trustee is responsible for carrying out the intentions of the grantor as expressed in the trust instrument. Therefore, the trustee must not only be willing and able, but must be familiar with the beneficiary and his or her needs. The trustee must also be qualified to handle all management, financial, and accounting duties necessary to properly administer the property of the trust.

The Successor Trustee

Before accepting or agreeing to such an appointment, you need to understand the potential responsibilities and liabilities that may exist.

The courts generally hold that a successor trustee is not responsible for a prior trustee's misdoings. However, once a successor trustee takes office, that trustee has a duty to ascertain the actions of his or her predecessor and take whatever steps are necessary to remedy any wrongs. Failure by a successor trustee to exercise due diligence may bring upon the trustee litigation as a result of a third party's misdeeds. The only real way for a successor trustee to avoid being trapped into such a situation is if the prior trustee accounted, formally or informally, settled by a release, or court order.

Accordingly, a successor trustee who fails to pursue his or her predecessor's actions or conduct an audit before assuming his or her responsibilities could find themselves at the end of a lawsuit for failure to act or breach of trust.

The Beneficiary

The "beneficiary" is the individual or group of individuals who receive(s) the primary benefits from the trust property. The primary beneficiary is usually entitled to any income the trust may earn. The "remainder beneficiaries" are those individuals or organizations who are entitled to the trust property (principal) after the entitlement of the primary beneficiary terminates in accordance with the terms of the trust agreement. If trust assets are mismanaged, the remainder beneficiary can, in addition to the primary beneficiary, assert claims against the trustee.

Primary and remainder beneficiaries may have conflicting investment interests with regard to the use of the trust property. The primary beneficiary will normally seek to receive as high a return as possible in order to maximize the trust's current income. In order to gain these higher rates of return, the trust property will be subject to a greater risk of being lost. Primary beneficiaries will be more than willing to take such risks if they do not have an interest in the principal itself. The main goal of the remainder beneficiaries, on the other hand, will be to preserve and protect the principal for their eventual inheritance. Therefore, the remainder beneficiaries would want the trust property to be invested in lower-yielding, lower-risk investments. Trustees must balance the interests of both classes of beneficiaries in order to fulfill their fiduciary obligations. Trustees, therefore, have a high degree of legal responsibility to the beneficiaries of a trust. They have, in most instances, the obligations of obtaining a reasonable income for the primary beneficiaries and a reasonable appreciation of the value of the trust's assets for those who will eventually receive those benefits.

The most common standard by which the investment decisions made by a trustee are evaluated is the "prudent man rule." This rule requires that a trustee act in the same manner with trust property as a person of prudence, discretion, and intelligence acts in the management of his or her own assets. The origin of this standard was an 1830 court case, *Harvard College v. Armory*. A restatement of this rule has been adopted that recognizes investment practices in the modern era. In 1992, a version of the prudent investment rule was adopted by the State of Illinois.

New York State passed the Prudent Investor Act. The new prudent investor rule represents a substantial shift in the standards of trust administration, investment, and trustee conduct. This is a departure from the long-established prudent man rule.

The underlying concept of the new prudent investor rule is that no type of investment or strategy is imprudent or prudent per se. Therefore, trustees are given wider latitude in analyzing their choices. Their prudence (or imprudence) will be assessed based on a broader range of factors, such as the terms of the trust, the risk tolerance of the trust, the beneficiaries' needs, and the amount of property in the trust. Another fundamental change is that the determination of a trustee's prudence is made on the entire portfolio of the trust and the strategy and investment techniques employed, rather than on isolated individual investments. According to the prior New York rule, a trustee's decision regarding one poor investment could be deemed imprudent even though the rest of the portfolio was properly allocated and performing well.

The Corpus

The property that the grantor of the trust transfers to the trustee is known as the "corpus" or "principal." It may be transferred in different ways, depending on the nature of the property. If the property is "personal property," such as stock, then either actual delivery or a transfer document is required. If the trust property is "real property," such as land, then a written instrument transferring it to the trust will be needed.

The Beneficiary/Trustee

A beneficiary who is also serving as a trustee may, under New York law, and serving as the sole trustee of a trust, engage in discretionary distributions of principal to himself or herself, provided that the purposes are limited to support, maintenance, and health (the ascertainable standard).

The value of all property over which a person possesses a general power of appointment is includable, at death, in the person's estate, whether they exercise it or not. The term "power of appointment" is applicable to a power given to the possessor by another (rather than to a power that has been created and retained by the same person).

In order to prevent the assets of a trust from being included in the gross estate of a person for transfer tax purposes, who is both a beneficiary and trustee, or having the exercise or failure to exercise a power by such a person treated as a gift, none of the powers granted to the beneficiary as trustee should fall within the purview of a "general power of appointment" as may be defined in a transfer tax system in effect at such time.

In other words, if a beneficiary is serving as trustee, and as trustee the beneficiary has the power to participate in decisions concerning the exercise of unrestricted discretion to distribute income or principal to himself or herself, the beneficiary could have a taxable general power of appointment and the assets of the trust could be included in his or her estate for transfer tax purposes, even if such power is never exercised. Similarly, if the beneficiary/trustee has the unlimited discretion to permit the use of the trust assets by the beneficiary, the beneficiary could also have a general power of appointment.

However, if under the trust instrument the beneficiary/trustee has a fixed right to income from the trust or an interest in income or principal of the trust, limited by an ascertainable standard, the beneficiary/trustee will have the power to participate in decisions with respect to the distribution of income or principal to himself or herself without adverse tax effects.

A power is considered limited by an ascertainable standard to the extent that the holder's ability to exercise or not exercise the power is reasonably measurable in terms of the possessor's needs for health, education, or support. Examples of powers limited by an ascertainable standard are powers exercisable by the beneficiary/trustee for his or her "support," "support and reasonable comfort," "support in his or her custom manner of living," "education, including college and professional education," "health," and "medical, dental, hospital and nursing expenses, and expenses of invalidism." However, a power to use property for the comfort, welfare, or happiness of the powerholder is not limited by the requisite standard.

Common Trust Provisions

Typically, a trust provides standard provisions setting forth the following:
- A description of the property transferred to the trust
- The name of the trustee and the powers of the trustee
- The names of the primary and contingent (remainder) beneficiaries and the conditions under which they are to receive the income and principal (discretionary, accumulated, or distributed)

3 1613 00469 2870

51

CALUMET CITY PUBLIC LIBRARY

- The powers of the trustee to distribute a portion of the principal of the trust for the support and maintenance of a beneficiary
- A provision that prevents the beneficiary from transferring his or her interest in the trust and states that the interest of the beneficiary is not subject to claims of creditors of the beneficiary (spendthrift)
- A provision setting forth the state rule concerning when the trust must terminate
- A provision stating that the named trustee/successor trustee is not required to post a bond
- A provision providing for the naming of a successor trustee or the method for the successor to be designated and the payment of compensation to the trustee
- The term or duration of the trust

The spendthrift provision imposes a restraint upon the equitable interest of the beneficiary. A spendthrift is a person who is incapable of managing assets prudently; so essentially, this type of trust provision prevents a beneficiary from selling or losing his or her interest in the trust to others. It imposes a disabling restraint on the beneficiary and creditors: the beneficiary cannot voluntarily transfer his or her interest, and his or her creditors cannot reach his or her interest. In New York State, all trusts are considered spendthrift unless the grantor expressly makes the beneficiary's interest transferable. There are, however, certain statutory exceptions to this presumption. For example, the Uniform Probate Code works the opposite way: A trust is not considered spendthrift unless the creator expressly makes the beneficiaries' rights in the trust property nontransferable.

Special Trust Provisions

Because a trust is usually set up for an extensive period of time, flexibility must be incorporated into its provisions. The trustee has to have the ability to respond to changing times and circumstances. Typical provisions providing for this flexibility are the following:

- A provision permitting the trustee the right to distribute or apply the income and even the principal of the trust to other persons. These are usually persons on the same level (siblings) but may also be descendants of the beneficiary.
- The discretion of the trustee to use the principal of the trust for the beneficiary and the standards under which such permission is given.

CALUMET CITY PUBLIC LIBRARY

- The power of the beneficiary to withdraw or invade the principal of the trust. Giving the beneficiary a limited power, such as the right to withdraw in any one year the greater of $5,000 or 5 percent of the value of the trust assets, will not leave the beneficiary completely at the mercy of a trustee's discretion when a need arises. Such a limited power should not place the beneficiary in a prejudicial transfer tax position either.
- If a beneficiary is disabled and could qualify for government assistance, special provisions must be incorporated.
- A clause permitting a change of "situs" of the trust for administrative convenience or favorable tax laws. Normally, the location or situs of the trust is where the trustee is located. The trust is usually therefore subject to the rules and regulations of the situs jurisdiction.
- A clause permitting the primary trust beneficiary to designate who will enjoy the remainder rights to the trust property. This is known as a power of appointment and can be general, specific, or limited.
- A clause permitting limited amendments of the trust to protect it against adverse tax consequences if subsequent changes in the law render certain provisions of an irrevocable trust undesirable or not within the original intention of the grantor.
- A power reserved by the grantor in an irrevocable trust to replace a trustee with another trustee (who normally cannot be the grantor).

Irrevocable Trusts

One of the main purposes of creating an irrevocable trust is the reduction of potential transfer taxes on such property, by removing the trust property from the owner's estate. Under a trust of this type, the grantor is not supposed to retain any right to amend, revoke, or alter the trust in any way. Additionally, the grantor cannot retain, directly or indirectly, any right to control the ownership or enjoyment of the property placed in the trust or the income generated by such property. As a result of these rules, the grantor in most instances should not act as a trustee.

Forms of Trusts

There are only two principal forms of trusts: the "inter vivos trust," which is created during lifetime, and the "testamentary trust," which is created under a will. An inter vivos trust may be revocable or irrevocable.

Inter Vivos Trust

An inter vivos trust is a trust agreement made while the grantor is still alive. A trust of this kind may be created in one of two ways. As grantor, you simply declare the holding of personal property for the benefit of another. This is known as a "declaration of trust" and the grantor becomes the trustee. Alternatively, as the grantor, you may transfer title in property to a trustee for the benefit of yourself or another person or group of persons.

The inter vivos trust may be revocable or irrevocable, depending upon state laws and the language of the trust instrument. Some states require that if a trust is to be revocable, there must be specific language in the instrument stating so. It is extremely important to consult the applicable state laws before setting up any type of trust.

The inter vivos trust has tax advantages, as it can permit a shifting of income from one person to another. The amount of control the grantor retains over the trust can raise questions regarding intent, and thus the validity of the trust. The validity of a trust where the grantor maintains the right to revoke the trust during his or her lifetime is usually accepted. However, where the grantor is the trustee and the sole beneficiary of the trust and no valid trust intent can be found, some courts have invalidated the arrangement. Generally, as long as an interest is created for a beneficiary other than the grantor, the trust will be valid even if the grantor retains extensive powers.

Amendment of a Trust: Decanting

Can you amend a trust? Most revocable trusts, if properly prepared, provide the authorization for the trust to be altered or amended, in whole or in part, during the grantor's lifetime. In most states, if the grantor is alive and competent and all of the interested parties to the trust are adults and consent to such a procedure, an irrevocable trust can be amended or revoked. If the grantor is not alive or his or her consent cannot be obtained, or if the consents of the other intended parties cannot be obtained, it would be practicably impossible to amend a trust. A testamentary trust is not amendable or revocable except by the courts under certain circumstances (i.e., tax reformation, mistakes in the drafting of the document, or under certain circumstances covering charitable gifts).

In 1992, the State of New York passed a statute that enables a trustee who has unlimited discretion to invade the principal of a trust to appoint that principal to the trustee of a different trust so long as the following conditions exist:

- There is no reduction in the income interest of the primary beneficiary
- There is no change in the beneficiaries of the trust
- The compensation of the trustee does not increase

In 2011, New York State broadened its decanting statute by granting trustees greater authority to alter the provisions of existing trusts. Under the revised statute, a trustee whose authority under the trust is limited now has discretion to alter the existing provisions of the trust to provide for a longer trust term. The trustee may also confer a power of appointment, as long as the marital deduction is not altered.

The new statute does not permit decanting by a trustee who has an interest in the trust, whether such interest is a present or a future one.

If a trustee wishes to proceed without prior court approval, the consent of all persons interested in the trust must be obtained, or the court provides notice to such persons. As such, by utilizing this procedure, an indirect amendment may be attained even though the rest of the provisions of the different trust are not the same.

Income Taxation of Trusts

Trusts and estates are income-producing entities recognized by the Internal Revenue Code. At one time, trusts were used as splitting devices by those in higher tax brackets to shift income to a lower tax bracket. The typical plan was to distribute income-producing assets to a spouse or child in trust, and the spouse or child in a lower tax bracket would pay less in taxes. The savings could be quite significant if one spouse was in the 50 percent tax bracket and the other was in the 20 to 30 percent tax bracket. Much of the tax advantage of this type of planning was removed by the tax revisions enacted in 1986.

The tax law (Revenue Reconciliation Act of 1993) sharply increased income taxes on trust funds commonly used by families to set aside money for minors and young adults. The change raised questions as to how existing trusts should be managed. Many people found that the income retained by a trust will now be taxed at a higher rate than if held by the grantor or beneficiary. It simply won't be worthwhile to accumulate much income in a trust. The tax rate was nearly doubled for some trust income. Under the present law, the maximum income tax rate of 39.6 percent is applicable on trust income over $11,950.

Parents who put money in a trust fund when a child is born and who make regular contributions over the years in anticipation of college and graduate school costs might easily find their funds in the highest tax brackets.

As a result of revision of the tax laws, a trustee must now consider shifting trust capital to investments that are expected to grow in value rather than to produce current income, such as stocks instead of bonds. Capital gains on stocks currently is taxed at a federal rate of 15 percent, while trust income, like dividends/interest, can be taxed at rates as high as 39.6 percent. This approach can be tricky, because investing for growth may mean taking on greater risk—something a cautious trustee does not like to do.

A trustee can distribute a portion of the income of the trust to the beneficiary, instead of retaining it in the trust. Investment income for a child under the age of fourteen is taxed at the parents' rate after the first few hundred dollars. But when they turn fourteen, children are taxed at their own individual rate, which is likely to be much lower than the trust's rate or their parents' rate.

Because trusts are the most flexible devices available in estate planning, they have to be considered in every person's plan. A trust not only can shield a beneficiary from third parties, but can provide characteristics that may not exist in the beneficiary, i.e., secure a beneficiary against his or her improvidence.

An Example of a Flexible Irrevocable Trust

HAVING YOUR CAKE AND EATING IT TOO

A grantor desires to create a trust for the benefit of his children, in which he and the trustee will have respective rights. His wife will be designated the trustee. The trust principal will eventually be distributed to his children, after the death of both parents. The trust property should not be included for potential transfer tax purposes in his estate nor the estate of his wife, provided there is no advance agreement between the grantor and the trustee, as to any distributions of principal and/or income to the grantor. The income of the trust will be taxed to the grantor, since the trust will be a "grantor trust."

The grantor will have:
1. the power to allocate receipts and disbursements as between principal and income;

56

2. the power to change the trustees, provided the grantor will not name himself as a trustee; and

3. the right to make the trusts as investments, vote the shares of stock held by the trust other than the shares of stock of a controlled corporation.

The trustee shall:

1. be granted broad discretionary powers over the distribution of the trust income and principal to the beneficiaries and others including the grantor, but the trustee cannot make any distribution that would satisfy a legal obligation of the trustee and/or the grantor;

2. have a special power of appointment that would allow the trustee to appoint the property to the grantor and/or others, but not to the trustee not the creditors or estate of the trustee or the creditors of the estate of the trustee;

3. If the trust is not a "grantor trust," the grantor can still retain certain additional trust powers;

4. The beneficiaries can be granted the power to appoint trust principal to the grantor and/or others.

As you see therefrom, a person can transfer assets, for the benefit of their children, and have persons of trust, including family members, maintain control over the property.

Transferring a Situs of a Trust

The location of a trust is significant in order to determine which state laws are applicable for administration and tax purposes. New York State laws provide that it is applicable to any trust created under the last will and testament of a domiciliary and a non-domiciliary if the will is admitted to probate in New York State or if, in the case of a lifetime trust, the trustee has a principal place of business or resides in New York State. It is also applicable, in the case of a lifetime trust, if it is created by a non-domiciliary, and if the trust holds real property located in New York State.

If the trustees wish to change the situs of the trust, they must first obtain, in the court of the state where they wish to relocate the trust, an order wherein such state will accept the jurisdiction over the trust. After obtaining such order, the trustees can petition the New York court for permission to change the situs of the trust.

Termination of a Trust

Under the terms of a complex trust, the trust terminates upon the death of beneficiary. The remaining trust principal is distributed to the remainder beneficiary or continued in trust, whichever the case may be. For trust accounting or income tax purposes, a terminating event does not cause the trust to terminate immediately as there is a reasonable period of time allowed to terminate the administration of the trust. During this period, legal title to the trust assets remains in the trustee until all the assets are actually distributed. A fiduciary cannot unduly prolong the windup period. If the distribution of the trust is unreasonably delayed, the trust will be considered terminated for federal income tax purposes once a reasonable period for the trustee to complete the administration of the trust has expired. In that event, if the trust continues to hold title to the assets, it will be treated as a grantor trust for federal income tax purposes.

CHAPTER 7

The Role of Trusts in Estate Planning

*M*ore than 125 years ago, Oliver Wendell Holmes was aware of the value of trusts when he said, "Put not your trust in money, but put your money in trust."

Trusts are the most useful and unique devices that are available in the field of estate planning. They can be used not only to span the gap between life and death, but to avoid and defer potential transfer tax.

There are a multitude of reasons why we create a trust. This chapter explains the different kinds of trusts and when they should be used. For example, in order to defer transfer tax when a noncitizen spouse is a surviving beneficiary, a trust must be used. Later on, I will focus on the creation of a trust for particular purposes, such as for asset protection purposes or for children with special needs.

Today, trusts have become the superstars of estate planning. They are usually created either for the benefit of the grantor or for the benefit of another person. They can be used to fund a child's education, provide for a spendthrift beneficiary, provide for a spouse that cannot manage or assume responsibility of property, provide for continuity in the event of incapacity, provide unusual tax benefits, provide for disabled persons in order to protect their entitlements, avoid probate, and hold property for elderly persons who cannot manage their own affairs. An important feature of a trust is the ability of its grantor to maintain postmortem financial control (ruling from the grave). The ability of a trust to span the void between life and death is probably its most extraordinary characteristic. Most states have laws placing limitations on the duration of such control. As a general rule, a trust may only last as long as any beneficiary named in it remains alive and for a certain period of time thereafter (twenty-one years after the last beneficiary dies). As of 2013, twenty (20) states have abolished the Rules Against Perpetuities (RAP). Seven states—Atlanta, Idaho, New Jersey, Pennsylvania, Rhode Island, South Dakota, and Wisconsin—have abolished the rule completely. Six (6) states have extended the permissible term of a trust as follows: Florida, 360 years; Nevada, 365 years; Tennessee, 360 years; Utah, 1,000 years; Washington, 150 years; and Wyoming, 1,000 years.

A trust affords unique tax and management benefits to both its creators and its beneficiaries. The property of an elder person's estate and his or her spouse's assets have to be integrated in the planning strategy for both lifetime management and transfer at death. In addition, consideration of potential needs like nursing home care and the support of children must be factored into the process. In the field of elder law, trusts are probably the most important devices employed.

Estate Taxes

The critical issue regarding trusts and estate taxes is whether the trust property will be includable in the gross estate and therefore subject to being taxed. It will be included in your estate for estate tax purposes in the following cases:

- If any power of revocation is retained
- If you hold a reversionary interest beyond a permissible amount (where the initial market value of the reversionary interest exceeds 5 percent of the value of the trust's assets, the trust would be considered a "grantor trust" for federal tax purposes)
- If you retain a power to direct the distribution of the assets of the trust or retain any enjoyment over the benefits of the trust

If, as the grantor, you retain simply administrative powers, the assets of the trust will normally not be included in your gross taxable estate. In a 1993 case, the United States Tax Court ruled that a grantor could replace a corporate trustee with another independent successor corporate trustee (even though the trustee's power to distribute income and principal was generally discretionary), and by doing so, the grantor did not retain any right of the enjoyment of the property. The tax court indicated that under the law of trusts, a trustee's primary obligation is to the interests of the beneficiary of a trust.

Particular Kinds of Trusts

There are various kinds of irrevocable trusts that may be employed in your estate plan. Each serves varied functions and has special income, gift, and may have potential transfer tax impact. One of the main purposes of these trusts is the saving of taxes. However, for many people, avoiding probate is a desired goal as well.

The Irrevocable Inter Vivos Trust

The main estate planning device to save and/or reduce potential transfer tax is the irrevocable inter vivos trust. In order to be able to benefit from this device, you must irrevocably transfer your property to the trust and must not retain any rights over it. Such a transfer could be subject to gift taxes and can be made available for the annual gift tax exclusion. If the grantor's spouse has a qualifying income interest in the trust, the marital deduction will be available.

The Pour-Over Trust

The pour-over trust is a trust into which assets are poured or added from another source. The addition could come from the estate owner's will or from a source completely outside the estate. It is useful as a receptacle for benefits from a qualified employee benefit plan or life insurance proceeds. Also, it may receive assets from other trusts or estates, such as from relatives.

The pour-over trust may be either revocable or irrevocable, having all the advantages and disadvantages of either type of trust. If the trust is revocable, as grantor, after watching it operate and seeing changes in circumstances, you may make whatever modifications are necessary. If it is irrevocable, later changes may be barred, and as grantor, you should initially provide provisions that are flexible enough to permit the trustee to deal with changed situations. However, in irrevocable form, the trust enables you to avoid probate of the trust property.

When benefits are payable to several beneficiaries, the trust form is usually the most effective way of making distributions in accordance with the wishes of the grantor and the needs of the beneficiaries.

The pour-over trust is helpful not only where there are multiple beneficiaries, but also where there are multiple assets. It permits the bringing together of these assets in one place and the development of a plan that coordinates and makes use of them in a way that will further the objectives of the grantor and the interests of his or her family.

When used with a will, the pour-over trust may be viewed as involving a testamentary disposition of property. It has long been recognized that a will may incorporate another document by reference. The courts have been able to sustain pour-overs on the basis of incorporation by reference, but implicit in the incorporation-by-reference theory is a requirement that the trust be in existence when the will is executed.

Since pour-overs may not have been fully tested in a particular jurisdiction, it may be advisable to include a fail-safe provision in a will to provide for an alternate disposition of the estate if the pour-over trust is invalidated. If such a provision mirrors the distribution provisions of the trust, one benefit of the pour-over will—avoidance of disclosure of the dispositions to be made—will be lost.

Coordination of revocable pour-over trusts and wills can be risky. There is the danger that the trust may not be in existence at the testator's death, having been revoked without any subsequent change to the estate owner's will. An intestacy problem may arise, perhaps with respect to the taxpayer's entire residuary estate. To avoid such a potentially disastrous result, the will might contain either (a) an express incorporation by reference of the provisions of the revocable trust, which would keep the trust "alive" (at least as part of the will) even after its revocation, or (b) some form of contingent testamentary bequest that will ensure that a will disposition preferable to intestacy can be made if the pour-over trust is revoked. These fail-safe provisions provide a degree of insurance in the event of lapse of omission in an estate plan.

The Pour-Up Trust

In a pour-over trust, assets are usually poured into a living trust. In another alternative, the assets of a living trust are poured into a testamentary trust or an estate, reversing the flow found in a pour-over trust. This form of trust is sometimes referred to as a "pour-up trust." A pour-up trust might be useful in the following situations:

- An elder family member has created a living trust with the prime purpose of achieving family income tax savings by removing income-producing property from his or her high tax bracket to the lower tax bracket of the trust or beneficiaries. On his or her death, the income-splitting advantage is lost.

- An individual has created a trust for the support of his or her parents (or other aged relatives). On the death of the beneficiaries, the trust will have served its purpose, whether these deaths occur before or after the death of the grantor.
- An individual has created a "standby trust" to manage his or her assets while he or she is traveling or disabled. On his or her death, such trust will have served its purpose.
- An individual has created a living trust to manage a portion of his or her estate with a view to observing how the trustee manages it before the individual dies and the trust becomes irrevocable.

In these and possibly other situations, a pour-up trust may prove appropriate. At the time of setting up a trust, you may not be in a position to determine the precise disposition of the trust assets. You may prefer to leave that determination to your living trust or will.

Providing for the Elderly

A trust may prove useful if you contribute substantial amounts to the living expenses of an elderly parent. Aside from whatever income tax benefit is available for claiming one's parent as a dependent, these contributions are expensive because they are made on an after-tax basis. An irrevocable trust with income payable to an elderly parent for life with remainder to your children can be used to reduce and/or save potential transfer tax and support a parent.

The use of a trust of this kind will succeed in shifting income, but it has disadvantages, the main one being that the trust property may not return to you. If you, as grantor, retain a reversionary interest in the trust, all of the trust income will be taxed to you unless, at the time of creation, your interest in the trust is worth less than 5 percent of the total initial value of the trust property. There are other powers you cannot retain if you want to avoid tax on the trust's income. You may not control the beneficial enjoyment of principal or income, such as by adding beneficiaries or varying the distribution of income. A third-party trustee, however, is permitted to exercise certain powers without tax jeopardy to the grantor. As grantor, you also may not retain any administrative powers exercisable primarily for your own benefit, such as the power to deal with the trust for less than adequate and full consideration or the power to borrow trust funds without proper interest or security.

A trust of this type may have other disadvantages as well: (1) potential gift tax liability may reduce the total tax benefits and may impact on the unified credit; and (2) start-up and administration costs of the trust may also reduce any potential tax savings.

It is possible for you to retain a testamentary power of appointment over the trust principal without having the income of the trust taxed to you. However, retention of this power will cause the trust to be included in your gross estate and may eliminate one of the advantages of creating this type of irrevocable trust. As long as the trust is not subject to inclusion in your gross estate, all future appreciation in value of the trust property will pass to the remainder beneficiaries free of potential transfer tax.

The Revocable Living Trust

The use of the living trust for estate planning purposes is discussed in detail in chapter 8.

Testamentary Trusts

A trust may be created in accordance with instructions contained in your will. Such trusts are known as testamentary trusts. They are used when you are unwilling to part with certain property during your lifetime, not even in a living trust, but want the control that a trust can provide, which you perceive as being in the best interests of your beneficiaries.

While the testamentary trust does not result in any immediate estate or income tax savings, when the will is executed or takes effect, it may. The trust can protect the trust property from successive potential transfer tax levies as it passes from one beneficiary to another. It may be characterized as a case of "pay now, save later." It may not always work out as planned, but if the trust can initially be funded with property of relatively low value but with strong appreciation potential, the savings for the family can be enormous.

The most common example of a potential transfer tax trust that can be created in a living trust or will is a "credit shelter" or "by-pass trust," which is used in conjunction with the unlimited marital deduction. The credit shelter trust may pay your surviving spouse income for life and possibly permit use of the principal for his or her defined and ascertainable needs. But it carefully avoids giving the survivor too much control over or rights in the trust property. In this way, the property will not be includable in the survivor's gross estate and can pass estate tax–free to the remainder beneficiaries.

The trustee may be authorized to accumulate income for specific purposes spelled out in the trust. Flexibility can be most important in a testamentary trust, and consideration should be given to the use of a number of special provisions designed to meet changes in the circumstances of the beneficiaries.

One of the most important things to consider in connection with testamentary trusts is that provisions can be made for a beneficiary that could not be made, if you were to set up a trust for yourself, without encountering income and potential transfer tax complications. For example, if you created a trust and retained the income rights for yourself, the trust property would be includable in your gross estate under the Internal Revenue Code. If, under the terms of the trust, income could be used to pay insurance premiums on your life or that of your spouse, the income would be taxable to you under the Internal Revenue Code and you would be treated as the owner of the policy and the proceeds would be includable in your gross estate. However, neither of these results would occur if you were the beneficiary of a testamentary trust.

The Support Trust

In a support trust, the trust provides that the beneficiary is only to receive as much of the income or principal as is necessary for support and education. This will ensure that the funds will be used to provide for the beneficiary in a sensible manner. Although the corpus of the trust may be invaded as necessary if the trust instrument contains such provision, it will also be controlled by necessity, not by the whim or desire of the beneficiary.

The Discretionary Trust

The discretionary trust places more responsibility upon the trustee in connection with the distribution of the income and principal of the trust. Under this type of trust, the trustee distributes to the beneficiary as much of the income or principal as he or she deems proper. However, in this type of trust, the trustee can be given the discretionary right to distribute the benefits of the trust to a number of beneficiaries, not just the primary beneficiary. This is the "sprinkling" or "spray" provision under which the trustee can make distributions to a number of beneficiaries without regard to equality as to amounts or as to times. However, the trustee may not avoid the fiduciary obligations imposed on trustees by distributing the funds improperly. In some instances, a court may step in to control a trustee if there has been a failure to observe the intent of the grantor. Improper distributions might be those favoring one beneficiary over another, unreasonably refusing to distribute assets, or failing to adequately provide for the beneficiary according to the wishes of the grantor.

The Grantor Trust

A grantor trust is one in which the income is taxable to the grantor because the grantor retains substantial control over the trust assets or retains certain prohibited administrative powers. An example of this would be a revocable inter vivos trust. By retaining the power of revocation, the grantor can terminate the trust at any time and reclaim the trust assets. When the purpose of setting up the trust is to benefit the grantor, directly or indirectly, and the grantor has control or advantage with regard to the trust assets, the grantor is taxed on the trust income.

Retirement Benefits

A trust can be designated as a beneficiary of a retirement benefit. This can be an important tool in estate planning in the case of a subsequent marriage. For a detailed explanation of this subject, see chapter 20.

Qualified Domestic Trust

The tax law that created the unlimited marital deduction for United States citizens created the qualified domestic trust (QDOT) for a noncitizen spouse. This type of trust defers estate taxes in the estate of a citizen until the death of the noncitizen surviving spouse. However, the terms of a trust of this kind is not as advantageous as a QTIP trust available for citizens. Under a QTIP trust, when the second spouse dies, the remainder in the trust is taxed in the second spouse's estate. Under a QDOT trust, the first estate is left open and when the second spouse dies, the assets in the QDOT trust are taxed in the estate of the first spouse to die.

On November 27, 1996, final regulations on a qualified domestic trust (QDOT) were issued by the Internal Revenue Service that (among other things) provide:

If the fair market value of the assets of the QDOT at the death of the first decedent exceeds $2 million, the trust instrument must require that:

(1) At least one U.S. trustee be a bank or (2) the U.S. trustee furnish

a bond or security to the IRS in an amount equal to percent of the fair market value of the trust corpus, determined as of the decedent's date of death. The regulations further provide that if the fair market value of the QDOT assets is $2 million or less, the QDOT need not meet the bank or bond requirements if, as an alternative, the trust instrument expressly provides that no more than a certain percent of the fair market value of the trust assets, determined annually, may be invested in real property that is not located in the United States. (3) For the purpose of the security arrangement, the value of a personal residence is excluded if its value is less than the exemption amount. (4) Potential transfer tax is not imposed on distributions to the surviving spouse for "hardship" reasons. Hardship includes distributions in response to an immediate and substantial financial need regarding the spouse's health, maintenance, education, or support, or that of any person the spouse is legally obligated to support.

The Taxpayer Relief Act of 1997 provides that in countries that do not permit a trust from having a U.S. trustee, the Treasury Department has the authority to waive the "U.S. trustee" requirement, if certain conditions are met.

The Dynasty Trust

A dynasty trust can be a unique device in estate planning. By transferring property to a trust and taking advantage of the unified credit and generation-skipping tax exemption (GST), you and your descendants could defer payment of any transfer tax (gift/estate) on the property in the trust for at least ninety years and possibly more.

A dynasty trust creates life income interests in successive generations of your family. Although the initial creation of the trust could be taxable (if the value of the property exceeds the exemptions), no estate or GST will be payable at the death of any of the succeeding beneficiaries during the term of the trust. Assuming no distributions of trust principal are made during the term of the trust, no transfer tax will be payable until the beneficiaries who receive the assets upon the trust's termination transfer those assets by gift or death.

To provide flexibility during the term of the trust, the beneficiaries can be given special powers to permit them to appoint trust principal to family members either during their lives or upon their deaths. The trustee can be given the right to distribute or apply the principal in order for the beneficiaries to accomplish lifetime goals and for their support, maintenance, and care.

As the baby boomers age and their own retirement approaches, estate planning for themselves and that of their parents becomes significant. The parents of baby boomers are interested in not only their children but their grandchildren as well. The dynasty trust therefore focuses on this multi-generational estate planning. The very nature of a dynasty trust dictates the flexibility required in the drafting of such an instrument. The sooner assets are placed into the trust, the quicker their growth is removed from one's estate. Today, estate planners without born grandchildren establish trusts for their children and their unborn grandchildren in order for the growth to be effective rather than upon the later birth of their heirs.

The provisions of a dynasty trust require flexible distributions clauses so as to anticipate future family circumstances at each generational level, encourage a beneficiary to be incentivized, i.e., trust income and principal distributions can be tied into a beneficiaries earned income or lump sum distributions can be tied to the attainment of a certain net worth or income level attained by a beneficiary or assist a beneficiary who is engaged in a worthwhile but non-compensating occupation, i.e., social worker, etc. Given the current divorce rates, the dynasty trust will protect the beneficiary's assets against being taken in a divorce proceeding or against the beneficiaries creditors. The trustee can be provided with a power to terminate or amend the trust if it becomes burdensome or otherwise not necessary, i.e., the potential transfer tax is eliminated.

The dynasty trust can be designed so that during the lifetime of the creator, all income tax associated with the trust, paid by the grantor, are not being charged with gift tax. In other words, the dynasty trust will grow tax-free.

One of the purposes of the transfer tax system is to ensure that there is a transfer tax at every generations level. A dynasty trust would only have a taxable distribution if the trustee were to make a distribution from the trust to a grandchild or more remote descendant of the grantor except if it was for the payment of a beneficiary's tuition and/or medical expenses.

However, the trust should be insulated from potential transfer tax if the grantor and spouse allocate whatever potential transfer tax exemptions are available at such time to the trust.

Some of the most interesting planning with dynasty trusts involves attempts to increase trust assets beyond the amount of the transfer tax exemptions that may be available at such time. One example of technique is the use of a life insurance policy. Suppose a grantor has $1 million of his or her remaining potential transfer tax exemption. The grantor could make a gift of that amount to a dynasty trust, which the trustee would use to purchase an insurance policy on the life of the grantor or, more commonly, on the joint lives of the grantor and his or her spouse. The grantor would allocate an amount potential transfer tax exemptions to the trust, sufficient to cause the trust to have no transfer tax consequences. Suppose, for illustration purposes, that the $1 million in the trust was sufficient to purchase a $10 million paid-up life insurance policy on the lives of the grantor and spouse. The result would be that the grantor would have leveraged $1 million of his exemption to remove $10 million in value from the transfer tax system. A similar leveraging benefit might be obtained if the grantor makes a gift to the dynasty trust of assets that are expected to increase significantly in value over time, such as an interest in pre-IPO shares of stock or a closely held business or in real property. Another example of exemption leveraging is for the grantor to sell highly appreciating assets to the trust in return for the trust's promissory note: The note could provide for payment of interest only for a specified period of years at the lowest rate permitted under the Internal Revenue Code. At the end of the note term, the note would provide for a balloon payment of principal to the grantor. If the assets in the trust produce a rate of return more than sufficient to service the interest and principal payments on the note, value will have been transferred to the dynasty trust free of transfer tax imposition. This technique is sometimes referred to as an "installment sale to an intentionally defective grantor trust."

Two techniques that generally do not work well to leverage a potential Generation Skipping Tax ("GST") exemption are the qualified personal residence trust (QPRT) and the grantor retained annuity trust (GRAT). A QPRT is a vehicle wherein a personal residence is the basis for a future gift to children or other beneficiaries at a discount. A GRAT is a gift technique for transferring other assets to children or other beneficiaries at a discount. Both techniques involve the grantor retaining the right to use trust assets for a set term, after which the remaining assets (the "remainder gift") pass to the grantor's designated beneficiaries. The value of the remaining gift is discounted by the value of the grantor's retained right to use the assets during the set trust term. Unfortunately, an allocation of potential GST exemption to the discounted value of the remainder gift at the inception of a GRAT or

QPRT will not inoculate the transfer from potential transfer tax because either of these trusts may abort if the grantor dies prior to the end of the term of the trust.

During the grantor's lifetime, the dynasty trust typically is structured as a single pot for the beneficial interests of all descendants of the grantor living from time to time. Upon the grantor's death, it is common for the trust to divide into separate shares for each of the grantor's children, with each child's trust lasting for his entire lifetime. The grantor could consider granting each child a nontaxable limited power of appointment, which gives a child the power to decide whether his/her trust should be continued for another generation and, if continued, whether it should be modified in any way. The grantor also could grant the trustee or a trust protector the power to make technical amendments to the trust or even the power to decant the trust into a new trust, usually with identical beneficiaries.

CHAPTER 8

The Living Trust

*T*here is no better method for you to hold assets than in a living trust. After reading this chapter, it will be clear to you that the living trust is the answer to just about every estate planning program. This chapter tells how it works and all of the advantages. The first living trust was written in this country approximately 230 years ago, and this chapter tells you its origin and how it arrived on our shores. Proper estate planning requires you to include other documents in your plan besides a living trust, which are the pour-over will and the power of attorney.

Where Did It Come From?

The origin of the living trust is rooted in English common law. In England, people used it to protect their assets from the Crown. By placing their assets in a trust, the general population prevented the English king and the lords from unjustly taking property away. The trust held title to land and thereby permitted land to pass from one generation to the next. The English courts upheld the validity of the trust, which thereafter became a part of English common law. The trust was then brought to this country by colonists. Today, the living trust is recognized in all fifty states as well as throughout the world.

Downsides to a Living Trust

There are no disadvantages to creating and using a properly prepared living trust. The incorrect perception that there is a downside to a living trust can result from preparing the living trust improperly or failing to properly fund it. A living trust that fails to consider all of the life situations of the grantor and the required tax concerns could be disastrous to a family. Furthermore, if you fail to fund your living trust, you have created an incomplete transaction and you leave your estate vulnerable to the probate process.

What Is a Living Trust?

The living trust is probably the most important legal device used in estate plans that are administered by banking institutions and trust administrations. The cost of creating a living trust may exceed that of creating a will but should be substantially less than that arising from a probate proceeding.

The living trust not only allows you continued total control over your affairs during your lifetime but also provides continuity in management and supervision in the event of your incapacity. This remarkable and unique device gives you the opportunity of seeing your "will" in operation while you are alive. It offers the avoidance of multiple probate proceedings where property is claimed in more than one state, as well as stronger insulation against attack on the basis of personal or undue influence or lack of capacity. The living trust ensures that after your death your survivors will have total control over your property, without depending on the sanction of the courts.

In the vast majority of estate plans, the living trust should be designated as its cornerstone. The lifetime trust, as it sometimes is called, is named as such because it is created during your lifetime. You can amend or revoke the trust at any time. It can be funded by the simple transfer of property or can remain unfunded until a specific event, e.g., your incapacity, at which time an attorney-in-fact, provided with the right, will transfer your assets. Thereafter, the assets will be managed by your trustee for your benefit.

Certain states do not allow the creation of a "springing" power of attorney (one that takes effect only upon the occurrence of a certain event, such as your incapacity). In such states, a living trust could be created with a provision that the successor trustee will act only in the event of your incapacity.

The living trust avoids many of the administrative procedures that are required in a guardianship proceeding, such as accountings, court permission to buy or dispose of the ward's property, and the posting of a bond.

How a Living Trust Works

Most people understand the significance of a will, but very few have any knowledge about trusts. A will is a legal document that transfers assets to heirs at death. A trust does the same thing. A will names an executor or personal representative to do this. A trust names a trustee to do the exact same thing—and that's where the similarity ends.

The living trust works as follows: You (the grantor/settlor) establish a written revocable trust agreement, naming yourself as the beneficiary (or one of the beneficiaries) while you are alive and family members or others as beneficiaries after your death. As such, you maintain full and absolute control over your assets and can revoke or change the trust at any time. The trust is funded during your lifetime by the transfer to it of your assets. Almost any kind of property you own can be placed in the trust—bank accounts, stocks, bonds, and real estate. You simply place the property in the trust by changing the name or title of the asset to the name of the trust. As such, no control is lost since you designate yourself as the trustee and therefore continue to manage and handle your property as before. Assets that have their own beneficiary designations, such as employee benefits, life insurance, IRAs, and the like are not transferred to the trust, but the trust can be named as the beneficiary of such items. However, before making any designations of such benefits, you should ascertain all potential transfer tax impacts in existence at such time.

As a general rule, you name yourself as the trustee or cotrustee of your living trust and you designate a successor trustee to take over upon your incapacity or death, at which time the trust becomes irrevocable. After your death, the trust makes provisions for the distribution of its assets to the beneficiaries you have designated, either outright or through the creation of further trusts that may qualify for all potential transfer tax benefits.

The living trust, therefore, is in effect a contract that is self-efficient and requires no approval by any third party to carry out its provisions after your death.

Formats

A living trust can take various forms, such as the following:

- A trust that is fully funded with assets, wherein you retain full authority until your incapacity or death, at which time its management is taken over by the successor trustees.
- A trust that is fully funded with assets, wherein you designate an additional or cotrustee until your incapacity or death, with full powers vested in the cotrustee.

- A trust that is fully funded with assets, wherein your sole authority is the right to amend or revoke the trust agreement. The trustee is not you (the trustee is a relative or a bank), and the trustee is given the full discretion to pay or apply the income and principal to or for your benefit.
- A trust that is totally unfunded (has no assets), sometimes called "standby trust," with a durable power of attorney authorizing the agent to transfer property to the trust in the event of incapacity.

Pour-Over

Provisions should always be made for a "pour-over" of your assets at the onset of your disability or death. The ability to transfer upon incapacitation is effectuated by a provision in the durable power of attorney. The power of attorney should be created at the time the living trust is created. Upon death, the transfer is completed with a pour-over will. The estate plan must coordinate both the nonprobate and probate devices to permit an orderly distribution of all of your assets at death. A pour-over will can cover those assets that are not transferred to the living trust during your lifetime and will therefore provide for the orderly administration of all of your affairs. Where there is a combined will and trust in the estate plan, the will normally provides for the probate estate to be poured-over, or added to the living trust when the administration of the estate has been completed. The entire estate is thereafter held and administered in accordance with the provisions of the living trust, allowing all assets to be distributed through the living trust after the death of the estate owner.

Incapacity

Since one of the important purposes of the living trust is to avoid court proceedings in the event of incapacitation, the trust must provide specific guidelines and conditions to determine the incapacity of the grantor. The determination procedure might be on the basis of either of the following methods:

- Certifications by two physicians (who are not on the team of the grantor's treating physicians) who could certify as to the lack of capacity of the grantor
- The existence of a court order certifying the incapacity of the grantor

Advantages of the Living Trust

Following is a list of advantages gained by using a living trust. The extent of all of these advantages will vary from state to state, depending on the laws of the applicable jurisdiction. The living trust will:

- Avoid the publicity, expense, and delay of probate.
- Avoid the interruption of income for family members on the death of the head of the family or on his or her becoming disabled or incompetent.
- Allow the grantor to view the trust in operation and to make changes as experience and circumstances suggest.
- Serve as a receptacle for estate assets and for death benefits from qualified employee benefit plans and insurance on the life of the grantor.
- Bring together assets scattered in two or more states or jurisdictions and place title in the trustee, thereby avoiding additional administrations of the estate owner's estate, particularly real estate, in places where such property is located.
- Make it easier to select the law that is to govern the trust than if this were attempted by will.
- Enable a going business to continue without interruption.
- Facilitate gifts to charities in states where there are restrictions on charitable gifts by will.
- Relieve the grantor of the burdens of investment management.
- Authorize the trustee to advance funds to the grantor's executor for certain purposes or to buy assets from the executor at a fixed price; thereby, it will avoid the forced sale of estate assets at depressed prices.
- Be less vulnerable to attack on the grounds of the grantor's lack of capacity, fraud, or duress than a will or a will-created trust would be.
- Require less accounting, administration, and judicial supervision than a trust created by will.
- Bar a surviving spouse's statutory right in some states to share in the deceased spouse's property.
- Place the property beyond the reach of the grantor's creditors, in some states.
- Assist in the management of assets for a young adult or spendthrift.
- Assist in the management of assets for an elderly or incapacitated

person. Rather than necessitate the appointment of a guardian, a trustee or successor trustee can immediately step in and manage the assets of the trust.

- Permit the purchase of U.S. Treasury bonds (flower bonds) when the grantor has or may become incompetent, provided that the trustee is required to use the bonds in payment of any potential transfer tax that may be due or when the trust terminates in favor of the grantor's estate.
- Permit trust property to be withdrawn by the grantor during his or her lifetime for the purposes of making gifts without making the gifted property includable in the grantor's estate.

The living trust may be amended at any time during your lifetime and before incapacity. This is usually accomplished by executing a written amendment setting forth the desired changes.

Avoiding Probate and Its Expenses

Assets held in the living trust at the time of your death are not subject to probate because they are not legally owned by you.

As has been discussed, probate is the process whereby a will is validated by a court (admitted to probate) and an executor or personal representative is appointed to conduct the affairs of the estate. The affairs include paying estate bills and collecting estate receivables; filing the income, estate, and other tax returns; paying any taxes due; and finally distributing the remaining estate assets according to the provisions in the will. This process can take years and can be costly. One of the main advantages of the living trust is that it passes assets on to your survivors without the involvement of this procedure. Probate fees can amount to anywhere between 1 and 9 percent of the total assets of the estate, which is substantially more than the cost of establishing a living trust.

The probate process covers only those assets that are solely in your name. It does not cover assets held in joint name, insurance payable to a named beneficiary, pension funds, IRAs, or assets held in trust. Thus, transferring assets into the living trust mainly avoids probate, the expenses of probate, and, in simple situations, the delay between the date of death and the final distribution of assets.

Trust Administration Expenses

By transferring assets into the trust, you will avoid the legal expenses of probate; the administration of a trust, however, involves some legal expenses, which should be minimal in amount. These could include the cost of transferring your property to the living trust. If stocks, bonds, and cash in a bank are involved, these assets can be transferred to the trustee by you without any cost.

Transferring real property requires the preparation and filing of a new deed. If the property is subject to a mortgage, the mortgage instrument must be examined to see if the property can be transferred without adverse consequences, such as the acceleration of the mortgage indebtedness. In some situations, consent of the mortgagee may be required.

Title insurance policies also should be examined to determine if there are any title insurance consequences due to the transfer.

Avoiding probate does not mean that your estate will avoid the administrative process of preparing and filing your final income tax return or filing and paying all potential transfer tax that may be due at such time. In many instances, it does not avoid preparing an inventory and accounting. In addition, someone has to collect any outstanding assets, pay your debts (if any), and finally make distribution to the beneficiaries. But this process is usually preferred by the successor trustees.

Multiple Probate Proceedings

Avoiding probate is particularly important if you live and own real property in more than one state. Each state exercises its own jurisdiction over its real estate. In these situations, each state where you live could claim that you were a domiciliary, or permanent resident, of that state and not only impose estate taxes but also make a claim against your estate for past-due state resident income taxes. If an additional or ancillary administration is required in the state where real property is located, the risk of income tax liability could be increased, since the income tax commission of the state is usually notified of the probate proceeding.

Each state has the power to determine the domicile status of its citizens. The fact that you claimed domicile and lived in another state or that your will is being probated in that other state is not determinative of your final domicile. Even if you acknowledged that you were a domiciliary or resident of a state, in an affidavit of domicile, voting in a particular state and other indications would not be in and of themselves binding in determining your domicile.

Avoidance of Publicity

When a will is admitted to probate, it becomes a public record and your assets become known to the public. In addition, the beneficiaries of your estate are made public as well as is what they have inherited. Trusts generally remain private and their terms secret. However, if in addition to the living trust, there is a will that is being probated and the will provides for a pour-over of assets into the living trust (which is common), the probate court may require that the living trust be filed with the court as part of the probate proceedings. In such an instance, the provisions of the trust may not remain secret.

Conversely, there are situations in which the probate court will seal the probate records so that even though there is a probate, publicity is avoided and the estate assets remain secret. Thus, it is possible for a person to establish a living trust for the purpose of secrecy and still have the trust instrument filed as public record, and for a person who has a will and not a trust to have the will terms remain secret.

Under the probate system, anyone can review the records of the probate court and the inventory, thereby knowing the assets of the estate, the identity of the beneficiaries of the estate, and the dispositions of the assets. No such opportunities are available when a living trust is established.

Protection against Incapacity

The living trust is an excellent method for protecting your assets in the event of incapacity. The trust can make specific provisions for the continuity of your affairs in the event of disability. The living trust can also be a "springing trust." Under such circumstances, the management of the living trust will only shift to the successor trustee when the incapacity occurs, as defined in the trust. Incapacity should only be determined by a certification method of independent individuals or by a court order and left to the judgment of the successor trustee or beneficiaries.

Many senior citizens place their assets into a living trust because they want to avoid court intervention if they become unable to manage their affairs. Court proceedings are both expensive and time consuming.

In the event of incapacity, the choice of the trustee becomes of vital importance. The trustee should not only be able to manage your assets but also have a sincere concern for your personal care.

Trusts that provide for incapacity should be supplemented by a durable power of attorney. That gives the attorney named power over any assets that are not held in trust even if the person granting the power becomes incapacitated. Such powers should provide for the ability of the agent or attorney-in-fact to transfer any of your assets not previously transferred by you to the trust. In many states, the durable power of attorney will become effective only in the event of your incapacity (a springing power of attorney) so that you retain all powers and authority until you become incapacitated.

Avoidance of Family Disputes

The establishment of a living trust should be considered if you believe that there may be a dispute among family members after death. In this instance, the living trust has several advantages over a will. No notice is required to be given to family members upon the death of the grantor, so they may not even be aware of—or ever become aware of—the existence of the trust. Even if they learn of the trust, the assets of the trust may in fact be distributed long before the heirs realize that a trust exists. Such a distribution would make a challenge more difficult.

Where there is a will, and therefore a probate proceeding, notice must be given to the heirs either before the will is admitted to probate or after the appointment of a personal representative, depending upon the laws of the state of domicile. The heirs would then have a chance to challenge the will before any assets were distributed. A challenge would also tie up the assets, with the result that no assets could be distributed until the challenge is resolved. Since there is no statutory method in existence for the challenge of a living trust, it's very difficult to challenge such an instrument.

A trust that operates and exists for some period during your lifetime is more difficult to challenge than a will, which takes effect after death. It is more burdensome to prove incapacity, fraud, or undue influence in the establishment of a trust if the trust was being managed during the lifetime of the grantor, especially where the grantor was a trustee. The courts of this country have fairly consistently protected living trusts from challenges by claimants.

In some states, "in terrorem clauses" (forfeiture in the event of a contest) are voided by statute so that an individual cannot protect his or her estate plan by providing for forfeiture of a bequest in the event of a challenge by an heir.

Common circumstances in which a will contest is likely are the following:

- Favoring one child. If a will gives one child a significantly larger legacy than other children, a contest may ensue.
- Favoring a second spouse. If a will gives a second spouse a share that seems disproportionate, the children of a prior marriage may be disposed to contest.
- Favoring children of a prior marriage. If a will favors the children of a prior marriage over those from a second marriage, the latter may be inclined to contest.
- Substantial charitable bequests. If there are large charitable bequests, heirs may be disposed to challenge.
- Bequests to a lover. Bequests to a mistress of the testator or to a male companion of the testatrix may evoke challenge.
- Bequests by homosexuals or lesbians. Bequests by homosexuals or lesbians to those with like preferences may be challenged as the product of undue influence.

If a will contest seems likely, consideration must be given to a revocable living trust as an alternative to a will.

Protecting Assets from Creditors

If you do not designate specific trust property in your living trust to pay your debts and taxes when you die, the trustee has the authority to designate which trust property will liquidate those obligations. The question of whether the trust assets are protected from the claims of creditors depends upon local law.

If the living trust is revocable by the grantor, most states will allow the creditors access to the trust assets while the grantor is alive. In addition, if a conveyance is made to a living trust and there are unpaid creditors, the transfer can usually be voided as a fraudulent conveyance, and the creditors can reach the assets.

In some states, the rules are more lenient and the courts look into the financial status of the person at the time the property is put into the living trust. The questions usually posed surround whether there is actual or unintentional fraud. Was the transferor solvent at the time the property was put into trust? Was the transfer made to avoid the payment of debts? If the answers are no, the trust is prepared to protect against the unexpected, and a "spendthrift" provision may in fact provide protection against creditors.

After the grantor dies, the trustee is not liable for distributions made prior to the time that the trustee is notified of the creditors' claims. With respect to federal taxes, however, the trustee would be liable for the taxes due if distributions were made prior to the payment.

Spouses

Most states give a surviving spouse elective rights or "common law dower" or "courtesy" (a right to a life estate), which is a statutory right to inherit a certain portion of the estate of the deceased spouse. For a more detailed discussion of this subject, see chapter 16. The question of whether the elective rights of a surviving spouse can be defeated through the use of a revocable living trust depends upon state law.

The Uniform Probate Code, which is applicable in many states, requires the elective right of a surviving spouse to apply the deceased's "augmented estate," which represents not only the property owned at the time of his or her death but the value of any property transferred during his or her lifetime, without consideration (gifts). For example, the New York rule (adopted in many states) holds that the elective right of the spouse cannot be defeated by a transfer to a revocable living trust or similar transfer over which the grantor retains control.

New York has included revocable lifetime transfers as part of the "net estate," which is counted in calculating a surviving spouse's share of the estate. Subject to certain exceptions, New York also includes as part of the net estate any transfer made without consideration within one year from the date of death and made in contemplation of death.

The Massachusetts rule holds that the elective right of the spouse can be defeated if the transfer to the trust is legally binding, regardless of whether the transfer was made to limit the spouse's elective share.

Uniform Probate Code

The Uniform Probate Code does not allow a spouse's right of election to be defeated. Its provisions do not limit a forced or elective share to the traditional probate estate, but instead extend the election to the "augmented estate," which includes the living trust's assets. Other states have limited the use of a living trust to defeat a spouse's share by court rules that have treated the trust as fictitious on the grounds that, when property is placed in a living trust, it has not been divested. In either type of state, the property in the living trust will be subject to the spouse's forced or elective share.

Spendthrift Trusts

Assets may also be protected from the claims of future creditors by transferring them to a trust established by a third party—for example, a spouse. Such a trust, however, is usually irrevocable and includes a spendthrift clause that insulates the beneficiaries' interests from being assigned to or attached by creditors. The law of the situs of the trust will determine the rights of the parties.

In all situations in which there is a transfer without consideration, the question of a fraudulent transfer always exists.

Interruption of Business

The death of an estate owner is a big blow to any business he or she may own or have an interest in. Probate delays could compound the issue and cause liquidity and management problems for the business. Proper structuring of the business and the use of key-man insurance can minimize the problem, but a living trust is another way to provide for the efficient continuation of the business. It allows the trustee to act in the deceased's stead without court approval and provides for a smooth transition to the survivors, the partners, or whoever inherits the business.

Special Assets

You may be better off not including certain assets in a living trust. It may be difficult to transfer an automobile into the trust since an insurance company may balk at insuring the beneficiaries of a trust. Similarly, you may not wish to transfer jewelry into a trust, which would require a listing of the jewelry and could give rise to insurance problems or questions in the event of a tax audit if the jewelry is disposed of.

There is also a question of whether a married person would want to transfer the family residence into a living trust, rather than have it pass to a surviving spouse. If the residence were transferred to a living trust, the trust provisions must provide for its maintenance and permit the surviving spouse to reside there rent-free. This would make the surviving spouse dependent upon the trustee's discretion in maintaining the residence, which may be an undesirable situation, especially where the trustee is a residuary beneficiary.

Further, you should consider that certain benefits might be lost after the death of the grantor, when the living trust becomes irrevocable. For example, in Florida and certain other states, a residence can qualify for the homestead exemption, which exempts a portion of the real estate taxes and immunity from creditors' claims, only if it is owned by a revocable trust.

In addition, many married people feel, for psychological reasons, that if one of them dies, the residence should pass to the survivor, rather than be held in a trust. In these situations, a joint tenancy with right of survivorship (which also avoids probate) might be a better alternative.

New York State Law

Most states specifically authorize by statute the creation of a revocable living trust agreement in which the grantor is the sole trustee and beneficiary during his or her lifetime. Prior to June 25, 1997, New York had no such statutory authority and only recognized living trusts through its case law.

On June 25, 1997, the governor of New York, George Pataki, signed into law a bill permitting the creation of a revocable living trust agreement in which the grantor is the sole trustee and beneficiary during his or her lifetime. The new law does require that after the current beneficiary's interest in the trust ceases, there must be provisions providing for the assets to pass to the next estate.

The bill requires that the trust be in writing, signed by the creator, and acknowledged in the presence of a notary public. This is the same formality that has to be observed for the recording of a deed. If the creator of a trust is not the sole trustee, at least one trustee must join in the execution. Any amendment or revocation must be signed in the same manner, and the trustee must be notified in writing. However, the law permits that, in place of the acknowledgment, a trust will be valid if it is signed in the presence of two witnesses. If a trust is a pour-over receptacle of a will, it must be acknowledged. The alternate method of legal execution of the trust instrument will facilitate families in situations where the creator may not be ambulatory or it is difficult to bring in a notary public to take the acknowledgment.

The new law makes express provisions concerning the funding of the trust by providing that the trust will be subject to and valid as to only those assets that have been actually transferred to it. This mandates that an asset transfer must be completed in order for it to be considered part of the corpus of the trust. However, for assets that are not registered, such as tangible personal property, the new law provides that an instrument of assignment setting forth a description of the assets will suffice for transfer purposes. As such, a provision in the trust instrument assigning to the trustee "the assets set forth in Schedule A appended hereto" is insufficient and does not accomplish the transfer of those assets.

The new law allows the creator of a living trust to revoke or amend it by a specific express provision in his or her will. As a result of the new law, there should be an increased usage of the revocable living trust as a will substitute.

The Successor Trustee

The selection of a successor trustee is an important planning decision. The successor trustee is the person or institution who normally succeeds after your death or incapacity. The trustee must, in addition to under-standing the structure of the family, be qualified to handle all the man-agement and financial-accounting duties necessary to properly administer the assets of the trust. You may decide to name a professional trustee. Banks and trust companies are the most typical sources of professional trustees. They offer stable, albeit conservative, money management.

However, such trustees may not be aware of the various needs of the beneficiaries of the trust; as such, where possible, a cotrustee should be named. Most elder family members will name a spouse or, if none exists, one or more children to serve as the successor trustees.

Income Tax Consequences of a Living Trust

There are no income tax savings to the grantor in establishing a living trust. The income generated by the trust assets will be taxable under the grantor-trust rules of the Internal Revenue Code. These sections provide that if the grantor retains the right to revoke, the power to control ben-eficial enjoyment, or the right to receive the trust income, then he or she is taxed as if the trust does not exist.

If the grantor is a trustee or cotrustee, the trust does not need a separate taxpayer identification number, nor must a separate federal income tax return be filed for the trust. If the grantor is not a trustee or cotrustee, then a separate taxpayer identification number is needed, and a separate federal tax return (1041) must be filed if the trust has taxable income, gross income of $2,450 or more, or a beneficiary who is a non-resident alien. All items of income, deduction, and credit, however, should be reported directly on the grantor's individual federal income tax return.

The Tax Reform Act of 1997 added section 645 to the Internal Revenue Code, which permits an executor and a trustee to elect that a qualified revocable trust be treated and taxed as part of a decedent's estate for income tax purposes. Section 645 therefore makes available to trusts some of the income tax advantages traditionally available only to estates. If the election is made, only one Form 1041 (fiduciary income tax return) is filed, rather than separate returns for the trust and the estate. The return is filed under the name and identification number of the estate. All items of income, deduction, and credit are combined. If there is no estate representative, the trustee files the Form 1041. Electing trusts may select a fiscal year. The election is made in a written statement attached to Form 1041 filed for the first taxable year of the related estate.

Income Tax Benefits

As grantor, you will also maintain certain income tax benefits, even if assets are transferred to the trust. Some of these benefits are as follows:

- Series EE bonds can be transferred to the trust without gain.
- The trust can hold S corporation stock because grantor trusts can be stockholders of S corporations.
- If the grantor owns a residence, all benefits of the income tax laws are available.
- A transfer of an installment obligation to the trust will not be deemed a disposition.
- The transfer of depreciable property to the trust will not cause depreciation recapture.

Cautions

There are several traps that have to be avoided with regard to certain special assets. If the living trust owns S corporation stock and if there is a litigated dispute that keeps the estate from being settled for more than two years after the grantor's death, the S corporation election may be lost. An estate has no such limitation.

With respect to passive activities for income tax purposes, after the grantor's death there is no provision to allow the $25,000 deduction for active participation in passive rental activities. An estate can claim such a deduction for a two-year period (subject to certain rules).

An executor can file a joint final income tax return with the surviving spouse, but a trustee cannot.

A trust must file calendar-year returns, while an estate can elect a fiscal year.

Trusts are subject to the throwback rule; estates are not. If property is distributed to a beneficiary and the distribution results in a loss, the loss could be disallowed. This does not apply to estates.

Gift Tax

If the trust is revocable, there are no gift taxes upon its creation because, as grantor, you maintain dominion and control over the trust.

However, a taxable gift can inadvertently be made if you become legally incapacitated during the term of the trust. In such event, the living trust then becomes irrevocable. The trust agreement can guard against this happening by providing that any power of revocation will continue to be exercisable after your disability by the holder of your power of attorney; or you can retain a special power of appointment that is set forth in the living trust. Further, it can provide for you to reserve the right to dispose of providing for your assets by your will.

Professional Asset Management

A lifetime advantage of a living trust is that it allows you to retain professionals to manage its investments. Although a professional trustee is not required, the option is open. If the beneficiaries are young or financially naïve, the attraction of professional management is even greater because, after your death, the trustee will be there to protect the assets until the beneficiaries are able to exercise responsible judgment on their own. Designating a professional trustee also gives you the opportunity to see how they will manage the living trust. If you do not like how it is being managed, changes can be made.

IRA as a Beneficiary

The living trust has no life expectancy since it is not a person but a trust. Therefore, when an IRA owner dies, if all the benefits are paid into the living trust, as the beneficiary, the total amount of the plan immediately becomes subject to income tax. However, on December 30, 1997, the Department of the Treasury issued a proposed modification to Proposed Regulation Section 1.401(2)(a)-1, D-5, which would allow a revocable living trust to be used in the same manner as irrevocable trusts—to be the beneficiary of a retirement plan if the requirements of the proposed regulations, as modified, are met. The proposed regulations require the following:

- The trust becomes irrevocable upon the IRA owner's death.
- A copy of the trust must be provided to the plan administrator.
- The IRA owner must agree to provide the plan administrator with any future trust amendments.
- A certified list of all trust beneficiaries must be provided to the plan administrator. The IRA owner must also agree to provide

any corrected certification when changes occur and must agree to provide a copy of the trust instrument if requested by the plan administrator. If there is more than one beneficiary, the life expectancy of the oldest beneficiary is used to calculate required minimum distributions. For further discussion on this subject, see chapter 22.

Funding the Living Trust

Title to property has to be transferred to the trust in its name. In other words, assets should not be transferred to the trustee but to the "trust." Trustees can change, which would require the reregistration of the property, whereas the trust continues its existence until it terminates according to its terms.

Property, such as tangible personal property, can be transferred by either listing it in a schedule attached to the trust or by executing a separate assignment of such property to the trust.

To transfer real property to a living trust, a deed has to be recorded setting forth the trust as the grantee of the property. To transfer securities, living interests, partnership interests, bank accounts, and other assets that have a title, specific documentation and instructions are required for each item.

Remember that any property you fail to transfer to your living trust, other than property held in joint tenancy or property that already has a designated beneficiary, will be probated. If your aim in setting up the living trust is to avoid probate, do not defeat yourself by omitting the crucial step of transferring your property to the living trust.

Marital Living Trusts

Since a living trust is revocable, it can be amended at any time by written document. A joint marital living trust created by both spouses can only be amended by both spouses. This is to safeguard each spouse against any wrongdoing by the other. In a joint spousal living trust, when one spouse dies, the deceased spouse's portion becomes irrevocable, while the surviving spouse's portion of the trust remains revocable, and he or she can amend such share as if it were a single person's trust.

A marital joint living trust can be revoked by either spouse at any time. Revocation restores both spouses to the same position they were in prior to the creation of the document.

Joint or Shared Ownership Property

In the eight community property states, where property is owned by spouses jointly or on a shared-owner basis, both spouses are equal owners of all property acquired after marriage.

Having separate living trusts for each spouse for joint or shared ownership property is generally not preferable. This is because each owner can transfer only his or her share of the property to his or her separate trust. To accomplish this, ownership of the joint property must be divided. Dividing shared marital property in half could lead to unfair and undesired imbalances; for example, one spouse's share could appreciate and the other's could depreciate.

As such, there is no need for spouses to divide property ownership as long as one trust is created to handle both spouses' shared interests. This can be done using a marital living trust. In it, each spouse has full authority to designate the beneficiaries of his or her portion of the property.

When the first spouse dies, the jointly owned or shared marital property is divided. The deceased spouse's portion of the property is transferred to the beneficiaries. One beneficiary is commonly the surviving spouse, but children, friends, and charities may also receive property. If the surviving spouse inherits property, he or she normally transfers it to his or her living trust, which continues in effect in its revocable form.

Beneficiaries and Trusts for Children

Beneficiaries are the persons or organizations that will receive the assets of the living trust after your death. In a joint marital living trust, each spouse can name his or her own beneficiaries.

Trusts for children who are beneficiaries under a living trust can be created as part of the living trust. In doing so, you can designate when the child will receive the trust property, who will manage it for the child, and what benefits the child will receive from his or her trust during its term. In such an instance, the trustee should be given broad powers to use the assets of the trust for the support, maintenance, and welfare of the child.

Using a Living Trust and a Will

In many instances, proper estate planning requires the creation of both a living trust and a will. This is especially true if not all assets can be placed into a trust or if there are special situations such as minors who need a guardian or litigation involving the estate owner.

To maximize planning goals, reduce potential transfer costs, fund a child's education, provide for an elderly parent, provide for a spendthrift beneficiary, provide for a spouse who cannot manage or assume the responsibility of property, avoid a contest, and provide for a continuity in your affairs, the living trust is the best means available.

Coordination between a living trust and a will is particularly important in situations involving payment of debts, taxes, and distribution. If a single bequest is to be made to a beneficiary, the living trust and the decedent's will must be coordinated so that the instrument making the payment has sufficient assets and that only one payment is made. Care must also be taken so as not to eliminate the bequest through cross-references between the trust provisions and the will provisions. If a marital deduction clause is used together with the establishment of a family trust, the will and trust documents must be coordinated so as not to eliminate or duplicate the amounts left to such trusts.

Questions about Living Trusts

Should everyone have a living trust?

Yes. However, certain young people who are really not thinking about their mortality and who will not die for a long time are really not interested in focusing on their form of estate planning. The main considerations of these people are the care of their minor children and an adequate distribution stream to their family. Financial security for their family is of permanent significance, and usually a will and a life insurance plan are the primary devices put into place. Probate avoidance and a continuity in the event of incapacity is not a current concern.

Where there are no potential transfer tax concerns and the assets can be passed on by the use of other nonprobate techniques such as joint ownership, life insurance, or pay-on-death accounts, the estate owner may not resort to the creation of a living trust. However, this can deny the estate owner the other features of the living trust such as providing continuity in the event of incapacity.

If, however, your estate is burdened with creditors, then you should consider the probate process. This is because the rules of the courts provide a cut-off time for creditors to file claims. If creditors fail to act, the beneficiaries can receive their property without concern about future claims. The living trust does not offer this kind of protection and the assets could therefore be subject to future claims of creditors for a longer period of time.

If you anticipate receiving property in the future, a living trust will really not be beneficial to you. This is because a living trust is effective to receive property you presently own. If your circumstances are as such, then you must create a backup will at the same time you make your living trust so that the assets to be received will flow to your beneficiaries through your living trust.

Where a guardian of a minor child is necessary, a will is required for this designation in most states. You can still have a living trust that would operate together with your backup will containing the designation. People with little or no estates need not be concerned with testamentary dispositions. They can implement the transfer of their assets by other devices.

How do you create a living trust?

A living trust is created by a written instrument that is often referred to as a trust agreement, trust indenture, or declaration of trust. The measure of the understanding necessary to execute a trust agreement is whether you understand the nature of the transaction.

How do you create a will?

A will must be written, witnessed, and executed with the formalities set by state law. The standard of capacity for signing a will is less than required for signing a trust agreement. When you make a will, you are only supposed to know who your heirs are and the nature of your assets.

Legal cases have held that less capacity is required for you to make a will than for you to execute any other legal document.

If you have a living trust, will there be any court proceedings when you die?

No. You will, however, have to seek the help of the courts for the appointment of a trustee if no successor to yourself is designated in the trust instrument or where the terms of the trust agreement are in dispute.

Should you have a durable power of attorney in addition to a living trust?

Yes. The agent can be given the right, among other things, to transfer to your trust any property you may not have transferred, both before and after, if you should become disabled.

During your lifetime, what taxes will a living trust avoid?

None. A living trust will not save any potential transfer taxes. Since the trust is revocable, the assets of your trust are included in your federal gross estate. The fact that they are to be included in the estate for tax purposes does not mean they are taxable upon your death. If the trust has provisions taking effect at death that either avoid (unified credit) or defer (marital deduction) taxes, the assets will not be subject to potential transfer taxes at that time. Income taxes are required to be paid on assets that are transferred to your living trust. For income tax purposes, under the "grantor trust" income tax rules, you are treated as the owner of the trust.

If you are the sole trustee or cotrustee, your living trust is not required to obtain a separate taxpayer identification number from the Internal Revenue Service (you can use your social security number). If you are not a trustee, besides obtaining an identification number, an annual fiduciary income tax return for the trust must be filed. No gift tax return will have to be filed nor will gift taxes have to be paid when you create your living trust.

If you should become mentally incapacitated, a gift tax question might arise due to the fact of the irrevocability of the trust. This would only arise if your beneficiaries were other than your spouse and their shares were in excess of the unified credit. The rationale behind this is the fact that your power to revoke the trust may no longer exist. This could cause all the transfers to take place after your death under the terms of the trust to be subject to gift tax. However, the use of a durable power of attorney, which survives your disability and authorizes and directs your agent (attorney-in-fact) to act on your behalf, with regard to a partial or complete revocation of the trust, will avoid this problem. This is yet another reason for you to engage only a professional advisor who is experienced in this field.

Can the living trust make distributions to persons other than the grantor?

Yes. The trustee can be authorized to make discretionary distributions to other persons.

Is the living trust valid in other states?

Yes. The living trust is used in every state and in many foreign countries as well.

If a residence is owned and thereafter sold by the living trust, are all income tax benefits available to the grantor?

Yes. The living trust can make use of the exemption provisions of the Internal Revenue Code.

Will the homestead exemption be lost if a home is transferred to a revocable living trust?

Usually, no. State homestead exemptions, which protect a homeowner's equity interest in a home from creditors, will not be lost because the house is transferred to a revocable living trust.

A "homestead exemption" is a legal device, available under the laws of most states, to protect the equity in a home from creditors up to an amount set by the laws of each state. If you qualify for a homestead, the home is protected against forced sale by creditors (other than mortgage holders) if the equity in the home is below the statutory limit. If the equity is larger than the amount protected by the homestead law, the home can be sold, but in many states, the protected amount is permitted to be invested in another home.

Is it expensive to transfer property into a living trust?

No. Except for deeds to real estate, which should be at minimal expense, transferring assets into a living trust should have no cost whatsoever. Your attorney should prepare the documents necessary to transfer your real property. All other assets can be transferred by letter of transfer, and no fee should be charged. Stocks and bonds should be transferred by your stockbroker, as a service to you, without fee. As a general rule, the cost of transferring your assets into your living trust should be nominal.

Must you go to court to amend a living trust?

No. If the trust so provides, you can revoke or amend your living trust simply by the preparation of a written instrument.

❖

CHAPTER 9

Gifts

*E*very complete estate plan should include a lifetime gift-giving program. The end result of making gifts while you are alive, and the use of the various strategies that are available, is the potential savings of substantial amounts of potential transfer taxes. Gift planning during your lifetime requires a multitude of considerations, the first of which is the tax consideration. Gift taxes, both federal and state, may be levied on certain transfers. The form of the intended gift is equally as important.

Whether the gift should be outright or placed in trust should be considered. Choosing which property to give away is another important consideration.

This chapter outlines this information in extensive detail, including what are allowable gifts and when you can make tax-free gifts. Charitable gifts and gifts between spouses, which are discussed at length, have important impacts because of their tax deductibility. Gifts to a noncitizen resident spouse require special planning in order to be effective.

The making of a gift and the establishment of a gift-giving pattern involve income, gift, and potential transfer tax considerations. All of these are explained in this chapter, in addition to the ability of a person to renounce a gift.

The new federal lifetime exemption allows each person $5.12 million against the gift tax, an amount that will be indexed for inflation. All gifts in excess of the exempt amount are taxed at the rate schedule determined by the new law, at a maximum rate of 40 percent. Gift taxes aren't actually paid until the exemption is used up. This means that until you've given away the amount of the lifetime exemption, if a person uses $1 million of the lifetime exclusion in the course of making taxable gifts, the estate tax exclusion will not be $5.12 million, but rather $4.12 million.

Definition of Gift

Transfer of property for less than adequate and full consideration is deemed a gift.

Completion of a Gift

Relinquishment of dominion and control over transferred property.

General Principles

1. A gratuitous transfer of an interest in property is not subject to the gift tax unless ownership of the property has shifted from the donor to the donee sufficiently to affect a completed transfer.

2. A gift is complete to the extent that the donor relinquishes all dominion and control over the transferred property. In other words, the donor retains no legal right or economic benefit in the transferred property. As a general rule, to the extent that the transferor retains any power to revoke the gift or to change the disposition of the property, the gift is incomplete.

Effect of State Law

To determine whether a donor has relinquished sufficient dominion and control over transferred property to effect a completed gift, state law determines that extent to which a donor has retained or relinquished control over the property.

Formalities of Transfer—Delivery of Transferred Property to Donee

Effective Delivery of Gift Generally Indicates Donor's Relinquishment of Dominion and Control

To complete a gift, a donor generally is required to do everything reasonably permitted by the nature of the property and the circumstances of the transaction to deliver the property to the donee. If actual physical delivery is impossible or impractical, constructive or symbolic delivery is sufficient to effect a completed gift, provided that the transfer is not subject to recall by the donor. In *Woolsey v. U.S.*, the district court held that mere credit entries on the donor's ledger account of alleged gifts to the donor's minor children, without the transfer of any stock, money, property, or property right to the donees, were not sufficient to constitute effective gifts.

In *Whitt Est. v. Comr.*, gratuitous transfers of real estate to the donor's children were held not to be completed gifts until the deeds to the property were recorded. Under the state recording statute, the deeds to the children could be defeated (prior to their recording) by the donor executing deeds to the same properties to bona fide purchasers for value without notice and also by the execution of mortgages on the property, if the mortgagees were without notice of the conveyances to his children.

Exclusions

Gifts made in a given calendar year are taxable minus the allowable exclusions and exemptions. The exclusions are (1) the annual exclusion and (2) amounts paid on behalf of another person for certain educational expenses and for medical care.

Presently, the annual exclusion permits you to exclude up to $14,000 in gifts to each separate recipient each year, or $28,000 if a husband and wife elect to split the gift. Generally, if a gift is split, a lower gift tax bracket is applicable to the total taxable gift. In addition the annual exclusion and exemption of each spouse applies to a split gift. If the gift is made in trust, you are entitled to the annual exclusion for each trust beneficiary. Where one spouse makes a gift, the spouses may treat the gift as having been made by both, and each may then claim the annual exclusion for that gift.

A gift of a "future interest" does not qualify for the annual exclusion. Any gift of an immediate interest in trust income is a gift of a "present interest." If, however, the power to divert the trust income to other beneficiaries or to accumulate or distribute the income is at the trustee's discretion, the gift is one of a future interest. Giving the beneficiary of a trust a "Crummey Power," i.e., the right to withdraw property from the trust when it is contributed to the trust, is considered a general power of appointment, and this thus gives a beneficiary a present interest in the trust. A contribution to a trust containing this provision would then qualify the gift for the annual gift tax exclusion.

Gifts to minors will also qualify for the annual exclusion, provided that all of the following apply:
- The custodian may expend principal and income for the benefit of the minor prior to the minor's reaching age twenty-one.

- The unexpended principal and income pass to the minor at age twenty-one.
- If the minor dies before age twenty-one, the property passes to the minor's estate or to persons appointed by the minor under a general power of appointment.

The annual exclusion may still be claimed if minors attain majority at age eighteen under state law. Gifts to minors made pursuant to the Uniform Gifts to Minors Act or the Model Gifts of Securities to Minors Act qualify for the annual exclusion as well.

An unlimited gift tax exclusion is allowed for tuition payments made directly to educational organizations and for unreimbursed payments made directly to health care providers for medical services, where these payments are made on behalf of another person. These exclusions are allowed in unlimited amounts in addition to the annual exclusion.

Charitable and Marital Deductions

The gift tax charitable and marital deductions have the same basic requirements as their potential transfer tax counterparts. The gift tax charitable deduction is also unlimited and available for gifts to the same recipients as would qualify as a bequest for the estate tax deduction. The same restrictions apply to gifts of property to charity where some of the interests in the property are noncharitable. These gifts must take one of a number of prescribed forms, such as a charitable remainder annuity trust or unitrust. For a more detailed discussion of charitable gifts, see chapter 10.

There is an unlimited marital deduction for gifts made between spouses. In other words, one spouse may transfer unlimited amounts of assets to the other spouse without worrying about gift tax liability as long as the transfer meets the requirements of the code for deduction; i.e., an outright gift or, if in trust, in the form of a QTIP trust or an estate trust in which the recipient beneficiary spouse is given the right to direct the disposition of the principal upon his or her death. A gift tax return need not be filed if a donor's gift qualifies for the marital deduction.

Disclaimers

A person may refuse to accept a gift by executing a qualified disclaimer, thereby causing the interest in the gift to transfer to another person. That transfer will not be considered as a gift if the formalities for a qualified disclaimer are followed. A qualified disclaimer must meet all of the following requirements:

- The disclaimer must be in writing—it must describe the interest disclaimed and must be signed by the disclaimant or his or her legal representative.
- The disclaimer must be received by the maker of the gift or executor (in the case of disclaimers of bequests) within nine months of the creation of the property interest (usually at the death of the estate owner) or nine months of the date the recipient of the gift turns twenty-one.
- The disclaimant must not have accepted the interest or any of its benefits.

Computation of Gift Tax

The rate of tax is determined by the total amount of all gifts you make during the calendar year in question and in all the preceding years since June 6, 1932.

The maker of the gift is responsible for paying the gift tax. If he or she dies before doing so, the executor or administrator of the estate must pay it out of the estate, or if there be no such person, the heirs are liable.

Considerations in Making Gifts

Strategies should be developed for lifetime giving. You may have a variety of personal and financial reasons for making gifts. You may want to experience the pleasure of sharing accumulated wealth with family members or a favorite charity. You may wish to assure that certain persons receive particular gifts now rather than risking uncertainty in distribution after your death. You may want to see firsthand the way a recipient handles a gift.

In order to select the most efficient and cost-effective way, you need to pose certain questions, such as the following:

- What should be given to one recipient rather than another?
- What is the most appropriate vehicle or instrument for making the gift?
- What time schedule for the gift is desirable?
- What are the financial and tax consequences of these choices?
- Are there less expensive alternatives available?

Net Gift Technique

The net gift technique involves a gift made on condition that the recipient of the gift pay the gift tax. However, it cannot be employed until the donor's exemption has been used up. In addition, when the person who receives the gift pays the federal gift tax, the maker of the gift might be required to pay income tax if the gift tax required to be paid by the donee exceeds the donor's cost basis in the gifted property.

Gifts to a Spouse

Gifts to a spouse may be made outright, in joint ownership, or in trust. Apart from your personal motives in making gifts to your spouse, the owner will find both advantages and difficulties in each of these respective methods of gift-giving.

Income Tax Considerations

Gifts between spouses consisting of income-producing property generally offer no income tax savings to the spouses. A couple filing a joint return is taxed at a lower rate than married persons filing separately with the same aggregate income. Moreover, the filing of separate income tax returns by an elderly couple might lead to additional tax liability with respect to half of their social security benefits. The only situation where tax savings can be realized by separate filings is where both spouses have taxable income and one has very high medical expenses, a substantial portion of which is not covered by Medicare or other health insurance.

A different picture, however, emerges in some states (e.g., New York) where tax rates for married spouses filing separate returns may be lower in the aggregate than the rate for a joint return. An elderly couple residing in such a state, particularly if its rates are high, might, therefore, reap some tax savings by transferring income-producing property to a spouse with a lower taxable income.

Gift and Potential Transfer Tax Savings

Gifts to a spouse may create a limited opportunity for transfer tax savings for some elderly persons, but obviously not for persons having estates not subject to potential transfer tax. The estate of an estate owner who has made no taxable gifts after 1976 may not be subject to potential transfer tax if he or she dies with an estate equal to an applicable potential transfer tax exemption, if same is in effect at such time.

Marital Deduction

Gifts between spouses enjoy an unlimited marital deduction for gift tax purposes and do not reduce the potential transfer tax marital deduction. In most cases, there is no tax advantage in a transfer of property to a spouse during lifetime as compared with a transfer to that spouse at death. In either case, there will be no tax liability for the spouse making the gift. Instead, the transferred property will be taxable as part of the other spouse's estate.

The Estate Tax Exemption

Gifts made to your spouse during your lifetime may produce potential transfer taxes savings if your spouse dies before you do and if you own substantially more property than your spouse does. This is particularly so if the estate of your spouse is less than the amount protected by the estate tax exemption.

Interspousal transfers may enable the estates of both spouses to take full advantage of potential estate tax exemptions. By making gifts to your spouse, you can ensure that you both will be able to fully utilize estate tax exemptions. Such transfers would not be taxable, as they are covered by the unlimited gift tax marital deduction. By utilizing the said estate tax exemptions in the combined estates of both spouses, the value of both exemptions potentially can be bequeathed to others, free of transfer tax.

In addition, if your spouse dies before you do and if the transferred property has a fair market value greater than the cost basis, the basis will be "stepped-up" to market value sooner than if it had been retained by you. The basis of transferred property will not be stepped-up if you gift the property to your spouse and he or she bequeaths the property to you and dies within one year of the gift transfer. There are some risks and disadvantages in this arrangement. The spouse who has received the gift might squander it. Divorce is sometimes possibility. If you die first, your spouse's cost basis in the gifted property will continue to be your original basis, rather than the basis at your death had you retained the property. Some risk can be reduced by making a QTIP gift in trust (see below) with the children receiving the remainder after the death of your spouse, or by purchasing life insurance on the life of your spouse with the children designated as both beneficiaries and owners of the policy.

QTIP Gifts to a Spouse

With certain exceptions, if you give your spouse a gift of anything other than an outright gift, the value of the gift will not qualify for the gift tax marital deduction. The one exception to this rule allows you to control who will receive the property when your spouse's interest terminates and permits a marital deduction for the property that is a gift of qualified terminable interest property (QTIP). QTIP is property that you transfer to a trust created by you (either during your lifetime or at the time of your death) in which your spouse has a qualifying income interest for life and with respect to which you make an election that the property in trust be treated as QTIP. A qualifying income interest for life gives your spouse the right to all income from the property for life, payable at least annually, and prohibits distributions of the property held in the trust to anyone other than your spouse during his or her lifetime. A QTIP gift to a spouse has the same advantage as any other spousal gift, in that it may augment your spouse's estate so as to take advantage of any available unified credit and marital deduction under the estate tax system while taking the property out of your estate.

- The amount of property in the trust at the time of your spouse's death equal to the credit amount could be passed on to remainder beneficiaries other than yourself.
- The balance could be retained in a marital deduction (QTIP) trust for your benefit without paying any potential transfer taxes on it at the time of your spouse's death. Upon your death, this portion of the trust may be includable in your estate for estate tax purposes.

A QTIP election is not always beneficial. It may be advantageous not to elect marital deduction treatment for lifetime gifts of a terminable interest. This alternative involves the donor's use of his or her unified credit to shelter the gift to the spouse and ultimately to permit the transfer of any appreciation in the property tax free to his or her children or grandchildren.

Gifts Made by an Attorney-in-Fact

As previously explained, through the use of the annual gift tax exclusion, your estate can be substantially reduced during your lifetime without paying any transfer tax costs.

If you were to become incapacitated, your ability to continue this kind of gift-giving would be severely restricted unless a properly prepared durable power of attorney were in effect. This document specifically authorizes your attorney-in-fact to make gifts on your behalf. Without this specific language, the Internal Revenue Service would not recognize any such gifts and would include any gifts made by your attorney-in-fact after the occurrence of your disability in your gross estate. The ability of an attorney-in-fact to make gifts, without specific authorization, depends upon state law. The state of Virginia authorizes an agent to perform any act that a principal could do without specific express authorization.

A Gift by a Nonresident Noncitizen

If you are neither a citizen nor a resident of the United States, the federal gift tax only applies to a transfer, by you, of property that is situated in the United States. The gift tax applies only to transfers of real and tangible property.

A Gift to a Noncitizen Spouse

For gifts made in the year 2013, the $143,000 annual exclusion for transfers by gift to a noncitizen spouse is allowed only for transfers that would qualify for the marital deduction if the recipient spouse were a U.S. citizen. Thus, a gift in trust would not qualify for the annual exclusion unless it were within one of the exceptions (QDOT) to the terminable interest rule. The $143,000 annual exclusion for gifts to a noncitizen spouse is available regardless of whether the donor is a citizen, resident alien, or a nonresident alien. On the other hand, a gift to a citizen spouse will qualify for a gift tax marital deduction regardless of the citizenship of the spouse making the gift.

There is no exemption against the gift tax imposed on transfers by nonresident noncitizens. However, the Applicable Exemption credit is available for transfer by resident noncitizens.

Deathbed Gifts

Generally gifts made within three years of death are usually not includable in your gross estate for potential estate tax purposes. The only gifts that would be includable in your estate would be the gift of a life insurance policy and gifts wherein certain rights or powers have been reserved by the donor. If the retained interest or power is transferred within three years of death, the property will be includable in the estate.

State Gift Taxes

Presently, there are a number of states and one U.S. possession that impose state gift taxes: In these jurisdictions, the gift tax regulations may be similar to the state's estate tax.

Gift Tax Advantages

There are tax advantages to making gifts during lifetime. A gift of property with potential appreciation will be removed from future appreciation in your estate, and gifts of income-producing assets remove future income from your estate.

Another advantage is that the gift tax is calculated only with regard to the value of the gift made and not the amount of the gift tax (provided that the gift is made more than three years before the donor's death). If property is transferred at death, the potential transfer tax is calculated with regard to both the value of the property transferred and the property used to pay the transfer tax.

Lifetime gifts can achieve many planning objectives, such as the following:

- Reduction of your taxable estate and therefore reduced estate taxes.
- Shifting of future appreciation of assets to the next generation.
- Shifting of future earnings on property.
- In those states that do not have a capital gains tax (e.g., Florida), a sale by the gift recipient would reduce income taxes.
- By making large intrafamily gifts, the transfer costs are less than passing the same property upon one's demise.
- Taking advantage of the current acknowledgment by the Internal Revenue Service that permits minority interests to be discounted for gift tax purposes.
- Control can be maintained by the donor through the creation of value-reduction devices. See chapter 22.
- Any portion of a gift that is deferred until January of the following year permits the donor to have the use of the gift tax until April 15 of the year following the year of gifting. However, any gift tax paid within three years prior to the demise of the donor will be included in the donor's estate for estate tax purposes.

A sale of property is another method of removing future appreciation from the estate of the owner. A sale also accomplishes the transfer of property while maintaining financial security to the former owner of the asset. The costs of such a transaction are (1) the income tax consequences to the seller, (2) the loss of control over the property sold, and (3) cash burden on the purchaser.

Bargain Sale

Property may be sold for less than its actual value. If the sale is bona fide, at arm's length, and there is no gift intention, there will be no gift. However, if property is sold at a price below fair market value, such a sale will be treated as part sale and part gift under the Internal Revenue Code. To the extent that the consideration received in money or money's worth is less than the fair market value of the property sold, there is a gift. A bargain sale that results in gift tax liability may also arise where the purchase price is equal to the fair market value of the property sold, but the notes given in exchange are worth less than their face amount, if they provide for low or no interest.

Payment of Gift Tax

Gift tax must be paid and reported on Federal Gift Tax Return Form 709 on or before April 15 of the year following that in which the gift was made.

Custodial Accounts for Minors

Under most state laws permitting the creation of custodian accounts of securities and other property for minors, the custodian generally has the discretionary power to distribute (apply) or withhold (accumulate) income, and to accelerate the distribution of principal for the minor's benefit.

This is the kind of power that, if reserved by the grantor of a trust, could lead to the inclusion of the trust funds in the grantor's gross estate. The Treasury Department has ruled that this rule is applicable to custodial accounts in the custody of the one who makes the gift (donor) if the donor is the custodian or successor custodian and dies while acting in that capacity before the minor attains majority. The same rule is applied by the Treasury Department to gifts under the Uniform Gifts to Minors Act and the Model Gifts of Securities to Minors Act. In other words, giving securities and other property to children through a custodial account may result in the transferred property being included in your gross estate, unless someone other than you is named as the custodian of the gift.

Trusts for Minors

Trusts can be created for minors to take advantage of the gift tax annual exclusion. In order to accomplish this, the trust must provide for the following:

- The income and principal of the trust may be used for the benefit of the minor until the minor reaches age twenty-one (21).
- Any income and principal not used for the minor will pass to the minor upon reaching twenty-one (21) years of age.
- If the minor dies before reaching twenty-one (21) years of age, the trust fund must be payable to his or her estate or to such persons appointed by the minor under a general power of appointment.

Revaluation of Gifts

Prior to enactment of the Taxpayer Relief Act of 1997 (the "Act"), as a result of federal court decisions (two of which were handed down in 1994), it could not be assumed that the statutory three-year limit protects a gift from being revalued by the Internal Revenue Service. This assumption was repudiated by these decisions. In those cases, the federal government was permitted to revalue gifts for estate tax purposes in spite of the fact that the three-year statute of limitations for reviewing a gift had long expired. The rationale of the courts was that if the value of the gifts affected the calculation of the estate taxes in the estate of the maker of the gift, the value of the gift originally made can be reviewed in the subsequent estate tax proceeding.

In the reported cases, the value of the gifts set forth in the filed gift tax returns did not result in the payment of any gift taxes because the value of the gifts did not use up the donor's unified credit. The makers of the gifts had made gifts of mineral rights, land, and/or closely held shares of stock to family members a few years before the respective donors died.

After the deaths of the donors, the Internal Revenue Service audited their respective estate tax returns and the government took the position that the gifts, as reported by the taxpayers, were substantially understated. The estates subsequently challenged the government's contention on the grounds that the three-year statute of limitations barred the review of these gifts. The courts, in handing down decisions in favor of the government, concluded that a revaluation could be made, even after the statutory limitation period, if it affected the calculation of the estate taxes in the estate of the maker of the gifts.

The Act provides that gifts made after August 5, 1997, cannot be revalued for estate tax purposes if the gift tax statute of limitations has expired, provided that the filed gift return is complete as far as the details and circumstances are concerned.

❖

CHAPTER 10

Charitable Contributions

*T*he benefits of a charitable gift can be divided between a beneficiary and a charity through the creation of a trust. This chapter describes the various forms in which charitable contributions can be made and the sophisticated strategy of combining the use of a charitable trust with an irrevocable life insurance trust.

Besides the use of the unlimited marital deduction under a potential transfer tax system in effect at such time, the charitable transfer tax deduction is really the only effective deduction that can completely shelter an estate from potential transfer taxes.

The Potential Transfer Tax Deduction for Gifts to Charity

Charitable contributions can generate not only income tax deductions but also for potential transfer tax deductions as well. The same contribution, if made during your lifetime, can generate both if it is includable in your estate by reason of your retention of a lifetime interest or powers over it. If the contribution is made by a living trust or a will, a transfer tax deduction may be available and distribution by the estate to the charity may qualify as a distribution deduction on the estate's income tax return. This, in effect, would amount to the estate receiving both an income tax deduction and a transfer tax deduction for the same charitable contribution. In any case, whether by living trust, will, or by a lifetime transfer, the charitable contribution is allowable only if the property is includable in your gross estate and there is in effect at such time, an estate tax permitting same.

In many ways, the potential transfer rules parallel the income tax rules for charitable contributions. This is generally true as to qualified recipients, the rules governing gifts of charitable remainders, and the valuation of gifts. There are, however, some differences. Most significant is the absence of the percentage limitations found in the income tax rules.

Charitable Trusts

Charitable trusts may be either inter vivos or testamentary in nature and may be set up to select charities as either income and/or remainder beneficiaries. For a charitable trust to be valid, it must serve some charitable purpose. Legitimate purposes include, but are not limited to, certain types of assistance for the financially disadvantaged, to advance a social interest of society, or assistance to help legally bring about a change in the law. The size of the group designated to benefit from the trust may vary. However, the larger the group of beneficiaries, the more flexibility there is.

One of the great differences between a charitable and noncharitable trust is that the former is not subject to the rule against perpetuities. This means that charitable trust arrangements may be perpetually in existence.

Charitable Remainder Trusts

If a person wishes to split the benefit of a bequest between a charity and a beneficiary, a trust will solve the problem. A charitable remainder trust will pay income to the beneficiary for a certain period and the assets remaining in the trust will pass to a charitable organization. The code defines the charitable remainder trust as one that provides periodic distributions to one or more noncharitable income beneficiaries for life or a term of years.

There are three types of charitable remainder trusts:
- Annuity trusts
- Ordinary unitrusts
- Income-only unitrusts

Charitable Remainder Annuity Trust (CRAT)

An annuity trust pays a fixed annual sum to the noncharitable income beneficiary without regard to current income yields of the trust. The amount to be received should not be less than 5 percent of the original value of the trust in order to preserve certain tax benefits to the creator of the trust. The present value of the donee's remainder interest, less the fair market value of the property placed in the trust, is the charitable deduction to the donor for federal income, gift, and potential transfer tax purposes, i.e., the actuarially calculated dollar value of the benefits of the trust to the noncharitable beneficiary as of the date the trust is created. The amount of the deduction would be less if the gift provides for a successor beneficiary to receive a benefit from the trust before the charity receives the remainder interest.

The annuity trust provides the income beneficiary with the greatest protection against loss in the value of the trust's principal. The beneficiary is not at the mercy of market or general economic fluctuations, since the fixed amount of the annuity must be paid even if the corpus of the trust must be consumed to satisfy the commitment.

The Charitable Remainder Unitrust (CRUT)

A charitable remainder unitrust pays out each year an amount generally equal to a fixed percentage (at least 5 percent), as selected by the donor, of the value of trust assets for the tax year. The trust assets are usually valued, as provided in the trust agreement, on the first business day of each taxable year.

This type of trust may also be designed to pay out either its net income for the year or the specified fixed percentage amount, whichever is less. This arrangement is commonly called a "net income" unitrust. With a net income unitrust, the trust agreement may provide that for the years in which trust income exceeds the specified unitrust amount, the excess income may be used to make up for past years in which the trust's net income was less than that amount. This type of net income unitrust is known as one with a "make-up" or "catch-up" provision.

The charitable remainder unitrust has the benefit of providing a hedge against inflation. In an inflationary economy, the value of the trust assets increase along with prices in general, thereby providing higher annual payments to the income beneficiary; on the other hand, when the market goes down, the payments decrease.

This trust is also flexible, since it can receive additional transfers of property subsequent to the initial transfer. Therefore, the same trust can be used for multiple charitable gifts, thus eliminating the costs of creating multiple trusts.

A possible disadvantage of the unitrust is the uncertainty of the amount of the annual payment to the income beneficiary. Accordingly, a donor whose primary concern is the certainty of the amount of income distributed to the income beneficiary should not utilize the unitrust for making a charitable remainder gift.

In such event, the donor's estate would receive a deduction for the value of the trust that will be received by the charity. The amount of the deduction would be determined by the size of the trust, the trust's terms, and the income to be paid to the charitable lead trust beneficiary.

Charitable Lead Trust

The scenario can be reversed by providing in the first instance for a charitable organization to receive income for a certain period with the remainder passing to the donor's beneficiaries after the set period. This is called a charitable lead trust (CLT). The CLT is an invaluable estate-planning tool because it affords the estate owner the opportunity to shift substantial assets out of the gross estate, at a significant discount, to individual beneficiaries with potentially little or no transfer tax.

The charitable lead trust is principally an income-shifting device designed to provide an income yield to charitable organizations. It has the following features:

- A charitable lead trust may be created by any taxpayer, individual, or corporation for the purpose of distributing an income yield to a qualifying charitable beneficiary.
- The trust may be created during the grantor's lifetime (inter vivos) or upon his or her death (testamentary).
- The instrument must be irrevocable and contain a payout obligation based upon a fixed percentage of the annual fair market value of the trust ("unitrust") or a fixed dollar amount or percentage of the initial fair market value of the assets conveyed to the trust ("annuity trust").
- The trust may last for any specified duration. There is no minimum or maximum period, although tax consequences will vary with duration.
- The charitable beneficiary may be designated in the instrument or be determined annually by the trustee or grantor.
- The remainder interest may revert back to the grantor or pass to a noncharitable third party.

The lead trust is really a combination of two gifts: an income interest and a remainder interest. The value of the annuity conveyed to a charity is determined with reference either to the gift tax or potential transfer tax regulations, depending upon how the trust is designed and when it becomes effective. Such a consequence will entitle the donor to an income tax deduction, a gift tax deduction, or an estate tax deduction.

If the remainder interest is conveyed from the grantor to a noncharitable beneficiary—for example, children or a trust for their benefit—a taxable gift will have occurred at the time of creation, valued as the difference between the fair market value of the property transferred in trust and the value of the charitable annuity conveyed. Therein lies the estate planning benefit of the lead trust. The Treasury tables that establish the value of the annuity interest are computed on the basis of the present worth of an annuity interest at a discount rate that floats from month to month for trusts created after April 30, 1989.

Example, Mr. Jones transfers $100,000 into a trust for 15 years, requiring 10 percent or $10,000 to be paid to a public charity during the trust term. At the end of the trust's duration, the remainder will be distributed to his children. Assuming a 10 percent discount rate, the present value of the charitable gift is $76,061. Thus, the present value of the remainder interest passing to the children is $23,939 ($100,000 less $76,061).

Charitable Remainder Trust (CRT) Strategy

Combining the use of a CRT with an irrevocable life insurance trust can provide for the replacement of an asset lost through the charitable gift. Removing an asset from an estate, replacing it with an asset outside the estate, and paying the insurance premiums with income tax savings is a positive strategy. If the CRT continues for the joint life of both spouses, then this plan would favor the use of an insurance policy payable on the death of the second spouse. If the CRT terminates on the death of one spouse, then the insurance would be placed on that individual's life. The insurance proceeds will replace the loss of the asset passing to the charity.

By transferring low-basis, low-yielding assets to a CRT, which in turn sells the assets and acquires high-yield assets, you can obtain a current charitable income tax deduction, increase current income, and avoid incurring tax on capital gains. The income tax savings and increased income stream can be used to purchase life insurance to replace the assets eventually passing to charity. You should not overlook, however, that in addition to potential transfer tax planning, CRTs can play a supporting role or even take center stage in retirement planning.

Who Should Consider a Charitable Remainder Trust?

Often, an individual holding highly appreciated assets will fund a charitable remainder trust during his or her lifetime. If these assets were sold by the individual, a capital gains tax would be imposed upon the proceeds, often significantly reducing the remaining base of wealth.

However, when appreciated assets are contributed to a charity and the assets are sold by the trustee, usually no tax will be imposed on the trust's gain, and a much larger base of wealth will be available to generate payments for the noncharitable beneficiaries of the trust. The Internal Revenue Service, in some circumstances, will impute the gain experienced by such a trust directly to the grantor (for example, where there was an understanding that the appreciated assets contributed to the trust would be sold by the fiduciary). Therefore, it is important if you are creating a charitable remainder trust with appreciated assets to seek the services of an experienced tax counselor to reduce the risk of having the gain attributed back to you.

❖

CHAPTER 11

Grits, Grats, and Gruts

$\mathscr{W}$hen a grantor retains certain interests in a trust for a period of time, the tax law sets forth special valuation rules at the time the trust is created. These devices are for gift tax purposes and leveraged gift transactions, and should be considered in every sophisticated estate plan. However, there is no step-up in basis to the beneficiary (donee) when the gift is made. For eventual capital gain purposes, the beneficiary of a gift takes over the basis of the donor. By establishing a trust, you can make a gift of the remainder interest to your beneficiaries with the value of the gift being discounted, because the value of your retained interest reduces the value of the remainder gift.

Grits, Grats, and Gruts are acronyms for grantor-retained income trusts and grantor-retained annuity and unitrusts. The concepts of all these devices are quite simple. The idea is that the value of a gift can be lessened by retaining or keeping an income interest, for a certain period of time, in the property gifted away. If all goes according to plan, the income interest expires before the donor or gift giver's death. As such, there is nothing left to include in the donor's estate. If the donor dies before the expiration of the income interest period, the value of the gifted property will be included in the donor's estate with a credit for any gift taxes that may have been paid, if at such time there is a transfer tax system, for estates, in effect at such time.

Retained Interests

For gift tax purposes, any retained interest other than a qualified retained interest will be valued at zero. Therefore, any gift of the remainder interest would be valued at the full value of the property transferred to the trust. For example, if a parent transfers $1 million of cash in trust for his children and retains the right to receive the income from the property for a period of years, the entire $1 million is subject to present gift tax. The grantor is not able to subtract the value of his retained income interest from the value of the gift. However, if the grantor retained, instead of mere income, a "qualified interest," then the value of his retained interest may be subtracted from the value of the gift and the harsh gift tax valuation rules may be avoided. Grits, Grats, and Gruts are such qualified interests. They permit the actuarial value of the grantor's retained interest to be deducted from the actual value of the property gifted in order to arrive at the value of the net gift.

How It Works

The grantor transfers assets to an irrevocable trust for a term of years with the retention of the income rights during that period of time. When the trust is established, a gift of the remainder interest is made to the beneficiary. Since this is a gift of a future interest, the annual exclusion is not available to offset the gift tax; however, the unified credit may be used for such a purpose. If the grantor survives the period selected, the assets are transferred to the beneficiary at the end of the term with no further transfer tax (estate or gift) imposed upon the property. If the grantor dies during the term of the trust (before the period ends), the entire trust could be included in the grantor's estate for transfer tax purposes in effect at such time. Thus, the selection of the term of the trust is very important.

For income tax purposes, the beneficiaries of the trust receive no step-up in basis for the assets placed in the trust. Their basis is the grantor's at the time of the transfer plus any gift tax paid at that time. Any gain on the sale of such property by the beneficiary will generate income tax. Presently, however, income tax brackets are still less than the higher estate tax brackets.

The tax benefit flows from the fact that, for gift tax purposes, the value of the interest retained by the grantor is deducted from the value of the asset placed in trust.

House Grit

If a $1 million residence is placed in a house grit, the value of the grantor's ten-year retained right is approximately 40 percent of the fair market value of the house for gift tax purposes. The value of the gift for gift tax purposes would be the remainder interest, or approximately one-half would be subject to gift tax.

The intra-family house transfer is probably most significant from an estate planning perspective if the residence is likely to appreciate over the term of the trust. What is important is that as grantor, you can manipulate the value of the remainder interest, and hence the value of the gift, by lengthening or shortening the term of the retained income interest. As the term of the income interest is lengthened, the value of the remainder interest decreases. However, there is a risk in making the term too long, since the trust property potentially could be included in a transfer tax proceeding if you should die before it ends.

It is often desirable for the grantor to decrease the value of the gift of the remainder interest even further. This can be accomplished by having the grantor or the grantor's estate retain a reversionary interest in the trust property in the event of the grantor's death during the term of the trust. The trust agreement would expressly provide that the trust property revert to the grantor's estate if the grantor dies before the term of the trust ends. Because this reversionary interest has value, the remainder interest is necessarily worth less. The reversion also gives the grantor the right to dispose of the property as part of the grantor's estate.

When interest rates go up, the value of the remainder interest in the Grit goes down, reducing the gift tax payable and increasing the tax savings.

In the Grit involving the grantor's personal residence, some important decisions will have to be made if the grantor survives the income term, which is the desired result. The grantor could certainly consider simply vacating the residence and turning it over to the trust beneficiaries. The grantor could also consider paying a fair market rent once the term has expired. The payment of rent could also be viewed as an additional way to transfer wealth at no estate or gift tax cost and might be entirely reasonable under certain circumstances.

In some cases, the grantor might even consider repurchasing the residence at the fair market value of the property at the end of the income term. The repurchase does not diminish the estate and gift tax benefits of the original transaction and amounts to nothing more than a substitution of cash for real property, leaving both the grantor and the trust beneficiaries in virtually the same position from a financial point of view. Only recently, the Internal Revenue Service has ruled that the existence of a lease or purchase residence option in the trust instrument upon the expiration of a qualified Grit will not disqualify the trust and will not affect the value of the remainder interest.

Grats and Gruts

In a Grat, the grantor transfers property to an irrevocable trust in return for the right to receive fixed payments on at least an annual basis based upon the initial fair market value of the property.

A Grut is the exact same concept, except the annual payments will fluctuate each year as the value of the property increases or decreases.

By using the technique discussed in this chapter, you are in effect betting that you will survive the term selected—as opposed to a private annuity, where you are betting that you are going to die sooner rather than later. See chapter 9 for a detailed discussion on this device.

Grat vs. Intentionally Defective Grantor Trust (IDGT)

Comparison

The Grat: A Grat is created by transferring assets to an irrevocable trust for the benefit of a beneficiary. The grantor retains an annuity interest for a term of years. The amount of the taxable gift is the fair market value of the property transferred minus the value of the retained interest (annuity). Any property remaining in the trust at the end of the term of the trust is distributed to the beneficiary with no further tax consequences. The annuity is calculated under Code Sec. 7520.

The IDGT: As opposed to transferring the assets to the Grat, the grantor creates a trust (Intentionally Defective Grantor Trust, "IDGT") for the benefit of the beneficiary and sells the assets to this trust. The trust is a grantor trust, and therefore, the grantor is treated as the owner of the trust for income tax purposes (no gain or loss is recognized on the sale) and the grantor is deemed for tax purposed to have sold the assets to himself. The interest rate on the note can be no less than the applicable IRC Sec. 1274 rate. At the end of the note term, the assets belong to the purchaser without further tax consequences. It is believed that the IDGT provides a greater economic benefit than the Grat because of the lower interest rate used for the IDGT. In the event the grantor of the Grat dies prior to the end of the term the transaction aborts and the assets are normally included in the grantor's estate. The IDGT can be used to leverage some portion of the transaction with a potential GST exclusion, whereas such an exemption cannot be applied in a Grat. One of the important reasons that the IDGT is superior to the Grat is that under the IDGT only interest payments need to be made during the term of the note with the principal being paid in a balloon payment at the end of the note term.

For the foregoing reasons, the IDGT is favored over the Grat.

The Grit: The Grit is an effective estate planning technique covering gifts to extended family members (niece or nephew), same-sex partners (whether or not married), and unrelated donees.

How a Grit works: The grantor of a Grit creates an irrevocable inter vivos trust, reserving the right to receive all the trust's income (typically interest and dividends) for a term of years or until his or her earlier death. The trust instrument provides that the remainder is payable to a named beneficiary who falls outside the statutory definition of "member of the family." The grantor has thus made a gift of the remainder, which is necessarily less than the value of the entire property place in trust. If the grantor survives the stated term of the trust, the trust principal will be distributed to the remainder beneficiary. Alternatively, the trust assets could be held in further trust for the remainderman's benefit and be paid at the remainderman's death to yet another permissible beneficiary. If the grantor dies within the trust term, the trust instrument typically provides that the trust property will revert to the grantor's estate. If that is the case, in addition to an income interest, the grantor will have retained a contingent reversion in the trust property, i.e., the trust property will revert to his estate if he fails to survive the trust term. Similarly, the grantor could retain a testamentary power of appointment over the trust property in the event that he does not survive the trust term. Although regulations provide that retaining a testamentary power of appointment renders a gift in trust incomplete for gift tax purposes, that rule appears not to apply when exercise of the power of appointment is subject to a contingency beyond the grantor's control, such as the grantor's death before a certain date. Likewise, retaining a contingent reversion does not render a gift in trust incomplete.

If the grantor dies during the trust term, the grantor could bequeath the trust property to the trust beneficiary (if the trust property is subject to a contingent reversion) or exercise his testamentary power of appointment in the beneficiary's favor. In this way, the trust property would be distributed to the same person as if the grantor had survived the trust term. In either case, provisions could be added to the trust and the grantor's will for payment of estate and inheritance taxes attributable to the trust's inclusion in the grantor's potential transfer tax estate.

Additionally, if disposition is by the exercise of a power of appointment, it may well be appropriate to include language in the will waiving any right of the grantor's executor to recover such taxes as are attributable to the exercise of the power of appointment. On the other hand, if the grantor has a living spouse of the opposite sex, consideration should be given to transferring the property to the grantor's spouse in order to take advantage of the marital deduction. If disposition is by exercise of a power of appointment, special care should be taken in the allocation of potential transfer taxes in the will.

If, upon the grantor's death during the trust term, the trust property will pass to the intended beneficiary in default of the grantor's exercise of a power of appointment, the grantor should consider adding language to his will or the trust instrument waiving any right of recovery of estate and inheritance taxes attributable to the inclusion of the trust assets in the grantor's potential transfer tax estate. In the absence of such language, the grantor's executor will be entitled to recover from the trust beneficiary those taxes that are attributable to the inclusion of the trust property by virtue of the grantor's retained interest.

Finally in some situations, the grantor may wish to retain flexibility over the ultimate disposition of the trust property if the grantor survives the trust term. To do so, the grantor may leave the ultimate selection of the remainderman in the discretion of an independent trustee, thereby, for example, protecting against the contingency that the grantor and a same-sex partner remainderman might separate before the conclusion of the term.

Valuing the gift element in a Grit: As described above, the typical Grit involves three distinct property interests, the grantor's two retained interests (grantor's income interest and contingent reversion or testamentary power of appointment) and the remainder, which is the gift component of the transaction. The value of the gift is the value of the property transferred, less the value of the grantor's retained interests.

CHAPTER 12

Life Insurance

$\mathscr{T}$he importance of life insurance in every estate plan cannot be overemphasized. In many estates, life insurance may be the largest single asset. The ability to remove the taxable aspect of property out of an estate is one of the most effective planning strategies.

Life insurance, unlike any other asset, develops its optimum value at the time of death. Therefore, any technique that permits such property to be transferred tax free has the highest of priorities and importance.

One of the most prominent purposes of life insurance is to improve estate planning by a family.

This chapter will cover these subjects as well as the reasons to consider life insurance, in what form it should be owned, and the different kinds of life insurance available.

The Need for Life Insurance in Estate Planning

Experts say that $7–$8 trillion is sitting in potential estates simply waiting to be passed on to the next generation. The amount of wealth that will be transferred in the decades to come staggers the imagination. However, as a result of potential transfer tax rates plus any state death tax, much of this property could be eroded by potential transfer tax.

As such, adequate life insurance coverage is one of the crucial components of a successful financial and estate plan. There are many specific reasons to acquire life insurance, including (1) to replace income lost by the death of a wage earner, (2) to provide liquidity for an estate and thereby prevent the forced sale of assets to satisfy potential transfer tax, (3) to shelter assets against potential transfer taxes and thereby maximize the transfer of property, and (4) to create assets in an estate. We often forget about the favored income tax treatment life insurance generally receives. This focuses on the deferral of tax on the internal growth that takes place with whole-life insurance. Apart from tax advantages, insurance borrowing features are usually favorable and are tax-free. Normally, a loan does not have to be paid back but is, however, eventually deducted from the death benefit.

Transfer Taxes

The existence of the unlimited marital deduction under a potential transfer tax system, in addition to other potential transfer tax exemptions, may lead many people to believe that the creation of an insurance fund may not be necessary. This can be a harmful misconception. Complete reliance on the foregoing may not prove to be in the family's best interests. This is a result of the dual impact of increasing longevity of the surviving spouse and the effect of inflation. The need for adequate protection is even more important where there is a loss of the marital deduction through divorce or death.

Incidents of Ownership

Life insurance proceeds are includable in your gross estate for estate tax purposes. This is true where they are payable to the estate or a named beneficiary when you die possessing any "incidents of ownership" in the insurance policy. Incidents of ownership include such powers as the right to change the beneficiary, the right to borrow against the cash value in the policy, or the right to assign or surrender the policy. An incident of ownership does not necessarily have to be a direct ownership. For example, if an insurance policy is owned by a corporation on the sole or controlling shareholder with the beneficiary being a third party, the incident of ownership would be attributed to the shareholder and would be included in his or her estate for potential transfer tax purposes.

Third-Party Ownership

The best way to ensure that the proceeds of an insurance policy will not be includable in a gross estate is to have someone other than the insured acquire and own the life insurance policy. A spouse can own an insurance policy on the life of the other spouse. Children can own a life insurance policy on the life of a parent. The owner of an existing insurance policy can transfer ownership of it and all incidents of ownership, and it will not be included in the transferor's estate, provided that person survives the transfer by more than three years. However, any such transfer could be subject to gift taxes.

Life Insurance Trust

To avoid the three-year rule and thereby have the insurance policy not included in the estate as a gift in contemplation of death, a new insurance policy can be acquired and be owned by an irrevocable life insurance trust.

A typical life insurance trust works in this way. You, as the grantor of the trust, name the trust as the owner and beneficiary of the insurance policies on your life. When you die, the trustee will collect the insurance proceeds, which will be free of potential transfer tax. He or she invests them prudently and makes distributions of income and principal to your beneficiaries according to the instructions you've set forth in the trust agreement. Your beneficiaries are thus spared the burden of financial management, but they will enjoy the fruits of your planning.

With an irrevocable life insurance trust, your trustee can purchase and own the policy for you (your connection to the transaction is limited to taking the physical and transferring funds to the trustee). Thus, if properly arranged, your life insurance trust can assure that your insurance proceeds will remain free of potential transfer tax.

One possible way to avoid the potential transfer tax includibility under a three-year rule on an existing policy could be a sale of the insurance policy. Suppose you own an insurance policy and want to put it into a trust to avoid it being subject to potential transfer tax. If you put it into a trust and die within three years, it will be includable in your estate for potential transfer tax purposes. Suppose instead you sold the insurance policy to your wife at its current fair market value (the cash surrender value). Your wife could then transfer the policy to a trust that she creates. The three-year rule will not be applicable since the transfer to your wife was a sale and not a gift. For income tax purposes, there is no taxable gain realized for a sale between spouses. In order to protect the legality of this transaction, there should be a substantial amount of time elapsing between these steps.

A life insurance trust will also allow you to:
- Determine when, in what amounts, and in what manner distributions will be made to your beneficiaries
- Give the trustee discretionary power to invade the trust in the event of a family emergency or a special situation (to finance a child's education, for example)

- Feel secure knowing your insurance proceeds will be professionally managed and invested according to your beneficiaries' needs and your own objectives
- Avoid the complexities of court-appointed guardianship if you name minor children as trust beneficiaries
- Avoid probate and the incidents thereto
- Unify your estate plan by having your estate assets "poured over" into your life insurance trust so that all of your assets can be administered by a single trustee

By having a life insurance trust acquire the policy in the first instance, the proceeds will be secure from potential transfer tax in both the estates of the insured and that of the beneficiaries. The funding of the trust to pay the annual premiums is usually accomplished by making annual gifts to the trust each year. However, gifts to an irrevocable life insurance trust of the amount of the annual premium payments, for gift tax purposes, are considered as "gifts of a future interest." This is so because the beneficiary will not enjoy the use of the property until the death of the insured. Such premium payments to the trust do not qualify for the gift tax annual exclusion. In order to circumvent this problem and have them qualify, the beneficiaries of the trust are given the right to withdraw (Crummey power) their proportionate share of any property gifted to the trust, which right is typically waived by the beneficiaries, thereby permitting the property to be used by the trustee to pay the annual premium. In setting up a trust of this kind, the insured person cannot serve as a trustee, otherwise the incidents-of-ownership rule will be attributable.

Change of Circumstances

What if you want to change the terms of the irrevocable trust? For example, estrangement of a child, a child develops special needs, or the death of a child. There are methods to deal with this type of situation.

You can allow the policy to lapse and replace it with a new insurance policy which is placed in a new irrevocable trust. If you are uninsurable, the grantor of the new trust could purchase the policy from the old trust for its cash surrender value. The Internal Revenue Service has ruled that a transaction of this kind is permissible, finding, however, that the trust would have a profit on the sale of the policy equal to the amount paid.

Survivorship Life Insurance

As a result of the unlimited potential transfer tax potential transfer tax deduction, the insurance industry developed a product called second-to-die or survivor insurance. This type of policy covers two lives and does not pay off until both insureds die. These policies, therefore, provide for lower premiums than a single life policy because they insure two persons. The proceeds of the "two life" insurance policy are traditionally used to pay the potential transfer taxes due when the surviving spouse dies. This type of insurance policy can be held in an irrevocable life insurance trust as well.

Business Split-Dollar Plan

Economic Benefit Regime

Treas. Regs. Section 1.61-22(b)(1) defines economic benefit split-dollar arrangements as:

"any arrangement between an owner and non-owner of a life insurance policy that satisfies the following criteria:

(i)   Either party to the arrangement pays, directly or indirectly, all or any portion of the premiums on the life insurance contract, including payment be means of a loan to the other party that is secured by the life contract;

(ii) A least one of the parties to the arrangement paying premiums under paragraph (b)(1)(i) of this section is entitled to recover (either conditionally or unconditionally) all or any portion of those premiums and such recovery is to be made from, or is secured by, the proceeds of the life insurance contracts; and

(iii) The arrangement is not part of a group-term life insurance plan described in section 79 unless the group-term life insurance plan provides permanent benefits to employees (as defined in Section 1.79-0)."

Regardless of what it is called (for example, private financing), you need to follow the regulations.

Treas. Regs. Section 1.61-2 also addresses the taxation of equity in economic benefit split-dollar arrangements. The section applies to all arrangements entered into after September 1, 2003, and any existing arrangement that is "materially modified" after that date. "Equity" refers to any part of the cash value (not including surrender charges) that is available to the non-premium paying party during life. That equity will be taxed at the time it accrues for income tax and transfer tax purposes (if that is also applicable).

The regulations define material modification by what it doesn't include. For example, it doesn't include minor administrative changes and changes made to comply with IRC Section 409(A). One of the things specifically not included as not being a material modification is an IRC Section 1035 exchange from an old policy into a new one (so, by inference, this type of exchange is a material modification).

What Rates Apply?

The value of the gift of the insurance premiums payments is based on the economic benefit to the person receiving the benefit. In Notice 2001-10, the IRS created Table 2001, which set new rates to measure the value of the insurance protection (that is, the economic benefit). The IRS had been unhappy with the way the insurance companies defined their "published" term rates available for sale. The rates used were unrealistically low and few, if any, policies were actually sold. While Notice 2008-2 revoked Notice 2001-10, it republished the Table 2001 rates so that they were (and are) still in effect. These new rates set out in Table 2001 apply to all new arrangements entered into after January 28, 2002. The regulations provide that the taxable term table can be changed at any time. The regulations allowed the continuation of the "Published" rates for older arrangements (that is, arrangements entered into on or before January 28, 2002, and not modified on or after that date). If the IRS changes the new rate, it is anticipated that the taxpayers with existing arrangements will have choice of which rates to use—that is, if the new rates are higher, taxpayers can continue to use the old rates and if the new rates are lower, they can switch to the new rates.

Family Split-Dollar Plan

What happens when a family member has a definite need for insurance protection, but there is no corporation to pay the premiums? In cases such as this, many have turned to a variation of the traditional employer-employee split-dollar plan to a "family" split-dollar plan. From a tax standpoint, family split-dollar may be one of the best-kept secrets in the entire financial planning arena. An example will demonstrate why.

Assume that a child needs financial help and the deferred tax buildup of cash value in a permanent policy could be more beneficial to the child's family over the long run, especially if they need to accumulate cash on a tax-deferred basis to pay for their child's future college expenses. Acquiring permanent coverage could take care of two needs with one policy.

Once the need is recognized for a permanent policy, the child could ask a parent to assist with the premium payments. The "split" of the family split-dollar plan would work as follows: The parent would pay the premiums, but enter into an agreement with the child under which the parent would retain the right to the policy's premium buildup of cash values. On the other hand, the child would be given the right to name his spouse as beneficiary of the balance of the death proceeds in excess of the premium buildup or cash value. Over time, the parent could give his or her interest in the policy's cash value to the child, allowing the child's family full access to the cash values to fund future college expenses.

As far as the tax consequences are concerned, the parent's premium payments under a family split-dollar plan result in no income being taxed to the child. Instead, the parent is deemed to have made a gift to the child measured not by the full value of the policy's premiums, but rather by the very low "economic benefit" cost used by the IRS to value the cost of permanent insurance protection in employer-employee split-dollar plans.

Since the parent's gifts of both the premiums and the cash values do not result in taxable income, the child should not have any reportable income from the family split-dollar plan. It is easy to see why a family split-dollar is a beneficial financial planning tool.

Living Benefit Policy

In answering the needs of terminally ill persons, insurance companies have developed products that allow their insureds to receive accelerated death benefits to pay for their medical costs. These "living benefits" permit the seriously ill to have access to life insurance benefits before death. This unusual approach has a dual role in our society. It not only helps individuals to meet these obligations but removes a portion of the responsibility of the state for whatever catastrophic long-term costs it may have to pay.

The growth of this industry has been fast moving and states are in the process of enacting legislation to regulate the companies offering this product.

Types of Insurance Policies

- *Term:* Although there are many variations on term insurance, the basic point to note is that term insurance is "pure" insurance that does not have an investment element. Its biggest advantage is its low cost; however, that is not the whole story. As an individual ages, the price of insurability goes up, and consequently, over the long run, term insurance may actually prove more costly than other investment types. It is perhaps best suited to young persons and those who need coverage for short periods of time. When you may need insurance coverage the most, it may not be there or if it is, it may be too costly to maintain.

- *Conventional Whole-Life:* Whole-life is the generic form of life insurance that adds an investment element. In a conventional whole-life policy, the death benefits are fixed, and there is a fixed maturity date, as well as fixed level premiums and a fixed progression of cash values, which grow tax free, against which you can borrow or cash in. It can cost several times more to have coverage under a whole-life policy than under a term policy, but it is a way of making forced savings. With whole-life insurance, no new physicals are required as the policy continues to be extended. During the recent economic crisis, whole-life insurance policies have been more successful in their conservative investments (bonds) than their competing products, a way to enhance returns is to buy a blended policy that includes term insurance and builds up the whole-life portion over the years. Commissions on this type of policy are lower than on a regular whole-life policy.

- *Variable Life:* Variable life is a variation of regular whole-life insurance that adds an element of flexibility to the choice of investment vehicles. Net premiums are invested in a fund or funds selected by the policyholder. If the fund earns more than a specified return, the death benefit and the cash value increase; the converse is true if the fund earns less, except the death benefit does not decrease below the original face amount. If financial markets decline, this form of policy can have adverse effects.

- *Universal Life:* This form of policy allows for flexibility of premium payments, as well as in the face amount of insurance. It has been a popular insurance product and combines the features of term and whole-life insurance. Part of the premiums are invested in a cash fund that is invested in fixed income assets, which means as interest rates go down, the premiums may go up. The rest of the premiums are used to finance renewable term insurance. This form of insurance permits you to not only vary the premium payments, but to increase or decrease the amount of the death benefit as well. Because there is no requirement that premiums are to be paid beyond the initial premiums, these policies afford great flexibility. However, universal life policies that fail to meet certain tests will be deemed to be modified endowment contracts, which could have adverse income tax effects to you. Over the life of the policy, the net cost to the policyholder may not exceed the cost of term insurance.

- *Universal Variable Life:* In an attempt to include the best of both worlds, these policies combine the investment flexibility of variable life with the premium and insurance amount flexibility of universal life. The caveat to this flexibility is that the policyholder must exercise control with a great deal of care.
- *Annuities:* Under this form of insurance, the company agrees to pay the policy amount to a beneficiary in installments, instead of a single payment. This is, in effect, a de facto trust arrangement. Establishing a trust to do the same thing may be less costly, more efficient, and have greater flexibility. You can be the beneficiary of your own annuity and as such receive installment payments during your lifetime.

Community Property

In a community property state, without an agreement to the contrary, one-half of the proceeds of an insurance policy are owned by the surviving spouse, notwithstanding the provisions in the policy as to who the beneficiary is.

Life insurance and the life insurance trust single-handedly satisfy a multitude of estate planning objectives simultaneously. The opportunity to benefit your heirs without death tax costs is so unique that it has to be considered a no-lose situation.

Transfers from Trust to Trust

The vast majority of insurance trusts are irrevocable because they are created for the purpose of eliminating potential transfer taxes. As such, the Internal Revenue Code precludes the grantor from having any incident of ownership over the trust, including the power to make trust modifications. Otherwise, the assets owned by the trust may be subject to transfer tax at the grantor's death.

Limited choices to alter a life insurance trust are available to the grantor who has supposedly severed all interests in the trust.

Options

The aim of each proposed choice is to transfer ownership of a life insurance policy from an existing trust to a new trust that provides current needs with the least tax risk or fiduciary exposure. Each strategy, however, except the last, results in some incidental value remaining in the existing trust, which indicates that these options are not intended to be a cure-all, but rather an exercise in damage control.

Practically speaking, the trustee of the existing trust and the new trust (which may be the same person) must be willing participants to the grantor's plans.

- *Purchase of Insurance Policy by New Trust.* Grantor establishes a new trust, funding the trust with $Y. Using the grantor's contribution of $Y, the trustee of the new trust purchases the insurance policy owned by the existing trust at its fair market value (i.e., the interpolated terminal reserve value of the policy plus the value of the unexpired premiums, assuming the insured grantor is in good health). If the new trust is a grantor trust with regard to the insured, there should be no transfer for value issue nor should the full value of the policy be included in the grantor's estate, because the transfer of the policy to the grantor trust is disregarded for income tax purposes and not considered a transfer for value. (Rev. Rule 2007-13 [I.R.B. 2007-11, 684])

The foregoing would be true to avoid the three-year inclusion rule under Section 2035 of the code on the distribution of an insurance policy on the life of a grantor from the trustees of a qualified retirement plan if the policy is distributed directly from the plan to an irrevocable trust created by the grantor which is a grantor trust.

- *Purchase of Insurance Policy by Grantor.* Grantor purchases the insurance policy held by the existing trust at its fair market value. Grantor then gifts the purchased life insurance policy to a new insurance trust.
- *Existing Trust Lends Money to New Trust.* Grantor creates a new trust. Trustee of the existing trust cashes in the current life insur-

ance policy and lends the proceeds to the new trust. The trustee of the new trust uses the proceeds from the loan to invest in a new life insurance policy.

- *Existing Trust Merges with New Trust.* Grantor establishes a new trust whose terms are substantially similar to the terms of the existing trust. Trustee of existing trust and trustee of new trust agree through a document of merger or by means of a court order to merge the existing trust into the new trust.

Each of these options involves a number of tax and fiduciary concerns and must be skillfully and professionally attended to.

Life Insurance Policy

Do not:

- provide in a life insurance trust a provision requiring the trustee to use the proceeds of an insurance policy to pay potential transfer taxes. If you do so, the insurance proceeds will be considered an asset of the estate and subject to potential transfer tax;
- leave the proceeds of a life insurance policy to your estate, otherwise the proceeds will be not only subject to claims of creditors but to potential transfer taxes as well (if not held in an irrevocable life insurance trust);
- borrow from the policy more than your cost basis, otherwise you will only pay income tax on the amount borrowed over your cost basis but the entire death benefit will be subject to income tax.

Long-Term Care Insurance

According to the Department of Health and Human Services, at least 70 percent of people over 65 will eventually need long-term care, either at home or in a nursing home, and that can be very expensive. The average stay for a woman entering a nursing home is almost four years; if she's in a semiprivate room, that costs about $270,000 total. A health insurance policy will not cover this kind of care, and Medicare offers very limited coverage. That's why you should consider long-term care insurance if you won't have ample retirement savings or other assets you could tap if needed. If you have long-term care insurance and must enter a nursing home at some point, the total cost of all your premium payments combined will almost certainly be less than the cost of a single year in the home—no matter how many years you've been paying premiums. Learn more at longtermcare.gov. If you want to pursue this coverage, work with an agent who specializes in it, and follow these rules:

- Buy only what is affordable. Do not stretch to buy a policy that covers 100 percent of anticipated future costs. It is far smarter to buy the amount of coverage for which you are sure you can keep making the premium payments. It makes no sense to buy a policy today that you will have to abandon in a few years because it is too expensive; you will get no benefit if that happens. Focus on what is safely achievable: Better to buy a policy that will cover 25 to 50 percent of future costs than no policy at all.
- Insist on an inflation adjustment. The cost of care rises each year; you need a policy whose benefit will also increase. Given the above-average inflation rate for health services, look for a 5 percent annual inflation adjustment.
- Aim for the shortest possible elimination period. This is the time before your policy kicks in; for example, if you have a 30-day elimination period, you'd pay for your first 30 days of care out of pocket. The shorter your elimination period (30 days is a typical minimum), the pricier the policy. If it's 90 days or longer, make sure you have other assets that you could use to pay for your care for that length of time.

CHAPTER 13

The Significance of Your Domicile

*W*here your legal residence is can be a most significant fact in estate planning. Today, many states will reach out to claim not only death taxes, but if they feel that you were a domiciliary there, they will review your income tax records.

This chapter tells you that you can only have one domicile (residence) and it spells out the various ways you can express your intentions so as to avoid potential conflicts. "Actions speak louder than words" is an important motto.

What Is a Domicile?

"Domicile" means whatever place you set up as your permanent residence and make the primary place for your affairs. You can have many residences but only one domicile, which is where you intend to return after you have been away. There is no single explanation that sets forth the criteria for all states. A single definition of domicile would be "a person's residence that is intended to be the permanent residence and not just a temporary one." If you own property in more than one state, you face the possibility of any of the states imposing domicile on you and the tax complications that can accompany it.

Usually, these issues are not raised during your lifetime. However, they can become a concern after your death. Problems can result in litigation and additional expenses to your estate. Once established, your place of domicile continues until your permanent residence is changed. The tax regulations of the states place the burden of proof upon the person asserting a change of domicile to show his or her intention of the change. Your actions, not your declarations, are controlling in determining the facts. The fact that you register and vote in one place is not necessarily conclusive, if in fact, this was done simply to avoid taxation in a jurisdiction. In determining your intention, the length of time spent at a location is significant but not necessarily controlling.

New York Law

The leading case in the state of New York was decided by a New York court in 1908 and still remains the law on the subject. This case provides that a written declaration of domicile shows an intent to establish domicile if it is honest and not given with the intent of deceit.

Florida Residence

When, for example, a retiree chooses his or her Florida residence as his or her domicile, there exists a method of expressing that intention in a very clear and convincing way. A written declaration of domicile is sworn to before a notary public and filed with the Florida circuit court. In the declaration, the individual states that it is to be taken as his or her declaration of citizenship, actual legal residence, and domicile in Florida. The retiree certifies the intent to register at the local Florida address when the registration books reopen and to comply with all other requirements of a legal resident of Florida. He or she certifies that he or she has no intention to return to the former domicile and intends to remain in Florida permanently.

What the Courts Consider

In determining domicile, the courts will look into various factors, including:
- Ownership of dwelling
- Percentage of time spent in the state where the dwelling is
- Homestead tax exemption in states where it applies
- Other real estate holdings
- Occupation or dual occupations
- Business interests and activities
- Filing of tangible and intangible property tax returns
- Voter registration and proof of actually having voted
- Automobile registration
- Driver's license

- Location of bank accounts and safe deposit boxes
- Location of a will
- Recital of domicile in a will
- Ownership of a cemetery lot
- Statement of residence via affidavit
- Church or synagogue membership
- Civic and fraternal club participation
- Union membership
- Charitable contributions
- Children's school attendance records
- Termination of residence by notice to the local taxing office, cancellation of voting registration, change of driver's license, change of auto license plates, and any of the activities showing a legitimate relocation from one state to another

Criteria for Florida

The following is a checklist of some additional actions a person can take to establish a Florida domicile:

- Obtain a Florida driver's license
- Use Florida license plates for the car
- File Florida intangible tax returns each year
- File federal income tax returns using a Florida address
- Use a Florida address for every occasion that an address needs to be given
- Avoid resident memberships in social clubs, religious organizations, and the like in the state of former domicile (those memberships should be converted to nonresident memberships)
- Obtain resident memberships in social clubs, religious organizations, and the like in Florida
- When able, file for Florida homestead exemption
- Maintain safe deposit boxes, bank accounts, and brokerage accounts in Florida and not in the state of former domicile
- Have credit cards and other bill statements mailed to Florida address
- Have Florida address printed on checks, business cards, and letterhead
- Transfer insurance to a Florida broker
- Maintain an office in Florida

- Spend more time in Florida than in other states
- Register and vote in Florida precinct

Probate and Domicile

A layman's inaccurate notions regarding his legal residence can result in his estate being devastated in probate. When holdings are sizable and located in two or more states, you can bet each state will be trying to secure its "probate allocation," unless precautionary steps are taken. Speaking of geography, estate planners often ask clients, Why don't you move to Miami Beach? While asked in jest, there is a serious rationale behind the question, because Florida doesn't have an inheritance tax or income tax, as so many states do. Yes, state death taxes can be a critical problem, but you should not relocate to Florida, or anywhere else, solely to avoid such tax problems.

If there looms a potential conflict, you should create a record containing documentation supporting your intention. Since the states are permitted to determine your permanent residence, you could face a determination from state tax authorities of multiple domiciles. This could mean multiple payments to more than one state of income and potential transfer tax and potential lawsuits.

All of this means that if you have a choice, choose the state with the better tax advantages, for example, Florida versus New York. If you do, you then have to alter your presence and affiliations with each. In one instance, you have to increase your contacts, and in the other, you have to reduce them with a measure of continuity in each case.

Changing your domicile is not simply a game where if you perform certain acts or make certain maneuvers, you are going to succeed. Where your permanent residence is situated is a question of fact, and this is why your actions and not your words are the determining factors.

CHAPTER 14

The Power of the Survivor

*W*hen it comes to an inheritance, the vast majority of our states protect a surviving spouse against receiving less than his or her statutory share of an estate. In most jurisdictions, it is difficult to disinherit a surviving spouse. Usually he or she has the right to make a claim against all of the "assets" of the owner's estate. The current trend of our states has been the widening of these rights by creating laws that add to the estate of a deceased spouse—assets that may have been transferred while he or she was alive solely for the purpose of defeating the surviving spouse's eventual statutory claim.

Today, the laws of the state of New York provide the most favorable treatment for a surviving spouse who does not receive his or her statutory share. Some states permit these rights to be defeated by the creation of certain kinds of trusts.

In order to avoid havoc, litigation, and unnecessary expenses, if you anticipate a problem, an agreement with your spouse specifically providing for his or her rights should be obtained during both spouses' lifetimes through a prenuptial or postnuptial agreement.

An important right provided for by state law available to a surviving spouse is the right to receive a statutory share of a deceased spouse's estate in lieu of, or in addition to, the provisions made in a living trust or will. Forty states and the District of Columbia grant a surviving spouse this right, commonly called the "elective right." Twenty-two of these states include some categories of nonprobate property in calculating the elective share, and twenty-five of these states permit the elective share to be satisfied in whole or in part by a trust or trust equivalent.

In addition, many states have laws that increase a decedent's estate by adding back to the estate certain lifetime transfers such as joint bank accounts, Totten trust accounts, and other revocable transfers against which a surviving spouse may elect. These forms of transfers are commonly called "testamentary substitutes," since they are transfers made during a spouse's lifetime that usually do not pass to the beneficiary of such an account until the death of the person who has created it.

The law of the particular state may exempt certain property such as life insurance proceeds or retirement benefits from the elective right. A survivor's share could be reduced if property that is not exempt is transferred into property that is exempt.

In most common law property states, a spouse is entitled to one-third of the property left by the other spouse. In a few, it's one-half. The exact amount of the spouse's minimum share often depends on whether the couple have children. In some states, the surviving spouse only has to be left a certain percentage of the estate transferred by will. In other states, property transferred by means other than a will, such as a living trust, is included when calculating whether a spouse has received his or her minimum legal share of property.

What happens if a person leaves nothing to a spouse or leaves less than the spouse is entitled to under state law? In most states, the surviving spouse has a choice of either taking what was provided or rejecting it and instead taking the minimum share allowed by state law. Taking the share permitted by law is called "electing to take against the will."

When a spouse elects to take against the will, the property taken comes out of one or more of the bequests given to others by the will (or in many states, other transfer documents such as a living trust, as well). In other words, somebody else is going to get less. So if you don't provide your spouse with at least the statutory share under your state's laws, your gifts to others may be substantially reduced.

The Augmented Estate

As mentioned above, in many common law states, all property of a deceased spouse, not just the property left by will, is considered in determining whether a spouse has been left the statutory share.

This is the concept adopted under the Uniform Probate Code. This is called the "augmented estate." It means that, in determining whether a surviving spouse has been adequately provided for in the estate of the deceased spouse, the courts in most common law property states look to see the value of the property the surviving spouse has received, specifically focusing on the following types of property:

- If a deceased spouse during the marriage transferred property to a third party, but retained a right to some enjoyment over it (possession of income/revocation)
- Property in joint name with a third party with the right of survivorship
- Gifts made in contemplation of death
- Gifts totaling more than a certified amount per year to any one person

These are the types of transfers that are added back for the purposes of calculating the elective right of the surviving spouse.

In most states, the traditional permissive method for funding the elective share is through the creation of an elective share trust. Under such a trust, the surviving spouse is entitled to the income from the trust for life based upon the minimum required amount. As such, if the will of the first spouse to die does not make at least such a provision, the surviving spouse has the right to elect to receive his or her legal portion outright.

In recognition of the rights of the surviving spouse to have direct access to a portion of the estate, many states have been modifying their laws to widen the rights of surviving spouses. In some states, such as New Jersey and Maryland, the spouse's share must be left outright. In other states, like Connecticut, Florida, and Maine, it can be left in trust. The community property states protect survivors' rights through their community property laws. The election afforded in these states centers around the right of the surviving spouse to receive his or her half of the shared property outright. The state of Georgia on the other hand has no protective provision for a spouse as it does not permit a surviving spouse to elect against the first spouse's will.

New York State

Recently, New York State changed its format. Its law is probably the most favorable to a surviving spouse and may lead the way for legislation in other states.

Prior New York law augmented an estate with testamentary substitutes, including gifts made in contemplation of death, Totten trusts, joint bank accounts, property held in joint tenancy, and revocable transfers in which the estate owner retained the power to consume, invade, or dispose of the principal. One purpose of making these nonprobate assets subject to the right of election was to limit the estate owner's ability to nullify the survivor's rights by disposing of assets outside of probate. Another purpose was to reduce the amount of the probate estate that could pass to the survivor under the right of election, if the survivor was also the beneficiary of nonprobate dispositions.

The new law adds to the existing ones the following categories of testamentary substitutes:

- Gifts made after August 31, 1992, and within one year of death that do not qualify for a federal gift tax exclusion and are made after the date of marriage
- For decedents dying after August 31, 1992, U.S. savings bonds held jointly with right of survivorship or held individually by the decedent and payable to a beneficiary other than the decedent or the decedent's estate
- For transactions entered after August 31, 1992, e.g., interests in pension, profit-sharing, individual retirement accounts (IRAs), and other retirement plan benefits (but only one-half of joint and survivor annuity and defined contribution plan benefits)
- Property over which the decedent held a lifetime general power of appointment
- Irrevocable lifetime trusts entered into after August 31, 1992, and the date of marriage, if the decedent retained an income interest or life estate

A sizeable loophole remains, however, due to lobbying by the insurance industry: the deletion of insurance proceeds from the expanded list of testamentary substitutes.

Many experts have suggested that a life insurance investment may be a safe haven under New York law since it is not considered a testamentary substitute. An argument may be made that, if a person obtains a life insurance policy and designates someone other than his or her estate as the beneficiary and the policy is retained until death, a distribution of property within the meaning of the law has been made (as a transfer with retained possession for life) and could be deemed to be a testamentary substitute and, as such, added back to the estate for elective rights.

Elimination of Elective Share Trusts

For decedents dying after August 31, 1992, the most significant change is that the surviving spouse may elect to take the elective share outright. An income interest in a trust or a life estate, such as the right to occupy the family residence for life, will no longer satisfy the survivor's right of election. The price of taking the elective share outright is that, unless the will or trust agreement provides otherwise, the survivor forfeits all beneficial interests in any "terminable interest" for his or her benefit to the extent that the interests exceed the amount of the elective share.

Example, Mary dies on September 1, 1994, with an estate of $900,000 consisting of a $150,000 interest in a house held in joint tenancy with her husband Jack; a $50,000 joint checking account; a $50,000 IRA of which Jack is the beneficiary; and $650,000 of securities. The securities pass to a trust in which Jack has an income interest and the couple's adult children have remainder interests. Under Mary's estate plan, the value of the property passing outright to Jack is $250,000, which is less than one-third of her estate. If Jack elects to take an additional $50,000 outright, he forfeits his income interest in the trust, thereby accelerating distribution of the trust to their children and prompt payment of estate taxes.

Planning Implications

Elimination of the elective share trust recognizes that the surviving spouse is entitled not only to financial support but also to compensation for contributing to the marriage partnership. It puts a surviving spouse in a position similar to that of a divorcing spouse. The similarity complicates estate planning. For example, estate plans calling for QTIP trusts may create a conflict of interest on the part of the person planning the estate for the spouses. The beneficiary spouse should be informed of the option to take a share outright, and a second estate planner may be necessary. Even harmonious relationships may require negotiation between each spouse's adviser in order to draft marital agreements waiving elective share rights.

Members of New York's estate planning bar also opposed the elimination of the elective share trust because it could create havoc with many existing estate planning strategies. For example, trusts designed to provide for children of a prior marriage or to hold the decedent spouse's interest in a closely held business could be sabotaged if the survivor elects to take an outright share.

A spouse's election to take a share outright can thwart marital deduction planning. Take the case of an illiquid estate consisting, for example, of a closely held business interest that is left in a QTIP trust for the transfer of the surviving spouse, thereby deferring potential transfer tax payments on the first spouse's death. The spouses have taken out a second-to-die life insurance policy, which meets the liquidity need for potential transfer taxes when the surviving spouse dies. If the surviving spouse elects to take his or her share of the estate outright (which he or she has the right to do), he or she will forfeit the balance of the interests in a QTIP trust. This could, therefore, accelerate potential transfer taxes to the first spouse's death, and if the forfeited portion is in excess of the applicable exemption, it might require partial liquidation of the estate to meet such potential transfer taxes. If a waiver of a surviving spouse's right of election cannot be obtained, the marital deduction can be preserved by amending a decedent spouse's plan to override the law's forfeiture provision. Thus, despite the survivor's election to take a share outright, the balance of the QTIP trust could remain in trust for the survivor's benefit.

Apparently, the state of New York did not take into consideration certain legitimate reasons for putting money in trust. Under the new law, an older couple cannot get married without a prenuptial agreement and be guaranteed that the property they bring to the marriage will pass to their own children from the first marriage. In addition, the spendthrift or incompetent spouse was not considered.

The most direct method to make sure the will of the first spouse is followed is to have the surviving spouse waive the right of election. The right of election of a surviving spouse is personal to him or her. As such, creditors have no involvement in it. If a spouse should die before exercising the right, the spouse will not have died possessing any property that would be subject to taxation.

The most secure method of limiting a spouse's right is through a prenuptial or postnuptial agreement. Without such an agreement, the only effective way to limit the election, in addition to the creation of exempt property, is the making of outright gifts to third parties.

Some states permit the right to be defeated by the creation of a revocable trust and placing assets in it. However, in the vast majority of states this form of trust will not defeat the right since the grantor maintains possession and control over the property placed in the trust. Some states permit the right to be defeated by transferring assets to an irrevocable trust even if an income interest is retained by the grantor.

It is the law of your permanent residence or domicile at the time of your death that will determine the rights of a surviving spouse with regard to real estate and personal property. With regard to property located outside of your domiciliary state, the law of the situs of the property will govern.

However, the use of a trust may afford you the opportunity to have the law of a jurisdiction other than your domicile apply to certain of your assets. To do this, you can create an irrevocable trust in your selected state and transfer assets located and kept in that state and other states. You can also recite that the law of the designated state will be applicable to the trust.

Percentages Allowed by States

The surviving spouse receives a right to enjoy one-third of the deceased spouse's real property for life in the following states: Connecticut, Kentucky, Rhode Island, and South Carolina.

The surviving spouse receives a percentage of the estate in the following states:

FIXED PERCENTAGE

Alabama	⅓ of augmented estate
Alaska	⅓ of augmented estate
Colorado	½ of augmented estate
District of Columbia	½ of estate
Florida	30% of estate
Hawaii	⅓ of estate
Iowa	⅓ of estate
Maine	⅓ of augmented estate
Minnesota	⅓ of estate
Montana	⅓ of augmented estate
Nebraska	⅓ of augmented estate
New Jersey	⅓ of augmented estate
North Dakota	⅓ of augmented estate
Oregon	¼ of estate
Pennsylvania	⅓ of estate
South Carolina	⅓ of estate
South Dakota	⅓ of augmented estate
Tennessee	⅓ of estate
Utah	⅓ of estate

PERCENTAGE VARIES IF THERE ARE CHILDREN (usually ½ if no children, ⅓ if children)

Arkansas	New Hampshire
Illinois	New York
Indiana	North Carolina
Kansas	Ohio
Maryland	Oklahoma
Massachusetts	Vermont
Michigan	Virginia
Mississippi	West Virginia
Missouri	Wyoming

OTHER

Delaware	$20,000 or ⅓ of estate, whichever is less.

CHAPTER 15

The Subsequent Marriage: Premarital and Postmarital Agreements

*W*hen people have been involved in multiple marriages and there are either more than one set of children or children from a prior marriage, the estate plan is even more complex. In such a situation, the conflict usually centers around the protection of the children from a prior union and the protection of the surviving spouse.

This chapter comprehensively informs you as to what strategies and devices are available, what your goals should be, what the tax ramifications are, and what the rights are of all of the parties.

One of the most common forms of protection and orderly distribution is the premarital agreement, which is universally recognized and in most states requires complete financial disclosure by each of the parties to it.

In finalizing an estate plan for people involved in this kind of situation, the choice of fiduciaries (executors, personal representatives, and trustees) and the application of the tax law is extremely important.

The conflict that can be presented by a subsequent marriage is the wish to provide an economic benefit to the surviving spouse, while making sure that property is available for the descendants of a prior marriage. To solve this dilemma, assets can be left in trust for the lifetime benefit of a surviving spouse with the children receiving the ultimate distribution after his or her death. However, in some instances where the spouse may not be much older than the descendants, the value of the money over a long period of time may mandate that the beneficiaries should get their inheritance, even after the impact of transfer taxes thereon, in the first instance. In this type of situation, probably the best method is providing an inheritance for each beneficiary of a specific sum or specific property based upon his or her needs without worrying about the tax aspect of the gift or having any relationship to the percentage of the entire estate.

The Choice of Fiduciaries

The choice of the executors or personal representatives and trustees in any estate plan is usually one of the hardest decisions faced by an estate owner. Naming a surviving spouse or child by a prior marriage can create conflicts. Usually, in this situation, some independent person is asked to serve either together with the family members or alone.

The Marital Deduction

From a tax deferral standpoint, most estates are helped by the use of the marital deduction. Since 1982, the tax law has permitted a marital deduction for qualified terminable interest property (QTIP). This allows the property to be placed in a trust for the benefit of the surviving spouse, who has a qualified income interest for life, with the guaranty that the ultimate disposition of the remainder balance will pass to those designated by the estate owner. One problem related to a QTIP is that, if the property in the trust is not productive, the surviving spouse has the right to demand that it be made so. A conflict can arise if, for example, property in the trust consists of an interest in a business that does not pay any dividends. See chapter 9 for a detailed discussion of the QTIP trust.

The Tax Clause

Who pays the potential transfer taxes when the subsequent surviving spouse dies is a very significant element in estates of this nature. This problem is obvious when different groups (spouse and descendants from a prior marriage) are sharing in the estate. Great caution must be taken to be sure that the potential transfer taxes are apportioned among the parties properly, especially when the surviving spouse controls the situation.

The following is a hypothetical example of how a situation can create a totally different result than the estate owner intended:

The estate owner desires to favor his surviving spouse with a lifetime interest in a QTIP trust that will pass to her children upon her death.

The will or living trust of the estate owner provides for the residuary or the rest of his estate to pass to his children. The estate owner's living trust or will provides that all potential transfer taxes will be paid out of the residuary of the estate without apportionment. If the executor or trustee does not elect to qualify the QTIP trust for the marital deduction, the property in the trust could be fully taxed in his estate and the residuary estate would bear the payment of the taxes. His children would wind up paying the potential transfer taxes on an inheritance that is to be eventually received by the children of the surviving spouse, who would inherit the same, free of transfer tax.

The Rights of a Surviving Spouse

In most common law states, the surviving spouse has a right to some portion of a deceased spouse's estate. Many states have rules requiring that at least a minimum share of the estate of the first spouse to die be transferred either outright or in a qualifying form to the surviving spouse. If the surviving spouse does not receive the minimum share, he or she would have a claim against the estate. The required percentage of the estate that is protected varies with each state. The net effect of these statutes is the limitation of the estate owner to transfer assets to others.

Life Insurance

An excellent way to protect children from a prior marriage and still provide an economic benefit to a spouse is through life insurance. This can be structured favorably insofar as potential transfer taxes are concerned by having a third party, such as an irrevocable trust, own and be the beneficiary of the insurance policy. Ownership of this kind will provide the surviving spouse with the benefits of the trust during lifetime and will pass on potential transfer taxes after the trust terminates to the children of the insured spouse. A trust of this kind must contain a provision that the benefits of the trust will only be paid to the spouse if he or she is married to and living with the insured spouse at the time of death. If the parties are not married or are separated at such time, the trust can provide for the benefit to revert to the descendants of the insured spouse.

Charitable Bequests

If there are no descendants and the first spouse to die is charitably inclined and wishes to guarantee that the property will eventually pass to a particular hospital, museum, or university on the second spouse's death, the living trust or will of the first spouse can be drafted to take advantage of both the marital deduction and the charitable deduction. This would completely shield the assets from potential transfer taxes. There are basically two ways to accomplish this, detailed below.

Annuity Trust or Unitrust

The will or living trust can create either a charitable remainder annuity trust or a charitable remainder unitrust. In either case, the income portion of the trust would be payable to the surviving spouse for his or her life. On the surviving spouse's death, the remainder must be paid to one or more "qualified charities" as defined in Section 501(c)(3) of the code. The decedent's estate will be entitled to a marital deduction for the surviving spouse's income interest and a charitable deduction for the remainder interest.

There are problems with this approach, however. The complicated rules of this type of trust limit the amount of income that may be paid to the surviving spouse, and the rules governing charitable remainder trusts prohibit any invasions of principal (other than to satisfy the income requirement).

QTIP Trust with Charitable Beneficiary

A simpler way is if one or more "qualified" charities are named as the remainder beneficiaries of a QTIP trust. All of the trust income is payable to the surviving spouse, and the decedent's will or living trust can provide that the principal be invaded under certain conditions for the surviving spouse's benefit. The first spouse's estate receives a potential transfer tax marital deduction for the full value of the QTIP. On the second spouse's death, the value of the trust is included in his or her taxable potential transfer tax estate but is offset by a full charitable deduction.

The unique issues that are raised by a subsequent marriage make it imperative that they be reviewed in advance. Waiting until after remarriage may be too late.

Premarital Agreements

A premarital agreement is often employed when the partners have been previously married. This type of agreement controls the distribution of assets in the event of death. It can also provide for financial and housing benefits in the event of a dissolution of the marriage. The use of premarital agreements should be considered whenever one of the parties is contemplating making a substantial gift to the other or where it is desirable to limit the statutory, common law, or community property rights of each party to the other's property or to limit or eliminate other claims of one against the other.

In some instances, the agreement does not focus on legal rights and duties, but rather, serves as a statement of the marital goals and relationship sought by the parties. This type of agreement may be incorporated into the more conventional type of premarital agreement.

In its common form, the premarital agreement involves a transfer, or the promise of a transfer, of property from a more affluent party to the other less affluent party. The promised transfer may be by living trust or will. If so, it does not preclude a larger gift than promised.

The agreement should really be considered as part of the estate plan of both parties and should be evaluated in terms of its legal estate, gift, and income tax consequences, the appropriate potential transfer tax reduction techniques, and general policy considerations. These considerations are discussed below.

Validity of Premarital Agreements

As a general rule, in order to be valid under state law, a premarital agreement involving property rights must be in writing, subscribed to by the parties, and acknowledged with the formalities required for the recording of a deed. In addition, it must be fairly arrived at and be fair and reasonable, both when entered into and at the time of any future trial involving the respective parties.

Because of the difficulty in defining "fairness" and "reasonableness," as well as the uncertainty created by the requirement that the agreement be fair at some future date, a number of states now require instead that the agreement not be "unconscionable." Proving unconscionability is harder than proving unfairness. The Uniform Premarital Agreement Act adopts the standard of unconscionability.

Both parties must make a full and fair disclosure of all their income and property. If one or both fail or refuse to make the required disclosure, any agreement entered into may be open to later challenge by the injured party. Even when disclosure has not been made, it has often been held that the party attacking the agreement had sufficient knowledge of the defendant's assets through other means.

An agreement may be challenged based on a claim of fraud, duress, or taking advantage by putting financial pressure on a less advantaged spouse, but these claims are not easy to prove. However, the closer to the date of marriage that an agreement is signed, the more likely it is that a claim of duress or overreaching will be upheld.

There is no requirement that each party be represented by a separate attorney. However, when one attorney represents both parties, the courts will scrutinize the agreement more carefully, particularly if the agreement is one-sided or if there was a lack of disclosure. The education and business experience of a party waiving separate representation is also taken into account.

It is becoming more common to videotape the actual signing of the agreement. The opposing attorneys examine each party to establish that the person signing read and understood the agreement, had the opportunity to consult with his or her attorney, and signed voluntarily.

Postmarital Agreements

Even if the parties marry without having entered into a premarital agreement, many states permit spouses to alter their rights through a properly executed postmarital agreement. The bargaining power of the "richer" spouse in a second or subsequent marriage, after the marriage has been solemnized, is diminished in contrast to the bargaining power of the "poorer" spouse. For this reason, the more advantaged spouse should generally strive for a premarital agreement.

Postmarital agreements may be much more useful where (1) neither spouse has been married before and the couple has been married (not necessarily happily) for some time, (2) no premarital agreement has been executed, and (3) the richer spouse controls nearly all of the marital assets. In these cases, both the "richer" and "poorer" spouses may have something to gain through a postmarital agreement. The richer spouse will be able to protect himself by reducing his or her estate's "exposure" in the event of death or divorce. The poorer spouse, for the first time during the marriage, will receive outright ownership of valuable assets without risking a divorce (so long as he or she waives state-law spousal rights). Though this might appear somewhat unattractive, a spouse who has control over very few assets might be willing to waive future assets in return for a sizeable sum of money or property that he or she could currently control or enjoy.

Another circumstance for a postmarital agreement is where one of the spouses believes that the premarital agreement may be defective and unenforceable (by reason, for example, of inadequate disclosure of the richer spouse's assets).

The Subsequent Marriage: Premarital and Postmarital Agreements

Still another circumstance where postmarital agreements make sense is where one spouse wishes to indicate that a particular asset of the marriage belongs to him or her, free from any interference by the other, either during the marriage or in the event of divorce. This is often done with interests in a family business. As compensation for giving up rights in the family business, the other spouse frequently will receive nonbusiness assets. These nonbusiness assets are usually less risky from an economic point of view but also less likely to produce income or gain.

It is imperative in this situation that each party be represented by separate counsel.

❖

CHAPTER 16

Planning for Minors

*P*lanning for minors (those under eighteen years of age) requires special estate planning. Since minor children cannot normally hold title to property, making gifts to, or for the benefit of a child, involves income, gift, and potential transfer tax considerations.

This chapter details the different options that are available and the ramifications as to whether to make a gift outright or place it in a trust.

If you have young children, you must be prepared in case a disaster should hit before they are capable of being legally and emotionally responsible for their affairs. A guardian might have to be appointed for their persons and property.

Guardians

In most states, a guardian of the person and property of a minor must be named in a will and cannot be designated in any other estate planning device, e.g., the living trust. The guardian selected by you must be approved by the court, which has the right to overrule your designation if it is in the best interests of the minor. An alternate guardian should be named in case the primary guardian does not serve.

Before designating a guardian, it is important to discuss your decision with the designated person to be sure he or she will serve if called upon.

In most states, minor children cannot own property outright. If you leave property outright to a minor child, the child will receive it when he or she is eighteen years old. However, you can designate a guardian to manage the property until the minor reaches eighteen years of age.

The guardian of the person, if financially responsible, can be designated to serve in the capacity of guardian of the property as well.

Trusts

You may also leave property to a child in a trust. If it is established in a living trust, the property avoids probate. If you leave property in a will, the property will go through probate before it is turned over to the trust.

Gifts to Children: Custodianship

Since minors cannot hold title to property, if you make a gift to a minor during your lifetime, it must be made pursuant to a state regulation. Many states employ the Uniform Gifts to Minors Act (UGMA), which permits you to give a gift to a minor by giving the gift to a custodian who holds title to the property for the benefit of the minor.

The UGMA covers gifts of money, securities, life insurance, and annuities. You can stipulate that the property is to be turned over to the minor at either age eighteen or twenty-one. In California (under the Uniform Transfer to Minors Act), it can be extended to age twenty-five. Some states also allow you to make gifts of realty, partnership interests, and tangible personal property in this fashion.

A custodian is given the power to invest, accumulate, or expend income or principal for the support, education, and benefit of the minor without regard to the parent's resources, obligation of support, or to the minor's other resources. Income from custodial property is taxed to the minor, but if used to discharge a parent's obligation of support, it will be taxed to the parent. In addition, the income tax effects are different for minors under and over the age of fourteen. (See "kiddie tax," discussed later in this chapter.)

A custodianship allows the minor access to funds at a relatively early age. If this is not your intention, you might prefer to set up a trust instead.

Unearned Income of Minor Children (Kiddie Tax)

The net unearned income of a child under age eighteen is taxed at his or her parent's top marginal rate. The source of the income is irrelevant. Therefore, gifts of income-producing property to minor children may not result in any overall income tax savings for you. However, all income of children age eighteen or older is taxed at the standard tax rates.

Unearned income is anything that is not derived from personal services. It includes the following:

- Social Security or pension benefits to the extent they are includable in gross income

- Income from assets held in a Uniform Gift to Minors Act custodianship
- Income from assets in a trust that is distributed to the child

Presently, the net unearned income for children under eighteen (18) is the amount of the child's unearned income generally taxed at the parents' top marginal rate if such income exceeds the sum of the $950 standard deduction and the greater of $950 or the itemized deductions directly connected to the production of such investment income (the "kiddie tax").

Because the unearned income of children age eighteen (18) and over is taxed at the child's lower rate, you should make gifts to them which defer taxable income until the child reaches age eighteen (18). These are some ways of deferring unearned income through gifts:

- Growth stock that typically pays little in current dividends but is likely to increase in value over the years. The child can sell the stock after age eighteen (18) and be taxed at the child's rate.
- U.S. government savings bonds (EE) with maturity dates after the child reaches age eighteen, unless the child already holds such bonds and has elected to treat each year's accrual of interest as income. This election is irrevocable, even for newly purchased bonds. If no such election has occurred, the child may defer the interest on the bonds until age eighteen (18) and then be taxed at his own rate.
- Since younger children will effectively be in the same tax bracket as their parents, investment strategies that make sense for you (e.g., municipal bonds) probably make equal sense for them.

Gifts to Children: Trusts

Trusts may accumulate income for a minor and still qualify for the annual exclusion ($14,000) as long as all principal or income is paid to the minor by the age of twenty-one (21). Trusts paying all income to the minor and trusts with withdrawal power also qualify for exclusion.

If you are planning to make gifts to minor children, you may find the flexibility of a trust more suited to his or her purposes than the custodianship discussed in the previous section. Tax considerations, as usual, must be taken into account. Several alternate forms of trusts are discussed below.

Section 2503(c) Trust

The Code Section 2503(c) provides a vehicle for creating a trust for the benefit of a minor that qualifies for the annual gift tax exclusion ($13,000). This section provides that a gift to an individual under age twenty-one (21) will not be treated as a gift of a future interest (a gift from which the beneficiary will not have any present enjoyment and is thus not eligible for the gift tax annual exclusion) if the gift meets these requirements:

- The trustee has the power to expend the gift property and its income for the benefit of the minor before he or she reaches age twenty-one (21)
- The minor has the right to receive the unexpended property and income at age twenty-one (21)
- If the minor should die before age twenty-one, the principal and income of the trust must be paid to the minor's estate or to persons he or she chooses (by will or otherwise)
- If you are concerned about potential estate tax liability, you should not name yourself as a trustee since the trust will be considered part of your estate if you die before the minor reaches the age of twenty-one (21)

While a trust offers certain advantages over a custodianship in some situations, these differences narrow in states that have expanded the class of property includable under a custodianship. For most middle-income older people contemplating modest gifts to grandchildren, the custodianship is probably preferable.

Section 2503(b) Trust

The Internal Revenue Code provides another method, under Section 2503(b), for making a gift to a minor (age 21) in trust that qualifies for the annual exclusion. This type of trust must be irrevocable and need only provide that all income be paid to the minor currently. The value of the gift is the value calculated under actuarial tables of the minor's right to the income of the trust during its term.

If you are a grandparent setting up such a trust, you may not wish to pay the income directly to the minor and, indeed, may have to pay it to a guardian in many states. Instead, the income can be made payable to the minor's parents to be expended for the minor's benefit, or the income could be paid to a custodial account for the minor.

Again, the expenses of setting up and administering this type of trust, as well as its advantages, should be compared with a custodianship.

Discretionary or "Crummey" Trust

An elderly grandparent may not find either of the preceding trusts to his or her liking. The Section 2503(c) trust requires distribution of the principal by age twenty-one (21) and sometimes earlier. The Section 2503(b) trust requires distribution of income from the outset. A third alternative gives the trustee discretion to distribute or accumulate income and, in addition, to give the minor the power to withdraw the property transferred to the trust for a reasonable period of time after the gift is made.

The minor's power to demand distribution of the property constitutes a present interest, and therefore, gifts to the trust qualify for the annual gift tax exclusion ($13,000).

As the grantor, you are required to alert the beneficiary of his or her power of withdrawal and to allow a reasonable time for its exercise or waiver of the right of withdrawal. Thirty days' notice is considered reasonable. There is no need to appoint a legal guardian on behalf of the minor beneficiary, but the trust must not present any legal barrier to such an appointment.

To be sure that there is no potential gift tax liability to a minor beneficiary if the withdrawal power is in excess of $5,000, the trust must provide that the minor will eventually receive the property upon the termination of the trust at his or her stated age or that the minor can control its disposition by his or her will (by a power of appointment) if he or she should die before the trust's termination date.

The Crummey trust offers the person seeking to provide funds for young children the greatest flexibility by permitting discretionary use of income and delaying distribution of the principal of the trust beyond majority without forfeiting the annual gift tax exclusion.

The best way to establish a trust for a child, which is to take effect after your death, is in a living trust. If you wish, you can create a separate trust for each of your children. Your successor trustee will manage the trust and use the trust's property for the benefit of the child until he or she attains the age you designate is the termination date, at which time the trust property is turned over to the child.

❖

CHAPTER 17

Estate Planning for Families with Children Who Have Special Needs

$\mathcal{E}$state planning for families that have a child with special needs must take into consideration a multitude of emotional, physical, and financial issues. This requires consideration not only of the child but of the family as a whole.

The only effective way to protect a special-needs beneficiary and ensure no loss of his or her government assistance is through the use of a trust fund. The type of trust fund and its important provisions are set forth in this chapter in detail. Included are sample trust provisions that should be contained in a trust of this kind for it to be legally and practically effective.

Each family must develop an estate plan that is tailored to the specific needs of all of its members, including the child with special needs. It is of particular importance to consult with professionals experienced in this unique kind of estate planning.

Who Is Going to Take Care of My Child?

The most important concern expressed by parents of a child with special needs is who will take care of their child when they are no longer here. Parents often find themselves asking questions such as, "What are my choices in designing a financial plan that can provide for my child in order to meet any possible future needs?" and "How can I establish a funding mechanism to pay for any needed services, and how can I be sure that these funds will be used for the benefit of my child without jeopardizing his or her entitlements to governmental benefits?"

If you die without a living trust or a will, your estate will be disposed of according to the laws of the state of your residence. If you have a spouse and children, the spouse will typically get a specific portion and the children the balance. If you have no spouse but only children, they will receive all of your property. When property passes to children in this manner, it is divided equally among them, whether or not they need it and whether or not they are competent and able to manage it. Thus, parents of a child with a disability are likely to wish for some different manner of distribution. These persons must have a living trust or a will.

Through their testamentary dispositions, parents can divide up their property however they think best, perhaps giving a larger share to the most needy child, which may be the one with a disability. There could be, however, several significant problems with this approach, such as the following:

- The disabled son or daughter may not have the capacity to manage property left to him or her outright.
- Property left outright to disabled persons will be counted as their assets and thus may make them ineligible for certain governmental benefits in which eligibility is based on need and a limitation of income and assets (SSI and Medicaid).
- With the additional assets counted as their own, disabled persons receiving governmental services may be subject to charges for care. Thus, in many ways, leaving assets directly to a handicapped person who would otherwise be eligible for governmental benefits is very much like making a gift to the government.

What Are the Goals?

In the creation of every plan by a family, there are two overriding and paramount considerations:

- The assurance that, no matter what is formulated, the disabled person does not lose or become disqualified for applicable entitlement programs
- To the extent legally possible, the family assets, including the disabled persons share, are kept out of the reach of governmental authorities providing services to that person

Planning Early

Successful family planning in this regard must begin at the time the family becomes aware of the handicapping condition, whether it be at birth, at the commencement of an illness, at the occurrence of an accident, or at the final diagnosis of a disability.

Creating a Fund

The focal point in the planning for a handicapped person's needs is a fund. The form and structure of this fund must be in such a manner that it will not be considered a resource that would disqualify the handicapped person from receiving entitlement benefits.

Federal Entitlement Programs

The most important federal programs are those based upon the recipient's financial need. The two most significant are (1) Supplemental Security Income (SSI), for aged, blind, or other persons with disabilities having limited income and resources, and (2) Medical Assistance, also known as Medicaid.

SSI and Medicaid Eligibility

Eligibility for SSI and Medicaid benefits rests not only upon the fact that the individual possesses some type of disability, but also upon the fact that the individual has limited income and resources. The vast majority of persons who qualify for SSI will automatically qualify for Medicaid. For a more detailed discussion of Medicaid, see chapter 23.

SSI Transfer of Assets

Federal legislation ("Legislation") establishes no penalty period for applicants or recipients of SSI who transfer or give away their resources similar to the one imposed on applicants for institutional Medicaid benefits. The SSA does, however, notify the local Medicaid agency of any transfer of assets by any SSI applicant.

The law also provides, however, that if the transfer is made to a Supplemental Needs Trust, no penalty can be imposed; therefore, SSI eligibility would not be jeopardized. (This planning opportunity applies only to people under sixty-five [65] years of age.)

"In-Kind" payments of food, clothing or shelter are considered income for SSI eligibility purposes. A recipient of payments of this kind may experience a substantial reduction in SSI benefits.

Although the Legislation does not specifically address transfers of income, the new system clarifies that a transfer of income in the month of receipt, such as an inheritance, is considered a transfer of resources.

SSI Income

The social security regulations define income as anything a person receives, in cash or in-kind, that he or she can use to meet his or her needs for food, clothing, or shelter. There are two types of income: earned income and unearned income.

The regulations exclude certain items from their definition of income, one of which is the proceeds of a loan.

Loans

Since the proceeds of a loan are not considered income for SSI purposes, support to a disabled person should be made in the form of a loan, rather than on a gift basis (which is considered unearned income). By treating this assistance as a loan, the person will avoid reduction in his or her SSI benefits. It is advisable to sign a loan agreement that reflects the understanding that the value of the assistance must be repaid, although a clear and provable oral agreement will suffice. However, local legal requirements for creating an enforceable loan must be observed.

For example, a disabled SSI recipient who may not have the legal capacity or ability to enter into a loan agreement may nevertheless be capable of receiving a loan, if state law holds that person liable or responsible for the reasonable value of necessities provided to him or her.

Any portion of borrowed funds that the borrower does not spend will be considered a countable resource or asset of the borrower, if he or she retains it into the month following the month of receipt. Therefore, in making advances to the disabled person under the terms of a loan agreement, caution should be exercised in not giving a larger amount than the person can spend before the end of the month. A loan should be made near the beginning of the month and the cash earmarked for certain monthly bills, which will also ensure that no carryover balance develops.

Resources

Resources or assets are defined as cash or other liquid assets or any real or personal property that an individual owns and could convert to cash to be used for his or her support and maintenance.

An individual is eligible for SSI benefits if his or her available resources do not exceed certain limitations, plus a burial allowance and all other eligibility requirements are met, which requirements include income limits for an individual living alone and, for a couple, living by themselves. If an individual lives with others, the income limit is different, as well as a couple who live with others.

Pursuant to the 1996 law passed by New York State, all preneed funeral agreements established on or after January 1, 1997, by SSI applicants or recipients must be irrevocable. Under the provisions of the law, any amount can be put into an exempt, irrevocable, preneed funeral agreement, and none of the funds will be counted by Medicaid or SSI as resources or income.

This prepayment must be deposited with the funeral director into a single irrevocable trust fund. The 1996 law removed the prior distinction between burial-space items, which could be prepaid in any amount, and non–burial-space items, which previously could be prepaid. At any time prior to the actual services being rendered, the funeral director or the arrangements can be changed.

It is important to note that resources of even $1 more than the threshold amount will result in the denial of benefits. Many times parents create an account for a child in the permissible amount, forgetting that very shortly, interest will accumulate and that the accumulation will render the individual ineligible. That $1 may result in the loss of $300 to $400 in benefits. If the individual is in a group home, even more may be lost in benefits.

Assets of the Handicapped Person

Due to the fact that qualification to obtain benefits under the entitlement programs is based upon the unavailability of income and resources, a person with special needs must, in effect, be disinherited so as to be able to qualify.

These limitations create complexities in dealing with resources that are actually owned by a handicapped person. These assets must be disposed of prior to that person's application for benefits. These problems become further complicated if the person has a substitute or surrogate decision-maker such as a guardian.

Guardianship

Many parents fear that their child will be unable to make decisions regarding his or her personal affairs or will be unable to protect his or her own legal and civil rights without help. They, therefore, consider guardianship. Guardianship results in either a total or partial loss of rights and decision-making power for the handicapped individual. Therefore, families must seriously consider the disadvantages, as well as the advantages, before requesting the appointment of a guardian.

Guardianship is a most serious measure for safeguarding a disabled person's welfare and should be resorted to only when no less drastic option (such as informal guidance and advice, a special bank account, a trust, or a representative payee) will work. Guardians are appointed by a court, and state law prescribes the standards that must be satisfied before a guardian is appointed.

Guardianships may be total or limited. In a total ("plenary") guardianship, the ward may lose many legal rights, including the right to vote, to make contracts, to sign checks, and to choose whether and where to go to school. The ward also may lose the right to manage any property and assets. When a total guardian is appointed, the ward loses all of his or her decision-making authority, even though there may be decisions he or she is capable of making.

Limited Guardianship

A limited guardian has powers only in the areas specified by the court's guardianship order. In order to properly limit the guardian's role, the court first determines where the disabled person needs help and then empowers the guardian to make decisions for the ward in those areas.

For example, in some limited guardianships, the guardian is given authority to make decisions regarding the ward's medical and educational needs, while the ward can still control the other areas of his or her life.

Unless the guardianship has been limited, the guardian will manage all of the person's personal and financial affairs. If the handicapped person is mildly or moderately disabled and capable of making some of his or her own decisions, guardianship may do more harm than good, as the loss of independence might undermine his or her efforts to manage his or her own life. However, if a person is severely or profoundly disabled, the loss of rights may be no loss at all, as he or she would not be able to exercise them anyway.

Third-Party Assets

In the family's development of a plan, assets that may pass to the disabled person upon the death of a third party must be traced and identified. These items can be in the nature of the following:

- Life insurance policies
- Pension benefits
- Bank accounts
- IRA accounts
- Stocks and bonds registered under the Gifts to Minors Act

Assets of this kind, like income and resources, have to be detoured and rerouted away from outright ownership and inheritance by a handicapped person.

Therefore, if a handicapped person is not to own resources or assets, gifts to such a person cannot be made whether by will or otherwise. If such a gift is made, the guardian of the ward could seek the authority of the court to remove the ward's share.

Renunciation of Inheritance

Can a special-needs person make a partial renunciation of an inheritance in order to retain medical eligibility? The answer used to be yes. Under OBRA 93, the answer is no.

Moral Gifts

Many parents and many planners believe that a simple way to approach the problem of disinheritance is to make gifts, either outright or by inheritance, to the siblings of the handicapped child. Such a transfer would be accompanied by a written expression on the part of the parents as to the use and purpose of these funds for the benefit of the disabled person during his or her lifetime.

For a multiple of reasons, many of them obvious, this process should be carefully considered before going forward. For example:

- These funds would be subject to all claims by creditors of the person to whom the funds are given.
- They can be the subject of matrimonial claims by a spouse of such a person.
- They can become involved in the business reversals of such a person.

- Lastly, temptations, even by the strongest of persons, might cause these funds to be used for purposes other than those originally intended.

Trust Fund

The best available alternative to ensure that there is a "contingency fund" in existence to care for and assist the handicapped person during lifetime is to create a discretionary trust fund, whether created by will or an inter vivos irrevocable trust. The fund must be structured with the view toward insulating it against the rights of the authorities seeking reimbursement for services rendered to the disabled person under the existing entitlement programs.

The trust can be established providing the disabled child with a lifetime interest (life estate) in the trust income and principal. Upon the death of the beneficiary, the balance remaining in the trust fund should pass to the children of the disabled beneficiary or, if there are none, to the beneficiary's siblings or, if there are none, to other designated beneficiaries. During the term of a trust of this kind, the grantor can provide in the trust agreement for the benefits from it (income and principal) not used for the beneficiary with special needs to be sprinkled or sprayed to the siblings of the disabled beneficiary or to other family members.

Who Should Be the Trustee?

The trustee should, if possible, have an understanding of the handicapped person's needs and also sufficient financial expertise to invest and manage the trust's assets intelligently. If there is no one person known with both of these qualities, a trustee who is close to the family should be given the right to consult with and retain expert financial advisors. If a substantial amount of money is involved, an institution with expertise in trust management can be named to act as the "financial or corporate cotrustee" and a trusted friend or relative to act as "personal cotrustee."

A family member who would be paid a fee is a preferable selection. The payment of the fee reduces the grantor's reluctance to impose the role of "surrogate parent" on the person. The fee can also operate to strengthen the person's sense of responsibility.

However, these same close relatives may well be the eventual recipients of the principal of the trust upon its termination. Sometimes, this can lead to an apparent conflict of interest, and such a selection must be given careful consideration.

The Grantor's Intention

The trust should contain a provision with language reciting the intent of the grantor of the trust. Such a clause would state:

> It is my intent that the beneficiary shall receive all government entitlements that the beneficiary would otherwise be entitled to but for distribution of income and principal from this trust. I recognize that in view of the vast costs involved in caring for a disabled person, distribution of income or principal to the beneficiary would be rapidly dissipated in the absence of the governmental benefits the beneficiary now receives or in the future would be entitled to. The trustees are strictly prohibited from distributing income and principal to the beneficiary if such distribution will serve to deny, discontinue, or reduce a government benefit which the beneficiary would otherwise receive. The income and principal shall thus only be used for those times of need of the beneficiary that will not be paid for by government entitlements. It is my intent that the beneficiary enjoy the maximum advantages of life and at the same time receive government entitlements.

A discretionary trust should clearly provide that the trustees are to use the assets to supplement and not to replace or supplant available government aid.

The Discretion of the Trustee

The basis upon which states rely when ordering a trustee to reimburse an agency or an institution for services provided deals with the scope of the trustee's discretion. The trust instrument, therefore, must provide that the trustees have absolute and uncontrolled discretion with regard to paying from the income or principal for the benefit of the beneficiary. Under a clause of this kind, a true discretionary trust is created, and the right of the beneficiary to receive any benefits does not exist. This protects both the undistributed trust income and the trust property from any third-party claims. Under this circumstance, an agency or institution would be unable to secure the aid of a court in compelling the trustee to reimburse it for services provided to the beneficiary, because the right of the beneficiary to these funds would not exist.

It is also difficult to predict over the beneficiary's lifetime (1) the cost of his or her care, (2) the amount of government aid he or she will receive, (3) what his or her state of health will be, and (4) the amount of the trust fund at the time of the demise of the grantor. Because the beneficiary's situation may change during his or her lifetime, it is additionally important that the trustees be able to provide for his or her changing needs. For these reasons, discretionary powers are more appropriate than imperative powers.

Escape Clause

In every trust instrument, a provision should be inserted which is called "an escape" or "fail-safe" clause. This clause would provide that the trust be made terminable upon any attempt by any creditors (including authorities seeking reimbursement for services provided) to reach the trust fund. This would revoke the trust if such an event took place and would distribute the principal of the trust to the remainder beneficiaries. Such a clause would state:

> If at any time the trustees are directed by a court of competent jurisdiction to distribute the income or principal to the beneficiary such that the beneficiary would lose a government entitlement, this trust shall be void ab initio (from inception), and all remaining principal and accumulated income shall be distributed forthwith to the remainder beneficiaries.

Such a clause protects and preserves the principal in case the law should change after the creation of the trust.

Predeath Termination Clause

If a highly functioning disabled adult may overcome the disability later in life, a predeath termination clause should be considered. Likewise, a "failed work" test clause should be provided to retrigger the noninvasion clauses of the trust and retain the principal if the disability is not overcome. A sample predeath termination clause would be as follows:

> The trust shall terminate, at the discretion of the trustee, prior to the death of the beneficiary, if the beneficiary is substantially gainfully employed, for a continuous period of two years, and the treating physician certifies in writing, that the disability no longer limits the beneficiary from being substantially gainfully

employed. At that time, 10 percent of the accumulated income and principal shall be distributed absolutely to the beneficiary. For each consecutive year of substantial gainful employment, an additional 10 percent of accumulated income and principal shall be distributed absolutely to the beneficiary. If there is a break in consecutive employment, the distribution test will be reinvoked. If there is no break in consecutive employment, in the last distribution year, the trust shall terminate with the distribution of all accumulated income and principal to the beneficiary, as the purposes of the trust will have been fulfilled.

Spendthrift Clause

The trust should also contain a provision preventing the beneficiary from pledging or encumbering the trust assets, thus preventing any creditor, including the state, from acquiring the assets in the trust. This is referred to as a spendthrift clause, and it is a valuable safeguard in the event that a beneficiary incurs significant debts.

Sprinkling Benefit Clause

The trust can provide the trustees with the ability to sprinkle or spray the benefits of the trust (income and principal) to other members of the family (siblings) or to organizations or persons providing services to the beneficiary. Such a clause would state:

> The grantor further authorizes the trustees, at their sole and absolute discretion, to pay or apply any income not so paid or applied to or for the benefit of a beneficiary, and/or members of his or her immediate family, to or for the benefit of the siblings of the beneficiary, per stirpes, for their support, maintenance, and care (and the children of the siblings if any sibling should not be living at such time); such payments or applications may be made in such amounts and proportions, without any obligations to make equal payments or applications, as the trustees shall, in their sole and absolute discretion determine, from time to time, to or for any facility, the beneficiary may be residing in and/or to any organization where the beneficiary may be a client or a participant in any program(s) sponsored by them, as the trustees shall determine, for the general uses of such facility and/or orga-

nization at such time or times, as shall be determined by the trustees, at their sole and absolute discretion. Any income not so paid over or applied as aforesaid shall be accumulated and added to the principal of the trust at least annually and thereafter held as a part thereof.

Housing Clause

With the current public policy toward deinstitutionalization, most disabled adults will not be institutionalized. Support groups across the country are working with government agencies to secure alternative housing for the disabled. Once this housing is established, the government entitlement programs will fund ongoing care through SSI or Medicaid. In the beginning, "start-up" monies may be needed, and trustees should be given the right to use trust funds for this purpose. Provisions related to this should be limited to "creating" housing and not "maintaining" housing, because SSI and Medicaid funds are not available for capital purchases of housing facilities.

To encourage nonprofit organizations or individuals to provide housing for the disabled adult child, the trust may include a special bequest to the provider of housing. Following is sample language for such a bequest:

> (_____ percent) to the organizations or persons who have provided appropriate housing for my disabled child in appreciation for those services. The total amount of this bequest or gift shall be equitably prorated by my trustee to such organizations or persons based on the number of years my disabled child was provided housing.

Irrevocable Inter Vivos Trust

Family members might consider establishing during their lifetimes an irrevocable inter vivos trust fund for a child with special needs. The fund could be set up with a modest or minimal sum. Upon the death of the grantor, additional assets could be added or poured over into the trust.

A device of this sort can serve two purposes: (1) it can be established, tested, and fine-tuned while everyone is alive, and by the time of the grantor's death, he or she will know that an ongoing functioning fund is in existence for a knowledgeable successor trustee; and (2) it can act as an existing fund to which legacies and gifts can be given by family members during their lifetimes and/or upon their deaths.

Supplemental Needs Trusts

The Supplemental Needs Trust discussed in this chapter is universally employed as a planning device for persons with disabilities in order to protect their government entitlements.

The states have protected these discretionary trusts from liability to the beneficiary's creditors and preserved eligibility for public assistance when the purpose of the trust has been found to provide the beneficiary with needs supplemental to those provided by governmental programs. Therefore, the trust instrument should state that its purpose is not to provide the primary care of the beneficiary, but rather for his or her supplemental needs and comfort. Examples of supplemental care needs might include grooming aids and other items relating to personal care; reasonable travel and related expenses to allow relatives and friends to visit the beneficiary and, if appropriate, allow the beneficiary to visit relatives and friends; reasonable expenses to assist the beneficiary in participating in recreational programs not otherwise provided where he or she resides; medical, dental, educational, therapeutic, and other professional services not paid for by private insurance or any governmental program; and expenses of a family member or friend to determine whether the needs of the beneficiary are being satisfied and, if necessary, to act as an advocate on his or her behalf. This last function may be very important if an appropriate person is available after the death of both parents. The advocate might visit the beneficiary at his or her residence to inspect living conditions; ensure that the beneficiary's educational, social, training, and medical programs are appropriate; evaluate additional needs; and ensure that trust funds or governmental entitlements are properly expended for the beneficiary.

At the end of this chapter are illustrations of an inter vivos Supplemental Needs Trust suggested by the Supreme Court of Kings County, State of New York, as well as language for a testamentary Supplemental Needs Trust that would be set forth in a will.

Insurance

In connection with funding a trust, families whose assets are limited should consider life insurance. Whatever the need for insurance is in a normal family situation, the presence of a disabled member, who will need perpetual care, totally changes the equation.

Life insurance can create an instant estate to provide adequate security, if governmental care is not desired or if the disabled person is, or for any reason may become, ineligible for governmental care. For many, life insurance will be the single most effective way of ensuring financial security for a dependent who needs a lifetime of care. After all, the government may someday reduce or do away with its funding, and only private funds would be available for a handicapped beneficiary.

Medicaid: OBRA 93

OBRA 93 recognizes the need to protect disabled persons during their lifetimes, even when they receive assets that would otherwise make them ineligible for Medicaid. The law protects proceeds received by a handicapped person from a successful lawsuit and provides for trusts to be created as follows:

- A trust containing the assets of an individual under age 65 who is disabled and which is established for the benefit of such individual by a parent, grandparent, legal guardian of the individual, or a court if the State will receive all amounts remaining in the trust upon the death of such individual up to an amount equal to the total medical assistance paid on behalf of the individual under a State plan under this title.
- A trust containing the assets of an individual who is disabled that meets the following conditions:

(i) The trust is established and managed by a nonprofit association. (Various not-for-profit organizations have established "master trusts" for this purpose.)

(ii) A separate account is maintained for each beneficiary of the trust, but for purposes of investment and management of funds, the trust pools these accounts.

(iii) Accounts in the trusts are established solely for the benefit of individuals who are disabled, by the parent, grandparent, or legal guardian of such individuals, by such individuals, or by a court.

(iv) To the extent that amounts remaining in the beneficiary's account upon the death of the beneficiary are not retained by the trust, the trust pays to the State from such remaining amounts in the account an amount equal to the total amount of medical assistance paid on behalf of the beneficiary under the State plan under this title.

These two sections present unusual planning opportunities for disabled persons who meet the defined criteria. Under these sections, it is permissible to fund these described trusts with "assets of a disabled individual." There is no limitation as to how those assets are acquired by the disabled person. Therefore, assets could be received from a settlement or a judgment from litigation, or an inheritance or assets acquired by the individual through earnings or investment prior to disability.

Pursuant to these provisions, upon the death of the disabled person, the trust funds will be applied to repay the state for its Medicaid outlay and any excess assets would pass to family members.

Trust Agreement

This TRUST AGREEMENT made this _____ day of _____, _____ (DATE), between (NAME), as Guardian of the property of (NAME) as "Grantor," and (NAME) as "Trustee" is established pursuant to an Order of the Supreme Court of the state of New York, (CNTY) County. The "Grantor" (NAME) currently resides at (ADDRESS). The "Trustee" (NAME) currently resides at (ADDRESS).

1.0   Trust Name: The Trust shall be known as the (NAME). The purpose of the Trust is that the Trust's assets be used to supplement, not supplant, impair or diminish, any benefits or assistance of any Federal, State, County, City, or other governmental entity for which the Beneficiary may otherwise be eligible or which the Beneficiary may be receiving. The Trust is intended to conform with New York State EPTL 7-1.12.

1.2   Declaration of Irrevocability: The Trust shall be irrevocable and may not at any time be altered, amended, or revoked without Court approval.

1.3   EPTL 7-1.6: EPTL 7-1.6 or any successor statute, or any similar statute of any jurisdiction, shall not be applied by any court having jurisdiction of an inter vivos or testamentary trust to compel against the Trustees' discretion, the payment or application of the trust principal to or for the benefit of (BENEFICIARY), or any beneficiary for any reason whatsoever.

2.0   Administration of Trust During Lifetime of Beneficiary: The property shall be held in trust for the Beneficiary, and the Trustee shall collect income and, after deducting all charges and expenses attributed thereto, shall apply for the benefit of the Beneficiary, so much of the income and principal (even to the extent of the whole) as the Trustee deems advisable in his sole and absolute discretion subject to the limitations set forth below. The Trustee shall add the balance of net income not paid or applied to the principal of the Trust.

2.1   Consistent with the Trust's purpose, before expending any amounts from the net income and/or principal of this Trust, the Trustee shall consider the availability of all Benefits from government or private assistance programs for which the Beneficiary may be eligible. The Trustee, where appropriate and to the extent possible, shall endeavor to maximize the collection and facilitate the distribution of these benefits for the benefit of the Beneficiary.

2.2   None of the income or principal of this Trust shall be applied in such a manner as to supplant, impair, or diminish any governmental benefits or assistance for which the Beneficiary may be eligible or which the Beneficiary may be receiving.

2.3   The Beneficiary does not have the power to assign, encumber, direct, distribute, or authorize distributions from this Trust.

2.4   Notwithstanding the above provisions, the Trust may make distributions to meet the Beneficiary's need for food, clothing, shelter, health care, or other personal needs, even if those distributions will impair or diminish the Beneficiary's receipt or eligibility for government benefits or assistance or if the Trustee determines that the distributions will better meet the Beneficiary's needs, and that it is in the Beneficiary's best interests, notwithstanding the consequent effect on the Beneficiary's eligibility for, or receipt of, benefits.

2.5   However, if the mere existence of this authority to make distributions will result in a reduction or loss of the Beneficiary's entitlement program benefits, regardless of whether the Trustee actually exercises this discretion, the preceding paragraph (2.4) shall be null and void and the Trustee's authority to make these distributions shall terminate and the Trustee's authority to make distributions shall be limited to purchasing supplemental goods and services in a manner that will not adversely affect the Beneficiary's government benefits.

2.6   Additions to Income and Principal: With the Trustee's consent, any person may, at any time, from time to time, by Court order, assignment, gift, transfer, deed, or will, provide income or add to the principal of the Trust created herein, and any property so added shall be held, administered, and distributed under the terms of this Trust. The Trustee shall execute documents necessary to accept additional contributions to the Trust and shall designate the additions on an amended Schedule A of this Trust.

3.0   Disposition of Trust on Death of Beneficiary: The Trust shall terminate upon the death of (BENEFICIARY) and the Trustee shall distribute any principal and accumulated interest that then remains in the Trust as follows:

3.1   The New York State Department of Social Services, or other appropriate Medicaid entity within New York State, shall be reimbursed for the total Medical Assistance provided to (BENEFICIARY) during his lifetime, as consistent with Federal and State Law. If (BENEFICIARY) received Medicaid in more than one State, then the amount distributed to each State shall be based on each State's proportionate share of the total amount of Medicaid benefits paid by all States on the behalf of the Beneficiary.

3.2   All remaining principal and accumulated income shall be paid to the legal representative of the Estate of the Beneficiary.

4.0   Trustee: (NAME) is appointed Trustee of this Trust. If for any reason, (TRUSTEE) is unable to or unwilling to serve as Trustee, then (NAME) shall serve as Successor Trustee, subject to the approval of the Supreme Court, (CNTY) County.

4.1   Consent of the Trustee: A Trustee shall file with the Clerk of the Court (CNTY) County, a "Consent to Act" as Trustee, Oath and Designation, duly acknowledged.

4.2   Bond: The Trustee shall be required to execute and file a bond and comply with all applicable law, as determined by the Supreme Court (CNTY) County.

4.3   Resignation: A Trustee may resign by giving written notice, a signed and acknowledged instrument, delivered to (i) the Supreme Court (CNTY) County; (ii) the Guardian of the Beneficiary, if any; and (iii) the Beneficiary. The Trustee's resignation is subject to the approval of the Supreme Court (CNTY) County.

4.4   Discharge and Final Accounting of Trustee: No Trustee shall be discharged and released from office and bond, except upon filing a Final Accounting in the form and manner required by Section 81.33 of the Mental Hygiene Law and obtaining judicial approval of same.

4.5   Annual Accounting: The Trustee shall file during the month of May in the Office of the Clerk of the County (CNTY), an annual report in the form and manner required by Section 81.32 of the Mental Hygiene Law.

4.6   Continuing Jurisdiction: The Court shall have continuing jurisdiction over the performance of the duties of the Trustee; the interpretation, administration, and operation of this Trust; the appointment of a successor Trustee; and all other related matters.

4.7   Powers of Trustee: In addition to any powers that may be conferred upon the Trustee under the law of the state of New York in effect during the life of this Trust, the Trustee shall have all those discretionary powers mentioned in EPTL 11-1.1 et seq., or any successor statute or statutes governing the discretion of a Trustee, so as to confer upon the Trustee the broadest possible powers available for the management of the Trust assets. In the event that the Trustee wishes to exercise powers beyond the express and implied powers of EPTL Article 11, the Trustee shall seek and obtain judicial approval.

4.8   Appointment of a Successor Trustee: Appointment of a successor Trustee not named in this Trust shall be upon application of the Court.

4.9   Compensation of Trustee: A Trustee shall be entitled to such compensation as may be allowable under the laws of the state of New York. In addition, the Trustee shall be entitled to be reimbursed for reasonable expenses incurred by the Trustee in the administration of this Trust.

5.0   Miscellaneous Provisions: [to be used as needed]

5.1   Governing Law: This Trust Agreement shall be interpreted and the administration of the Trust shall be governed by the laws of the State of New York; provided, however, that Federal law shall govern any matter alluded to herein which shall relate to or involve government entitlements such as SSI, Medicaid, and/or other Federal benefit programs.

5.2   Notifications to Social Services District: The Trustee shall provide the required notification to the Social Services District in accordance with the requirements of section 360-4.5 of Title 18 of the Official Regulations of the State Department of Social Services, and any other applicable statutes or regulations, as they may be amended. These regulations currently require notification of the creation or funding of the trust;

notification of the death of the beneficiary; and, in the case of trusts exceeding $100,000, notification in advance of transactions that substantially deplete the trust principal (as defined in that section).

5.3   Savings Clause: If it is determined that any provision hereof shall in any way violate any applicable law, such determination shall not impair the validity of the remaining provisions of the Trust.

5.4   Usage: In construing this Trust, feminine or neuter pronouns shall be substituted for those of the masculine form and vice versa, and the plural for the singular and vice versa in any case in which the context may require.

5.5   Headings: Any headings or captions in the Trust are for reference only, and shall not expand, limit, change, or affect the meaning of any provision of the Trust.

5.6   Binding Effect: This Trust shall be binding upon the estate, executors, administrators, and assigns of the Grantor and any individual Trustee, and upon any Successor Trustee.

IN WITNESS WHEREOF, the undersigned have executed this Agreement as of the date and year first above written.

DATED: GRANTOR:

                                                _____

                                                (NAME) as Guardian of the Property of (NAME)

DATED: TRUSTEE:

                                                _____

                                                (NAME) (TRUSTEE)

STATE OF NEW YORK   )
) ss.:
COUNTY OF NEW YORK   )

On the _____ day of _____, in the year __, before me, the undersigned, personally appeared _____, personally known to me or proved to me on the basis of satisfactory evidence to be the individual(s) whose name(s) is/are subscribed to the within instrument and acknowledged to me that he/she/they executed the same in his/her/their capacity, and that by his/her/their signature(s) on the instrument, the individual(s), or the person(s) upon behalf of which the individual(s) acted, executed the instrument.

                                                _____

                                                NOTARY PUBLIC

STATE OF NEW YORK   )
) ss.:

COUNTY OF NEW YORK   )

On the _____ day of _____, in the year 200__, before me, the undersigned, personally appeared _____, personally known to me or proved to me on the basis of satisfactory evidence to be the individual(s) whose name(s) is/are subscribed to the within instrument and acknowledged to me that he/she/they executed the same in his/her/their capacity, and that by his/her/their signature(s) on the instrument, the individual(s), or the person(s) upon behalf of which the individual(s) acted, executed the instrument.

_____

NOTARY PUBLIC

SCHEDULE "A" To Supplemental Needs Trust

Schedule of Assets

Suggested Language for Last Will and Testament

[ARTICLE #]: I give and bequeath (the sum of $_____ or _____ percent) of my estate to my Trustee hereinafter named as a Supplemental Needs Trust for the benefit of (name of beneficiary). My Trustee shall hold, manage, and reinvest the same bequest and shall have the sole and absolute discretion to expend or not expend principal and/or income for the benefit of said beneficiary, subject to the following purposes, terms and conditions:

A.   My Trustee shall hold, manage, invest, and reinvest these funds and collect the rents, interest, dividends, and other incomes therefrom. My Trustee, in consultation with the lifetime guardian of said beneficiary, shall pay the income and/or principal from this trust fund after proper charges and expenses to the guardian of the person or property of said beneficiary, or directly to a service or property provider for the benefit of said beneficiary, as requested by [his/her] guardian. My Trustee is authorized to pay from the income and corpus of this trust any sums that may be needed or useful in enhancing the lifestyle of said beneficiary, or for any costs or expenses [he/she] deems of extraordinary or compelling necessity. Any distribution from this Trust shall be at the sole discretion of the Trustee and not subject to court review.

B.   Payments by my Trustee for the benefit of the person or property of said beneficiary shall be made subject to the following uses and conditions:

1 (a) It is the testator's intent to create a Supplemental Needs Trust that conforms to the provisions of section 7-1.12 of the New York Estates, Powers, and Trusts law. The testator intends that the trust assets be used to supplement, not supplant, impair, or diminish, any benefits or assistance of any Federal, State, County, City or other governmental entity for which the beneficiary may otherwise be eligible or which the beneficiary may be receiving. Consistent with that intent, it is the testator's desire that before expending any amounts from the net income and/or principal of

this trust, the Trustee consider the availability of all benefits from government or private assistance programs for which the beneficiary may be eligible and that, where appropriate and to the extent possible, the Trustee endeavor to maximize the collection of such benefits and to facilitate the distribution of such benefits for the benefit of the beneficiary.

C. None of the income or principal of this trust shall be applied in such a manner as to supplant, impair, or diminish benefits or assistance of any Federal, State, County, City or other governmental entity for which the beneficiary may otherwise be eligible or which the beneficiary may be receiving.

D. Neither income nor the principal in the hands of my Trustee, before the interest and/or principal is actually paid or delivered to the guardian of or for the benefit of said beneficiary, shall be subject to voluntary or involuntary anticipation, encumbrance, alienation, or assignment, either in whole or in part, nor shall such interest be subject to any judicial creditors or claimant of said beneficiary.

E. The beneficiary does not have the power to assign, encumber, direct, distribute, or authorize distributions from this trust.

F. Certain needs of said beneficiary may be provided for by my Trustee from the income and/or principal, including additional food, clothing, or health services not provided; stereos, tape recorders, VCRs, television sets, or other electronic items; vacations; trips; and birthday and holiday gifts, or similar tangible items, if they are not otherwise provided by governmental financial assistance and benefits or by the provider of services.

G. Notwithstanding the provisions herein, the Trustee may make distributions to meet said beneficiary's need for food, clothing, shelter, or health care even if such distributions may result in an impairment or diminution of said beneficiary, receipt or eligibility for government benefits for assistance but only if the Trustee determines that (i) said beneficiary's needs will be better met if such distribution is made, and (ii) it is said beneficiary's best interests to suffer the consequent effect, if any, on said beneficiary's eligibility for or receipt of government benefits or assistance.

H. However, if the mere existence of the Trustee's authority to make distributions pursuant to this subparagraph shall result in the beneficiary's loss of government benefits or assistance, regardless of whether such authority is actually exercised, this subparagraph shall be null and void and the Trustee's authority to make such distributions shall cease and shall be limited as provided in paragraphs two and three above, without exception.

I. In making any distribution to or for the benefit of said beneficiary, the Trustee should consider what benefits said beneficiary may be entitled to from any governmental agency, including but not limited to Social Security Administration benefits, Veterans Administration benefits, Medicaid (including medical assistance and day-treatment program assistance), and Supplemental Security Income benefits. I request that my Trustee assist said beneficiary in collecting, expending, and accounting separately for all such governmental assistance benefits but not commingle them with the trust fund.

J. This trust shall terminate upon the death of said beneficiary. Upon the termination of this trust, my Trustee is directed to pay such portion of the burial costs and expenses including the cost of a burial lot and a marker of said beneficiary, not covered by insurance or otherwise from [his/her] property other than the income and principal of this trust and to pay over and distribute the remaining principal and any accrued and accumulated income as follows: (Insert provisions for distribution of the remaining assets in the trust.)

Sample Language to Dispose of Remaining Assets in the Trust

(A) If not otherwise provided for, a sum to cover burial expenses, including plot and grave marker.

(B) The balance of the principal and remaining income of the trust shall be paid in equal shares to my other children then surviving and to the issue of my deceased children, per stirpes and not per capita.

CHAPTER 18

Persons with the Risk of Acquired Immune Deficiency Syndrome (AIDS)

*T*here are a multitude of factors that must be taken into consideration with regard to the special interests of persons with AIDS. These include the mental state of the individual, the special relationship that partners have, and the nature of their relationships with their families.

Safeguarding the estate from potential challenges (will contests) from other family members has to be a primary goal. The living trust can be the foundation for an effective plan and will serve to dissuade potential claims.

The Need to Plan Is a Must

The AIDS virus attacks the immune system. Therefore, the individual becomes vulnerable to a host of other potential diseases, such different forms of cancer, pneumonia, and diseases that invade the nervous system and eventually cause brain damage. Approximately two-thirds of AIDS victims develop dementia, which is an impairment of the intellectual function of the mind in the areas of language, emotions, and judgment. However, these problems taken individually do not mean that a person afflicted with this disease lacks testamentary capacity (the ability to create a legal will). Testamentary capacity is a legal standard. It is incumbent upon every attorney to determine if his or her client is capable of making a will. Most of the persons who contract this disease are relatively young (approximately only 10 percent are over sixty [60] years of age).

The ever-increasing number of persons afflicted by this disease calls for a special focus on estate planning in this segment of our population. In this category, one of the main goals is to protect against successful challenges. Homosexual males are the principal victims of AIDS. Drug users and some heterosexual individuals are victimized as well, but under normal conditions, they will not require a special focus on their estate plans beyond their providing for incapacity. The need for special planning arises out of the relationships that homosexuals have with their companions. A 1990 U.S. Census survey of the nation's 91 million households shows that 2.6 million are unmarried heterosexual couples, and 1.6 million are couples of the same sex. In the vast majority of situations, the laws of this country do not afford these people any rights at all except on an isolated basis. Therefore, unmarried couples have a greater need to address estate planning than married couples. For a married couple, in most instances, laws of the state take over when no planning has been done.

In the main, our states have no laws that authorize a marriage between homosexuals. The courts of some states have permitted the legal adoption of one homosexual by another. Some state courts have refused adoption to take place where it is discovered that there exists a homosexual relationship. The rationale is that if the court granted an adoption, the person seeking the adoption could be subject to criminal liability for abuse or incest of the adoptee. Adoption legally granted would provide the adopted person with the status of a child with respect to inheritance rights. In certain communities housing is subject to rent control and only family members may succeed to the benefits of the original tenant. In 1989, New York State's highest court held that a long-lasting relationship between homosexuals living together in a rent-controlled apartment satisfied the family succession requirement of the law. In the same year, the City of New York extended city-employee insurance coverage to homosexual companions. In San Francisco, laws provide for the registration of homosexual couples, giving those registered insurance and other benefits that they would not otherwise be entitled to. In Austin, Texas, a recent policy permitted health insurance benefits to be extended to domestic partners. This is further indication that estate planning for unmarried couples is quite different than for married couples.

Legal and Liability Considerations

The requirements and concerns in this kind of estate planning include, but also go far beyond, the status of the relationship between the individual and his or her family—whether it be good, caring, or strained. There are also potential liability questions that have to be considered. It has been reported that the estate of Rock Hudson was held accountable for large damages for failure to disclose to his companion that he suffered from AIDS. This may lead to the legal responsibility of disclosure not only to long-term partners but to short-term relationships as well.

Financial Concerns

Due to the prospect of extremely large medical costs throughout all phases of the disease, including hospital and custodial care costs, and the loss of earnings that will accompany the disabling effects of the disease, the following should be considered:

Cash value life insurance acquired while the person is insurable can later be withdrawn to fund these costs. Policies that have recently emerged offering living benefits should be investigated. Health care providers can be designated as beneficiaries of the insurance policies to pay for the costs of care while the person was alive.

Retirement plans can be invaded to generate cash flow. A person should consider the use of these vehicles to the extent allowed and should create these funds as well and take advantage of the tax benefits. Medicare covers those aged sixty-five and older and is not available to the vast majority of this population.

The availability of Medicaid is dependent on financial need. Benefits and eligibility requirements vary from state to state. As set forth elsewhere in this book, there are minimum levels of financial assets one can own before qualifying. This program is for the indigent. However, one can qualify after impoverishing oneself once the appropriate penalty period has transpired.

Advanced Directives

Many victims of AIDS accept their terminal prognosis and express a desire to limit medical treatment. As such, living wills and health care proxies are extremely important to permit their wishes to be carried out and to have no extraordinary procedures prolong their lives (see chapter 21). In addition, much emotion and pain will be avoided if the question of the disposition of the remains of the person are addressed during his or her lifetime. In most states, the directions of a person as to his or her funeral and burial arrangements will generally be strictly followed. A durable power of attorney should be in place in anticipation of the time when a victim of AIDS will not be able to manage his or her affairs.

Wills

If disinheritance of a family is the main theme of the will, it must be properly drafted and executed to achieve this result. If a homosexual is legally married, the rights of a surviving spouse have to be addressed so that he or she will not take action against the will. This can be dealt with in advance by a waiver.

Challenges

The main challenge to a will is focused on the failure of proper execution. Therefore, all of the formal requirements of the state in which it is made should be observed and documented. The second most frequent challenge is that the estate owner was unduly influenced to make out a will that resulted in a distribution in favor of the person doing the influencing. Given the fact of the many biases that are rampant in this country, the estate owner has to anticipate that the rationale employed by a court will be on traditional social standards and attitudes as opposed to what is becoming socially acceptable today.

An attorney should prepare and supervise the execution of the will. The execution should be memorialized in a memorandum. If the testator is hospitalized or is known to be ill, and because the disease in many instances brings on dementia and depression, a physician might be present and attest to the competency of the testator in a signed statement. If at all possible, the physician should be one who has known the testator over a period of time and has some experience with AIDS. Witnesses to the will should not be related to the testator, and they should at the same time execute an affidavit attesting to proper signing of the will in accordance with the laws of the state in which it was signed. A film or video could be made of the execution of the will.

A challenge may be brought on the grounds of undue influence on the part of the companion of the testator. In other words, the question that could be raised is, Is that the will of the testator or is it the will of someone else? It must always be established that the will is the voluntary independent expression of the person. If the attorney was selected by the testator, so much the better, but if the beneficiary/companion recommended the attorney, care must be taken to establish and show the lawyer/client relationship that exists is with the person whose will is executed and not the beneficiary. The beneficiary should not participate in conferences with the attorney. Meetings should take place at the attorney's office with office associates as participants and witnesses, and whatever can be done should be done to document that the will was the independent act of the person who created it. The establishment of a bequest to a possible challenger with a disinheritance clause if that person challenges the will is an effective will provision and an effective technique to discourage a will contest.

Trusts

The use of a living trust is an important consideration. It is more difficult to upset a trust than a will.

AIDS victims, in making dispositions of their property, usually have two main testamentary objectives: (1) the provision of security for the victim's companion for a period of time (life or a term of years); and (2) after this period, to provide benefits for remainder persons (relatives or charity). An irrevocable trust for a term of years or life of the companion, followed by a gift to other beneficiaries, can serve this purpose. The nature of the relationship of the parties will determine the term of the benefits.

If an irrevocable trust is created, gift taxes based on the full value of the property at the time the trust is created will be due, but they may be offset or reduced by the unified credit. If the beneficiary is an AIDS victim, his or her interest may be short-lived, and by the same token, the vesting of the trust property in the remaining beneficiaries will be sooner than might otherwise be expected.

Life Insurance

Life insurance may be important for several reasons. It is a way of providing benefits to the victim's companion without costs and probate.

There may be a question of insurability if the insured person dies within the contestable period. As with a will, a challenge could be made on grounds that the beneficiary designation was made under undue influence, having been made at a time when the insured was mentally impaired as a result of his or her disease. The timing of the making of the beneficiary designation is therefore important.

Certain kinds of group term insurance offered under company plans or by professional groups may be obtained without evidence of insurability. This kind of life insurance can accomplish the desired goal.

Joint Purchase of Property

A joint purchase of property by the AIDS victim and beneficiary may be extremely significant. The property is purchased from a third party with the AIDS victim acquiring a life income interest and the other party a remainder interest. Each party pays out of his or her own funds the full value of his or her interest actually determined. The transfer tax benefit lies in the victim's shorter actual life expectancy as against the life expectancy assigned by Internal Revenue Service tables for the purpose of determining the value of the life and remainder interests.

Lifetime Gifts

If the AIDS victim holds or is about to acquire property or funds in his or her own name, he or she might want to consider placing it in joint ownership with his or her companion. The gift would be subject to gift tax and the full value of the property would then pass to the survivor at death. Probate would be avoided, and the gift would be voidable only if the challenger were able to prove fraud on the part of the companion.

Lifetime gifts under the umbrella of the $13,000 annual gift exclusion and the unified credit are other options open to the AIDS victim. Both the creation of a joint tenancy and an outright gift of property under the annual exclusion ($13,000) can serve to save potential transfer tax.

Standard Guardianship

The AIDS situation stresses the requirement of the designation of a guardian for a child of a parent who has a terminal or incapacitating disease. To settle this problem, the state of New York in 1992 enacted legislation that permits an individual who is dying, incapacitated, or is at risk becoming so, to petition the court for a standby guardian. The authority of the guardian covers both the activities of the relative of the incapacitated person (a child) during his or her lifetime (the incapacitated person) and after his or her death. The state of Florida has also enacted comparable standby guardian legislation.

This kind of law affords comfort to a single parent who, anticipating this kind of debilitating situation, can witness the designation of a guardian during his or her lifetime.

The basic formats and devices that are involved in estate planning for persons with AIDS are, in most instances, similar to planning for any other person. Special needs in estate planning arise because laws that are not applicable to same-sex partners create a difference between their legal rights and those of the rest of the people in this country.

For the professional who reads this chapter, remember that "an ounce of prevention is worth a pound of cure." The anticipation of a "contest" starts with the first visit to your office and must be anticipated from that moment on.

The GRIT

There are several devices that are suitable to same sex couples under current Federal Law. One of the most significant is the grantor retained income trust (GRIT). The technique affords an ability to transfer assets, at a discount, to a less wealthier spouse or partner. The gift is of a remainder interest and the applicable gift tax credit may be used in calculating the gift tax. If the grantor survives the term of the trust the trust assets pass to the beneficiary with no further gift or potential transfer tax, as there is no retained interest. If the grantor dies during the term of the trust, value is included in the grantor's estate. Any applicable credit previously used in computing the gift is restored to the estate of the grantor.

If a reversion factor is included (the grantor's earlier death) in computing the value of the gift, the value of the gift is reduced by the value of the reversion.

❖

CHAPTER 19

Surrogate Planning for the Senior Citizen

*T*he graying of America means that many more people are facing the issues of aging. It was anticipated that by the year 2000, 35 million people (approximately 13 percent of the total population) will be over the age of sixty-five. Furthermore, in approximately thirty years, this group could make up over 20 percent of the national census. It is, therefore, important to consider nonfinancial aspects of estate planning.

The process of estate planning encompasses more than mortem and postmortem decisions. A complete estate plan will include the preparation of surrogate instruments or advance directives. These lifetime tools provide advanced planning in the event of your losing the capacity to make decisions. This is all the more important in today's society as a result of the medical advances that are allowing many of us to outlive our mental capabilities.

Competent adults have the right to make decisions regarding their own health care, including the right to refuse life-sustaining treatment. This right is based upon the common law right to give or withhold consent based upon the Fourteenth Amendment's right to liberty. Advance directives such as health care proxies or living wills afford these rights to a person who does not have the capacity to make such decisions by designating a surrogate or an agent to make medical and health care decisions for them.

If you become incapacitated and cannot make health care or financial decisions, another person will have to make these decisions for you. Therefore, you have a few choices. If you do nothing, the people closest to you will have to seek legal help by petitioning the court for the appointment of a guardian or conservator. This type of proceeding, because of the costs and time delay, should be avoided if at all possible.

The second choice is to create the advance directives while you are healthy and select those who will act for you when you cannot act for yourself. If nothing else, the cost savings, in comparison to the court costs, is enough of an impetus for you to act when you are able.

Health Care Decisions

Living trusts, like health care proxies, are types of advance directives. The rationale behind giving a third party the right to make your health care decisions is that when you are mentally incapacitated, you are entitled to the same rights you had when you were competent. These rights include the right to refuse medical care services. No one can be required to undergo any particular surgical procedure or be forced to take a medication. This is true, as well, as far as life-sustaining measures are concerned. A person who has capacity can refuse all life-sustaining procedures. Our courts have upheld an individual's right to refuse food and hydration.

Most of our states have created, by statute, a special durable power of attorney for health care decisions. A few states have created a general durable power of attorney that permits you to authorize your agent to make your health care decisions in the event that your mental capacity deteriorates.

Property Management

If you no longer have the mental capacity to act in a competent manner, the management of your property is at risk. The techniques that will ensure the orderly management of your assets center around the durable power of attorney, joint tenancy, and the living trust.

Most of the problems created by powers of attorney that lack appropriate powers can be circumvented by the creation of a living trust. In addition, even though the states generally recognize each others' laws, on powers of attorney, there are differences. In Florida, only blood relatives can serve as an attorney-in-fact. Certain states do not permit springing powers. In Georgia, a power of attorney automatically survives incapacity unless provided otherwise, whereas in most states it is not durable unless specifically set forth in the instrument.

To avoid the costly problem of guardianship and court intervention, there is no better method to deal with the orderly management of your entire affairs than the living trust. The assets are in place and no marshaling is necessary. Your trustees can act from the moment of your incapacity and the trust will continue in existence until after your death and be used to distribute the assets thereafter. This is quite different from a power of attorney, which automatically terminates upon your death.

Because of potential tax liabilities (gift and income), joint tenancy should only be implemented between nonspouse cotenants and between spouses for small bank accounts. With the durable power of attorney and living trust, there is no transfer of assets and no such exposure to transfer and income tax liabilities.

The Family Limited Partnership ("FLP") is also a useful planning device. By retitling assets out of your name, both the living trust and Family Limited Partnership avoid the necessity of probate and the need for a guardian. Both of these techniques provide a vehicle for succession planning. Assets such as real estate and securities and even life insurance may be placed into the FLP. A person's residence should not be transferred to an FLP because of the potential loss of the availability of income tax benefits, such as deductions of interest and real estate tax and the sheltering of gains through the available exemption. One method of avoiding loss of those benefits is to transfer the residence to the FLP subject to a retained life estate with the reservation of a special power of appointment. In such a case, the income tax benefits would be applicable and the heirs of the estate owner would receive an asset with a stepped-up basis, and it would be includable in the estate for potential transfer tax purposes.

Advance Directives

The vast majority of deaths in this country occur in institutions. This creates the distinct possibility of being kept alive by artificial means when there is no hope of survival except by those methods. Most people prefer to die with dignity rather than subject themselves and their families to this process. By the use of advance directives, you can set the stage for a time when you cannot act yourself, as to the use of life-support systems.

The alternatives are as follows:
- Do or say nothing (This will require the use of life-support systems to keep you alive as long as possible)
- Clearly direct that artificial means should not be employed to prolong life
- Create a durable power of attorney or health care proxy and designate to an agent the authority to make such decisions
- You can set up thresholds for discontinuing artificial life support in your living will or health care proxy

What Is a Living Will?

A living will is not a will in the sense that we understand that term. It is nothing more than an instrument that expresses your intentions regarding the use of life-support systems if you are terminally ill and there is no hope for recovery.

State laws vary and the document may have other powers. A living will is directed to medical decisions. Under it you do not designate anyone to make decisions; you simply express your wishes if certain circumstances were to exist. The application of the living will is narrowed to the use of life-support systems. As states have developed durable powers of attorney or health care proxies, the use of living wills has been reduced, as these documents allow you to express your wishes and designate someone to be sure they are carried out.

Most people, to be certain that their wishes are understood and carried out, will create both a living will and a health care proxy. In such cases, the living will serves as a guide and supplement to the agent under the proxy instrument.

Many states have adopted statutes to honor the living will. The state of New York has not done so, but recognizes the contents of them by case law. Living wills have been accepted by courts of various states in dealing with health care matters for an incompetent individual.

Where Should a Living Will Be Kept?

A living will should be kept separate from the health care proxy but accessible to friends and family. Friends and family members who are likely to stay in touch with the patient, despite his or her incapacity, are desirable custodians for a living will, in addition to the appointed health care agents.

A related question is how to keep living wills current. Periodic review is desirable because values and feelings about what constitutes an acceptable existence may change over time. Maintaining living wills among tax files or other routinely handled documents helps to keep them visible for annual review and revision as desired. If you travel extensively, you might want to take a copy with you.

Health Care Proxies

A health care proxy is a document that provides for all health care aspects, not just life-sustaining measures. Many states have adopted health care proxy or surrogate decision-making statutes. These documents permit an agent to make a broad range of health care decisions for a person. The living will and the health care proxy are not incompatible documents. Depending upon state law, the provisions of a living will outlining life-prolonging measures can be incorporated into a health care proxy.

In New York, a properly appointed health care agent can be authorized to make any or all health care decisions for a particular person by the use of a simple document known as a health care proxy. It can be exercised without any need for clear and convincing evidence of the person's wishes, a notable change in New York law.

A health care proxy is a type of advance directive. Advance directives are oral or written directions concerning the health care desired once a person has lost the capacity to make decisions.

The New York State statute mandates that the following four elements be in the proxy document:

1. Names of principal and agent
2. Statement of intent that the agent is to have authority to make health care decisions on behalf of the principal
3. Signature and date by the principal or another acting on the principal's behalf
4. Two witnesses who observe the execution and sign below the statement that "the principal appeared to execute the proxy willingly and free from duress"

The statute provides a form that has been adopted and distributed by the State Department of Health. It also permits the use of customized documents, as long as they include the above elements.

Capacity Presumed

Almost any adult can execute a health care proxy, because the capacity to do so is legally presumed.

In New York, an agent's authority can take effect only during periods of the principal's temporary or permanent decisional incapacity. Unlike some other states, New York does not allow for a person to authorize the agent to act at a time when he or she has decision-making capacity.

The New York statute permits you to limit the agent's authority by including health treatment instructions. Such instructions might limit the agent's authority in decisions involving surgery or might specify the agent's powers regarding the use of artificial nutrition and hydration.

If you want to grant an agent unlimited discretion concerning, for example, artificial feeding, you need only indicate that the agent "knows my wishes concerning artificial nutrition and hydration."

At a minimum, copies of health care proxies should be distributed to the named agent, substitute agent, and personal physician. It is preferable to distribute them also to family members and friends. If others are likely to be involved in treatment, such as a local hospital or treating specialists, copies should be delivered to them for inclusion in your medical records. A note taped to your driver's license or wallet card can be used to indicate the existence, name, and telephone number of the health care agent.

Agent decision-making procedures are wholly inconsistent with both the underlying doctrine of self-determination and agency principals. If your wishes are "reasonably known," the agent must make decisions consistent with your wishes. If your wishes are "not reasonably known and cannot with reasonable diligence be ascertained," with one exception, an agent must make treatment decisions consistent with your best interests.

The exception to the use of the "best interests" test applies to decisions about artificial nutrition and hydration. If your wishes are not reasonably known or ascertainable, the agent may not decide on your behalf about the use of this kind of treatment. The "best interests" test may not be applied in this situation.

Because an agent makes a treatment decision, the agent is entitled to receive sufficient medical information to give an informed consent.

Power of Attorney

A power of attorney is a document that deals with financial affairs. It is a relatively short and uncomplicated instrument. It can be used to protect your property during a period of incapacity without the need of court intervention. The power of attorney is simply a document wherein another person (the "attorney-in-fact") is authorized to act in place and on behalf of the person (the "principal") with regard to the property of the principal. An alternate agent can be designated as well. All of the states have adopted the "durable" power of attorney, which makes the power of attorney survive your incapacity and can continue after such an event. A power of attorney can be created for a singular purpose with the agent authorized to act in a limited fashion, such as purchasing or selling real property. Many people are hesitant to confer the management of their affairs to another and therefore provide that the authority to act may only be effective when incapacity is confirmed by their physician. Many states, however, do not have such "springing event" statutes.

Many states do not permit gifts to be made on your behalf unless such authority is expressly stated in the power of attorney. The ability of the agent to transfer assets of a mentally disabled principal is significant for estate planning purposes. This right can continue the principal's program of lifetime giving and maximize the use of the unified credit and the annual exclusion during the period of incapacity. Under such a right, charitable gift-giving programs can continue as well.

A power of attorney can be revoked at any time prior to your incapacity. The nature of the creation of a power of attorney does not require the transfer of title to any assets for it to take effect. There are no filing or recording requirements. Usually spouses or partners are given the authority to act for each other. When there is no spouse, children are normally designated, and if there are none, then usually a trusted friend or professional is designated as the agent.

The New York Power of Attorney

On January 27, 2009, Governor David A. Paterson signed into law the amendment to Article 5, Title 15 of the General Obligations Law (GOL) effective September 1, 2009.

A power of attorney (POA) executed prior to the new law's effective date is still valid.

The important changes:

(i) Authority to make substantial gifts and transfer other property must be set forth in a supplemental rider.

(ii) The agent is given the authority to obtain medical records under HIIPA Privacy Rule for billing and payment purposes.

(iii) New procedures for revoking a POA.

(iv) The ability of the principal to appoint a third party with regard to the agent's accountability in the event the principal becomes incapacitated.

(v) A third party cannot unreasonably refuse to accept the POA.

(vi) If the principal is desirous of giving gifts, other than those which are cumulatively less than $500 per recipient ("major gift") under the new law, the principal needs to expressly grant such authority in a separate rider.

(vii) The POA must be signed by the agent and acknowledged.

(viii) The agent does not have the power to add a beneficiary or change the existing beneficiary to a retirement plan unless granted specific authority.

(ix) The agent acting under a POA has a fiduciary duty to the principal which duty includes a number of fiduciary obligations, such as the keeping of records, keeping property separate.

(x) In order for an agent to resign, written notice thereof is required.

(xi) An agent is not entitled to receive compensation unless the principal specifically provides for same in the POA.

(xii) If an agent fails to make the principal's records available, a special proceeding may be bought.

The aims of the amendments to the new law serve to eliminate certain financial abuses, adopt certain changes in the Internal Revenue Service Code under the HIPPA (Health Insurance Portability and Accountability) Privacy Rules, clarify ambiguities, and add clearer directions for both the principal and the agent.

Coordination with the Living Trust

As has been discussed in detail in chapter 8, the power of attorney and the living trust are documents that require coordination.

Even if you use a durable power of attorney, property in your living trust remains subject to your trustee, not your attorney-in-fact. However, a properly prepared durable power of attorney will serve you in many other areas, such as the ability of your agent to make gifts to your family, file your income tax returns, commence litigation on your behalf, create trusts for you and your beneficiaries, and a whole list of other important financial and estate planning measures and procedures.

CHAPTER 20

Retirement Benefits

*T*he Internal Revenue Service has ruled that taxpayers may pass money in individual retirement accounts, stretching out the income tax liabilities for many, many years. By doing so, an estate can be maximized through the tax deferred growth of this property. Unfortunately, most financial advisors do not understand the applicable rules and, as a result, are improperly advising their clients.

This chapter sets forth the ABCs on how these rules work and how you can best take advantage of them. You can even set up a trust to serve as a beneficiary of your retirement plan and thereby create both estate and income tax shelters. In addition, this chapter explains some of the latest new proposed regulations on Required Minimum Distributions issued by the Internal Revenue Service.

In a subsequent marriage, a trust can be used not only to provide benefits for a surviving spouse but also to protect the principal for children of a different marriage. These trusts must be irrevocable, yet many estate planners make the error of recommending a revocable living trust to be the beneficiary thereof.

Taxes Involved

Tax-deferred retirement accounts like IRA, Keogh, and 401(k) plans are governed by three possible tax consequences and various distribution rules. Potential transfer tax can be assessed unless some transfer tax exemption is available. Income taxes are due as benefits are withdrawn from the plan. If an estate is subject to potential transfer taxes, any income taxes due at that time can be reduced by certain credits for potential transfer tax paid. The Taxpayer Relief Act of 1997 eliminated the 15 percent excise tax on inter vivos "excess distributions" from retirement plans and repealed the excise tax on "excess accumulations" upon the death of a plan participant.

Estate Plans for Retirement Assets

Retirement assets are actually illiquid at death. This means that since income taxes have to be paid when they are withdrawn, they are really not—in dollars—what they seem to be. In order to pay estate and excise taxes, which are usually triggered when the second spouse dies, distributions must be made from the retirement plan or IRA, which will be subject to income tax at such time (an asset of this kind is called "income in respect of a decedent"). After taking into account the deduction for any potential transfer tax paid, the effective income tax bracket is 15–20 percent.

This 15–20 percent loss factor is analogous to the loss that occurs when real estate or business interests must be liquidated to pay such transfer taxes, hence the concept "illiquid retirement plan assets." For retirement plans of $1 million or more, the total loss factor (estate, income, and excise taxes) can be 70–80 percent.

A simple and cost-effective way to plan for the loss is to purchase a life insurance policy on the husband or wife or both ("second-to-die"). There are three ways to fund the insurance premium: (1) a portion of the annual retirement distributions is gifted to an irrevocable trust that owns the policy, (2) a single life policy is owned by a subtrust in the qualified plan, or (3) a single life or second-to-die policy is owned by a profit sharing plan.

Decisions

Payments from a qualified retirement plan or IRA must commence in the year the participant reaches seventy and a half years of age (by April 1 of the following year). This is your required beginning date (the "RBD"). The Small Business Job Production Act of 1996 defers required distributions until retirement for those who continue to work. However, this rule does not apply to IRAs or to owners of 5 percent or more of a business.

Therefore, at age seventy and a half, certain decisions have to be made that combine both estate and tax planning:

- How much money should be withdrawn each year?
- Who should be named as a beneficiary for any funds left in an account after the account holder's demise? It is important to note that you can now change your beneficiary at any time.

Distributions can be taken in one of the following ways: (1) a lump sum distribution (the entire distribution would be subject to income taxes), (2) in periodic installments over a specified number of years, or (3) in periodic installments over a specified number of years based upon the table that provides for same.

Income Tax Consequences

Retirement benefits are subject to income taxes when distributed. If someone receives a lump sum distribution as a result of the participant's death, the overall tax consequences will be substantial.

For example, if your child receives a lump sum distribution as a result of your death, the proceeds from the plan are deemed income in respect of decedent (IRD). This means that the entire benefits will be included in your estate for potential transfer tax purposes and that your child will have to report the distribution on his or her income tax return—however, receiving a credit on this return for a portion of the transfer tax paid on this asset.

Spousal Rollover

If a surviving spouse receives a lump sum distribution as a result of the participant's death, the proceeds may be rolled over into the surviving spouse's IRA account. This is known as a "spousal rollover." Only the spouse of a participant has this option. Once rolled over, the funds are subject to IRA rules (they cannot be withdrawn without penalty until age fifty-nine and a half), but the surviving spouse need not take any distributions until age seventy and a half. Income taxes, therefore, will be deferred until the funds are actually withdrawn. After the death of the account holder, the surviving spouse must by December 31 of the year following the owner's death elect the rollover and choose new beneficiaries.

Roth IRA

Besides a regular IRA account, a second option for contributing to an IRA—the Roth IRA—was established under the Taxpayer Relief act of 1997. Contributions to this IRA will be nondeductible, but distributions will not be includable in income if certain conditions are met: The distribution must be made after the first five years of establishing a Roth IRA and either after the individual reaches fifty-nine and a half years of age, because of death or disability, or for first-time-home-buyer expenses.

In addition, amounts invested in existing IRAs can be converted to a Roth IRA without AGI limitations, at a tax cost. Amounts converted that would have been includable in income had they been withdrawn are currently taxed. If the conversion was made prior to January 1, 1999, this amount can be included in income over four years. Married persons filing separately cannot take advantage of the conversion provision.

The New Regulation for Required Minimum Distributions

On January 11, 2001, the Internal Revenue Service issued proposed regulations that establish new guidelines for determining required minimum distributions from IRAs and other certain qualified plans. The new regulations represent a major modification of the former regulations that were proposed in 1987 and never finalized. The brand-new proposed regulations restate and replace the 1987 proposed regulation, although many of the concepts and rules set out in the 1987 proposed regulations are contained in the revised proposed regulations. The regulations became final for calendar years beginning on or after January 1, 2002.

Distributions During Lifetime

The regulations provide a table, referred to as the "Uniform Table," under which a uniform distribution period can be determined. This table is based upon the life expectancy of the IRA holder. The table is the same that was used under the former proposed regulations when a nonspouse beneficiary was named who was more than ten years younger than the owner (the MDIB Table). The table recalculates life expectancies each year.

The table is available to any holder without regard to the identity of the beneficiary, or no beneficiary if none has been named. This means that a single holder of an IRA who designates a nonperson (a charitable organization) as a beneficiary can have the deferrals heretofore available only to a holder who had designated a younger person as a beneficiary. The age of the holder is the only ingredient necessary for input into the table. The Uniform Table is presented at the end of this chapter.

There is one exception to the use of the table, which is where the sole named beneficiary is the holder's spouse who is more than ten years younger than the owner. In such a situation, the actual joint life expectancies of the owner and the spouse must be used and recalculated.

The latter would create smaller minimum distributions than under the table.

The rules do not permit the appointment of a designated beneficiary after the holder's death. However, the named beneficiary or beneficiaries have the opportunity to recast who would receive the benefits for purposes of the required minimum distributions and the manner in which they would be received. A disclaimer by a beneficiary would make such adjustments.

Death of the Holder before Required Beginning Date

Once the designated beneficiary has been clarified, if a single person is the named beneficiary, that person is required to commence receiving distributions under the five-year rule or over his or her life expectancy. Under the five-year rule, the entire IRA must be distributed by the end of the fifth year following the holder's death.

If there is more than one (1) named beneficiary, the distributions will then be based on the life expectancy of the oldest beneficiary.

Death after the Required Beginning Date

Distributions, if the holder dies after his or her required beginning date for the year of death, the difference must be distributed by the end of the calendar year of his or her death, and the five-year rule does not apply.

Spouse Named as the Only Beneficiary

Where the spouse is named as the only beneficiary of an IRA, the most advantageous plan for him or her is to roll over the IRA into his or her own IRA or elect to treat the inherited IRA as his or her own. The benefit of the spousal rollover is to obtain smaller distributions on the life of the surviving spouse under the table, with the right to designate the beneficiary thereof.

If the holder has not reached his or her required beginning date at the death of the owner, a spouse has the options of doing the following:

- Electing the five-year rule.
- Wait until whichever date is later, either the end of the year in which the owner would have reached his or her required beginning date or until December 31 of the year following the year of the holder's death. At the later of the two dates, the spouse must then commence to receive distributions over his or her expectancy.

Important Provisions

- *Subsequent Beneficiary*. The regulations provide that a named beneficiary, after the holder's death, can name a subsequent beneficiary in the event of death of the named beneficiary. However, the required distribution period is the life expectancy of the original named beneficiary.
- *Trust as Designated Beneficiary*. The rules regarding a trust as a designated beneficiary remain mostly the same:
    - The trust must be valid under state law.
    - The beneficiaries of the trust must be identifiable.
    - The trust must be irrevocable, or will be at the plan owner's demise.
    - Trust documentation information must be provided to the administrator of the plan.

Caveats

- The Internal Revenue Code requires that you start drawing from your IRA (and paying tax on the distributions) the year that you reach seventy and a half. Usually, the payments must be made by the end of each year (December 31), but in the first year, you are entitled to a three-month grace period.
- You can change the beneficiary of your IRA at any time.
- IRAs and certain other retirement plans can be used in your estate plan to take full advantage of potential transfer tax impositions such as the use of an applicable exemption and that of your spouse by the funding of a qualified marital deduction trust (QTIP) so as to defer the potential transfer tax or of a credit shelter trust that will permit you to control the ultimate disposition of the principal of the trust.
- If you intend to make any charitable gifts, use your IRA. Not only will you receive a potential transfer tax deduction, no income taxes will be required to be paid by the charity when it receives the gift.
- A taxpayer who inherits an IRA may have to pay potential transfer tax on the gift. This can be totally avoided by the implementation of charitable planning. Plans such as IRAs, 401(k)s, 403(b)s, and defined contribution plans can be used for charitable gifts. To save taxes, all you have to do is change the allocation of your assets among your beneficiaries.
- A profit-sharing plan can be used to purchase life insurance. As a general rule, if whole life insurance is purchased, the cumulative

premium cannot be more than a certain percent of the cumulative employee's contribution attributed to the participant's account. If term insurance is purchased, the amount that can be used cannot exceed half the foregoing amount. The purchase of life insurance with profit-sharing-plan contributions can only be accomplished if the plan permits it. If the life insurance in the plan is owned in a manner so that the participant has no "incidents of ownership," the proceeds of the life insurance should not be included in the participant's estate for tax purposes. If the life insurance proceeds are part of a trust that is set up to exclude it properly from a spouse's estate, the proceeds will escape taxation in two estates.

Inherited IRAs

A few good rules should be observed regarding inherited IRAs:

- Since all movement of the funds must be from one IRA custodian to another—all transfers should specify a "Trustee-to-Trustee Transfer." Unless the transfer is from a deceased sponsor, the IRA must be retitled, which new title should include the original owner's name and an indication that it is inherited, i.e., "Samuel Smith, deceased, inherited IRA for the benefit of John Smith, beneficiary."
- In order to ensure maximum stretch-out flexibility, the beneficiary form on file with the custodian of the IRA must be completed.
- A spouse who is the beneficiary has more options available than other inheritors, i.e., a spouse who has not reached 59½ at the time of inheritance can wait until after age to do the spousal rollover and the spouse does not have to make any withdrawals until he or she reaches 70½ years of age.
- Distribution requirements—if the deceased IRA owner was 70½ or older, the mandatory distribution for the year in which the deceased died must first be withdrawn. Furthermore, if any potential transfer taxes are paid, an itemized deduction may be taken in order to offset some part of the IRA income. The minimum distribution request to be taken is calculated by the balance of December 31 of the previous year divided by the beneficiary's life expectancy listed on the IRA "single life expectancy" table as opposed to the table by IRA owners. The following year the same life expectancy table is used, less 1 year.

The Downsides of Roth IRA Conversions

- The income tax cost is too great and eats into the retirement savings.
- The age of retirement is too near.
- Tax brackets change in retirement.

Suggestions

The rules governing retirement benefits are complicated. Sometimes there is a conflict between income tax planning and estate planning.

(1) A common misunderstanding is that by creating a retirement plan, you are converting capital gains to ordinary income, or giving up the opportunity to take advantage of the 15 percent tax rate on qualified dividends and capital gains.

(2) The need to convert to a Roth IRA. You must have funds to pay the income tax on the conversion, converting to a Roth IRA, which is nothing more than making an additional contribution to your retirement account. Under a Roth IRA, there are no required distributions during lifetime. You can easily fund a credit shelter trust or a generation-skipping transfer tax exempt disposition with a Roth IRA.

(3) Benefits should not be withdrawn too soon.

(4) Sometimes a beneficiary collects the benefits before realizing that he or she could have stretched them out over his or her life expectancy.

Got Stretch-Out?

A stretch-out is accomplished if the death beneficiary's life expectancy is allowed for the purpose of calculating required minimum distributions (RMDs) after the plan owner's death under Internal Revenue Code Section 401(a)(9) and the regulations thereunder.

But the life expectancy of a beneficiary of a trust may be recognized if, and only if, the trust meets a number of complicated requirements. Such a trust is often called a "see-through trust" or a "pass-through trust."

To qualify, a trust must include a provision that directs the trustee to distribute to the trust beneficiary any amounts the trustee withdraws from the plan. Plan distributions may not accumulate, which makes the trust a conduit for directing plan distributions to the individual beneficiary. Such a trust is also often called a "conduit trust."

The RMD rules effectively impose two steps of analysis when a trust has been designated as death beneficiary of a retirement plan account:

- Rollovers of inherited accounts from qualified plans by nonspouse beneficiaries

A spousal beneficiary of a participant in a qualified retirement plan is permitted to roll over the prior deceased participant's plan benefit to the surviving spouse's IRA or other qualified plan. Under law, however, a nonspouse beneficiary was not allowed to roll over an inherited retirement plan account to an IRA or any other plan. Often, this had the effect of requiring the nonspouse beneficiary to collect the inherited retirement plan account (and pay income tax on the account) faster than the tax law would otherwise require.

To remedy the situation described, new IRC Section 402(c)(11) allows a non-spouse beneficiary—beginning in 2007—to transfer an inherited qualified retirement plan, Section 457 plan, or Section 403(b) annuity death benefit to an IRA established for the purpose of receiving the inherited retirement plan account. To effectuate this, the beneficiary must use the trustee-to-trustee transfer mechanism. The beneficiary may not receive the distribution and then roll the distributed amount over to a qualifying IRA (as would ordinarily be allowed for a regular IRA rollover).

Assuming that the inherited retirement plan account has been properly transferred to an IRA established for this purpose, the IRA will be treated as an inherited IRA and the beneficiary will be subject to the minimum distribution rules that apply to a nonspouse beneficiary of an inherited IRA. Thus, generally, the beneficiary will be able to receive the distribution of the inherited account over his or her life expectancy and will be able to designate his or her own beneficiaries for the inherited IRA (although the subsequent beneficiaries will not be able to further extend the life expectancy if the initial beneficiary dies prior to attaining his or her life expectancy).

Restrictions on Inherited IRA

1. A nonspouse beneficiary may not roll over a distribution from an inherited IRA into an IRA in the beneficiary's own name, or make rollovers to an inherited IRA. A spouse beneficiary may roll over all or any part of the deceased spouse's IRA into another IRA in the spouse beneficiary's name.
2. A nonspouse beneficiary may make a direct transfer of assets in the inherited IRA to another IRA only if the transfer IRA is maintained

in the name of the deceased taxpayer, or in the name of the name of the beneficiary as a beneficiary of the deceased IRA owner. If the nonspouse beneficiary inadvertently makes a rollover from the deceased owner's IRA to another IRA, the rollover is taxable. The beneficiary may not correct the rollover by redesignating the rollover as a transfer.

3. The beneficiary may make the transfer even if the beneficiary was receiving required minimum distributions prior to the transfer. However, the nonspouse beneficiary may not transfer the minimum distribution amount that the beneficiary was required to receive for the year of transfer. The transfer does not change the amount or timing of minimum distributions that the nonspouse beneficiary is required to receive.

4. A nonspouse beneficiary may not change the name on an inherited IRA. The nonspouse beneficiary is immediately taxed if the nonspouse beneficiary changes the name of the owner from the deceased person to the nonspouse beneficiary.

5. A nonspouse beneficiary may not make additional contributions to an inherited IRA. Contributions to an inherited IRA are nondeductible. A spouse beneficiary may make additional contributions to the deceased spouse's IRA, in which case the spouse will be treated as the owner rather than the beneficiary of the IRA.

6. A nonspouse beneficiary may not elect to receive distributions as owner of the IRA. Only a spouse beneficiary may elect to receive as owner, and thereby delay minimum distributions until the surviving spouse attains age 70½.

7. The inherited IRA must be treated separately for purposes of determining the taxable amount of a distribution and the nontaxable return of basis. This differs from the rule applicable to other IRAs in which all of the taxpayer's IRAs are aggregated in determining the taxable portion of a distribution and nontaxable return of basis.

Custodian

The IRA trustee or custodian must be a qualified trustee or custodian. The IRA owner may not act as the trustee or custodian.

Penalties for Failure to Receive Minimum Distribution

General Rule

If an IRA fails to make the required distributions, there is a 50 percent excise tax on the minimum amount that the IRA should have distributed each year. Excess distributions in one year do not reduce the required minimum distributions or penalty taxes in subsequent years.

The penalty is imposed in the calendar year containing the last day by which the amount must be distributed. It is not imposed in the year for which the required minimum distribution must be made unless the distribution must be made by the last day of that year.

Roth IRA

The account balance in a Roth IRA must be distributed to the death beneficiaries within the same time periods that apply to a traditional IRA.

When electing the method and amount of required minimum distributions, the beneficiary should take into account the five-year holding period that must be met in order to avoid taxation of the earnings portion of the distribution. A distribution after the death of the IRA owner is nontaxable if the distribution is made after the taxable year during which the deceased IRA owner first made an initial Roth IRA contribution. The five year holding period for a beneficiary I determined independently of the five year period for the beneficiary's other Roth IRAs. However, the beginning of the five year holding period is not redetermined on the death of the IRA owner. The period of time that a Roth IRA is held in the name of the beneficiary includes the period of time in which the deceased IRA owner held the Roth IRA. There is a special rule for a spouse beneficiary who takes as owner.

Payment Methods

The post-death distribution rules for a nonspouse depend upon whether the deceased owner was receiving required minimum distributions as of the date of death.

(i) If the IRA owner died prior to April 1 of the year following attainment of age 70½ (the required beginning date for minimum distributions), then the remaining amount in the IRA must be distributed within one of the following time periods:

• *Rule 1—Five-Year Payout.* The account balance may be distributed by December 31 of the fifth year following the owner's death. The IRS refers to this distribution option as "Rule 1." For example, if an IRA owner dies on January 1, 2003, the entire interest must be distributed by December 31, 2008, in order to satisfy the five-year rule.

- *Rule 2—Payment over Life or Life Expectancy.* Distributions may be made over the remaining life or life expectancy of the designated beneficiary commencing by December 31 of the year after the date of death. The IRS refers to this as "Rule 2." Under this rule, the minimum distribution amount each year is the account balance on December 31 of the prior year divided by the remaining life expectancy of the oldest individual beneficiary.

(ii) *Death after Age 70½ Year*

If the IRA owner died after April 1 of the calendar year following attainment of age 70½, then the five-year rule does not apply. The maximum payout period is the longer of (i) the remaining life expectancy of the designated beneficiary, or (ii) the remaining life expectancy of the deceased IRA owner. Distributions must commence by December 31 of the calendar year following the year of the IRA owner's death.

(iii) *Death after Age 70½ and Prior to Required Beginning Date*

The IRA owner may die after attaining age 70½ and prior to the required beginning date (April 1 of the calendar year following attainment of age 70½). The IRA owner may or may not have already received required minimum distributions for the first two years. In such case, the IRA trustee is not required to make minimum distributions to the estate of the IRA owner for the age 70½ year. Instead, the beneficiaries are required to receive minimum distributions under the same rules that apply to beneficiaries of IRA owners who die prior to age 70½. The nonspouse beneficiaries must receive distributions either by December 31 of the fifth calendar year following the death of the IRA owner, or over the remaining life expectancy of the oldest individual beneficiary commencing by December 31 of the year after the date of death.

Tax Planning

If the spouse is younger than the deceased IRA owner and has substantial assets, the rollover alternative would allow the spouse to prolong distributions from the IRA. In addition, it would permit the spouse more time to designate his or her own beneficiaries. It would allow the surviving spouse to consider circumstances that may arise after the death of the IRA owner in designating beneficiaries.

If the spouse is the designated beneficiary, and is younger than the IRA owner and less than age 59½, then by electing to be a beneficiary, he or she can receive funds sooner, without penalty unlikely using the rollover alternative.

A third alternative is that the spouse beneficiary may choose the five-year option whereby the entire amount of the IRA must be distributed by the end of the fifth year following the year in which the IRA owner died.

A third alternative is that the spouse beneficiary may choose the five-year option whereby the entire amount of the IRA must be distributed by the end of the fifth year following the year in which the IRA owner died.

Uniform Table

AGE OF THE OWNER	DISTRIBUTION PERCENT
70	27.4
71	26.5
72	25.6
73	24.7
74	23.8
75	22.9
76	22.0
77	21.2
78	20.3
79	19.5
80	18.7
81	17.9
82	17.1
83	16.3
84	15.5
85	14.8
86	14.1
87	13.4
88	12.7
89	12.0
90	11.4
91	10.8
92	10.2
93	9.6
94	9.1
95	8.6

AGE OF THE OWNER	DISTRIBUTION PERCENT
96	8.1
97	7.6
98	7.1
99	6.7
100	6.3
101	5.9
102	5.5
103	5.2
104	4.9
105	4.5
106	4.2
107	3.9
108	3.7
109	3.4
110	3.1
111	2.9
112	2.6
113	2.4
114	2.1
115 and older	1.9

❖

CHAPTER 21

Medicare and Medicaid and Supplemental Security Income

*W*hat are Medicaid and Medicare? Who is entitled to the benefits of these programs?

The thought of being impoverished as a result of long-term care haunts people. Asset-preservation strategies are important to individuals who want to protect their estates from financial decimation. Medicaid is the only government program that offers an alternative to the disastrous financial results that can come from long-term nursing home care. This chapter discusses these available entitlements and what the requirements are for eligibility.

Medicaid is a program for needy persons and is jointly funded and administered by the federal government and the states. All of the states participate in this program. The federal government contributes about half the costs. Each state administers its program and can set its own standards. Medicare on the other hand is totally under the federal system and is for the population who are aged or for persons with disabilities.

The Omnibus Reconciliation Act of 1993 (OBRA 93) changed many of the rules relating to Medicaid. In this chapter, you will find out how to create a trust and, thereafter, transfer your assets into it and qualify for Medicaid benefits.

Overview

Medicare is a government health insurance program for the aged and people with disabilities. The Medicare system does not make provisions for sheltering a family from the catastrophic costs of nursing home care.

It is not a long-term care plan and does not begin to cover all of one's health care needs.

For example, it does not cover prescription drugs, vision, hearing, dental care, custodial care, and private duty nursing. Despite Medicare's limitations, it is the foundation for all other health insurance. It is virtually impossible for senior citizens to obtain any health insurance without Medicare coverage.

Medicare is divided into two parts. Part A, Hospital Insurance (HI), covers hospital, skilled nursing facility, home health, and hospice services. Part B, Supplemental Medical Insurance (SMI), covers physician services, durable medical equipment, ambulance services, therapy service, and laboratory tests.

Medicare enrollment is automatic for all persons—regardless of income—who are (1) sixty-five or older and eligible for social security or railroad retirement benefits, (2) have been receiving social security disability income for at least twenty-four months, or (3) have end-stage renal disease (ESRD). However, a person who does not meet these eligibility requirements but who is sixty-five or older and a U. S. citizen or a legal alien residing in the United States for at least five years may elect to enroll in Parts A and B or Part B alone.

Medicaid

The only available source to defray home or nursing home care expenses is the Medicaid system. Because individuals can qualify by meeting the minimum threshold requirements, people will plan their estates to achieve these levels. By transferring their assets and subsequently meeting the qualifications standards, the assets are preserved for the next generation.

Medicaid is a joint federal-state program of medical assistance for needy persons who are aged, blind, or disabled or who qualify for cash benefits under the Aid to Families with Dependent Children (AFDC) program. Each state operates its Medicaid programs according to general standards set by Congress but administers them by a state agency, with the costs of administration split roughly fifty-fifty between the state and the federal government.

Besides being an American citizen or a permanent resident alien, an applicant for Medicaid must show that he or she is (1) aged, blind, disabled, or the parent of a minor child; and (2) financially needy according to program criteria. Persons age sixty-five and older meet the first standard. Those who qualify for Supplemental Security Income (SSI) benefits in many states satisfy the criteria for both SSI and Medicaid. (See chapter 19 for a detailed discussion on SSI benefits.)

Financial Need

Financial need is established when an individual's (or couple's) income and resources fall below Medicaid ceilings. For 2010, the monthly income limit for an eligible individual was $767 or $1,117 for an eligible married couple. The resource or asset limit level, effective January 1, 2010, is $13,800 per person plus any amount in an irrevocable preneed funeral arrangement. Aged, blind, or disabled persons whose incomes and resources are above these limits may nevertheless qualify for Medicaid if their net income and resources, after their medical bills are paid, fall below these limits.

What counts as income for Medicaid purposes is different from the definition of income used by the Internal Revenue Service for income tax purposes. For Medicaid, it means anything that a person receives in cash or in-kind that can be used to meet the person's needs for food, clothing, or shelter is considered income.

An applicant with resources in excess of the permissible limit is required to spend them down, give them away, or sell them until the balance is within the allowable limits.

Financial Responsibility of Spouses for One Another

Medicaid considers the income and resources of each spouse to be available to the other (a process called "deeming") when the spouses live together in the community and one applies for Medicaid.

If spouses separate but neither is institutionalized and one of them applies for Medicaid, deeming ends at the close of the month in which they separate. Deeming continues for six months, however, if both of the separated spouses apply for Medicaid.

When one spouse is institutionalized and the other remains in the community, the "community spouse" is permitted to retain or acquire a minimum monthly maintenance needs (income) allowance of up to $2,739 (New York) for the institutionalized spouse. A community spouse can also retain up to $74,820 or one-half (½) of the couple's resources to a maximum of $109,560) in nonexcluded resources without affecting the institutionalized spouse's Medicaid eligibility. Any excess income in the community spouse's name is considered not available to pay for the institutionalized spouse's care. Assets acquired by the community spouse after the month

Medicaid eligibility for the institutionalized spouse is established is not considered available. If the community spouse has more than $2,739 in income per month, Medicaid might suggest that he or she contribute 25 percent of the excess to the institutionalized spouse's medical care.

New York couples with substantial unearned income (for example, interest and dividends) who anticipate that one spouse is likely to enter a nursing home and apply for Medicaid might be advised to transfer this income to the community spouse's name. If this income exceeds the community's spouse's allowance of $2,739, that spouse will be allowed to keep the excess, subject only to the voluntary contribution option. The same result could be obtained by purchasing an annuity in the community spouse's name.

Uncooperative Community Spouses

New York State rescinded its previous policy of denying the monthly income allowance to a community spouse who refused to use excess resources for the care of the institutionalized spouse.

The state will, however, deny Medicaid to an institutionalized spouse where the community spouse does not reveal income and resource information, unless the denial causes "undue hardship." The state, however, has never denied Medicaid to a spouse because the other spouse refuses to contribute to the costs of care of the applicant spouse.

Exempt Transfers

Certain assets or resources are exempt from the coverage of the transfer rules and therefore their transfer for less than fair market value is not penalized. The term "resources" has the same meaning here as it does under the SSI program, except for the person's home. Thus all resources that are exempt for SSI purposes are also exempt from the transfer penalties. Therefore, the total value of an exempt resource (e.g., a car or a life insurance policy) can be transferred without penalty.

The law does not penalize the transfer of a home during the thirty-six month look-back period if the residence is transferred for the sole benefit of the institutionalized person's spouse, or to a blind or disabled child, or to any of the following:

- A dependent child
- A sibling with an equity interest who had resided in the home for one year prior to the applicant's admission to a medical institution or nursing facility

- The son or daughter of the individual who had lived in the home for two years prior to the institutionalization and who had cared for the individual

In addition, no transfer of any asset is penalized to the extent that:
- The asset was transferred to the community spouse or a blind or disabled child.
- A satisfactory showing is made to the state that the individual intended to dispose of the asset either at fair market value or for other valuable consideration, or the asset was transferred exclusively for a purpose other than to qualify for medical assistance.
- The state determines that denial of eligibility would cause an undue hardship.

Some important aspects of the rules are listed below:
- Transfers of assets in order to qualify for SSI benefits are not penalized, regardless of how close they occur to the date of SSI eligibility.
- Many states do not consider the resources of the community spouse to be available to the institutionalized spouse after the month in which the institutionalized spouse establishes eligibility for Medicaid. As such, a transfer of assets by the community spouse after this time will not affect the institutionalized spouse's benefits. A person could, therefore, transfer an exempt asset, such as a residence, to the ownership of the community spouse (an exempt transfer), and once Medicaid eligibility is established, the community spouse would be free to transfer the exempt asset without penalty.
- Transfers of assets in order to qualify for Medicaid also are not penalized, regardless of when they occur, provided the eligible person receives only home- or community-based Medicaid services and only those Medicaid services that are not equivalent to the level of care provided in a nursing facility.

Transfer of Assets

Where assets are transferred, prior to the date a person applies for Medicaid, the state will look back to 60 months. If assets are transferred for less than fair market value, the State will withhold services for a period of time (the "penalty period"). The length of the penalty period is determined by dividing the value of the transferred assets by the average monthly private-pay rate for nursing facility care in the state where applied, i.e., a person transfers assets having a value of $90,000, divided by $3,000, the average monthly private-pay rate, results in a thirty-month penalty period. There is no limit to the length of the penalty period.

There are certain types of transfers where the penalties are not applied, which are:

- Transfer to a spouse, or to a third party for the benefit of the spouse.
- Transfer by a spouse to a third party for the sole benefit of the spouse.
- Transfer to certain disabled individuals or to trusts established for those individuals.
- Transfer for a purpose other than to qualify for Medicaid; and transfers when imposing a penalty would cause undue hardship.

Disclaimers and Forced Shares

Can an institutionalized spouse disclaim an inheritance without jeopardizing Medicaid eligibility? The issue can arise either after the person is receiving Medicaid, making the inheritance an available resource, or prior to application for Medicaid, making the renunciation a transfer of assets (if the testator died within a certain period prior to the person applying for Medicaid).

The decisions regarding this issue are few and split. North Dakota holds that the disclaimer is not a transfer of assets. However, New York and Connecticut courts have ruled to the contrary. New York has reached a similar result in a case involving a surviving spouse who failed to exercise her statutory right of election against the will of her deceased husband.

Lifetime Uses of a Personal Residence

If the transferor retains only a lifetime right to the use and occupancy of a residence, rather than a life estate, some states do not count this interest as an asset for Medicaid purposes, even though it is still part of the transferor's estate. A clause should be placed in a gift deed of the personal residence retaining the right to the use and occupancy of the property.

It has also been reported that many jurisdictions are treating the life estate, for Medicaid purposes, as an available resource for the transferor while institutionalized. In these situations, the state assumes that the premises can be rented, and therefore, it imputes the fair market rental value of the home and thus requires contribution to the costs of care.

To avoid this result, one of two strategies can be adopted:

- Argue that the home must be kept vacant for the possible return of the person to live there.
- At the time of the original transfer, limit the life estate to the use and occupancy of the person, thereby preventing its rental to others.

Effective October 22, 1993, the New York State Department of Social Services changed the treatment of the home of a Medicaid applicant or recipient who leaves the home to enter a nursing home. As a result, in this state, Medicaid will no longer include the homes of institutionalized Medicaid applicants or recipients as a countable resource if they clearly express their intent to return home at a future date. The "intent to return home" need only be a written statement from the individual (or authorized representative) expressing the intent to eventually return home.

Upon the death of a nursing home resident, Medicaid will be entitled to reimbursement from the estate of that person for any services provided, including recovery against any home which the Medicaid recipient owns individually at the time of his or her death.

OBRA 93 confirmed that for Medicaid purposes the disclaimer of an inheritance is considered a disqualifying transfer.

Treatment of Trusts

Where an individual, his or her spouse, or anyone acting on the individual's behalf, establishes a trust using at least some of the individual's funds, that trust can be considered available to the individual for purposes of determining eligibility for Medicaid.

In determining whether the trust is available, no consideration is given to the purpose of the trust, the trustee's discretion in administering the trust, use restrictions in the trust, exculpatory clauses, or restrictions on distributions.

Certain trusts are not counted as being available to the individual. They include the following:

- Trusts established by a parent, grandparent, guardian, or court for the benefit of an individual who is disabled and under the age of 65, using the individual's own funds.

- Trusts established by a disabled individual, parent, grandparent, guardian, or court for the disabled individual, using the individual's own funds, where the trust is made up of pooled funds and managed by a non-profit organization for the sole benefit of each individual included in the trust.
- Trusts composed only of pension, Social Security, and other income of the individual, in states that make individuals eligible for institutional care under a special income level, but do not cover institutional care for the medically needy.

In all of the above instances, the trust must provide that the state receives any funds, up to the amount of Medicaid benefits paid on behalf of the individual, remaining in the trust when the individual dies.

A trust will not be counted as available to the individual where the State determines that counting the trust would work an undue hardship.

Living Trusts

Transfers of assets by an applicant or the spouse to a revocable living trust do not trigger a period of ineligibility because the assets are still considered to be available to the grantor, but the use of the trust funds for any other purpose than for the spouses' benefit is considered a transfer. Assets transferred to an irrevocable trust that could be paid to or used for the benefit of either spouse are also considered a countable resource, and any actual payments to them are income, while the balance of the trust assets are subject to the transfer rules.

"Income Only" Medicaid Rules Clarified

OBRA 93 sets forth rules governing "income only" trusts, which are irrevocable trusts that reserve to the grantor income on the principal of the trust for life, but do not allow the grantor any access to the principal of the trust during his or her lifetime.

If a person establishes an irrevocable trust guaranteeing the income of the trust to himself or herself for life but excludes the distribution of the trust corpus to himself or herself, the corpus of the trust will not be considered an available resource to the individual after the applicable transfer-of-assets waiting period (60 months). If the trust permits the grantor the right to appoint the remainder of the trust (after his or her death) to a limited class of people, then no gift tax is payable at the time the trust is created. An individual who places his or her residence in an "income only" trust and retains a testamentary "limited power of appointment" will also preserve the income tax benefit from capital gains upon the sale of the property permitted under the Internal Revenue Code. This benefit would not be available if the property were given away. When such a trust is created and the individual enters a nursing home, the state will receive the income from the trust, which is an indirect incentive or a way for the state to fund these costs.

Tort Settlements

Disabled persons whose disabilities were caused by a third party may be able to obtain a substantial settlement or judgment. If the settlement or award is used to fund a Supplemental Needs Trust (SNT), it will not disqualify the recipient from qualifying for Medicaid.

The Omnibus Budget Reconciliation Act of 1993 (P.L. 103-66, OBRA '93) exempted assets placed in SNTs from Medicaid eligibility determinations. Thus, a Special Needs Trust ("SNT") funded with the assets of a disabled individual under sixty-five years of age is not treated as an available resource for purposes of Medicaid qualification, and the transfer of the disabled person's assets to the trust is not considered a disqualifying gift. Upon the death of the beneficiary, however, the remaining trust principal must be used to reimburse the state for medical assistance paid on the beneficiary's behalf. If the disabled person is over age 65, the assets may be placed in a "pooled" trust established by a not-for-profit organization, but the usual transfer of asset penalty rules will apply. However, the New York courts have determined that the sum to satisfy the lien can be derived only from that portion of the recovery "that it intended to compensate each plaintiff for past medical expenses" and instructs the courts below to allocate the portion of the settlement for medical expenses. Thus, the portion allocated to pain and suffering and economic loss can still be earmarked for the SNT.

Strategies

It is only uncompensated transfers that generate a penalty for Medicaid-planning purposes, while transfers for valid consideration may be freely made without penalty. An annuity transaction is a transfer for valid consideration that can result in the transferor's immediate eligibility for Medicaid without really surrendering the transferred asset.

An annuity is a fixed annual payment for the duration of a person's (the annuitant's) lifetime. The usual annuity contract involves a transfer of funds in return for specified annual payments based on the annuitant's reasonable life expectancy. The trend in using annuities for Medicaid planning has been to purchase a Medicaid compliant annuity (e.g., through an insurance company).

Typically, the private annuity will be between members of a family, but this is not a requirement. As with a commercial annuity, it can be for the life of the purchaser or for the joint lives of the purchaser and another (such as husband and wife), or any other form that an annuity may customarily take. The typical private annuity, however, will not have a term certain so that payments will cease on the annuitant's death and the contract performance will be completed; therefore, no part of the transferred property is included in the annuitant's estate for estate tax purposes.

For Medicaid purposes, the transfer of property in return for a private annuity is treated identically to the purchase of a commercial annuity. That is, the projected value of payments must be actuarially sound-based on the annuitant's life expectancy and the applicable interest rates.

Caveats

- Medicaid provides long-term benefits to persons sixty-five or over or disabled persons who qualify under the financial requirement rules. In certain situations, even a high income will not bar the obtaining of Medicaid.
- Medicaid is available in all states.
- Medicaid does not pay cash benefits to its recipients.
- Limitations.

Providers of health care throughout the country are not required to be members of the Medicaid programs. This means that in certain areas it may be difficult to find a medical specialist who will accept Medicaid. If your physician refuses to accept Medicaid payments (because of the lower reimbursement than other providers and because of the amount of paperwork), you will be required to find a new personal physician.

Medicaid cannot afford to provide you with the amount of in-house services (nurses, care-givers, attendants) you may require or wish for. Only your money can purchase these options. This may mean a dissipation of your property, but the quality of your life should be paramount.

A trust created under your living trust or will to take effect after your death, for the benefit of your surviving spouse, or a handicapped child, in the form of a discretionary special-needs trust, which prevents the principal from being considered a resource or asset for Medicaid purposes and which applies the income from the trust at the discretion of the trustee, will not only permit the person to qualify for Medicaid but will preserve the principal of the trust for the next generation!

The format for such a trust (set forth in living trust) for the benefit of a surviving spouse could be in the following form:

Trust for Surviving Spouse That Preserves Medicaid Eligibility

(1) To hold, invest, and reinvest the same, to collect and receive the income, and after paying all expenses incidental to the management of the trust, pay to my spouse, or apply for the benefit of my spouse, _____ during his/her lifetime so much of the income and principal as the Trustees, in their absolute discretion, determine to be advisable for his/her support, comfort and maintenance and for his/her final funeral expenses upon his/her death.

(2) In the event that my spouse should enter a medical institution, the Trustees shall apply the principal and income of the trust for his/her comfort but not for his/her food, clothing or shelter.

(3) In making such payments and expenditures, the Trustees shall take into account any funds or assistance the Trustees know to be available to my spouse from governmental and private sources.

(4) The interest of my spouse in the income or principal of this trust shall be free from the control or interference of any of his/her creditors or of any government agency providing aid or benefits to him/her and shall not be subject to attachment or susceptible of any anticipation or alienation.

(5) In making such payments and expenditures, the Trustees need not consider the effect such distributions may have upon the interests of the remainder of the trust.

(6) The Trustees shall consult regularly with my children to ascertain my spouse's needs and desires and may follow his/her recommendations in making payments and expenditures in my spouses behalf.

(7) Upon my spouse's death or in the event that the terms and conditions of this trust are challenged in court by any governmental agency, the trust shall terminate and the corpus of the trust, together with any accumulated income thereon, shall be paid absolutely to my children in equal shares, per stirpes.

Medicaid Seeks Recovery from All Refusing Spouses

Since a recent court decision, described below, New York City and some other countries are seeking recovery from all refusing spouses of the cost of care provided to their Medicaid recipient spouses. Recovery is being sought whether the sick spouse is in a nursing home and the community spouse is refusing to contribute income or resources in excess of the community spouse allowances or the sick spouse is receiving community services or home care and the well spouse is refusing to contribute income or resources. Previously, Medicaid waited until the death of the second spouse to seek recovery from that spouse's estate for the cost of care furnished to the Medicaid-eligible spouse. Now, New York City Medicaid and some other counties are sending letters to all refusing spouses requesting that they reimburse Medicaid for the cost of their sick spouse's medical care. If no response is sent to this letter, Medicaid files a lawsuit for payment of an outstanding debt in the amount paid by Medicaid for the care of the sick spouse. These lawsuits are based upon a 1998 case brought by New York City Medicaid against a community spouse who refused to contribute his resources in excess of the community spouse resource allowance to the care of his sick spouse on nursing home (*Medicaid Commissioner of the DSS of the City of New York v. Benjamin Spellman*). Both the original court and the Appellate Division of the First Department ruled that Medicaid could seek reimbursement from refusing spouses during their lifetimes without waiting to seek recovery from their estates after death.

Supplemental Security Income

Supplemental Security Income (or SSI) is a monthly stipend provided to aged (legally deemed to be 65 or older), blind, or disabled persons based on need, paid by the United States government. The program is administered by the Social Security Administration. Payments are made from the US Treasury general funds, not the Social Security trust funds. The payments are generally paid on the first of the month for the current month (as opposed to social security benefits which are paid for the prior month). The program was created in 1974 to replace various state-administered programs that served the same purpose, as a way to standardize in the level of benefits through the addition of Title XVE (Title 16) of the Social Security Act.

Eligibility

In order to be eligible to receive SSI benefits, an individual must prove the following:
- They are 65 or older, blind, or disabled.
- They legally reside in one of the 50 states, the District of Columbia, Northern Mariana Islands, or are the child of military parent(s)

assigned to permanent duty outside of the U.S., or are a student (certain restrictions apply) temporarily abroad.
- They have income and resources within certain limits (see sub-sections).
- They have applied for the benefits.

The decisions as to whether an individual is disabled is made by the various state Disability Determination Services (DDS), which contract with the federal government to make such determinations. Although the DDSs are state agencies, they follow federal rules. This arrangement arose from the inception of OASDI, when some key members of Congress considered the Social Security Disability program should be administered employing federalism, fearing expansion of the federal government.

Aged, Disabled, or Blind

In order to be eligible for SSI, a person must meet the definition of being aged, disabled, or blind.

Aged—Being deemed aged consists of attaining the age of 65 or older. The Social Security Administration, like the United States government in general, follows English common law and considers a person to attain an age the day before their birthday.

Disabled—Being deemed disabled consists of meeting the general disability definition used by the Social Security Administration:

> Disability means inability to engage in any SGA (significantly gainful employment) by reason of any medically determinable physical or mental impairment which can be expected to result in death, or has lasted or can be expected to last for a continuous period of not less than 12 months.

Income

One of the requirements to receive SSI is that the individual's income must be below certain limits. These limits may vary based on the state the individual lives in, his/her federal living arrangements, the number of people living in the residence, and the type of income. The limit varies on all of these factors and is described in the below section on benefit computation.

Resources

Another requirement for SSI is that the individual's resources are below a certain limit. Generally, this amount is $2,000 for a single individual and $3,000 for an individual and their spouse (whether the spouse is eligible for SSI or not). However, conditional benefits may be paid if a substantial portion of the resources are considered nonliquid, resources that cannot be sold within 20 working days, if they agree to sell the resourced at their current market value within a specified period and repay the money after the nonliquid property is sold.

However, not all actual resources are counted in calculating an individual's or couple's resources for SSI purposes.

The resource limits were originally set at $1500 for an individual and $2,500 for couples in 1974, and were not linked to inflation. In 1987 the limits were raised to $1,800/$2,700, in 1988 to $1,900/$2,850, and in 1989 to $2,000/$3,000. Under current law, they will remain at present levels indefinitely.

Benefit Details

Payments for SSI are made for the first day of the month, unless the first of the month is on a weekend or a legal holiday, in which case the payment is made on the first day prior that is not a weekend or a legal holiday. The minimum benefit is $1.

The SSI program, or Title XVI of the Social Security Act, provides monthly federal cash assistance of up to $674 (as of 2009) for an individual to help met the costs of basic needs of food, shelter and clothing. In most states, SSI eligibility usually assures concurrent access to important medical coverage under the various state Medicaid programs and sometimes access to Section 8 housing benefits. In some states, supplemental payments are made by the state, increasing the cash assistance available through SSI. For example, the state of California increases the cash assistance by up to $233 per month as of 2007.

❖

CHAPTER 22

The Protection of Assets

*T*he explosion of litigation in this country has been caused by many factors: the growth of the legal profession, the contingent fee system, the expansion of theories of legal liability, and the large awards returned by juries including the granting of punitive damages. These changes have given rise to the need for asset protection devices.

With proper planning, assets can be forever insulated and protected against claims of third parties.

Popular devices that afford protection over and above liability insurance are:

Limited Liability Companies and Family Limited Partnerships

Irrevocable Trusts—Domestic and Offshore

Offshore Trusts

For expatriates and the citizens of many countries, one of the principal benefits of offshore trusts is low taxes. Since assets are held offshore and are not part of an individual's estate, they can often appreciate free of domestic taxes. For the same reasons, offshore trusts are also frequently exempted from inheritance taxes.

Under U.S. law, however, offshore trusts owned by citizens of this country, whether expatriate or resident, are subject to the same taxes as any other assets.

What does make offshore trusts attractive is the protection they provide from legal challenges. For example, in common law countries, spouses can successfully contest the terms of wills if they can convince juries that they have been inadequately provided for. However, according to Nicholas Landor, a trust administrator at Hill Samuel in London: "Trusts established in offshore centers have never been challenged successfully on such grounds because legal precedents make it clear that the wishes of a trust's creator are primary to all other concerns."

No matter how controversial or complicated the terms of an inheritance may be, they are just about inviolable to claims by a third party when property is held in an offshore trust. In the United States today, it is risky for professionals to own all of their assets outright. Malpractice awards are substantial and, in many instances, cannot be covered by insurance. But if a professional transfers assets to an offshore trust, they can be protected. The offshore trust strategy would also be useful for a businessman contemplating substantial personal guarantees or becoming involved in an unsure business venture.

The key to successful offshore asset protection is a clear no-liability condition at the time the trust is created. All offshore jurisdictions have rules against financial fraud, the deliberate avoidance of creditors, or other attempts to avoid legitimate financial claims. If there are no questions about solvency or debt at the time the trust is established, then these jurisdictions consider trusts as separate entities that are free from all future claims on the assets held by the trust.

Certain offshore centers such as the Cayman Islands, the Bahamas, and the Cook Islands have taken steps to further strengthen the protection of these trusts. To clarify questions about the timing of claims made against a trust, these countries have passed statutes of limitations beyond which legal challenges to the trust cannot be made. In the Cook Islands, for example, challenges to the trust must occur during the first three years of the life of the trust. In the Bahamas, lawsuits must be brought within the first two years. And in the Cayman Islands, challenges are only valid within the trust's first six years of existence.

An offshore trust brings with it the further advantage that it removes litigation out of local courts. The foreign jurisdiction will normally not enforce a foreign court's decision without relitigating it.

Certain foreign jurisdictions do not recognize the judgments of American courts. As such, and in order to make a claim on the assets in the trust, a new case has to be brought in the foreign court based upon the local law. The claim has to be victorious, and then a fraudulent conveyance proceeding has to be brought against the trust. This would require the claimant bringing to the foreign jurisdiction witnesses, exhibits, and all other evidence required to sustain the claim. This of course assumes that the foreign court will accept jurisdiction over the matter in the first place. This entire process tends to discourage third parties from proceeding in such a fashion. Also, most of the jurisdictions that permit the creation of the asset-protection trusts do not permit contingency fee arrangements. As such, local attorneys are required to represent a claimant and have to be compensated accordingly.

Generally, in foreign jurisdictions, transfers of assets may be open to challenge under two sets of legal rules, one being known as fraudulent conveyance rules. The second set of rules deals with bankruptcy law. Once an offshore trust is created, its assets can be moved anywhere. The advantage of having an existing offshore trust is that if someone files a claim against your personal assets, the trust is not subject to the fraudulent conveyance restrictions. In fact, the trustees are obligated to take whatever action is necessary to preserve trust assets, including moving the assets anywhere in the world. Today, transactions with foreign countries are no more complicated than conducting business in another state.

Although title to the asset is held overseas, it is not necessary for the owner to part with control of the transferred property. The property may be protected by transferring it to a domestic limited partnership. The owner can receive a 99 percent interest in the property as a limited partner and a 1 percent interest as a general partner. The owner can then transfer his or her 99 percent limited partnership interest to a foreign trust. As the general partner, control of 100 percent interest of the assets is effective while owning only a 1 percent interest. Although the owner has parted with ownership of 99 percent of the interest in the assets, the foreign trustees do not directly control the assets; rather, they hold a passive interest in the limited partnership and the property will remain in the United States.

In the event creditors pressure the owner and question the structure of the trust and partnership in a U.S. court, the assets held at the limited partnership level may be transferred offshore to a foreign entity, which will substitute for the domestic limited partnership, over which the owner exercises a similar level of control.

Reporting Requirements

The grantor of an offshore trust must file certain tax returns—or else.

Form	Type of Return	Due Date
3520	Creation of and transfer of property to offshore trust	April 15
3520-A	Information return with respect to operations of the offshore trust	March 15

Form	Type of Return	Due Date
SS-4	Application for federal tax identification number	At time of creation of Offshore trust
1041	Fiduciary trust tax return. Complete only the first block and attach a separate statement as required by Treas. Reg. Section 1.671-4 that includes the name, address, and taxpayer identification number of the grantor with a statement of the income, deductions, and credits.	April 15
56	Notice concerning fiduciary relationship	Upon creating of a fiduciary relationship or with first Form 1041
709	Gift tax return	April 15
1040	Individual federal income tax return	April 15
1040, Schedule B, Part III	Interest in foreign financial account; grantor or beneficiary of Foreign trust.	April 15
TD F 90-22.1	Interest in foreign financial account.	June 30

Domestic Protection

Most of the states in this country have laws designed to protect creditors that invalidate asset transfers made at certain times or made with the intent to defraud creditors, such as when someone who has liabilities, contingent or otherwise, transfers property for less than its full value.

Planning to protect one's property can also have significant estate planning advantages. Protection devices can include trust gifts, life insurance, qualified retirement plans, and marital property division.

Recently, the U.S. Supreme Court ruled on the question as to whether state law permitting access by creditors to pension plan assets of a bankrupt individual could be preempted by federal law. The court decided favorably for plan participants by protecting funds set aside in Keogh and qualified plans. In addition, today most states now protect all IRAs from the claims of creditors in the event of bankruptcy.

In many states, property held jointly by married couples is not subject to seizure by creditors unless both spouses are obligated and then only by particular creditors. Furthermore, in most states, if a deed to real property is in the name of husband and wife, a tenancy by the entirety is presumed to be created. In such a case, if the debtor-spouse dies first, the other spouse will own the property free and clear. If the non-debtor spouse should die first, creditors could then proceed against the property to satisfy debts of the surviving spouse. When creditors face these type of situations, they will often attempt to settle claims as opposed to waiting for the death of a spouse.

Many states have homestead exemptions that protect a certain amount of the equity in a residence from creditors. In most instances, the only requirement to obtain such protection is simply filing a form requesting it. In the states of Florida, Kansas, Minnesota, South Carolina, and Texas, the dollar amount of homestead protection is not limited. At the end of this chapter is a schedule of the homestead exemptions available in the various states.

Properly prepared trusts can also protect assets from creditors. As previously discussed in chapter 14, integrating a life insurance policy with an irrevocable trust can protect the policy owned by the trust and, under the proper circumstances, will shelter it from potential transfer tax imposition.

Outright gifts to family members can be a form of asset protection if made at the appropriate time. This, however, may not be possible if recipients are minors or persons who are unable to manage investments. In such situations, trusts can be created wherein control is retained and the donor can even be the trustee and retain full control over the management and distribution of the property.

The Alaska Trust

Effective January 1, 1997, the state of Alaska established itself as an important situs for the creation and administration of irrevocable trusts for both protection against creditors and estate planning purposes. The Alaska statute provides that so long as the creator of a trust has not retained the rights to revoke the trust, the trust will be valid against creditors unless the assets transferred to the trust are intended to delay or defraud the creditors or unless the transfer was made at a time when the creator was in default by thirty days or more in making child support payments.

The Alaska statute also provides that an Alaska trust may continue in perpetuity. Under the new law, four requirements must be met for the laws of Alaska to govern the administration of the trust:

- One of the trustees must be a "qualified person," meaning that one of the trustees must be a trust company with its principal place of business in Alaska, a bank with trust powers with its principal place of business in Alaska, or an individual resident of Alaska.

- At least some part of the trust assets must be deposited in Alaska, either in a checking account, time deposit, certificate of deposit, brokerage account, trust company fiduciary account, or other similar account located in Alaska.

- The Alaskan trustee's duties must include both the obligation to maintain trust records and the obligation to prepare or arrange for the preparation of the trust's income tax returns, although neither of these duties must be exclusive to the Alaskan trustee.

- Part of the trust's administration must occur in Alaska, including physical maintenance of the trust's records in Alaska Prior to the passage of the Alaska Trust Act, there was no domestic jurisdiction wherein a grantor could "retain" the discretionary right to trust income or principal and yet have the transfer considered a completed gift for federal transfer tax purposes, and therefore not have the property included in the grantor's estate. In most jurisdictions, trust doctrine provides that where a person creates a trust for his or her own benefit, a trust for support, or a discretionary trust, his or her creditors can reach the maximum amount which the trustee under the terms of the trust could pay to him or her or apply for his or her benefit.

Alaska now provides creditor protection to a qualifying trust notwithstanding the grantor's right to receive discretionary distributions, and thereby avoids the necessity of making substantial inter vivos gifts in order to reduce the amount of one's taxable estate. The Alaska Trust was amended in the year 2006.

The State of Hawaii

On June 30, 2010, the State of Hawaii enacted a statute designed to provide for self-settled spendthrift trust protection. The law is comparable to the trend in trust law permitting discretionary asset protection trusts to be created by a settlor. The Permitted Transfers in the Trust Act are designed to increase state tax revenues by encouraging high net worth persons to create such entities for both funding and management of wealth in the State of Hawaii.

The Hawaii statute provides inter alia:

1. The trust agreement must be irrevocable and must be bound by the laws of the State insofar as its administration.
2. The settlor, among others, can reserve the following rights under the trust agreement:
   (i)   veto distributions
   (ii) execute a power of appointment by will, in favor of the settlor, not his estate
   (iii) receive the income
   (iv) receive the principal
   (v)   remove a trustee
   (vi) appoint a new trustee
   (vii) appoint a trust protector

There are approximately ten (10) other states that permit the creation of a self-settled discretionary domestic asset-protection trusts including the states of Nevada, Delaware, South Dakota, Rhode Island, and Alaska.

Domestic Family Limited Partnerships

Domestic family limited partnerships have become a popular technique for protecting accumulated wealth, as well as for potential transfer tax planning (see chapter 25). As useful as they are, there are disadvantages for potential asset protection purposes:

- The partnership entity continues to be subject to the local system of law
- Free access to the partnership assets will be prevented if a creditor obtains a court order to attach and freeze the partnership assets
- The potential ability of a creditor to establish that the purpose of the creation of the partnership was for reasons other than estate planning

The FLP can establish two distinct positives in the protection of a family's assets. One of which is a discount that can be obtained in the gift and potential transfer tax planning area as a result of transferring an interest that is both not marketable and is a minority interest thereby having no voting control. The limited partnership interest in a FLP can have the foregoing characteristics. Usually the sole remedy of a creditor of a person who holds limited partnership interests is to file a charging lien against the interests. The court can foreclose on a charging lien, which only means that the creditor receives a permanent right to receive the debtor's distributions from the limited partnership, if that is made. The partnership income attributable to the partnership interest that has been foreclosed upon will be taxed to the creditor whether it is distributed or not. Therefore, the charging lien in many instances can lead the parties to effectuate a settlement favorable to both sides.

Another strategy to protect assets is the limited liability company (LLC). For a detailed discussion of this entity, see chapter 25.

Trusts

Domestic trust law generally restricts the nature and extent of benefit and/or control that a creator of a trust can retain. Our laws generally provide that if you do not place the assets of the trust out of your reach (irrevocable trust), the trust property will not be placed out of the reach of a creditor.

If you create a trust at a time when there is absolutely no fraudulent conveyance issue, it could be attacked years after its creation if you have retained any benefit or control from or over the property placed in the trust.

An asset-protection trust integrated with an overall estate plan can accomplish everything a typical inter vivos living trust can accomplish, including avoidance of probate, confidentiality, asset administration in the event of the creator's disability, continuity upon the creator's death, and potential transfer tax planning.

These trusts can be either domestic or offshore. A spendthrift trust is one that does not permit the beneficiary to assign his or her rights to the income and principal of the trust. Under New York law, every irrevocable trust is automatically a spendthrift trust. If one creates a trust in another country the laws of that country will be applicable to the trust. These laws in certain instances may be more favorable to the debtor than local U.S. law, i.e., attorneys in many foreign countries are not permitted to engage on a contingency basis; the foreign country's laws may require a shorter period for bringing a claim of fraudulent transfer; the foreign country is usually not obligated to recognize a U.S. judgment or claim; once a lawsuit is threatened the situs of the trust may be moved to another jurisdiction. In other words, offshore trusts complicate the ability of a creditor to satisfy a claim.

Prior to 1997, offshore trusts were the only place that offered a protection of assets if a person created a self-settled irrevocable trust. In 1997 the states of Delaware, Nevada, Utah, Rhode Island, and South Dakota enacted laws recognizing self-settled irrevocable trusts. Alaska also adopted a protection of assets statute and amended in 2006. Most of the statutes of these states are similar, however, under Alaska law a creditor has four years after a trust has been established to bring a claim for it to be recognized, whereas, under Nevada law the period is two years. Under Delaware law, the creator of an irrevocable trust can retain a right to receive income of the trust. However, the Supreme Court of the United States has not as yet ruled on whether a state must give full faith and credit to the laws of a sister state regarding wealth-protection trusts.

The foregoing items are just a few of the routes that can be taken in seeking the protection of assets from creditors.

Homestead Exemptions

STATE	EXEMPTION ($)
Alabama	5,000
Alaska	27,000
Arizona	100,000
Arkansas	2,500
California	Limited
Colorado	30,000
Connecticut	None
Delaware	None
District of Columbia	None
Florida	No limit
Georgia	5,000
Hawaii	30,000
Idaho	50 over the mortgage
Illinois	7,500
Indiana	7,500
Iowa	Unlimited (but does not apply to debts dated preownership)
Kansas	No limitation
Kentucky	5,000
Louisiana	15,000
Maine	12,500
Maryland	None
Massachusetts	100,000
Michigan	3,000
Minnesota	No limit
Mississippi	75,000
Missouri	8,000

STATE	EXEMPTION ($)
Montana	40,000
Nebraska	10,000
Nevada	95,000
New Hampshire	30,000
New Jersey	Yes
New Mexico	20,000
New York	2,000
North Carolina	Yes (Value is set by statute)
North Dakota	80,000
Ohio	None
Oklahoma	5,000
Oregon	15,000
Pennsylvania	None
Virgin Islands	30,000
Rhode Island	None
Virginia	5,000
Tennessee	5,000
Washington	30,000
Texas	No limit-acreage limit
West Virginia	5,000
Utah	8,000
Wisconsin	40,000
Vermont	30,000
Wyoming	10,000

CHAPTER 23

Family Limited Partnerships and the Limited Liability Company

*F*or wealthy families, the family limited partnership can be the cornerstone of their estate plan. The ability to do business in partnership form and limit your liability can be very significant. This chapter discusses in great detail limited liability companies, what they are and their benefits.

There are at least eighteen states that have laws permitting the creation of limited liability companies (LLC). The purpose of this kind of entity is the avoidance of unlimited liability on the part of the general partners in a general partnership. Under general partnership law, general partners are liable for all of the obligations of the partnership, to the extent that the partnership assets are not sufficient to satisfy the same. In a limited liability company, none of the members of the company have any personal responsibility for the obligations of the company. In a professional limited liability company, each member is liable for his own misconduct, and it is only the property of the negligent party and his supervisor that is available to a damaged third party.

In a general partnership, the injured third party can look to the personal property of all of the partners to the extent that the partnership assets are not sufficient to satisfy his or her claim.

Overview of the Family Limited Partnership (FLP)

Currently, one of the most exciting topics in the field of estate planning is the use of the family limited partnership for the purposes of wealth transfer.

Under such a plan, an individual contributes property to a limited partnership, in exchange for general and limited partnership interests.

Thereafter, gifts of limited partnership interests are made to family members or trusts for their benefit, with the individual donor retaining the general partnership interest.

In a limited partnership, the general partner is the individual who has the exclusive management and control over the partnership assets. This includes the determination of the timing and the amount of distributions to all of the partners as well as the compensation to the general partner for services rendered to the partnership.

Even though the general partner has retained control over the assets of the partnership, the gifts of the partnership interests will not be included in his or her estate. The values of the transferred limited partnership interests for gift tax purposes, due to lack of marketability and minority discounts, will be less than the value of the same partnership assets.

The discounts represent a recognition by the government that a minority interest in a business is not readily saleable and that the owner of a minority interest has no control over the property owned. Depending upon certain factors, the amount of the discount may vary between 10 percent and upward of 50 percent. In addition to the use of the $1,000,000 exemption in making gifts of these interests ($2,000,000 if the gifts are split between spouses), the family limited partnership can be used to take advantage of the generation-skipping transfer tax exemption in effect at such time.

Assets that are subject to a large discount could therefore be transferred, not only avoiding gift taxes, but generation-skipping transfer taxes as well, which are taxed at the rate of 35 percent of the value of the gift.

Until the Internal Revenue Service issued a ruling in 1993 permitting these discounts, it had maintained that if members of a family owned all of the entity, the family controlled it, and any gift or sale of a minority interest was not entitled to be discounted in value for gift tax or sale purposes.

A byproduct of the family limited partnership is a lower tax bracket for the limited partners through income shifting. Another advantage of the family limited partnership is that creditors of the limited partners cannot touch the assets of the limited partnership.

What Is It?

The term "family" implies that the partnership is owned by family members. A limited partnership has both "general partners" (who run the partnership) and "limited partners" (who as passive investors have no vote nor any voice in the management). General partners have unlimited personal liability for partnership obligations, while limited partners have no liability beyond their capital contributions.

The partnership ownership can be divided among the general and limited partners in any way the partners designate. In a family limited partnership, the interest of the general partner is usually 1 percent and the balance of the interests is owned by the limited partners. Since the general partner has the only vote on partnership business decisions, it makes no difference how small that interest is for voting and, therefore, control purposes.

In a family limited partnership, both general and limited partners share income, loss, tax attributes, and cash flow based upon their ownership percentage interest in the partnership.

How It Works

The general partner transfers property to the partnership in exchange for the ownership of the entire limited partnership interests. He or she thereafter will eventually, on an annual basis, transfer limited partnership percentage interests of the limited partnership to members of his or her family by taking advantage of the annual exclusion ($10,000). This process may go on for years, depending upon the value of the assets, the number of beneficiaries, and the amount he or she wants to transfer.

The Advantages

There are many tax and nontax benefits to the family limited partnerships. They include:
- Reduced asset values for transfer tax purposes through valuation discounts
- General partner's ability to make substantial gifts and also maintain control of the assets
- Sheltering of gifts from the creditors of the recipients of the gifted interests
- Continuing control of income from transferred assets, since distributions from the partnership must be authorized by the general partner

- A means to segregate partnership assets as separate assets and not marital assets
- Gifts of limited partnership interests will qualify for the annual gift exclusion since they are present interest gifts
- Reduced probate costs with respect to real estate located in other states
- The advantage of enjoying tax, management, and operational flexibility that may not be available in other formats

What Assets Should Be Funded in the Partnership

The most advantageous would be those that are most likely to appreciate in value. Real estate interests, marketable securities, and cash can be transferred to the partnership. The reason that the gift of a limited partnership interest is discounted for transfer tax purposes is due to the fact that the recipient receives a minority interest, which is nonvoting, and as such cannot exercise any control over the investment nor realistically can he or she sell it in the open market. In addition, the partnership agreement usually places restrictions upon the limited partner's transfer of his or her partnership interest without first offering the interest to a group usually consisting of close family members.

If the senior members of a family do not wish to have the next generation own their interests in the family limited partnership outright, an irrevocable trust can be formed. Their partnership interests can be gifted to it. A parent could even serve as the sole trustee without having any beneficial interest in the trust, and the powers of the trustee could be limited to an ascertainable standard, which means that the income from the principal in an FLP would be applied on a discretionary basis, for the health, maintenance, and welfare of the beneficiary.

For those who have significant assets, family limited partnerships may be the best answer to reducing transfer taxes. The ruling by the Internal Revenue Service that minority interest discounts for closely held business interests can be claimed, even when related family members own the entire entity, has opened the door to wide use of this very significant strategy.

Asset Protection Trusts and Family Limited Partnerships

The best of both worlds can be accomplished when asset-protection trusts (APT) and family limited partnerships (FLP) are combined. The combination can be achieved merely by one or more gifts to the trust of a limited partner's interest. Control over the partnership assets can be maintained by the general partner. If a general partner of a family limited partnership is facing potential creditors, choices may be available that might otherwise not exist. These could include having an offshore trustee remove the domestic trustee of an APT and cause the liquidation of the FLP. In this instance, the assets of the partnership would be distributed to the APT based on its ownership share. Thereafter, and in the exercise of the trustee's legal responsibility to preserve the assets in the interests of the beneficiaries, the foreign trustee could place the distributed assets out of the jurisdiction of the general partner's residence, which then places the battle over those assets in the foreign court.

Limited Liability Companies (LLC)

The LLC is really a hybrid partnership-corporate entity. It has the flow-through income tax characteristics of a partnership and the limited liability qualities of a corporation. It has been described as a limited partnership with no general partner and an S corporation without partnership restrictions.

The background for this form of organization comes from the desire and need for a business structure that is taxed as a partnership, yet protects its owners from unlimited liability. The general and limited partnerships offer the desired flow-through tax treatment, but the general partner (or partners) in each instance have unlimited personal liability for partnership debts. This corporation form limits the liability of its owners but does not offer the flow-through tax treatment of the partnership. The S corporation comes closest to the desired objectives, but the S corporation is less flexible than the partnership and is subject to certain restrictions that render it impractical in many situations.

The first limited liability company statute was enacted in Wyoming in 1977. Today, about forty states have approved this form of entity, including the states of New York and New Jersey.

LLC Basics

The LLC is an unincorporated entity with two or more members formed under state law. The LLC is formed by filing articles of organization with the appropriate state agency. Those articles of organization state the name of the entity, the date of creation, the names of the managers, if any, and the nature of the business. These articles of organization are similar to the certificate of limited partnership for a limited partnership.

Structurally, then, the LLC has the look of a partnership. The LLC does not issue stock certificates; the interests of the members are described in a document known as the operating agreement, a document that looks and works much like a partnership agreement. The operating agreement describes the interest of each member in LLC profits, liabilities, and capital.

Owners of the LLC are referred to as members. All the members will be responsible for the management of the LLC unless the operating agreement specifies one or more managers to manage its affairs. The manager need not be a member of the LLC and there is no restriction with respect to who can be a manager. Therefore, members can consist of corporations, partnerships, nonresident aliens, trusts, or any other legal entity in addition to individuals. Members should consider entering into agreements with each other, similar to buy/sell or shareholder agreements providing, among other things, for the management of the business and the division of its profits and losses.

The obvious advantage of the LLC over the partnership is the absence of personal liability of any of the principals. In the general partnership, all the partners have personal unlimited liability for the debts of the partnership. Even the limited partnership must have at least one general partner and that general partner is personally liable for the debts of the limited partnership. In the LLC, none of the members, whether they are managers or not, are personally liable for the LLC debts. In fact, the members of an LLC can participate in the management of the LLC without exposing themselves to personal and unlimited liability. In contrast, if a limited partner takes on management responsibilities, he or she also takes on the personal liability of a general partner.

Estate Planning Considerations

The members of the LLC face all the estate planning problems and challenges encountered by other owners of closely held businesses. While there has not been a great deal of experience with LLCs, the issues with respect to the valuation of the interest of a member should be identical to those of the partner in a partnership and a stockholder in a corporation.

For estate planning purposes, the LLC has advantages over an S corporation with regard to certain step-up in basis provisions, and because an LLC is subject to partnership tax provisions, it is not subject to what is commonly called the "Anti-Byrum" Amendment. This amendment is very technical and covers what happens when a donor transfers an interest in property consisting of shares of stock of a corporation, and retains certain rights over the property. In a 1995 case, the following took place.

On May 1, 1995, Jack Green owned 250 shares of stock in Greenco, his family's closely held business. The 250 shares represented 25 percent of the outstanding stock of Greenco and had a fair market value of $2,500,000. Jack's brothers Harold, Mike, and Bob each owned a 25 percent interest in Greenco. Greenco's value had been increasing rapidly, and Jack wanted to transfer some of his shares to his son, Roy, so that the appreciation on these shares would avoid taxation in Jack's gross estate. At the same time, however, Jack did not feel Roy was ready to have a voice in corporate decisions and wanted to keep the right to vote the shares he transfers.

On May 2, 1995, Jack transferred one hundred shares to Roy, but retained the right to vote these shares for the rest of his life. When Jack dies in 2005, the family members still have the same respective ownership interests in Greenco. Assume that at the time of Jack's death, the 10 percent interest held by Roy has increased in value to $2,000,000.

On these facts, the full $2,000,000 value of the stock in which Jack retained the voting rights would be included in his gross estate under Code Sec 2036(b). Although Jack owned only 15 percent of the Greenco stock directly during the last three years of his life, the 85 percent owned by Roy, Harold, Mike, and Bob are attributed to him under Code Sec. 318, and he is deemed to own 100 percent of the Greenco stock at the time of his death.

The problem illustrated in this example might not have been encountered if Greenco had been an LLC instead of an S corporation. Code Sec. 2036(b) applies to stock in corporations and not to ownership interests in a partnership. Because LLCs are subject to the partnership tax provisions and not the corporate tax provision of the code, the "Anti-Byrum" Amendment would presumably not be applicable to them.

Recent Governmental Developments

Revenue Ruling 93.12, which permitted the use of cutting-edge estate planning devices, has caused the Internal Revenue Service in recent times to go public in the areas of discount planning. The government wants to block abuses that are taking place and stop the sham transactions that are being created. These are occurring in circumstances where discounts are being taken for 50 percent to 80 percent on portfolios consisting only of readily marketable securities in false family limited partnerships or where the sole function of the creation of the FLP and the taking of the discount on transfers is to reduce the potential transfer tax.

There is presently no stated Internal Revenue Service position with respect to the acceptable range of discounts, nor is there any specific standard being employed by the government to stop the taxpayer from overreaching.

Some examples of the egregious situations that have been reported are detailed below:

The Service recast the transfer of FLP units as a sham in a marketable securities partnership formed two days prior to the death of a ninety-two year old, where transfer was made by a power of attorney holder, and disallowed a claimed 50 percent discount.

In another case, a physician was advised that he could establish an FLP and transfer all his real estate to the partnership (with himself as a 1 percent general partner and trusts for the benefit of his three children owning 99 percent limited partnership interests), when at the same time he was negotiating a settlement of substantial income tax liability with the Internal Revenue Service pertaining to other matters. The doctor was denied a discharge of his indebtedness to the government and the transfer to the FLP of his real estate, at a time when the government was pursuing collection, constituted a willful attempt to evade or defeat the taxes he sought to be discharged.

In another case, the FLP was formed two days before the decedent's death when the decedent was terminally ill and had been removed form life support. The Internal Revenue Service took the position that the valuation discounts should be disallowed. One theory was that the formation of the partnership and the transfer of the partnership's interests should be treated as a single testamentary transaction and therefore the partnership should be disregarded for purposes of potential transfer tax valuation under the sham transaction doctrine.

In another case, the Internal Revenue Service held that the value of transferred property is included in a decedent's gross estate if there is an express or implied understanding at the time of transfer that the transferor will retain the economic benefits of the property. In this situation, the decedent created three family limited partnerships and transferred interests in them to her children. A partnership bank account was created for each partnership, but partnership income was not deposited into this account. Instead, in violation of the partnership agreements, it was deposited into the decedent's personal checking account and commingled with her other assets. Thus, the decedent was managing the assets exactly as she had before the transfer. This fact, combined with the acknowledgment by the children that formation of the partnership was merely a way to allow the decedent to assign interests in partnership assets, indicated that there had been an implied understanding that the decedent would retain the enjoyment of the property for her life.

The FLP is certainly a valid and significant device in the estate planning process. In addition to the preservation of wealth and reduction of estate, gift, and generation-skipping taxes, it offers an asset protection feature. This technique and other value reduction devices should be used under proper circumstances. "Deathbed" eve filings for bankruptcy transfers are cases of misuse and improper situations. For future planning, a solid foundation needs to be constructed to insure that the vehicle is viable.

Family Limited Partnerships (FLPs) Update

The government's campaign against the FLP has been both unsuccessful and successful in the courts. A federal district judge in San Antonio, Texas ruled in the Matter of E. Church Estate that the decedent's holdings could be valued at less than half of the fair market value for estate tax purposes. There were three other cases in the same year that rejected the challenges of the government to the FLP discounts and sustained the taxpayer's valuation discounts.

In 2007 the courts held that FLP assets were subject to estate tax under Section 2033 when taxpayers failed to complete the transfer of assets properly and Section 2036(a)(1) when there were implied agreements to retain enjoyment on the income from the transferred assets. In examining the situation the total facts will be examined by the court. If partnership formalities are not followed there is a retained interest in the economics of the transaction, the full value of the property transferred will be included in the transferor's estate for potential transfer tax purposes. In the transfer of assets, where the full control is not relinquished and certain rights are retained, such as the right to receive the income until the death of the transferor, the transferred property will be included in the gross estate.

In 2008 there were several important cases regarding the inclusion of FLP partnership interests in the estates of decedents under Internal

Revenue Code Section 2036 and the valuation of gifts of partnership interests, which cases indicate:

- For the bona fide sale exception of IRC Section 2036 to apply, you must have a legitimate non-tax purpose for forming the FLP.
- There must be active management of the assets of the partnership.
- Gift-giving can be a legitimate non-tax purpose for forming an FLP (although it cannot be the sole purpose).
- Formation by one person who received 100 percent of the partnership interests does not prevent the application of the bona fide sale exception.
- Management strategies for limited liability partnership (LLP) assets should be documented and implemented.
- No assets of the partnership can be used for personal expenses; the partnership cannot be treated as a bank account.

Unless Congress enacts rules to the contrary, some recent court cases in the tax court of the United States afford the ability to obtain reductions in values (discounts) in the valuation of family limited partnership assets. The rules in the courts have set forth that if the appropriate prior steps and procedures are followed in the valuations, the properties involved should be discounted. The recent court cases have also provided an alert that all of the steps involved in a valuation discount transaction should not be effectuated at the same time. In other words, the Internal Revenue Service has maintained where each of the transactions (gift/sale, etc.) were done at the same time they merged into one (1) larger transaction and resulted in one large gift of the underlying assets. The recent cases have held that 6–12 days was a sufficient time period between transactions.

2036 Inclusion

Under IRC Section 2036(a)(1), a decedent's gross estate includes the fair market value (FMV) of transferred assets to the extent that the decedent retained possession or enjoyment of, or the right to income from, the assets for his or her life or for any other period that does not end before death. In order not to have a retained interest described in Section 2036(a)(1), a person must have completely and irrevocably parted with all of their title, possession, and enjoyment of the transferred assets. No express or implied agreement among the parties at the time of transfer that the donor will retain the possession or enjoyment of, or the right to the income from, the transferred property, can exist.

Under IRC Section 2036(a)(2), a decedent's gross estate includes the fair market value of transferred assets if the decedent died with the right, either alone or in conjunction with any person, to designate the persons who shall possess or enjoy the property or the income therefrom (as a general partner or manager, for example). Section 2036(a) includes an exception if the decedent's transfer of the assets to the partnership constituted a bona fide sale for adequate and full consideration. In the context of FLPs, this requires that the transfer was made for a legitimate and significant non-tax business purpose; that is to say, there were non-tax reasons for establishing the partnership and that the transferor retained partnership interests proportionate to the value of the property transferred.

In 2009 there were four important cases that were won by the taxpayers. The estates were able to prevail against challenges by the Internal Revenue Service on the basis of the bona fide sale exception to Code Section 2036. In the foregoing cases, the estates were able to establish, with the satisfaction of the court, that the transfer's contribution of assets into the FLP was made in furtherance of appropriate non-tax business purposes.

These cases serve to reinforce the structuring of the FLP to the extent that in addition to establishing legitimate non-tax purposes for creating the FLP:

- for a transfer of FLP interests to constitute bona fide sale the taxpayer should retain sufficient assets to support his or her lifestyle;
- all appropriate business operations should be observed and respected after the FLP is created;
- active investment/management of the assets of the FLP must be observed.

In addition to meeting the technical requirements in the formation of an FLP, the following should exist:

- The partners should follow all the procedures required by state law and the partnership agreement in all actions they take with respect to the partnership.
- The general partner should retain only those rights and powers normally associated with a general partnership interest under state law, and no extraordinary powers.
- The partnership should hold only business or investment assets (or both) and not hold assets for the personal uses of the general partner.

- The general partner should report all partnership actions to the limited partners, and the limited partners should act to ensure that the general partners do not exercise broader authorities over the partnership affairs than those granted under state law and the partnership agreement.

The points in the following list should be considered in planning and administering an FLP:

- The partnership should be formed first and interests transferred at a later date.
- A professional, independent appraiser should be used to value the underlying partnership assets (with the exception of liquid assets, i.e., cash and marketable securities).
- The FLP should be created when the donor is healthy. Before his death in 1992, Sam Walton wrote a biography wherein he explained how his family beat potential transfer tax. In 1953, he put his business into an FLP and gave shares—at very low values—to his children.

In the partnership agreement, make reference to the non-tax purposes for its formation, such as:

- Asset protection.
- Bringing assets together for common management.
- Permitting the donees to observe the donor's management philosophies.
- Limiting the transfer of assets outside of the family.
- Reducing probate costs.
- Making it easier to make gifts of various assets in a group of assets
- For the state of jurisdiction of the partnership, choose a state with favorable partnership laws, such as Delaware (it does not automatically allow a limited partner to withdraw from the partnership).
- The partnership agreement should deny a limited partner the right to withdraw.
- The partnership term should be of a long duration.
- The general partner can be a corporation.
- The partnership agreement should provide for the annual distribution of the net income.

- The transfer of partnership interests should be subject to restrictions and the consent of the general partner.
- A donor should not give shares of voting stock in a closely held corporation to an FLP in which the donor is the general partner.
- Do not use the partnership funds for personal use.
- Do not put your residence into a partnership. If you do, you must pay rent (the partnership is supposed to be set up for business purposes).
- Try to put a mixture of assets into the partnership.
- Do not mix an offshore trust with a partnership.
- Do not set up the partnership on your deathbed.
- Be careful in mixing charitable transactions and partnerships.

The Charging Order

A creditor of a limited partner can petition the court for a charging order which gives the creditor the right to attach distributions made to the partner. In such event, all distributions that would have been made to the partner will be made to the creditor. The creditor receives no voting rights and has no method to force distributions to be made. Furthermore, a creditor would not have the right to succeed to any of the ownership rights of a partnership interest. Problems can arise when attempts are made to circumvent a creditor's charging order by making loans or other payments to the debtor partner.

❖

CHAPTER 24

Estate Planning for the Business Owner

*I*f you have an interest in a business, you have to take into consideration a variety of factors that will affect this interest during your lifetime and at the time of your death.

This chapter outlines what must be contemplated. This includes whether such an interest will be sold when you die, who will succeed to the management after your death should you place this interest in trust to be managed by your trustees, how will it be valued, and how the taxes will be paid.

In this chapter, you will learn about important strategies that should be considered during your lifetime, such as the buy/sell agreement, the use of life insurance, and avoiding probating your business interests.

Today, as a result of a recent revenue ruling (1993), minority business interests can be gifted away or sold at a discounted value for gift tax purposes. These very important methods are discussed, as well as the significance of structuring your estate in order for it to qualify for an estate tax payment deferral (which can be up to fifteen [15] years).

If you own an interest in a business, no matter the form of ownership—sole, partnership, or corporate—you must have an estate plan. It is important to make provisions for the succession of management and future ownership. It has been said that many closely held businesses fail to survive past the first generation due to lack of proper planning. If a business is to be sold or liquidated, arrangements for these events have to be considered. If there is to be a continuity, a decision has to be made on the method of transfer to the survivors, whether outright or in trust. The assets of a business should be sheltered from potential transfer tax to the extent possible, and probate should be avoided to ensure a prompt continuity at the least amount of expense.

Usually, it is not advantageous to discontinue a business immediately upon the death of the sole owner, unless it is a single-person business. Some flexibility should be afforded to the survivors to continue its operation until it can be liquidated or sold by them on the most favorable terms. This can be done by ensuring that there are key employees in place who will agree to continue to operate the business for a period of time on an agreed compensatory basis, usually for something more than just a salary—for example, a participation in the profits.

If there is more than one owner inheriting the business, and there may be a conflict on whether to keep, sell, or liquidate the business, having in place an estate business plan will help to deal with an issue of this kind. The beneficiaries of an interest in a business who continue as owners usually do not have any input into the management of the affairs of the business. This is usually left in the hands of the other surviving owners. As such, the beneficiaries have to rely on the controlling owners for a return on their investment.

Following are three concerns all family business owners must address as they plan their estates:

- Who will take over the business if I die? Owners often fail to develop a management succession plan. It is essential to the survival of the business that successor management, whether from the family or otherwise, be available to take over the stewardship.

- Who should inherit my business? This may not be an asset that should be split equally among children. For those active in the business, inheriting it may be critical to their future motivation. To those not involved in the business, the interest may not be seen as valuable. Perhaps the entire family feels entitled to equal shares in the business. This issue has to be resolved to avoid discord and possible disaster later on.

- How will the Internal Revenue Service value the business? Because family-owned businesses are not publicly traded, it is usually impossible to know the real value of the business. The final value placed on the business for potential transfer tax purposes is often determined only after a long and tedious battle with the Internal Revenue Service. It is critical that the owner plan ahead and make sure there is enough liquidity in his or her estate to pay estate taxes, in addition to providing support for heirs.

Transfer Tax Breaks for Family Businesses

With the potential severity of potential transfer tax, Congress recognized that family businesses might have to be sold just to pay the bill. To help lessen the tax burden, Congress provided two types of relief for business owners.

Section 303 Redemptions

The company can buy back shares of stock from an estate without the risk of the distribution being treated as a dividend for income tax purposes. Such a distribution must, in general, not exceed the potential transfer taxes imposed, funeral, and administration expenses of the estate. To qualify, however, the value of the business interest included in the estate must exceed 35 percent of the value of the adjusted gross estate.

If the redemption qualifies under Section 303, there will be no negative income tax consequences to the distribution, and cash from the corporation can be made available to pay expenses. This is an excellent way to pay potential transfer tax.

Real Estate

Real estate that is used for a business can be valued for potential transfer tax purposes on a "special use basis": As such real estate can be valued at its "present use" rather than the "highest use" yield, so that farm property can be valued as its use as a farm rather than a potential location for a commercial development (shopping center, etc.). In order for this rule to apply, the following conditions must exist:

- The value of the family business must equal 50 percent of the gross estate.
- The value of the real estate of the business must be at least 25 percent of the overall estate.
- The decedent or a member of his or her family must have used the real estate for the business during five of the preceding eight years.
- There also exist certain restrictions on the sale or mortgage of the property for a period of up to fifteen years after the receipt of the tax considerations.

Using Life Insurance

Instead of paying the tax in installments, heirs can use life insurance proceeds to pay potential transfer taxes. There are several advantages to this method. Insurance provides an immediate source of guaranteed liquidity and avoids a forced sale of business or other estate assets.

The estate must have cash to pay interest on the deferred tax installments. This amount can be quite substantial, particularly if the liability is paid over the full deferral period. An additional "hidden" obligation is keeping the estate open during the deferral period. By paying the tax with insurance proceeds, the legal administrator avoids any additional administration costs. Provided that ownership is structured properly, it is possible to have the proceeds available to pay taxes, yet not have them taxed at the estate owner's death (see chapter 14).

Gifting the Family Business

The key to reducing potential transfer tax is to limit the amount of appreciation in the estate. As an example, assume that a business is worth $500,000 today but is likely to be worth $1 million in future years. By giving away the business interests today, the future appreciation will be kept out of the estate owner's taxable estate.

There may be no better gift than an interest in the family business, which may be the fastest appreciating asset owned.

Minority Discount

Those who plan to make a gift of an interest in a family business should be aware of a recent ruling by the Internal Revenue Service that makes it possible to transfer a larger share of a family business without paying tax because a minority stake in the business can be valued at a discount.

The Internal Revenue Service revenue ruling said that a gift to a family member can be made at a "minority discount." The discount is a recognition that a minority interest, which is an interest that has either no vote or is less than a controlling (usually 51 percent) interest, in a parcel of real estate or other property may be worth less than face value because it cannot easily be sold and the owner may have little control over the whole property.

Although the Internal Revenue Service has long recognized minority discounts, it had excluded family businesses, reasoning that when the entire business was held by family members, the family controlled it and there was, in effect, no minority. A number of court decisions over the years, however, found in favor of the discounts for family members, and the Internal Revenue Service reversed itself 1993.

This ruling means the Internal Revenue Service has recognized that family members, too, have their fights and their disagreements and that just because people are related does not mean they have the same idea about running a business. Here is how the ruling might help save on potential transfer taxes which can be substantial, when transferring shares in a family business. Each taxpayer is entitled to give $13,000 a year to any number of people without paying gift taxes. A couple can give $26,000 to each of their children, or others. By making use of the minority discount, then, an individual or couple can transfer a larger percentage of the business without the involvement of potential transfer taxes.

Although the Internal Revenue Service did not authorize a particular percentage discount in its ruling, most courts feel that 30 percent is reasonable for transfer tax planning purposes.

Furthermore, a couple need not be the sole owners to take advantage of the minority discount. The Revenue ruling stated that the discount would be permitted, "whether the donor held 100 percent or some lesser percentage of the shares of stock immediately before the gift."

The minority discount has applications beyond the $13,000 annual gift provision. Anytime a business is broken into pieces, the discount may apply. Consider the example provided by the Internal Revenue Service: One person owns all the shares of stock in a corporation. He or she transfers 20 percent to each of his five children. Even though the family still has 100 percent of the company, the value of the shares can be discounted.

Advantage of the discount can be taken through a sale of property as well as through the gift technique. Let us say a person plans to use the minority discount to sell some commercial property. The property is valued at $400,000 and generates $40,000 a year in income. The person plans to sell it to his or her four children for a total of $280,000.

The children will pay a parent a purchase price of $280,000, with interest, over twenty years, so he or she will receive income from the property. Because the property was sold for less than its market value, incurring a capital loss, the parent will get the return of principal tax-free, although he or she must pay income tax on the interest. If the parent still owned the building, he or she would have to pay tax on the income in any event. The estate owner in this situation would sell the shares separately to the four children, each receiving a one-quarter interest and paying $70,000 for his or her respective share.

Part of any gift-giving program should include the family entering into a buy/sell agreement (see below). Such an agreement could prevent a spouse of a child from owning the shares of the family business. In addition, and at the time of the gift giving to the children, shares could be given to the grandchildren in trust. The trust, with its income, could purchase life insurance on the life of the parent of the grandchild and if the parent should predecease the grandparent, the trust could purchase the shares of stock of a predeceased child of the estate owner.

Estate Freeze

A flexible strategy for the business owner was reinstated in late 1990 when Congress retroactively repealed the "estate freeze" legislation that had become law in 1987. Prior to the enactment of this law, it was common for business owners to recapitalize their business, retain a preferred stock interest, and give all of the common stock interest to their beneficiaries. This way, they remained in control of their company and "froze" the value of their stock for potential transfer tax purposes. All future appreciation affected only the common shares, not the owner's preferred stock.

Congress recognized the estate tax loophole and created Section 2036(c) in an attempt to prevent future estate freezes. The section was under constant attack since its creation and was finally repealed retroactively in 1990. In its place, Congress passed legislation that once again permits the use of estate freezes, but only if certain requirements are met.

Gifting family business interests can be a very effective potential transfer tax saving strategy. Caution has to be taken because of some of the problems involved. The value of the gift can have both gift and potential transfer tax ramifications. The Internal Revenue Service may challenge the value placed on the gift and try to increase it substantially.

The Buy/Sell Agreement

When a business has multiple owners, whether it be a partnership or corporation, its owner must create a plan that is consistent with the owner's business plan.

A powerful tool to help keep control of the future of a business is the buy/sell agreement. This is a contractual agreement between the shareholders and their corporation, between a shareholder and other shareholders of a corporation, or among partners in a partnership. Without such an agreement, chaos can arise among the business owners. In such an event, the law of the state where the business is located will be applied. This can produce disastrous results. For example, the law of most states provides that, upon the death of a partner, the partnership must be dissolved, unless an agreement among the partners provides to the contrary.

If a sole proprietor wants his or her business to continue after death, a designee, if possible, should be named to continue the business for the benefit of the survivors. The agreement controls what happens to a business interest in the event of a specific event, such as the disability or death of a shareholder. For example, the agreement might provide that, at the death of the partner or shareholder, or upon a permanent disability, his or her interest is bought back by the business entirely.

As an alternative, the agreement might provide that the other individual owners purchase the partners interest or that the business is to be sold or liquidated.

A well-drafted buy/sell agreement can solve several estate planning problems for the closely held business owner:

- It can provide a ready market for the interest in the event the owner's estate wants to sell upon death.
- It can set a price for the shares. In the right circumstances, it can also fix the value for potential transfer tax purposes.
- It can provide for a stable continuance of the business by avoiding unnecessary disagreements caused by an unwanted new owner.
- The valuation of the decedent's interest in the business has valuable meanings to the beneficiaries. In the first instance, it sets a standard for either the purchase of it by the surviving owners or a sale to third parties if the agreement among the owners permits such a transaction. The value is required to be known for estate tax purposes even if the estate is not subject to potential transfer tax. Even though the government is not bound to accept a value set by partners, it can view it as a basis if the valuation method is reasonable.

These methods for determining value are usually set forth in the agreement of the owners, which agreement could provide, inter alia:

- The establishment of a flat dollar amount for the disabled or deceased owner's interest.
- Setting up an appraisal method to value the business.
- Agreeing on the method to establish a book value of the business.
- Providing a capitalization of net earnings method to determine the value of the business.

- In most instances, providing that if the disabled or deceased owner's interest is not purchased by the remaining owners, the business is to be liquidated and the net proceeds distributed to the owners, including the disabled owner and the estate of a deceased owner.

Life Insurance and the Buy/Sell Agreement

Life insurance may serve a major role in funding a buy/sell agreement because it provides the ready cash to finance a transaction in the event of death of a shareholder. Proceeds may be received free of income and potential transfer tax. The proceeds are paid to the deceased shareholder's estate, and the executor then assigns the stock to the remaining shareholders or corporation.

However, watch out for a tax trap that may exist in buy/sell agreements. For example, assume a corporation funds a buy/sell agreement by buying $1 million worth of life insurance for each shareholder. The life insurance proceeds paid to the corporation are free from regular income tax but subject to the alternative minimum tax (AMT), a flat tax designed to ensure that corporations pay their fair market share of taxes. Under the AMT rules, 75 percent of the insurance proceeds, or $750,000, is taxed at a 20 percent rate, yielding a tax bill of $150,000. As a result, the company actually holds only $850,000 worth of life insurance net of taxes, not the $1 million policy face value.

To avoid this potential problem, the insurance policies should be owned individually rather than through the corporation. In this instance, each owner owns a life insurance policy on the other, subject to the terms of the buyout agreement among them. For individuals who conduct their business as S corporations, the AMT is not an issue, because the insurance proceeds flow through directly to the individual shareholder's income tax returns.

Probate Avoidance

In most instances, in order to keep a business free of outside involvement, the probate process should be avoided. Subjecting a business to probate, in many jurisdictions, places the management of the business in the hands of the court during the probate administration. This can be avoided by the use of the living trust, which for most tax and administrative reasons is usually the best choice.

The owner of the sole proprietorship should likewise consider selecting a living trust as the best way to avoid probate. If a business is owned by more than one individual, whether it be in partnership, corporate form, or joint venture form, the living trust is certainly the best probate avoidance device. Each business agreement among the owners would provide for the ability of each owner to transfer his or her interest to a living trust. Each of the owners would therefore incorporate into his or her living trust provisions that are consistent with the business plan, for example, rights of the surviving owner to purchase the interest of a deceased owner.

Unless lifetime planning has taken place providing for an orderly continuity of affairs, the business owner and especially the owner of a sole proprietorship runs the risk of his survivors encountering a potential decimation of this asset because of the problems that might arise.

The Job Protection Act of 1996

The Job Protection Act of 1996 (the "Act") expanded the type of trust that is eligible to own shares of stock in a Subchapter S corporation.

Under prior law, only a certain type of trust such as a Qualified Subchapter S Trust (a "QSST") could be a shareholder in an S corporation. A QSST is a trust under whose terms (1) only one current income is permitted, (2) the principal of the trust can only be distributed to that beneficiary, and (3) the income of the trust must be distributed to the beneficiary.

These requirements prevented a QSST from sprinkling or spraying its benefit among more than one beneficiary or accumulating the income.

The Act expanded the type of trust allowed to own shares of stock in an S Corporation to include the "electing small business trust" (an "ESBT"). To qualify as an ESBT, all beneficiaries of the trust must be either individuals or certain charitable organizations and all interests in the trust must have been acquired by it either by gift or bequest. Each beneficiary of the trust will be counted as a shareholder, the number of which was increased by the Act to seventy-five from thirty-five. The trust can have multiple beneficiaries, and its benefits can be distributed among its beneficiaries, or its income can be accumulated. The remainder beneficiaries can be different from the income beneficiaries, i.e., income to spouse for life with remainder to children.

A downside to the use of this trust is that the income that is received by the trust from the S corporation will not be taxed to the beneficiary but to the trust at its maximum individual rate. Income received by the trust from sources other than the S corporation is subject to the normal rules of trust taxation.

Significant Recent Trends

What follows is a discussion of significant recent trends:

Blockage Discount

Blockage discounts in a gift transaction represent the adverse effect upon fair market value arising from the additional competition that real properties create if offered concurrently on the market. If a portfolio of properties is sufficiently large within an applicable market so that a concurrent offering of the properties would reduce the value, then a blockage discount for residential apartment property within a prescribed neighborhood of a major city is applicable.

Capital Gains Tax Liabilities

A taxpayer can reduce the fair market value of a gift of an interest in a corporation to take into account potential capital gains tax liabilities that may be incurred if the corporation were liquidated or distributed or its assets were sold, even in the absence of any plans for a liquidation, sale, or distribution.

Estate Freezing Techniques: Grantor Retained Annuity Trusts

A grantor retained annuity trust (GRAT) is an irrevocable trust to which a business owner can transfer shares in his or her business (typically Subchapter S stock or interests in an LLC or FLP) but retain the right to a fixed annuity (payable not less than annually) for a stated term of years. At the end of the stated term, which must expire during the business owner's lifetime, the property remaining in the GRAT (i.e., the appreciation and income in excess of the annuity amount that is to be paid to the business owner) will pass to the beneficiaries (children). Only the value of the remainder interest (passing to the children) is subject to gift tax. Thus the larger the annuity, the longer the stated term, and the lower the IRS assumed interest rate, the smaller the gift to the children. For gift tax purposes, the Internal Revenue Service has indicated that it intends to do away with a (a zero gift tax value) "zeroed-out" GRAT, a gift that produces no gift in excess of the annuity amount payable to the business owner. If the GRAT fails to produce a return in excess of the annuity amount the remainder beneficiaries will receive nothing and the assets are returned to the grantor. As such there is no gift tax cost to the business owner. From a gift tax point, a GRAT can be an excellent estate planning device. The downside of a GRAT is that the business owner fails to survive the term of the GRAT and it aborts with his or her death during the term thereof.

Installment Sales to Intentionally Defective Grantor Trusts

Technique

The plan calls for an installment sale of nonvoting property (FLP or LLC interests) to an irrevocable trust (grantor) in exchange for a balloon promissory note. The purchase price may be significantly discounted, depending on the nature of the property sold. Prior thereto, a trust is created which will be treated as owned by the grantor for income tax purposes, but not for transfer (gift and estate) tax purposes. The taxes paid by the grantor on the trust's income and capital gains, if any, are tax free gifts to the beneficiaries of the trust.

In order to avoid characterization of the transaction as merely a gift with a retained interest, it is generally suggested that the trust be "seeded" with an initial gift of assets equal to at least ten (10%) percent of the value of the property ultimately to be purchased from the grantor. It has been suggested that a guaranty of the debt due by the beneficiaries of the trust or if possible collateral be given (mortgage or security interest) that could serve as a substitute for the seed funds.

Certain types of property will tend to maximize the estate freezing potential of this technique. The sale of an interest in a family limited partnership or LLC will allow for substantial discounts for minority interests and/or lack of marketability. Potential for post-transfer appreciation will also enhance the estate freeze, as will the ability to funnel income into the trust.

Conclusion

Business succession planning is critical to ensure the continuation of a family owned business, particularly if the owner plans to retire within a reasonably short period of time. An effectively developed succession plan provides for a smooth transition in management and ownership with a minimum of transfer taxes. Additionally, a business succession plan can provide financial security and freedom to the retired business owner and his or her spouse. Once completed, the business succession plan will provide peace of mind for the business owner and its employees, personal satisfaction for family members and new opportunities for the business itself.

❖

CHAPTER 25

Estate Planning for the Surviving Spouse

$\mathcal{E}$state planning for the surviving spouse can involve a number of issues, including appropriate election in the first estate, the proper use of the marital deduction, disclaimers, and income tax planning. This chapter discusses a few of these considerations.

Disclaimers by the Surviving Spouse

A qualified disclaimer made by the surviving spouse is treated as if such interest had never been transferred to him or her. A disclaimer may be desirable in the following circumstances:

General Disclaimers

If the estate of the surviving spouse is large so that the acceptance of a bequest would result in increasing the potential transfer tax payable on death, in excess of what could be saved by accepting the bequest and thereby reducing the potential transfer tax of the estate of the first to die, then a disclaimer should be considered. The loss of the use of money used to pay the higher potential transfer tax in the estate of the first to die must be considered in such a situation.

Disclaimer by Surviving Spouse to Save the Applicable Credit

In the situation where the entire estate provides for an unlimited marital deduction, the decedent's applicable credit would be wasted. However, the waste can be avoided by having the surviving spouse make an appropriate disclaimer of a fractional part of the amount passing to him or her under the unlimited marital deduction bequest. The amount disclaimed would fall into the nonmarital trust and ultimately would pass to the remainder beneficiaries.

Disclaimer of Applicable Credit Amount

A surviving spouse may disclaim his or her life interest in an applicable credit trust. By doing so, the applicable credit bequest will pass to the decedent's alternate beneficiaries (usually the children of the decedent and the disclaiming spouse). If only the applicable credit amount is disclaimed by the surviving spouse, no added tax will be due, unless, under state inheritance tax laws, nonspousal beneficiaries are given lower exemptions or are subject to higher rates of tax than spousal beneficiaries. No potential transfer tax will be due by reason of a shift in ownership of an applicable credit legacy. Disclaimers of an applicable credit trust interest by the surviving spouse can be useful if the surviving spouse decides that sufficient assets exist so as to provide his or her lifetime support.

Disclaimer of Pension Benefits and IRAs

The Internal Revenue Service has ruled that a disclaimer of benefits under a qualified employee retirement plan is allowable and is not treated as an alienation of plan benefits.

In a letter ruling, a surviving spouse transferred her one-half interest in the decedent's IRA, which was community property, to an IRA in her own name with her children as beneficiaries. She then disclaimed the maximum amount of her interest in the decedent's one-half interest that would incur no potential transfer tax and transferred the undisclaimed portion of the decedent's one-half interest to her own IRA by a direct trustee-to-trustee transfer. The disclaimed portion of the decedent's interest in the IRA was ruled not to be includable in the surviving spouse's estate.

In another letter ruling, disclaimers were used successfully to permit a surviving spouse to roll over IRAs originally payable to the decedent's estate. Under the decedent's will, the IRAs passed to a residuary qualified terminable interest property (QTIP) trust. The spouse, the decedent's children, and the minor and unborn issue of the decedent—through their guardian ad litem—executed qualified disclaimers of a pecuniary amount of the residuary estate equal to the value of the IRAs and, in the case of the children and the minor and unborn issue, all their interest in any property passing under state intestacy law. The personal representative then funded this amount passing to the spouse with the IRAs. The government ruled that the IRAs passed directly from the decedent to the surviving spouse and qualified for the marital deduction.

Disclaimer of Community Property

A surviving spouse can make a "qualified disclaimer" of a decedent's rights in community property, regardless of the fact that she may have retitled certain of the community assets to her own name. So long as the survivor did not draw any funds or income from the accounts listed on the disclaimer (and made the disclaimer within nine months of the decedent's death), the act of retitling the assets did not constitute acceptance of the decedent's share of the community property interest or its benefits.

Disclaimer in Favor of the Surviving Spouse

A person other than the surviving spouse may make a disclaimer that results in the property disclaimed passing to the surviving spouse. In such a case, the disclaimed interest is treated as passing directly from the decedent to the surviving spouse and would increase the marital deduction. The increased marital deduction, in turn, would reduce the decedent's potential transfer tax, while possibly increasing the taxes of the survivor's estate.

Such a disclaimer might be effected, for example, where bequests to children exceed the exemption equivalent of applicable credit. The children could disclaim that portion of their bequests that would eliminate or reduce the potential transfer tax as much as possible. Children might do this for a variety of reasons, including concern for the spouse's needs. But they may also do so with the reasonable hope that gifts in the amount of their disclaimed bequests will later be forthcoming, in installments if need be, to minimize or eliminate gift taxes. Also, depending on a variety of circumstances, they may benefit by the potential transfer tax savings.

Disclaimer of Marital Property

The Internal Revenue Service has increased the use of disclaimers by surviving spouses that allow joint marital property to be disclaimed. Code Section 2518 allows disclaimers of one-half the property held as joint tenants if the surviving spouse disclaims within nine months after the death of the joint tenant, regardless of when the joint tenancy was created.

Use of Disclaimer to Create a Marital Deduction Trust (QTIP)

The tax court of the United States has ruled, in a memorandum decision, that an estate was permitted to elect QTIP treatment for a trust that by its strict terms permitted the accumulation of income. The *Lasiter Est. v. Comr.* case involved the estate of Henry Lasiter, a Georgia resident, who left a 1970 will that provided that the decedent's residuary estate was to be divided into two trusts: (1) a general power of appointment marital trust, the funding of which was limited to a pre-1982 marital deduction; and (2) a residuary trust, which provided for income and principal to be distributed among the decedent's wife and descendants. Specifically, the trustee of the residuary trust was to pay "such part of the income and/or principal . . . as it [deemed] necessary to provide for the support in reasonable comfort" of the decedent's wife, as well as "to provide for the support and education of [the decedent's] children and the descendants of any deceased child. . . ." In addition, the decedent's wife was given an inter vivos and a testamentary limited power of appointment over the residuary trust principal.

Through a series of disclaimers, the family sought to convert the residuary trust into a QTIP marital trust and thereby avoid having to limit the marital deduction to one-half of the decedent's adjusted gross estate. Therefore, the children and the court-appointed guardian for the decedent's minor child, et al., claimed their respective interests in the residuary trust during their mother's lifetime, including any rights as possible beneficiaries under the decedent's wife's inter vivos power of appointment. The decedent's wife, who was also the decedent's personal representative and trustee, also executed a disclaimer in which she disclaimed her inter vivos power of appointment over the trust as well as any various fiduciary powers.

There are several vehicles, such as a family limited partnership (FLP) or a limited liability company (LLC), that can be used for gift-giving purposes while the donor retains control of the investment as a general partner and reduces the value of the gift by way of a discount (by providing the gifted interest as non-voting). Grits, Grats, and Gruts are available as well for inter vivos transfers.

One offsetting consideration in making lifetime gifts instead of testamentary transfers is that the donor pays a gift tax now to save potential transfer tax later. Thus, the lower tax on large lifetime transfers over large testamentary transfers must be weighed against the lost use of the money, also taking into account (1) income tax savings from income shifting and (2) potential transfer tax savings from removing the future appreciation and the gift taxes paid from the donor's gross. If the donor dies within three years of having made the gift, however, the gift taxes are included in the donor's gross estate, and the computational advantages of the lifetime transfer are lost.

Life Insurance

Depending on the needs of the family, life insurance should be investigated for purposes of providing additional family wealth. The age and health of the spouse are significant in the availability of this kind of property.

Remainder Interests

Under the code, the remainder interest in a QTIP trust will be subject to potential transfer tax in the surviving spouse's estate. In a recent case, the surviving spouse purchased the remainder interest from the remainder beneficiaries, causing a merger of the two properties' interests (income and remainder) and, as a result, extinguishing the trust. The Internal Revenue Service has not ruled that the amount paid in the acquisition of the remainder interest was a gift since the surviving spouse "in effect" already owned the property in the trust.

Closely Held Interest

If the surviving spouse is in a controlled position as the managing member of a limited liability company or general partner of a limited partnership, consideration should be given to dilute and/or surrender this interest for restriction or elimination of the eventual potential transfer tax impact purposes.

Charitable Interests

The surviving spouse may also wish to consider creating charitable interests upon his or her demise or during his or her lifetime, with remainder interests to charity. These types of transfers and/or trusts can provide potential transfer tax deductions upon the death of the surviving spouse. A charitable remainder trust created during lifetime, will provide a lifetime income and an income tax deduction for the value of a charity's interest in the remainder. A testamentary charitable lead trust (CLAT) could be considered. The establishment of a CLAT at the time of death allows the decedent's heirs to benefit from any appreciation in value of the trust assets while the charity receives six annual payments of annuity income during the term.

IRA Planning

The Internal Revenue Service ruled in Revenue Ruling 2005-36 that a surviving spouse could disclaim a portion of an IRA even after having received from the IRA the required minimum distribution for the year of the decedent's death.

If the IRA owner had not yet reached age 10½ at the date of death; the required beginning date for the surviving spouse, a beneficiary, to begin taking minimum distributions may be postponed until the end of the year in which the IRA owner would attain 70½.

The surviving spouse has the right to rollover into his or her own name, which means that the spouse-beneficiary becomes the participant of the IRA and is treated as such under the minimum distribution rules.

Asset Allocation

The failure of ensuring that each spouse owns a sufficient amount of property to apply the available potential transfer tax exemptions and credits could result in a greater potential transfer tax after both are deceased. As a general rule, it is proper planning to be sure that each spouse has sufficient assets in his or her name for such use. Since there is no gift tax between spouses, this can be accomplished by inter vivos transfers from the more advantaged spouse, whether outright or in trust.

Conclusion

The surviving spouse needs to contemplate the use of other potential transfer tax-saving devices, such as charitable transactions and the use of gift-giving exclusion and exemption, all of which are discussed in greater detail in this book. Lifetime gifts provide not only a method of avoiding probate and eliminating administration costs but also help protect the assets of the estate. They can produce savings and afford benefits for the entire family in the following ways:

- All appreciation will never be subject to potential transfer tax.
- If the gift is made more than three years before the donor's death, any gift taxes paid will not be included in the donor's estate.

- If the gift is to a family member in a lower income tax bracket, there will be a reduction of family income taxes.
- The income earned on the gifted property, after taxes, will be excluded from the donor's gross estate.
- Death taxes will be reduced.
- The annual exclusion and exemption gifts can remove assets from the donor's estate without potential federal and state transfer tax There should be no hesitation in the surviving spouse to implement an estate plan that has as a goal of the conservation of the estate and the protection of wealth that has taken a lifetime to accumulate.

CHAPTER 26

The Cutting Edge: Value-Reduction Strategy in Discount Planning

*A*n estate faced with a large potential transfer tax calls for highly aggressive estate planning. The following are a few of the "hottest topics" created in estate planning today.

The Family Limited Partnership: Various Techniques

A family limited partnership (FLP) can be used to transfer property interests all within one (1) family unit, but at significant discounts from what otherwise would be fair market value. The thrust of the FLP is to make lifetime transfers of property at significant reductions in the tax otherwise payable on the transfer of property at death. The use of the FLP requires a substantial inter vivos taxable gifting program. The latter calls for a deep concern about saving taxes for the beneficiaries and a willingness to make significant gifts during the estate owner's lifetime.

Technique. The family member contributes property (real estate, cash, marketable securities) to the FLP in return for an ownership interest in the capital and profits of the partnership.

The partnership interests are broken down into general partnership (GP) interests and limited partnership (LP) interests. The GP assumes management responsibility and personal liability for partnership obligations not satisfied by the FLP's assets. The personal liability of the LP is limited to their investment.

Typically, the family member receives a 1 percent GP interest and a 99 percent LP interest. Gifts are then made of LP interests to children and grandchildren (in trust).

The transfer (gift) tax value of the LP interests are substantially less than the underlying asset value. The reduction in value or discount is a result of lack of a ready market and the LP's inability to make decisions regarding the management of the FLP, to demand distributions, and to force a liquidation of or withdrawal from the partnership. The leverage of valuation discounts can be further enhanced by selling LP interests to a defective grantor trust.

Sale to a Defective Grantor Trust

Technique. This plan calls for an installment sale of property (LP interests) to an irrevocable trust (grantor) in exchange for a balloon promissory note. Prior thereto, a trust is created that will be treated as owned by the grantor for income tax purposes but not for transfer (gift and estate) tax purposes.

In order to avoid characterization of the transaction as merely a gift with a retained interest, it is generally suggested that the trust be "seeded" with an initial gift of assets equal to at least 10 percent of the value of the property ultimately to be purchased from the grantor. As an alternative to seeding a trust, the beneficiaries of the trust can guarantee the note or the noteholder can take back a creditor's lien on the trust property, i.e., UCC-1 or mortgage lien.

The grantor then sells property to the trust in exchange for a promissory note usually calling for payments of interest-only during the term of the note with a "balloon" payment at the end. The purchase price may be significantly discounted, depending on the nature of the property.

Certain types of property will tend to maximize the estate-freezing potential of this technique. The sale of an interest in a family limited partnership (FLP) will allow for substantial discounts for minority interests and/or lack of marketability while enabling the grantor to maintain effective control of the business. Potential for post-transfer appreciation will also enhance the estate freeze, as well as the ability to funnel income into the trust.

Generally, the note would call for annual interest payments by the trustee to the grantor. However, the interest can be accrued. Payments may be made from the "seed" money (or additional gifts made by the grantor to the trust) or investment earnings thereon or from income generated by the purchased property or, if necessary, by return of some portion of the property in kind to the grantor.

Upon maturity of the note, principal is repaid to the grantor (or his or her estate or heirs) in cash or in kind. Repayment in the event of death may be facilitated by life insurance on the grantor's life owned by the trust. Use of life insurance also reduces the need to sell low-basis assets and may provide the trustee with cash to acquire other assets from the estate.

One of the other advantages of the grantor trust is that all trust income would be taxable to the grantor, not the trust, which results in additional tax-free gifts being made to the trust's beneficiaries. By paying the tax, the grantor is reducing his or her taxable estate by the amount of the tax paid plus the appreciation thereon.

The most important benefit derived from a transaction that includes a grantor trust is that it is not recognized for income tax purposes, but will be acknowledged for transfer tax purposes. Once assets are placed in a grantor trust their appreciation will accumulate free of income, gift, and potential transfer tax. Therefore, a grantor has a way to commence transfer tax free growth by selling assets to a grantor trust.

FLP: Estate Discount

Technique. An FLP is formed by the estate owner. The general partner would be a Sub S Corporation formed by the estate owner. The estate owner would sell to his or her children controlling voting shares of the corporation, and the corporation would thereafter, as a general partner, manage the limited partnership. The estate owner would subscribe for the entire limited partnership interest and would thereafter continue his or her investment in the partnership, which would have investment activities, etc. No gift is made by the estate owner, and the purpose of the transaction would be to obtain a discount in the estate owner's estate of at least 40 percent of the date-of-death value of his or her interest in the partnership. The larger the investment, the greater the size of the discount and the more the potential transfer tax savings.

During the estate owner's lifetime, the partnership will need to invest and have activities (purchasing/selling, etc.).

Be aware of the imposition of Section 2036 of the code as follows:

- In a sale, it might be better to make sure some principal payments are made before the due date of the note.
- Make sure there is a valid business non-tax purpose; relinquish all rights to the interests in the properties transferred that motivated the creation of the entity; make sure that there is an active ongoing management of a mix of property; engage a reputable appraiser to value the discounts that you seek.

- Examples if non-tax purposes are:
  - (i) succession of the management of the assets;
  - (ii) protecting the entities assets from divorce claims, creditor's claims, inheritance claims;
  - (iii) maintaining a family's investment principles;
  - (iv) consolidation of a families assets for estate administration purposes.
- Observe the step transfer theory. Do not fund, gift/sell, the interests in the entity on the same day. A period of time between the two should be observed. If not, the Internal Revenue Service may look to call the entire transaction as a gift of the underlying assets. In recent cases, at least 6–12 days was acceptable.

Family Split Dollar

The Family Split Dollar planning possibilities are numerous. Family Split Dollar arrangements are particularly well suited for estate owners with taxable estates who do not wish to give up control over their life insurance policies. Many individuals with taxable estates die owning their personal life insurance policies. They fail to transfer the ownership of the policies out of concern that they may need access to the policies' cash values. Family Split Dollar may be the perfect solution.

What Is Family Split Dollar?

In general, Family Split Dollar is a shared premium arrangement between two parties in a nonemployment context. Typically, the owner of the policy will be an irrevocable trust. Rather than contributing to the trust an amount equal to the entire required premiums, the grantor can avoid potential transfer tax, gift, and potential generation skipping taxes on the funding of a life insurance policy by obtaining the necessary cash from any available source. The only gifts required to be made to the trust are smaller amounts equal to the annual economic benefit cost of the life insurance death benefit that will be paid to the trust. In other words, rather than having to gift the entire life insurance premium to the irrevocable trust, the grantor will only have to gift the federally published annual P.S. 58 table rates (or the so-called P.S. 38 costs for a survivorship policy) or the insurer's alternative term rates into the trust each year.

In Private Letter Ruling 9636033, the Internal Revenue Service ruled favorably for the first time on the validity of a Family Split Dollar arrangement.

The arrangement in the private letter ruling was an agreement between the insured's spouse and the insured's irrevocable trust. The insured's irrevocable trust applied for, owns, and is the beneficiary of a life insurance policy on the life of the insured. The trust will contribute toward the annual policy premiums an amount equal to the economic benefit cost (the P.S. 58 table rate or the insurer's alternative term rate in accordance with Rev. Ruls. 64-328 and 66-110). The amount of the economic benefit cost will be gifted to the trust each year by the insured.

The insured's spouse will pay all of the policy premiums in excess of the economic benefit cost, in accordance with the split dollar agreement signed by the spouse and the irrevocable trust. The split dollar agreement provides that the insured's spouse owns all of the cash value of the policy.

The policy is collaterally assigned by the trust to the spouse as security for the spouse's interest. The collateral assignment utilized gives the assignee (the spouse) the right to execute policy loans and surrenders (partial and full), and the right to change the dividend option. As long as the parties' marriage is stable and as long as the spouse does not predecease the insured, the economic unit of the insured and spouse always have complete unencumbered access to the cash value of the policy. The pure death benefit in excess of the policy cash value is owned by and is payable to the irrevocable trust and therefore escapes taxation in the estates of both the insured and the insured's spouse.

The Service ruled in PLR 9636033 that as long as the irrevocable trust contributed an amount equal to the economic benefit cost of the insurance coverage, there would be no estate or gift tax (and presumably no income tax) consequences resulting from the split dollar arrangement (assuming that gifts into the trust are covered by the annual gift tax exclusion).

Owner of Life Insurance: FLP versus Irrevocable Trust

Family limited partnerships are entities that may be used to further business and family planning objectives while at the same time providing gift and potential transfer tax benefits through the application of marketability and minority interest discounts. Given the right circumstances, the family limited partnership may be a viable alternative to the irrevocable life insurance trust.

The real and perceived disadvantages of irrevocable life insurance trusts have prompted many financial and tax advisers to recommend that their clients consider the use of a partnership as an alternative ownership vehicle for needed life insurance coverage. We all know the general problems with life insurance trusts. Generally, these arrangements are irrevocable in nature, which means that changes in family and financial situations may not be adequately met by the inflexibility of in most trust agreements.

Since trusts are creatures of state law, they normally require a judge's approval for modification, which translates into added legal costs. In addition, the insureds should probably not serve as their own trustees because having some personal decision-making power over how trust assets are distributed may result in potentially adverse tax consequences. These issues of "irrevocable commitment" and "surrender of control" are two of the major reasons why many life insurance trusts are never completed.

In addition, the Crummey clause provisions for irrevocable life insurance trusts are under continued intense scrutiny by the Internal Revenue Service. It is the Crummey power language that allows the premium payments to be characterized as present interest gifts eligible for the gift tax annual exclusion.

Thus, many individuals have begun to speculate on how long it will be before congressional action either eliminates, or severely restricts, this approach to life insurance planning. Although predicting what Congress might or might not do is at best a chancy proposition, there's no denying that the loss or severe limitation of the Crummey powers could bring into question the continued viability of the irrevocable life insurance trust as an estate planning technique.

For all these reasons, the use of a family limited partnership (FLP) should be considered. What we are talking about, of course, is a bona fide partnership that has legitimate business purposes and has not been established solely for tax avoidance purposes or simply to hold life insurance policies.

Typically, the life insurance need is for estate liquidity or to permit an orderly business continuation program. This need remains the same under either approach. We are simply substituting partnership ownership for trust ownership. In doing so, however, there are numerous advantages to the partnership that are not available when an irrevocable trust arrangement is used.

Partnerships do not require judicial involvement to make changes in ownership, management, or even in distribution patterns for profits and losses. Thus, all parties to the transaction—even senior family members—retain some control over being able to revoke or modify the terms of the partnership arrangement. Since the partnership is the owner of the life insurance policy(ies), these powers give the individuals indirect control over the life insurance policy(ies). Further, partnership tax provisions have many advantages over tax provisions for estates and trusts.

If the FLP Owns the Coverage

In effect, a bona fide family limited partnership (FLP) becomes the vehicle for investing in the same needed life insurance coverage that would have been purchased under the irrevocable life insurance trust. Generally, the insured (or insureds) would be the senior family member(s) who will also be acting as the managing partner(s) of the FLP but who would own only a small equity interest. The FLP itself, however, is the owner and beneficiary of the policy and would pay the premiums from its funds.

The partnership form of ownership also assures that there will be no potential transfer-for-value problems if the ownership of the policies needs to be restructured within the terms of the FLP itself. Transfers of life insurance policies to and from the FLP itself or among the various partners are statutory exceptions to the transfer-for-value rules. This exception would also apply to transfers of any other life insurance policies outside the FLP among the various partners. Thus, the income tax–free nature of the insurance death proceeds is not in danger of being lost because of potential changes in policy ownership.

The Flexible Irrevocable Trust

These devices, in addition to the basic estate planning tools, such as the bypass or credit shelter trust, irrevocable life insurance trust, family limited partnership, and the qualified personal residence trust, are the basic programs being used in sophisticated estate planning today. The gross estate of every individual includes not only property owned at death but also property the person gave away during his or her lifetime, over which particular rights or benefits were retained so as to be included under various sections of the code.

The two common thrusts of the two important provisions of the code (Sec. 2036 and Sec. 2038) are that (1) the estate owner gratuitously transferred property (gift) and (2) the estate owner kept some right, benefit, or power prohibited by the code.

Section 2038 causes property to be included in the decedent's gross estate if he or she transferred property by gift and, at the date of his or her death, the enjoyment of the property was subject to change through the exercise of a power by the decedent alone or in conjunction with others to amend, revoke, or terminate.

Section 2036 requires the decedent to possess the prohibited powers and does not cause inclusion if any family member of the decedent has such powers.

The code, the cases, and the revenue rulings are clear that potential transfer tax inclusion under Sections 2036 and 2038 can be avoided if the decedent does not keep (1) any right to enjoy or possess the property; (2) any income from the property; (3) any right to determine who will enjoy or possess the property; (4) any right to determine who will receive the income; and (5) any right to amend, revoke, or terminate the trust.

Giving Rights to Others

Nothing in the code prohibits a person from giving such rights to another person (i.e., your spouse) and not having these sections apply.

Accordingly, if one wishes to "have his or her cake and eat it too" and not have the property included in his or her estate and that of his or her spouse, one can establish a trust for the benefit of his or her children, and the grantor and the trustee may have the following powers:

The grantor may have:
- The power to substitute assets of an equivalent value without the consent of the trustee
- The power to allocate receipts and disbursements as between principal and income, even though expressed in broad language
- The power to change the trustees, but cannot name himself or herself as a trustee
- The right to direct investments and vote stock held by the trust other than stock of a controlled corporation

The trustee may:
- Be a spouse and be granted broad discretionary powers over the distribution of the trust income and principal to his or her children, but he or she cannot make any distribution that would satisfy a legal obligation of either spouse

- Be granted discretionary powers to distribute trust income and principal for his or her health, education, support, and maintenance
- Have a broadly stated limited power of appointment that would allow him or her to appoint the property (income and principal) to the grantor but not to himself or herself, his or her creditors, his or her estate, or the creditors of his or her estate

In addition, the children may have the power to appoint trust principal to the grantor.

In summary, one would not have the right to dictate or control what is to be done with the property given away. There must be no existing agreement between the spouses to exercise a power that has been given to the trustee.

The potential transfer tax laws have historically permitted spouses to act in concert and allow a spouse or other family members to hold powers over property that the estate owner (decedent) could not hold.

Trust and Leaseback

The potential transfer tax impact on a family can be reduced by creating a trust, for the benefit of the family, and transferring to it, by gift or sale, a business asset. After the property has been transferred, the trust will lease back the property to it. Thereupon the rental payments the lessee has to pay must be reasonable rent. In order for the transaction to be valued from an IRS viewpoint, there must be a valid business purpose to it. Asset protection from the transferring point of view is sufficient reason to establish a valid of purpose.

Charitable Lead Trust (Testamentary)

The use of this type of estate freeze technique is usually when the taxpayer is alive. However, it can be established at the time of death in order to continue the appreciation value of the assets. A charitable lead annuity trust is a GRAT equivalent except that the annuity for the trust term is paid to a charity instead of retained by the grantor of the trust. An advantage of the CLAT is that it can be used testamentary, as offset to a GRAT, which is for lifetime use. The testamentary CLAT provides the vehicle to ensure that any appreciation in value passes to the descendants of the grantor and not to a charity. A testamentary CLAT cannot be a grantor trust and is a separate taxpayer for federal income tax purposes.

An example of a testamentary CLAT is as follows:

Decedent intends to leave $1 Million to charity at her death. If she leaves it outright, her estate will receive a potential transfer tax $1 Million charitable deduction, subject to the potential transfer tax which could be $500,000 (if no charitable bequest).

If instead a CLAT was established at death, to pay $100,000 per year to the charity for 10 years, with the remainder, if any, to pass back to the decedent's family, then assuming as Sec. 7520 rate of 4% and a total return of 1% it would require that the trust be funded with only $811,090, to produce annual payments of $100,000. Furthermore, at the end of the trust term of the decedent's heirs would receive $510,027 free of potential transfer taxes, plus an additional $98,000 at the decedent's death ($1,000,000 − 811,090 × 52%).

The premises of the annuity are based upon the dual effect of the potential transfer tax charitable deduction and the ability to appreciate the CLAT corpus at a rate in excess of the annuity rate, results in the enhancement in value of the ultimate distributions of the trust to or for the benefit of the decedent's family. The price paid for this benefit is the ability of the family members to the use of the assets of the CLAT during the term of the trust.

Life Estate

A life estate is a popular estate planning technique. It usually will avoid probate and achieve the decedent's goals. The technique to create a life estate in most instances is through the provisions set forth in a will or trust. A life estate in real property affords the life tenant with all of the benefits and responsibilities of ownership of the property. This means that the life tenant not only possesses the use and enjoyment of the property but has the required duty to maintain the premises. The instrument creating the life estate must be clear and unequivocal as to the terms of the life estate and the obligations of the life tenant during the term thereof. Usually if the life tenant chooses to have the premises sold, the net proceeds are placed in trust for the benefit of the life tenant for the balance of the term. With regard to personal property, a life estate can be created, however, a tenant who is granted a life estate in personalty will have the responsibilities of a trustee over the property in his or her possession.

Trust Decanting

Decanting is a technique that can be available to amend the provisions of an existing irrevocable trust that needs to be changed. Seven of our states—New Hampshire, Florida, South Dakota, Tennessee, New York, Alaska, and Delaware—allow trustees by statute to modify an irrevocable trust. Modification of an irrevocable trust means the trustee of a trust can take part or all of the assets of an existing trust and transfer them to a new trust that has provisions different from the original trust agreement.

Some of the main reasons for amending a trust agreement are changing the termination date of a trust; to the degree permitted, modify the distribution provisions; provide for successor trustees; change the situs of a trust; change the administration clauses; modernize an outdated trust, which would include bringing it up to date with the current transfer tax laws.

The statutes of the various states that permit modification require that the trustee of the trust agreement to be amended must have discretion to invade the principal of the trust. It has been accepted in all of the foregoing states that the designated beneficiaries under the original trust agreement need not benefit under the newly created trust agreement. Under New York law, a trustee may invade the principal of a trust for the benefit of one or more proper objects of the exercise of the power. It has been interpreted that "proper objects" means that beneficiaries under the original trust agreement may not be included in the modified trust agreement but that beneficiaries not set forth in the original trust agreement may not be included in the amended trust agreement.

The Delaware statute does not require a trustee to have absolute authority to invade the principal of a trust but only requires the trustee to have the authority to invade the principal of a trust. Under Delaware law, a trustee can expand the beneficiary class beyond the beneficiaries designated in its original trust agreement but which cannot be accomplished by granting a trustee a power of appointment.

The New York decanting statute was the first of its kind in the United States. It was enacted in 1992 and revised in the year 2000. The different states who have adopted trust remodeling each have particular unique provisions. New York has not revised its statute since its last revision. The ability to revise a trust agreement can now be a routine step in a family's planning especially where there are changes in circumstances, whether they are motivated by family or financial causes.

As of the date of this book, Pennsylvania and Ohio were considering whether to enact their own respective decanting statutes.

A Perpetual Trust

The various purposes of creating a trust (1) reduce overall taxation on the property held in trust and/or the income it produces (2) to guarantee professional objective management of the assets and (3) protect the beneficial interests of the beneficiaries from claims of creditors. Where the law permits, in today's world, it is not inappropriate to create a trust to last as long as the law it is subject to permits. However, powers to terminate and/or distribute its assets, sooner, can be given to the trustee and/or the beneficiary.

A perpetual trust can be created by providing that the trusts assets, at each generational level, shall continue to be held for the then living descendants, upon the same terms and conditions. Therefore, each descendant for whom a share in trust is created, becomes the primary beneficiary until his or her death, when the trust assets pass in trust to his or her descendants.

In selecting who should serve as trustee, a primary beneficiary should be considered together with a professional trustee. However, the primary beneficiary should be given the right to replace the professional trustee (with or without cause).

In a perpetual trust, the primary beneficiary, at each level, should be granted certain powers of appointment such as (1) the right to change the manner of the dispositive provisions, which could include the right to direct that a portion of the trust property may be distributed outright and (2) the right of a primary beneficiary to withdraw a certain limited amount of trust property during each year of the term of the trust. These rights can be granted to the trustees rather than the beneficiary.

Each family, given health circumstances, potential creditors, claims, etc., given their particular circumstances, needs to decide how long a trust should last. It is easy to terminate a trust but impossible to get the assets back into a trust, if they have been distributed.

CHAPTER 27

Overview of the U.S. Estate and Gift Taxes as Applied to Nonresidents Not Citizens

Domicile

For purposes of the U.S. estate and gift taxes, an alien is considered a U.S. resident if he or she is domiciled in the United States at the time of his or her death or at the time of a gift. If an alien enters the United States for even a brief period of time, with no definite present intention of later leaving the United States, her or she is deemed to be domiciled in the United States and, therefore, is considered a U.S. resident for estate and gift tax purposes. Thus, an alien may be considered a nonresident for potential transfer tax purposes and a U.S. resident for income tax purposes, or vice versa, since the potential transfer tax residency test is the more subjective domicile test just described, while the income tax residency test is met if the alien satisfies an objective day count test known as the "substantial presence test" or holds a green card (i.e., is a lawfully admitted permanent resident of the United States).

Under the estate and gift tax domicile rules discussed above, a person acquires a domicile in a place by living there, for even a brief period of time, with no definite present intention of later leaving. This determination is a factual issue that focuses on many factors, none of which is determinative. Some of the factors on which the IRS and court focus are (i) the length of time spent in the U.S. and abroad and the amount of travel to and from the U.S. and between other countries; (ii) the value, size, and locations of the donor's or decedent's homes and whether he or she owned or rented them; (iii) whether the alien spends time in a locale due to poor health, for pleasure, to avoid political problems in another country, etc.; (iv) the situs of valuable or meaningful tangible personal property; (v) where the alien's closed friends and family are situated; (vi) the locales in which the alien has religious and social affiliations or in which he or she partakes in civic affairs; (vii) the locales in which the alien's business interests are situated; (viii) visa status; (ix) the places where the alien states that he or she resides in legal documents; (x) the jurisdiction where the alien is registered to vote; (xi) the jurisdiction that issued the alien's driver's license; and (xii) the alien's income tax filing status.

Assets Subject to U.S. Estate and Gift Tax

Generally, nonresident aliens are subject to potential transfer tax only on "U.S.-situs" property, with no credit for foreign death taxes paid. The foreign country may allow a credit against its death taxes for transfer tax paid. Nonresident aliens are also subject to federal gift tax on lifetime gifts of U.S. situs property, but not on gifts of U.S. situs intangible property.

U.S. situs property includes the following: (i) real property located in the United States; (ii) tangible personal property located in the United States (including cash, U.S. Treasury Bills, cars, furniture, jewelry, artwork, etc.); (iii) shares of stock issued by a U.S. corporation; (iv) subject to certain exceptions (set forth below), any debt obligation, the primary obliger of which is a U.S. person or the United States, a state or any political subdivision of the United States, or the District of Columbia, or any agency or instrumentality of any such government; (v) property that is gratuitously transferred by a nonresident alien decedent while he or she is alive, by trust or otherwise, if (A) the nonresident alien decedent retained for his or her life (or for a period that cannot be ascertained without reference to his or her death) some type of possession, control, or enjoyment of said property or its income or the right to designate who will possess or enjoy the property, (B) possession or enjoyment of the property could be obtained only by surviving the decedent and the decedent retained a reversionary interest in the property that exceeds 5 percent of the value of the property at the time of the decedent's death, (C) said property was, on the date of the nonresident alien decedent's death, subject to his or her right to alter or revoke the transfer (or if such power was relinquished by the NRA decedent within three years of the date of his or her death), or (D) if the decedent transferred within the three-year period prior to his or her death an interest in property that would have been included in his or her estate under any of the foregoing rules, and if the property so transferred was situated in the United States at the time of the transfer or at the time of the decedent's death; and (vi) and interest in a partnership, if (A) the partnership does not qualify as a separate legal entity under the law of the jurisdiction where it was established or is dissolved on the death of one partner, and the underlying assets of the partnership are situated in the United States, or (B) if the partnership is a separate legal entity under the laws of the jurisdiction where it was established and it survives the death of a partner and the partnership carries out its business in the United States.

Examples of assets that are deemed to be situated outside of the United States are (i) shares of stock issued by a foreign corporation; (ii) deposits with persons carrying on the banking business, deposits or withdrawable accounts with a federal or state chartered savings institution (if the interest on such accounts is withdrawable on demand subject only to customary notice requirements), and amounts held by an insurance company under an agreement to pay interest thereon, as long as, in each case, the interest on such deposits or amounts is not effectively connected with the conduct of a trade or business in the United States by the recipient thereof; (iii) deposits with a foreign branch of a domestic corporation or partnership engaged in the commercial banking business; (iv) "Portfolio Debt Obligations," as long as the decedent was a nonresident alien for income tax purposes (a Portfolio Debt Obligation will be considered U.S. situs property if the decedent was a resident for income tax purposes, even if he or she was a nonresident alien for potential transfer tax purposes); and (v) proceeds from a life insurance policy on the nonresident alien decedent's life.

Although nonresident aliens are also subject to gift tax on gifts of U.S. situs property, gifts of U.S. situs intangible property by a nonresident alien generally are exempt from the gift tax. Property that is not considered intangible property and is therefore subject to federal gift tax when given away by a nonresident alien, includes (i) real property situated within the United States; (ii) tangible personal property situated within the United States at the time of the gift; and (iii) U.S. or foreign currency or cash situated within the United States at the time of the gift.

Property that is considered intangible personal property and is therefore not subject to federal gift tax when given by a nonresident alien includes: (i) shares of stock issued by a U.S. or foreign corporation; and membership interests in a limited liability company; (ii) debt obligations, including a bank deposit, the primary obligor of which is a U.S. person, the United States, a state, or any political subdivision thereof, the District of Columbia, or any agency or instrumentality of any such government; and (iii) interest in U.S. or foreign partnership (although there is some debate on whether partnership interest are intangible personal property).

Estate and Gift Tax Credits and Deductions

The estate of a nonresident alien receives a credit of only $13,000 against the potential transfer tax (the equivalent of a $60,000 exemption). There is no credit for gifts made during the lifetime of a nonresident alien. Nonresident aliens do, however, receive the benefit of the so-called annual exclusion from gifts (currently $13,000 per donee).

The estate of a nonresident alien may deduct from the gross estate the value of property passing to the decedent's surviving spouse, to the same extent that as the estate of a resident alien or U.S. citizen. Consequently, if the nonresident alien decedent's spouse is a U.S. citizen, a marital deduction will be permitted if all of the requirements of 2056 (covering bequests to surviving spouse) are satisfied. If the surviving spouse is not a U.S. citizen (regardless of whether he or she resides in the United States), as with the estate of a resident alien or U.S. citizen, in order for the estate of the nonresident alien to take advantage of the marital deduction, the provisions of 2056(d) must be satisfied (which provides that a bequest to a surviving spouse will not qualify for the marital deduction unless the property is held in a qualified domestic trust, as provided in 2056A, or unless the surviving spouse becomes a U.S. citizen within a specified period of time after the decedent's death). In addition, the gift tax marital deduction is generally not allowed for property passing to a spouse who is not a U.S. citizen, except that a donor can give his or her non-U.S. citizen spouse up to $100,000 per year (indexed for inflation to $120,000 for 2007) without the imposition of any gift tax.

Treaty Impact

The United States has estate and gift tax treaties with the following countries: Australia, Austria, Denmark, Finland, France, Germany, Ireland, Italy, Japan, Netherlands, Norway, South Africa, Sweden, Switzerland, and the United Kingdom. Each of these treaties alters in some respect the rules discussed above with respect to the application of the estate and gift taxes to nonresident aliens who reside in these countries and should, therefore, be reviewed before rendering any estate or gift tax advice for such persons. By way of example, this paper will focus on the estate and gift tax treaties between the United States and Austria, France, Germany, and the United Kingdom, all of which are domicile-based treaties.

❖

CHAPTER 28

Generation-Skipping Tax

*I*n order to prevent you from passing your property to persons two or more generations below you without the imposition of a transfer tax, a tax is imposed called a "generation-skipping tax" (GST). Under the 2012 Act, the GST exemption is $5 million, which is indexed for inflation and capped at the top rate of GST tax at 40 percent. This chapter will detail the different types of transfers that can result in the imposition of this tax and what you can do to minimize it.

The generation-skipping tax is assessed in addition to any gift or estate tax required to be paid on all transfers. The GST exemption that is applicable to many transfers to our descendants shelters them against this kind of tax. There are methods for maximizing the use of this exemption that are discussed in this chapter.

Since the GST is frequently misunderstood, familiarizing yourself with the series of questions and answers at the end of this chapter will afford you a better understanding of the GST and its implications.

The Generation-Skipping Tax

In addition to federal estate and gift taxes, a tax is imposed on transfers for the eventual benefit of persons two or more generations below the donor (a "skip person"). Presently, the rate of tax is 40 percent of the value of the property transfer. Every individual has a $5 million generation-skipping tax exemption.

The generation-skipping transfer tax (GST) is designed to eliminate most tax advantages that resulted from transfers of property that skipped a generation. The tax is imposed, in addition to the estate and gift tax, on direct or indirect transfers to beneficiaries who are at least two generations younger than the transferor.

Examples of generation-skipping transfers include:
- A lifetime gift to a grandchild.
- A bequest by will to a grandchild.
- A gift, either during your lifetime or at death, to be held in trust for the lifetime of a child with the remainder interest passing to a grandchild. The generation-skipping transfer will occur when the child's interest terminates or when assets are distributed to a grandchild.

The GST tax allows the government to collect transfer tax as if the property had not skipped a generation. For example, if a grandparent bequeaths property to a grandchild rather than a child, there is an estate tax on the transfer, as well as a GST tax. The end result is as if the property had passed from grandparent to child to grandchild, incurring two separate transfer taxes.

Exemption

The exemption from the GST tax per-transferor will protect many transfers against taxation. The exemption amount may be allocated to any property with respect to which you are the transferor.

Married couples can elect to "split" the use of their exemptions, much like the case of the gift tax, so that a married couple under the new law have a $10 million combined GST exemption. The $5,000,000 exemption per transferor applies to both lifetime and death transfers. Like the gift tax exemption, the GST exemption is not transferable between spouses, but the statute makes provision for gift-splitting. The Internal Revenue Code provides that a gift will be treated as if made one-half by each spouse if the spouses elect such treatment. This means that a spouse can make the gift out of his or her property and the other spouse can elect to treat the gift as being made one-half by him or her.

A complicated set of rules governs the election of property to be covered by the exemption; the allocation of the exemption if the transferor does not elect to apply it, and the taxation of property that is only partially covered by the exemption.

The GST tax is levied upon "taxable terminations," "taxable distributions," and "direct skips" to "skip persons" (a party two or more generations below the generation of the transferor).

Taxable Terminations

Taxable terminations occur when, immediately after the happening of an event, a skip person has an interest in property; and at no time after such event may a distribution be made to a person who is not a skip person. As an example, where a parent creates a trust for a child, with remainder to a grandchild, a taxable termination will occur on the event of the child's death and the termination of the trust.

Taxable Distributions

Taxable distributions occur when distributions that are not taxable terminations are made to skip persons. For example, a taxable distribution will be made when a trust permits distributions of income and principal to any descendant of a parent during the lifetime of his or her child, such as a distribution of income to a grandchild or great-grandchild. GST tax on taxable distributions is levied (after a deduction of expenses) on the full value of the property received and is payable by the beneficiary receiving the distribution.

Direct Skips

Direct skips are transfers to skip persons, subject to estate or gift tax. For example, a direct skip will occur where a parent makes a gift or leaves a legacy to a grandchild. The transfer will be subject to both the gift tax or estate tax and to the GST tax. Subject to an exception explained below, GST tax on direct skips is levied on the full value of the property received by the beneficiary on a tax-exclusive basis (the base for computation does not include the GST tax to be paid).

Transfers to a trust in which all the income beneficiaries are skip persons is deemed to be a direct skip, even if the remainder beneficiaries are nonskip persons. For example, the entire value of real property is subject to GST tax if you leave a life estate in property to a friend who is forty years younger (a "skip" person) with the remainder in the property to your daughter (a "nonskip" person).

An important way to maximize the use of the GST exemption is to create multiple trusts to ensure that at least one of the trusts will be completely free of GST tax.

Questions and Answers

What is the generation-skipping transfer tax?

It is a tax levied in addition to federal estate or gift taxes. In many cases, the same transfer, such as a lifetime gift, can be subject to both federal gift tax and generation-skipping transfer tax.

What are examples of generation-skipping transfers?

A generation-skipping transfer is usually either a lifetime gift or an amount passing to a beneficiary at death that skips a generation. Classic examples are lifetime gifts by a grandparent to a grandchild or outright bequests by a grandparent to a grandchild under a will. Such transfers "skip" the middle generation (the child of the grandparent who is the parent of the grandchild).

Why is a special tax needed for such transfers?

In the absence of a generation-skipping transfer tax, there is a loophole in the federal estate and gift tax system for wealthy individuals. The estate and gift tax system is intended to impose a tax on the transfer of wealth from one generation to the next. People of "normal" wealth usually abide by traditional rules and leave their property outright to their children in a transfer subject to gift or estate tax. The children either spend it or add to it during their lifetimes, and then pass it to their children, subject to another gift or estate tax, and so on.

The tax policy concern has been that the very wealthy have the means to avoid these rules. Instead of passing their wealth outright to their children, they set up trusts for their children, even grown children. These trusts are large enough that the income from them is sufficient to provide comfortably for the children's generation. At the children's death, however, the trust assets are not included in the children's estate for estate tax purposes. These trusts can stay in existence from generation to generation, subject only to the rule against perpetuities, and thereby avoid transfer taxes at the intervening generational levels.

The purpose of the generation-skipping transfer tax system, therefore, is to impose a special tax when a transfer is made that skips a generation in order to "make up" for the tax that would have been paid at the skipped generational level or levels.

What is the definition of a skip person?

The Internal Revenue Code defines a direct skip as a transfer, subject to federal gift or estate tax, to a "skip person." The requirement that the transfer be subject to gift or estate tax essentially means that the generation-skipping transfer tax applies only to gratuitous transfers and not to sales or exchanges or compensation payments or other types of transfers.

A skip person can be either a natural person or a trust. A natural person is a skip person if he or she is two or more generations below the transferor. Thus, a grandchild is a skip person to a grandparent because the grandchild is two generations below the grandparent. A child is not a skip person to a parent because the child is only one generation below the parent.

A trust can be a skip person under some circumstances. These include situations where the only beneficiaries of the trust are skip persons.

A grandparent sets up a trust in which a grandchild is the sole beneficiary. Gifts to such a trust constitute direct skips and are potentially subject to generation-skipping transfer tax at the time they are made.

What is a taxable termination or taxable distribution?

This essentially deals with distributions from a trust to skip persons, whether while the trust is in existence (a taxable distribution) or at its termination (a taxable termination).

You cannot, therefore, avoid the generation-skipping transfer tax through the use of a trust. That is because either the transfer to the trust will itself be a generation-skipping transfer or, if not, subsequent transfers from the trust to skip persons will be.

Example, Grandmother sets up a trust in her will for her only son. Under the terms of the trust, upon the son's death, any remaining trust property will pass to the son's surviving children. The transfer to the trust upon Grandmother's death is not a direct skip because the testamentary trust is not a skip person (that is because the son is a nonskip person beneficiary of the trust). When the son dies, the transfer of the remaining trust property to the grandchildren is a taxable termination which is a generation-skipping transfer potentially subject to generation-skipping tax liability.

What is the generation-skipping transfer tax rate?

The generation-skipping transfer tax rate is presently 35 percent, subject to adjustment based on the portion of the transfer that qualifies for the $5 million GST exemption.

Are all transfers to grandchildren subject to the generation-skipping transfer tax?

No. There are two important exceptions:
1. The first exception is that any lifetime gift that is a direct skip and that is not a taxable gift for gift tax purposes is essentially nontaxable for generation-skipping transfer tax purposes as well. This

means that annual gifts to grandchildren that qualify for the $13,000 annual exclusion per donee (which can increase to $26,000 per donee if a husband and wife join in the gift under the gift split-ting rules) are also exempt from the generation-skipping transfer tax.

2. The second exception is, as previously mentioned, for transfers that qualify for the $5 million GST exemption. For example, if the transferor's GST exemption is allocated to a direct skip, there is no generation-skipping transfer tax liability for the transfer.

Are there any planning ideas that can maximize the amounts that can be transferred to grandchildren and later generations using the $5 million GST exemption?

Yes. It is possible to "leverage" the $5 million GST exemption and thereby transfer significant additional amounts to those generations. One of the most effective methods of doing so is with an irrevocable insur-ance trust.

The key concept is that the generation-skipping transfer tax is based on the inclusion ratio of the trust. The inclusion ratio defines what per-cent of the property in the trust is subject to the GST tax (after applying the exemption). As long as that inclusion ratio can be kept at zero, there is no generation-skipping transfer tax on any amounts, regardless of how large, distributed from the trust.

The way to keep the trust's inclusion ratio at zero is to make sure that all contributions to the trust have the $5 million GST exemption allo-cated to it. This means that as long as total contributions to the trust do not exceed $5 million and as long as the grantor's GST exemption is allocated to those contributions, all amounts distributed from the trust are exempt.

Another exemption applies to a direct skip if the member of the skipped generation is deceased at the time of the transfer. In determining whether a transfer is a direct skip, a grandchild of the transferor, whose parent (the child of the transferor) is deceased, will be treated as if he or she were a child of the transferor in lieu of the predeceased parent. In such a case, the grandchild and all succeeding lineal descendants of the grandchild are moved up a generation.

The Taxpayer Relief Act of 1997 extended the "predeceased parent exception" of the generation-skipping transfer tax to include collateral heirs, such as grandnieces and grandnephews, provided the transferor has no lineal descendants at the time of the transfer.

It is very important in the estate-planning process for your professional advisors to review every trust that is being administered or that (revocable or irrevocable) you have created to identify any possible GST problems. If there is any exposure to GST, because the trust does not provide the ability to amend it to divide the trust into separate parts, the aid of the courts can be sought. The courts will permit a reformation so that the trust may not only be divided and the exemption allocated to a particular part, but in certain cases, permit the utilization of a spouse's exemption.

GST Trap

There are gifts that do not count toward the gift tax annual exclusion ($14,000) and do not count for GST tax purposes, i.e., direct payment of a grandchild's tuition and direct payment of a grandchild's medical expenses or medical insurance premiums to an insurance provider.

In some instances, the gift tax annual exclusion applies as well to a generation-skipping transfer, i.e., the grandparent writes a check to grandchild in the amount of $14,000. However, with a trust, the gift tax exclusion and the GST tax annual exclusion do not overlap. Transfers to trusts that qualify for the gift tax annual exclusion do not automatically qualify for the GST tax annual exclusion. In order for a transfer to a trust to qualify for the GST tax annual exclusion, the following circumstances must exist:

- The transfer is a direct skip.
- The trust can have only one beneficiary during the beneficiary's lifetime.
- The assets of the trust will be included in the gross estate of the beneficiary upon his or her death, if the trust is still in existence at such time.

Dynasty trusts and most life insurance trusts do not meet the above requirements. As a result, gift tax returns are required covering the transfers to such trusts with allocations taken for GST exemptions equal to the amount of the entire gifts.

❖

Chapter 29

The Estate, Gift, and Generation-Skipping Tax

$\mathcal{O}$ n January 1, 2013, the United States Senate passed HR 8, the American Taxpayer Relief Act of 2012. Late on January 1, 2013, the House of Representatives passed the bill, and on January 2, 2013, the president of the United States signed the bill (the "Act").

The amendments to the Act take effect as if they were included in the amendments made under Section 303 of the prior law, entitled the Tax Relief Unemployment Insurance Reorganization and Job Creation Act of 2010.

- The new law applies to estates of decedents, generation-skipping transfers, and gifts made after December 31, 2012.
- The new law sets the exemption at $5 million, indexed for inflation, for estate and gift tax purposes, which means that the amount of the applicable exclusion for the year 2012 is $5,120,000. It also provides for a $5 million exemption, also adjusted for inflation, for generation-skipping transfers. The IRS also recently released the inflation-adjusted amount for the exclusions in 2013: $5,250,000. Under the new law, the top rate for transfer tax purposes is 40 percent. The estate and gift taxes will be determined by a single flat rate once the donor or decedent's transfers (gift and estate) exceed the applicable exclusion amount. For example, if a donor uses $1 million of his or her applicable exclusion to make taxable lifetime gifts and dies thereafter, the unused applicable exclusion for his or her estate, for transfer tax purposes, will be $4 million rather than $5 million. Therefore, the lifetime gift tax exemption and the estate tax exemption are expressed as a total

amount of $5 million per person. However, annual gifts of up to $14,000 per donee can be given without reducing a donor's lifetime exemption. In a case of this kind, a married couple can split a gift so that each will be deemed to have given one-half (½) thereof, which gift-splitting will increase the amount of the applicable exemption available for each of the spouse's estates.

- Transfer of deceased spouses' unused estate tax exemption ("portability") was made permanent as a result of the Act. "Portability" means that, beginning in the year 2011, a deceased spouse's unused portion of his or her $5 million estate tax exemption is transferable to a surviving spouse's unused estate tax exemption. Portability of a deceased spouse's unused estate tax exemption (i) applies to decedents dying after the year 2010 and (ii) is limited to the unused estate tax exemption of the last deceased spouse of the surviving spouse. In order for portability to be effective, the election is made by the executor; if there is no executor, the election is made by the person in actual or constructive possession of the property of the deceased spouse. This is done by filing a complete and properly prepared Form 706 (federal estate tax return), whether or not the return is required. The return must document and complete the fact that the deceased spouse's taxable estate was less than his or her basic exclusion amounts.

- The exemption for the generation-skipping transfer ("GST") tax, which is applicable to transfers, whether by gift or estate, from a person to remote descendants who are at least two (2) generations younger that the transferor, the GST exemption will permanently be the same as the estate tax exemption. The maximum GST tax rate is set permanently at 40 percent.

Miscellaneous

Other provisions of the 2012 Act include the following.

- The state death tax deduction permanently replaces the state death tax credit.
- Existing provisions affecting family-owned business interests and the payment of the estate tax in installments for closely held business interests are extended.

The technical provisions of the Economic Growth and Tax Relief Reconstruction Act of 2001 are made pertinent as follows:

(i) Liberalization of the rules on the estate tax deduction for conservation easements under Section 2031(c).

(ii) Automatic allocation of GST exemption to transfers to GST trusts.

(iii) Permitting certain retroactive allocations of GST exemption.

(iv) Permitting qualified severance of trusts for GST tax purposes.

(v) Permitting the IRS to allow late allocations of GST exemption.

(vi) Adopting substantial compliance rules for allocation of GST exemption.

(vii) Slight easing of the rules on the deferred payment of estate taxes on closely held business interests under Section 6166.

(viii) Waiver of the statute of limitations on certain special use valuation of farm real estate under Section 2032(a).

None of the Administration's following proposed changes ("loopholes") were adopted:

(i) Modification of the rules pertaining to Grantor Retained Annuity Trusts (GRATs) (the modification sought by the Administration was to require a minimum ten-year term for a GRAT and the negation of a "zeroed-out GRAT").

(ii) Changes in the provisions pertaining to family limited partnership (FLPs).

(iii) Revisions to sales to intentionally defective grantor trusts ("IDGTS").

(iv) Modifications to the Grantor Trusts rules as follows:

(a) The assets of the trust would be included in the gross estate for estate tax purposes.

(b) Distributions from the trust to beneficiaries during the Grantor's life would be subject to gift tax.

(c) If during the life of the Grantor, the Grantor ceased to be treated as the owner of the trust for income tax purposes, any remaining trust assets would be subject to gift tax.

The Gross Estate

All property in which you have an interest at the time of your death is included in your gross estate. This includes the following:

- One-half interest in community property.

- Joint interests.
- Annuities.
- Property subject to a general power of appointment.
- Life insurance proceeds.
- Life interest in property for which QTIP marital deduction was elected.
- Property gifted during your lifetime. The gross estate does not include interests in property that terminate at the time of your death, as do some life estates.

The gross estate includes the full value of all property of a U.S. citizen or resident no matter where the property is situated. If property is taxed by a foreign country, a credit for foreign death taxes may be available to reduce the federal estate tax.

Certain income is included in the gross estate, such as dividends, interest, rents, and compensation, including contingent fees. Income accrued prior to death but not reportable on your final income tax return is known as "income in respect of a decedent" (IRD). There is a special income tax deduction for estate taxes attributable to the inclusion of IRD in the gross estate.

Community Property

In community property states (Arizona, California, Idaho, Louisiana, Nevada, New Mexico, Texas, Washington, and Wisconsin), all property acquired by the spouses during their marriage is regarded as owned in equal shares by the spouses, and, therefore, each spouse has a vested interest in one-half of the shared property. The one-half interest is acquired while the spouses are domiciled in a community property state and continues even if the couple subsequently moves to a non–community property state. However, each spouse may also acquire property separately by gift or inheritance. At the death of one spouse, therefore, only one-half of the community property and all of the separately acquired property are included in that spouse's gross estate.

Joint Interests

Included in the gross estate is the entire value of property held by you and any other person as joint tenants with a right of survivorship at your death. The value of your interest in the property, however, will be reduced to the extent that your estate can show that the surviving joint tenant (1) had an original ownership interest never transferred for full consideration to the decedent, or (2) made an original contribution to the cost of acquiring the property, unless this contribution came from your own funds.

If the joint tenants are spouses, unless one of the spouses is not a U.S. citizen, only half the value of the asset is included in the deceased spouse's gross estate at his or her death, regardless of who furnished the original consideration. There is an exception to this provision involving real property acquired by a married couple as joint tenants. Pursuant to a 1981 amendment to the code, the estate of a decedent who died after 1981 is entitled to a full-basis step-up under a tenancy by the entirety ownership of real property purchased before 1977 and for which the surviving spouse supplied none of the consideration. Significant tax planning opportunities are therefore available for married individuals with pre-1977 jointly held real estate.

Annuities

The gross estate includes the value of an annuity that still has residual value after your death, for example, one which is payable to a beneficiary who survives you. Also included in the gross estate are payments from qualified pension, stock bonus, or profit-sharing plans; tax-deferred annuities; individual retirement accounts (IRAs); and certain military retirement plans. The amount included in the gross estate is the proportion of the annuity attributable to your contributions to the purchase price. Contributions made by your employer or former employer are deemed to be contributed by you if made by reason of your employment.

Powers of Appointment

Any property over which you have a general power of appointment at the time of your death is included in your estate. A general power of appointment allows you to appoint property to yourself or your estate, your creditors, or the creditors of your estate. A power of appointment is not general, and as such is not included in your estate, if it can be exercised only in favor of specific persons or a limited class of persons.

Proceeds of Life Insurance

Generally, the proceeds of an insurance policy on your life, whether payable to your estate or to other beneficiaries, are included in your gross estate. This rule does not apply, however, if at the time of your death you retained no incidents of ownership in the insurance policy and the proceeds were not payable to your estate or to be used for the benefit of your estate. For avoidance of estate taxes on life insurance, see chapter 14.

QTIP Marital Deductions

A marital deduction is allowed for the value of all property in which a surviving spouse receives a lifetime "qualifying income interest." This property is known as a "qualified terminable interest property" (QTIP) and is includable in the gross estate of the surviving spouse if the estate of the first spouse takes a marital deduction with respect to this property.

Property Transferred during Decedent's Lifetime

The gross estate includes (1) transfers effective at decedent's death, (2) transfers with a retained life estate, and (3) revocable transfers. These types of transfers, together with gifts of life insurance and all gift taxes paid within three years of death, are included in gross estates, as well.

Gifts Made within Three Years of Death

Generally, the value of property transferred as a gift prior to your death is not includable in your gross estate but may be subject to gift tax. However, certain gifts, such as a gift of life insurance, a transfer effective at your death, a transfer with a retained life estate, or a revocable transfer, are included in your gross estate.

Transfers Effective at Death with Reversionary Interests

The gross estate includes the entire value of property transferred by you as a gift if you retained a "reversionary interest" in the property (a right to receive the property back at some future date). This is so if the value of such right is in excess of 5 percent of the value of the entire property immediately before your death. For example, you create a trust to pay income to your brother for his lifetime. Upon your brother's death, your brother's son is to receive the principal of the trust. If the son is not living at the time of your brother's death, the trust principal reverts back to you. If there is a greater than 5 percent chance that you will outlive your brother's son, the trust principal is included in your gross estate. In order to determine the potential "chance," the ages and health of all of the significant parties is evaluated actuarially.

Transfer with a Retained Life Estate

The gross estate includes the value of all property to the extent of your interest therein, which you have transferred at any time, by trust or otherwise (unless by a sale for full consideration) and in which you have retained an interest for life or for a shorter period. These retained interests are the possession, enjoyment, or right to the income of the property, or the right to designate the persons who will possess or enjoy the property or the income from it.

For example, say you create a trust to pay income to your descendants during your lifetime and you retain the power to determine from year to year which of your descendants will actually receive the income and in what proportions. This retained power will cause the entire trust property to be included in your gross estate.

Revocable Transfers

The gross estate includes the value of any interest in property transferred by you to another for less than full and adequate consideration if you possess at the time of your death the power to alter, amend, revoke, or terminate the transfer in favor of anyone, such as the power to change a beneficiary.

How Is the Property of the Estate Valued?

The property included in the gross estate is valued as of the date of your death, unless your legal representative elects a date six months after the date of your death (the "alternate valuation date"). The alternate valuation date may be chosen only when it reduces both the value of the gross estate and the federal estate tax liability. The alternate valuation applies to all the includable assets of your estate. The amount of the marital and charitable deductions, which depend on the value of property passing to a spouse or charity, must also be adjusted to the alternate value. The value of property that is sold between the date of death and the alternate valuation date is, for estate tax purposes, its sales price. There is usually a trade-off between estate and income tax savings when choosing the alternate valuation date. The estate tax values of estate assets become the inherited cost basis for income tax purposes. The alternate valuation should only be used if the reduction in estate tax exceeds the present value of the additional income tax. The decision regarding the alternate valuation election depends upon many factors, including the estate tax rate, the income tax rates of the beneficiaries, and their investment goals.

Fair Market Value

The values of assets includable in the estate is their fair market value on the valuation date. Fair market value is the price at which the property would change hands between a willing buyer and a willing seller, neither being under any compulsion to buy or sell, and both having reasonable knowledge of relevant facts. If the item is one generally sold at retail, the fair market value is the price at which the item or a comparable item would be sold.

What Are the Deductions Allowed?

Once the value of the gross estate is determined, the next step is to subtract from it a number of allowable deductions. The difference is the taxable estate. The two most significant deductions are the marital and charitable deductions. They are important because they can be planned for in advance and can substantially reduce or eliminate the estate tax altogether.

In addition, the following deductions are also allowable:

- Funeral expenses, including the costs of a tombstone, monument, or mausoleum; funeral services; and a burial plot for the decedent or his or her family, including the reasonable cost of its future care.
- Administration expenses actually incurred in administering the estate, i.e., collecting assets, paying debts, and distributing property among the people entitled to it. These expenses include executor's commissions, revocable trustee's commission's attorneys' fees, court costs, accountants' and appraisers' fees, and the like.
- Claims against the estate that were allowable and enforceable as personal obligations of the decedent under local law. A pledge to a charity is deductible if it would have qualified as a bequest and is enforceable against the estate. Accrued but unpaid taxes may also be deducted. State and foreign death taxes and the federal estate tax are not deductible.
- Unpaid mortgages and debts, such as the expenses of the decedent's final illness.
- The value of losses incurred during the settlement of the estate from fires, storms, shipwrecks or other casualties, or from theft, to the extent that they are not compensated by insurance or other sources.

Charitable Deduction

A bequest to a qualifying charity is deductible from the gross estate. There is no limit on the amount of this deduction. An estate will pay no estate tax if it is all left to charity. A charitable deduction is also possible if a charity is an income or remainder beneficiary of a trust. The new American Taxpayer Relief Act of 2012 renewed the ability to make tax-free distributions from Traditional or Roth Individual Retirement Account assets to qualified charitable organizations for both 2013 and retroactively for 2012. The maximum amount that may be transferred in any one year is $100,000. The provisions permitting same applies to persons age seventy and a half or older at the time the transfer is completed. It must be completed by February 1, 2012, in order for the transfer to qualify for the tax year 2012 and by December 31, 2013, for the tax year 2013, without being reported as taxable income. See chapter 10 for a discussion of charitable trusts.

Marital Deduction

An unlimited marital deduction is allowed for property included in a gross estate that passes outright to your spouse. Transfers of terminable interests or interests that terminate upon the happening of a certain event, such as the remarriage of a surviving spouse, or with the passage of time, do not qualify for a marital deduction. Exceptions to these include qualified terminable interest property (QTIP), power-of-appointment trusts, and if the period of time that a spouse must survive the deceased spouse does not exceed six months.

Property passing to the surviving spouse as a joint tenant by right of survivorship, through dower or curtesy interests, under powers of appointment, and by transfers made during your lifetime that are included in your gross estate, all qualify for the marital deduction. The deduction also applies to life insurance proceeds paid outright to the surviving spouse or to a trust, which itself qualifies for the marital deduction.

A transfer of property to a trust under which all beneficial interests pass to the surviving spouse may also qualify for the marital deduction.

No marital deduction is allowed for property passing to a surviving spouse who is not a U.S. citizen unless the property passes in the form of a qualified domestic trust (QDOT). For a discussion of this type of trust, see chapter 7.

QTIP Transfers

Transfers of a life estate in qualified terminable interest property (QTIP) to a spouse is an exception to the terminable interest rule and qualifies for a marital deduction. Your spouse must have a "qualifying income interest" for the property to be so designated. This means that he or she must be entitled to receive all the income from the property at least annually, and that no person can appoint the property during your spouse's lifetime to anyone other than your spouse. The transfer may be in the form of a life estate for your spouse or a trust. You may retain or create powers over part or all of the QTIP corpus, but only if they are exercisable on or after your surviving spouse's death. Thus, your surviving spouse need not be given a general power of appointment. In order to qualify a transfer as QTIP, an election to take the marital deduction for a QTIP transfer is made by your legal representative on the estate tax return and is irrevocable. Property thus qualified is subject to a gift tax, if transferred during your spouse's lifetime, or subject to an estate tax upon your spouse's death as part of his or her estate.

International Estate Planning

Federal estate taxes are imposed on all property owned by U.S. citizens worldwide and by residents of the United States whether they are citizens or not. The United States does have estate tax treaties with various countries, which, in some instances, provide for full credits for estate taxes paid to another nation. If no treaty exists, the foreign country could tax its citizen and if that citizen resided here, the United States could tax the same assets as well. A foreign citizen who may not reside here could be subject to U.S. estate tax laws if he or she owns property here. Property is considered located here if it is:

- Real property located in the United States
- Tangible personal property located in the United States—this includes clothing, jewelry, automobiles, furniture, or currency
- A debt obligation of a citizen or resident of the United States, a domestic partnership or corporation, any estate or trust (but not a foreign estate or trust), the United States, a state or a political subdivision of a state, or the District of Columbia
- Shares of stock issued by domestic corporations

Property Not Located in the United States

Notwithstanding the above rules, property of a nonresident, noncitizen decedent is not considered located in the United States if it is:

- A deposit with a U.S. bank, if the deposit was not connected with a U.S. trade or business and was paid or credited to the decedent's account.
- Stock issued by a corporation that is not a domestic corporation, even if the certificate is physically located in the United States.
- An amount receivable as insurance on the decedent's life.

If you are a foreign citizen residing outside of the United States and if you own shares of stock in a domestic corporation, such as Ford Motors, you would be subject to federal estate taxes on those shares. These estate taxes might be avoided by the creation of an offshore entity.

There are certain government securities that are exempt from federal estate tax, such as Treasury bonds that mature longer than six months from inception. The rationale for making them estate tax free is to encourage their purchase by foreign nationals.

Transfers from Expatriates

Beginning on June 17, 2008, a U.S. citizen or resident is subject to a special transfer tax upon receipt of property by gift, devise, bequest, or inheritance from an expatriate. The tax rate is the highest gift tax rate. The special transfer tax is applied to gifts and bequests that exceed the annual gift tax exclusion ($14,000 for the year 2013). The tax is reduced by any estate tax paid to a foreign country with respect to such gift or bequest.

A covered gift or bequest does not include property that:

- is a taxable gift by a covered expatriate that is reported on a timely filed gift tax return;
- is included in the gross estate of a covered expatriate and reported on a timely filed estate tax return;
- would be eligible for an estate or gift tax charitable deduction or marital deduction if the transferor were a U.S. person.

A covered expatriate for the purposes of the Internal Revenue Code is defined as an individual who has either relinquished U.S. citizenship or ceased to be a lawful permanent long-term resident of the United

States and who meet the requirements needed to be subject to the alternative tax required under Code Sec. 877(a)(2).

A covered gift or bequest made to a domestic trust is subject to tax in the same manner as a U.S. citizen or resident above described, and as the recipient, the trust is required to pay the tax imposed.

IRS Form 708 is required to be used by taxpayers to report "covered gifts or bequests" from covered expatriates.

Disclaimers

If your surviving spouse disclaims a bequest, it is treated as if it did not pass to him or her and therefore does not qualify for the marital deduction. Similarly, an interest disclaimed by a beneficiary that passes to a surviving spouse does qualify. A disclaimer is not the same as acceptance of the property and subsequent disapproval of it. A formal "qualified disclaimer" must be executed in writing and communicated to the legal representative within nine months after the transfer or, in the case of a minor, by the age of twenty-one.

Applicable Credit for State Estate Tax Saving

For a married couple, the way the exemption is utilized can have a positive result for any state estate tax savings. This tax can be avoided by creating a trust in the amount of the state estate tax exemption for the benefit of the surviving spouse, who would receive all income therefrom and the principal, if necessary. Upon the death of the second spouse, the property in the trust will pass to the next generation state estate tax free. The benefits from the trust can also be sprinkled or sprayed among children and grandchildren in addition to the surviving spouse. If both spouses create such a plan, then upon the death of the survivor of them, they can effectively pass property having a value equal to both state estate tax exemptions to their heirs.

Credit for Gift Tax

A credit against the estate tax can be allowed for gift taxes calculated on gifts made after December 31, 1976, for any portion of such a gift that is later included in a decedent's gross estate. The gift taxes allowed for credit purposes will be those that are due based upon the gift tax exemption and rates that exist in the year of death of the decedent and not the year of the gift.

Credit for Estate Tax on Prior Transfers

A credit against the estate tax is allowed for federal estate tax paid on the transfer of property to the present decedent from a person who died within ten years before or after the present decedent's death. The original transferred property need not be identified in the present decedent's estate nor be in existence at the time of his or her death. It suffices that the prior transfer of property was subject to federal estate tax in the prior person's estate and that the prior person died within the prescribed time. If the transferor died within two years before or within two years after the transferee's death, the credit allowed for the tax on the prior transfer is 100 percent of the maximum amount allowable. If the transferor predeceased the transferee by more than two years, the credit allowed is a reduced percentage of the maximum amount allowable. The percentage allowable may be determined by using the following table:

PERIOD OF TIME		% ALLOWABLE
EXCEEDING	NOT EXCEEDING	
—	2 years	100
2 years	4 years	80
4 years	6 years	60
6 years	8 years	40
8 years	10 years	20
10 years	—	none

Credit for Foreign Death Taxes

A credit against the federal estate tax is allowed for any estate, inheritance, legacy, or succession taxes actually paid to any foreign country on property located in that country that is included in the decedent's gross estate. The credit cannot exceed the federal estate tax attributable to such property. The credit must be claimed within four years after the filing of the estate tax return.

Computation of the Estate Tax

The federal estate tax is computed as follows:
1. Determine the gross estate.
2. Subtract from the gross estate the permissible deductions.
3. Add the value of taxable gifts made after 1976.
4. Apply the unified rate schedule to the taxable estate.

The result is the tentative estate tax. Next:

5. Subtract from the tentative estate tax any gift taxes paid on post-1976 gifts.
6. Deduct the following applicable credits:
   - The unified credit
   - State death taxes paid
   - The credit for gift tax on all post December 31, 1976, gifts included in the gross estate
   - The credit for tax on prior transfers
   - The credit for foreign death taxes

The result is the net estate tax.

Method of Paying Estate Taxes

Without question, one of the largest burdens that can be placed on your estate is paying the federal estate taxes, which is due within nine (9) months from the date of death. However, an automatic extension to file the estate tax return for an additional six (6) months can be requested. It does not extend the time for the payment of the estate tax which is due at the end of the nine (9) month period. If your estate is not liquid, it could encounter adverse financial effects to meet these obligations. This could even erode or reduce the value of the potential inheritance of your survivors. Of course, as you have read elsewhere in this chapter, with proper planning, married couples can completely avoid and postpone all estate taxes until the surviving spouse dies. In addition to death taxes, your death triggers other obligations, such as funeral expenses and professional fees for attorneys, accountants, and appraisers where necessary. If property passes through probate, the court fees and expenses of probate will be incurred as well.

If the state of your domicile imposes a death tax, this will have to be paid as well, and usually within the same time frame. Some states do not even have the same estate tax structure as the federal government. This is often found in the area of the unlimited marital deduction. In such an event, the state may impose a state inheritance tax even though there may be no federal estate tax.

A sound estate plan must not only include strategies for reducing the amount of estate tax ultimately payable by the estate and/or beneficiaries, but also should include techniques for providing for the payment of the tax that will be due.

Generally, funds to pay the estate tax can come from:

- The maintenance of liquid investments by the decedent.
- The sale of assets to raise the funds necessary. This may not be advantageous due to the possibility that a forced sale may generate lower prices. If you have an interest in a closely held business, a buy-sell agreement could ease a liquidity problem. In such a case, usually the business or the co-owners would purchase the interest. In many instances, the purchase is funded with life insurance proceeds on the life of the deceased owner.
- The purchase of life insurance. Life insurance, besides providing liquidity for the payment of estate taxes, is also a method of reducing estate tax, since it can be kept out of the taxable estate. One of its advantages is that the receipt of the death benefits from a life insurance policy comes at approximately the same time the obligations of the estate owner accrues. For a more detailed discussion of life insurance and its vital role in estate planning, see chapter 12.
- Borrowing, including borrowing from the federal government under Section 6166 of the Internal Revenue Code. Borrowing to pay estate tax is an alternative that may be available to create liquidity to pay for transfer costs. It can make economic sense if the after-tax cost of the loan is less than the return after tax on the funds. A problem that occurs sometimes with this approach is the ability of furnishing proper collateral satisfactory to the lender in order to obtain the needed financing. Normally, estate taxes are due within nine (9) months of death. However, if a closely held business interest is included in the gross estate and if its value exceeds 35 percent of the adjusted gross estate, the estate may qualify for a deferral of tax payments. Under this arrangement, only interest on the tax due is paid until four (4) years after the normal due date for estate taxes on the value of the business. The estate tax related to the closely held business interest can then be paid in ten (10) equal annual installments. As such, a portion of the estate tax is deferred for as long as fourteen (14) years from its original due date. Interest is charged on the deferred payments but at a low rate on the estate tax related to the closely held business interest. The interest rate on the remaining deferred amount is the rate charged for underpayment of taxes.
- Section 303 Redemption. If the value of a closely held corporation is included in the gross estate and if the value exceeds 35 percent

of the adjusted gross estate, the corporation can buy from the estate its shares of stock. The distribution from the corporation cannot exceed the amount of the estate taxes and the funeral and administration expenses. If the redemption qualifies under the appropriate section, there is no negative income tax to the shareholders (dividend) resulting from the distribution. There are time requirements during which a Section 303 redemption can occur. Distributions by a corporation in redemption of its shares of stock must take place within three years (3) and ninety days after the filing of the estate tax return to qualify under Section 303. If the estate has a dispute with the Internal Revenue Service in the tax court of the United States, the redemption must be completed within sixty days following the date on which the decision becomes final. Furthermore, if an extension of time is elected under Section 6166, the redemption must be completed during the time determined for the payments of the installments.

The Applicable Credit

The use of the applicable credit in estate planning is important. Even though there is portability of a spouse's unused estate tax credit, to the extent possible, the credit should be availed of in the estate of the first spouse to die for the following reasons: suppose the surviving spouse fails to take advantage of the circumstances in the desired manner (in Trust), for reasons beyond his of her control, such as incapacity. Creating a credit shelter trust in the estate of the first spouse to die will avoid an unintended or unsatisfactory result after the demise of both spouses.

Postmortem Planning

There are often effective methods of reducing estate taxes after the demise of a spouse. The estate can select a fiscal year for income tax purposes. The benefits to this are twofold: income taxes on the income of the estate can be delayed, and the distributions received from the estate by a beneficiary will be included in that persons income tax return for the following year (as opposed to the year of receipt).

An estate can choose to deduct most of the expenses it incurs during the administration of the estate on either its income or estate tax return. In order for the beneficiaries to get the benefit of certain losses and deductions of the estate in excess of the income for the final year, these should be paid in the year of termination.

If a noncitizen spouse receives an inheritance that is not in the appropriate form of a qualified domestic trust, he or she can create such a trust and contribute the inheritance to it and, in that way, preserve the marital deduction and the deferral of the estate taxes until his or her demise.

Disclaimers can be filed in order to both increase and decrease the marital share.

QTIP and QDOT treatment can be elected. If a spouse becomes a U.S. citizen before the estate tax return is filed, the QDOT format will not be necessary.

There are certain income tax elections that a surviving spouse must consider, such as:

- Not claiming any commissions (compensation) as an executor or personal representative
- Making a rollover of a lump-sum retirement plan distribution
- Electing to file a joint final income tax return for federal and state purposes with the deceased spouse
- An election has to be made to step-up the basis of an interest inherited in a partnership.
- An election can be made to report interest on government savings bonds on the final income tax return of the deceased person.

In connection with generation-skipping trusts that are subject to generation-skipping tax distributions to a grandchild for medical expenses or to pay tuition will not be subject to this type of tax. A beneficiary who might inherit property subject to GST could renounce an amount over the exemption level ($5 million in the year 2011).

Private Annuities

A private annuity is a transfer of property in exchange for an unsecured promise to pay a fixed amount for the lifetime of the transferor.

In response to what may be the creation of abusive private annuity trusts the government has declared obsolete Revenue Ruling 69-74, which described the transferor's gain.

Under the proposed regulations the transferor's gain is now recognized at the time of the sale and is not deferred over the term of the annuity agreement.

Estate Tax Advantages

Transferring property in exchange for annuity payments removes the property from your taxable estate for estate tax purposes. Unless your death is imminent at the time of the transfer, this result will be achieved even if you die shortly after the transfer.

The annuity payments that you receive will be included in your taxable estate. You can avoid this result, however, by using the payments to make tax-free annual gifts to children, grandchildren, and other beneficiaries.

Income Tax Advantages

A private annuity offers an income tax advantage if you are transferring a capital asset that already has increased in value from the time you acquired it. Unlike an ordinary sale, with an annuity you do not pay tax on the entire capital gain in the year of the transfer. Instead, your gain is spread out over your lifetime. This may reduce your taxes in other ways, such as by keeping your income below a level that would trigger the reduction or loss of itemized deductions or other tax benefits or that would trigger taxation of social security benefits.

A private annuity also has an advantage over an installment sale. With an installment sale, depreciation recapture income is taxed in the year of the sale, regardless of when payments are made, and a resale of the property by the purchaser could accelerate the seller's deferred gain. With a private annuity, any recapture is taxed as payments are made, and a resale of the property by the child has no impact on the annuitant's tax situation.

Practical Advantages

Private annuities also offer practical advantages. A private annuity can relieve you of a burden of managing business or investment property. In addition, private annuities can save estate administration costs because the transferred property is removed from your probate estate.

The estate tax and other advantages outlined above can be achieved only if the property is transferred in exchange for your child's (or other individual's) unsecured promise to make the annuity payments. The estate planning benefits may be lost if you retain any interest in the property or if the payments are tied to the property's income.

Estate Tax versus Gift Tax

The method by which the gift tax is actually computed has a direct bearing on the advisability of making intra-family gifts since it may cost less total transfer tax to give away an amount of property than to leave it to someone at one's demise. The gift tax is computed on the amount of the transfer to the recipient. The estate tax is computed on the amount of the property held by the estate owner on the date of death, including that portion of the estate tax that will be used to pay the tax and, thus, not received by the beneficiaries. Therefore, one of the differences between subjecting property to estate tax as opposed to gift tax is that the potential transfer tax system is inclusive and the gift tax system is exclusive. It may be better for a family, for the surviving spouse, having inherited property, free of taxation and fleshed up in basis, to give such property to descendants, thereby subjecting it to lower gift taxes.

One offsetting consideration in making lifetime gifts instead of testamentary transfers is that the donor pays a gift tax now to save estate taxes later. Thus, the lower tax on large lifetime transfers over large testamentary transfers must be weighed against the lost use of the money, also taking into account (1) income tax savings from income shifting and (2) estate tax savings from removing the future appreciation and the gift taxes paid by the donors. If the donor dies within three (3) years of having made the gift, however, the gift taxes paid are included in the donor's gross estate, and the computational advantages of the lifetime transfers are lost.

IRAs and the Alternate Valuation Method (AVM)

Individual retirement accounts have been with us since 1974, but there is still no official or informal Internal Revenue Service guidance or any other authority regarding how the AVM applies to IRAs.

- *Distributed*
  Distributing assets out of an IRA within six months after the date of death would not freeze the value of such assets for alternate valuation purposes unless such distribution is considered an "other disposition."

- *Sold*
  The question is whether the IRA is treated for alternate valuation purposes as an asset itself (so all the executor needs to do is compare the value of the IRA on the date of death with its value six months later to determine which is lower), or whether the IRA is treated as a collection of individual securities, so that the beneficiary's sale of a security inside the IRA within six months after the

date of death would cause the AVM period to end for that security (with the results of reinvestment of the proceeds of the sale being irrelevant for estate tax valuation purposes). Sometimes, using the collection-of-securities approach would favor the taxpayer; in other cases, it would favor the IRS.

- *Transfer to a different custodian*
  An IRA beneficiary can cause his or her inherited IRA to be transferred, by direct "plan-to plan transfer," to a different IRA custodian.

  If the exchange involves no selling of securities and no taxable distribution, just an intact transfer of the inherited investments to a different IRA provider, there would not appear to be any basis for an argument that the transfer was a "disposition."

- *Division of the account*
  It can be to the advantage of multiple beneficiaries of a single inherited IRA to divide it into separate inherited IRAs, one payable to each of them.

  An argument could be made that this is a "mere change in form," and not a disposition.

  If the beneficiaries did not take proportionate shares of each and every security in the account, query whether they have engaged in an exchange of inherited assets, triggering closing of the AVM period.

Exclusion for Qualified Family-Owned Businesses

This exclusion permits the fiduciary of an estate to elect special estate tax treatment for qualified "family-owned business interests" if such interests comprise more than 50 percent of a decedent's adjusted gross estate and certain other requirements are met. For decedents dying after December 31, 1997, this provision in combination with the applicable credit, can effectively shield $1.3 million of value in qualified family-owned business interests from a taxable estate.

To qualify for this exclusion, a family-owned business interest is any interest in a business principally located in the United States and owned at least 50 percent by one family, 70 percent by two families, or 90 percent by three families, as long as the decedent's family owns at least 30 percent of the business. Each business owned by the decedent and members of the decedent's family is subject to separate testing to determine if it is a qualified business interest. The benefit of this exclusion is generally recaptured if no qualified heir remains active or the business is disposed of within ten years of the decedent's death. This exclusion is available for estates of persons dying after December 31, 1997.

Gift Revaluation

In calculating prior taxable gifts for estate tax purposes, the Act provided that for gifts made after August 5, 1997, a gift for which the statute of limitations has passed cannot be revalued for purposes of determining the applicable estate tax bracket and available unified credit. However, the statute of limitations will not run on inadequately disclosed gifts made in calendar years ending after August 5, 1997, regardless of whether a gift tax return was filed for other transfers in that same year. The timely filing of a gift tax return starts the running of the statute of limitations for assessment of additional gift taxes. The code provides that the amount of any tax imposed severally must be assessed within three years after the return is filed. This can be extended to six years if the gift tax return omits items that are properly included having a value in excess of 25 percent of the total amount of gifts set forth in the return.

The statute of limitations will run only if a gift tax return is filed. If no return is filed or if a fraudulent return is filed with the intent to evade tax, there is no period of limitations and a deficiency may be assessed at any time.

The estate and gift taxes are now unified. The new rates for both transfers are as follows:

ESTATES AND GIFTS TAX RATE SCHEDULE
2013 and Later

Amount subject to tax equal to or more than –	Amount subject to tax less than –	Tax on amount in column (A)	Rate of tax on excess over amount in column (A) Percent
$	$	$	%
	10,000		18
10,000	20,000	1,800	20
20,000	40,000	3,800	22
40,000	60,000	8,200	24
60,000	80,000	13,000	26
80,000	100,000	18,200	
100,000	150,000	23,800	30
150,000	250,000	38,800	32
250,000	500,000	70,800	34
500,000	750,000	155,800	37
750,000	1,000,000	248,300	39
1,000,000		345,800	40

❖

Net Worth Worksheet

*D*etermining your net worth is the first step in preparing an estate plan. This worksheet will help you to organize your inventory for easy reference.

ASSETS	IN YOUR NAME	IN SPOUSE'S NAME	IN JOINT NAMES
Residence (current market value)	$ _____	$ _____	$ _____
Other real estate	$ _____	$ _____	$ _____
Bank accounts (checking and savings)	$ _____	$ _____	$ _____
Other cash accounts (money market funds, savings bonds, CDs, credit union accounts, etc.)	$ _____	$ _____	$ _____
Stocks, bonds, and mutual funds	$ _____	$ _____	$ _____
Life insurance (face value)	$ _____	$ _____	$ _____
Disability insurance (monthly benefit)	$ _____	$ _____	$ _____
Business partnership interests	$ _____	$ _____	$ _____
Retirement plan accounts:			
Pension plans	$ _____	$ _____	$ _____
Annuities	$ _____	$ _____	$ _____
IRA and Keogh accounts	$ _____	$ _____	$ _____
Stock option or savings plans	$ _____	$ _____	$ _____
Other (such as 401(k), profit-sharing, and deferred compensation plans)	$ _____	$ _____	$ _____
Personal property (replacement value of jewelry, vehicles, boats, household furnishings, etc.)	$ _____	$ _____	$ _____
Receivables, trusts, tax shelters, and other assets	$ _____	$ _____	$ _____
Collectibles (market value of antiques, fine arts, precious metals, etc.)	$ _____	$ _____	$ _____

ASSETS	IN YOUR NAME	IN SPOUSE'S NAME	IN JOINT NAMES
Other assets (specify)	$ _____	$ _____	$ _____
TOTAL ASSETS	$ _____	$ _____	$ _____
LIABILITIES			
Mortgages	$ _____	$ _____	$ _____
Life insurance loans	$ _____	$ _____	$ _____
Notes and trust deeds	$ _____	$ _____	$ _____
Other loans or debts (personal loans, credit cards, etc.)	$ _____	$ _____	$ _____
TOTAL LIABILITIES	$ _____	$ _____	$ _____
NET ESTATE (assets minus liabilities)	$ _____	$ _____	$ _____

Glossary of Terms

abatement: A priority system of reducing or eliminating bequests that an estate cannot afford to pay.

actuary: One who calculates various insurance and property costs; particularly, one who computes the cost of life insurance risks and insurance premiums.

ademption: Property left to a beneficiary in a will that is no longer in the decedent's estate upon death.

adjusted gross estate: During administration, debt administration expenses and losses are deducted. What is left is the adjusted gross estate.

administration of the estate: When the court supervises the distribution of the probated estate.

administrator: A personal representative appointed by the court to administer the estate of an intestate.

alternate valuation date: A date six months after the date of the decedent's death.

alternative minimum tax: A way of computing income tax disallowing certain deductions, credits, and exclusions.

annual exclusion: Under gift tax laws, each person may give as much as $10,000 per year to whomever he or she wishes.

annuity: A right to receive fixed, periodic payments, either for life or for a term of years, payable at specific intervals.

ascendant or ancestor: A person related to an intestate or to a claimant to an intestate share in the ascending lineal line.

attested will: A will signed by a witness.

augmented estate: Property owned at the time of a person's death as well as the value of any property transferred during his or her lifetime without consideration (gifts).

basis: What one has invested or put into property, real or personal. For tax purposes, subtract the basis from the proceeds of a property sale to determine the net gain.

beneficiary: A person or entity selected by the testator to receive a portion of the estate upon the testator's death.

bequest: A clause in a will directing the disposition of personal property.

bypass trust: Also known as a credit shelter trust. This is an estate tax-skipping trust used in conjunction with the unlimited marital deduction.

charitable lead trust: Trust in which a charitable organization receives income for a certain period with the remainder passing to the donor's beneficiaries after a set period.

charitable remainder trust: Trust created to pay income to beneficiary for a certain period and assets remaining in the trust pass to a charitable organization. There are three types of charitable remainder trusts.

charitable trust: A trust created for the benefit of a charitable organization. There are several different kinds of charitable trusts that can be created.

closely held corporation: A corporation with less than twenty-five shareholders. Usually, all the issued shares are held by only those who work in the corporation.

codicil: A testamentary instrument, which, after it has been properly executed, is added to the will.

community property: A property system premised on the belief that everything acquired during marriage belongs equally to each spouse.

compromise settlement: In a civil action, where two or more persons mutually bind themselves to refer their legal dispute to a third-party arbitrator.

contingency beneficiary: An alternative beneficiary selected by the testator in case the primary beneficiary dies prior to the testator.

contingent remainder: A remainder interest that does not become possessory until a certain specified event takes place.

corpus: Property the settlor/transferor places in the trust. (Also known as the trust res or trust principal.)

credit shelter trust: Also known as the bypass trust. This is an estate tax-skipping trust used in conjunction with the unlimited marital deduction.

Crummey power: The right of a beneficiary of a trust to withdraw a portion of a gift made to the trust equal to the lesser of the annual exclusion ($10,000) or the value of the gift made to the trust that year.

custodian: General term to describe anyone who has charge or custody of property. Also, person named to care for property left to minor under Uniform Gift to Minors Act.

death taxes: Taxes on the estate of the decedent. Federal death taxes are called estate taxes and state death taxes can be termed inheritance taxes, among other names.

devise: A clause directing the disposition of real property in a will. The person named to take the real property is called the devisee.

discretionary trust: A trust that allows the trustee to distribute as much trust income to the beneficiary as he or she deems proper.

disinheriting: When a testator cuts someone out of his or her will. A spouse cannot legally disinherit another spouse, but a parent can disinherit a child or another by stating so specifically in his or her will or living trust.

distributee or next of kin: That person or persons who are or who may be entitled to the property of an intestate.

domicile: The permanent residence of a person or the place to which he intends to return even though he may reside elsewhere.

dower or curtesy: A statutory right to inherit a certain portion of the estate of the deceased spouse.

elective share: A portion of the estate that a surviving spouse is entitled to by statute.

escheat: A reversion of property to the state if no relatives are living to inherit.

estate planning: The development of a plan to provide for effective and orderly distribution of an individual's assets at the time of death.

estate tax: Tax imposed on the fair market value of the net asset value of a decedent's estate.

execution: Making a written document complete by meeting the legal requirement of the completion, usually signing, witnessing, and notarizing.

executor or personal representative: The administrator named in a will.

executory interest: Interests that will take place in the future.

exemption: A deduction allowed to a taxpayer because of his status (i.e., over sixty-five, being blind, particular dependents, etc.)

fair market value: The average value that can be placed on an asset as determined by market forces.

family limited partnership: A legal entity that can provide asset protection and allows for management and control of assets.

fee simple absolute: The complete, outright right to ownership of land, present and future.

fiduciary: A person having a duty created by his, her, or its undertaking to act primarily for the benefit of others, such as an executor, personal representative, or trustee.

generation-skipping tax: Tax imposed to prevent you from passing property to two or more generations below you without paying a transfer tax.

gift tax: A tax imposed on transfers of property by gift during the donor's lifetime.

grant: Formal transfer of real property.

grant of probate: The actual validating of a will.

grantee: Person to whom grant is made.

grantor: The person by whom the grant is made.

grantor retained annuity trust (Grat): Irrevocable trust into which the grantor transfers property in return for the right to receive fixed payments on at least an annual basis based upon the initial fair market value of the property.

grantor retained income trust (Grit): Trust created so that the value of a gift can be lessened by the grantor retaining an income interest, for a certain time, in the property gifted away.

grantor retained unitrust (Grut): Same as a Grat, except that annual payments will fluctuate each year as the value of the property increases or decreases.

grantor trust: A trust where income is taxable to grantor because he or she retains substantial control over the trust assets or retains certain prohibited administrative powers.

gross estate: The value of all property left by the deceased person required to be included in his or her estate for estate tax purposes.

guardian: A court-appointed person who is legally responsible for the care and well-being of a minor. The only device parents can use to select a guardian for their child or children upon their deaths is a will.

heir: A person entitled by statute to the assets of the intestate is called an heir at law.

holographic will: A will entirely in the handwriting of a testator.

homestead: That part of a homeowner's real property that is exempt from attachment or sale by a creditor for the homeowner's general debts.

honorary trust: Not a legal trust. Some states allow people to leave part of their estate to an animal "in honorary trust."

individual retirement account: A tax-deductible savings account that sets aside money for retirement.

inheritance tax: A tax levied on the heir of a decedent for property inherited.

insurance trust: A trust created to own and be the beneficiary of an insurance policy.

inter vivos trust: A trust made during one's lifetime. Intestacy: If one dies owning assets and does not have a valid distribution instrument, the property will pass to the closest blood heirs of the deceased person.

intestate: Dying without a will or with a will found not to be legally valid.

irrevocable trust: A trust that cannot be revoked or amended by the creator of the trust.

issue: Offspring, children, and their children.

joint ownership: Property owned by two or more persons. Upon the death of one joint owner, ownership is transferred to the surviving owners.

joint tenancy: Property held by two or more persons with the right of survivorship between them.

keogh plan: A retirement plan established by a self-employed individual.

kiddie tax: The federal income tax code provision that any unearned income of a child is taxed at the child's parent's rate.

lapse: An inheritance "lapses" when the intended beneficiary predeceases the testator.

legacy: A clause in a will directing the disposition of money.

life estate: An estate in property held by a person for his or her lifetime or measured by the life of another; the estate ends upon the death of the holder or the measuring life, whoever dies first.

life insurance trust: Trust that collects and holds proceeds of life insurance for distribution to beneficiary and investment so as to exclude these monies from insured's estate for tax purposes.

living trust: A trust established by a person during his or her lifetime.

living will: A document that states that a person does not want his or her life prolonged by artificial means.

marital deduction: A deduction allowed by estate law for all property passed to a surviving spouse. Use of this deduction allows estate tax to be computed only after the death of the second spouse.

material provision: A provision that is important and necessary to a will or trust.

multiple probate: This occurs when decedent owns real estate or other property in more than one state that becomes subject to probate in each state at time of death.

no-contest clause: A clause in a will attempting to disinherit a person who attacks the will's legal validity.

noncupative will: An oral will.

nonprobate asset: Property that you have transferred during your lifetime, except that you have retained the total right, at anytime during your lifetime, to alter the distribution upon your death.

per stirpes: In Latin, "through or by the roots." Gives a beneficiary a share in the property to be distributed, not necessarily equal but in proportion to which, the person through whom he claims from the ancestor would have been entitled, i.e., a child claiming through his or her predeceased parent.

personal property: Holdings such as furniture, jewelry, stocks, cash, and other items of personal possession.

pickup tax (sponge tax): Permits the state in which one dies to receive a portion of the estate taxes that would have been paid to the federal government.

pooled income fund: A fund among multiple donors, wherein each reserves a pro rata share of its assets. The amount of income paid to each donor is determined by the performance of the fund and the individual's proportionate share.

pour-over trust: A trust into which assets are poured or added from another source.

pour-over will: A will used in conjunction with a revocable living trust to "pour-over" or transfer to the trust any assets that were not transferred to the trust before death.

pour-up trust: Assets of a living trust are poured into a testamentary trust or an estate, reversing the flow found in a pour-over trust.

power of attorney: A document by which one person grants to another the legal right to act on his or her behalf with regard to specific situations.

preliminary distribution: Assets distributed prior to the close of the estate.

probate: The procedure by which a transaction alleged to be a will is judicially established as a testamentary disposition, and also applies to the administration process of an estate.

qualified disclaimer: Acceptance of bequest and subsequent disapproval. Must be executed in writing and communicated to the executor or administrator within nine months after the transfer or, in the case of a minor, by the age of twenty-one.

qualified domestic trust (QDOT): Trust for a noncitizen that defers estate taxes in the estate of a citizen until the death of the noncitizen surviving spouse.

qualified terminable interest property (QTIP): Trust created for the benefit of a spouse and entitled to a marital deduction.

remainder: Property left over after all will distribution provisions have been satisfied.

remainder beneficiary: A beneficiary named in the will or trust to receive the remainder property.

res or principal: The property the settlor/transferor places into a trust.

residuary beneficiary: General legacy to persons or organizations that will receive the balance of property not specifically given or legacies that have lapsed.

residuary clause: Provides for a distribution of the remainder of the estate after all of the other specific and cash bequests have been made.

retained income trust: A trust created to give a gift of a future interest whose value is discounted for gift tax purposes.

reversionary interest: A right to receive property back at some future date provided that the value of such a right immediately before death is in excess of 5 percent of the value of the entire property.

revocable trust: A trust that can be changed or revoked by the creator.

rule against perpetuities: The rule that no contingent interest is good unless it must vest, if at all, no later than twenty-one years after the death of all the beneficiaries who wer in being (alive) at the time of the creation of the interest.

self-proving procedure: Adopted by majority of states. Affidavit stating that all the requisites for due execution have been complied with.

settlor: The person who creates a trust.

spendthrift trust: A trust established by a third party to protect the interests of another party (i.e., spouse) from claims of future creditors.

sponge tax: In a state such as Florida, where there is no estate tax per se, the state receives from the estate the credit calculated in a taxable estate as its state death tax.

springing trust: When the management of a living trust will only shift to a successor trustee when incapacity or other specified event occurs, as defined in the trust.

sprinkle trust: Trustee has the discretion to distribute income to a number of beneficiaries. Also known as a discretionary trust.

sprinkling or spray provision: Provision in discretionary trust that allows trustee to make distributions to a number of beneficiaries without regard to equality as to amounts or times.

standby trust: A trust created to manage a person's assets while he or she is abroad or disabled.

statute of descent and distribution: The law that sets forth the order of distribution of the property of a decedent that is not disposed of by will or trust.

statutory will: Form will with fill-in-the-blanks; authorized in a few states.

stepped-up value: The value property is increased to (fair market value) at the time of the owner's death that will reduce or eliminate capital gains taxes upon its eventual sale.

stopgap: Additional tax designated as the generation-skipping transfer tax that prevents property from passing over a generation without estate taxes being imposed on such a transfer.

succession: Process by which the property of a decedent is inherited by will or through descent.

support trust: Trust created to provide beneficiary with only as much principal or income as necessary for support and education.

tenancy by the entirety: Ownership of property by a husband and wife together. Neither spouse is allowed to alienate any part of the property so held without consent of the other.

tenancy in common: When each co-owner owns an undivided fractional interest in the property.

terrorem clause: Provides for forfeiture of legacy in the event of a challenge by a beneficiary.

testamentary capacity: Criteria established by the laws of our states required to be met by you in order for you to create a legally valid will.

testamentary substitute: Transfers usually made during a spouse's lifetime but which usually do not pass to the beneficiary of such an account until the death of the person that created it.

testamentary trust: A trust created in accordance with instructions contained in your will. Takes effect only after death.

testate: One passes "testate" when he or she leaves behind a valid will.

testator (male) or testatrix (female): Name for person who has created a legally valid will.

throwback rule: Rule that applies only to trusts, not estates. If property is distributed to a beneficiary and the distribution results in a loss, the loss could be disallowed.

Totten trust: A bank account created that prevents a joint owner from withdrawing any funds before your death. If the beneficiary of such an account predeceases you, the account will pass under the residuary clause of your will.

trust: A legal entity created to control the distribution of property.

trustee: The person holding legal title to a trust for the benefit of a beneficiary.

Unified Credit against Estate and Gift Tax: Credit up to $1,730,800 (equivalent to $5,000,000 in property) that can be credited against the federal estate and gift tax.

Uniform Gifts to Minors Act: Law that permits you to give a gift to a minor by giving the gift to a custodian who holds title to the property for the benefit of the minor.

uniform marital deduction: Unlimited amounts of property that can pass or be gifted to a surviving spouse without estate or gift tax consequences.

Uniform Probate Code: A model statute governing distribution of estate assets. This may be adopted, used as a guide, or wholly ignored by the various states.

unitrust: A qualified trust in which the grantor retains certain income rights.

will: An expression, either written or oral, of a person's intentions concerning disposition of property at death.

Index

Books from Allworth Press

Allworth Press is an imprint of Skyhorse Publishing, Inc. Selected titles are listed below.

Your Will and Estate Plan: How to Protect Your Estate and Your Loved Ones
by *Harvey J. Platt* (6 x 9, 224 pages, paperback, $16.95)

Living Trusts for Everyone: Why a Will Is Not the Way to Avoid Probate, Protect Heirs, and Settle Estates
by *Ronald Sharp* (5 ½ x 8 ½, 160 pages, paperback, $14.95)

Estate Planning and Administration: How to Maximize Assets, Minimize Taxes, and Protect Loved Ones, Second Edition
by *Edmund T. Fleming* (6 x 9, 288 pages, paperback, $16.95)

Estate Planning for the Healthy Wealthy Family
by *Stanley D. Neeleman, Carla B. Garrity, and Mitchell A. Barris* (6 x 9, 256 pages, paperback, $22.95)

Legal Forms for Everyone, Fifth Edition
by *Carl W. Battle* (8 ½ x 11, 240 pages, paperback, $24.95)

Winning the Divorce War: How to Protect Your Best Interests, Second Edition
by *Ronald Sharp* (5 ½ x 8 ½, 208 pages, paperback, $16.95)

Spend Your Way to Wealth: A Complete New Approach to Retirement and Investment Planning That Really Works
by *Mike Schiano* (6 x 9, 208 pages, paperback, $21.95)

Feng Shui and Money: A Nine-Week Program for Creating Wealth Using Ancient Principles and Techniques
by *Eric Shaffert* (6 x 9, 256 pages, paperback, $16.95)

To see our complete catalog or to order online, please visit *www.allworth.com*.

**Praise for the novels of *New York Times* and
USA TODAY bestselling author Diana Palmer**

"Diana Palmer is an amazing storyteller, and her long-time
fans will enjoy *Wyoming Winter* with satisfaction!"
—*RT Book Reviews*

"The popular Palmer has penned another winning novel, a
perfect blend of romance and suspense."
—*Booklist* on *Lawman*

"Palmer knows how to make the sparks fly....
Heartwarming."   —*Publishers Weekly* on *Renegade*

"Sensual and suspenseful."   —*Booklist* on *Lawless*

"Diana Palmer is a mesmerizing storyteller who captures the
essence of what a romance should be."   —*Affaire de Coeur*

"This is a fascinating story.... It's nice to have a hero wise
enough to know when he can't do things alone and willing
to accept help when he needs it. There is pleasure to be
found in the nice sense of family this tale imparts."
—*RT Book Reviews* on *Wyoming Bold*

"Readers will be moved by this tale of revenge and justice,
grief and healing."   —*Booklist* on *Dangerous*

"Lots of passion, thrills, and plenty of suspense... *Protector* is a
top-notch read!"   —*Romance Reviews Today*

P9-DEF-652

Praise for the novels of
***USA TODAY* bestselling author Naima Simone**

"Simone balances crackling, electric love scenes with
exquisitely rendered characters."   —*Entertainment Weekly*

"Passion, heat and deep emotion—Naima Simone is a gem!"
        —*New York Times* bestselling author Maisey Yates

"Simone never falters in mining the complexity of two
people who grow and heal and eventually love together."
        —*New York Times* bestselling author Sarah MacLean

"Simone is always a good bet."   —*All About Romance*

"I am a huge Naima Simone fan. With her stories, she has
the ability to transport you to places you can only dream of,
with characters who have a realness to them."
        —*Read Your Writes*

"[Naima Simone] excels at creating drama and emotional
scenes as well as strong heroines who are resilient survivors."
        —*Harlequin Junkie*

DIANA PALMER

DANGEROUS

&

Naima Simone

A KISS TO REMEMBER

If you purchased this book without a cover you should be aware that this book is stolen property. It was reported as "unsold and destroyed" to the publisher, and neither the author nor the publisher has received any payment for this "stripped book."

HQN®

ISBN-13: 978-1-335-45436-2

Dangerous

Copyright © 2022 by Harlequin Books S.A.

Dangerous
First published in 2010. This edition published in 2022.
Copyright © 2010 by Diana Palmer

A Kiss to Remember
First published in 2021. This edition published in 2022.
Copyright © 2021 by Naima Simone

All rights reserved. No part of this book may be used or reproduced in any manner whatsoever without written permission except in the case of brief quotations embodied in critical articles and reviews.

This is a work of fiction. Names, characters, places and incidents are either the product of the author's imagination or are used fictitiously. Any resemblance to actual persons, living or dead, businesses, companies, events or locales is entirely coincidental.

This edition published by arrangement with Harlequin Books S.A.

For questions and comments about the quality of this book, please contact us at CustomerService@Harlequin.com.

HQN
22 Adelaide St. West, 41st Floor
Toronto, Ontario M5H 4E3, Canada
www.Harlequin.com

Printed in Lithuania

Recycling programs for this product may not exist in your area.

MIX
Paper from responsible sources
FSC® C021394

For a complete list of titles available by Diana Palmer,
please visit www.dianapalmer.com.

Also by Naima Simone

The Road to Rose Bend
Christmas in Rose Bends

Trust Fund Fiancé
Ruthless Pride
Back in the Texan's Bed

For additional books by Naima Simone,
visit her website, www.naimasimone.com.

CONTENTS

Dear Reader,

Of all the books I've written in recent months, this one has taken the biggest toll on me emotionally. I knew from *Heart of Stone* that some of Kilraven's family had been murdered. I knew from *The Maverick* that his little three-year-old girl was one of the victims. But actually dealing with the emotions that arise from such tragedy, even in a novel, can be difficult.

I have, thank God, never lost a child. But as I wrote the scenes dealing with Kilraven's loss, I developed a whole new relationship with boxes of tissues. This seemingly steel-hard man has a very soft center, and discovering it was fascinating.

I also dealt with an unexpected and shocking reality when I got to the last few chapters. The man I had fingered as the murderer informed me quite bluntly that he had nothing to do with it. So I had to go back and rethink my strategy, and my plot. I didn't really mind. It was kind of fun.

Winnie started out as a meek woman who wouldn't even stand up to her own brother. During the course of this book, in which she works as a 911 operator, she became a fountain of calm and quiet knowledge, and the courage she had always possessed was revealed to her. She did, in fact, become a "little blond chainsaw," as her new mother-in-law dubbed her.

I had a lot of help with this novel from a lovely lady who actually is a 911 operator, Cindy Angerett. She gave me great insight into the job, and I have dedicated the book to her in gratitude. Please note that I do make mistakes, more than ever these days as my mind ages with me. But the mistakes are my own, and I take full responsibility for any you may find. I owe my life to a diligent 911 operator. They are a gift from God in times of great danger. I love them all.

Thank you all, again, for being so kind and so loyal for all these years. The greatest joy I have in my profession is the friends I make in the course of following it, and in the readers who have become my extended family.

Love to all from your greatest fan,

Diana Palmer

DANGEROUS

Diana Palmer

To Cindy Angerett, 911 dispatcher,
Beaver County, Pennsylvania, and to emergency services
personnel everywhere, who give their time generously,
both on and off the clock, to help someone in need.

CHAPTER ONE

KILRAVEN HATED MORNINGS. He especially hated mornings like this one, when he was expected to go to a party and participate in Christmas gift-giving. He, the rest of the police, fire and emergency services people in Jacobsville, Texas, had all drawn names around the big Christmas tree in the EOC, the 911 emergency operations center. Today was the day when presents, all anonymous, were to be exchanged.

He sipped black coffee in the Jacobsville Police Station and wished he could get out of it. He glared at Cash Grier, who smiled obliviously and ignored him.

Christmas was the most painful time to him. It brought back memories of seven years ago, when his life had seemed to end. Nightmarish visions haunted him. He saw them when he slept. He worked his own shifts and even volunteered to relieve other Jacobsville police officers when they needed a substitute. He hated his own company. But he hated crowds far more. Besides, it was a sad day, sort of. He'd had a big black Chow keeping him company at his rental house. He'd had to give it away because he wasn't allowed to keep animals at his apartment in San Antonio, where he would be returning soon. Still, Bibb the Chow had gone to live with a young boy, a neighbor, who loved animals and had just lost his own Chow. So it was fated, he guessed. He still missed the dog, though.

Now, he was expected to smile and socialize at a party and enthuse over a gift that would almost certainly be a tie that he would accept and never wear, or a shirt that was a size too small, or a book he would never read. People giving gifts were kindhearted, but mostly they bought things that pleased themselves. It was a rare person who could observe someone else and give just the right present; one that would be treasured.

At his job—his real job, not this role as a small-town police officer that he'd assumed as part of his covert operation in south Texas near the border with Mexico—he had to wear suits from time to time. Here in Jacobsville, he never wore a suit. A tie would be a waste of money to the person who gave him one for Christmas. He was sure it would be a tie. He hated ties.

"Why don't you just string me up outside and set fire to me?" Kilraven asked Cash Grier with a glowering look.

"Christmas parties are fun," Cash replied. "You need to get into the spirit of the thing. Six or seven beers, and you'd fit right in."

The glare got worse. "I don't drink," he reminded his temporary boss.

"Now isn't that a coincidence?" Cash exclaimed. "Neither do I!"

"Then why are we going to a party in the first place, if neither of us drink?" the younger man asked.

"They won't serve alcohol at the party. And for another, it's good public relations."

"I hate the public and I don't have relations," Kilraven scoffed.

"You do so have relations," came the tongue-in-cheek reply. "A half brother named Jon Blackhawk. A stepmother, too, somewhere."

Kilraven made a face.

"It's only for an hour or so," Cash said in a gentler tone. "It's almost Christmas. You don't want to ruin the staff party now, do you?"

"Yes," Kilraven said with a bite in his deep voice.

Cash looked down at his coffee cup. "Winnie Sinclair will be disappointed if you don't show up. You're leaving us soon to go back to San Antonio. It would make her day to see you at the party."

Kilraven averted his gaze to the front window beyond which cars were driving around the town square that was decorated with its Santa, sled and reindeer and the huge Christmas tree. Streamers and colored lights were strung across every intersection. There was a tree in the police station, too, decked out in holiday colors. Its decorations were, to say the least, unique. There were little handcuffs and toy guns and various emergency services vehicles in miniature, including police cars. As a joke, someone had strung yellow police tape around it.

Kilraven didn't want to think about Winnie Sinclair. Over the past few months, she'd become a part of his life that he was reluctant to give up. But she didn't know about him, about his past. Someone had hinted at it because her attitude toward him had suddenly changed. The shy smiles and rapt glances he'd been getting had gone into eclipse, so that now she was formal and polite when they spoke over the police band while he was on duty. He rarely saw her. He wasn't sure it was a good idea to be around her. She'd withdrawn, and it would be less painful not to close the distance. Of course it would.

He shrugged his broad shoulders. "I guess a few Christmas carols won't kill me," he muttered.

Cash grinned. "I'll get Sergeant Miller to sing you the one he composed, just for us."

Kilraven glared at him. "I've heard it, and please don't."

"He doesn't have a bad voice," Cash argued.

"For a carp, no."

Cash burst out laughing. "Suit yourself, Kilraven." He frowned. "Don't you have a first name?"

"Yes, I do, but I don't use it, and I'm not telling it to you."

"I'll bet payroll knows what it is," Cash mused. "And the bank."

"They won't tell," he promised. "I have a gun."

"So do I, and mine's bigger," Cash returned smartly.

"Listen, I have to do concealed carry in my real job," he reminded the older man, "and it's hard to fit a 1911 Colt .45 ACP in my waistband so that it doesn't show."

Cash held up both hands. "I know, I know. I used to do concealed carry, too. But now I don't have to, and I can carry a big gun if I want to."

"At least you don't carry a wheel gun, like Dunn does." He sighed, indicating Assistant Chief Judd Dunn, who was perched on the edge of his desk talking to a fellow officer, with a .45 Ruger Vaquero in a fancy leather holster on his hip.

"He belongs to the Single Action Shooting Society," Cash reminded him, "and they're having a competition this afternoon. He's our best shot."

"After me," Kilraven said smugly.

"He's our best resident shot," came the reply. "You're our best migrating shot."

"I won't migrate far. Just to San Antonio." Kilraven's silver eyes grew somber. "I've enjoyed my time here. Less pressure."

Cash imagined part of the reduced pressure was the absence of the bad memories Kilraven still hadn't faced, the death of his family seven years ago in a bloody shooting. Which brought to mind a more recent case, a murder that was still being investigated by the sheriff's department with some help from Alice Mayfield Jones, the forensic expert from San Antonio who was engaged to resident rancher Harley Fowler.

"Have you told Winnie Sinclair about her uncle?" Cash asked in a hushed tone, so that they wouldn't be overheard.

Kilraven shook his head. "I'm not sure that I should at this stage of the investigation. Her uncle is dead. Nobody is going to threaten Winnie or Boone or Clark Sinclair because of him. I'm not even sure what his connection to the murder victim is. No use upsetting her until I have to."

"Has anyone followed up on his live-in girlfriend?"

"Not with any more luck than they had on the first interview," Kilraven replied. "She's so stoned on coke that she doesn't know the time of day. She can't remember anything that's of any use to us. Meanwhile, the police are going door to door around that strip mall near the apartment where the murder victim lived, trying to find anybody who knew the guy. Messy murder. Very messy."

"There was another case, that young girl who was found in a similar condition seven years ago," Cash recalled.

Kilraven nodded. "Yes. Just before I...lost my family," he said hesitantly. "The circumstances are similar, but there's no connection that we can find. She went to a party and disappeared. In fact, witnesses said she never showed up at the party, and her date turned out to be fictional."

Cash studied the younger man quietly. "Kilraven, you're never going to heal until you're able to talk about what happened."

Kilraven's silver eyes flashed. "What use is talk? I want the perp."

He wanted vengeance. It was in his eyes, in the hard set of his jaw, in his very posture. "I know how that feels," Cash began.

"The hell you do," Kilraven bit off. "The hell you do!" He got up and walked off without another word.

Cash, who'd seen the autopsy photos, didn't take offense. He was sorry for the other man. But there was nothing anybody could do for him.

Kilraven did go to the party. He stood next to Cash without looking at him. "Sorry I lost my temper like that," he said gruffly.

Cash only smiled. "Oh, I don't get ruffled by bad temper anymore." He chuckled. "I've mellowed."

Kilraven turned to face him with wide eyes. "You have?"

Cash glared at him. "It was an accident."

"What was, the pail of soapy water, or the sponge in his mouth?"

Cash grimaced. "He shouldn't have called me a bad name when I was washing my car. I wasn't even the arresting officer, it was one of the new patrol officers."

"He figured you were the top of the food chain, and

he didn't like people seeing him carried off from the dentist's office in a squad car," Kilraven said gleefully.

"Obviously, since he was the dentist. He put one of his prettier patients under with laughing gas and was taking advantage of her when the nurse walked in and caught him."

"It does explain why he moved here in the first place, and settled into a small-town practice, when he'd been working in a major city," Cash mused. "He'd only been in practice here for a month when it happened, back in the summer."

"Big mistake, to start raging at you in your own yard."

"I'm sure he noticed," Cash replied.

"Didn't you have to replace his suit...?"

"I bought him a very nice replacement," Cash argued. "The judge said I had to make it equal in price to the one I ruined with soap and water." He smiled angelically. "She never said it had to be the same color."

Kilraven grimaced. "Where in hell did you even find a yellow and green plaid suit?"

Cash leaned closer. "I have connections in the clothing industry."

Kilraven chuckled. "The dentist left town the same day. Think it was the suit?"

"I very much doubt it. I think it was the priors I pulled up on him," Cash replied. "I did just mention that I'd contacted two of his former victims."

"And gave them the name of a very determined detective out of Houston, I heard."

"Detectives are useful."

Kilraven was still staring at him.

He shrugged.

"Well, I'm never talking to you when you're washing your car, and you can bet money on that," Kilraven concluded.

Cash just grinned.

The 911 operations center was full. The nine-foot-tall Christmas tree had lights that were courtesy of the operations staff. The LED bulbs glittered prettily in all colors. Underneath, there was a treasure trove of wrapped packages. They were all anonymous. Kilraven glared at them, already anticipating the unwanted tie.

"It's a tie," Kilraven muttered.

"Excuse me?" Cash asked.

"My present. Whoever got me something, it will be a tie. It's always a tie. I've got a closet full of the damned things."

"You never know," Cash said philosophically. "You might be surprised."

Amid the festive Christmas music, the staff of the operations center welcomed their visitors with a brief speech about the hard work they put in all year and listed some of their accomplishments. They thanked all the emergency services personnel, including EMTs, fire and police, sheriff's department and state police, Texas Rangers and state and federal law enforcement for their assistance. The long refreshment tables were indicated, and guests were invited to help themselves. Then the presents were handed out.

Kilraven was briefly stunned at the size of his. Unless it was a very large tie, or camouflaged, he wasn't sure what he'd snagged here. He turned the large square over in his hands with evident curiosity.

Little blonde Winnie Sinclair watched him out of the corner of her dark eyes. She'd worn her blond, wavy hair long, around her shoulders, because someone had said Kilraven didn't like ponytails or buns. She wore a pretty red dress, very conservative, with a high neckline. She wished she could find out more about their enigmatic officer. Sheriff Carson Hayes had said some of Kilraven's family had died in a murder years before, but she hadn't been able to worm any more information out of him. Now they had a real, messy murder victim—actually their second one—killed in Jacobs County, and there was a rumor around law enforcement circles that a woman in San Antonio had known the victim and died for it. There were even more insistent rumors that the cold case was about to be reopened.

Whatever happened, Kilraven was supposed to leave and go back to his federal job in San Antonio after Christmas. Winnie had been morose and quiet for days. She'd actually drawn Kilraven's name for that secret present, although she had a hunch her coworkers had arranged it. They knew how she felt about him.

She'd spent hours trying to decide what to give him. Not a tie, she thought. Everybody gave ties or handkerchiefs or shaving kits. No, her gift had to be something distinctive, something that he wouldn't find on any store shelf. In the end, she put her art talent to work and painted him a very realistic portrait of a raven, surrounded by colorful beads as a border. She didn't know why. It seemed the perfect subject. Ravens were loners, highly intelligent, mysterious. Just like Kilraven. She had it matted at the local frame shop. It didn't look bad, she thought. She hoped he might like it. Of course, she couldn't admit that she'd given it to him. The gifts were supposed to remain anonymous. But he wouldn't know anyway because she'd never told him that she painted as a hobby.

Her life was magic just because Kilraven had come into it. Winnie came from great wealth, but she and her brothers rarely let it show. She enjoyed working for a living, making her own money. She had a little red VW that she washed and polished by hand, bought out of her weekly salary. It was her pride and joy. She'd worried at first that Kilraven might be intimidated by her monied background. But he didn't seem to feel resentment, or even envy. In fact, she'd seen him dressed up once for a conference he was going to. His sophistication was evident. He seemed at home anywhere.

She was going to be miserable when he was gone. But it might be the best thing. She was crazy about him. Cash Grier said that Kilraven had never faced his demons, and that he wasn't fit for any sort of relationship until he had. That had depressed Winnie and affected her attitude toward Kilraven. Not that it squelched her feelings for him.

While she was watching him with helpless delight, he opened the present. He stood apart from the other officers in his department, his dark head bent over the wrapping paper, his silver eyes intent on what he was doing. At last, the ribbon and paper came away. He picked up the painting and looked at it, narrow-eyed, so still that he seemed to have stopped breathing. All at once, his silver eyes shot up and pierced right into Winnie's dark ones. Her heart stopped in her chest. He knew! But he couldn't!

He gave her a glare that might have stopped traffic, turned around and walked right out of the party with the painting held by its edge in one big hand. He didn't come back.

Winnie was sick at heart. She'd offended him. She knew she had. He'd been furious. She fought tears as she sipped punch and nibbled cookies and pretended to be having a great time.

KILRAVEN WENT THROUGH the motions of doing his job until his shift ended. Then he got into his own car and drove straight up to San Antonio, to the apartment of his half brother, Jon Blackhawk.

Jon was watching a replay of a soccer match. He got up to answer the door, dressed in sweatpants and nothing else, with his loosened black, thick hair hanging down to his waist.

Kilraven gave him a hard stare. "What are you up to?"

Jon made a face. "Getting comfortable. Come in. Isn't this a little late for a brotherly visit?"

Kilraven lifted the bag he was carrying, put it on the coffee table and pulled out the painting. His eyes were glittering. "You told Winnie Sinclair about the raven pictures."

Jon caught his breath when he saw the painting. Not only was it of a raven, Melly's favorite bird, but it even had the beadwork in the same colors framing it against a background of swirling oranges and reds.

He realized, belatedly, that he was being accused. He lifted his dark eyes to his brother's light ones. "I haven't spoken to Winnie Sinclair. Ever, unless I'm mistaken. How did she know?"

The older man's eyes were still flashing. "Somebody had to tell her. When I find out who, I'll strangle him."

"Just a thought," Jon pondered, "but didn't you tell me

that she called for backup on a domestic dispute when you didn't call and ask for it?"

Kilraven calmed down a little. "She did," he recalled. "Saved my butt, too. The guy had a shotgun and he was holding his wife and daughter hostage with it because the wife was trying to get a divorce. Backup arrived with sirens and lights blaring. Diverted him just long enough for me to subdue him."

"How did she know?" Jon asked.

Kilraven frowned. "I asked. She said she had a feeling. The caller hadn't told her about the shotgun, just that her estranged husband had walked in and made threats."

"Our father used to have those flashes of insight," Jon reminded him. "It saved his life on more than one occasion. Restless feelings, he called them."

"Like on the night my family died," Kilraven said, sitting down heavily in an easy chair in front of the muted television. "He went to get gas in his car for the next day when he had a trip out of town for the Bureau. He could have gone anytime, but he went then. When he came back..."

"You and half the city police force were inside." Jon winced. "I wish they could have spared you that."

Kilraven's eyes were terrible. "I can't get it out of my mind. I live with it, night and day."

"So did Dad. He drank himself to death. He thought maybe if he hadn't gone to get gas, they'd have lived."

"Or he'd have died." He was recalling Alice Mayfield Jones's lecture of the week before. "Alice Jones read me the riot act about that word *if*." He smiled sadly. "I guess she's right. We can't change what happened." He looked at Jon. "But I'd give ten years of my life to catch the guys who did it."

"We'll get them," Jon said. "I promise you, we will. Had supper yet?" he added.

Kilraven shook his head. "No appetite." He looked at the painting Winnie had done. "You remember how Melly used her crayons?" he asked softly. "Even at the age of three, she had great talent..." He stopped abruptly.

Jon's dark eyes softened. "That's the first time I've heard you say her name in seven years, Mac," he said gently.

Kilraven grimaced. "Don't call me...!"

"Mac is a perfectly nice nickname for McKuen," he said stubbornly. "You're named for one of the most famous poets of the seventies, Rod McKuen. I've got a book of his poems around here somewhere. A lot of them were made into songs."

Kilraven looked at the bulging bookcases. There were plastic bins of books stacked in the corner. "How do you ever read all those?" he asked, aghast.

Jon glared at him. "I could ask you the same question. You've got even more books than I have. The only things you have more of are gaming discs."

"It makes up for a social life, I guess," he confessed with a sheepish grin.

"I know." Jon grimaced. "It affected us both. I got gun-shy about getting involved with women after it happened."

"So did I," Kilraven confessed. He studied the painting. "I was furious about that," he said, indicating it. "The beadwork is just like what Melly drew."

"She was a sweet, beautiful child," Jon said quietly.

"It isn't fair to put her so far back in your memories that she's lost forever."

Kilraven drew a long breath. "I guess so. The guilt has eaten me alive. Maybe Alice is right. Maybe we only think we have control over life and death."

"Maybe so." Jon smiled. "I've got leftover pizza in the fridge, and soda. There's a killer soccer match on. The World Cup comes around next summer."

"Well, whoever I root for will lose, like always," he replied. He sat down on the sofa. "So, who's playing?" he asked, nodding toward the television.

WINNIE WAS SICK at heart when she left after the party to go home. She'd made Kilraven furious, and just before he was due to leave Jacobsville. She probably wouldn't ever see him again, especially now.

"What in the world happened to you?" her sister-in-law, Keely, asked when she came into the kitchen where the younger woman was making popcorn.

"What do you mean?" Winnie asked, trying to bluff it out.

"Don't give me that." Keely put her arms around her and hugged her. "Come on. Tell Keely all about it."

Winnie burst into tears. "I gave Kilraven a painting. He wasn't supposed to know it was me. But he did! He looked straight at me, like he hated me." She sniffed. "I've ruined everything!"

"The painting of the raven?" Keely recalled. "It was gorgeous."

"I thought it looked pretty good," Winnie replied. "But he glared at me as if he wanted to tear a hole in me, and then he just walked out of the party and never came back."

"Maybe he doesn't like ravens," the other woman suggested gently. "Some people are afraid of birds."

Winnie laughed, nodding thankfully as Keely put a paper towel in her hands. She dried her eyes. "Kilraven's not afraid of anything."

"I suppose not. He does take chances, though." She frowned. "Didn't you send backup for him after some attempted shooting lately? They were talking about it at work. One of our girls is related to Shirley, who works with you at the 911 operations center," she reminded her.

Winnie grimaced. She took her purse off her shoulder, tossed it onto the bar and sat down at the table. "Yes, I did. I don't know why. I just had a terrible feeling that something bad was going to happen if I didn't. The caller didn't say anything about the perp having a gun. But he had a loaded shotgun and he was so drunk, he didn't care if he killed his estranged wife and their little girl. Kilraven walked right into it."

They were both remembering an earlier incident, when Winnie was a new dispatcher and she'd failed to mention a gun involved in a domestic dispute. Kilraven had been involved in that one, and he'd given her a lecture about it. She was much more careful now.

"How did you know?" Keely persisted.

"I really couldn't say." Winnie laughed. "I've had feelings like that all my life, known things that I had no reason to know. My grandmother used to set the table for company when we didn't even know anybody was coming. They'd show up just when she thought they would. The second sight, she called it."

"A gift. I've heard them say that Cash Grier's wife, Tippy, has it."

"So have I." Winnie shrugged. "I don't know, though. I just get feelings. Usually they're bad ones." She looked up at Keely. "I've had one all day. I can't shake it. And I don't think Kilraven's reaction to my gift was the reason. I wonder…"

"Who's that coming up the driveway?" Boone Sinclair asked, joining them. He brushed a kiss against Keely's mouth. "Expecting someone?" he asked her, including Winnie in the question.

"No," Winnie said.

"Me, either," Winnie replied. "It isn't Clark?"

He shook his head. "He flew up to Dallas this morning for a meeting with some cattle buyers for me." He frowned as he went to the window. "Old car," he remarked. "Well kept, but old. There are two people in it." His face tautened as a woman got out of the driver's seat and went around to the passenger side. She stood in the edge of the security lights because it was already dark. Boone recognized her just from the way she walked. She spoke to someone in the car, was handed a briefcase out the window. She smiled, nodded and turned toward the house. She hesitated just for a minute before she started up the steps to the front door. Boone got a good look at her then. She was, he thought, the spitting image of Winnie. His face went harder.

Keely knew something was going on from their expressions. Winnie was staring out the window next to Boone, her dark eyes flashing like sirens. Before Keely could ask a single question, Winnie exploded.

"Her!" she exclaimed. "How dare she come here! How dare she!"

CHAPTER TWO

WINNIE STORMED OUT into the hall. Her face was taut with anger.

"Who is she?" Keely asked Boone, concerned.

His own face had gone hard. "Our mother," he said bitterly. "We haven't seen her since she left. She ran away with our uncle and divorced our dad to marry him."

"Oh, dear," Keely said, biting her lip. She looked up at his angry expression. "I think I'll go on upstairs. It might be better if the two of you saw her alone."

"I was thinking the same thing myself. I'll tell you all about it later," Boone said gently, kissing her.

"Okay."

WINNIE HAD ALREADY thrown open the front door. She looked at the older version of herself with seething hatred. "What do you want here?" she demanded hotly.

The woman, tall and dignified, her blond hair sprinkled with gray but neatly combed, wearing a dark pantsuit, blinked as if the assault was unexpected. She frowned. "Winona?" she asked.

Winnie turned and stormed back into the living room.

Boone's eyes narrowed. "If you're here looking for money," he began in a cold tone.

"I have a good job," she replied, puzzled. "Why would I want money from you?"

He hesitated, but only for a moment. He stood aside, stone-faced, and let her in the door. She was carrying a briefcase. She looked around, as if she didn't recognize her surroundings. It had been a very long time since she'd lived here.

She turned to Boone, very businesslike and solemn. "I have some things for you. They belonged to your father, but your uncle took them with him when he…when he and I," she corrected, forcing the words out through her teeth, "left here."

"What sort of things?" Boone asked.

"Heirlooms," she replied.

"Why didn't our uncle come with you?"

Her eyebrows arched. "He's been dead for a month. Didn't anyone tell you?"

"Sorry," he said stiffly. "It must be sad for you."

"I divorced your uncle twelve years ago," she said flatly. "He's been living with a woman who makes her living as a low-level drug dealer, selling meth on the streets. She's an addict herself." She indicated the briefcase. "I told her these things belonged to her boyfriend's family and that legal proceedings might ensue if she didn't hand them over." Her expression was determined. "They belong here."

He motioned her into the living room. Winnie was sitting stiffly in an armchair, as welcoming as a cobra.

The older woman sat down gracefully on the sofa, her eyes going to the mantel, over which hung a painting of Boone and Winnie and Clark's late father. Her gaze lingered on it sadly, but only for seconds. She put the briefcase on the coffee table and opened it. She drew

out several items, some made of gold, including pieces
of jewelry that were worth a king's ransom.

"These belonged to your great-grandmother," she
told the other occupants of the room. "She was a high-
born Spanish lady from Andalusia who came here with
her father to sell a rancher a prize stallion. Your great-
grandfather was a ranch foreman who worked for the
owner. He had very little money, but grand dreams, and
he was a hard worker. She fell in love with him and married him. It was her inheritance that bought this land
and built the house that originally sat on it." She smiled.
"They said she could outride any of the cowboys, and
that she once actually fought a bull that had gored her
husband, using her mantilla as a cape. Saved his life."

"There's a painting of her in the upstairs guest bedroom," Boone said quietly, lifting one of the brooches in
his strong, dark hands.

"Why did you bother to bring them back?" Winnie
asked coldly.

"They'd have been sold to buy drugs," she replied simply. "I felt responsible for them. Bruce took them when we
left." Her face hardened. "He felt that he was deliberately
left out of your grandfather's will. He was furious when
your father inherited the ranch. He wanted to get even."

"So he corrupted you and forced you to run away with
him," Winnie said with an icy smile.

"I wasn't forced," the older woman said kindly. "I was
naive and stupid. And I don't expect to be welcomed back
into the family because I returned a few heirlooms." She
picked up her briefcase and stood up. Her eyes went from
her son to her daughter. "Is Clark here?"

Boone shook his head. "On a date."

She smiled sadly. "I would like to have seen him. It's been so long."

"Your choice, wasn't it?" Winnie demanded. She stood up, too, dark eyes blazing. "Dad hated you for leaving, and I look like you, don't I? I paid for his pain. Paid for it every miserable day he was alive."

"I'm sorry," the older woman said haltingly.

"Sorry. Sorry!" Winnie jerked up her blouse and turned around. "Want to see how sorry you should really be?"

Boone caught his breath at the marks on her back. There were scars. Two of them. They ran across her spine in white trails. "You never told me he did that!" Boone accused, furious.

"He said that if I told, you and Clark would have similar souvenirs," she bit off, pulling her blouse down.

The older woman winced. So did Boone.

"I've wanted to see you for years," Winnie said, reddening. "I wanted to tell you how much I hated you for running off and leaving us!"

She only nodded. "I don't blame you, Winona," she said in a steady, calm voice. "I did a terrible thing, to all of you." She drew in a long breath and smiled sadly. "You won't believe it, but there was a price that I had to pay, too."

"Good," Winnie bit off. "I'm glad! Now please leave. And don't come back."

She whirled and ran up the staircase.

Boone walked his mother to the door and opened it for her. His expression was unrelenting. But his eyes were curious, especially when he saw that she had a passenger in her car. It wasn't a new car, but it was well kept.

He noted her clothing. Not from upscale stores, but serviceable and not cheap. Her shoes were thick-soled and laced up. She was immaculately clean, even her fingernails. He wondered what she did for a living. She seemed a sensible woman.

"Thank you for bringing the heirlooms home," he said after a minute.

Gail Rogers Sinclair looked up at him with quiet pride. "You look like your father, as he did when we were first married." She frowned. "Didn't I read that you married this year?"

"Yes. Her name is Keely. She works for a local vet."

She nodded. "Her mother was killed."

He blinked. "Yes."

"At least that crime was quickly solved," she replied. "This new murder in Jacobsville is getting a lot of attention from the Feds. I don't think it's going to be as easy to catch the perpetrator." She searched his eyes. "There may be a tie from the case to your uncle," she said calmly. "I'm not sure yet, but it could mean some bad publicity for all three of you. I'll try to keep it quiet, but these things have a way of getting out. There's always some resourceful reporter with a reputation to build."

"That's true." He was curious about her familiarity with the case. "How are you involved?" He wanted to know.

"That's need to know, and you don't," she said, gentling the words with a smile. "I understand that Winnie works as a dispatcher with emergency services. I'm very proud of her. It's a generous thing she does, working for her living. She would never have to."

"Yes. How is our uncle concerned with the murder?"

"I don't know that yet. It's still under investigation. Messy," she added. "Very, very messy, and it may involve some important people before it's over. But it shouldn't cause any problems for you three," she added. "The murderer doesn't have anything to fear from you." She glanced at her watch. "I have to go. I came down to confer with a friend, and I'm late. I'm sorry I didn't get to see Clark. What does he do?"

"He works with me on the ranch," Boone said. He was adding up her attitude and her indifference to their wealth and her sadness. "Someday," he said, "maybe we need to talk."

She smiled at him with quiet eyes. "There's nothing more to be said. We can't change the past. I made mistakes that I can't ever correct or atone for. Now, I just get on with my job and try to help where I can. Take care. It was very good to see the two of you, even under the circumstances." She looked at him for a moment more, so much pain in her eyes and in her face that it made him feel guilty.

Finally, she turned and walked down the steps toward the car. Boone watched her, scowling, his hands in his pockets. She got into the car, spoke to a shorter person in the passenger seat, started the engine and slowly drove away.

WINNIE CAME BACK down after the car was gone. Her eyes were wet, her face red with bad temper despite Keely's comforting upstairs. "She's gone, then. Good riddance!"

Boone was pensive. "I wish you'd told me what Dad did to you."

She managed a wan smile. "I wanted to. But I was

afraid of what he might do. He really hated me. He said that I was the image of my mother, but he was going to make sure that I never wanted to follow in her footsteps."

"He kept you in church every time it was open," he replied quietly.

"Yes." She wrapped her arms around herself. "And threatened every boy who came here to see me. I ended up with a nonexistent social life." She sighed. "I suppose I'm very repressed."

"You're also very nice," Boone said. He put his arms around her and hugged her fondly. "You know, despite the misery of our childhoods, we've done pretty well, haven't we?"

"You certainly have," she said, wiping away the tears. She smiled. "I love Keely. She's not only my best friend, now she's my sister-in-law."

He was somber. "You saved her life after the rattlesnake bit her," he said quietly. "She would have died, and I would have been responsible." His face hardened. "I can't imagine why I believed such lies about her."

"I'm sure your ex-girlfriend's detective was convincing," she said. "You shouldn't look back. Keely loves you. She never stopped, not even when she thought you hated her."

He smiled. "I was a hard case."

"Well, we're all victims of our childhood, I suppose. Dad was tough on you, too."

"He couldn't beat me down," he recalled. "He got furious at me, but he respected me."

"That was probably what saved you from the treatment I got." She sighed. "It was twelve years ago when she left. I was ten. Ten years old."

"I was technically an adult," he recalled. "Clark was in junior high." He shook his head. "I still don't understand why she left Dad for our uncle. He was a shallow man, no real character and no work ethic. It's no surprise to me that he was dealing drugs. He always did look for the easy way to get money. Dad bailed him out of jail more than once for stealing."

"Yes." She looked at the heirlooms lying on the coffee table. "It's surprising that our mother brought those back. She could have sold them for a lot of money."

"Quite a lot of money," Boone said. He frowned, recalling what she'd said about their uncle's possible connection to people suspected in the local murder. He looked at Winnie, but he didn't say anything about it. She was too shaken already. It could wait. "I wonder who she had with her in the car?" he added suddenly.

She turned. "A boyfriend, maybe," she said curtly. "I could tell he was male from upstairs. But he looked pretty short."

"Not our business," Boone said. He picked up a brooch with a tiny painting of a beautiful little Spanish girl, in her middle to late teens by the look of her, dressed all in black with a mantilla. Her red lipstick and a red rose in her hair under the black lace mantilla were the only bright things in the miniature. Her hair was long, black and shiny. She had a tiny, strange little smile on her lips. Mysterious. He smiled, just looking at it. "I wonder who she was?" he mused aloud.

"Turn it over. Maybe there's initials or something," she suggested, dabbing at her eyes with a handkerchief.

He did. He frowned. "It's labeled with a piece of tape. Señorita Rosa Carrera y Sinclair." He whistled. "This was our great-grandmother, when she was first married! I should have known, but the portrait of her upstairs was painted when she was older."

Winnie looked at it, took it from his hands and studied the lovely face. "She was very beautiful." She laughed. "And she fought bulls with a mantilla! She must have been brave."

"If what I remember hearing from Dad about our great-grandfather is accurate, she had to be brave."

"Truly." She put the brooch down and looked at the other treasures. "So many rubies," she mused. "She must have loved them."

"You should pick out some of those to wear," he suggested.

She laughed. "And where would I wear expensive jewelry like this?" she chided. "I work for Jacobs County dispatch. Wouldn't the girls have a hoot seeing me decked out in these? Shirley would fall out of her chair laughing."

"You should get out more," he said somberly.

She gave him a long, sad look. "I'll never get out, now. Kilraven is leaving after Christmas," she said. Her face fell. "I gave him the raven painting at the party. He glared at me as if I'd committed murder under his nose and stormed out without even speaking to me." She flushed. "Nothing that ever happened to me hurt so much."

"I thought the presents were anonymous."

"They were. I don't know how he knew it was me. I've never told him that I paint."

"He's a strange bird," Boone commented. "He has feelings. Sort of like you do," he added with a grin. "Sending backup when you thought he was going to a routine domestic fight with no weapons involved."

She nodded. "He was furious about that, too. But it saved his life."

"You really ought to see Cash Grier's wife, Tippy. She has those intuitions, too."

"She knows things," Winnie replied. "Whatever sort of mental gift this is, I don't have her accuracy. I just feel uncomfortable before something bad pops up. Like today," she said quietly. "I felt sick all day. Now I know why."

"You do look like her." He was going to add that their mother used to have odd feelings about things that later happened, but he didn't.

"Yes," she said curtly. She looked at the jewelry. "I shouldn't have been so mean. She did a good thing. But it will never make up for leaving us."

"She knows that. She said she didn't come for forgiveness."

She frowned. "Why did she come?"

"She's meeting someone."

"A boyfriend here in Jacobs County?" she asked curtly.

"No, she said it was business." He frowned, too. "You know, she seems to know a lot about that recent murder here."

"Why would she?"

Boone grimaced. "I wasn't going to tell you, but it seems our uncle may have had ties to the case."

She let out a breath. "Oh, that's great. Now he's not just the man who stole our mother, he's a murderer!"

"No, not that sort of involvement," he replied. "I think he might have had some connection to the people involved. From what she said, he was a heavy drug user."

"Not surprising. I never liked him," she confessed. "He was always picking on Dad, trying to compete with him in everything. It was sort of sad to me at the time because anybody could see he wasn't the equal of our father at business or ranching or anything else."

"Our father had some good qualities. Hitting you like that wasn't one of them," he added coldly, "and if I'd known about it, I'd have knocked him through a wall!"

"I know that. It was only the one time," she said quietly, "and he'd been drinking. It was just after he and our mother met that time, when he thought she wanted to come back. It wasn't long after she'd gone away with our uncle. He came back home all quiet and furious, and he drank like a fish for about two months. That was when he hit me. He was sorry afterward, and he promised never to do it again. But he hated me, just the same, because I looked like her."

"I'm sorry."

"Me, too," she said with a sigh. "It sort of turned me against men, at least where marriage was concerned."

"Except with Kilraven."

She flushed and glared at him. "He'll probably never speak to me again, after what happened at the party. I don't understand why he was so angry." She sighed. "Of course, I don't understand why I painted a raven for him, either. It's not one of my usual subjects. I like to do flowers. Or portraits."

"You're very good at portraits."

"Thanks."

"You could have made a name for yourself as a portrait artist, even an illustrator."

"I never had the dedication," she replied. "I really do love my job," she added.

"So does Keely," he replied with an indulgent smile. "It's not a bad thing, working when you don't have to."

"You'd know," she accused, laughing. "You work harder on the ranch than your men do. That reporter for *Modern Ranching World* had to learn to ride a horse just to interview you about your new green technology because he could never find you unless he went out on the ranch."

"They're putting me on the cover," he muttered. "I didn't mind doing the article—I think it helps ranching's public image. But I don't like the idea of seeing myself looking back at me from a magazine rack."

"You're very good-looking," she said. "And it is good PR. Not that you'll ever sell the idea of humane beef cultivation to vegetarians," she added with a chuckle.

He shrugged. "As long as people want a nice, juicy steak at a restaurant, there's not much chance that ranchers are going to turn to raising house cattle."

"Excuse me?"

"Well, you could put a diaper on a calf and bring him inside..."

She hit him. "I'm going to bed," she said. "And when I get upstairs, I'm going to tell Keely what you just said."

"No!" he wailed. "I was only kidding about it. She'd actually do it!"

She laughed. "There wouldn't be room. Bailey's as big as a calf."

The old German Shepherd looked up from his comfortable doggy bed by the fireplace and wagged his tail.

"See?" she asked. "He knows he's a calf."

He shook his head. He bent to ruffle the dog's fur. He glanced at Winnie. "You going to be okay?"

"Sure." She hesitated. "Thanks."

"For what?"

"Being my brother. Don't leave the jewels lying

around," she advised. "If Clark comes home and sees them, he'll beg some of them for whatever girl he's crazy over at the moment."

"Good thought," he said, grinning. "I'll put them in the safe and drive them to town Monday and lodge them in the safe-deposit box."

"She could have sold them and we'd never have known," she replied quietly. "I wonder why she didn't? She's not driving a new car. Her clothes are nice, but not expensive."

"There's no telling why," he said.

"Did she say anything about where she was going?"

He shook his head. "Just that she was meeting a friend."

"At this hour? I wonder who she knows here?" she mused. "She used to be friends with Barbara, who runs the café. But Barbara told me years ago that she hadn't heard a word from her."

"It might be some newcomer," Boone said. "Not our business, anyway."

"I guess. Well, I'm going to bed. It's been a very long day."

"For you, it sure has," he said sympathetically. "First Kilraven, now our mother."

"Things can only get better, right?" she asked, smiling.

"I hope so. Tell Keely I'm going to make a couple of phone calls, and I'll be up. You sleep well."

She smiled. "You, too."

KILRAVEN HAD JUST pulled up in the driveway of his remote rental house in Comanche Wells when he noticed a sedan sitting there. Always overly cautious, he had his .45 automatic in his hand before he opened the door of his car. But when he got out and saw who his visitor was, he put it right back in the holster.

"What the hell are you doing out here at this hour of the night?" he asked.

She smiled. "Bringing bad news, I'm afraid. I couldn't get you on your cell phone, so I took a chance and drove down."

He paused by the car. "What's wrong, Rogers?" he asked, because he knew it had to be something major to bring her from San Antonio.

She didn't correct him. Her last name had been Sinclair, but she'd taken her maiden name back after she divorced Bruce Sinclair. Now she went by the name Gail Rogers. She leaned against the car and sighed, folding her arms over her chest. "It's Rick Marquez," she said. "Someone blindsided him in an alley near his apartment and left him for dead."

"Good Lord! Does his mother know?"

She nodded. "She's at the hospital with him. Scared her to death. But he looks worse than he is. Badly bruised, and a fractured rib, but he'll live. He's mad as hell." She chuckled. "Whoever hit him is going to wish they'd never heard his name."

"At least he'll walk away," Kilraven said. He grimaced. "This case just keeps getting more and more interesting, doesn't it?"

"Whoever's behind these murders seems to feel that the body count no longer matters."

"He's feeling cornered and he's desperate," Kilraven agreed. His eyes narrowed. "You watch your back. You're in as much danger as Marquez. At the very least, they should put you on administrative until we get some sort of lead on what's happening."

"I won't sit at a desk and let everyone around me take risks," she replied calmly.

"Still..."

She held up a hand. "Give up. I'm stubborn."

He sighed. "Okay. But be extra cautious, will you?"

"Of course. Has forensics turned up anything interesting about the DB down here?" DB referred to dead body.

"Alice Jones is handling the case. She's got a piece of paper that they're teasing secrets out of, but she hasn't told me anything new. Senator Fowler's actually cooperating, though. It shook him up when one of his female employees turned up dead. Somebody tried to make it look like suicide, but they didn't do their homework. Had the pistol in the wrong hand."

"I heard about that," she said. "Sloppy. Real sloppy."

"That's what worries me." He bit his lower lip. "I'm going to ask for some time off to work this case. Now that our newest Junior Senator Will Sanders has stopped putting obstacles in our path, maybe we can catch a break. With Marquez sidelined, you're going to need some help. And I have good contacts."

"I know." She smiled. "We might actually solve your case. I hope so."

"Me, too." His face was taut with pain. "I've spent the last seven years waiting for something to help crack the case. Maybe this latest murder is it."

"Well, it's going to be slow," she said. "We're no closer to the identity of the man found dead in Jacobs County, or to the people who killed Senator Fowler's employee. Now we've got Marquez's attack to work on, as well."

She shook her head. "I should have gotten a job baking cakes in a restaurant."

He gave her a look of mock surprise. "You can cook?"

She glared at him. "Yes, I can cook. On my salary who can afford to eat out?"

He laughed. "Come work for me. I have an expense account."

"No, thanks," she said, holding out both hands, palm up. "I've heard about some of your exploits."

"Lies," he said. "Put out by jealous colleagues."

"Hanging out of a helicopter by one hand, firing an automatic weapon, over an *ocean,*" she related, emphasizing the last word.

"I did not," he said haughtily.

She just stared at him.

"Anyway, I was not hanging on by my hand." He hesitated. Then he grinned. "I wrapped one of my legs around a piece of cargo netting and held on that way!"

"I'm going home," she said with a laugh.

"Keep your doors locked," he advised firmly.

"You bet."

She climbed in under the wheel and shut the door. Beside her, a shadowy figure waved. He waved back. He wondered who her companion was. He couldn't see him clearly in the darkness, but he looked young. Maybe a trainee, he thought. He turned back toward his house.

CHAPTER THREE

KILRAVEN FELT UNCOMFORTABLE when he remembered how upset Winnie Sinclair had been at the Christmas party. When he got over his initial anger, he realized that she couldn't possibly have known about his daughter's fascination with ravens. After all, who could have told her? Only he and Jon knew. Well, his stepmother—Jon's mother—knew. But Cammy had no contact with Winnie.

There was another thing. How had he known that Winnie had painted the picture for him? It was all secret. It was disturbing that he'd felt it so certainly, and that he'd been right. Her tears at the sight of his angry face had made the connection for him. He was sorry about his behavior. The deaths were still upsetting for him. He couldn't find peace. In seven years, the pain hadn't eased.

Winnie had feelings for him. In another time, another place, that would have been flattering. But he had no interest in women these days. He'd dated Gloryanne Barnes before she'd married Rodrigo Ramirez, but that had been nothing more than friendship and compassion. Winnie, though, that could be a different matter. It was why he tried not to let his attraction to her show. It was why he avoided her. If only, he thought, avoiding her had kept him from wanting to get closer to her.

He was going back to San Antonio soon. He was going to take a leave of absence and try to help solve the cold case that had haunted him for seven long years. Perhaps he might finally have peace, if the killer could be brought to justice.

It was good that Senator Fowler and his protégé, Senator Sanders, had stopped fighting them about reopening the case. It was bad that some powerful politician might be involved, even on the fringes of the crime. Their names would make it a high-profile case, and the tabloids would have a field day. He cringed at the thought of seeing the autopsy photos while he was standing in line at the supermarket, where the tabloids were displayed at the checkout counter. These days, some reporters thought nothing of the family's right to privacy. After all, a scoop was still a scoop.

He put the case to the back of his mind, as he tried to most every day. He only had a few days left in Jacobsville. He was going to do his job and then pack up and go home. In between, he was going to try to explain to Winnie Sinclair why his attitude toward her had been so violent at the Christmas party. He didn't want to encourage her, but he couldn't leave with the image of her hurt expression in his mind.

WINNIE HAD JUST spent a harrowing half hour routing two police cars to a standoff at a convenience store. In fact, it was one of only three convenience stores in the entire county. The perpetrator, a young husband with a history of bad decisions, had gotten drunk and decided to get some quick cash to buy a pretty coat for his wife. When the clerk pulled out a shotgun, the young man had fired and hit the clerk in the chest. He'd holed up in the store with the wounded man when patrons had called the police.

Winnie had dispatched a Jacobsville police officer to the scene. Another officer had called in to say he was going to back up the first officer. It was a usual thing. The officers looked out for each other, just as the dispatchers did.

There was no hostage negotiator, as such, but Cash Grier filled the position for his department. He talked the young man out of his gun. Thank God, the boy hadn't been drunk enough to ignore the chief and come out shooting. Cash had disarmed him and then had Winnie tell the paramedics to come on in. It was routine for paramedics to be dispatched and then to stage just outside the scene of a dangerous situation until law enforcement made sure it was safe for them to go in. It was just another example of how the emergency services looked out for each other.

THE CLERK WAS BADLY INJURED, but he would live. The young man went to the detention center to be booked and await arraignment. Winnie was happy that they were able to avert a tragedy.

She drove her little VW back to the ranch, and she felt happy. It was hard to go through the day after Kilraven's pointed snub at the Christmas party. She was still stinging, and not only from that. Her mother's visit had unsettled her even more.

When she got home, she found Keely and Boone waiting for her in the living room.

"There's a carnival in town. We're going," Keely said,

"and you're going with us. You need a little R and R after all that excitement at work."

"How did you know…?" Winnie exclaimed.

"Boone has a scanner," Keely pointed out, grinning.

Boone grinned, too.

Winnie laughed, putting the coat she'd just shrugged out of back on. "Okay, I'm game. Let's go pitch pennies and win plates."

Boone threw up his hands. "Honey, you could buy those plates for a nickel apiece at the Dish Barn downtown!"

"It's more fun if you win them," Winnie said primly. "Besides, I want cotton candy and a ride on the Octopus!"

"So do I," Keely said. "Come on, sweetheart," she called to Boone as they went through the back door. "The cotton candy will be all gone!"

"Not to worry," he said, locking up. "They'll make more."

THE CARNIVAL WAS loud and colorful and the music was heady. Winnie ate cotton candy and went on the Octopus with Keely, laughing as the wind whipped through their hair and the music warbled among the bright lights.

Later, ankle deep in sawdust, Winnie stood before the penny pitching booth and the vendor gave her a handful of change in exchange for her two dollar bills. She was actually throwing nickels or dimes, not pennies, but she always thought of it in terms of the smaller bits of change. Just as she contemplated the right trajectory to land a coin on a plate, she spotted Dr. Bentley Rydel standing very close to Cappie Drake. Behind them, and closing in, was Officer Kilraven, still in uniform. Winnie paused to look at him. He spoke to the couple and laughed. But then he saw Winnie over their heads and his smile faded. He turned abruptly and walked right out of the carnival. Winnie felt her heart sink to the level of the ground. Well, he'd made his opinion of her quite clear, she thought miserably. He hadn't forgiven her for the painting. She turned back to the booth, but not with any real enthusiasm. The evening had been spoiled.

CASH GRIER CALLED Kilraven a few days later and asked for his help. Cappie Drake and her brother were in danger. Her brother had been badly beaten by Cappie's violent ex-boyfriend, just released from jail on a battery conviction stemming from an attack on her. Now he seemed to be out for blood. Eb Scott had detailed men to watch Cappie, but Kell was going to need some protection; he was in a San Antonio hospital where he'd just undergone back surgery to remove a shifted shrapnel sliver that had paralyzed him years ago. Cash asked Kilraven to go up and keep an eye on Kell until San Antonio police could catch the perp.

Kilraven went gladly. It was a relief to get out of town, even for a couple of days. But it was soon over, and he was back in Jacobsville again, fighting his feelings for Winnie. He was still no closer to a solution for his problem. He didn't know how he was going to deal with the discomfort he felt at leaving Winnie Sinclair behind forever. And there was still that odd coincidence with the painting. He really needed to know why she'd painted it.

In the meantime, Alice Jones had called him with some shocking news. The bit of paper in the dead man's hand in Jacobsville had contained Kilraven's cell phone number. Now he knew he'd been right to ask for that time off to work on his cold case. The dead man had known something about the murders and he'd been trying to contact Kilraven when he'd been killed. It was a break that might crack the case, if they could identify the victim and his contacts.

THE NEXT WEEK, Winnie worked a shift she wasn't scheduled for, filling in for Shirley, who was out sick. When she got off that afternoon, to her surprise, she found Kilraven waiting for her at the door.

She actually gasped out loud. His silver eyes were glittery as he stared down at her.

"Hello," she stammered.

He didn't reply. "Get in your car and follow me," he said quietly.

He walked to his squad car. He was technically off duty, but still in uniform. Officers in Jacobsville drove their cars home, so that they were prepared any time they had to be called in. He got in his car and waited until Winnie fumbled her way into her VW. He drove off, and she drove after him. Glancing to one side, she noted two of the operators who were on break staring after them and grinning. *Oh, boy,* she thought, *now there's going to be some gossip.*

Kilraven drove out of the city and down the long, winding dirt road that led to his rental house. The road meandered on past his house to join with a paved road about a mile on. His house was the only one on this little stretch. *He must like privacy,* Winnie thought, *because this certainly wasn't on anybody's main route.*

He pulled up at the front door, cut off the engine and got out of his car. Winnie did the same.

"I'll make coffee," he said after he unlocked the door and led her into the kitchen.

She looked around, curious at the utter lack of anything personal in the utilitarian surroundings. Well, except for the painting she'd done for him. It was lying on the counter, face up.

She felt uncomfortable at his lack of small talk. She put her purse on the counter near the door that led down the hall to the living room. "How's Kell Drake?" she asked.

He turned, curious.

"We heard about it from Barbara last week," she said, mentioning the café where everybody ate. Barbara was the adoptive mother of San Antonio homicide detective Rick Marquez. "She has Rick at home. He's getting better, but he sure wants to find whoever beat him up," she added grimly.

"So do we. He's one tough bird, or he'd be dead. Somebody is really trying to cover up this case," he added.

"Yes. Poor Rick. But what about Kell?"

"That ended well, except for his bruises. He's going to walk again," he said. "I guess you also heard that they caught Bartlett in the act of knocking Cappie Drake around," he added. "It seems that Marquez and a uniformed officer had to pull Dr. Rydel off the man." He chuckled.

"We, uh, heard that, too," she said, amused. "It was the day before Rick was jumped by those thugs. Poor Cappie."

"She'll be all right. She and Rydel are getting married in the near future, I hear."

"That's fast work," she commented.

He shrugged. "Some people know their minds quicker than other people do." He finished putting the coffee on and turned to glance at her. "How do you take it?"

"Straight up," she said.

His eyebrows lifted.

"I don't usually have a lot of time to stand around adding things to it," she pointed out. "I'm lucky to have time to take a sip or two before it gets cold."

"I thought Grier gave you one of those gadgets you put a coffee cup on to keep it hot," he said. "For Christmas."

"I don't have a place to put it where it wouldn't endanger the electronics at my station," she said. "Don't tell him."

"I wouldn't dream of it." He set out two mugs, pulled out a chair at the table and motioned her into another one. He straddled his and stared at her. "Why a raven?" he asked abruptly. "And why those colors for beadwork?"

She bit her lower lip. "I don't know."

He stared at her pointedly, as if he didn't believe her.

She blushed. "I really don't know," she emphasized. "I didn't even start out to paint a raven. I was going to do a landscape. The raven was on the canvas. I just painted everything else out," she added. "That sounds nuts, I guess, but famous sculptors say that's how they do statues, they just chisel away everything that isn't part of the statue."

He still didn't speak.

"How did you even know it was me?" she asked unhappily. "The gifts were supposed to be secret. I don't tell people that painting is my hobby. How did you know?"

He got up after a minute, walked down the hall and

came back with a rolled-up piece of paper. He handed it to her and sat back down.

Her intake of breath was audible. She held the picture with hands that were a little unsteady. "Who did this?" she exclaimed.

"My daughter, Melly."

Her eyes lifted to his. He'd never spoken of any family members, except his brother. "You don't talk about her," she said.

His eyes went to the picture on the table. They were dull and vacant. "She was three years old when she painted that, in preschool," he said quietly. "It was the last thing she ever did. That afternoon, she and her mother went to my father's house. They were going to have supper with my father and stepmother. My father went to get gas for a trip he was making the next day. Cammy hadn't come home from shopping yet."

He stopped. He wasn't sure he could say it, even now. His voice failed him.

Winnie had a premonition. Only that. "And?"

He looked older. "I was working undercover with San Antonio PD, before I became a Fed. My partner and I were just a block from the house when the call came over the radio. I recognized the address and burned rubber getting there. My partner tried to stop me, but nobody could have. There were two uniformed officers already on scene. They tried to tackle me." He shrugged. "I was bigger than both of them. So I saw Melly, and my wife, before the crime scene investigators and the coroner got there." He got up from the table and turned away. He was too shaken to look at her. He went to the coffeepot and turned it off, pouring coffee into two cups. He still hesitated. He didn't want to pick up the cups until he was sure he could hold them. "The perp, whoever it was, used a shotgun on them."

Winnie had heard officers talk about their cases occasionally. She'd heard the operators talk, too, because some of them were married to people in law enforcement. She knew what a shotgun could do to a human body. To even think of it being used on a child... She swallowed, hard, and swallowed again. Her imagination conjured up something she immediately pushed to the back of her mind.

"I'm sorry," she said in a choked tone.

Finally, he picked up the cups and put them on the table. He straddled the chair again, calmer now. "We couldn't find the person or persons who did it," he said curtly. "My father went crazy. He had these feelings, like you do. He left the house to get gas. It could have waited until the next morning, but he felt he should go right then. He said later that if he'd been home, he might have been able to save them."

"Or he might have been lying right beside them," Winnie said bluntly.

He looked at her in a different way. "Yes," he agreed. "That was what I thought, too. But he couldn't live with the guilt. He started drinking and couldn't stop. He died of a heart attack. They said the alcohol might have played a part, but I think he grieved himself to death. He loved Melly." He stopped speaking and drank the coffee. It blistered his tongue. That helped. He hadn't talked about it to an outsider, ever.

Her soft, dark eyes slid over his face quietly. "You think this may be linked to the body they found in the river," she said slowly.

His dark eyebrows lifted. "I haven't said that."

"You're thinking it."

His broad chest rose and fell. "Yes. We found a small piece of paper clenched in the man's fist. It took some work, but Alice Jones's forensic lab was able to make out the writing. It was my cell phone number. The man was coming here to talk to me. He knew something about my daughter's death. I'm sure of it."

His daughter's death. He didn't say, his wife and daughter. She wondered why.

His big hands wrapped around the hot white mug. His eyes had an emptiness that Winnie recognized. She'd seen it in military veterans. They called it the thousand-yard stare. It was the look of men who'd seen violence, who dealt in it. They were never the same again.

"What did she look like?" Winnie asked gently.

He blinked. It wasn't a question he'd anticipated. He smiled faintly. "Like Jon, actually, and my father," he said, laughing. "She had jet-black hair, long, down to her waist in back, and eyes like liquid ebony. She was intelligent and sweet natured. She never met a stranger..." He stopped, looked down into the coffee cup, and forced it up to his lips to melt away the hard lump in his throat. Melly, laughing, holding her arms out to him. "I love you, Daddy! Always remember!" That picture of her, laughing, was overlaid by one of her, lifeless, a nightmare figure covered in blood...

"Dear God!" he bit off, and his head bent.

Winnie was wary of most men. She was shy and introverted, and never forward. But she got up out of her chair, pulled him toward her and drew his head to her breasts. "Honest emotion should never embarrass anyone," she whispered against his hair. "It's much worse to pretend that we don't care than to admit we do."

She felt his big body shudder. She expected him to jerk away, to push her away, to refuse comfort. He was such a steely, capable man, full of fire and spirit and courage. But he didn't resist her. Not for a minute, anyway. His arms circled her waist and almost crushed her as he gave in, momentarily, to the need for comfort. It was something he'd never done. He'd even pushed Cammy away, years ago, when she offered it to him.

She laid her cheek against his thick, soft black hair and just stood there, holding him. But then he did pull away, abruptly, and stood up, turning away from her.

"More coffee?" he asked in a harsh tone.

She forced a smile. "Yes, please." She moved to the table and picked up her own cup, deliberately giving him time to get back the control he'd briefly lost. "It's gone cold."

"Liar," he murmured when she joined him at the coffeepot and he took the cup from her. "You'd blister your lip if you sipped it."

She looked up at him with a grin. "I was being politically agreeable."

"You were lying." He put the cup on the counter and gathered her up whole against him. "What a sweetheart you are," he ground out as his mouth suddenly ground down into hers.

The kiss shocked her. He didn't lead up to it. It was instant, feverish passion, so intense that the insistence of his mouth shocked her lips apart, giving him access to the heated sweetness within. She wasn't a woman who incited passion. In fact, what she'd experienced of it had turned her cold. She didn't like the arrogance, the pushi-ness, of most men she'd dated. But Kilraven was as honest in passion as he was otherwise. He enjoyed kissing her, and he didn't pretend that he didn't. His arms forced her into the hard curve of his body and he chuckled when he felt her melt against him as he ground his mouth into hers.

Her arms went under his and around him. The util-ity belt was uncomfortable. She felt the butt of his auto-matic at her ribs. His arms were bruising. But she didn't care. She held on for all she was worth and shivered with what must have been desire. She'd never felt it. Not until now, with the last man on earth she should allow herself to feel it for.

He felt her shy response with wonder. He'd expected that a socialite like Winnie would have had men since her early teens. The way of the world these days was experi-ence. Virtue counted for nothing with most of the social set. But this little violet was innocent. He could feel it when she strained away from the sudden hardness of his body, when she shivered as he tried to probe her mouth.

Curious, he lifted his head and looked down into her flushed, wide-eyed face. Innocence. She couldn't even pretend sophistication.

Gently, he eased her out of his arms. He smiled to lessen the sting of it. "You taste of green apples," he said enigmatically.

"Apples?" She blinked, and swallowed. She could still taste him on her mouth. It had felt wonderful, being held so close to that warm strength. "I haven't had an apple in, well, in ages," she stammered.

"It was a figure of speech. Here. Put on your coat."

He helped her ease her arms into it. Then he handed her the cup.

"Am I leaving and taking it with me?" she asked blankly.

"No. We're just drinking it outside." He picked up his own cup and shepherded her out of the door, onto the long porch, down the steps and out to a picnic table that had been placed there, with its rude wooden benches, by the owner.

"We're going to drink coffee out here?" she asked, astonished. "It's freezing!"

"I know. Sit down."

She did, using the cup for a hand warmer.

"It is a bit nippy," he commented.

A sheriff's car drove past. It beeped. Kilraven waved. "I'm leaving next week," he said.

"Yes. You told us."

A Jacobsville police car whizzed by, just behind the sheriff's car. It beeped, too. Kilraven threw up his hand. Dust rose and fell in their wake, then settled.

"I had some sick leave and some vacation time left over. I can only use a little of it, of course, for this year, because it's almost over. But I'm going to have a few weeks to do some investigating without pay." He smiled. "With the state of the economy what it is, I don't think they'll mind that."

"Probably not." She sipped coffee. "Exactly what do you do when you aren't impersonating a police officer?" she asked politely.

He pursed his lips and his silver eyes twinkled. "I could tell you, but then I'd have to—"

A loud horn drowned out the rest. This time, it was

a fire truck. They waved. Kilraven waved back. So did Winnie.

"Have to what?" she asked him.

"Well, it wouldn't be pretty."

"That's just stonewalling, Kilraven," she pointed out. She frowned. "Don't you have a first name?"

"Sure. It's—"

Another loud horn drowned that out, too.

They both turned. Cash Grier pulled up beside the picnic table and let down his window on the driver's side. "Isn't it a little cold to be drinking coffee outside?" he asked.

Kilraven gave him a wry look. "Everybody at the EOC saw me drive off with Winnie," he said complacently. "So far, there have been two cop cars and a fire truck. And, oh, look, there comes the Willow Creek Police Department. A little out of your jurisdiction, aren't you?" he called loudly to the driver, who was from northern Jacobs County. He just grinned and waved and drove on.

Winnie hadn't realized how much traffic had gone by until then. She burst out laughing. No wonder Kilraven had wanted to sit out here. He wasn't going to have her gossiped about. It touched her.

"If I were you, I'd take her to Barbara's Café to have this discussion," Cash told him. "It's much more private."

"Private?" Kilraven exclaimed.

Cash pointed to the road. There were, in a row, two sheriffs' cars, a state police vehicle, a fire and rescue truck, an ambulance and, of all things, a fire department ladder truck. They all tooted and waved as they went by, creating a wave of dust.

Cash Grier shook his head. "Now, that's a shame you'll

get all dusty. Maybe you should take her back inside," he said with an angelic expression.

"You know what you can do," Kilraven told him. He got up and held out his hand for Winnie's cup. "I'm putting these in the sink, and then we're leaving."

"Spoilsport." Cash sighed. "Now we'll all have to go back to work!"

"I can suggest a place to do it," Kilraven muttered.

Cash winked at Winnie, who couldn't stop laughing. He drove off.

Winnie got up, sighed and dug in her coat pocket for her car keys. It had been, in some ways, the most eventful hour of her life. She knew things about Kilraven that nobody else did, and she felt close to him. It was the first time in their turbulent relationship that she felt any hope for the future. Not that getting closer to him was going to be easy, she told herself. Especially not with him in San Antonio and her in Jacobsville.

He came back out, locking the door behind him. He looked around as he danced gracefully down the steps and joined her. "What, no traffic jam?" he exclaimed, nodding toward the deserted road. "Maybe they ran out of rubberneckers."

Just as he said that, a funeral procession came by, headed by none other than the long-suffering Macreedy. He was famous for getting lost while leading processions. He didn't blow his horn. In fact, he really did look lost. The procession went on down the road with Winnie and Kilraven staring after it.

"Don't tell me he's losing another funeral procession," she wailed. "Sheriff Carson Hayes will fry him up and serve him on toast if he does it again."

"No kidding," Kilraven agreed. "There's already been the threat of a lawsuit by one family." He shook his head. "Hayes really needs to put that boy behind a desk."

"Or take away his car keys," she agreed.

He looked down at her with an oddly affectionate expression. "Come on. You're getting chilled."

He walked her back to her car, towering over her. "You've come a long way since that day you went wailing home because you forgot to tell me a perp was armed."

She smiled. "I was lucky. I could have gotten you killed."

He hesitated. "These flashes of insight, do they run in your family?"

"I don't know much about my family," she confessed. "My father was very remote after my mother left us."

"Did you have any contact with your uncle?" he asked.

She gaped at him. "How do you know about him?"

He didn't want to confess what he knew about the man. He shrugged. "Someone mentioned his name."

"We don't have any contact at all. We didn't," she corrected. "He died a month ago. Or so we were told."

"I'm sorry."

Her dark eyes were cold. "I'm not. He and my mother ran away together and left my father with three kids to raise. Well, two kids actually. Boone was in the military by then. I look like my mother. Dad hated that. He hated me." She bit her tongue. She hadn't meant to say as much.

But he read that in her expression. "We all have pivotal times in our lives, when a decision leads to a different future." He smiled. "In the sixteenth century, Henry VIII fell in love with a young girl and decided that his Catholic wife, Catherine of Aragon, was too old to give him a son anyway, so he spent years finding a way to divorce her and marry the young girl, whom he was certain could produce a male heir. In the end, he destroyed the Catholic Church in England to accomplish it. He married Anne Boleyn, a protestant who had been one of Catherine's ladies, and from that start the Anglican Church was born. The child of that union was not a son, but Elizabeth, who became queen of England after her brother and half sister. All that, for love of a woman." He pursed his lips and his eyes twinkled. "As it turned out, he couldn't get a son from Anne Boleyn, either, so he found a way to frame her for adultery and cut off her head. Ten days later, he married a woman who could give him a son."

"The wretch!" she exclaimed, outraged.

"That's why we have elected officials instead of kings with absolute power," he told her.

She shook her head. "How do you know all that?"

He leaned down. "You mustn't mention it, but I have a degree in history."

"Well!"

"But I specialized in Scottish history, not English. I'm one of a handful of people who think James Hepburn, the Earl of Bothwell, got a raw deal from history for marrying Mary, Queen of Scots. But don't mention that out loud."

She laughed. "Okay."

He opened her car door for her. Before she got in, he drew a long strand of her blond hair over his big hand, studying its softness and beautiful pale color.

Her eyes slid over his face. "Your brother wears his hair long, in a ponytail. You keep yours short."

"Is that a question?"

She nodded.

"Jon is particularly heavy on the Native American side of his ancestry."

"And you aren't?"

His eyes narrowed. "I don't know, Winnie," he said quietly, making her name sound foreign and sweet and different. "Maybe I'm hiding from it."

"Not you," she said with conviction. "I can't see you hiding from anything."

That soft pride in her tone made him feel taller. He let go of her hair. "Drive carefully," he said.

"I will. See you."

He didn't say anything else. But he did nod.

With her heart flying up in her throat, she got in and drove away. It wasn't until she got home that she realized she still didn't know his first name.

CHAPTER FOUR

WINNIE WAS BACK at work the next morning almost walking on air. Kilraven had kissed her. Not only that, he seemed to really like her. Maybe San Antonio wasn't so far away. He might visit. He might take her out on a date. Anything was possible.

She put her purse in her locker and went to her station. It was in the shape of a semicircle, and contained a bank of computers. Directly in front of her was a keyboard; behind it was a computer screen. This was the radio from which she could contact any police, fire or EMS department, although her job was police dispatch. There were separate stations for fire, police and EMS. Fire had one dispatcher, EMS had two. She, along with Shirley at a separate console, handled law enforcement traffic on her shift for all of Jacobs County. Beside her was a screen for the NCIC, the National Crime Information Center. Behind the computer screen, on a shelf, sat three other computer screens. One, an incident screen, noted the location of the units and their current status. The middle was CAD, or computer aided dispatch, which featured a form into which information such as activity code and location were placed; typing in the location brought up such data as prior calls at the residence, the nearest fire hydrant in case of fire, the name and address of a key holder and even a box to fax the incident to the police department. It also had screens for names and numbers of law enforcement personnel, including cell phone and pager numbers. There was a mobile data terminal from which dispatch could send messages to law enforcement on their laptops in their cars. The third computer screen was the phone itself, the heart and soul of the operation, through which desperation and fear and panic were heard daily and gently handled.

This information came through two call takers. Their job was to take the calls as they came in, put them into the computer and send them to the appropriate desk: fire, police or EMS. Once the location and situation were input, the computer decided which was the appropriate agency or agencies to be dispatched. For a domestic incident with injuries, police were sent first to secure the scene, and an ambulance would stage in the area until it was deemed safe for the EMS personnel to enter the house to assist the injured. Often the perpetrator was still inside and dangerous to anyone who attempted to help the victim. More police officers died responding to domestic disputes than almost any other job-related duty.

Winnie had just dispatched a police officer to the scene of a motor vehicle accident, along with fire and rescue, and was waiting for further information.

In between the calls, Shirley leaned over while the supervisor was talking to a visitor. "Did you hear about the break in the murder case?"

"What break?"

"They found Kilraven's cell phone number clenched in the victim's hand."

"Oh, that. Yes, Kilraven told me."

Shirley's eyes twinkled. "Did he now? Might one ask what else he told you, all alone at his house?"

"How do you know we went to his house?" Winnie asked, blushing.

"A few people told us. There was a sheriff's deputy, Chief Grier, a fireman, a funeral director..."

Winnie laughed. "I should have known."

"They did all just mention that you and Kilraven were drinking coffee at a picnic table, outside in the freezing cold," Shirley added.

"Well, Kilraven felt that we shouldn't start gossip."

"As if." Shirley chuckled. "What were you talking about?" she added slyly.

"The murder case," Winnie said with a grin. "No, really, we were," she added when she saw her coworker's expression. "You remember Senator Fowler's kitchen help died mysteriously after she gave some information to Alice Jones, the coroner's investigator from San Antonio, about the victim? Now there's gossip the murder might be linked to other murders in San Antonio." It was safe to tell her that. No way was she going to add that Kilraven's family might be involved.

"Wow," Shirley exclaimed softly.

"Heads up," Winnie whispered, grinning, and turned away before Maddie Sims came toward them. The older woman never jumped on them about talking because they only passed remarks back and forth during lulls in the operations, but she did like them to pay attention on the job. She would know what they did anyway because everything was recorded when they were working. Maddie would be diplomatic about it, though.

Winnie smiled as Maddie passed. A message from the police officer responding to the wreck was just coming in, requesting a want and warrants on a car tag. She turned back to her console and began typing in the numbers.

IT WAS A BUSY NIGHT. There was an attempted suicide, which, fortunately, they were able to get help dispatched in time. There were assorted sick calls, one kitchen fire, several car versus deer reports, two domestic calls, a large animal in the road and three drunk driver reports, only one of which resulted in an arrest. Often a drunk driver was reported on the highway, but no good description of the vehicle or direction of travel was given and it was a big county. Occasionally, an observant citizen could provide a description and tag number, but not always. Unless a squad car was actually in the area of the report, it was difficult sometimes to pursue. You couldn't pull an officer off the investigation of an accident or a burglary or a robbery, she mused, to go roaming the county looking for an inebriated driver, no matter how much the officers would like to catch one.

At break, she and Shirley worried about the assault on Rick Marquez.

"I hope he's not going to be attacked again, when he goes back to work. Somebody wants this case covered up pretty badly," Shirley said.

"Yes," Winnie agreed, "and it looks like this is only the tip of the iceberg. We still have that mangled murder victim in our county. Senator Fowler's hired help told Alice Jones something about him and the poor woman was murdered in a way that made it look like suicide. Now there's an attempt on Rick, who's been helping investigate it."

"He's lucky he has such a hard head," Shirley said.

"And that his partner went searching for him when

he didn't turn up to look at some paperwork she'd just found. Yes, I heard about that from Keely," Winnie said. "Sheriff Hayes," she added with a grin, "is Boone's best friend, so they know more than most people about what's going on. Well, except for us," she added wryly. "We know everything."

"Almost everything, anyway. You know, we used to live in such a peaceful county." Shirley sighed. "Then Keely lost her mother to a killer who was friends with her father. Now we get a murder victim dead in our river and his own mother wouldn't recognize him. This is a dangerous place to live."

"Every place is dangerous, even small towns," she replied with a smile. "It's the times we live in."

"I guess so."

They had homemade soup with cornbread, courtesy of one of the other dispatchers. It was nice to have something besides takeout, which got old very quickly on ten-hour shifts. The operators only worked four days a week, not necessarily in sequence, but they were stress-filled. All of them loved the job, or they wouldn't be doing it. Saving lives, which they did on a daily basis, was a blessing in itself. But days off were good so that they had a chance to recover just a little bit from the nerve-racking series of desperate situations in which they assisted the appropriate authorities. Winnie had never loved a job so much. She smiled at Shirley, and thought what a nice bunch of people she worked with.

Kilraven was pumping his brother for information. It was, as usual, hard going. Jon was even more tight-lipped than Kilraven.

"It's an ongoing murder investigation," he insisted, throwing up his hands. "I can't discuss it with you."

Kilraven, comfortably seated in the one good chair in Jon's office, just glared at him with angry silver eyes. "This is your niece and your sister-in-law we're talking about," he said icily. "I can help. Let me help."

Jon perched on the edge of his desk. He was immaculate, from his polished black shoes to the long, elegant fingers that were always manicured. His black hair was caught in a ponytail that hung to his waist. His face grew solemn. "All right. But if Garon Grier asks me, I'm telling him that you stood on me in order to get this information."

Kilraven grinned. "Should I stand on you, just for appearances?" He indicated his big booted feet. "I'm game."

"I'd like to see you stand on me," Jon shot back.

"Come on, come on, talk."

Jon sighed. "I don't have much, but I'll share." He punched the intercom. "Ms. Perry, could you bring me the Fowler file, please."

There was a pause. A light, airy, sarcastic feminine voice answered. "Hard copy is kept in your filing cabinet, Mr. Blackhawk," she said sweetly. "Lost our password again, have we?"

Jon's face tautened. "What I am losing, rapidly, is my patience. For your information, Garon took out the files to show Agent Simmons. They're in your filing cabinet."

There was a dead silence. A filing cabinet was opened and then closed, and impatient high heels came marching into Jon's office with a pleasant face, blue eyes and jet-black hair, cut short.

She put a file on the desk. "We do have electronic copies of this, password-protected, if your password ever presents itself again," she said sweetly.

Jon glared at her. "You were an hour late for work two mornings this week, Ms. Perry," he said, his tone as bland as her own. "So far, I haven't reported it to Garon."

She stiffened. Her blue eyes had blue shadows under them. She didn't shoot back an excuse.

"Perhaps it would help your present attitude if you knew that Ms. Smith has an extensive rap sheet, of which my mother is unaware. With your, shall we say, proclivities for sneaking in the back door of protected files, I should think you could dig out the rest of the information all by yourself. If," he added with dripping sarcasm, "you can manage to keep your present job long enough to look for it."

She reddened. Her blue eyes shot ice daggers at him, but her voice was even when she spoke. "I'll be at my desk if you need anything further, Mr. Blackhawk." She left, without even looking at Kilraven. Her back was as stiff as her expression.

Jon got up and closed the door behind her with a little jerk. His own eyes, liquid black, were smoldering. "Ever since my mother sent Jill Smith in here to vamp me, it's been like this."

"You did have Ms. Smith arrested for harassment," Kilraven pointed out with barely suppressed amusement. "And taken out in handcuffs, if I recall?"

Jon shrugged. "A man isn't safe alone in his own office these days."

"You're safe from that particular woman, I'll bet," Kilraven replied, nodding toward the direction Joceline Perry had taken.

"Most men are."

"Care to say why?"

Jon went back to the desk and picked up the file folder. "She has a little boy, about three years old. His father was killed overseas in the military. She can freeze a man from half a block away."

"Not necessary in your case, bro, you're already frozen."

Jon glared at him. "Don't call me that disgusting nickname, if you please."

"Excuse me, your grace."

Jon glared even more.

Kilraven sobered. "All right, I'll try to act with more decorum. Is Mom still speaking to you?"

"Only to tell me how poor Ms. Smith is suffering from my rejection. I've tried to tell her that her newest candidate for my affections is one step short of a call girl, but she won't listen. Ms. Smith's mother is her best friend, so naturally the daughter is pure as the driven snow."

"She might not be, but you certainly are." His brother grinned.

Jon's black eyes narrowed. "And you certainly would be, if you hadn't been conned into marrying Monica."

Kilraven's amused expression fell. "I guess so. I never planned to get married in the first place, but she knew her way around men. Funny, I never even wondered why, until we were already married and she was pregnant with Melly. She had boyfriends that actually showed up at the house from time to time to see her."

"Which didn't go over well."

"I was young and jealous. She was experienced, but I wasn't." He gave his brother a quiet appraisal. "You could still charm unicorns. Don't you think you're old enough to consider getting married?"

"No woman could live with me. I'm married to my job. And when I'm not at work, I'm married to the ranch."

"I miss it from time to time," Kilraven mused. "I guess I'll forget how to ride a horse eventually."

"That's a joke. You've got more trophies than I have."

They were both expert horsemen. In their youth, they participated in rodeo and stood undefeated at bulldogging in southern Oklahoma until they retired from the ring.

"But all this is beside the point," Jon said. He handed the file to Kilraven. "You'll have to read it here and you can't have photocopies."

"Fair enough." He started reading. Jon took a phone call. By then, Kilraven had enough information to form an uncomfortable hypothesis.

"Senator Fowler's protégé, Senator Will Sanders, has a brother, Hank, one of the more dangerous career criminals and a man who has his hands in every illegal operation in the city," Kilraven murmured as he read. "Two attempted murder charges, both dropped for lack of evidence to convict, and at least one accusation of rape."

"For which he drew a suspended sentence when the lady recanted." Jon's eyes narrowed thoughtfully. "In fact, his brother, Senator Sanders himself, has a statutory rape charge that was dropped for lack of evidence. He has a taste for virgins, and since a good many women are experienced even by their mid-teens, he's looking for them younger and younger."

"Pervert," Kilraven muttered. "The victim in this case was fourteen. Fourteen years old! He gave her an illegal substance and had her in a guest bedroom in his own house. He even filmed it for the amusement of his friends." He frowned. "There was a dead teenage girl

seven years ago, remember? It was just before Melly..."
He cleared his throat. "The girl was found in a similar
condition to our murder victim in Jacobsville. I've always
felt there was a connection, but we were never able to put
our finger on one."

"Just coincidence, probably," Jon agreed. "They do
happen."

Kilraven tossed the file back onto Jon's desk with utter
disdain. "He filmed himself assaulting a fourteen-year-
old. And they couldn't prove it? There was film!"

"It's not called film anymore, it's digital imaging, but
I get your meaning. No, they couldn't prove it. The cam-
corder was erased in the police property room, by persons unknown, conveniently before arraignment. We
can't accuse anybody, but Senator Sanders has a long-
time employee who did hard time for a violent crime.
He's violently protective of both brothers, and he has a
cousin who works for SAPD."

"How convenient. Can we put some pressure on the
cop?" Kilraven asked.

Jon gave him a wry look. "We've got enough problems.
We're having him watched by internal affairs. That will
have to do. Now, to get back to the case involving the living fourteen-year-old, the assistant D.A. in the case was
hopping up and down and using language that almost got
him arrested in his own office when they told him. That
was just after the girl's parents called and said they were
refusing to let her testify."

"They didn't want the creep prosecuted?" Kilraven
exclaimed.

Jon's expression was eloquent. "The week after that,
the girl's father was driving a new Jaguar, one of the

high ticket sports models, and he paid off all his gambling debts at once."

Kilraven was quiet. "Those cars run to six figures. The file says the father worked as a midlevel accountant."

"Exactly."

"If Melly had been fourteen, and someone had done that to her, I'd have moved heaven and earth to put the man away for life. If I didn't break his neck first."

"Same here. Money does talk, in some cases."

"In a lot of them." Kilraven was thinking. "The senator's wife started divorce proceedings a few years ago, and then stopped them and started drinking. Her husband still has lovers and she can't seem to get away from him. They have a beach house in Nassau where she spends a lot of time."

"And the senator's family has a ranch one property over from our own near Lawton," Jon replied, naming the Oklahoma town where both boys were born.

"Maybe the wife knows something about her brother-in-law that she'd be willing to share," Kilraven thought out loud.

"Don't go harassing the senator or his wife," Jon said firmly. "We've finally got something that might give us a clue to our own cold case. Garon Grier has someone working undercover on this, as well. If you put somebody's back up, we could lose all the ground we've gained. Not to mention that we could be facing some real heat from higher up."

"I'm on leave of absence," Kilraven pointed out.

"Yes, but you still have a boss who won't like your involvement in a case that isn't connected to your present employment."

"I have a great boss. He'd understand."

"Sure he would, but he'd still fire you."

"I've been fired before."

"You've been reprimanded, too. Don't pile up too many demerits, boy scout," Jon teased. "You'll get yourself kicked out of any federal work."

Kilraven sighed and stuck his big hands in his pockets. "I guess I could be a small-town cop in Jacobsville for life if I had to."

"You'd never manage it. Cash Grier told Marquez that he's already one step closer to nailing you in a barrel and sending you down the Rio Grande."

"He'd have to get me in the barrel first and drive me all the way to the Rio Grande. By the time he got there, I'd have extricated myself from the barrel, appropriated his truck and had local authorities arrest him for kidnapping."

Jon didn't say anything. He just smiled. He knew his brother well enough to believe it.

"That said, he's a good man to work for. He goes to the wall for his officers."

"So does Garon Grier, here."

Kilraven nodded. "They're both good men." He frowned. "Don't they have two other brothers?"

"Yes. One of them is also in law enforcement."

"Like the Earp brothers," Kilraven mused.

"There were five of them. There are only four Grier brothers." He got up. "We're still running down leads on the murder victim," he said. "I've got Ms. Perry checking parole files to see if we can find a match there. Maybe the victim was just out of prison and between jobs when he was wasted."

"If he has a rap sheet, he'll be easier to identify," Kilraven agreed. "And if they cheek-swabbed him, which I imagine they did, Alice Jones can use all that high-tech stuff at the forensic lab to discover his identity."

Jon nodded. "DNA is a blessing in cases like this where the DB is unidentifiable under conventional means."

"Makes our job easier," was the bland reply, "but good police work still largely consists of wearing out shoe leather. Speaking of which, I want to have a talk with Marquez. He might have gotten a look at his attackers."

"We've already asked. He didn't."

"I want to talk to him anyway."

"He isn't back on the job yet. He'll be at his mother's house in Jacobsville."

"Thanks," Kilraven said drily. "I did know that, living in Jacobsville myself."

Jon's black eyes twinkled. "I understand that you had a visitor recently at your house. A blonde one."

"Good Lord. You heard that all the way up here?"

"You were seen by a substantial number of uniformed people."

"Who drove by my house just to spy on me," Kilraven said with mock disgust. "What is the world coming to when a man can't have a cup of coffee with a guest?"

"A cup of coffee at a picnic table, outdoors, in freezing temperatures. Something wrong with the sofa in your living room?"

"If people can't see you, they guess what's going on and they're usually wrong. I didn't want Winnie subjected to gossip," he added quietly. "She's an innocent."

Jon's eyebrows went up over twinkling eyes. "And how would you have found that out?"

Kilraven glowered at him. "In the usual way."

Jon pursed his lips. "Imagine that!"

"It's not serious," came the short reply. "She's a friend. Sort of. But I asked her to the house because I wanted to know why she painted that picture that was a dead-ringer for Melly's raven drawing."

Jon sobered at once. He remembered his brother's visit that night with the painting. "And?"

"She said she started to paint a landscape," Kilraven replied with a puzzled expression. "She didn't know why she painted a raven, or those colors on the beads. She didn't know how I knew it was her, either. I've never even told her that our ranch is called 'Raven's Pride.'"

"We have those flashes of insight because it runs in our family," Jon reminded him. "Our father had a cousin who was notorious for his very accurate visions of the future."

Kilraven nodded. "I wonder where Winnie's gift comes from. She doesn't know. Funny," he added, "but Gail Rogers, the detective who's helping me with our case, has those premonitions. She gets some gossip when she pegs a suspect that nobody else connected with a case."

The intercom buzzed. Jon answered it.

"Agent Wilkes is on his way in with Agent Salton, and you're all due for a meeting in ASAC Grier's office in ten minutes," Joceline said in a voice dripping with sugar. "Would you like coffee and donuts?"

Jon looked surprised, as he should have. Ms. Perry never volunteered to fetch snack food. "That would be nice."

"There's a Dunkin' Donuts shop around the corner," she reminded him. "If I were you, I'd hurry."

"I'd hurry?" he repeated.

"Yes, because my job description requires me to type

and file and answer phones. Not be a caterer," she added, still sugary. She hung up.

"One day, so help me, she'll drive me to drink and you'll have to bail me out of some jail where I'll be surrounded by howling mad drug users," Jon gritted.

Kilraven patted him on the shoulder. "Now, now, don't let your blood pressure override your good sense."

"If I had good sense, I'd ask for reassignment to another field office, preferably in the Yukon Territory!" he said loud enough for Ms. Perry to hear him as he opened his office door.

"Oooh, polar bears live there," she said merrily. "And they eat people, don't they?"

"You wish, Ms. Perry," he shot back.

"Temper, temper," she chided.

Jon was almost vibrating, he was so angry. Kilraven smothered laughter.

"I'll call you," he told his brother. "And thanks for the information."

"Just don't go off half-cocked and get in trouble with it," Jon said firmly.

"You know me," Kilraven said in mock astonishment. "I never do anything rash!"

Before Jon could reply, Kilraven walked out the door.

RICK MARQUEZ STILL had his arm in a sling and he was like a man standing on a fire ant hill. "They won't let me come back to work yet," he complained to Kilraven. "I can shoot with one hand!"

"You haven't had to shoot anybody in years," Kilraven reminded him.

"Well, it's the point of the thing. I could sit at a desk

and answer phones, but oh, no, I have to be at 100 percent before they'll certify me fit for duty!"

"You can use the free time."

"Yeah? For what? Watering Mom's flowers?"

Kilraven was studying the dead bushes at the front porch. "They look dead to me."

"Not those ones. These ones." He let Kilraven into the living room, where huge potted plants almost covered every wall.

Kilraven's eyebrows lifted. "She grows bananas and coffee in the house?" he exclaimed.

"Now how do you recognize coffee plants?" Marquez asked with evident suspicion. "Most people who come in here have to ask what they are."

"Anybody could recognize a banana plant."

"Yes, but not a coffee plant." Rick's eyes narrowed. "Been around coffee plants somewhere they don't grow in pots?"

Kilraven grinned. "Let's just say, I'm not a stranger to them, and leave it at that."

Rick was thinking that coffee grew in some of the most dangerous places on earth. Kilraven had the look of a man who was familiar with them.

"I know that expression," Kilraven said blandly, "but I've said all I'm going to."

"I know when I'm licked. Coffee?"

"I'd love some." He gave Rick a wry glance. "Going to pick the beans fresh?"

Rick gave the red berries a curious look. "I do have a grinder somewhere."

"Yes, but you have to dry coffee beans and roast them before you can use them."

"All right, now you're really making me curious," Rick told him.

Kilraven didn't say a word. He just kept walking.

They went into the kitchen where Rick made coffee and Kilraven fetched cups. They drank it at Barbara's kitchen table, covered by a red checkered cloth with matching curtains at the windows. The room was bright and airy and pretty, like Barbara herself.

"Your mother has good taste," Kilraven commented. "And she's a great cook."

Rick smiled. "Not a bad mother, either," he chuckled. "I'd probably be sitting in a cell somewhere if she hadn't adopted me. I was a tough kid."

"So was I," Kilraven recalled. "Jon and I kept our parents busy when we were boys. Once, we got drunk at a party, started a brawl and ended up in a holding cell."

"What did your parents do?"

"My stepmother was all for bailing us out. Our father, however, was an FBI agent," he added quietly. "He told her that rushing to our defense might make us think we could get away with anything and we might end up in more serious straits. So he left us there for several days and let us sweat it."

"Ouch," Rick said, wincing.

"We were a lot less inclined to make trouble after that and I only recall getting drunk and going on a bender once in my adult life." That had been after he found his wife and child dead, but he didn't elaborate. "Of course, we were really mad at Dad. But now, looking back at it, I'm sure he did the right thing."

"Life teaches hard lessons," Rick agreed.

Kilraven nodded. "And one of those lessons is that we

don't go alone to a meeting with a potential informer. Ever."

Rick flushed. "First time it ever came down like that," he said, defending himself.

"There's always a first time. When I was just a kid, during my first month with San Antonio P.D., one of the detectives went to a covert meeting with a crime boss and ended up in the morgue. He was a friend of my father's."

"It does happen. But if we don't take chances from time to time, we don't get clues."

"True enough."

"Not that I mind the company—I'm going stir crazy down here—but why are you here?"

Kilraven glanced down at the coffee cup. "Two reasons. First, I want to know if you got a look at your attackers."

"They blindsided me," Rick said with disgust. "I don't even know if it was one guy or two. I woke up in the hospital." He raised his eyebrows. "Second reason?"

"I want to know what you know about Senator Will Sanders's brother, Hank."

"Him." Rick sat back in the chair. "He was a navy SEAL. Decorated, in Operation Desert Storm," he said, surprising Kilraven. "Since he got out, however, he's made real strides in taking over mob territory in San Antonio. But his brother, the senator, is the real weird one."

"Weird, how?"

Rick's dark eyes twinkled. "Well, he's about one beer short of a six-pack."

"Dangerous?"

Rick shook his head. "Stupid," he corrected. "He doesn't seem to be malicious, but he's protective of his younger brother and it's always a frame. The police don't like Hank, that's why they keep arresting him for things he didn't do."

"Give me a break!"

"From what I gather, the senator uses his brother for menial tasks like intimidating other politicians or enticing teenage girls to his house to meet the senator. The amazing thing is that he's never been charged with anything," he added, "except the one statutory rape offense, which was dropped."

"Jon told me about that one. How is it that he hasn't become a media feeding frenzy?"

"The senator employs an older former gangster who, in turn, employs professional bouncers. One was sent to make veiled threats about the journalists' families."

"That's low," Kilraven said coldly.

"Sure is, but it works. We've tried to cooperate with journalists to catch the guy at it, but it's hard to find a journalist who's willing to risk his family in order to put the senator's right-hand man away. You might notice just recently what happened to that young woman who worked for Senator Fowler when she divulged information to Alice Jones about the Jacobsville murder victim. Nobody's been charged in that case yet, and probably won't be."

"I heard that Senator Sanders was at that party at Senator Fowler's house when Alice Jones asked the questions," Kilraven said. "He probably figured what was going on. He may be stupid, but he's also shrewd."

"Most politicians are. I think we're going to find that Senator Sanders's younger brother is up to his ears in this case, somehow. What I don't know, yet, is exactly how."

"Winnie Sinclair's late uncle has been mentioned as having some peripheral involvement."

Rick nodded. His eyes narrowed on Kilraven's bland expression. "I haven't said anything about it. The detective we're working with on the case mentioned it to me."

"She came to see me recently."

Rick's face was thoughtful. "I hope she's not in any danger," he said. "She's been closer to the investigation than I have, spent a lot of free time going over records, looking for clues. She's angry that she was taken off the case and demoted to traffic."

"Senator Fowler intervened to get her reinstated to his favor," Kilraven replied. "And he talked to his protégé, Senator Sanders, about the political dangers of trying to stifle a murder investigation, regardless of whether or not his younger brother was involved."

"I just hope she doesn't push too hard," Rick said. "Gail's a fine detective, with an honorable record in the department. She's had a lot of personal problems, but it's never affected her job performance."

"We all have a lot of personal problems."

Rick pursed his lips. "Yours seems to be blonde."

Kilraven glared at him. "She is not a personal problem. She's a friend."

"If you say so."

"I do." He sipped his coffee. "I'm taking some time off to work on the cold case. I thought I might go up to San Antonio and see her."

"Give her my regards, and tell her I swear I'll never try to meet with any more so-called informants in any alleys late at night," Rick advised, indicating his arm in the sling.

Kilraven chuckled. "I'll do that."

CHAPTER FIVE

JON WAS IN THE middle of a long telephone call about a pending case when Joceline stuck her head in the door. Her blue eyes had some sparkle in them, rare for her these days, but when she saw that he was on the phone, she held up a hand and went back out.

Curious, he ended the conversation and walked into the outer office.

"Something?" he asked.

She grinned, holding out a sheet of paper.

He took it. His eyebrows lifted in surprise. "Dan Jones?" He stared at her. "Who is Dan Jones and why am I reading his rap sheet?"

"He's your DB in the Little Carmichael River in Jacobsville," she said. "I checked the state records for anyone recently paroled, narrowed it down to ten possibles who haven't checked in with their parole officers lately, and requested DNA evidence to be sent to Alice Jones to compare with the DNA they pulled off the victim. And there he was. Dan Jones."

He smiled. It was rare for him to do it and extraordinary that he smiled at Joceline, who was his nemesis. She stared at him as if she didn't recognize him; the smile made him look so different. His black eyes sparkled. His white, perfect teeth gleamed.

"Remind me to put in a request for a raise in salary

for you, Ms. Perry," he said. "I'll note your contribution to the case, as well."

"Thanks," she stammered.

"Dan Jones." He turned and went back into his office, his mind working in overdrive. "Get my brother on the phone, will you?"

"Yes, sir."

KILRAVEN WAS ON fire with the news, once he got it. He spent the next two hours trying to track down Rick Marquez's partner, Gail Rogers. She'd gone to the scene of a suicide, dispatch said, and gave him the address after he told them, not quite truthfully, that he was working the case with her. The uniformed officers at the apartment door tried to stop Kilraven, but he just waved his federal badge at them and kept walking.

The victim was lying facedown on the sofa. There was a very large knife sticking out of his back.

Kilraven glanced at the female detective sergeant. "I thought they said you were at the scene of a suicide, Rogers," he remarked.

"Sure. Suicide. He obviously stabbed himself in the back." She rolled her eyes.

"Sure. You can do that, you just have to have really long arms," Alice Jones—whose last name was now Fowler—told her, walking into the room with an evidence bag she'd just collected. Behind her was the photographer who was recording the scene. Another crime scene technician was using a vacuum collection system to suction possible trace evidence in the form of hair and fiber from the carpet around the body, and still another had an ultraviolet flashlight with which he was searching for traces of blood and bodily fluids on nearby surfaces. "What are you doing in here messing up my crime scene, Kilraven?" she added with a grin. "This isn't a federal suicide."

"From where I'm standing, this isn't a suicide, period," Kilraven returned.

"His wife says it is," Alice murmured. "In fact, she saw him do it."

His eyes narrowed. "She did."

"Yes. That was just before the two-headed cat flew in the window and attacked her."

He whistled.

"They took her down to county," the detective said, "by way of the hospital."

"For a psych evaluation?" he asked.

"For detox. She'd snorted enough meth to put two men in the morgue, from the look of it."

"People who make meth should be hung up by their noses and left to rot," he said coldly.

"Create a need, and then supply it, that's how the song goes," Gail said solemnly. Her dark eyes were cold. "My ex-husband knew every drug known to man, and used most of them. I had no idea until we were on our honeymoon and he tried to get me to shoot up. I left him that very week."

"Love does blind us," Alice interjected.

"You'd know, Newly-Married Alice," he teased.

She grinned. "Harley and I have calves," she said. "His boss, Cy Parks, gave us a seed bull and several heifers, and they were filled ones."

Kilraven blinked. "Excuse me?"

"Well, if a heifer is open when she's not pregnant, doesn't it make sense that she's filled when she is?" she asked.

Kilraven just shook his head. "We learn something new every day."

"Know what the difference is between a bull and a steer?" she continued with a cocky grin.

He gave her a droll look. "I own half of the biggest cattle ranch in Lawton, Oklahoma, Alice. I grew up on a horse."

"Did you really?" she exclaimed.

"My brother just called me with the news about Dan Jones," Kilraven told her. "Nice work."

"I told you I had skills," Alice reminded him. "It's amazing to me that I'm not in demand as technical advisor to any number of programs about autopsies on television." She frowned thoughtfully. "Heck, I'm amazed that they aren't after me to star in one of them. I'm young, I'm gorgeous, I'm…is anybody listening to me?" She opened her arms wide.

"We're trying not to, Alice," Kilraven said with a wry grin.

"Fine. I'll just go about solving crimes on my own, unappreciated, unloved…"

"Shall I tell Harley you said that?" he asked.

She made a face at him and left the room.

"That DNA match was really good work, Alice," he called after her.

"No need trying to butter me up, Kilraven, I'm not listening!"

"It was good work, but it doesn't help much, yet," Detective Rogers said a minute later. "We have a name and a rap sheet, but there's a lot of work left to do in order to connect him with anybody."

"We'll get there. I wanted to know if you've had any

luck questioning witnesses around the motel where the victim lived."

"Nobody knows anything." She sighed. "Well, let me rephrase that, nobody knows anything for free and I'm broke until payday."

"I can bankroll you, if you're willing to go back," he said.

"I hate paying informants, but I can't really see any straight-up way to get information in this case. And I'm not really sure that they'll say anything if we pay for it," she added. "One of the guys I talked to said we were sticking our noses in places even cops shouldn't go."

"That sounds interesting."

"I'd take bullets, if I went," Alice suggested from the other room.

"I always take bullets," Kilraven informed her.

"When I finish up here," Rogers said, "we can go back to the motel and see if a few photos of Ben Franklin on currency will open any mouths."

"You're on. See you, Alice!" he called to the woman in the other room, who waved a hand in his general direction.

THE MOTEL WHERE Dan had been living was a seedy, sad little affair on the wrong side of town. Its one enticement to the poor was the low cost of housing. On the other hand, customers had to share space with any number of small furry rodents or long-legged bugs.

There were five men living in the motel, only two of whom were longtime residents. One of them knew Dan Jones, but it took several photos of Ben Franklin to get inside his room and several more to overcome his survival sense.

He was elderly, looked half-starved and wore glasses

so thick Kilraven was dubious about his ability to even see his visitors.

"Bad people he was mixed up with," the old man told them. "Real bad. He said he couldn't stay anyplace long, because they were trying to shut him up. He knew things, see. He wouldn't say what, but he said he wanted to go straight and they weren't going to let him. He had a girl, nice girl, he said. She was real religious and wanted him to go to church with her. He liked it. Said he thought he could make up for some of the things he did." He shook his head. "I knew he'd never live. Once he said that name, I knew they'd kill him." He gave Kilraven a hard look. "You just make sure you say I never told you nothing, or they'll find me in some alley."

"I won't tell anyone," Kilraven promised. "What name did he say?"

He hesitated.

"What name?"

He sighed. "Hank Sanders," he said finally.

Kilraven's jaw tautened. "Senator Sanders's little brother," he muttered.

"That's the one. Law can't touch him. He's got powerful friends. You watch, they'll never get the guys who killed Dan. They can cover up any crime they want to. You just watch your own backs, or they'll get you, too."

"Nobody smart kills a cop," Kilraven told him.

"Yeah, well, these guys don't build rockets," came the wry reply.

Kilraven handed him another Franklin and walked out with the detective.

"Now what?" she asked with a sigh.

"Now what, indeed. How do we investigate the brother of a senator for a possible homicide?"

"Call some reporters...?"

"Oh, no," he interrupted. "I'm not going to be a nightly news snack. Once they latch on to this cold case, there will be autopsy photos of my wife and child on every tabloid from here to New York City," he added grimly. "No, we have to play this close to the chest. I'll see what I can dig up on the senator's brother. Suppose you see if any of your informants know anything about Dan Jones and his pals."

"I'll do that." She was quiet and thoughtful for a minute. They stood just outside the motel in the chilly night air with the neon sign missing two letters of the word *motel.* It seemed to emphasize the hopelessness of the building, old and in need of much repair that the owner obviously couldn't or wouldn't effect.

"I hope I never end up in a place like this," Kilraven said glumly.

"Me, too, although I've lived in worse places in years past," she said with a soft laugh. She looked up at the night sky. "I want to do something dangerous."

"Like dive off a building or something?" he asked with a twinkle in his eyes.

She shook her head. "No. I mean, I want to reopen the case of that teenager who was found in a similar condition to our Jacobsville murder victim seven years ago."

He was instantly somber. "You think there may be a link to our cold case?"

She nodded. "Just a hunch. I don't have inside information or anything, but I've got a feeling..."

"I have a friend in Jacobsville who has those same hunches. Saved my life once," he recalled, thinking about Winnie.

"Mine might end in tragedy," she said with a sudden

flash of insight. "It's very risky. But I think it might be a piece in the puzzle."

His eyes narrowed. "You think there may be a tie to the senator."

"I don't have a scrap of evidence that points to him. Just a hunch. She was very young," she recalled. "She went off supposedly to meet a boy she was dating and turned up dead in an unspeakable condition, just before you lost your family, and looking like our mysterious Dan Jones when his body was found. It may be a coincidence. On the other hand…"

"It never hurts to play the odds," he agreed.

"I'll get right on it. You watch your back," she added with a grin. "I'd hate to have to identify you by your DNA."

"So would my brother," he replied, smiling.

She nodded. "I'll be in touch."

WINNIE KNEW SOMETHING was going on with Kilraven, but she didn't know exactly what. He'd gone to San Antonio to see his brother and Marquez's female partner. Before that, he'd spent time with Rick at his house. She wished she knew Kilraven well enough to ask him what was happening. They weren't getting any inside information at dispatch and that alone was disturbing. They usually had some tidbits about any case that was being worked, even ones up in San Antonio.

She was still floating on air from that hard, sweet kiss, and hoping it wasn't going to be an isolated incident. He was the first and only man she'd ever had such feelings for. She'd hoped that he felt the same way. But he hadn't phoned her or looked in at Barbara's Café where she had lunch most days. In fact, he was conspicuous by his absence.

The holidays were over. She and Keely had taken down the beautiful old Christmas ornaments and packed them away, along with the other decorations and the tree. The house looked cold and bare. Jacobsville still had its tinsel and bells and Christmas trees on light poles, along with garlands of fir and holly. But those artificial leftovers generally didn't come down until the middle of January. They made Winnie sad. She'd hoped she might see Kilraven during the holidays. But if his cold case was heating up, she could understand that he'd want to be in the middle of it.

She should have realized how single-minded he was about the past. She didn't.

Kilraven had barely noticed Christmas Day. Jon came by and brought him a diamond tie tack. He returned the gift with one of his own, a rare print of running horses that Jon had been looking for. Kilraven had found it on the internet months ago and bought it, then had it framed and kept it in a closet for the big day.

"Don't you even put up a tree in your apartment?" Jon had exclaimed, looking around at the bare apartment. There wasn't even a photograph on display, no paintings, nothing personal at all. Just gym equipment in one bedroom, job-related computers and monitors in another, gaming consoles, and the bare necessities of furniture in the living room and dining room, with a fully-equipped kitchen where Jon sometimes whipped up gourmet dishes for both men.

"It's just a place to sleep. I've been busy trying to run down leads."

Jon's eyes had narrowed. "What I hear is that you've

been driving people nuts trying to get them to work your cold case above pressing new murders."

"Hey, it's the first break we've had in seven years," he said defensively, and his face hardened. "It should have been worked until it was solved when it was fresh!"

"I won't argue that, but you know what it's like, trying to give your best to two dozen cases at a time, all with grieving relatives who want blood and tears from the perps."

"I know that," Kilraven said tightly. "But this is personal."

Jon moved closer. "Don't start obsessing again," he said quietly. "It took over your life for three years after it happened. I don't want to see you falling back into that abyss."

"I'm going to solve it," he told his brother. "No matter what the cost. Whoever killed my little girl is going to pay for it with his blood!"

Jon understood how he felt. He didn't know what to say. It was such a personal matter.

"They've had weeks!" he burst out. "They know the guy's name, where he lived, that he was involved with a woman who worked for Senator Fowler, that he went to a church nearby...for God's sake, there are church members, other employees who worked for the senator, people who lived at the motel he stayed at...!"

"I heard about the resident who was, shall we say, compensated for information," Jon said curtly. "That's not good police work."

"Hey, whatever works," he shot back. "He was the only man my detective could find who was willing to say anything at all and he was scared to death even to whisper certain names."

"Like the name of the junior senator's brother?" Jon queried.

"Exactly."

Jon stuck his hands in his pockets. "Mac, I'm not saying it's a bad lead, but if the case ever comes to trial, that paid informer is going to come back to haunt you. One broken link in a chain of evidence can let a murderer walk."

Kilraven's silver eyes were lawless. "Who says he'll ever get to trial?" he asked in a tone so soft with menace that it made the hair on the back of Jon's neck stand up.

"If you act outside the law, you'll go to prison," Jon said quietly. "Don't do it. Don't even think about it. We have the rule of law, and it works."

"Not all the time."

"Vigilante law has been known to kill innocents," Jon reminded him. "You don't want to run off half-cocked and finger the wrong person. Do you?"

Kilraven's face was like stone. "I want justice."

"Good. So do I. Stop talking like some Old West desperado."

Kilraven lifted an eyebrow.

"Have you ever read a real history of the old Texas lawmen on the border in the early 1800s?" Jon asked.

"Who hasn't?"

"One Texan with a badge could walk into a town across the border and residents would run away screaming when they saw just the badge," he replied.

"Those old-timers had to be tough to stay alive," Kilraven defended them.

"You're missing the point."

"Which is?"

"You can carry a threat so far that instead of respect for the law, you create panic and fear."

"Whatever works," the older man repeated.

Jon sighed irritably. "I can talk to you about a dozen other subjects and you're the soul of rationality. On this one, you aren't even coherent."

"Look at the autopsy photos. I'll give you coherent."

Jon had moved closer and laid a big hand on his brother's shoulder. "Nobody knows better what you went through than I do," he said quietly. "I'll help you, any way I can. But if you step outside the law, nobody will be able to. You understand?"

Kilraven softened, just for a minute. Jon was a hard case, but he really cared about his sibling, and Kilraven knew it. He managed a smile. "I could have done worse for a brother than you," he said.

Jon chuckled. "Yes. Me, too."

It was the closest they came to expressing the real affection they had for each other. Neither man was known for public displays of private emotions.

Now it was January, cold and barren and dry. Kilraven glared at the flat horizon with its gray skies and stark trees lifting bare limbs over frosty ground. It felt dead, as Kilraven felt dead inside. He was sorry he hadn't at least phoned Winnie over the holidays, but every new lead in the case kept him pacing the floor and waiting for phone calls. Not that he waited long. Every homicide detective in San Antonio recognized his cell phone number by now and they hung up the minute it flashed on their screens.

"Damn it!" he muttered, throwing the phone at his leather sofa after his latest attempt at communication got him a quick click followed by a busy signal.

No sooner had it hit than it started ringing.

He grabbed it up. Maybe one of the detectives was psychic.

"Hello?" he said.

"I have news," Jon said smugly. "Remember I told you that I had Ms. Perry researching Dan Jones's known associates?"

"Yes. You found something!"

"I did, indeed. The junior senator's brother engaged Mr. Jones as a gofer," he replied.

"The connection. Finally!"

"Okay, hold it right there," Jon said firmly. "You can't jump in and blow the whole investigation. We have to go slow, to gather evidence, to—"

"Damn!"

"I know how impatient you are," Jon told him quietly. "But you don't want us to blow a murder case by intimidation and threats, do you?"

Kilraven was silent.

"Do you?"

"Of course not," he said on a heavy sigh.

"Good. Now take a deep breath and promise me you won't go rushing over to the evil brother's lair and start knocking him through walls trying to pin the murders on him."

Kilraven let out the breath. "I promise."

"We have to go at him sideways. First we pin down exactly what tasks Dan Jones was known to do for him, whether any of them involved intimidation or worse. Then we have to find witnesses who saw it and are willing to talk."

"The informant at the motel might know more."

"Anything you get with bribes will be a banquet for the perp's defense team," Jon said sternly.

Kilraven quieted down. "I guess so," he said irritably.

"You know so. What you can do is find a way to talk to the senator's wife," Jon added. "We know that she's afraid of her husband's brother. We don't know why. We need some way to dig information out of her without making her suspicious."

"They have vacation property in the Bahamas," Kilraven said. His eyes narrowed. "I could fly down there…"

"She won't talk to you," Jon said. "I know, because I've tried. It's going to take a woman."

Kilraven's heart jumped. "The Sinclairs own property in Nassau."

"Yes, they do," Jon said. "In fact, their property sits just down the beach from the senator's. I had Ms. Perry dig that out for me."

"And we have a ranch in Lawton, near the senator's homeplace, where his grandfather was born. They vacation there sometimes, as well. Winnie Sinclair might be willing to help. We could go down there together."

Jon's voice chilled. "If you take her down to Nassau and share her beach house, gossip would get back to Jacobsville. Her reputation is spotless. It would be a shame to put a blemish on it."

Kilraven was thinking, not quite rationally. "We could get a nice ceremony at city hall the day before we left for the Bahamas, followed by a nice annulment the day we came home."

Jon glared at him. "The woman's crazy about you from what I hear. Even you couldn't be that cold-hearted, to think of marrying her temporarily just to help in a murder investigation!"

"I was kidding," Kilraven lied. "Look, I might ask her to fly down there and accidentally run into the senator's wife and have lunch or something. She might be able to find out something we can't."

"It might put her in the line of fire, too," Jon argued.

Kilraven pursed his lips. "More reason that I should be on hand, just in case."

Jon threw up his hands. "I can't talk to you!"

"Sure you can. It's a great idea. I'll go work on it."

"I didn't mean it that way," Jon said. "Mac, you can't use people who care about you."

"Why not? Everybody else does." His face hardened. "My daughter is dead. Somebody killed her and walked away, like it never happened. I want somebody to pay for it. Somebody is going to pay for it, no matter what I have to do to get an arrest in the case!"

"No matter who you have to sacrifice to do it?" Jon asked softly.

"You're twisting what I said."

"Not really."

Kilraven squared his shoulders. "Winnie's got a crush on me. She's too young to feel anything stronger than that," he said, dismissing her feelings. "She'd be thrilled to have a marriage license in her hands, even if it was for only a couple of weeks. We'd solve the case, get an annulment and go back to our own lives."

"Mac...!"

"Like a date, only we'd live together, briefly."

"She has a brother who eats live snakes," Jon shot back. "I know Boone Sinclair. You do not want him on your neck. He was spec ops in Iraq, and he has skills that could match yours. He's very protective of his sister."

"I'm not going to hurt Winnie," Kilraven raged. "For God's sake, we'll have a vacation together. What's sinister about that?"

"A vacation where you'll troll her as bait to catch the senator's wife."

"You said we can't get her to talk because we're men. Okay. Winnie's a female."

"You don't even know if she'll do it," Jon said. "But if you ask her, for God's sake, tell her the truth. And tell her it's risky. Because it is. You could be putting her life on the line."

"Just for talking to a senator's wife?" he scoffed. "Don't be so alarmist."

"I have to be. You're not thinking straight. You're too bullheaded about this case to be logical."

"And you're too logical to feel revenge."

Jon shook his head. "No, I'm not. I saw them, too," he added quietly. "Melly was a very special child. I may not have liked her mother, but I loved her. Just as you did. I don't want somebody to get away with killing her, either."

Kilraven relaxed, but only a little. "I'll talk to Winnie."

"Do that. But be honest. Okay?"

"Okay."

ALL THE WAY to Jacobsville, he was thinking of ways to sell Winnie on the idea without telling her too much. Jon was all business, but Kilraven's heart was bleeding all over again from the memory of what he'd seen that long-ago rainy night when he intercepted a homicide call and found his family dead. He'd had nightmares for years. He heard Melly call for him, scream for him to save her, and he tried to get up, but he was held down by ropes and he couldn't get loose. The same dream, night after night, with her screams in his ears.

He'd dived headfirst into a whiskey bottle for several

weeks afterward. Jon had saved him from going even further downhill by getting him into a treatment facility. Fortunately, his bosses had understood his behavior. Counseling and time off had given him the opportunity to pretend to the world that he was over the deaths, well-adjusted and ready to go back to work. Nothing was further from the truth, but he learned to hide his feelings. He was good at it by now.

He'd taken some of the most dangerous jobs he could find in a futile effort to get the horrible pictures out of his mind. The CIA had taken him on with reservations, but discovered that he was an asset with his knowledge of foreign languages. Like his brother, Jon, he spoke Farsi and several Arabic dialects, in addition to Spanish, French, Russian, German and even Lakota Sioux. If he wore colored contacts, he was olive-skinned and dark-eyed enough to pass for someone Middle Eastern, and he had, working covertly and sometimes with foreign governments to ferret out information vital to national security.

His specialty had become kidnapping cases, which was why he'd gone undercover in Jacobsville about the time General Emilio Machado went missing and showed up in Mexico. The general had nabbed first Gracie Marsh and then Jason Pendleton in an effort to regain his government in South America. He was friendly to the U.S. and not the same sort of tyrant who held power there, now. Kilraven had been looking for him, but hadn't realized where he was until he got involved with Rodrigo Ramirez and the DEA on a drug case. And voilà, there was Machado. He'd solved that case.

Now he had something much more personal to pursue during his leave of absence. All he needed were the tools to solve it. One of them was Winnie Sinclair. And he was going to get her to help him. No matter what he had to do—even if it meant using her own feelings for him in the process. The only thing that mattered was bringing his daughter's killer to justice any way he could.

He could still see her, the last day of her little life. She'd started toward the car where her mother was waiting impatiently to take her to day care. But she'd turned suddenly. She ran back to Kilraven with her black hair flying, laughing, her arms outstretched. He'd picked her up, swung her around and kissed her.

"I love you, Daddy," she'd whispered, and kissed him back. "Always remember."

He could barely see the road for the film in his eyes. "Always remember." They were the most painful words of all now because he remembered what had happened just a few hours later. He would never see those black eyes sparkle, or hear that musical little laugh, or open his arms for Melly to run into. He drew in a harsh breath and swallowed down the hard lump in his throat. His hands went white where they gripped the steering wheel. Three years old, and some heartless intruder had killed her. Somehow, he swore, someday, someone was going to pay the price for that murder. And he was going to make it happen. He didn't care if it cost him his job, or even his life. The killer was going to be brought to justice.

CHAPTER SIX

WINNIE WAS HAVING a quick lunch at Barbara's Café on her way home from work. She'd been on a split shift, working five hours of her ten-hour shift before midnight and going back in at 3:00 a.m. to pick up the rest of it. The EOC was organized so that each operator worked a ten-hour shift, and because someone was arriving as someone else was leaving, there was overlap. It allowed the incoming operators to know what was going on and saved long explanations of existing or developing situations.

She loved her job. There were times when she was so stressed that she had to take breaks in the EOC "quiet room," a place set aside for people who needed a brief moment of solitude after hectic periods of time to come down off the ceiling. It was a high-pressure job, with lives in the balance. The training had been intensive, but after her internship she felt capable of handling most any situation that arose. And if she needed help, it was all around her. These dedicated, good-hearted people made her proud to be a part of their group.

"You look worn out," Barbara mentioned as she put a plate of salad and a grilled cheese sandwich in front of Winnie, along with a cup of hot coffee. Winnie put cream and sugar in the coffee, something she only did when she had grilled cheese.

"Bad night," she replied with a wan smile. "I worked

a split shift to accommodate one of our other operators who had a death in the family. It was hectic. Much more than usual."

Barbara sat down with her for a minute. "The Tate boy?" she asked gently.

Winnie hesitated, and then nodded. It was useless to deny her involvement. In Jacobsville, everybody knew what was going on. Besides, it would be in the newspaper the next day. Operators never talked about incidents at work otherwise. "Tragic," she said heavily. "His poor mother."

"She has friends. She'll cope."

"Yes, but it was so senseless," Winnie said.

Barbara put a gentle hand on hers. "Nothing is really senseless. Sometimes we just don't understand the reasons things happen. Like Rick getting beat up." She shook her head. "Thank God he has such a hard head."

Winnie nodded. "He was lucky. But this boy was only fifteen years old," Winnie said. "He thought it would be funny to steal a car and go for a joyride. He allegedly ran over a ten-year-old child and crippled her for life, and then couldn't avoid a power pole and killed himself." She shook her head. "I don't understand anything."

"That's what I mean," Barbara said. "I don't think we're meant to understand, sometimes." She looked up. "You need cheering up."

"That would take more than a salad and coffee, I'm afraid."

"How about something six feet tall and very good-looking?"

"Hmm?"

"How about bringing me what she's having?" Kilraven asked as he pulled up a chair and sat down beside Winnie, whose heart leaped up into her throat even as tired as she was. "Except I want my coffee black."

Barbara smiled. "Coming up."

She left and Kilraven gave Winnie a bold appraisal. She was wearing a pair of dark slacks with a blue polo shirt, her blond hair in a neat braid. She looked very young, tired and disillusioned.

"I heard," Kilraven said.

She met his silver eyes. He was wearing slacks and a black polo shirt with a wool jacket. He looked expensive and worldly out of uniform. She managed a smile. "We're all still reeling. Up until the ambulances got there, we had hope."

"You did everything possible. It was a good effort."

"We did everything possible and he still died."

"That's not your call," he replied quietly. "People die. We all do, eventually."

She managed a weary smile. "So they say."

Barbara came back with his salad and sandwich and coffee. "You have to learn not to take things so much to heart, baby," she told Winnie gently.

The endearment was comforting. Winnie sighed. "I do try."

"It's no bad thing to have a heart," Kilraven interjected.

"Yes, it is," Winnie murmured. She drew in a long breath and pushed back her plate. "It's very good, Barbara, I'm just sleepy and worn out. I almost went straight home, but I haven't had anything since supper early yesterday evening."

"You have a canteen at the EOC," Kilraven pointed out.

"Yes, but in order to eat, you have to have time to eat,"

she reminded him. "That wasn't the only emergency we had. It was the busiest night we've had this month."

"It was a full moon," Kilraven said as he dug into his salad.

"It was," Barbara exclaimed. "But what does that have to do with it?"

"Beats me," he said. "But it really does bring out the worst in some people."

Barbara just shook her head. "If you need anything else, let me know."

It was an indication of how depressed Winnie was that she wasn't dropping utensils or spilling coffee from nervousness at Kilraven's unexpected company. She sipped coffee and stared at her discarded salad blankly.

After a minute, she glanced at him and frowned. "What are you doing down here?" she asked suddenly. "We heard you were in San Antonio, working with detectives to find connections to our DB in the Little Carmichael River."

"I was, and I have," he said. "I need a favor."

Her heard did jump, then. "What?"

"Not now. Finish your coffee and we'll take a ride."

She glanced around at the lunch crowd. They were eating and shooting covert glances at Winnie and Kilraven.

"If I go for a ride with you, we'll be the talk of the town all weekend," she said.

He chuckled. "I don't care." He looked into her dark eyes. "Do you?"

She shrugged. "I guess not."

"While they're talking about us, they're leaving somebody else alone," he pointed out.

"I suppose." She finished her coffee. "Do you think it's going to tie into your own cold case?" she asked abruptly.

His face tautened. "I think it may. We've got a lead. It's a small one, but it may pay dividends down the road. Before this is over, some big-time feathers are going to get ruffled."

She cocked her head. "Now, I'm curious."

"Good. Let's go." He swallowed the rest of his coffee and picked up her lunch tab, despite her protests, as well as his own. Then he shepherded her out the door and toward a black late-model Jaguar sports car.

She was taken aback. Used to seeing him in a prowler, this was new.

"Don't tell me you haven't ever seen one." He chuckled.

"Of course I have. I just never pictured you driving one."

"Out of curiosity, what did you picture me driving?" he queried at the passenger door.

"A squad car," she said with a smile.

He chuckled. "Point to you, Miss Sinclair." He started to open the door and then hesitated, frowning. "Sinclair. Do you know your family history?"

"Sort of," she said, disconcerted. "My people came from Scotland."

His silver eyes twinkled.

"Why does that amuse you?"

"Lord Bothwell married Mary, Queen of Scots after the suspicious death of her husband, Lord Darnley. Bothwell's mother was a Sinclair."

"Why are you so interested in Bothwell?" she asked.

He pursed his lips. "My ancestors were Hepburns."

"Well, isn't it a small world?" she exclaimed.

"Getting smaller by the day. Climb in."

He went around and got in beside her, approving the fact that she fastened her seat belt at once. So did he.

"Where are we going?" she asked.

"Someplace without video cameras and an audience," he said with a grim nod toward the faces peering out of the café.

"We could go to my house," she said.

"Keely may be at work, but I expect your brothers are around the house somewhere."

"Boone is. Clark's up in Iowa, looking at cattle for Boone."

"My point, exactly. I want to talk to you without an audience."

She turned her purse over in her hands. "Okay. I'll try to stay awake."

"Poor kid," he said sympathetically. "You work hard for minimum wage. You don't have to work at all, do you?"

She shook her head. "It's just that we were all raised with a strong work ethic. We're not the sort of people to sit around and play cards or go to parties."

"Your father has been dead for some time, hasn't he?"

She nodded. "He was a good man, in a lot of ways. But he had some terrible flaws. I suppose they were because our mother ran off with his brother. He never got over it."

"That would shatter a man's pride," he had to agree. He glanced at her set features. "No curiosity about where she lives, or with whom…?"

"No," she blurted out. She flushed at his sudden scrutiny.

"People make mistakes, Winnie," he said gently.

The visit from her mother still stung. "Yes, they do, and we're supposed to forgive them. I know that. But I could have happily gone my whole life without seeing her again."

"Has she remarried?"

She glanced at him, frowning. "Remarried?"

"You said she was married to your uncle. Your uncle died."

"Wait a minute," she said. "How do you know that?"

"It's one of the reasons I came down here to talk to you. Your uncle may have been on the periphery of this case."

"Boone said something about that, but not that he was actually involved. Our uncle was a murderer?" she exclaimed, horrified.

"We don't think he killed the DB," he said at once. "But they found a thermos bottle at the site where the car went into the Little Carmichael River. It was a match for one that your uncle was said to have in his house. A San Antonio detective who's working with us on this case went to his house to check it out. She spoke with his roommate."

Winnie was stunned. It had never occurred to her that her uncle might be involved in murder.

"His roommate." She blinked. She looked at him. "Our mother said that his roommate was strung out on drugs."

He looked surprised. "That's right. Well, I guess she had to go over there if she recovered your heirloom jewelry, right? Anyway, our detective also paid the roommate a visit and checked out the thermos. She was barely lucid—the roommate I mean—but she did identify a photograph of the thermos."

"My uncle's thermos was on the bank of the river next to the car of a murder victim, and you don't think he was involved?" she asked, blank from lack of sleep and shock.

He drew in a breath. "That's why I said I think he was on the periphery. I think he might have known the murderer."

She sat back in her seat, wondering at the connection and interconnection of lives. She frowned. "Do you think my uncle was murdered?" she asked.

He didn't speak for a minute. "Now, isn't that an interesting question. I don't think we considered that his death might not have been natural. He was a heavy drug user."

"Sheriff Hayes's brother was killed by an overdose that he didn't know he was taking," she said. "So was Stuart York's wife's sister. They were given a pure form of the drug instead of a diluted one and didn't realize it."

"We'll look into that," he said at once.

Winnie looked down at the purse in her lap. "So many dead people. What did they all know that got them killed?"

"I don't know, Winnie," he said quietly. "But I'm going to find out."

He pulled into a small roadside park. It was deserted at this time of year. It was a pretty place in the other seasons, beside a tributary of the Little Carmichael River, where kids played in warm weather. The trees were bare and stark against a gray sky. The whole world looked dead. Even the grass.

"It will be cold, but I don't think we'll be a tourist attraction here," he chuckled as they got out.

Winnie pulled her gray Berber coat closer because the wind was sharp and cold. She walked beside Kilraven, in his dark wool jacket, to the stream. She noted as she looked down that he was wearing black boots, so highly polished that they reflected the sky. She smiled. It was like him to be fastidious.

"What are you smiling at?" he asked.

"Your boots," she said. "Not a speck on them. You're elegant for a cattleman turned law enforcement officer."

He chuckled. "I guess so."

She wondered why. She was too polite to ask.

He stared at her with a faint smile. "You're curious, but you won't ask. I like that about you."

"Thanks."

He put his hands in his pockets and looked at the bubbling stream in between the shallow banks. "My mother was white," he said shortly. "She left my father when I was about two years old. She took me with her, but she liked to party. She couldn't afford a housekeeper, but she didn't consider that it was dangerous to leave a child alone. In fact, she seemed to forget that she had me from time to time. My father came looking for me after he got a call from the police in a little town outside Dallas. A neighbor had heard screaming from inside a deserted house that my mother had rented. The police broke in and found a card with his name and telephone number on it, and they called him."

She waited. She didn't insist.

He drew in a breath. "My mother had been partying with a man, apparently one who liked alcohol and didn't especially like women. He beat her to death. I guess I was lucky that he didn't kill me, but he probably assumed that I was too young to identify him. He locked the door and left us both inside. It was two days before I got hungry enough to scream."

"Dear God," she whispered.

He glanced at her with hollow eyes. "My father carried me home and cleaned me up. He was going with a younger woman who loved kids. She latched on to me as if I were the only child on earth." He chuckled. "He married her, and they had Jon. But I never felt as if I were his half brother. My earliest memories are of Cammy. My stepmother."

"Cammy?"

"Her name is Camelia, but nobody calls her that." He drew in a long breath. "She's very conservative and deeply religious, so Jon and I had a strict upbringing. Our father was out of town, sometimes out of the country working for the FBI, so Cammy basically raised us both." He glanced at her with some amusement. "She'd probably make mincemeat out of you, little canary bird. She's hard-going, as at least one of our former girlfriends could attest."

"Your, plural?" she queried.

"Jon and I once had an attachment to the same girl. It ended in a rather enthusiastic altercation, from which we both emerged with dental bills. The girl, predictably, discovered that she was really in love with her former boyfriend. Too late to do us any good." He laughed.

"Your stepmother must be one nice lady," she commented.

"She is. Difficult to live with, but nice."

"I'm sorry about your mother."

"I'm sorry about yours," he replied. He turned to her

and moved closer. "I've never told anyone about my mother."

She was flattered. She smiled. "I've never told anybody about mine, either. Just family."

"Does she look like you?" he asked, curious.

"Pretty much. She's older."

"She must live somewhere nearby."

"I wouldn't know." She closed up.

"Now, don't do that," he teased gently. He drew her against him. "We were making progress and then you turned into a sensitive plant and closed your leaves up."

She smiled. "Sorry." She flattened her hands against his broad chest, under the jacket. She could feel the warmth of his body through the soft fabric of his shirt.

The touch, light as it was, built fires deep inside him. His breathing changed. The scent of her body was in his nostrils, seducing him. It had been years since he'd felt a woman's body against him in the darkness, since he'd known what it was to be a man. And here he was with a woman who didn't even know what happened when the lights went out, except for what she'd heard or read.

She looked up. "What's wrong?"

His eyebrows lifted. "Well, I was just considering how nice it would be to lay you down on the grass and…" He cleared his throat. "Sorry."

She laughed, delighted. "Were you really?"

He cocked his head. "Not offended?"

"Oh, no. I have all these deep questions about how it feels and what happens," she confided. "I did almost find out, once, but my brother Boone walked in and knocked the boy down the front steps into a mud puddle." She sighed. "I was fifteen. Boone felt I was too young to be the target of a twentysomething cowboy. So the cowboy went to work for somebody else and I went back into cold storage, and so did my physical education."

He burst out laughing. "Good for Boone."

"He's always looked out for me. So has Clark, in his way." She sighed. "Neither of them knew what it was like at home when they were gone, and I couldn't tell. My father hated my mother, hated her more than ever after they met and talked a few weeks after she left. He came home cursing her. We weren't told what happened."

"Sad that they couldn't work it out."

"I would have liked having a mother," she agreed. She looked up at him. "I was horrible to her when she showed up at the house. I guess I could have been more forgiving."

"It's hard to forgive people who sell us out," he said.

She nodded. She drew in a long breath. "All of this is very interesting, but it doesn't have much to do with why you came looking for me. Does it?"

He framed her face in his hands and lifted it. "Maybe it does." He looked at her mouth for a long time, so long that her heart raced. "Sorry," he murmured as he bent his head, "but I'm having withdrawal symptoms…"

His mouth hit hers like a wall, opening and twisting, hungry and insistent, warm against the cold that whirled around them on the bank of the stream. She melted into him, sliding her arms around his broad chest. Her fingers dug into his back, feeling the solid muscle there, drowning in the hunger he raised in her so effortlessly.

He liked her response. It was immediate, unaffected, totally yielding. He loved the way she felt in his arms. He drew her closer, feeling the sudden, familiar surge of desire that corded his powerful body, no longer hidden from her.

She gasped as she felt it. His hands went lower and pressed her hips into his.

He lifted his head and stared into her wide, shocked eyes. He didn't say a word. But he wouldn't let her step back, either.

"We mustn't…!" she whispered.

"What happened to all that talk about wanting to know how it felt?" he asked, pursing his lips. He wasn't smiling, but his eyes were.

"Well, I do," she stammered. "But not right now."

"Not right now."

She nodded. She flushed.

He chuckled wickedly and let her move away a discreet distance. He liked her high color. He liked a lot of things about her. "Chicken," he teased.

"Chook, chook, chook." She imitated a hen and grinned up at him.

"Actually," he said, looping his arms around her waist, "I was thinking of a way for you to indulge some of that curiosity."

"You were?"

"Not to excess," he said then, feeling cautious. It would be too easy to go in headfirst, and have to repair the damage later. "You have a summer house in Nassau."

The sudden shift in subject matter hit her like a brick in the head. "Uh, yes."

"It borders on property owned by the junior senator from Texas."

"Yes, it does."

"His wife doesn't like him. He plays around with very

young girls and it hurts her pride, so she goes to the summer home to escape the media spotlight. And the senator."

"That's what I've heard."

"Have you ever met her?" he asked suddenly, hopefully.

"Actually, I have," she replied. "We were at a party once, thrown by the American embassy, and I've gone to parties at her house, before her husband was a senator. She's very nice."

He smiled. "How would you like to go down to Nassau with me and stay in the summer home while we see if she might be even more talkative about her brother-in-law?"

She cooled down at once and pulled away. "I'm not like that."

"Excuse me?" he asked, disconcerted.

"I mean, I flirt a little too hard with you, and maybe it looks like I'm worldly and I'm leading you on. But I'm not. I can't, I mean, I won't… My brother would kill you," she added, blushing.

He understood at once and burst out laughing.

"It's not funny," she muttered, glowering at him.

"That's not why I'm laughing. I don't have an illicit weekend in mind," he assured her. His eyes smiled, too. "I'm pretty conservative myself, in case you haven't noticed. I don't have women. In fact," he said with a sigh, "I've only ever had one woman and I was married to her."

She really blushed then. "Oh."

"So I think as much of my reputation as I think of yours," he added. "I was considering that we might get married in the probate judge's office. Just for the trip," he said emphatically. "I'm not in the market for a long-term wife or a new family. I can't... I won't risk that again. But we can be married long enough to do some investigating."

She was gaping at him. "We'd get married so that you could ask a senator's wife a few questions in the Bahamas?" she asked blankly.

He laughed. "It sounds bad, when you put it that way."

"But it's what you want to do."

"No, it isn't." He gave her a considering look. "I won't mention what I'd like to do. But it's why I think we should get married. Just in case."

Her eyebrows arched. Her eyes began to twinkle. "Just in case what?"

"In case I can't resist the temptation to do what I'd like to do," he said wryly. "In which case, it wouldn't be an annulment, it would be a divorce."

She cocked her head up at him. "You might like me."

"I'm sure I would. But I'm not getting married again."

"You just said you wanted to," she pointed out.

"Temporarily," he emphasized.

"You're afraid I'd get temporarily pregnant if we went down there as an unmarried couple," she mused.

He glared at her. "I don't get women temporarily pregnant."

"You sure wouldn't get me that way, because I believe very strongly that if babies get made, they should get born," she said firmly.

He sighed. "Winnie, I've had a traumatic seven years," he said. "Right now, the only thing I want to do is find out who killed my wife and child. I'm not emotionally sound enough for a new relationship of any kind."

She felt doors closing. He was brutal. But perhaps

he felt he needed to be. He didn't want to give her any false hope.

His silver eyes narrowed. "This is how you looked that morning when you found me and Sheriff Hayes in bed with your brother and Keely," he said.

"Excuse me?"

"You stopped playing with me," he said somberly. "You stopped looking at me with those big, soft brown eyes as if you'd die to have me."

"I never looked at you that way," she defended herself. "I thought you were dishy. So have a lot of other women, I'll bet."

"I minded when other women did it," he said surprisingly.

"You did?"

"You're just a little violet, blooming under a stair," he said softly, touching her face with the tips of his fingers as he looked down at her intently. "Twenty-two to my thirty-two, Winnie. That's almost a generation."

"It's ten years and I'm old for my age."

He pursed his lips. "Not old in the right way, kid," he insinuated.

She glared at him. "Nobody learns things without somebody teaching them," she said flatly. "My father and my big brother made sure nobody got close enough."

"Good for them," he repeated.

"Listen, I have the makings of a femme fatale if I could just learn the basics," she told him. "Books don't tell you anything. They assume you already know."

"What sort of books have you been reading?" he asked in mock surprise.

"The same sort boys hide under their mattresses,

I imagine, but I need more than just pictures! You're changing the subject." She pushed against his chest. "I'm not marrying you temporarily. You can find some other woman to go with you to the Bahamas and I'll loan you our vacation home."

"I'm not shacking up with a total stranger," he said curtly.

"Well, you're not shacking up with me, either, Kilraven," she told him.

"That's why I'm trying to get you to marry me!"

She pulled away and walked closer to the stream. She felt sick to her stomach. He wanted a no-strings marriage so that he could help solve the case. She was a means to an end for him. He didn't feel anything for her, really. He never would. He lived with ghosts. She felt more chilled by that realization than from the cold weather. She wrapped her arms around her chest.

He watched her with growing irritation. It was just like a woman to start fishing for emotional involvement. All he needed was her company so that he could get to the senator's wife. Why was she making it so hard? It was because she had feelings for him, he thought irritably. As if he could see a future with a woman only a few years out of high school. He didn't want children, so there was no point in staying married.

"You're making this complicated," he said shortly, ramming his hands into his pockets. "Why can't we just look on it as a lark? We get married, have a holiday on the beach, and build some memories that don't require anything heavy."

She turned and looked at him, horrified.

"We could enjoy each other," he said, losing ground.

"We can have separate bedrooms and behave like un-married people," she said. "Or I'm not going."

"What the hell sort of vacation is that?"

"The only sort you're getting with me," she returned, coloring. "You think you can have fun with me and just walk away. I'm not built like that. I can't...damn it, I won't!" She turned away. "You can take me back to the café, right now!" She started walking toward the car.

He just stared after her. "What the hell did I say?" he asked the tree beside him.

"That's it, talk to the trees," she muttered when she was out of earshot of him. "Look out. They may start answering you!"

CHAPTER SEVEN

KILRAVEN THOUGHT ABOUT her reactions. Maybe she was right. If they could go together to Nassau and just have a few days of sun and sand and ocean, and he didn't pressure her into something she didn't want, it might pay off in a better working relationship. Working, as in courting the senator's wife. Because whatever he said, his only intent was to find out if there was a skeleton in the closet of the senator's brother. He wanted the people who killed his family. That was more important than the future, or Winnie's feelings or any other consideration. Maybe he was using her, but he didn't care. It was an obsession, just as his brother had said. He was going to catch the killer, no matter who he had to hurt to do it.

He walked behind her to the car. "Okay," he said as he unlocked the car and helped her inside. "We'll do it your way. But if I jump off the roof of your summer home in frustration and die, it will be on your conscience."

"It won't," she returned.

"Heartless girl."

She glanced at him. "And I'm not wearing anything provocative the whole time."

"Amazing willpower," he murmured. "Good for you."

She sighed. "And I'm not telling Boone. You'll have to."

His face froze. That was not a prospect he was looking forward to. He knew Boone, and that Boone had been in the military. It was going to be tricky telling him why he was marrying his baby sister. He didn't need to be told that Boone was going to be angry.

"Surely, you're not afraid of him," she said with faint malice.

He drew in a breath. "No, not afraid," he replied.

"You can tell him how you want to marry me so that we can frolic from bedroom to bedroom in the Bahamas and you can use me to dig information out of the senator's wife," she continued.

He glared at her. "You're twisting it," he muttered.

"I'm twisting it?" she exclaimed. "You want me to marry you for a few days so that you can get information that will lead you to whoever killed your family." She sobered. "I don't blame you. If it were me, I'd do anything to find out, too. But I'm the one being used. It feels dirty."

He really glared now. "Dirty."

She grimaced. "That was a poor choice of words," she said slowly.

He closed the passenger door without another word. He went around, got in under the wheel and shot the car out onto the highway. His face might have been carved from stone.

Winnie felt tears threatening. She wasn't used to confrontations since the death of her father. She didn't fight with her brothers. She was a little afraid of Boone, but she didn't advertise it. Men were frightening in a temper. She glanced at Kilraven and thought of glaciers. She knew so little about him. Most of what she'd learned was from other people, although he'd been forthcoming with her on some level. But he kept his true feelings to himself. He seemed happy to be a loner.

She looked out the window uncomfortably as he sped down the road toward Barbara's Café, where her car was parked. She was already regretting her hasty words. What would it hurt to marry him, even if it was temporary? She was crazy about him. Maybe she could store up enough memories to get her through the rest of her life, because she knew she'd never love another man like this.

But he didn't look like he was contemplating a second proposal. In fact, he looked as if he wished he'd never met her.

She wanted to apologize. She knew it was useless. She'd offended him. Not that he hadn't offended her first. What sort of woman did he think she was?

Her lips made a thin line. She knew that he'd never have mentioned a holiday with her if it hadn't been for the senator's wife living near the Sinclair beach house. She was a means to an end, and it was impersonal. He liked her. Maybe he liked kissing her. But there was no feeling behind it, except maybe a physical one. The chemistry was definitely there. He felt it, as surely as she did. But he didn't love her. Perhaps he couldn't love anyone again. The trauma of his loss had turned him cold, made him afraid to try again. He didn't want another child. He didn't want another wife, either. Winnie was a tool. He'd use her to get the information he needed, then he'd put her back on the shelf and forget her very existence. It hurt, knowing that.

He pulled up in front of Barbara's Café where she'd left her car and sat with the engine idling.

She wanted to say something. She couldn't think of anything that would express her confused emotions.

He wanted to say something, too, but he was angry. Anything he said would be too much.

Her hand went to the car door. "Thanks for the ride," she said tautly.

"Sure."

She waited for a minute, but he didn't say another word. He didn't even look at her. She opened the door, got out and closed it behind her. She walked to her own car without looking back. She could barely see it through her tears when she heard him drive away.

"YOU LOOK LIKE death warmed over," Keely said gently later, when they were fixing supper.

Winnie managed a smile as she made a pasta salad. "That's how I feel."

"Want to talk about it?"

Winnie put the finishing touches on the salad and covered the bowl before she put it in the refrigerator to chill. "It wouldn't help," she said finally.

"Well, if you do want to talk, you know where I am," Keely said.

"You're the best friend I've ever had," Winnie told her. "It was the best day of my life when Boone married you." She hugged her warmly.

"I could return the compliment. You saved my life when the rattler bit me. I thought I was a goner."

Winnie laughed. "Poor old snake," she said, fighting back the tears that the hug had provoked.

"He never should have bitten me in the first place."

"He wouldn't have, if you hadn't sat on him," Winnie said.

"I guess so."

"You won't tell Boone, if I tell you?" she asked.

Keely's green eyes twinkled. She crossed her heart.

"Kilraven wants me to marry him."

"Winnie! That's great news…!" Keely began.

Winnie held up a hand. "It's not. He wants me to marry him and spend a few days at our summer house in Nassau so that he can have me pump Senator Sanders's wife for information about her crooked brother-in-law. Then he wants an annulment when we get back. Unless I'm willing to, how did he put it, enjoy our time together, in which case we can get a divorce when we come home."

Keely just stared at her. "That silver-eyed devil," she exclaimed. "I hope you told him where to go!"

"Not in so many words, no," Winnie replied quietly. "But I did tell him no."

"Good for you. I can't believe he asked you to do such a thing!"

"Neither can I."

"You poor thing," Keely said. "I know how you feel about him."

"So does he." She sighed. "That's part of the problem. I shouldn't have been so obvious."

"It's not as if you could help it."

"Well, that's true."

"Men are a lot of trouble. Even the best of them."

Winnie leaned back against the counter with her arms folded over her chest. "I really thought he was beginning to like me. He seemed to. Then he came up with this cock-eyed plan." She glanced at her friend. "I do understand how he feels. He loved his little girl…"

"Little girl?" Keely exclaimed. "He's already married?"

Winnie's eyes were sad. "He was. Someone killed his daughter and his wife. The little girl was just three years old. She drew him a picture. It looked just like the painting I did for him, as a Christmas gift."

Keely went quiet. "You really do have something extra in your brain, Winnie."

"I must." She laughed softly. "It made him furious. That's why he took me to his house that time, to find out why I painted a raven. I didn't even know myself. When he showed me the finger painting, I almost passed out."

"It wasn't the first time you've had odd connections. You knew Kilraven was in danger and sent backup long before he asked for it."

"Eerie, isn't it?"

"Not eerie," Keely said gently. "It's a gift. You probably saved Kilraven's life when you sent another squad car to assist him."

"He gave me strange looks after that."

"I think he's conflicted about how he feels," Keely said. "A man who's gone through a trauma like that has to work through it."

"He's had seven years."

"Yes, but he hasn't really faced it, has he?" Keely asked. "He wants revenge. It's all he lives for. But revenge is a hollow thing."

"He'll find that out."

"Yes, he will." Keely hugged her. "But it doesn't help you, does it?"

Winnie hugged her back. "Not a lot."

"Give him time," Keely advised. "Just be there when he needs someone to talk to. He seems to have told you things that he hasn't shared with anyone else. He really is a loner."

"Yes."

"Why did he want to marry you to go to the Bahamas?" Keely wondered.

"We'd have to stay in the house together. He was worried about his reputation," she added facetiously.

"His?"

Winnie flushed, when she recalled what he'd told her. "Well, his and mine," she amended without elaborating. "He said it wouldn't look right for us to be staying together, alone, when we're not married."

"Talk about a throwback to an earlier generation," Keely exclaimed.

"So says the woman who offered to send my brother packing because she thought he was looking for a good time," Winnie said and grinned.

Keely grimaced. "Touché. I guess Kilraven's like us. He doesn't move with the times. That's not a bad thing. I don't like promiscuous men any more than I like promiscuous women, and I don't care if it's supposed to be acceptable behavior to the whole world."

"Want me to get you a soapbox and a placard?" Winnie mused.

Keely laughed. "I sound like a crusader, don't I? I don't preach to people about my personal beliefs, I don't tell people what I think they should do. But I never was one to go with the crowd. Neither are you."

"We live in a whole community of dinosaurs," Winnie pointed out. "Including Kilraven."

Keely smiled. "He'll come around."

"Do you think so?" she asked miserably. "He didn't even look at me when he let me out at Barbara's. He just drove away."

"He'll think about it and then he'll call you."

"Not a chance in the world."

Keely pursed her lips. "I'll bet you some homemade rolls."

"You can't make homemade bread," Winnie pointed out.

"That's how sure I am that Kilraven will be back," she returned. "Wait and see."

Winnie only smiled. But she didn't believe it.

KILRAVEN WENT TO see Jon. He was fuming about Winnie's refusal and at a loss as to how to change her mind. Maybe Jon had some ideas.

But Jon didn't. Worse, he kept grinning, as if the whole thing was a joke.

"It's not funny!" Kilraven growled.

Jon glanced at him from his lounging position on his sofa. "Yes, it is."

Kilraven sat down in the easy chair. There was a soccer game on, two European teams slugging it out with feet, heads and shoulders on the huge green field.

"You have to see it from her point of view," Jon said gently. "She's lived a sheltered life. She doesn't really know much about men. If you know her brother, Boone, you've already figured that out. I imagine that protective attitude of his kept a lot of men away from Winnie when she first started dating. Most grown men are afraid to stand up to him. From what you've told me about her, I can guarantee you that Winnie won't even try."

Kilraven sat back in the chair and crossed his long legs. He let out a frustrated sigh. "This is the best chance I'm going to get to see if the senator's wife knows something," he said. "All I want Winnie to do is go down to Nassau with me for a few days."

"No, you want her to move in with you and do what comes naturally for a few days. She isn't buying it. She's the sort of woman who won't settle for anything less than marriage, but a permanent marriage, not a pretend one. She sees right through you. That's what you can't take."

He shrugged. "It's damned inconvenient."

"What is?"

Kilraven looked at the television screen. "She's attractive."

"But you don't want anything permanent."

"That's part of it."

"Is there another part?"

He nodded. "She's twenty-two, Jon."

"Oh. Now I begin to see the light."

"Twenty-two to my thirty-two," he continued. "She's already learned about the generation gap from her parents. Her mother was twelve years younger than her father. She ran off with his younger brother. Winnie saw the dangers."

"Then why is she still interested in you?"

"God knows. I'm an old, worn-out, used-up lobo wolf," he said heavily, staring at his shoes. "She's innocent and unsophisticated." He laughed. "Funny. When I first met her, I had this idea that she was a bored debutante playing a game, pretending to be naive. But it was a far cry from the truth. She's very naive, but she doesn't play games and she's greener than grass. I don't know how she's managed to stay so innocent for so long in the circles she and her family travel in."

"Which brings us back to big brother Boone, who would knock your teeth in for playing around with his baby sister."

Kilraven smiled. "I guess I wouldn't blame him. It was a stupid thing I suggested to her. Still, I'm not taking her to Nassau and staying in the house with her without some legal ceremony. She's a fine young woman. I don't want to mess up her reputation."

"Or your own," Jon mused.

Kilraven shot him a glance. "At least I don't have the police lead women out of my office handcuffed."

He shrugged. "What can I say? She tried to bend me back over my own desk." He shook his head. "My mother needs therapy."

"I would never have said that," Kilraven replied. He grinned. "But I'm glad you did."

"We should have taught Cammy how to recognize a call girl."

"Too late now." He pursed his lips. "Ms. Perry still giving you hell at the office?"

"Come to think of it, no." Jon frowned. "I can't figure out why. I did praise her for doing such a good job of digging up info on our murder victim. She's been different since then."

"Different, how?"

"You know, I haven't really thought about it," Jon said. "She's stopped sniping at me. She smiles once in a while. Things like that."

"Look out."

He chuckled. "No need. She's not interested in me. She doesn't like men."

"She has a child."

"Strange thing about that. She seems afraid of men, if they come too close physically."

"Where's her husband?"

"He wasn't her husband," Jon replied somberly. "He went overseas and got killed. Maybe there was some violence in the relationship. But before she got involved with him she didn't date much, either."

"She might have other preferences."

"She might, but she doesn't. She keeps to herself."

"What's the little boy like?"

"Don't know," Jon said. "I've never seen him."

"Don't you have those Bring Your Child to Work days?"

Jon glared at him. "We have an FBI office—we don't encourage employees to use it as a day-care center."

Kilraven held up both hands.

"I don't like children."

Kilraven was giving him an odd look. "Why?"

"I just don't."

"Oh. I remember. The soap thing."

"It was not a soap thing," Jon corrected him. "The kid wrote obscene words all over the passenger side of my car, and I didn't notice until one of my coworkers was rolling in the aisles laughing about it."

"I thought you had to be observant to work for the FBI," Kilraven said innocently.

"Observant? Who looks at the passenger side of his car every morning?" Jon asked belligerently.

"CIA personnel, checking for bombs," Kilraven replied.

"In your case, I'd even be checking the paint for C-4," his brother pointed out. "But nobody ever tried to blow me up."

Kilraven chuckled. "It wasn't much of a bomb." He recalled the incident his brother was alluding to. "The brown envelope he'd shoved it into was torn and you could see the wires sticking out."

"Lucky for you."

"Lucky for him, too. He's only doing five to ten for attempted murder. He could be facing the needle for a capital crime."

"I believe the defense attorney was insinuating that we need a better educated class of criminal and looking straight at you when he said it?"

"So I cost him a couple of gold stars on his defense record as a public defender," Kilraven scoffed. "One of the lowlifes he got off raped a girl one day after he was acquitted. The pissant knew he was guilty—he defended him anyway and got him off. I just made sure the prosecutors knew that the public defender had 'encouraged' a witness not to testify at the first trial. He got a reprimand from the bar association." He glanced at Jon. "Pity we don't still have the rack and public stocks."

"You need to lay off that sixteenth-century Scottish history," Jon advised. "Why don't you read something modern?"

"I do. Combat manuals and books on antiterrorism."

Jon threw up his hands.

BUT JON HAD, at least, convinced Kilraven that he wasn't going to get anywhere with Winnie if he continued with his present plan. He went back home to his apartment downtown to think about his next move.

It was a nice apartment, roomy and open. He had three bedrooms, one of which he used as an office. It contained all his high-tech equipment, weight-lifting bars and traveling accessories, including a bag that remained packed year-round in case he was sent overseas on a mission with a few minutes' notice. That had happened in the past. It wouldn't anytime soon because he was officially on a leave of absence.

There was a bed in the room, also a desk where his laptop stayed connected to the internet—hard-wired and monitored, to make sure he had no hackers on board.

There was a guest bedroom next to his own, with the minimum of amenities. It was just a place to stay, in case some out-of-town agent needed a secure place to bunk down.

His own bedroom was Spartan, just a double bed, because he liked room to turn over, and a chest of drawers and bookcase. The bookcase was almost the size of the bed, and chock-full of historical tomes. In a corner was a big Schmidt-Cassegrain telescope, which he rarely had time to use.

In the living room was a spacious white-leather-covered sofa and matching chair. In front was a fifty-inch TV with the latest technology, a satellite receiver and three complete gaming systems, his favorite of which was the Xbox 360, which he accessed with Xbox Live. He had most of the newer games, but his favorite was *Call of Duty*, followed by the *Halo* series. He had one sword and sorcery game—*Elder Scrolls IV: Oblivion*—and played it for variety.

He plopped down on the sofa and activated the television. He had access, through the Xbox, to all the latest movies on download. He'd just put on the latest *Star Trek* film before he went to see Jon. Now he keyed it up, popped the lid on a wine cooler he'd brought from the fridge, and settled down to watch Kirk, Spock and McCoy begin all over again for a new generation. He grinned as he watched. The original *Star Trek* was his favorite retro TV series.

THE NEXT DAY, he got into his car and drove down to Jacobsville again. He wasn't sure how he was going to convince Winnie to go to Nassau, but he was going to try one last time. He couldn't afford to give up now, when he was so close to finding that one vital clue that would finally solve the tragic murder of his family.

He drove up to her front door. He'd already checked with the EOC center to make sure she wasn't working this morning. Sure enough, when he rang the doorbell, she came herself to answer it.

She looked at him warily. She was dressed in jeans and a red T-shirt that said President of the Jacobsville Dog Chasing and Cursing Society.

He read the T-shirt and burst out laughing.

She hadn't realized what she was wearing because she was still drinking her first cup of coffee of the day, so the laughter surprised her. Then she looked down and recalled the legend on the shirt, and she laughed, too, breaking the ice.

"Where the hell did you get a shirt like that?" he asked.

"Had it made," she said simply. "It was after one really bad day, when I got yelled at by three different callers for not sending an officer to deal with a stray dog." She smiled. "It was the day the branch bank was robbed and we had every officer dealing with it. Not a lot of time to go looking for a stray dog."

"Especially a giant German Shepherd Chihuahua that was gray, black, off-white and had three legs, they thought," Kilraven quoted the report.

"That's the one." She shook her head. "You wonder why eyewitness testimony is supposed to be so valuable when you get calls like that."

"Exactly."

She opened the door. "Come on in. But if you came to try and convince me to go with you on a trip, Boone's in the living room." It was a threat.

"I didn't. I need to talk to him, though."

Surprised, she waved him through to the next room.

Boone was watching the news. He looked up when Kilraven walked in. He pursed his lips and turned off the television. "I know why you're here," he told him. "And the answer's no."

Kilraven dropped into an armchair across from him. "She's over twenty-one," he pointed out. "Old enough to decide for herself."

Boone leaned forward. He looked formidable. "You want someone to help you open a can of worms. This is a big can, and it might contain pit vipers instead of worms. Just by asking her to go with you, you could be putting her life in danger."

Kilraven's face was impassive. "I know your background. I think you should know mine. I've spent the past few years as a special operative. They send me in when the situation is considered too dangerous for unskilled personnel. I'm trained in every method of combat known to man, and a few I made up as I went along. I've had four partners, one of whom I saved three times from certain death. I can defuse a bomb, build one, disarm an armed man, blow up a bridge and recruit men to work for me in some countries that are barely on the map. I'm also a skilled negotiator. I'm trained in weaponry, martial arts and my specialty is innovation. There isn't a man alive your sister would be safer with. Possibly, not even you. And if you think I'd permit anyone to harm her, despite my own interest in solving this case, you are grossly mistaken."

He sat back and waited for Boone to take that in and reply.

Boone was surprised at the admissions. He knew very little about Kilraven, except that he worked undercover for some federal agency. Now he knew more. He respected the man for laying it on the line. But he was still uneasy about letting Winnie become involved in this.

While he was debating his next sentence, Winnie came walking in with two mugs of coffee. She handed one to Kilraven and sat down beside her brother.

"You can decide whatever you like," she told her brother without actually meeting his eyes, and her hands shook. "But I'm going with him."

Kilraven and her brother wore the same perplexed expression.

"It's dangerous," Boone said gently.

Her hands became steadier. She'd been bluffing, but it seemed to have worked. Boone wasn't trying to dominate her, as he had most of her life. She was scared to death of him, but she kept seeing Kilraven's eyes when he spoke of his little girl who had been killed. That look, more than any of his words, had changed her mind. She'd been waiting, hoping, that he'd ask her again. Keely had been right. Kilraven had come back.

"Life is dangerous," Winnie said. "I do know Senator Sanders's wife, and she won't think it strange if I show up in our beach house. Even with a husband." The word made her color slightly. She'd dreamed, hoped, wished that someday Kilraven might want to marry her. She'd never expected that it would be a sham marriage. But even a few days was more than she might have expected in the normal run of things. She had to take the chance that he might like her enough to stay with her.

Boone glanced at Kilraven, who was watching her with an impassive face. His silver eyes, however, were glittery with feeling. He could feel the man's anguish. Cash Grier had told him quite a bit more about the case than Winnie knew. He didn't have the heart to interfere, even if his gut instinct was to do just that. Anyway, if there was a threat, he knew how to deal with it. So did Kilraven. It wasn't right to let the men who'd killed a child walk.

"Keely and I can stand up with you, if you need witnesses," he said finally.

Winnie smiled at him. "Thanks. But first, he and I need to discuss the parameters of our new relationship," she told Kilraven bluntly.

He grinned. "Okay. We'll drive up to San Antonio and I'll show you how to get past the Hunters in *Halo: ODST*."

"Nobody can get past those damned Hunters," Boone scoffed.

"I can," Kilraven said, grinning.

"You'd better teach me," Boone told Winnie, smiling.

She laughed. "That's a deal. I'll just get my coat." She couldn't believe it. For the first time in her adult life, she'd told Boone what she was going to do. She'd actually gotten away with it. Maybe all it took was enough courage to say no. Even if your knees knocked together and your teeth chattered while you said it!

CHAPTER EIGHT

WINNIE AND KILRAVEN were almost to San Antonio when he got a call on his cell phone. He activated the phone from the steering wheel, putting it on the speakerphone.

"Kilraven," he said.

"Marquez," came the reply. "Thought you might like to know that it's open season on detectives investigating your case."

"Somebody else got mugged?" Kilraven asked.

"Shot," Marquez said flatly. "My partner. They just took her to the Marshall Medical Center. I'm on my way there right now."

"I'll be right behind you." He shut off the phone and glanced at Winnie. "Sorry, but this concerns me. She's a friend of mine."

"Let's go!" she said, waving him on.

He floor-boarded the gas pedal.

Fortunately, he didn't have to stop and explain why he was breaking speed limits. He arrived at the hospital and parked as close to the emergency room as he could get. He and Winnie ran for the entrance.

Marquez was waiting in the hall, looking morose. He looked up when they entered.

"Any news?" Kilraven asked.

Marquez shook his head. "All they could tell me was

that it didn't look lethal," he said. He shrugged. "Like you can tell. I've seen so-called flesh wounds take a man out."

"So have I," Kilraven said quietly.

Marquez glanced at Winnie. "Hi."

"Hi," she returned.

"Do you know her?" Kilraven asked. When Marquez frowned, he said, "This is Winnie Sinclair."

"Oh!" Marquez exclaimed. "You work at the EOC center," he added, just when she thought he was going to come out with something about her family and its wealth.

Pleasantly surprised, she grinned. "That's me. I work with Shirley. And I have lunch at your mother's café most days. She's a great cook."

"She is." He started to add something, but the doctor came toward him, still in his surgical greens.

Marquez stepped forward. "Well?"

The doctor grinned. "She's a tough one," he said. "We got the bullet out. She came to and looked at me and said, 'You get me patched up quick, I'm going after the blankety-blank fool who did this to me!'"

Marquez chuckled. "That sounds just like her. She'll be okay?"

He nodded. "A few days in the hospital—she won't like that, either—and she'll be on sick leave for another couple of weeks." He cocked his head at Marquez. "Any chance the two of you could give up ticking off criminals in my city? I could use some rest!"

"Complaints, complaints, when we give you the opportunity to practice your craft and perfect it," Marquez taunted.

The physician chuckled. "So you do."

"When can I see her?"

"In about an hour. They'll wheel her down to a room. She breezed through the surgery." He shook his head. "Wish all my patients did half that well."

He walked away.

"We'll wait with you," Kilraven told him, glancing at Winnie to make sure she agreed, which she did. "I feel responsible."

"What for? It was my idea, and hers, to reopen the case. You were the holdout," Marquez reminded him.

Kilraven still felt guilty. She was a good woman. A good investigator. She'd been helping him. He hadn't realized what she was risking until now. And he wanted to put Winnie in the line of fire. What if she got shot? What if the perp had a better aim next time? He felt sick to his stomach.

A noise behind them heralded the entrance of two uniformed officers and another plainclothes detective, who went straight to Marquez to find out the patient's condition. They relaxed when told that she was out of surgery and had a good prognosis.

"That's like Rogers," one of the policemen chuckled. "She's tough as army leather!"

"You ought to know," Marquez joked back, "she was your training officer before she was bumped up to homicide."

"Bumped up, the devil," the plainclothes detective muttered. "You patrol guys get to take coffee breaks and sleep all night. We get dragged out of bed every time they find a body, even if we're not on duty."

"Always on call, that's us." Marquez chuckled.

The detective glanced at Kilraven and frowned. "Don't I know you?"

"Ought to," Kilraven said, stepping forward with his hand out. "You trained me back when I worked for SAPD."

"Kilraven? Damn, you've got old!" the man joked.

"Fine wine ages," Kilraven said haughtily, "it doesn't get old."

"What are you doing up here? You know Rogers?"

Winnie listened idly, not participating in the conversation. Her mother's maiden name was Rogers. What a strange coincidence. But it was a common enough name. Anyway, she was sure it wouldn't be a relation of hers. Her mother had no relatives in Texas. They were all in Montana, and only cousins.

"Marquez called me on his way to the hospital. Rogers has been working my cold case with him," Kilraven said. "Stubborn woman. Knowing what happened to Marquez here just made her dig her heels in harder. She's a good detective."

The detective sobered at once. "Damned shame about that case. I wasn't on homicide then, I was just a patrol officer, like you. But at least one detective quit the force because he couldn't continue on the case. He said it broke his heart."

"It broke mine, too," Kilraven said heavily.

The detective clapped him on the shoulder. "Even the coldest cases get solved. You wait. When Rogers gets out of here, she'll turn San Antonio red looking for clues. They'll wish they'd sent a better shot."

"They won't get a second chance at her, or me," Marquez said solemnly. "I promise you."

"He's good at his job," the suited man told Kilraven, "but he chases crooks in the nude." He shook his head as Marquez started to protest. "Brings down the tone of the whole department."

"The perp stole my laptop right out of my own apartment!" Marquez protested. "What was I supposed to do, get dressed before I started chasing him?"

"You could have called for backup, Marquez," came the droll reply.

"I could have, if I hadn't left my cell phone in my car!"

"See?" the detective told Kilraven. "Back in our day, we'd have called on a landline. I don't guess you've got one of those, do you, boy?" he asked Marquez blithely.

Marquez glared at him. "Who needs a landline? It's like carrying a telephone booth around!"

"You need a landline to save L.E.O.'s butts," Winnie piped in when the local law looked her way, surprised. She was using the term for law enforcement officers. "I work at our county's emergency operations center. I'm a 911 dispatcher."

"Nice work, Kilraven," the plainclothes detective said admiringly as he grinned at Winnie. "If you need saving, here she is."

Kilraven chuckled. "She did save me," he said. "Sent backup before I asked for it, and spared me a face full of buckshot from a drunken perp."

"Good woman," the detective said, nodding.

"Oh, he's worth the effort," Winnie joked, smiling at Kilraven. "We hate losing him down in Jacobsville."

"Losing him?" the detective asked, surprised. "You working small towns these days?"

Kilraven shook his head. "I was involved in some undercover work, breaking up a kidnapping ring."

"I heard about that. General Machado was up to his ears in it, wasn't he?" Marquez asked.

Kilraven chuckled. "He was. Last we heard he took the ransom he got for Jason Pendleton and went back to South America to retake his country."

"More power to him," the detective said somberly. "There are some barbarians heading up the junta who ousted him. My niece married a professor from over there. He's one of the people Machado's opposition put in prison. She's hoping she can generate enough publicity to make them turn him loose, but no luck so far."

"How about some coffee?" Marquez asked. "I had to get out at 4:00 a.m. to investigate an attempted murder in the south side apartments. I'm about to go to sleep standing here."

"What's unusual about that?" the detective asked with a grin. He held up both hands. "Okay, I'll stop. In fact, I'll buy you a coffee, Marquez."

"No, Hicks, I'll buy you one," Marquez said, moving toward the canteen. "That way, it goes on my expense account!"

Kilraven led Winnie along, her small hand tucked into his big one, down the hall to the canteen. She was in her element among uniforms. The feel of his fingers linking into hers made her heart race. She looked up into warm silver eyes that smiled at her. She felt closer to him than she ever had.

IT WAS ALMOST two hours later when Marquez went to check on Detective Rogers and came back to announce that she was in a room and complaining about the doctor's assessment of her condition.

"We'd better get up there before she breaks out a window and tries to leave." Marquez chuckled.

"Will they let us all in?" Kilraven asked.

"Sure they will," Hicks drawled. "One of us can divert the nurses at the duty station while the rest of us sneak into Rogers's room."

"I have a better idea," Kilraven mused. "I'll flash my badge and tell them it's federal business."

"Just like a Fed, isn't it?" Hicks asked. "They always want to steal the show."

"Okay, flash your badge and tell them it's police business and see how far you get," Kilraven dared.

Hicks chuckled as they filed into the elevator. "The way my luck's been running, I'd get arrested for impersonating a detective. We'll do it your way."

KILRAVEN COULD LIE with a straight face and sound very sincere, Winnie thought with admiration. He got them past the nurses, although Winnie got odd looks from the staff as she followed behind the men.

She was curious about this detective, who was so brave and dogged about Kilraven's case that she was willing to risk her life to solve it. Her own life hadn't been overfull of women as role models, but this one sounded interesting. She was keen to meet her.

"There you are, all dolled up and looking pretty," Hicks told the woman in the bed.

"There you are, looking like a vulture dressed up in a suit," came the sarcastic reply. "Will you get me the hell out of here? I want to find the SOB who shot me!"

Winnie was behind the tall men and couldn't see the

woman, but she was surprised at how familiar her voice sounded.

Then she moved around Kilraven and got the shock of her life. There, in the bed, bandaged and bruised and indignant, was her mother!

Detective Rogers didn't see Winnie, and she was furious that a little flesh wound was keeping her off the job.

"He says I can't come back to work until he certifies me fit for duty!" she raged, alluding to the doctor. "Meanwhile, that slimy lowlife who shot me is all over San Antonio bragging about it to his lowlife friends!"

"I was in the same boat and you weren't overflowing with sympathy for me," Marquez pointed out.

"You got manhandled, Marquez. I got shot!" she flung back. She took a deep breath and ran a hand through her unkempt hair. "I can't stay in here! I have to get home…"

"You get right back in that bed," Marquez said with authority, and moved closer to force her if he had to. "You're probably still in shock. You're certainly foggy from the anesthetic."

"He's home by himself," she said miserably. "The sitter will have to go to work. Good Lord, what time is it?"

"Eight," Marquez said.

"She'll leave in half an hour. He can't stay by himself!"

"Who can't?" Kilraven asked, moving forward, curious. "Your boyfriend?"

"My son," she said heavily. "Matt."

Her son? Winnie felt her head spinning. Her mother was a police detective and she had a son. Her uncle's son. None of the family had known. She recalled the passenger in her mother's car at the house, a short man. It had been the boy!

She moved into view. Her mother glanced at her and glowered. "Great. Just what I need to make this day perfect."

Winnie didn't know what to say. She was shocked speechless.

Kilraven didn't connect the odd phrase with Winnie, so he ignored it. "I'll go by your apartment and arrange for someone to stay with him," Kilraven said, still unaware who Rogers was or Winnie's connection to her. "You just get well."

Rogers studied Winnie's pale face. "Why are you here?"

"I'm with him," Winnie said in a small voice, indicating Kilraven.

"Yes. We're getting married," Kilraven told her, curious at Rogers's response to his blonde companion.

Rogers's eyes widened. "You're marrying him?" she exclaimed. "Are you out of your mind?"

"Thanks a hell of a lot," Kilraven growled.

"You're not in any shape to be marrying anybody, least of all my daughter!" Rogers muttered.

Kilraven went very still. "Your daughter?" He glanced at Winnie. Slowly, he added up the similarity and odd bits of information. "Your daughter."

"Yes. I left her father twelve years ago."

"And married my uncle," Winnie said coldly.

"Briefly," Rogers replied with faint humor. "I divorced him six days later."

Winnie gaped at her.

Rogers shrugged. "He was so strung out on coke, he didn't know his name."

"Right up until the end," Kilraven agreed. "But I'm

still not sure he wasn't helped into the next world. He might have known something, too."

"Indeed. But that has to be looked into before we'll know for sure." Rogers regained her composure. "There's a Hispanic woman, Señora Del Rio, who lives two doors down from my apartment. She's Juana's grandmother. Juana's sitting with Matt today." She gave him the address. "Ask her if she'll keep Matt until I get out of here, and I'll make it right with her. Juana's got six kids," she added with a wan smile, "and they love Matt. He lets them play games on his old Nintendo. But she can't keep him at night. She works. The kids stay with her aunt."

Games. Kilraven's eyes lit up. "I'll find her. You stop worrying."

Rogers lay back on the pillows and grimaced. "I hate bullets."

"So do I," Kilraven said heavily. "I remember how much they hurt. Don't you do something stupid, like trying to escape from here. We'll just hunt you down and bring you back."

She made a face at him. "Okay."

"Can I talk to you for a minute?" Marquez asked Kilraven.

"Sure."

The uniformed officers said their goodbyes and filed out while Marquez and Kilraven were in the hall. Winnie moved closer to the bed to stare at her mother.

"You didn't say what you did for a living," she told her mother.

Rogers stared at her without smiling. She looked terrible, washed-out and pale and in pain. "You didn't need to know."

"You have a son," she began hesitantly. "Dad never told us…"

Rogers stared at her with icy brown eyes, the same shade as Winnie's. "My life is none of your business. I made a mistake and paid for it. I'm still paying for it. You don't need to stick around to rub it in. You made your opinion perfectly clear the last time I saw you."

Winnie hesitated. She'd been so sure of herself, of her righteous indignation. Now she felt oddly in the wrong.

"Do you need anything from your apartment?" Winnie asked politely.

"If I do, I'll ask one of the officers to get it for me."

It was a cold rebuff, but Winnie was too shocked to take offense. She was reeling from the revelations of the night.

Kilraven walked back in. "We'll get on the road. Need anything?"

Rogers shook her head. "Just to get out of here. I guess you don't take bribes?"

He raised an eyebrow. "What would you bribe me with?"

"I'm broke until payday, so you'll have to do it for affection." Rogers laughed. "Tell Matt to get me a couple pairs of pajamas, my robe and my slippers. I'll ask one of the boys to pick them up tomorrow."

"I'll bring them back tonight," Kilraven told her firmly. "But you owe me."

She made another face.

Kilraven caught Winnie's hand. "I'll be back later," he told the detective.

"They won't let you in," Rogers told him.

"I'm a Fed. They'll let me in."

"Snob," Rogers murmured, but the aftereffects of the anesthetic were catching up with her. She closed her eyes and nodded off. Winnie was still reeling from the news that she had a half brother that neither she nor her brothers knew about, and that her mother was in law enforcement. It was a shock.

THEY WERE HALFWAY to the apartment before Kilraven spoke. "You never told me she was your mother."

"I didn't make the connection," she said. "The last we heard, she was living with my uncle in Montana. Then she showed up at the house with the jewelry. I was horrible to her," she said quietly. "I didn't mean to be. I thought she came to see us to get money." She shook her head. "And she's a cop. I can't believe it."

"She's a detective," he corrected. "A damned good one, too."

She wasn't handling this well. She wasn't ready to have a new member of her family, and she hated being put in the position of having to deal with a child.

"I wonder how old he is?" she said aloud.

"Who?"

"My mother's son."

He glanced at her with narrow silver eyes. "Your brother," he corrected. "Jon and I don't share a mother, but that doesn't make us less related."

Her jaw tautened. "Yes, well, you've had your whole life to get used to having him around. I only found out about mine a few minutes ago."

He sighed. "Point taken. I guess it was a shock."

She shook her head. "Dad never said a word! He must

have known, especially if she's been living in San Antonio all this time!"

"Maybe it was too much for his pride to admit that his brother had a child with his ex-wife," Kilraven ventured.

"Her son was with her at the house," she said dully. "We saw someone in the car with her, but he didn't come in."

"She came to see me later that same day, I guess. I saw him, too, but I didn't make the connection that he was her child. I knew she'd been married and that she'd had some personal problems. Marquez didn't elaborate." He glanced at her. "I don't suppose he connected her with your family, either. Certainly, she never told us that she was related to anyone in Jacobsville."

Almost, she thought, as if her mother was ashamed to admit it. Perhaps she was. She'd said that she made a mistake that she was still paying for. Winnie had only thought of her own ordeal because of her mother's desertion, and Boone's and Clark's. It had never occurred to her that her mother wasn't happy, or that she might have divorced her new husband so quickly.

"How strongly was my uncle connected to your case?" she wondered aloud, remembering their talk about her uncle.

"I don't know. The thermos is a strong indication that he might be," Kilraven told her. "I just can't be certain how he would have fit into this, unless he had some connection with Hank Sanders, the senator's criminal brother." He glanced her way. "Given your uncle's apparent drug use, Hank might have been his supplier. Or he might have done odd jobs for Sanders. I don't know yet."

"It's a sick feeling, to think that a member of my family might be responsible for someone's death."

"Winnie, it doesn't mean that you're in any way responsible for it," he said gently. "Don't think like that."

She bit her lower lip. "Sorry. I'm just nervous." She watched cars whiz by in the other lane. Neon signs flashed past as they drove. "Her son is going to be scared to death when he finds out what happened to his mother."

"Obviously."

"But she'll have to stay in the hospital for several days, won't she? What if the woman can't take care of him?"

"Let's cross bridges when we get to them, okay?" He turned a corner. "If she's not available, I'll find someone who is. He can't be left alone."

"No. Of course he can't."

Kilraven drove slowly down the street, looking for the apartment number Rogers had given him. He stopped in front of a unit and cut off the engine.

It wasn't a good neighborhood. The apartments needed a paint job. The number signs on them were faded. It looked as if the shingles hadn't been replaced in recent memory. The street sign nearby had gang graffiti.

Winnie was taking all that in, thinking what a comedown it must have been for a woman who lived with a millionaire to find herself here, in this type of neighborhood.

"Let's go in," Kilraven said, opening his door.

They walked up on the concrete front porch, what little there was of it, and knocked on the door.

"¿Quién es?"

"Somos amigos de la señora que vive aquí," Kilraven replied in his elegant Spanish.

The door was opened, just a crack, by a dark-haired young Hispanic woman. Her black eyes surveyed the two people outside. She must have decided that they looked trustworthy, because she undid the chain latch and opened the door.

There were three children gathered around a small color television set, playing an old Xbox game. Two were Hispanic. The third had thick, dark brown hair and brown eyes, and an olive complexion. He was wearing jeans and a faded black T-shirt. He looked up.

"Hello," he greeted them, curious. "Did you come to see my mom? She's not home yet. Juana and her kids were staying with me, but she has to go to work soon."

Winnie was shocked at the boy's appearance. Her uncle had been almost blond, like her mother. The boy was the spitting image of Boone and Clark.

"Are you Matt?" Kilraven asked.

The boy seemed to sense something. He put the controller down and lifted his chin. "It's my mother, isn't it? Something's happened to her." He waited, stiff-lipped, for the reply.

"She's been shot, but she's all right," Kilraven said quickly.

"Shot?" The boy seemed to crumple for a minute, but then he rallied. He took a deep breath, as if to steady himself. "Shot. But she won't die?" he added quickly, hopefully.

Kilraven smiled. "Not a chance. She's one tough bird."

Matt caught his breath. He smiled back, hesitantly. He had perfect white teeth. That smile changed his whole look. "Okay." He glanced at the little woman next to him. "Juana has to go. She's already late for work and she has to take her kids to her aunt's house. It's all right," he told the little woman. "I can stay by myself. I'm twelve."

"You cannot," Juana argued.

"His mother said that a Señora del Rio who lives a couple of doors down might be able to stay with Matt," Kilraven began.

"But, no," Juana said at once. "That is my *abuela,* my grandmother. She went to see her sister this morning! Her sister is in Juarez!"

"I told you, I don't need babysitting," Matt argued. "I've stayed by myself after school, until Mom got home. I know not to answer the door unless I know who it is."

"You cannot be alone," Juana argued. "You are not able…"

"I am so!" Matt flashed back. "I'm perfectly all right!"

Juana looked at the newcomers with anguish.

"Everybody makes such a fuss," Matt muttered. He shifted on the sofa, dragging himself toward the arm.

That was when Winnie noticed the wheelchair. Matt pulled it toward him, placed it within reach and propelled his small body into it with efficiency. "I can do everything except walk," he muttered. "I can even cook. And there's a phone. I can call for help if I need to."

Winnie felt her pride drop to her ankles. The boy was proud, and he didn't like being thought of as handicapped. But he certainly couldn't stay by himself.

"I must go," Juana said. "I'm so sorry."

"We'll take care of Matt," Kilraven said easily. He smiled. "I'm sure his mother is grateful that you stayed so long."

"It was nothing. She sat with me when my husband was in the hospital. Here, in this neighborhood, we look out for each other. Tell her I pray for her, okay?"

"I'll do that," Kilraven said.

She and her children left, but not before Juana bent to hug Matt and assure him that his mother would be all right.

The door closed behind her.

"Who are you?" Matt asked his guests. "Law enforcement?"

"I am," Kilraven said. "She's a 911 dispatcher." He indicated Winnie.

"I'm going to be a detective when I grow up," Matt assured the tall man. "There's nothing I can't do, if I want to. Mom taught me that. She's really going to be all right?"

"Honest," Kilraven said. He glanced at the game console. "That's an old one."

"Yeah," Matt said, grinning, "but it still works pretty good. Mostly I play the original *Halo* and it's great for that one."

"You play online?"

Matt shook his head. "Can't afford that," he said easily. "Do you play?"

Kilraven grinned. "Everything," he said. "I've got three game systems and about three dozen gaming discs."

"Wow," Matt said. "It must be nice," he added with a wistful smile. He moved the wheelchair away from the sofa. "I had a nice motorized one that Mom bought for me last Christmas," he said, "but Dad came by and said he needed to borrow it for a friend of his. He just sold it to buy drugs," he added. "Was Mom furious! But she couldn't get him to replace it, so she borrowed this one from a neighbor whose father had used it before he died."

Winnie felt sicker by the minute. "Your father took the wheelchair away?" she asked, shocked.

"Yeah. He was always coming by and taking things, usually he didn't even ask. He sold anything he could get to buy drugs with." He shook his head. "I'm never using drugs. I don't ever want to end up like him."

"How did that happen?" Kilraven asked the boy, indicating his legs.

"Dad had this idea that he'd wreck the car so he could get insurance money," he replied. "He ran out in front of a semi and it hit on my side of the car. Mom said he had a big insurance policy on me and he meant to kill me." He avoided looking at them. "He didn't get a dime. Mom tried to have him arrested, but they wouldn't take my word for what he did."

Winnie was hearing her mother talk about paying for her past and now it made terrible sense. She couldn't believe her uncle would treat a child like that. But people on drugs weren't especially reasonable.

"You look like my mom," Matt said suddenly, staring at Winnie.

"I guess I should," Winnie said, smiling despite the lump in her throat. "I'm your sister."

CHAPTER NINE

MATT STUDIED HER with open curiosity. "We went to see you down in Jacobsville," he recalled. "Mom said I might get to meet you, but when she came back out, she was all quiet. She said it wasn't a good time."

Winnie could have gone through the floor. While she'd been shouting at her mother and cursing her for the past, this young, disabled boy had been hoping to meet his family. Nobody knew anything about him. She and her brothers hadn't even known that he existed. She felt her sins line up and laugh at her. She'd never felt quite so low.

"It wasn't a good time," Winnie said, swallowing her regret.

He cocked his head as he looked up at her. "Mom said I had brothers."

"You do. Two of them." Winnie pulled out her cell phone. "I think it's time you met them, too." She started punching in numbers.

WHILE THEY WAITED for Boone, Keely and Clark to show up, Kilraven sat down with Matt and played one of the games with him. Matt had a spare controller, a present from one of his mother's coworkers.

"Hey, you're pretty good." Matt laughed when Kilraven fought him to a draw.

"Sometimes my job takes me to places where there isn't much in the way of entertainment."

"What do you do?"

Kilraven grinned. "Sorry. Classified."

Matt was impressed. "Can you tell me who you work for?"

"Sure. CIA."

"Wow! You're a spy!"

"Not really," Kilraven said easily. "I do all sorts of covert jobs. Last one was trying to break a kidnapping ring."

"Did you have to shoot anybody?"

"I don't shoot people," Kilraven assured him.

"Then why do you carry a gun?" came the wry reply, because the holster of a small automatic handgun was visible under Kilraven's jacket when he used the controller.

"So people won't shoot me," the tall man replied with a grin.

Matt laughed and they went back to another round of the game.

Winnie watched, sitting on the wreck of a sofa. The whole place was no-frills. The pictures on the walls were cheap, like all the furnishings. The only expensive thing in the room was that used game console and the games for it. Her mother's priorities were obvious—Matt came first. It touched her and made her feel very guilty that she had anything she wanted while her half brother and her mother were living almost at subsistence level on a police detective's salary. It was a good-paying job, she knew from talking to Marquez; but anyone with a disabled child had more expenses than parents of healthy kids.

The knock at the door was surprising. Boone must have flown up from Jacobsville.

She went to open the door. She grinned at Boone. "What did you do, put a jet under that Jaguar?" she asked.

He chuckled. "Just about. I noticed Kilraven's car out front, too." He paused. "Where is the boy?"

She opened the door. Matt stopped playing in midjump and turned to look at his visitors with wide, surprised eyes.

"You look like me," he said when Boone moved into the room, dark-haired and dark-eyed, very imposing in his boots and white Stetson.

"I do," Boone said, surprised. He moved closer, his eyes on the wheelchair.

"Don't let the wheels fool you," Matt said easily, when he perceived the big man's reaction to the wheelchair. "I'm faster than you are."

"You like video games, huh?" Clark asked, moving forward. He smiled at Matt. "We haven't introduced ourselves. I'm Clark. That's Boone," he indicated the tall man. "That's Boone's wife, Keely." He introduced the smaller woman who was hugging Winnie. "We're Sinclairs."

"I guess I'm your brother," Matt said hesitantly.

"I guess you are," Boone replied. His glance around the room took in everything Winnie had already learned about their half brother.

"Why didn't you know about me?" Matt asked reasonably.

"Because we weren't on speaking terms with your mother," Winnie said for all of them. "Something I'm really sorry about now, Matt. We made assumptions."

"Yeah, because she ran off with your uncle," Matt replied, grimacing. "She said it was the stupidest thing she ever did. She knew what he was the day they got married, when he started shooting up on their honeymoon. She left him. Then your father came to see her, later, but I was on the way and he thought I was Dad's child."

The three older Sinclairs went very still.

"What do you mean?" Winnie asked for them.

"Well, see, she never slept with Dad," Matt said in a very grown-up way. "She said he was so repulsive to her that she couldn't let him touch her."

Which meant, obviously, that Matt was their father's child. Their true brother.

"Oh, boy," Clark said heavily. He was thinking, they all were, that their mother had gone through years of hell with a child alone, trying to support them, because of a mistaken belief.

"Here it comes," Matt told Kilraven with some sarcasm. "Now we'll get the hugs and the gushing about how I look like my real father and everybody will feel guilty. Give me a break!"

Boone burst out laughing. "Okay. Now I know he's a Sinclair."

Matt lifted an eyebrow. "Well, you don't look like the gushing type," he told Boone.

"He's not," Clark assured him. "He was in Special Forces in the army."

"Wow," Matt said admiringly. He glanced at Kilraven. "Does that mean he's better at hand-to-hand than you are?"

Kilraven gave Boone an apologetic grin. "No. I was part of a SWAT team at SAPD before I became a Fed. I'm also a master trainer in hand-to-hand combat."

"SWAT? Really? I watch these shows on TV about

SWAT teams all over the country. They're real brave," Matt said. He sighed. "I wish I could do stuff like that when I grow up, but I guess I'll be a desk guy. Anyway, I'm going to be in law enforcement, like my mom. Except I hope I don't get shot, like she did."

"Your mom got shot?" Boone asked, shocked.

Then Winnie realized that she hadn't said much when she told them about Matt and that they should come up to San Antonio on the double.

"Yes, but not lethally," she said quickly. "His mother—our mother," she corrected, "is a sergeant of detectives with SAPD," she said. "She works homicide. She was shot in the line of duty. She's in the hospital, but she's going to be okay."

Boone was surprised, as were the others.

"She's good, too," Matt said. "Sometimes she gets these hunches, feelings, about cases, and she can solve them when other detectives can't. They say she's spooky."

Winnie flushed because she had the same kind of hunches, and now she knew where the gift came from.

"Do you get them…feelings?" Boone asked him.

"Sometimes," Matt said. "I knew something was wrong tonight, but I didn't know what."

"He's going to be here alone," Winnie said. "Someone who doesn't want that cold case reopened—" she didn't name it in front of Matt "—is assaulting people on the case. Marquez got beaten up, our mother got shot. She'll be okay, but she's going to be in the hospital for a few days. Matt needs someplace to stay."

"He can come to the ranch," Boone said, glancing at Matt. "We've got plenty of horses. You can go riding with me."

"I can't ride," Matt exclaimed. "I mean, look at me!"

Boone smiled. "We have disabled kids out riding one day a week. It's therapy for them. We have the means to put you on and keep you on, safely, and the horses are very tame. Not that you'd go out unsupervised."

Matt rolled his wheelchair closer to Boone. "I would really like that," he said quietly. "I've never even seen a horse close up. Do you have cattle, too?"

"Sure do."

"I wouldn't be in the way?"

"Not at all," Keely assured him with a smile.

"You can play video games with me," Clark said. "I've got all the *Halo* series, including *Halo: ODST...*"

"The new *Halo?*" Matt exclaimed, all eyes. "Oh, I read about it in some of the gaming magazines Mom brought from the office after the guys finished with them. I'd love to play the new ones, but this won't play anything much except the old games. I don't mind," he said quickly, defending his mother. "Mom does her best for us."

The Sinclairs exchanged guilty glances.

"Yes, she does," Winnie said. "She's very brave, Matt. They had to force her back into the bed." She chuckled. "She was trying to climb out and go after whoever shot her."

Matt laughed. "Yeah. She's like that. Some guy down the street tried to take our new push lawnmower off the front porch last summer and Mom saw him. She chased him down, jumped a hedge to get to him quicker, threw him down, cuffed him and called for backup to take him down to booking." He laughed. "She's my role model. Not that I want to be a woman when I grow up," he was quick to add, and they all laughed.

"Let's get you packed, if you're coming with us," Keely said.

"Okay!" Matt said with enthusiasm. He wheeled into his bedroom, leaving her to follow.

The Sinclairs moved into a group, all morose-looking. "I wish I'd known any of this twelve years ago," Winnie said heavily.

"You aren't the only one," Boone agreed.

"We've been willfully blind." Clark sighed.

Kilraven joined them. "He's a great kid," he said. "I wish I'd realized the connection before this, but Rogers never spoke about her family. We only knew that she'd had a lot of personal problems. Her ex-husband hounded her, you see," he added, "always trying to get things from her to buy drugs with. He carried off Matt's new motorized wheelchair and sold it."

"What a bum," Winnie said angrily.

"We'll get Matt a new one," Boone said. "No problem."

"We can get him an Xbox 360, too, and some games for it," Kilraven said. He glanced at the tiny television. "And a bigger TV to play them on."

"Maybe an Xbox Live gold card, too," Clark suggested.

Kilraven was thoughtful. "He can stay with Winnie and me for a few days, after we're married," he said. "I have a three-bedroom apartment. We won't be able to go down to Nassau for a couple of weeks. The senator's wife had a change of heart and went to visit her sister in New York, but she's supposed to be going to the Bahamas week after next."

"You spies know everything," Clark said.

Kilraven grinned. "Of course we do."

Winnie moved closer to him. "We could wait to get married…."

"No, we couldn't," Kilraven said firmly, looking down at her.

She averted her eyes, but the reply pleased her. Maybe he was getting used to the idea, and just maybe he wouldn't want a divorce at the end of the pretense.

MATT WAS BUNDLED into Boone's big Jaguar, along with a ratty suitcase full of things he thought he'd need, and the apartment door was locked.

"We'll bring you up to the hospital tomorrow to see your mother," Boone assured Matt. "I want to see her, too."

The others voiced their assent.

"I'll bring Winnie home in a little while," Kilraven told them. "We still have things to talk about."

"We'll leave a light on," Keely said with a smile.

They waved the Sinclairs off and got back into Kilraven's own Jaguar.

"This has been a very strange night," Winnie said heavily. "I have a brother I didn't know about, and a mother who's a well-known police detective. I feel as if my life just turned on its axis."

"I can understand that." He moved out into traffic. "He's quite a boy," he said, smiling.

"Yes, he is. It's amazing, how easily he speaks of his handicap."

"It's only a handicap if he makes one of it. I had a friend in Iraq who had lost both his legs to a rocket attack. He was fitted with artificial ones and he wins races now. He said that as long as he still had his life, he wasn't bothered by trifles. Trifles!" He laughed. "Can you imagine?"

"Soldiers are tough," Winnie said. "Boone came out of the service with wounds much worse than he ever told us about. Keely said some of them were bone-deep. He never said anything, and we never knew."

"We all have scars of one sort or another."

She glanced at him. "You said you'd had bullets dug out of you."

"I have." His tone was grim. "One out of my lung, another out of my hip and one out of my arm. When I'm older, I'll probably have some arthritis because of the way the bullet went in. They did repairs, but no repair is as good as the original part."

"Battle scars," she said quietly.

"Yes."

Her eyes narrowed. She looked at him evenly. "You wanted the most dangerous assignments you could find," she said aloud, speaking as if she were accessing information from some intangible source. "You asked for them. One took you right into an enemy encampment and you walked straight at a man firing a machine gun…!" She broke off because he slammed on the brakes. Thank goodness they weren't in traffic.

"Who told you?" he asked curtly. "Who?"

She was disconcerted. "Nobody," she said at once.

His eyes narrowed. He wasn't buying it.

"I don't know anyone who was with you overseas, Kilraven," she said reasonably.

"Then how did you know that?"

She grimaced and looked away. "I don't know."

He was remembering what they said about her mother's intuition, and then came the memory of Winnie painting the raven and sending backup when he was in great danger in Jacobsville.

"You have the same ability your mother does," he said aloud.

She grimaced. "I guess so. I didn't know where it came from. Not until tonight." She glanced at him apologetically. "It's freaky, huh?"

He sighed and started the Jaguar forward again. "Not so much. It just takes a little getting used to."

"And you don't like talking about personal things."

"No," he replied at once. "I don't." He glanced at her. "But I've told you more than I've ever told anyone else, except Jon, about my private life. So I guess I trust you."

She smiled. "Thanks."

He pulled into the parking lot at his apartment building and led her inside, where a security guard kept watch from a desk.

He walked to the desk. "Kilraven," he said. "Apartment 5A. I brought a woman here for illicit purposes...." He indicated Winnie, who gasped and flushed and started protesting.

"It's okay, ma'am," the security guy chuckled. "He says the same thing when he brings other male agents home with him. We're used to it."

Winnie burst out laughing and slapped Kilraven on a big, muscular arm. "You beast," she muttered.

"Actually, we're getting engaged," Kilraven told the security guy with a grin. "You can see why. She's a trouper. She's a 911 operator in Jacobsville."

"I'm impressed," the security guy said. "My sister is

one for San Antonio EOC. Tough job. You have to love it to do it."

"Isn't that the truth," Winnie agreed.

"We won't be here long," Kilraven said. "I just need enough time to convince her that I'm a good prospect. She's reluctant."

"Well, if you didn't go off on secretive missions, shooting people and coming home with wounds, I might try to help you convince her. She probably thinks she'll be a widow in a few months," the guy replied.

"You shut up, or I'll tell everybody who comes in here that you wear women's lingerie under your uniform."

"You wouldn't dare," the security guy said indignantly.

"Just try me."

The security guard gave him an international signal with one hand.

"Yeah, and the horse you rode in on." Kilraven chuckled.

They went into the elevator and up, silently. Kilraven opened his apartment with two keys and invited her inside.

It was amazingly elegant and neat for a man's living space. There were original paintings on the wall and the furniture was good quality leather, white and spotless. The television was state-of-the-art. Several gaming consoles were connected to it. The carpet was beige, and the curtains were earth-toned.

"You said you didn't watch television," she accused.

He chuckled. "I don't. But I have two, one here and one at the rental house in Jacobsville, to play games on." He looked around. "How do you like the apartment?"

"It's very nice," she said, surprised.

"Did you think I lived in a cave?" he asked.

She grinned. "It wouldn't have shocked me."

"Well, this is my cave, and you'll notice that I can pick up after myself."

"I did notice that. Good job."

"Don't be condescending or I won't marry you," he assured her. "Coffee?"

"I'd love some."

"Come on."

He led her into a spacious kitchen with built-in appliances. There was a microwave, and sitting next to it, a huge coffeepot.

"I drink a lot of it," he explained as he made coffee. "Most nights, I don't sleep."

She could see why, but she wasn't keen to bring up his past. "It's a nice kitchen."

"Spacious," he agreed. "And bright. I don't use half the gourmet appliances I've got, but my brother comes over once in a while and cooks something for us. He's a gourmet chef, very accomplished."

"I heard that."

He put out mugs and sat down at the kitchen table with her. "You've got a brother you didn't even know about."

"It came as a shock. Like my mother's profession. I've spent years hating her for what Dad did to me," she said heavily. "He hated her. I guess he thought the child was my uncle's and he couldn't forgive her for it. I'm sure she tried to tell him that Matt was his. Obviously, he didn't believe her. My father was a proud man, but inflexible. He didn't forgive people. Boone's a lot like him, but less judgmental."

"I like your brothers."

"Me, too."

The coffee was ready. He poured it, black, into two mugs and handed her one as he sat back down. "Down to business. We can get married by a probate judge here or in Jacobsville. Where do you want to do it?"

"Jacobsville," she said without thinking about it.

"No frills," he added firmly. "It's a temporary marriage."

She nodded. "Got you."

"And no roomful of witnesses. Just Boone and Keely. I might have asked Jon, but he's going to be out of town."

"Okay."

He scowled. "You're taking this very calmly for a woman who wanted to beat me up a few days ago when I suggested it."

"I changed my mind," she replied.

He sipped coffee. "I won't change mine, Winnie," he said suddenly. "If you're thinking I'll be reluctant to end the marriage when this case is closed, don't. I meant it when I said I didn't want to remarry or have a child."

"I know all that."

He drew in a long breath, and suddenly he looked older, worn. "Rogers got shot working this case. Marquez got assaulted. A man who wanted to tell me about it was murdered and left unrecognizable." He glanced at her worriedly. "I'm not sure it's a good idea to involve you at all. Maybe Boone was right. I could be putting you in the line of fire."

That was flattering, that he was worried for her. "You also told Boone that there was no man around who could protect me better than you could."

"Well, that's true."

"Of course it is. And it's not like I'm going to be walking into a machine gun," she added wryly. "I'm just going to help you get in touch with the senator's wife."

He sipped coffee again, thinking. "She's the only hope we have of getting any inside information. The junior senator has already tried to stop the investigation. If it wasn't for Senator Fowler's help, we'd already have been forced to give it up. But I'm still not sure we won't face more roadblocks. If the junior senator's brother is involved in these murders, he'll probably go the limit to try and save him. It's just human nature," he added solemnly. "I'd do anything to protect Jon, although he'll never need it. He's as honest as any man I know."

"So are you," Winnie said.

He smiled. "Thanks."

"Why did you offer to let Matt stay with us?" she wondered.

He gave her a sardonic look. "Birth control."

She flushed.

He chuckled. "Nothing gets by that young man. He'll keep us honest. Besides," he added, "he's great at video games."

"So am I," she pointed out.

"Suppose you prove it?" he challenged with a grin.

He turned on the television and his game console and loaded the newest *Halo* game. They sat down and took up twin wireless controllers, and the game began.

But, as always, the dire Hunters started taking Winnie out the minute she encountered them. Kilraven gave her a sympathetic look and proceeded to take down the Hunters as if they were the humorous little grunts in the game instead of the sturdiest villains.

"How do you do that?" she exclaimed, breathless.

"It's not that hard. Watch." And he proceeded to show her his tricks.

Two hours later, they were still playing, except now Winnie wasn't getting blown away by the Hunters every few steps.

She glanced at the clock and gasped. "It's two o'clock!"

"Aww, and the coach turned back into a pumpkin, didn't it?" he sympathized, blasting his way through a barricade.

"You don't understand, I have to be at work at eight!"

He blinked. He looked at her. "Eight?"

She nodded.

He sighed and turned off the console. "Bummer."

She chuckled. "It is, but I have to go."

He put the controller down. Then he turned her into his arms and looked down at her with quiet, piercing silver eyes while her heart hammered up into her throat.

"Pretty and brave and plays video games," he murmured. His eyes dropped to her mouth. "And tastes delicious…"

He bent and kissed her. It wasn't like any way he'd kissed her before. It was soft, tender, teasing. And then, quite suddenly, it was fierce and hungry and demanding. He wrapped her up in his big arms, riveted her to his hard body that grew harder by the instant. He groaned, his mouth insistent as it pressed her lips apart.

Seconds later, she was stretched out on the leather couch with Kilraven's body over hers. One long leg was in between both of hers and his hands were all the way under her blouse and bra, bent on exploration.

She would have protested. She just couldn't get her

mouth away from his long enough. Then he had her bare to the waist and he was poised over her, looking down at small, firm, pretty pink breasts with hard little dusky tips, and the expression on his face stopped the words in her throat.

He touched her as carefully as he'd have touched a butterfly's wings. "My God," he whispered, and the words sounded reverent.

She was breathless. She watched him, watching her, and her eyes were dark and soft.

He traced around a hard nipple, propped on one elbow, fighting for control. "I wondered what you'd look like," he whispered deeply. His silver eyes glittered as he studied her with soft appreciation.

"I'm...small," she managed.

He laughed. "I like small." He bent and brushed his lips very softly over the warm flesh, drawing a shocked gasp from her. He lifted his head and searched her eyes. "You haven't done this before," he said, surprised.

"I told you I didn't believe in that sort of thing," she managed.

"Yes, but most women indulge in petting at some point."

She swallowed. "I've been rushed, grabbed, lunged at..." She searched his eyes. "You make it feel..."

"Dirty?" he asked shortly.

She remembered what she'd said to him, at the roadside park, and she winced. "I didn't mean that," she said. "I was scared."

"Of me?" he asked, shocked.

"You're a steamroller, Kilraven," she told him. "You walk right over people. I was afraid you'd rush me into something I wasn't ready for, and I fought the only way I knew how. It's not dirty when you touch me," she whispered. She managed a self-conscious smile. "I like it."

He raised an eyebrow. "You do?"

She nodded. "I might point out that I am lying here naked," she began.

"No, no," he said, "naked is when you have all your clothes off." He grinned. "Shall I demonstrate that?" he asked with gleaming eyes.

She slapped his hands when they went to her slacks, but she was laughing. "Don't you do it!"

"Spoilsport." He sighed. "Okay, I'll do my best to exercise some restraint." While he was saying that, he was stripping off his shirt.

Winnie's breath caught at the wide, thick wedge of curling black hair that covered him to his belt buckle, and probably beyond.

He pursed his lips. "Impressed?"

"Oh, yes," she said, far and away gone from hope of subterfuge.

"And I will tell you, it feels as good as it looks," he murmured, easing down over her, so that she got the full impact of the soft, curling hair as it tickled her breasts before it settled down on them. He nudged her legs apart. "No, no, you mustn't discourage me, you'll hurt my feelings," he chided as he bent to her mouth. "You wouldn't want to make a grown man cry...?"

She couldn't have answered him if she'd wanted to. He was immediately passionate. He never seemed to lead up to it. He didn't need to. The impact of his sexuality was so intense that it just blew away all her defenses at once. She arched up into his hard body and slid her arms around him, her nails digging into his muscular back as he kissed her, as if he never meant to stop.

At the same time, she felt his hips shift. There was a hardness where their bodies met, and the feverish motion of his hips brought a surge of pleasure so unexpected and intense that she cried out, gasping.

He felt that explosion of breath against his mouth and lifted it. She was shivering. Her eyes were wide. He looked into them, seeing her innocence, her shock, her enjoyment as he moved sensually against her.

"Feel it?" he whispered.

She gasped. Of all the outrageous things to ask…!

"Now, think how it would feel, pushing slowly down into your body," he whispered at her lips, "into that warm, moist darkness, hard and deep!"

"Kilraven!" she gasped at the outrageous comment.

He laughed. But the need was growing by the second. His hips curled down into hers, hard, emphasizing how capable he was. He groaned softly and shivered. "There's a big soft bed just a few feet down the hall."

She groaned, too, but her hands were pushing, not pulling. "No," she managed in a husky little voice. Her face was flaming, and not only from the intimate position. She hadn't dreamed that men would say such blatant things to women! "I'm not on the Pill!"

That stopped him dead. His mind wasn't working. It was enslaved to the throbbing hunger in his lower extremities. He dragged in a harsh breath, and then another. He didn't have anything, either. He didn't carry around prophylactics because he never slept with women. She could get pregnant. Just for an instant, he thought about a baby in her arms and his whole soul felt grief like a lance. No! Never again!

He dragged himself up into a sitting position, his head in his hands as he fought down the nausea and pain. He'd almost let it go too far. He didn't dare look at her. She was even more perfect than he'd imagined, under her clothes.

She hurried back into her things, swallowing down her embarrassment. But she realized, belatedly, that he was still struggling to regain his composure. It made her feel better about the loss of her own. She sat back down beside him, a little uneasy.

He lifted his head and met her wide, worried eyes.

"I know. I'm a bad man. Luring you in here with video games, seducing you with promises of cheats and victory codes..." He chuckled when she hit him playfully.

"Seducing women with video game cheats," she accused, relieved that he wasn't mad. "You villain."

"Hey, whatever works," he teased.

"Take me home, so I can get enough sleep to do my job." She chuckled, getting up.

She got her purse and waited until he turned off the television and the lights and opened the door.

"It amazes me," he said.

"What?" she asked.

"How very innocent you are," he remarked quietly, staring straight into her dark eyes.

She colored prettily. "I'm getting less innocent by the day," she said tautly.

He grinned. "Didn't know men said such blatant things to women?"

She colored even more. "Kilraven!"

He laughed. "I shouldn't tease you. I can't help it. You

fascinate me," he said involuntarily. He caught her hair at her nape and drew her face up to his. "Pretty little breasts," he whispered, and brought his mouth down on hers, hard, before she could protest. "We'd better go."

They were on the way to the car. He studied her admiringly. "You're richer than sin, your whole family is, but you work at a minimum-wage job."

"The work ethic was pounded into us at an early age," she said simply. "Boone works on the ranch with his men."

"I know. I read the magazine article in *Modern Ranching World*." He chuckled. "In fact, there's a copy of it on my coffee table. Your brother is unique. So is Clark, in his way."

"Clark is always trying to be Boone, and knowing that he never will be," she said sadly. "I think it must be terrible, to be the younger sibling of an overachiever."

"Don't tell my brother that. He'd never understand."

She laughed. "Your brother is like you, an overachiever with an abundance of intelligence and courage. He could never feel like a second son."

"No, he doesn't," Kilraven agreed, warmed by her opinion of him. "He's excelled in his chosen profession."

"So have you."

He shrugged. "I had reasons for overachieving, though."

"Yes, I know you did," she said with sympathy. She stopped at the Jaguar and turned to face him. "You'll break the case," she said. "I'm sure of it."

He touched her cheek gently. "Blind trust or some secret knowledge of the future?" he teased.

"I don't know. Both, maybe."

He sighed. "Maybe. We'd better go."

He drove her down to the big Sinclair mansion in Comanche Wells and let her out at the front door.

"I won't come in," he said from behind the wheel. "It's too late."

She noted the lights still on in Clark's room. "I guess they'll be up all night playing video games," she said enviously. "Clark has the new *Halo*, too. So does Boone."

"You can tell Boone how to get past the Hunters," he chuckled.

"And I will. See you."

"Tomorrow," he said. "I'll drive you and Matt up to see your mother. What time do you get off?"

"Four, tomorrow," she said. "It's usually a longer shift, but one of the girls wanted to be home when school's out for a teacher workday, so she's doing the night shift for me."

"Nice."

She grinned. "Very."

"I'll see you at four. We never did set a date for the wedding," he added. "How about Friday?"

Her heart jumped. She was thinking of all the arrangements and invitations and a gown and flowers. Just as quickly, she remembered that she wasn't going to have any of those traditional things. Not for a sham wedding. A temporary affair.

She managed a smile anyway. "Okay. Friday it is."

"See you tomorrow."

"See you."

He didn't move. He waited. She realized that he wasn't leaving until she was inside. It was flattering. She went into the house and closed the door. Only then did she hear the car drive away.

On her way to bed, she went through a dark house. The only room alive in it was Clark's. She poked her head in the door. Matt was sitting in front of the game console, in his chair, while Clark perched on a beanbag chair beside him. They were whacking grunts in *Halo*.

"Having fun?" she asked.

The two males grinned at her, looking so much alike they could have been twins.

"Never mind. Watch out for sticky grenades," she advised.

"We've been sticking them on Hunters," Matt told her.

"Does it work?" she asked, never having tried it.

"Watch," Matt said. His avatar tossed one at the huge Hunter. The next minute, the fearsome creature was on the ground.

"Excellent," Winnie said, giving him a thumbs-up. "I'll have to try that. Kilraven's coming up to take us to see Mom tomorrow just after I get off work at four," she told him.

"Your brother… I mean, Boone, called to check on her. They said she's sleeping and doing well," Matt replied.

"Good. Sleep well."

"Eventually," Clark promised.

She shook her head and went to bed.

CHAPTER TEN

WINNIE HAD A boring day at work. It was the norm to have a few days of routine calls and then one that taxed personnel to their very limits. On a difficult shift, there could be terrible wrecks, attempted robberies, suicides and futile foot chases after suspects that ended in frustration. There could be officers injured. There could be suspects who resisted arrest. There could be drunks with guns daring police to evict them from an abused wife's house. There could even be dog attacks or wild animal attacks. But this day was uneventful, except for a chase after a stolen car that finally resulted in an arrest.

"Guess who made the collar?" Winnie asked Kilraven when she and Matt were in the Jaguar with him, headed for the hospital in San Antonio.

"I'll bite," Kilraven said.

"Macreedy," she replied.

He gaped at her. "Him?"

"Him," she said. She glanced at Matt in the backseat, who was frowning, curious. "He's a deputy with the sheriff's department. He's famous for losing funeral processions in inaccessible places. He has no sense of direction. So when he does something like this, we're all surprised."

Matt grinned. "I get it."

"Maybe Carson Hayes was right, and all he needed was a little self-confidence," Kilraven said.

"Maybe so." Winnie laughed.

THE HOSPITAL WAS CROWDED. Kilraven maneuvered Matt's wheelchair through the crowds with Winnie following close behind as they made their way to Detective Gail Rogers's room.

"Mom!" Matt exclaimed, reaching up.

She laughed and leaned over, grimacing at the painful effort to hug him. "You're okay, then?" she asked, fighting tears.

"Of course I'm okay," he scoffed. He sat back down and grinned at her. "You look pretty good," he said. He was fighting tears, too, although he tried to hide it.

"I just got shot," she said. "No big deal."

"Right," Matt drawled.

Rogers looked past him at Winnie and Kilraven. "I think I may have missed something. The nurses said he went home with the Sinclairs. How did he end up at the ranch?"

"We knew who his father was the minute we saw him," Winnie said quietly. "I would try to apologize, but I don't know where to start. Boone and Clark feel the same way."

Gail lay back on her pillows and looked at her daughter with quiet pride. "I never tried to explain," she said after a minute. "Your father was furious when he knew I was pregnant. I tried to tell him the child was his, but I couldn't get him to listen. Finally, I just quit trying. I knew it was no use to try and contact any of you kids. He would have stopped any attempt and he'd have made you pay for it. I had Matt and got on with my life. He's been a joy," she said, glancing at her youngest child with a smile.

"That's in between being a holy terror." Matt laughed. "That's what she calls me."

"He likes to take the chair for rides down hills," she

said, making a face at him. "See these gray hairs," she asked him, pointing at the top of her head. "You gave them all to me."

"I like going fast," Matt protested. "Not that I get much speed in this old thing," he muttered. "I'm not complaining," he added quickly. "It helps build up my arm strength."

"We've got a motorized one ordered," Winnie said, surprising everyone in the room. She smiled. "Boone had them do a one-day ship. We'll have it tomorrow."

"Well!" Gail exclaimed.

"You can't argue," Winnie added firmly. "You know how the Sinclairs are when they get the bit between their teeth. Boone and Clark want to see you," she said then. "But they won't come until you say it's okay."

She bit her lower lip. She was hesitant, and Winnie understood why. She moved closer to the bed. "We've all had a rough time," she said slowly. "It isn't going to be easy, trying to put our family back together. But we all want to. Especially me."

Gail took in a long breath. "We can try."

Winnie smiled. It was a genuine smile. "Yes. We can."

"When do I get to come and stay with you?" Matt asked Kilraven. "Not that I don't like the ranch, I like it a lot," Matt said. "But he works for the CIA," he said in a loud whisper. "Maybe he can use his influence to get them to hire me when I get out of college."

Kilraven laughed. "Maybe I can. If I still have any by then."

"I'll bet you've got all sorts of top secret gadgets, too, don't you?" he persisted.

"A few," Kilraven admitted. "But some of them are classified."

"Darn."

"You can see the ones that aren't."

"When?"

Kilraven glanced at Winnie. "We're getting married Friday."

"Wow! Will it be in a church with a minister and everything? Can I come?"

"It will be in a judge's office," Winnie said calmly. She smiled. "Of course you can come."

"Oh." Matt seemed very disappointed.

Kilraven felt uncomfortable. "I want coffee."

"I want hot chocolate," Matt said. "Can we go get some and bring it back here?"

"I guess so. You want something?" he asked the women.

"Coffee would be nice," Winnie said.

Gail shook her head. "They'll never let you give me caffeine. I know. I tried to bribe one of the nurses to bring the pot in here. Vicious girl," she muttered. "Made all sorts of threats. If I just had my service weapon…!"

"Now, now, no shooting up hospitals," Kilraven chided. "What would people think of the department if Marquez had to bail you out of jail, and you in a hospital gown?"

Gail glowered at him. "I hate hospitals."

"Yes, well, they save a lot of lives," Kilraven reminded her.

"So they do."

"We won't be long," Kilraven said. He pushed Matt ahead of him out of the room.

Winnie stared at her mother with wide, soft eyes. She

was trying to reconcile the memories of twelve years ago with the woman in the hospital bed.

"You've changed," Winnie said finally.

"Yeah," her mother said with a chuckle. "I've gotten older and meaner."

"I meant, you…" She bit her lip. "It's hard to put into words. I remember you always waiting on Daddy, bringing him things that he could have gotten for himself. He wouldn't even make himself a sandwich. You were always jumping up, every time he called. You aren't docile like that anymore. You're like, well, you're like the people I work with in Jacobs County," she said with a faint smile. "They're hard people, because they do a hard job. But they're always there when you need them. They never let you down. That's what I mean."

"I let you down, though, didn't I, baby?" she asked sadly. "I was such a wimp, Winnie. I let your father walk all over me, from the day I was sixteen and we got married. I was raised thinking that's what women are supposed to do." She smiled. "Your uncle Bruce was a high roller. He was flamboyant and full of dreams, funny and fun to be with. I'd never met anybody like him. He came to see your father twelve years ago and made a dead set at me. I'd been dominated and ignored and taken for granted for so many years…" She broke off. "I didn't know he hated your father and wanted to score off him. I didn't know that's why he'd kept his distance from us, except for Christmas cards once a year. I fell, and fell hard. So we ran away together." She shook her head. "We went to Vegas and I got a divorce, then we got a quickie wedding and went to the Bahamas. That was when I knew why he was always so hyper. He was a drug user. He shot up in the room, and wanted me to join him." She lay back on the pillows, agonizing over the memories. "I used my ticket and came back to the States. I wouldn't sleep with him. He came to see me and confessed that he'd only wanted me because he hated your father for, as he said, cheating him out of the ranch. It didn't happen that way, but that's another story."

"You never slept with him?" Matt had told her as much, but she needed to hear it from her.

She shook her head. "I found him repulsive when I saw him using drugs. I could never do that. You know, I never even had a parking ticket my whole life. My grandfather was a U.S. Marshal."

"Wow," Winnie said, impressed. "That would be my great-grandfather."

Gail nodded. "He was quite a guy. I used to have clippings of some of his exploits, but I wouldn't know where to look for them, after all this time. I imagine your father threw all my things out."

"Actually, he didn't get the chance to," Winnie told her. "You remember old George, who drives the cattle trucks for us?"

"Yes."

"Daddy put the stuff out and told him to carry it off, but George hid it in the attic while Daddy was gone hunting."

Gail was surprised. "And you didn't throw it out, Winnie? You had good reason to."

"I didn't think about it," Winnie confessed. "I was just ten years old. George said we had to keep it, and he was a grown-up, so I kept the secret." She smiled. "I hadn't thought about it in years! All those things, even your trunk, they're still up in the attic." She hesitated. "You might like to come down and look at them sometime."

Gail smiled hesitantly. "I might."

"What happened after you got home from the Bahamas?" Winnie asked.

"I had no money, your father had cut off my credit card and emptied our joint bank account," she said with a sigh. "I had a little savings account that he couldn't touch, just a few thousand dollars, but it was enough to get me an apartment and some clothes to wear. I didn't know how I was going to make a living, but I thought about Granddaddy, and I knew I might have a future in law enforcement. I was athletic and healthy and strong for my height, and I looked younger than I really was. So I applied, and they accepted me. I did the police academy thing, graduated with honors, and got a job with the San Antonio Police Department. Last year, I got promoted to homicide detective sergeant. It's the best job I've ever had. I love it."

"I worked as a clerk for the Jacobsville Police Department for a while, before I got the job as a 911 operator," Winnie told her. "I figured I was too soft to be a cop."

Gail laughed. "So did I. But I seemed to fit right in."

"Our uncle… He lived in San Antonio, didn't he?"

"Oh, yes, he did," she said heavily. "He was a pest, always needing money, wanting loans, wanting me to go back to your father and make it all up to him so that he could get forgiven and back in your father's good graces." She shook her head. "All those dreams he had, but the drugs got in the way of anything he tried to do. In the end, they killed him. But not before he'd done permanent damage to Matt."

"Matt told us about that," Winnie said coldly. "I couldn't believe a man would be so coldhearted as to do that to his own nephew."

"He could do that, and more," she said. "He got mixed up with Senator Sanders's hoodlum brother," she added. "I thought he was just a 'gofer,' just an extra hand for the local bad guys. But he might have had his hand in more than that. I didn't want anything to do with him, but especially after he crippled Matt and almost killed him. I swear to God, if I could have proved it, I'd have had him sent to prison for life for attempted murder. But it was only Matt's word against his." She shook her head. "He always could talk his way out of anything." She lay back on the pillows with a grimace. "Then he had the gall to come to the apartment when I was working and tell Matt that he needed to borrow the motorized wheelchair. Matt's so good-hearted, he said sure." She winced. "He sold it to buy drugs. I saved every extra dime I had for almost a year and a half just to afford it, and then my coworkers put in the last couple of hundred dollars I was short…" Her voice trailed off.

"Matt will have a new one tomorrow," she said gently. "It's all right."

Gail looked at the ceiling, fighting tears. "One stupid mistake. I made one stupid mistake, and I've paid for it, over and over again. If I could only go back and change it." She shook her head. "But there's no way. You kids paid a higher price than I did for that one mistake I made. I'm so sorry, Winnie. So sorry…!"

She was sobbing. Winnie ran to her, pulled the blonde head into her arms and rocked it, crying, too.

"It's okay, Mama," she whispered. "It's okay."

The sobs grew louder. Gail had gone so long without hope, missing her children, wanting to see them. It had been impossible. Now here was her daughter, forgiving her, comforting her. It was like a new start. It was even worth getting shot.

Winnie laughed, because she'd said that last bit aloud. "Please don't get shot again," she said gently.

"I'll do my best, baby," Gail promised. She drew back, dabbing at her eyes with the sheet.

Winnie pulled out a paper towel and dabbed at her own eyes.

Kilraven appeared in the doorway and hesitated.

"Women's Terrorist and Sobbing Society?" Kilraven quipped.

"What a great legend for a T-shirt," Winnie exclaimed. "I'll have some made up right away." She glanced at her mother and laughed. "You can have one, too."

"I'll wear it to work and drive my lieutenant bonkers," Gail promised, laughing.

Kilraven handed Winnie a cup of coffee in a plastic cup. "It looks weak."

"I don't care. It's still coffee," she said.

Gail shook her head. "What I wouldn't give for a cup of that."

"I'd let you share it, but the nurses would probably smell it on your breath and have us thrown out," Winnie reasoned.

"Evil girls," Gail muttered.

"I understand from the night nurse that you've been an interesting patient," Kilraven said with pursed lips and twinkling eyes. "Sneaking out the door and down to the street in your gown and a robe to have a cigarette?"

She glared at him. "You can't smoke in here, they won't let you."

"You could quit," he pointed out.

"You know what you could do, too," Gail shot right back.

He chuckled as he glanced at Winnie. "See? That's you in twenty years."

"God forbid!" Gail said.

"Stop that," Winnie told her. "You're not bad."

"I guess I ought to quit smoking, sure enough. But it won't help my other shortcomings. I yell at people, I do terrible things to uniformed officers," Gail began.

"What do you do to uniformed officers?" Kilraven wondered.

"Only if they threaten to mess up my crime scene," Gail said defensively.

"What?"

"I send them to other precincts to question people I think might be involved in my cases."

"Oh? That doesn't sound too bad," Winnie commented.

"I give them false names of people in lockup," she confessed.

"And you're calling the nurses evil?" Kilraven asked.

She glowered at him. "They won't let me smoke and drink coffee."

"You should quit smoking," Kilraven pointed out.

"Oh, sure, it's easy, I'll start right now," Gail said sarcastically. "Have you ever tried to quit?"

"Sure. I quit two years ago." He frowned. "And I quit five years before that. And I quit seven years ago." He smiled.

"Have you ever stayed quit?" she persisted.

"I've been clean for two years," he pointed out. "And as long as I don't have anything traumatic to upset me, I probably can stay quit for the rest of my life."

Gail was looking at him curiously. "That's a big if."

He shrugged. "I like cigars." He glared at Winnie when she made a face. "I'm not the only person around who likes a good cigar. They say the governor of California likes them, too."

"Smelly, stinky things," Winnie scoffed.

He lifted his eyebrows. "Yes? Well, if you marry me, you'll just have to get used to them, won't you?"

"Not for long," she said under her breath.

He leaned back in his chair. "Yes. Not for long."

"I wish I could come to the wedding," Gail said heavily. "But they won't let me out for another few days. I don't even know how many. The doctor won't come in here anymore so I can ask him."

"I saw him in the hall," Kilraven told her. "He says he's never coming back in here, because you grill him like a murder suspect."

"I do not," she said haughtily. "I only wanted to know when I could go home."

"It's the way you asked him," Kilraven said. "Need to work on your people skills, Rogers," he pointed out.

"Blow my people skills," she returned hotly. "I can't sit around here in my underwear while whoever shot me goes from bar to lowlife bar, bragging about it! I want to lock him up and throw away the key, as soon as I find out who the hell he is!"

"He may not be bragging about it."

"Of course he's bragging about it, he shot a cop and got away with it," she said, smoldering. Her dark eyes narrowed. "But not for long. I'll track him down if it takes me five years!"

"See?" Kilraven said, nodding toward Winnie's mother. "That's why she makes a good detective."

"Speaking of detectives, are they any closer to finding out who blindsided Marquez?" Gail asked, diverted.

"No," Kilraven told her. "They're still working the case. They'll add yours to it. I'd bet half my pension that they're connected, somehow."

"It's all connected," Gail said. "The murder of your family, the DB in the Little Carmichael River in Jacobsville, the death of Senator Fowler's employee, Marquez's mugging and my wounds. All tied together. Something else, Kilraven—I seriously think we should reopen the case of that young girl who was found murdered just before your family was killed."

Kilraven's silver eyes glittered. "You still think there's a connection. Why?"

"Look at the cases," she said intently. "Both victims were found in such a condition that only DNA could identify them. The killers have never been found. I heard that the killer left a thermos near the submerged car that the perp was driving. Left it out in the open, wiped clean of prints." Her eyes narrowed. "Bruce Sinclair, my ex-husband, had one just like it. My question is, how did it wind up in Jacobsville?"

"Did your ex give it to someone?" Kilraven asked.

"I don't know. But we need to find out. You might go to see that hophead girlfriend of his, the one who was living with him," Gail suggested. "I don't know if she's sober enough to remember anything, but it's worth a try.

Just be careful," she added. "Somebody's targeting people connected with this case."

"This isn't the time to be careful," he replied. "It's time to put the heat on the perps, take the fight into their own territory. I have a hunch that Senator Will Sanders's brother is up to his neck in these cases."

Gail nodded. "So do I. How do we prove it?"

Kilraven leaned back in his chair. "I'm going to put the word out on the street that Hank Sanders is being looked at as a potential suspect in two assaults on law enforcement officers. Let's see what happens."

Gail's dark eyes sparkled. "What original thinking."

"Thank you," he replied with a chuckle. "It just might flush somebody out."

"Or he might sacrifice somebody to get the heat off himself," she replied.

"Or he might tell his brother the senator, and the two of you might be out of a job," Winnie said solemnly.

"In which case," Kilraven told her, "we'll go to Senator Fowler and plead our cases. He had Sanders back off before when he took your mother off the case and busted her back to traffic duty."

"Senator Sanders had you demoted?" she asked Gail, shocked.

Gail nodded. "I didn't know it at the time, not until Alice Jones let something slip about her fiancé's father. That's Senator Fowler," she added.

"Yes, Harley's father." Winnie nodded.

"Who?" Gail wanted to know.

"Harley Fowler. He works for Cy Parks on his ranch."

Gail shook her head. "That's after my time, I'm afraid. I don't know Mr. Parks."

"He's very nice."

"Nice." Kilraven chuckled. He glanced at her. "Listen, that old lobo wolf may be married and have kids, but don't think he's tame."

"I forgot," she told Gail with a smile. "Mr. Parks was a professional soldier, a mercenary, for many years before he settled in Jacobsville. We all thought he was just another rancher until drug lords started setting up camp nearby. He and Dr. Micah Steele and Eb Scott went after the drug lords with Harley, and shut down the whole operation."

"I did hear about that," Gail replied, smiling. "It was in all the papers, even on the television news. No interviews, though."

"That would take magic," Kilraven commented. "None of those dudes likes publicity, even now that they've retired. Well, maybe Eb Scott wouldn't mind. He runs a state-of-the-art training camp for counterterrorism in Jacobsville. We use his firing range for practice. It's formidable."

"So is Mr. Scott, from what we hear." Winnie laughed. "He got married, too, a few years back. He and his wife have a son, I believe."

Kilraven had that faraway look in his eyes. He thought of his little girl, the last time he'd seen her. His face hardened. Too many people were getting away with murder. That teenage girl—he and Jon had commented on it.

He looked at Gail and frowned. "You were talking about reopening that case, the one with the teenage girl. That was just before you got shot. Did you mention it to anyone downtown?"

She blinked. "Well, to a couple of people, I guess," she said.

"The senator's little brother probably has an ear in your department, otherwise how would the senator have known that you were reopening my cold case?" he asked.

"Good point, Kilraven."

"So what if this dead teenager is the case they don't want anyone looking at? What if there's a connection?"

"I was thinking that, too," Gail replied.

"You may be onto something. There's another thing—there was a statutory rape case against Senator Sanders some years ago, remember it?"

Gail frowned. "Yes. A teenage girl, fourteen, I believe. Her father and mother refused to let her testify against him. The charges were dropped."

"Yes, and the next day, Daddy was driving a new convertible Jaguar. How ironic," Kilraven said sarcastically.

"That was a case I wanted to reopen," Gail muttered, "just so I could tell her father what I thought of him."

Kilraven was adding up clues in his head. "That might be the way to break the case wide-open," he said, thinking aloud. "Maybe you could talk to the girl."

Gail nodded slowly. "She might be able to tell me something about how the senator handled her. Or rather how his brother handled her. That might give us a lead into how he operates when he wants something hushed up."

"We're getting close, but in a way we didn't even realize," Kilraven said. "When you get out of here, that has to be your priority." His eyes narrowed. "There's one living witness who could testify to Senator Sanders's tactics with teenage girls. The teenager would be a woman now. She might talk to you."

"It's been some time since the case was dropped," she mused. "Anything could have happened in the meantime. The girl is grown, and living on her own, I'd imagine. Away from her father's influence, she really might be willing to talk to me. It's worth a try."

"Yes," Kilraven said. "Well worth it. But first you have to get well."

She grimaced. "I can't believe I was stupid enough to let myself get shot."

"That's what Marquez keeps saying, although he got beaten up instead of shot," Kilraven commented.

"Either way, we're sidelined," she said heavily. She shifted and groaned. The pain medicine was wearing off. She reached beside her and jiggled the drip catheter. She sighed. "That's better. Damned thing gets sluggish from time to time. They put the painkiller right in it," she added. "Beats having to call them in here four times a day to put it in me manually." She sighed. "I really hate drugs, you know. But right now, I can't say much against them. It really helps with the pain."

"I know," Kilraven said solemnly. "But it gets better. It just takes time."

"Time." She nodded. Her eyes closed. "I'm so tired."

"You should get some rest," Winnie said. She stood up and moved to the bed, bending to kiss her mother's forehead and smooth back the blond hair. "I'll come back to see you tomorrow. We'll bring Matt..." She stopped, looking around. "Where is Matt?" she asked, realizing that he hadn't come in with Kilraven.

"He met a girl about his age in a wheelchair down at

the drink machines. They both love video games." He chuckled. "He was going to have his hot chocolate with her."

They heard wheels rolling about that time and turned to see Matt coming in the door.

"Sorry," he told them. "I forgot the time. There was this girl, nice girl. I got her email address," he added. He grimaced. "If I ever get email, I can send her one," he corrected.

"I have email," Kilraven said easily and smiled. "You can use mine."

"Thanks!" He moved the chair beside Gail's bed. "Sorry I wasn't in here. I was supposed to be visiting you. But that girl has an incredible score at Super Mario Brothers," he exclaimed. "She got busted up in a car wreck, too, but it was really an accident, not deliberate like mine. Are we leaving already?" he added when Winnie slipped into her coat.

"Your mother's tired," Kilraven said gently. "She needs rest, so she can get well quicker."

"Yes, I do," Gail agreed. She smiled and held out her arms to hug Matt. "You be good for your brothers and sister," she said.

"I'm being very good, aren't I, sis?"

It took Winnie a minute to realize it was her he was addressing. She flushed a little and laughed. "Yes, you are, little brother," she replied, and felt warm inside with the words.

He grinned. "Trying to be, anyway," he amended. "We'll see you again tomorrow. Won't we?" he asked the other adults.

"You bet," Kilraven promised.

"See you tomorrow, Mom," he told Gail. He hesitated. "You know, they're right about the smoking," he said unexpectedly serious. "I know you do it outside, so it won't affect me. But it's affecting you. I don't want to lose you. See?"

She held out her arm, fighting tears, and hugged him close. She drew in a long breath. "Okay, kid. If that's what you want, I'll do it."

"Really?"

"Really." She looked past him at the two adults. "Just don't be surprised when you all have to come and bail me out of jail for climbing walls and threatening other police officers."

Kilraven pursed his lips. "There are new products that deal with the side effects."

"I could buy a yacht for what they cost," Gail muttered.

"That isn't a problem, and don't argue," Winnie said at once. She gave her mother a firm look.

"Well!" Gail exclaimed. She glanced at Kilraven. "She's me in twenty years, huh?"

Kilraven nodded.

"No wonder he's planning on a short marriage," she told Winnie.

Winnie laughed. It was easier to joke about it than face it. "You get well. We'll see you again, soon."

"Take care."

The others said their goodbyes, too, and left.

Winnie ruffled Matt's hair. "You'd better be good, or I'll tell Boone," she threatened.

"Horrors!" he said, but he laughed.

Winnie looked up at Kilraven and smiled. "Thanks for driving us."

He slid his hands into his pockets and shrugged. "I'm not overburdened with work right now. I enjoyed it. Your mother's in a class of her own."

"Yes," Winnie said proudly. "She is."

THE WEDDING WAS a quiet affair. Boone and Keely stood up with Winnie and Kilraven, while Matt and Clark and a few local citizens who'd heard about the wedding filled the benches near the doors outside the probate judge's office.

The judge, a woman, looked from one of them to the other. "You ready?" she asked.

They nodded.

"Please join hands." She looked at her book. "Do you, Winona Sinclair, take McKuen Kilraven for your husband…"

"McKuen." Winnie said it softly, surprised.

"I was named for a famous poet," he said, glowering at her.

She smiled. "I noticed. It suits you. I like it."

He smiled back. "Thanks."

"Ahem."

They glanced at the probate judge.

"Sorry," Winnie said.

She laughed, shaking her head, then she continued.

And they were married. Kilraven bent to brush his mouth gently over Winnie's, but not with any great enthusiasm. He looked uncomfortable in his dark suit, distinguished and almost untouchable. Winnie was certain he was remembering his first wedding, and she was positive it wasn't in some probate judge's office. Probably his first wife had had all the trimmings, including a beautiful gown and flowers and...

"Congratulations, Mrs. Kilraven!" Keely laughed, and hugged her.

"Mrs. Kilraven," Winnie said, shocked at the sound of the name that was now hers.

"Hey, that's you," Keely teased.

"Sorry. I was just thinking," she replied, and then flushed. She couldn't admit she'd been regretting her wedding.

"Don't," Keely advised. "Just be happy."

"It's only temporary," Winnie whispered.

"Is it?" Keely replied in a whisper, and winked.

Boone bent to kiss his sister's cheek. "You made a pretty bride," he said, admiring her neat figure in the white suit she was wearing with a pillbox hat and a tiny veil.

She was clutching a small bouquet that she'd had made up, of white roses and baby's breath. Kilraven hadn't even noticed her suit or the bouquet. She was certain he hadn't thought of offering her one. He was somber and quiet and introspective. She knew it wasn't the happiest day of his life. But it was exciting to her. She was married! Even if it only lasted a few weeks, she was Kilraven's bride. She smiled so radiantly that the newspaper photographer covering the private affair was almost too stunned by her beauty to snap the picture. But he managed.

CHAPTER ELEVEN

KILRAVEN PULLED HIMSELF together and tried to stop thinking back to his first wedding. He should have offered Winnie a bouquet, at least, but he hadn't even done that. He'd been resentful that he had to marry her just to question a senator's wife. It was his own idea; why was he blaming her for it?

No, the pain came when he remembered Monica walking toward him down the aisle, dressed in a lavender gown with a bouquet of lilac. It wasn't traditional, but neither was she. She'd been lovely. The most beautiful woman alive, with her long wheat-colored hair and her laughing blue eyes. He'd been in love. Deeply in love. The wedding had been the happiest day of his life, at least until little Melly was born. Then his life began, even as Monica was finding other partners for her sensual adventures. Kilraven had lived for his little girl. Until that night...

He heard voices around him and realized that he'd been staring into space while people were trying to congratulate him. He smiled and returned handshakes. He wasn't being fair to Winnie. Whatever his own feelings, she was in love with him. It wasn't right to treat her so coolly on her wedding day.

He moved to her side and curled her fingers into his. She looked up at him, surprised.

"You really do look beautiful," he said softly, studying the way her long, thick, wavy blond hair radiated around her face, the way her dark eyes seemed to smolder in her face with its oval shape and peaches-and-cream complexion.

She flushed. "Thanks," she stammered.

He bent and brushed his mouth over her forehead, just below the tiny veil she'd pushed up when they were saying their vows. "I should have offered to buy you a bouquet," he whispered. "That's the groom's part of the deal."

She smiled. "It's okay. I had this one made up."

"I like it."

"Thanks."

"Well, where's the reception?" Cash Grier asked, moving up to the front of the office.

Kilraven blinked. "We aren't having a reception."

"I guess I can go home, then." He chuckled. "It's only at the receptions that we have to arrest people."

"What are you talking about?" Winnie asked.

"Don't you remember Blake Kemp's wedding?"

"Oh," she said, nodding. "Yes, I do. Cake and punch went flying and several of the witnesses ended up in jail."

He grinned. "Best reception I was ever at," he commented. He glanced at Kilraven. "You're sure you're not having a reception?"

"Sorry. No time."

"Oh," Cash mused. "In a hurry, are you?"

Kilraven glowered at him. "It's not that sort of marriage, and please get your mind above your belt!"

"Whatever do you think I meant?" Cash asked with an angelic expression. "I was only going to offer to give you a police escort out of town. All the way to San Antonio, if you like."

"No, thank you," Kilraven said firmly. "You'd have Hayes send Macreedy, and we'd all end up driving the back roads of Florida or some other state hoping to be rescued."

Cash shook his head. "You have a suspicious mind."

"Absolutely." Kilraven nodded.

"Well, I do wish you the best." He extended his hand. "I've enjoyed working with you, for the most part. But there were times I wanted to put you in a barrel and float you down to Mexico." He added with a grin, "I guess we can overlook those times."

Kilraven laughed as he shook hands. "I won't mention that I've had the same impulses about you."

"Have you really?" Cash asked. "Thing is," he added in a conspiratorial tone, "we don't have any barrels in Jacobsville."

"Oh, I think we could find one if we really looked," Kilraven murmured.

"Are we ready to go?" Winnie asked her new husband. "We're on our way to the hospital to see Mom," she added with a smile. "She wanted to see me in my wedding suit."

Kilraven felt guilt stab at him. It was Winnie's first wedding, and he'd cheated her. It should have been a religious service, in a church with a pastor. The thought stung.

"Yes, we'd better go," he said, in a harder tone than he meant to.

"You okay?" Matt asked, frowning.

He patted the boy's shoulder. "Sure!"

But Winnie knew better. He was regretting the impulse that had made him ask her to marry him. It was all a sham, a pretense. They were going to interrogate a politician's wife and it had to look natural, so they were married. But it wasn't going to be happily ever after, and she wouldn't keep him for long. It was just temporary.

"Now you look all gloomy," Matt said, eyeing his sister.

Winnie perked up. "Do I?" she asked, smiling at him. "I don't feel gloomy," she lied.

He smiled. "Okay. Just checking."

HER MOTHER MADE a fuss over the pretty white suit and protested when Winnie got a vase from one of the nurses and made a bouquet for Gail out of her bridal bouquet.

"No, you'll want to save that," Gail protested.

"What for?" Winnie asked, smiling. "It's just flowers. Our marriage probably won't last much longer than they will."

Kilraven felt those words like a stab in the heart. He looked at Winnie as if he thought she was needling him, but he realized quite suddenly that she wasn't. Maybe he was taking the lack of frills at their wedding harder than she was. Winnie was a realist.

His hands were clenched in his pockets as he watched her move around the room. She had an easy grace in her walk, elegance personified. She was pretty and sweet and intelligent; she'd finished two years of college before she quit and went home to work for the Jacobsville Police Department as a clerk. He frowned. Why had she dropped out of college? he wondered. He'd never asked.

Of course, he'd never talked to her long enough to get around to personal questions. He'd tried to be remote and inaccessible, to discourage her from daydreaming about him. This marriage wasn't going to do much to cure that crush she had on him, that was for sure.

Still, if anything happened down in Nassau, he wouldn't be taking advantage of a single woman. He pursed his lips as he studied her trim figure, her slight breasts, her long, pretty legs. He loved that long, blond hair. He remembered the feel of it, clenched in his fingers while he kissed her. He remembered the taste of her bare breasts... His body made a sudden and visible statement about how it had enjoyed that long, sweet taste of her. It wanted more.

"Going for coffee. Want any?" he asked Winnie, as he started toward the door.

"Yes, please," she said.

He waved a hand and kept walking.

"He's acting very oddly," Winnie remarked. She grimaced. "I think he's comparing me with his first wife," she told her mother, "and I don't imagine I compare well."

"You don't know that," Gail said soothingly. "It's hard for men to get married. He's got a lot on his mind, too."

"Yes. This case." She perched on the chair by her mother's bed. "I painted a picture of a raven and gave it to him for Christmas. It was supposed to be an anonymous present, but he knew immediately that I'd done it, and he was furious. He walked out without saying a word to me." She sighed. "Then he took me to his house and showed me a picture just like it. His daughter had drawn and colored it just before she was killed. They were identical. He wanted to know how I knew to paint something like that. I don't know."

"I've had that ability all my life," Gail told her. "I can

crack cold cases that other detectives can't. I get feelings, intuition. I can feel it when something's not right."

"So it runs in the family."

"I don't know. I don't recall my parents or their parents ever knowing something was going to happen before it did." She smiled. "I guess you inherited it from me. So did Matt," she added. "He knows when I'm in trouble."

"And you know about him."

Gail nodded. "He's quite a boy."

"Dad would have been proud of him," Winnie told her. "I'm so sorry he wouldn't listen to you."

"Baby, you're not half as sorry as I am," Gail said. "But the past twelve years have taught me to be self-sufficient, to take care of myself. I went from my home straight into marriage, at an age when most girls are just learning about boys and dating. I missed so much." She smiled sadly. "Your father was handsome and charming. He convinced me that marrying him was the smart thing to do, so I did it. He was twelve years older than me. That's not a lot, but it's almost a generation."

"I know," Winnie said quietly. "That's the argument Kilraven uses with me. He's ten years older than me."

"He's dangerous," Gail said, her voice quiet and intense. "I don't mean that he'd ever hurt you, I know he wouldn't. But he takes chances. He lives on the edge. He's done things you wouldn't believe in the line of duty."

"Warning me off him?" Winnie teased.

"It's far too late for that," Gail replied. "Just try not to go in headfirst, okay? You may be hoping for a long-term commitment, but that man isn't ready for one. He hasn't faced his own tragedy. Until he does, he's a walking time bomb, waiting to self-destruct."

"I couldn't say no," Winnie replied. "I love him," she confessed, averting her eyes.

"I know that. I'm sorry."

Winnie shifted in the chair. "He might discover that he can't live without me."

"That's a very long shot."

"Well, we have to have goals to aim for," Winnie said, trying to rally her sense of humor. "Some women want to go to Mars, I just want to keep Kilraven."

"The women going to Mars will get their wish long before you get yours," Gail assured her.

"You are so cynical." Winnie laughed. "Just like Kilraven."

"We're L.E.O.s," she replied with a wan smile. "The job makes us that way."

"I do understand, a little," Winnie said. "I work with people in law enforcement. I know what you go through, what you have to look at. I know how hard you work, and how unrewarding it can be. I know how critical the public is of you. The media notices every tiny slip you make, and ignores the big drug busts and the simple acts of kindness and the danger you endure just to do the job. I think it's a great job," she added with a smile. "And I'm proud that you're one of those people."

"Thank you," Gail said softly. "That means a lot."

There was a metallic sound, followed by a loud hum, and Matt came into the room. "Finally got here!" he exclaimed. "I got stuck on an elevator going up and I couldn't get to the front in this to press the button for your floor. Kilraven and I got separated downstairs at the elevators. Where is he?" he asked suddenly.

"Gone after coffee," Winnie said with a grin. She

looked at her mother. "How do you like it? You should have seen Kilraven trying to disassemble it to get it in the trunk of the Jaguar! It's complicated."

"Yes, but he's a whiz at machinery," Matt enthused. "I wish I had the gift."

"Don't we all." Gail sighed. She grinned at her son. "I do like the chair."

"I hugged Boone," he said. "He's the greatest."

"Yes, he is," Winnie agreed.

"I like Clark, too," Matt said quickly. "He's great at video games!"

"And, of course, that's the best character reference he can give," Gail said drolly.

Matt made a face at her. "Video games are my life, what can I say?"

"In about five years, girls will be your life, so enjoy it while you can," his mother told him.

"Girls. Yuuck." He hesitated. "Although, that girl in the wheelchair sure was pretty. I still have her e-mail address," he added, and levered his eyebrows up and down.

"He's going to be a ladykiller." Winnie sighed.

"I am not killing women when I grow up," Matt said indignantly.

"That's not what it means," Gail told him, and explained.

He grinned. "That wouldn't be so bad. I could charm women out of their video games."

"I think you have a problem," Winnie told her mother.

"I know I do," Gail replied.

Kilraven came back with coffee and they had a short visit. Matt was keen to get to Kilraven's apartment and see those game consoles he'd heard about; not to mention the collection of first-person shooter games.

"Bloodthirsty boy," Kilraven accused when they'd said goodbye to Gail and were on their way in the car.

"I'm not bloodthirsty, I just like to kill monsters," Matt defended.

"Me, too." Kilraven chuckled. He glanced over the backseat. "There's this game, *Elder Scrolls IV: Oblivion,*" he began.

"I played that at a friend's house once. Everything in it looks so real!"

"Yes, it does. Well, every so often when I play it, I go to a tavern, get drunk, slug an Imperial Guard and steal his horse and ride it away." He sighed. "I usually get halfway down the hill before they catch up with me and shoot me full of arrows." He glanced at Matt, who was laughing. "Of course, I make a save just before I do all that, so I can go back to the save and it never happened. I do like to be law-abiding on record."

Winnie was laughing, too. "That's evil!" she charged.

"No, it's evil if I do it in real life." He leaned toward her as he stopped at a red light. "Not many Imperial Guards riding horses around San Antonio," he added.

She laughed again. "I guess not."

He pulled into his parking lot and reassembled Matt's wheelchair, grabbing his overnight bag before they went into the lobby.

"I have returned with two people," Kilraven began, addressing the security guard, "and I intend to take them upstairs for illicit purposes…"

"Oh, for God's sake, Kilraven, get out of here!" the guard groaned.

Kilraven glared at him. "Have you no sense of honor at all? Will you sully the name of this fine establishment by allowing me to…"

"Out!" The guard gestured, standing. "Or I call the cops."

"But I am the cops!" Kilraven wailed. "And I just got married!"

"A likely story!" the guard retorted.

"No, I did. Look." He tugged Winnie's hand toward the guard and displayed the pretty gold ring he'd put on her finger.

"Well!" the guard exclaimed. He smiled at Winnie. "My condolences, Mrs. Kilraven," he said formally. "You have put your neck in a guillotine that…"

"That's enough," Kilraven huffed. "Peasant!"

"Schwartzriter!" the guard shot back.

Kilraven grinned, took Winnie's hand, motioned to Matt and headed for the elevator.

"What's a swartz…whatever he said?" Matt asked.

"Black rider. It's German. They were famous in the sixteenth century," Kilraven told him as they crowded into the elevator. "They carried several braces of pistols and rode in formations of columns. The first men on the line would fire and ride to the back of the line and reload. Their comrades would follow suit. They were like light artillery. Brave, cunning and deadly. He can call me a black rider anytime he likes."

"I've got other names!" the security guard called as the door closed.

Kilraven chuckled. It was an ongoing battle of words and insults that he enjoyed. The security guard was also a history nut, and he was as deep into the sixteenth century as Kilraven was.

"You know a lot about that stuff, don't you?" Matt asked.

"I do. I was a history major in college," he confessed. "I still love it."

"I hate history. It's all dates and boring things."

"Boring!" Kilraven exclaimed, horrified. "History?"

"Well," Matt began, hesitating.

"When Lord Bothwell was falsely accused of insulting the queen of Scotland, he was sent into exile in England, where he was arrested. He wrote a note to an enemy of his, an earl who lived on the northern border of England and Scotland, asking for refuge. He was notorious for raiding the earl's lands, mind. Well, the earl was so amused by the request that he honored it and invited Bothwell to stay at his estate and agreed to be his keeper. In the process, he discovered that Bothwell was intelligent and, as the Earl of Northumberland said, 'not the man he was rumored to be.' Does that sound boring?"

Matt laughed. "Not really. But don't you have to memorize dates?"

"I do it for love of it, not because I have to," Kilraven said, smiling at the boy.

"You like that Lord Bot... Bottle...?"

"Bothwell. James Hepburn, Earl of Bothwell. He was the son of the 'Fair Earl' who was a suitor of the mother of Mary, Queen of Scots. Bothwell had no legitimate children, but his nephew—who was the son of his sister and the half brother of Mary, Queen of Scots—inherited his title and estates. He was a bitter enemy and sometimes supporter of James the First of England. James was the son of Mary, Queen of Scots."

"Wait, wait," Matt pleaded. "Too much information! My brain is exploding!"

Kilraven chuckled. "Sorry. I do tend to get carried away."

"I'll bet you've got every book ever written on the subject," Winnie guessed.

He winked at her, smiling when she colored prettily. "I have, including a number of out-of-print ones. We're home."

He opened the apartment door and let Matt go in first.

"Hey, this is nice!" Matt exclaimed.

"Very nice, indeed. Come here, woman," he told Winnie and abruptly bent and scooped her up in his arms. "I'm carrying you into my cave, in the best macho fashion."

She clung to his neck, laughing. He was fun to be with.

"I like your cave," she remarked.

He swung her around, making her hold on tighter. Then he bent his head and kissed her with muted hunger, mindful of small eyes watching.

"You're home, Mrs. Kilraven," he said, and he made the words sound new and bright.

She caught her breath. Her heart was racing like a wild thing. "Thanks, Mr. Kilraven," she replied, smiling.

He rubbed his nose against hers. "Can you cook?"

"Can I cook!" she exclaimed haughtily. "I can make real bread. My sister-in-law taught me how."

He was surprised. "Real bread? Honestly?"

"Honestly."

He put her down. "Prove it."

"Do you have yeast?"

He blinked. "Yeast what?"

"Yeast, like you put in bread, to make it," she exclaimed.

He frowned. "I don't know." He moved into the kitchen and began rummaging through cabinets. "Jon made some sort of sourdough starter once. I think he used yeast... yes! Here it is. We've got plain flour, too."

"How do you know the difference between plain and self-rising?" she asked curiously. "I don't think of you as a cook."

He grinned at her. "I'm not. I can do a few dishes, but I mostly get takeout. Jon is a gourmet chef," he reminded her. "He can make anything. Well, mostly anything. He accidentally got the self-rising flour when he was making biscuits with baking soda. It was a disaster. He used some very bad words."

"What bad words?" she teased.

"Oh, no, I'm not using them in front of a minor," he said, indicating Matt, who was listening and grinning.

"I am not a miner," Matt told him. "I don't even own a shovel or a pick."

"Smart mouth," Kilraven muttered.

"It runs in the family," Winnie told him. "Now if you have an apron, and you'll leave the kitchen and stop distracting me, I'll make yeast rolls."

"Heaven," Kilraven said, almost groaning with pleasure. "I haven't had them since Cammy stopped making holiday dinners."

"Cammy?" Winnie asked, surprised. "Who is she?" She was hoping it wasn't some shadowy girlfriend.

"My stepmother," he said, grinning when he realized

what she was thinking, especially when she flushed. "Her name is Camelia, but we always called her Cammy. Remember? I told you when we were standing in the roadside park."

She'd been thinking of other things and had forgotten. "Oh."

"She wants to meet you," he said hesitantly.

"That would be nice," Winnie replied, busy with her bread materials.

"Oh, I'm not sure you'll think so, after you meet her. She's very possessive. She'll probably give you a hard time."

She glanced at him. "I can take care of myself."

"Okay. But I warned you." He went into the living room and turned on the television, and then the game consoles. In minutes, he and a fascinated Matt were in the middle of the new *Halo* game, so involved that they didn't stir until Winnie insisted that cold bread and chicken weren't good.

"This is delicious," Kilraven said as they plowed through the homemade bread, heavily buttered, served with a simple chicken dish and asparagus tips with hollandaise sauce. "I didn't know you could cook like this!"

She smiled. "I learned from one of our housekeepers. She was a wonderful cook. That was when I was in my teens."

"You're good," he said.

"You really are," Matt seconded. "This is great chicken!"

She laughed. "Glad you like it."

MATT WAS BACK at the game console, and Winnie and Kilraven were having second cups of coffee when the doorbell rang.

He went to answer it. As he opened the door, he gave Winnie a concerned look. A tall, dark-haired, dark-eyed woman in a tailored suit with her long hair in a bun came into the apartment, wearing spiked high heels and an attitude. She gave Winnie a long look that didn't soften the ice in those eyes.

"This is your new wife?" the woman asked haughtily.

"Yes, Cammy," Kilraven said. "Don't I get a hug?"

She did hug him, warmly, laughing. "You look wonderful. Who's that?" she asked, frowning at the boy in the wheelchair.

"I'm Matt," he said with a grin. "I'm Winnie's brother. Don't let the wheels fool you, I'm dangerous. I shot five Hunters!"

"Halo," Cammy groaned. "Is there any male in Texas who doesn't play that game?"

"Not many, including my brother, who has his own copy," Kilraven assured her. "Come and meet Winnie Sinclair. She works for Jacobs County EOC as a 911 operator."

"Does she?" Cammy went into the kitchen, her arms folded tight across her breasts. She gave Winnie a cold appraisal.

"It's nice to meet you," Winnie began apprehensively.

Cammy made a sound in the back of her throat. "Mc-Kuen hasn't said anything about you at all. This is a very quick wedding. Are you pregnant?"

Winnie gave her an astonished stare. "Well, if I am, we'll call the local television stations and offer them interviews. It will make headlines everywhere!"

"Excuse me?"

"A woman getting pregnant without having sex," Winnie said in a low voice so that Matt wouldn't hear.

"You won't sleep with him?" Cammy asked, shocked. "Well, some wife you're going to be! Did you trick him into marrying you when you found out he had a big ranch and was rich?" she continued doggedly. "You're after his money, aren't you?"

Winnie stood up to her full height, which was almost a head shy of Cammy's. "For your information, Mrs. Kilraven…"

"Blackhawk," came the terse reply. "My name is Blackhawk. So is his," she indicated Kilraven, "but he won't use it."

"My choice, Cammy," came the droll reply.

"For your information, Mrs. Blackhawk," Winnie continued haughtily, "my brother is Boone Sinclair of Comanche Wells. You might have seen his photo on the cover of the national ranching magazine this month? The issue about going green on the range?"

Kilraven retrieved his copy of *Modern Ranching World* from the coffee table and helpfully handed it to Cammy. His eyes were twinkling with amusement.

Cammy read ranching magazines. She loved the ranch. And she knew exactly who Boone Sinclair was the minute she saw his face on the cover of the magazine. "Those Sinclairs?" she asked hesitantly.

"Yes," Winnie said icily. "Those Sinclairs. My people are related to every royal house in Europe. My great-grandmother was the daughter of a titled Spanish don, and quite wealthy. Her mother was the niece of the King of Spain!"

Cammy wanted very badly to throw a loftier genealogy back at Winnie, but her ancestry had produced no person more elevated than a grain merchant in Billings, Montana. She went red in the face.

"As for marrying your stepson for his money," Winnie added cuttingly, "I could probably buy and sell you on my inherited oil and gas holdings alone!"

Cammy swallowed. Hard. She glared at Winnie furiously, looking for a comeback.

"If you'll excuse me now, I have to do the dishes," Winnie said with a huff, and turned back into the kitchen. "By the way, I can make homemade bread, too. Can you?"

Cammy marched back into the living room, grabbed her purse and coat, and glared at her stepson, who was trying his best not to laugh. She slammed the magazine into his outstretched hand.

"I am never coming back to this apartment in my life as long as you're married to that…that little blonde chain saw!" she exclaimed with a furious dark glare toward the kitchen. "Goodbye!"

She stormed out of the apartment and slammed the door for effect.

Kilraven burst out laughing. He kept it up until his eyes teared. "Well, that's a first," he told Winnie, hugging her affectionately. "Cammy used to send women running. Jon and I couldn't keep a girlfriend when we were in high school. I thought she'd cut you up like fish bait. And you send her running out the door." He hugged her again, rocking her in his big arms. "My little blonde chain saw," he murmured at her ear, and kissed it.

"You're not…mad?" she faltered.

He lifted his head. He smiled at her. "I'm not mad."

"I didn't mean to be so unkind," she began.

"Cammy will conveniently forget everything you said and come back with a wedding gift in a day or two, then she'll try to make friends with you." He grinned at her dubious expression. "You'll see. She's all bluff. What she dislikes most is people she can run over."

"I used to let people do that," she confessed. "Working with you inspired me to greater heights."

He bent and nuzzled her nose with his. "I'm inspired, too. Cammy ran like a scalded cat. I've got to call Jon and tell him. He's in New York on a case," he added, reminding her why his brother had missed the wedding.

Matt winked at her. He'd heard all that, but didn't comment.

Kilraven pulled out his cell phone. Winnie, feeling elated and proud of herself, walked back to the kitchen.

"Hey, Jon," Kilraven said into his cell phone, "guess who married a little blonde chain saw today!"

CHAPTER TWELVE

WINNIE SETTLED DOWN with Matt and Kilraven after she'd put the dishes in the dishwasher and stored the leftovers. There were only two controllers and they were using a split screen to battle each other. But when Winnie came in, Matt relinquished his and sat coaching her. It was fun.

About midnight, Matt said good-night and wheeled himself into Kilraven's equipment room where a bed had been made up. Kilraven walked Winnie to hers, making it obvious that he had no intention of sharing it with her, wedding night or not.

"We agreed," he said gently. "Didn't we?"

She smiled. "Yes." She tried not to sound disappointed. She'd had sleepless nights since their interlude on his sofa.

He caught her waist and lifted her up so that he could put his lips to her ear and wouldn't be overheard. "But just in case, are you on the Pill?"

She shivered at the deep, husky note in his voice. She cleared her throat. "Yes. The doctor started me on it two days ago."

"Good."

"We aren't going to," she began.

His lips slid from her ear down to her soft mouth and claimed it suddenly with a hunger and intensity that made her shiver from head to toe. His big hands lifted her hips up into his and ground them into the sudden hardness.

A surge of heat throbbed down her stomach and made
her breath catch under his mouth as he rotated her thighs
against his and she moaned helplessly. She felt him smile
as he suddenly lifted his head and looked straight into
her shocked eyes.

"We aren't going to?" he mused. "Are you sure?"

Her face flamed. He was driving her mad, but she had
to consider where this was going to end. He was going
to take her to Nassau to get him a conversation with a
senator's wife, and then he was going to toss her out the
door. She had to keep that in mind.

"Yes," she said quietly. It didn't help when she shivered.

His eyebrow jerked. He set her back on her feet and
studied her for a long, somber moment.

"Addictions are hard to cure," she said with as much
dignity as she could muster. Hard, considering that her
knees were shaking and her voice was unsteady. "The
best way to avoid them is not to create them."

"Sensible," he agreed. A corner of his very sensuous
mouth curved up. "Little blonde chain saw," he added in
a soft, amused tone as his silver eyes glittered posses-
sively over her flushed face. "Sleep well."

She managed a smile. "You, too."

He turned and left her. He didn't seem particularly
disappointed, because he went right back to his game as
if nothing had happened.

Winnie went into the guest bedroom, put on her pajamas and crawled under the covers. It must be the strang-
est wedding day any woman ever had.

SHE GOT UP early the next morning after a viciously sleepless night and cooked a nice breakfast. Matt wheeled into
the kitchen a few minutes later, grinning.

"Smells good," he said. "I'm not used to anybody cooking breakfast, especially since Mom got back on homicide," he added. "She gets called out at all hours of the night. Sometimes she doesn't even get home until I'm ready to leave for school."

"What do you eat?" she wondered.

"Cereal, mostly," he said. "I like it, you know. I wasn't criticizing. Mom works hard."

She smiled at him. "Matt, you've got to be the nicest boy I ever met," she told him sincerely. "I'm glad you turned out to be my little brother."

"Thanks," he replied, surprised.

"Oh, it's not what you think," she teased. "The older ones always picked on me because I was the baby. Now you're the baby!"

He chuckled. "I get it. I'm the lowest link in the food chain."

"Or thereabouts." She laughed.

"Where's Kilraven?" he wondered.

"Probably still asleep," she said. "I'm sure I heard plasma rifles going off around daylight."

"Poor guy. I guess he doesn't get much time to play games when he's really on the job."

"I guess not," she agreed.

"It was a nice wedding," he said.

She nodded. "I thought so, too."

"You sure you're really married?" he asked in a deliberately discreet tone.

She glanced at him and smiled. "You ever hear about going undercover?"

"Sure. Mom knows a narc who does that."

"When you go undercover, sometimes you do things

so they appear to be one thing, when they're really another thing," she continued.

He was quick. "So you're pretending to be married, but you have a license to prove it if anybody asks."

Her eyebrows lifted. "You're good," she said.

"My mom's a homicide detective," he reminded her. He frowned. "Our mom's a homicide detective," he corrected.

She smiled. "I forgot."

"We going to see her today?"

"You bet," she said enthusiastically. "When do you go back to school?"

"Did you have to bring that up?" he groaned.

"Sorry. I did."

"Monday." He sighed. "I've got homework for it, too, can you imagine? Over the weekend!"

"Education is not for the weakhearted," she pointed out.

"I guess so. Did you like school?"

"Not really," she confessed. "I went to college for two years, but I got sick one winter and failed a course when it was too late to do an 'incomplete.' Blew my GPA. I didn't really like my major, anyway, so I went home and got a job working as a clerk for the Jacobsville Police Department. That's where I met Kilraven."

"His first name's McKuen," he reminded her. "Why don't you call him that?"

"I'm not sure it would be safe," she said thoughtfully.

"You could always call him Mac."

"Going to loan me some body armor first?" she asked dubiously.

He laughed. "Right."

"One of us had better tell him breakfast is ready," she said when she put biscuits and eggs and bacon on the table. She started to set the table.

"One of us. He's your husband."

"Yes, but he's your brother-in-law," she replied. "I think you should call him. He might throw things."

He shot her a grin and turned the wheelchair. "No guts, no glory," he called over his shoulder.

She sighed with relief. She hadn't wanted to mention that Kilraven might sleep raw, and she wasn't walking into that bedroom if he did. Prude, she told herself, you're married. Yes, she answered herself, but remember what you told yourself about addictions?

She turned right back to the cabinets and pulled out silverware.

KILRAVEN DRAGGED IN five minutes later, fully dressed, his hair immaculately combed. But he was red-eyed and half-asleep.

He pulled out a chair, yawning, and sat down, smiling at Winnie when she put a cup of hot coffee under his nose. "Thanks," he said. "I didn't go to bed until the early news came on."

"I heard," she said.

"Excuse me?"

"Plasma rifles, sniper rifles, grenades…"

"Sorry," he said as he sipped coffee.

She laughed. "Don't feel guilty. When I have days off, I do the same thing. I wasn't really sleepy, either," she confessed, avoiding his suddenly amused glance, "but I finally drifted off myself. Matt slept like a rock."

"I always sleep like a rock," Matt said with a grin.

Kilraven didn't reply. He slept fitfully, and it was rare even now that he spent an entire night asleep. The past haunted him.

Winnie saw the pain in his face that he couldn't quite hide, and she felt a stab of conscience that she couldn't be the person he wanted her to be. She couldn't spend a night in his arms and go on with her life, she thought miserably, even if he could.

He sipped coffee, ignoring the food.

"Aren't you hungry?" Matt asked. "These biscuits are really good."

Kilraven glanced at him, frowning, then at the platters of food. "Good Lord," he exclaimed, looking at Winnie. "You made biscuits?"

She nodded. "I can do all sorts of breads."

He reached for one, pulled it apart, buttered it and put on strawberry jam. He bit into it and his eyes closed. He almost groaned. "I haven't had a homemade biscuit since I was a kid," he confessed, smiling. "We had this cook, Laredo, who could do almost anything with flour, even cakes. He made the most delicious biscuits, but these are even better."

Winnie smiled. "Thanks."

He reached for the platters of bacon and eggs. "I'm not used to a hot breakfast, but I'll bet I could adapt, if I tried."

Matt chuckled as he reached for another biscuit. "Me, too. Homicide detectives don't have time to do a lot of cooking."

"Neither do Feds," he pointed out.

"Or 911 operators." Winnie raised her hand.

"This lady at dispatch saved Mom's life last year," Matt related. "She went to interview a witness in a homicide and he turned out to be the perp. Mom managed to hit 911 on her cell phone, inside her coat while the guy was threatening her with a gun." He grinned. "She had two squad cars in less than two minutes, believe it or not, with sirens and lights going full tilt. While they were diverting the suspect, Mom disarmed the perp, knocked his legs out from under him and cuffed him, all this before the uniformed officers even got to the door!"

"Wow," Winnie said, impressed.

"The dispatcher knew Mom," Matt continued, "and she found two squad cars in the vicinity on her computer and sent them."

"Quick thinking," Kilraven said. He grinned at Winnie. "Your sister saved my butt in a similar manner."

"You did?" Matt asked, waiting to be told how.

Winnie shrugged. "I just had a hunch that he needed backup."

"Yes, and sent it before I was able to call and ask for it," he added pointedly.

"Mom knows stuff before it happens, too," Matt said. "She was at the hospital when they brought me in, after her ex-husband tried to kill me." His face was somber. "She said she knew. She saw it, in her mind. It's sort of scary, sometimes."

"Yes, it is," Winnie confessed. "I see things that I wish I couldn't see."

"Well, I'm glad you saw that I needed help," Kilraven informed her, "or we wouldn't be having this conversation."

She grinned at him. He grinned back.

HE FINISHED BREAKFAST and pulled out his cell phone. "I've got to call my brother and find out if there's any new intel on the case."

He moved into the next room. The phone rang and Joceline Perry answered it.

"Hi, Perry," he said, using her last name, as he always did. "Is the boss in?"

"I understand that he doesn't do many concerts these days," she cracked, referring to the real "Boss," Bruce Springsteen.

"Funny girl," he muttered.

"And that was a movie with Barbra Streisand," she said with mock excitement.

"Give me my brother or I'll come down there and anoint you with India ink."

"Terroristic threats and acts!" she exclaimed.

"Joceline…!"

"That's more like it," she told him.

There was a click. "Blackhawk," Jon's voice came over the line.

"Can you do something for me?" Kilraven asked.

"Sure. What do you want?"

"Go out into the waiting room, find something wet and dump it over Joceline's head."

"Let me check the deductible on my medical insurance first," Jon mused. "What do you want? Advice on how to manage the 'little blonde chain saw' or how to calm Cammy down?" he added with a chuckle.

"Cammy's been talking to you," he replied.

"Not talking so much as shouting," Jon replied complacently. "I'd just turned my cell phone on when I got back from New York and walked into my apartment, and it was already ringing. I gather that Cammy's sense of superiority was temporarily displaced by feelings of inadequacy." He chuckled. "I have to meet Winnie. She must be a firecracker."

"Actually, she's not," Kilraven replied pensively. "She's shy and quiet around people she doesn't know. But Cammy was pretty overbearing, especially when I mentioned that Winnie was a 911 operator. I'm sure she knew that Boone Sinclair was recently on the cover of the nation's top cattle magazine because we all subscribe, but she didn't connect Winnie with him until I put the magazine in her hand." He chuckled. "She does now."

Jon chuckled, too. "I've never known my mother to be at such a disadvantage with anybody."

"Me, either," Kilraven replied. "But let me give you some advice, if you ever get engaged, make sure she wears body armor. If Cammy's that bad about me, just imagine how she'll be about you."

"No worries there. I've got too much work on my desk to be thinking about women. Plus Giles Lamont is due for parole soon," he added darkly.

Kilraven felt uncomfortable at the mention of the man's name. Jon was the arresting officer in a federal case that had put Lamont, a gambler with underworld ties, behind bars for five years. He'd sworn that he'd kill Jon if he ever got out of prison, even if it meant going back in stir forever, or getting the needle. "You could go to the parole board," Kilraven began.

"And do what?" Jon asked curtly. "Do you know how many death threats I get a week? He's just one more. Like they're going to keep a man in prison just because he threatened a federal officer!"

"Terroristic threats and acts," Kilraven began.

"Without witnesses," Jon replied.

Kilraven cursed under his breath. "Listen, you watch your back. You're the only brother I've got."

"Thanks, I'm fond of you, too," Jon quipped. "On a more cheerful note, guess who just bought a first-class plane ticket to Nassau?"

Kilraven's heart skipped. "Senator Sanders's wife?" he asked hopefully.

"The same. She's leaving tonight."

"Then we're leaving first thing tomorrow," Kilraven told him. "Keep me in the loop if you hear anything else, okay?"

"Will do. Have a nice trip, and don't seduce Winnie."

"What?"

"If she stood up to Cammy, your opinion must be important to her," came the quiet reply. "Don't break her heart trying to solve the case."

Kilraven felt his temper bristling. "My daughter was murdered," he reminded Jon. "I'll do anything, hurt anybody, whatever it takes to find her killer. I can't help it. She was my whole life," he gritted.

Jon drew in a long breath. "I know how much you loved Melly," he said gently. "I'm working as hard as I can on the case. But you just remember that several people are already dead because they knew too much, and the people responsible have assaulted two police detectives assigned to the case. Get my drift?"

"I'll watch my back," Kilraven promised. "Keep digging. If we can get anything on Hank Sanders, anything that connects him to the DB in Jacobsville or the assaults, we can hang him out to dry. Then we have a way to bargain with him."

"Bargain with a killer?"

"I'm not convinced that he is one," Kilraven said suddenly. "It doesn't sound like a decorated navy SEAL, does it? His big brother likes young girls and he has enough money to buy and sell them. I can't get that fourteen-year-old girl he drugged out of my mind. Rogers is going to try to find her and talk to her when she gets out of the hospital. If we can get her to talk to an assistant D.A., maybe she'll implicate the senator. He might plead to lesser charges and confess something."

"You're assuming that the Sanders boys were responsible for Melly," Jon said quietly. "You have no evidence, not a shred, to base that assumption on. Just because one man operates outside the law, it doesn't mean he kills people."

"I know that."

"So walk softly," Jon continued.

"I will."

"Sure you will, wearing steel-toed combat boots with spikes." Jon sighed. "Remember when we were on the FBI Hostage Rescue Team together?" he added, smiling at the memory.

"I do," Kilraven said. "Those were good days, while they lasted."

"You jumped in and got shot, thumbing your nose at proper procedure," Jon reminded him. "That's why they threw you out."

"Well, the CIA caught me when the FBI tossed me," Kilraven mused. "They like people who think outside boxes."

"Just don't do any more jumping. Okay?"

"Hey, if I lose it all, I can go back to the ranch and be a cowboy," Kilraven said. "Or move to Jacobsville and work for Cash Grier."

"You'd never fit in a small town or on a ranch," Jon said quietly. "You live for the adrenaline rush."

"It's the only thing that keeps me sane," Kilraven said heavily. "I don't need a lot of time to sit around and think."

"That's why we have video games," Jon replied. "I've got a new one for Xbox 360, *Dragon Age Origins*, and I just signed up for *World of Warcraft* on the PC."

"I'm still working my way through *Halo: ODST*," came the amused reply. "In fact, I was up until daylight playing it."

"Gamers are not sane."

"Speak for yourself." Kilraven chuckled.

"You take care," Jon told him. "And if you need help, call me."

"Hey, I'm taking my own personal dispatch person along with me," Kilraven replied. "If I need help, she can get it for me immediately!"

Jon chuckled, said goodbye and hung up.

Joceline stuck her head in the door. "I'm going to lunch," she said. "Would you like a sandwich?"

Wary of her, because she never offered to bring him food, his eyes narrowed as he stared her way. "Would I like...?"

She nodded. "They make great ones at Chuck's, near the airport road. But if you're going, you should go now, it gets crowded early," she told him, grinned and closed the door again.

He threw a book at the door.

"I saw that!" she called back, and kept walking.

KILRAVEN WALKED BACK into the kitchen. "I've just booked us on a flight to the Bahamas, first thing in the morning," he told Winnie, who looked stunned. He glanced at Matt. "Sorry, sport, but you'll have to go back to the ranch for a while."

"That's okay," Matt said. "Boone's going to teach me how to ride a horse!"

Winnie grinned. "You couldn't be in better hands," she assured him. "I'll miss you."

"You could take me along," Matt told her, grinning.

"Oh, sure, we're pretending to be on a honeymoon with my kid brother tagging along. I'm sure everyone would believe that," Winnie mused.

"Just kidding," Matt said. He shook his head. "Life's funny, isn't it? A few days ago it was just Mom and me. She got shot and now I have a whole family." He looked at Winnie affectionately. "It's nice."

She smiled. "Very nice."

Kilraven glanced at his watch. "If we're going to see your mother, we need to leave pretty soon. We'll have to have time to get the future *Halo* champ moved."

"Me?" Matt asked. "I've only gotten past the first level."

"In one day," Kilraven said with mock disgust. "Took me three."

"Wow!" Matt enthused.

"Let's go," Kilraven told his companions.

"But the dishes," Winnie began, nodding toward them, stacked in the sink.

"The dishes can wait," he said. He wasn't rude, but he said it with an odd note in his voice, as if he didn't like having her work around his apartment.

She held up both hands. "Okay. It's your apartment," she said, and managed a smile. "I'll just grab my purse and my coat. Matt, can you get yours…?"

"Sure." He buzzed off toward the spare bedroom.

KILRAVEN WAS SOMBER all the way to the hospital. He smiled at Matt and talked video games with him, but there was a sudden coolness in his manner toward Winnie. She couldn't help but notice it. She wondered if she'd offended him by making breakfast.

They found Gail sitting up in bed, but less animated than she had been.

"Third day," Kilraven said, nodding. "It's always the worst one."

"I'm finding that out," Gail replied after she'd hugged Matt and her daughter lightly. She was favoring the arm on the side where she'd been shot. "It hurts like hell and I'm running a temp. The doctor is gloating. I tried to make him let me go home yesterday, and he wouldn't. Now I see why. It would be all right if he wasn't so damned smug about it," she muttered.

Kilraven chuckled. It was the first hint of humor in him since they'd left the apartment. "He was the same way with Marquez," he told her. "But he might have a case on you. He's divorced."

"He's years too old for me," Gail said haughtily.

Kilraven lifted both eyebrows. "He's a year older than you are."

"Exactly," Gail said.

Winnie burst out laughing.

Gail's eyes twinkled at her. But she was feverish and subdued because of the pain.

They didn't stay long. Winnie and Matt didn't want to tire their mother. Winnie made sure she had Boone's cell phone number.

"Yes," Gail said softly. "He and Clark and Keely came to see me last night. I didn't realize how much Clark and Matt favor each other."

"Boone was probably reserved, wasn't he?" Winnie asked, nodding when her mother looked surprised at the comment. "He's always like that until he gets to know you. It's been a long time."

"He's very much like your father," Gail said. "He has the same strength and he's just as reserved, but you always know you can depend on him."

"Yes," Winnie said, and she smiled.

"Clark's a great gamer," Matt told her. "He's been showing me new ways to use grenades! It'll be great training for when I grow up and join a rolling SWAT team," he added with twinkling dark eyes.

Gail groaned. "No! You are not joining a SWAT team, and I don't care how fast you are in that thing!" she indicated the wheelchair.

"That's just jealousy," Matt told his sister. "She tried to get into SWAT, but they said she was too old."

"Too old!" Gail burst out. "Can you imagine?"

"Delicately aged wine requires careful handling," Kilraven said smoothly, repeating one of his favorite adages.

Gail looked at him. "You drunk?" she asked sharply. He glowered. "I was trying to make you feel better."

"Good idea. Go find the so-and-so who put me in the

hospital and lock him up for twenty years, that will make me feel better!"

"Sorry, we have another priority right now. Winnie and I are flying down to Nassau tomorrow."

Gail's eyes narrowed. She turned to Matt. "How about taking a dollar and getting me a soft drink at the canteen?" she asked him.

"Sure! You want a Coke?"

She nodded. She started to reach in her drawer, but Kilraven was quicker. He handed Matt a dollar bill. "Don't use it to impress girls," he teased.

"Some impression this would make," Matt scoffed. "These days, it takes a Jaguar." He pursed his lips. "You're my brother-in-law. How about loaning me the Jag in four years when I start dating?"

"Get out of here," Kilraven said in mock anger.

Matt chuckled all the way out the door.

Kilraven moved closer to the bed, all teasing gone out of him. "The senator's wife is on her way to her beach house. It sides on property the Sinclairs own," he said. "Winnie's going with me so that we can get to know her, in hopes that she might feel confident enough to share some information about her brother-in-law."

"You got married to pump a suspect's relative?" Gail exclaimed.

Kilraven glared at her. "I'm not ruining Winnie's reputation by having her live with me for several days while we court the senator's wife."

Gail smiled. "You're not a bad guy, Kilraven."

"Yes, he is," Winnie mused, but her eyes twinkled.

Kilraven gave her a wink, laughing when she flushed.

"Well, both of you be careful," Gail cautioned. "These people play for keeps."

"You're good with hunches," Kilraven said. "What do you think? Are we following a cold trail, or could the senator's brother have a stake in this case?"

Gail was silent for a minute. "I don't really know. I think the senator's up to his ears in parts of it," she said. "I want to talk to the mother of that young girl who was found dead."

He was somber. He'd thought about questioning the teen who lived, but never about asking the mother of the girl who was found dead. "You think she might know something more than she told the police at the time it happened?"

"Could be. She supposedly went on a date and turned up dead in a condition where her own family wouldn't have recognized her, just like our DB on the Little Carmichael River. Her car was even found next to a river. It just seems too close to be a coincidence."

"I agree. But it would be a long shot."

"I'm famous for long shots."

"You won't get out of here for several days," Kilraven said.

"Not unless I can K.O. the doctor." Gail sighed.

"When we get back, maybe we'll have some new information to work with. Meanwhile, I've got a buddy watching out for you, just in case your assailant comes calling again."

"I'm a cop," she pointed out.

"Yes, and your department's budget is less than my annual video game allowance," he said sarcastically, "so I don't imagine they're lining up for overtime to trail you."

She grimaced.

"My buddy is between jobs and he loves catching crooks. You won't see him or know who he is, but he'll be around."

"Thanks, Kilraven," she said.

"You're my temporary mother-in-law." He chuckled. "It's the least I can do."

"Don't turn your back, even in Nassau," Gail cautioned them. "The senator's wife may accept you being there on face value, but I'm betting her husband wouldn't. One thing I did find out before I was shot—there's an old family retainer, Jay Copper. He's very protective of Senator Sanders. There's been gossip that he's really the senator's father. He was in prison for several years for a messy homicide, got out on a technicality. Anyway, he was charged at least once with intimidating a reporter who was digging into that statutory rape case. Threatened to have his family blown up with a shotgun."

Kilraven's intake of breath was audible.

"Yes, I thought that might sound familiar." Gail nodded, her eyes cold. "Copper doesn't like Hank Sanders or the senator's wife, Patricia. One of my contacts said that the main reason Patricia stays out of the senator's way is because she's afraid of Copper."

Kilraven's eyes narrowed. "I heard something about that old guy. They called him Copperhead, back in the seventies, when he was supposedly involved in drug trafficking in Dallas."

"That's the one. He's still on the job, intimidating everybody he can to keep the senator nice and safe."

"What about Hank Sanders?"

She pursed her lips. "Now isn't that an interesting

question. I went to see Garon Grier down at the Bureau a few days before I was shot, and guess who was waiting for him in the parking lot, trying not to be seen?"

Kilraven's heart jumped. "Hank Sanders."

She nodded. "Why is a notorious criminal keeping company with one of the more notorious conservative FBI agents?"

"There's another curious fact. Hank was a decorated navy SEAL."

She pursed her lips. "That turns us in a whole other direction. And I have a theory."

"So do I," Kilraven replied. "But we'll keep that between us until Winnie and I get back from the Bahamas. Maybe we can find out more."

"Even if Jay Copper didn't go with Patricia Sanders to the Bahamas, ten to one he's got one of his goons there keeping an eye on her," Gail added. "Word was that she was trying to divorce the senator, until Copper mentioned that it would hurt the senator in the polls and he wouldn't like her to try it. She backed off at once."

His eyes narrowed. "I get the idea."

"Be careful," she told him firmly.

"I'm always careful." He smiled as he glanced at Winnie. "And don't worry. I'll take care of your daughter."

Winnie smiled, but she wished he'd said "my wife" instead of Gail's daughter. Still, it was early days yet. She had time to make an impression. He was quite obviously hungry for her. And where there was smoke, there was fire.

CHAPTER THIRTEEN

THEY GOT OFF the plane in Nassau with the rest of the business-class section and even though it was winter back in the United States, it was perpetual summer in the Bahamas. They looked out the window of the terminal as they came onto the concourse. People were walking around in shorts.

"Why did I wear a coat?" Winnie groaned.

"Because you were cold?" Kilraven mused. "Come on. Let's get in the line for customs."

"It will be slow. It always is."

"Are we in a race?" he asked.

She hit him.

THEY LOOKED LIKE a society couple. Winnie was wearing a trim, very expensive cream-colored couture pantsuit with designer high heels and purse. Kilraven was wearing silk slacks and shirt and an expensive jacket. He made a point of telling the customs official that he and Winnie were newlyweds on their honeymoon. They walked out of the terminal past a steel drum band, unconsciously moving to the rhythm of the music.

A limousine that Kilraven had hired when he made the reservations was waiting for them. It whisked them along the winding road that led from the airport, past Cable Beach, to the road that led to the exclusive section of New Providence where so many millionaires had summer homes.

"Isn't it beautiful?" she asked, looking out the tinted window. "The first time we came here, I must have been about four years old. I saw the white sand and all the incredible shades of aqua and turquoise of the water and asked my parents if it was a painting."

"I know what you mean," he said. "Those colors look too vivid to be real."

"Have you been here before?" she asked.

He laughed. "I've been through here," he replied. "I've seen airports and hotels all over the world, but my experience with open country has been mostly in the dark."

She understood the reference at once. "You never talk about it, do you?"

"Wouldn't dare," he replied. "Most of it is classified." He pursed his lips and smiled at her. "I trust you, but you'd need a government clearance to know particulars."

She made a face. "I tell you everything," she countered.

His eyebrows arched. "You do?"

"I told you about my mother and my father," she pointed out.

His eyes grew sad. "And I told you about my daughter. I've never spoken of her to anyone outside my family, except people directly involved in the case."

"I'm sorry you lost her in such a way."

He averted his gaze to the scenery passing the windows, tall casuarina pines and royal palms lining the narrow paved road. "So am I."

She pressed a wrinkle out of the soft fabric of her

slacks. "Haven't you ever thought about having another child?"

"No," he said at once, and with ice dripping from the tones.

The violence of the reply disconcerted her. She met his eyes and almost flinched at what she saw in them.

"I won't go through it again," he assured her.

"But just because you lost one child in such a horrible way…!"

He held up a hand. "I won't discuss it, either," he said coldly. His silvery eyes were glittering like metal. "I appreciate your help, I really do. But if you have any illusions about why we're here, let me disenchant you. We're here to ask questions and get answers, not spend a few torrid nights in each other's arms. I could walk away after and never look back. You couldn't. You're too young and too innocent for a casual affair. So we'll do what we came here to do, go back to the States and get a quiet annulment. And there won't be any complications. Least of all a pregnancy. Period."

She felt as if he'd stuck a pin in her. He was intimidating like that. She was used to him being amused or teasing around her. He'd never been really harsh, except that one time when she messed up at dispatch and nearly got him killed. This was the real man behind the banter, and he was scary. No wonder Gail had said he was dangerous.

He realized that he was upsetting her and he forced himself to calm down. She was a normal, loving woman who wanted a home and family. Her feelings for him were getting in the way of her common sense, and that was only infatuation. She'd get over it. She was, as he'd already said, very young. Twenty-two to his thirty-two.

"Sorry," she said, and managed a smile.

"No, I'm sorry," he replied quietly. "I forget your age sometimes." He forced a smile. "You'll find a man who wants to settle down and have a family with you, one day. But it won't be me. You know that already."

She nodded. She wasn't really agreeing, but it seemed safer to appear to acquiesce. At least he wasn't looking at her with that icy glare anymore.

"Now there's a dangerous method of travel," she said to divert him, pointing to mopeds zipping past in the other direction.

He chuckled. "I had to appropriate one of those in another country for emergency transport once," he confessed. "Rounded a curve and went right over the handlebars." He shook his head. "That's how I ended up with a steel pin in my leg. It's a lot harder than it looks."

"And you drive a Jaguar?" she chided.

He frowned. "Jags are built to be stable on the road at extremely high speeds. Mopeds aren't."

"Well, my brother thinks Jags can fly. He's never been able to convince state troopers that he should be allowed to fly them on the interstate."

He chuckled. "Me, either."

"I wish we were going downtown. I'd love to see the old British Colonial hotel," she mused.

"The what?"

"Oh, that's not what they call it now," she said. "It's the Hilton Hotel these days. It's right downtown, next to the wharf. It was the site of old Fort Nassau and the scene of many battles in the seventeenth century. It was also the place to be seen socially at the turn of the twentieth century. The Duke and Duchess of Windsor even attended parties there when he was governor of the Bahamas during the Second World War." She smiled. "There's a statue of the pirate Woodes Rogers right out in front of the hotel. Ironically, he was the first governor of the Bahamas."

"Just as Henry Morgan, the pirate, was the first governor of Jamaica," he chuckled. "His grave was lost in the late seventeeth century during a devastating earthquake that sent most of Port Royal to the bottom of the ocean."

She shivered. "Yes, there was an earthquake in Portugal in 1755 that sent a stone quay into the sea, killing people who'd rushed there for refuge. They estimated that over 20,000 people perished in Lisbon in a matter of minutes, from the earthquake and the tsunamis that followed it."

He stared at her. "You follow earthquake history."

She laughed self-consciously. "Well, yes," she confessed. "I practically live on the United States Geological Survey site."

"So do I," he exclaimed.

"Really!"

"Really. There and the Weather Channel and at www. spaceweather.com," he added. "I follow sunspots and meteor showers and..."

"...and near-earth asteroids on Spaceweather," she laughed. "Yes. Me, too."

His eyes were twinkling. "You have a telescope."

"How did you know that?" she asked, startled.

"A lucky guess. I have one, too. You didn't see it because it's in my bedroom. It's a composite, a..."

"Schmidt-Cassegrain," she guessed, smiling sheepishly when he laughed. "How big is the aperture?"

"Eight inches."

"Mine's ten," she bragged.

"Yes, but you live out in the country." He sighed. "I'm in town, and the eight-inch lets in less light pollution."

"You'll have to come look at astronomical events with me, when we get through with our undercover stuff," she said. "Boone had a small observatory built for me in the back patio. I can leave my telescope out in all weathers, because it's waterproof."

"I'd like that," he said seriously. He was looking at her oddly. "In all the time we've known each other, you never mentioned liking natural events or astronomy."

"It never came up," she said.

"I guess not." He liked what he was learning about her. But she was still far too young, especially for what he'd been thinking about when he first proposed this trip. He was vaguely ashamed of himself, more so when he recalled her recent turmoil in finding that she had a brother she didn't even know about and that her uncle might be involved peripherally in the recent murder. Then, too, her mother had been shot. Perhaps that wouldn't have bothered her some weeks ago, but since discovering her mother's true situation, it had hit her hard. And he'd been thinking of a holiday romp with her, a sexual escapade that he could forget, but that she couldn't. She cared about him. She really did. It was disturbing, on several levels.

Monica, his late wife, had liked his family's wealth. Despite his job as a policeman at the time, she knew his family had money and she'd decided she might as well marry for money as love. Perhaps she'd been fond of him, but it had never been more than that. She'd been mostly unconcerned with Melly after her birth. Kilraven had doted on the child, taking her places with him, showing her off. He clamped down on the memory. It was painful. He recalled that Cammy, his stepmother, hadn't liked Monica at all. Not that she liked any women her son and stepson brought around. But she'd often said that there was something dark and cold lying curled up in Monica's brain.

"Deep thoughts?" Winnie asked gently.

"What?" He laughed humorlessly. "I was thinking about Monica. My wife," he added when she looked puzzled. "She lived in Neiman Marcus and Saks. She loved clothes and diamonds and parties."

"She must have loved her family, too," she said.

"She loved my money." He sighed. "But she never bought a dress or a pair of shoes or even a toy for Melly. If I gave her money to buy stuff for Melly, she bought clothes for herself with it. I finally learned to shop for my daughter myself."

Winnie was surprised. In the other woman's place, she'd have been showering her daughter with presents, cuddling her, taking her places, taking photos of her night and day... She averted her eyes and her hands gripped her purse hard. "That's sad," she said.

"I asked her once why she didn't ever play with the baby," he recalled solemnly. "She said it was her job to have the child, mine to raise it. She'd done her part. She didn't even like children, she just got tired of me badgering her about having kids." He dropped his eyes to the floorboard. "Cammy might not be your idea of the perfect mother," he added with a deep laugh, "but she was a hell of a stepmother. She was always taking me places, doing things with me, buying me stuff. When Jon came along, he was my brother, plain and simple—she treated us both just alike. Heaven help any teacher or bully who gave us trouble at school. Cammy would be on them like a duck on a june bug. Even Dad wasn't ever so protective of us."

"I'm sure she improves on closer acquaintance," Winnie said stiffly. "I'll see if Boone will loan me a cattle prod to carry if I have to talk to her again..."

He gave her an affectionate look. "Little blonde chain saw," he said with pure amusement.

He made it sound like a caress. She felt warm, safe, secure. She smiled. "I'm not like that, usually."

The smile faded. "I know. You don't assert yourself enough. People will walk all over you, if you let them."

"You'd know." She sighed.

"I'm used to walking on people," he pointed out. "You have to stand up to me."

"I'm still trying to stand up to Boone," she said, wincing. "It's not easy."

"You did very well, convincing him to let you come down here with me," he said somberly. "I was proud of you."

She lifted her eyes to his. "You were?"

He nodded. "Stick around with me for a while and I'll have you eating tigers with just a little hot sauce, raw."

Oh, give me the chance, she thought. But she only smiled. "I'll follow your sterling example."

The car was slowing. It pulled up to a wrought-iron metal gate, very ornate, and Winnie jumped out and punched a code into the computerized access panel. She got back in. The gate opened.

"Boone had it installed," she said. "We had a break-in a few years ago. Now we're very security conscious."

He nodded. He was going to make sure the security

was top-notch while they were in residence. He didn't
want any surprise visits, just in case they ruffled enough
feathers to invite unwanted visitors.

THE HOUSE WAS white with a red ceramic tile roof. It sat
well back from the beach, on a plot of land that was covered with casuarina pines and palms. Around the long
front porch were hibiscus and lantana, and brilliant bougainvillea climbing the patio balcony.

"Nice," Kilraven said as they walked up onto the
porch, the driver following with their luggage. He had
the driver set the bags down and gave him a substantial
tip, with thanks. The man saluted with a big grin, and
went back to his vehicle.

Winnie was putting her key in the door. She'd already
disabled the security pad.

She opened it and sighed at the beauty of the inte-
rior. The furniture was pristine, the floors spotless and
highly polished wood. There were original paintings on
the walls, one of Boone and Clark and Winnie as children.
The house had been in the family for two generations.

Kilraven walked to the portrait and studied it. Winnie had long, wavy hair. She was wearing a white dress
and holding a red hibiscus flower, laughing. She was
very pretty.

"I was five years old when that was painted," she said,
looking at it from beside him. "My parents were still together. We used to come here for several weeks in the
summer."

He nodded. He looked around. The furnishings were
nice, but they looked new. "These aren't very old," he
remarked.

"No. The last big hurricane that hit the island got the original house," she said sadly. "The painting survived because it was on loan to a local gallery, which survived. We lost everything, except the shell of the house. Boone had it rebuilt. It's a replica of the original, but without the things that gave it a history."

"The painting survived, at least," he commented.

"Yes. But we learned a hard lesson. Now we don't bring heirlooms down here anymore. Just in case." She turned. He was still looking at the painting. "I'll bet you've lived through hurricanes at least once."

He smiled faintly and dug his hands into his pockets. "Hurricanes, typhoons, tornadoes, sandstorms and enemy attacks with blazing guns."

She grimaced. "I've never even been in a tornado, although one went right by the house not too many years ago." She laughed. "And I've never had to face an attack by anybody armed."

"No reason for you to have to," he pointed out.

"Thank goodness." She went toward the kitchen. "I phoned down here before we left San Antonio and had Marco come up and turn on the electricity and stock the fridge. He acts as part-time caretaker for us. He also owns a local art store." She laughed. "He's the reason we still have that painting. He has strict instructions to rush right down here and put it in storage if there's even a gale warning."

"You could take it to Comanche Wells," he said.

"It belongs here," she replied simply. "But we did have it copied."

"Good thinking."

"Are you hungry?" she asked.

"Starved." He sighed. "Peanuts don't do a thing for me."

"In defense of the airlines," she said, "they have to feed the monkeys something."

"Why can't they feed us real meals? I was on this flight to Japan," he recalled with a smile, "and I asked for Japanese cuisine. It came in several stages, just as it does in Osaka at a good restaurant. I loved it."

They went into the kitchen and Winnie opened the refrigerator. She reached in and then turned with a ham platter in one hand and a mayonnaise jar in another. "I've never been to Asia. How do they serve food?"

"In tiny bits," he said. "On one plate, you might get a morsel of meat with a small slice of fruit. On another, a spoonful of salad. Dessert comes on a plate in the form of a walnut-size scoop of plum ice cream with a small leaf and a drizzle of syrup for decoration. It's edible art."

"Wow."

"Like they do gifts," he said, moving to the counter to find plates and bread and in a drawer to pull out a knife for the mayonnaise. "It doesn't matter what the present is, they're concerned with the way it's wrapped. The more elegant, the better."

"You liked it there," she commented.

He nodded. "Very much." He chuckled as he watched her make ham sandwiches.

"What's funny?"

"I was thinking that I could never commit a crime on the streets of Osaka without being immediately taken into custody. I'm more than a head taller than most people I met."

She grinned. She looked down at his shoes. "And with bigger feet, I imagine."

"That's another thing, if you think you may need a second pair of shoes, you're advised to take them with you. You won't find a size to fit you unless you have feet the size of yours." He was looking at her little feet in the high heels and his expression was almost affectionate. "What do you wear, anyway, about a five?"

"Five and a half," she corrected.

"Tiny little feet," he mused. "Pretty in those strappy high heels."

She flushed. "Thanks."

He took the knife out of her hand and put it on the table. His expression was unreadable as he suddenly lifted her by the waist, right up to his eyes. "You promised not to wear anything suggestive," he said.

She gasped. "Listen, I'm covered from head to mid-calf…!"

His mouth brushed hers, sending shivers of pleasure down her spine. "Those sexy little feet aren't covered," he whispered. He nibbled her upper lip.

"My…feet…aren't covered?" she faltered.

"Sexy feet," he whispered. His tongue slid under her top lip and explored the soft, moist flesh. His big hands tightened on her waist. He moved just a few steps to the counter and lifted her there, so that she was almost on a level with his eyes. His lips whispered over her face, from her cheek to her nose, down to the corners of her mouth.

While he was exploring her face and enjoying her helpless little gasps, his hands were busy on her jacket and the front clip of the bra under it. She didn't realize it until she felt the air on her bare skin, until she saw his eyes dropping down, until she heard his breath catch.

She would have jerked at the bra, but the way he was

looking at her made her heart stop. His hand traced over the high, firm swell of her breast, his fingers smoothing down over the suddenly taut nipple. It was like the night on his sofa all over again, and she was helpless.

"Beautiful breasts," he whispered tautly. "As pink as the inside of a conch shell. Soft. Silky. Delicious."

As he spoke, his head bent. His lips took the place of his fingers in a light, whispery caress that was so tender it made her whole body clench.

"Sweet as honey," he whispered. His other hand smoothed up her rib cage, over the breast he wasn't kissing.

Winnie was on fire. She'd never been touched like that voluntarily before Kilraven came along. Once a boy had grabbed her on a date and hurt her when she fought her way out of his arms. No other man had ever been allowed to go this far.

She arched her back in helpless response to the sensations he was arousing.

"You like this, do you?" he murmured. "I know something you'll like better."

As he spoke, his mouth opened and he took almost her whole breast inside it, teasing the nipple with his tongue as the soft suction caught her in the grip of a hunger she'd never felt before.

She moaned, a high-pitched little skirl of sound that brought Kilraven's blood up, hard. His mouth became insistent, almost violent, on her soft skin. All at once, he lifted her again, only to rivet her hips to the rising hardness of his body, to show her the desire that raged in him from the contact.

His mouth bit at hers. "I had a buddy in Iraq," he whispered roughly. "He came home on leave and his wife was walking around in a short gown with nothing under it. He dropped his pants, lifted her onto him and walked around the house, bouncing her against him. He said the climax was so violent that they fell down the steps into the sunken living room and had to go to the emergency room after." His mouth ground into hers. "He said it was worth a broken ankle."

She shivered. The mental imagery made her even hotter than she already was.

His hands ground her hips into his and he groaned.

Her hands were also busy, pulling at buttons until she reached hard muscle and thick hair. She rubbed her breasts against his chest in a fever of need, moaning again at the sensation it produced.

"I don't want to...stop," he bit off. "It's been too long!"

"I don't care," she whimpered. She wrapped her legs around him, shivering. "Please..."

He didn't need to be asked twice. He carried her into the first bedroom he came to, put her on the bed and stripped.

Her eyes widened as she saw him without the protection of clothing. He was incredible-looking, all muscle and tanned skin, all man. She was too aroused to feel embarrassed, even when he stripped her as efficiently and tossed her back onto the coverlet.

He covered her with his body, his face taut and grim, rigid with the desire that was consuming him. He moved her legs apart and lowered himself between them.

"Are you really a virgin?" he whispered roughly.

"Sorry. Yes," she managed as she felt him against her.

He slid a hand under her hips and lifted her. His eyes held hers as he impaled her suddenly.

She cried out, shocked and hurt.

His teeth clenched. He held her still when she tried to move back away from him. "It won't hurt for long," he promised gruffly.

But it did. She bit her lower lip until blood dropped, salty and hot, on her tongue. She closed her eyes, aware of his harsh breathing, the downward push of his hips as he drove for satisfaction, blind and deaf to everything except the need to overcome the anguish that consumed him. The tension snapped very quickly, in a red rush of sensation that made him cry out with its intensity. He shuddered over her, ramming his hips down against hers as he filled her body with his in one final, insistent surge of passion.

He felt her tears as his face slid against hers, felt her shivering. He kissed the tears away. His hand smoothed tenderly over her hair, brushing it away from her wet, pale face.

He looked down into her eyes. "It's been seven years," he whispered quietly.

She couldn't stop shivering. "Seven years?" she whispered, surprised.

He nodded. He bent and brushed his mouth over her closed eyelids, sipping away the wetness. "I'm a prude, just like my brother," he whispered. "I think people should be married before they have sex."

She swallowed, trying to cope with the pain. "So do I."

He propped himself on an elbow and studied her face quietly. "I've never been with a virgin," he confessed.

She frowned. "Your wife…?"

"She was a party girl," he said heavily. "I thought all women were like you, that they waited for marriage. I had a shock on my wedding night, when she shared the benefit of her sensual education with me." He managed a brief smile. "I was shocked and mad and couldn't even express it, because she got me so hot I'd have died to have her. She kept me that way for three years."

She searched his eyes. Incredible, to be lying together with him in such intimacy and talk to each other like this. "I don't know anything about men," she confessed shyly, "except what I've read in books and seen in movies."

"And heard from girlfriends?" he prompted.

"Actually, I've only ever had one real girlfriend, my sister-in-law, Keely, and we don't ever talk about such things," she told him. "So I guess I'm a prude, too."

He moved the hair away from her ear and studied it. "You have tiny little ears."

She smiled. "They match my tiny little feet."

"Sexy feet," he said again. "Some men like breasts, others like legs. I like feet."

"My goodness!"

He lifted his head. "How bad is it, when I do this?" He moved his hips, very slowly.

She caught her breath.

He lifted up and then pushed down again.

She caught her breath again. But this time, her fingernails bit into his muscular arms and pulled.

He smiled. "I thought it was best to get the pain out of the way first," he whispered. "Because I know a few things that I can teach you."

"You...do?" She was shivering, but not from pain.

"Mmm-hmm," he murmured. He slid his hand under

her hips and lifted her, tenderly, into the slow thrust of his body. "Put your legs together. That's right."

She moaned harshly.

"See?" His head bent and he brushed her mouth open with his lips while he moved lazily against her, each movement more arousing, more sensual than the one before.

Her fingernails bit into him again.

"Move your hands down my back and do that," he whispered.

She slid them over his hips and onto the firm muscles, digging in.

He groaned and arched, increasing his possession of her.

She gasped.

He looked straight into her eyes and shifted. The pleasure bit into him like a sweet knife. He could see the echo of it in her own face. She started to close her eyes, faintly embarrassed at watching something so intimate.

"No, don't close your eyes, Winnie," he whispered. "Watch me. Let me watch you."

She flushed as she met his silver eyes. He shifted again, catching one of her silky thighs in his hand and positioning her again, so that she groaned and shivered.

"Now," he whispered, "I'm going to show you why the French call a climax the 'little death.'"

He slid one hand under her nape and clenched it in her hair. His silver eyes glittered as he moved in and his body thrust hard and fast down into hers, each movement deep and quick and passionate. It only took a few seconds for her to go over the edge. She gaped at him and suddenly cried out.

"That's it," he whispered huskily when she arched up. "That's it, baby, come up and get me. Come on, come on, push, push, push!"

She was screaming. The pleasure was like a vice. Her eyes were wide-open and he was watching her, seeing it, laughing as she clawed at his hips and ground hers up into his in a rhythm that was faster than her own heartbeat.

"Get it, baby," he gritted. "Get it now!"

She shuddered and shuddered, twisting up, arching up, pleading in a voice that she only vaguely recognized as her own, while the pleasure suddenly built to a crescendo and exploded in her body like a rush of molten magma. She gasped almost in shock as it overwhelmed her. She shivered and sobbed, clinging to him while she was buffeted by the most incredible pleasure she'd ever experienced in her life.

His face, above her, clenched and he bit off something explosive as satisfaction shook his powerful body like a feverish chill. He arched his hips down into hers and cried out hoarsely, his head thrown back in pure ecstasy as he shuddered with her in a climax so hot that he almost passed out.

She was aware of her own heartbeat, going like a drum, of her sobbing breaths as she tried to drag in air. She felt Kilraven still shuddering against her, his voice breaking as he felt the tension explode.

Her eyes were intent on him. She'd never seen an expression like that. His face was clenched and flushed. His eyes were closed. His whole body shuddered again and again and when his eyes opened and he saw her watching, he groaned and the shudders seemed to deepen.

"Dear... God!" he cried, and shuddered again.

She was fascinated. All her reading hadn't prepared her for what she was seeing. He wasn't pretending, he was really blind with pleasure that she was giving him. Impulsively, she lifted against him and moved sensually. He sobbed and the shuddering increased. She loved pleasing him. It made her own body throb all over again. She moved feverishly, arching up to him, twisting, watching him cry out as pleasure brought him into uncharted realms of passion.

It took a long time. She shivered again with surprise as another climax tightened her muscles. Watching him, pleasing him, was giving her fulfillment again and again.

He felt her body clench over and over, felt her tighten around him, as he drowned in pleasure. He was letting her see, letting her enjoy him. He was enjoying her. He couldn't remember a time with Monica when he let himself lose control to this extent. He'd always held something back, vaguely ashamed of the way she could manipulate him with sex. This was different. Winnie loved him. It was all right if she saw him helpless, if she watched him achieve satisfaction in her soft body.

He was shuddering. He made a sound in his throat, and his body ground down into hers as the last silvery rush of pleasure began to fade away.

She felt him relax. She took his full weight, hungry for the contact to continue, so satiated that she could barely get her breath.

"The little death," she whispered, and shivered one last time.

"Yes."

She closed her eyes as she felt exhaustion leave her

limp and boneless under his hard, damp body. The hair on his chest felt wet against her breasts.

His cheek slid against hers with a long, heavy sigh. "Little blonde...chain saw," he whispered. And, incredibly, he fell asleep.

So did she, in the aftermath of something so explosive and unexpected that she knew nothing would ever be the same again.

CHAPTER FOURTEEN

WINNIE CAME AWAKE SLOWLY, aware of discomfort in an odd place. She moved and winced. Then memory came flooding back and she knew why she was uncomfortable. She was under the covers, but without a stitch of clothing on. Kilraven was nowhere in sight.

In the absence of passion, nudity was embarrassing. So were her poignant memories of what she had said and done with him. Her face flamed as she jumped out of bed, still clutching the sheet, and looked for her clothes.

She had a vague memory of feeling them stripped off and tossed onto the floor, but now they were draped across a chair. On a table, her suitcase was open.

She dragged the sheet with her, pausing every couple of steps to listen, to make sure Kilraven wasn't coming through the door. She grabbed underwear, jeans and a T-shirt and made a rush for the bathroom, almost tripping over the sheet.

A FEW MINUTES LATER, clean but still uncomfortable, she walked out into the bedroom with damp hair. She'd forgotten to pack a hair dryer and she couldn't remember where one was to be found in the summer house.

Well, it was thin hair and the heat was enough to dry it without any help, she reasoned. She went back into the kitchen. It was deserted. Kilraven had apparently put away the ham and bread and mayonnaise, and stacked the dishes in the sink. Remarkable, she thought, how neat he was.

She looked out the window and was surprised to see the sun going down in the distance. It had been early afternoon when they'd arrived from the airport. She flushed again, recalling how that time had been spent. Kilraven was nothing if not gifted in bed. If he could make a screaming, clawing passionate woman out of someone as sedate as Winnie, he could certainly lay claim to incredible skills.

She went back into the bedroom and unpacked. She wondered where Kilraven had gone.

HE WAS WALKING along the beach, barefooted, wearing tan Bermuda shorts and nothing else. He felt like the worst sort of betrayer. He'd promised himself, and Winnie, that he'd take care of her and that nothing would happen to make an annulment impossible. The minute he'd touched her, all those resolutions had gone into eclipse and he'd reacted like a sex-starved adolescent.

Still, he recalled with some pride, he hadn't made a total hash of the thing. He had the marks on his back to prove it, too. He winced a little and then laughed, recalling her nails biting into him as she moaned.

He didn't want to have to go back and face her. Was she going to think he'd changed his mind about staying with her? He hadn't. She was sweet to teach and he'd enjoyed her. But sex was a poor foundation for a marriage. And he should know. It was the only thing he and Monica ever had in common.

At least Winnie was on the Pill. But he should have had

more self-control. He kicked at a shell that had washed up on the sugar-sand beach and cursed. He could have kicked himself.

"What did that poor shell ever do to you?" a female voice inquired amusedly.

He turned his head and looked into the eyes of Senator Will Sanders's wife.

She was a brunette. She had long hair down to her waist. She was wearing a neat one-piece black bathing suit with oversize sunglasses, carrying a book, a towel and some tanning lotion in a bottle.

He frowned. "Am I trespassing?" he asked curiously.

She laughed. "Afraid so. Although I don't know if we own the beach just because we own the house it's in front of."

He shrugged a broad shoulder. "Why not? We think we own our beach," he said, and smiled.

She moved forward with self-confidence and a charming smile. "I'm Patricia Sanders," she said, extending a hand.

He shook it firmly. "Kilraven," he said.

The smile faltered. "You're the FBI agent..."

He gave her a horrified look. "Not me!" he exclaimed.

"But someone said," she began.

"My brother, Jon Blackhawk. He's the FBI agent," he said. "I'm a Fed. But with another bureau."

She was suspicious. "Why are you walking along my beach, federal agent?"

He smiled self-consciously. "Hiding from my wife. Hoping she won't be waiting with a baseball bat when I go back to the house. It's that one," he added, playing the role for all he was worth as he indicated the Sinclair summer house nearby.

"That's the Sinclair place," she said more suspiciously.

"Yes, and Winnie Sinclair is my wife." He sighed.

The suspicion was gone at once. "Winnie?"

He nodded. He sighed again, loudly. "At least she's my wife right now. I don't know how long that will last, however. We may have the shortest wedding in Comanche Wells's history."

She began to smile. "Made her mad, did you?"

He winced. "Furious!"

"I would never have thought of her as a woman with a temper."

"That's because you've never known her since she was married to me," he said with resignation. "We've been married for two days, six hours and," he looked at his watch, "thirty minutes. As of right now."

Her dark eyes were twinkling. "I see."

"How do you know Winnie?" he asked, frowning.

She gave him an exasperated look. "I have a summer home next door to hers," she said with slow deliberation.

"Oh. Oh!" He shook his head, laughing. "Sorry. I'm a bit slow at the moment."

"Arguments will do that to people," she agreed. She looked haunted for a minute.

"I'd better go back and face the music," he said heavily. "Nice to meet you. We probably won't see each other again. I'll be dead."

She laughed, and it had a delightful sound. "I don't think she'll really kill you. You're on your honeymoon, then?"

He nodded and smiled. "I'm taking a few weeks off.

We can't stay long, though. She works as a 911 operator back home, and they'll need her. She only gets two weeks."

"A 911 operator? Winnie Sinclair?" she exclaimed, shocked.

"They all work," he said. "Rich may be nice, but the Sinclairs all have an exaggerated work ethic. Especially Winnie." He chuckled. "That's how I met her. I was working in Jacobsville and she was on dispatch. Almost got me killed one night, but I calmed down when she started crying. She's quite a woman."

"I like her," the senator's wife said. "She's very sweet."

"Yes, well, she's not mad at you, is she? My stepmother calls her a little blonde chain saw."

Mrs. Sanders burst out laughing. "What a description!"

"Sometimes it's very accurate."

She hesitated. Her dark eyes gave him a curious appraisal. "I'm throwing a party for some local friends Wednesday night. If you and the chain saw aren't otherwise occupied, you might come over."

"Thanks, but I don't drink," he said.

She gaped at him. "You don't? Now you have to come. I've never met a man who didn't drink. My husband can go through a fifth of whiskey in one sitting!" She laughed.

"Well, if we're free, we might come over for a few minutes. Thanks," he said, trying to sound reluctant.

"I'll make sure you have something nonalcoholic. And I've got a world-class chef preparing the buffet. You don't want to miss that."

He smiled. "Sounds nice."

"Never turn down free food," she told him in a conspiratorial tone. "I grew up very poor in Oklahoma. I got a job as a small-town newspaper reporter because I learned that if you went to cover events where food was served, you got fed for free."

He chuckled. She looked wicked when she smiled like that. "I see your point."

She tossed the towel over her shoulder and pulled down her sunglasses. "We'll start about six," she said. "But it's not on the clock. You can show up anytime before midnight."

"All right. Thanks again."

She shrugged. "I get tired of the same faces day after day." The way she said it, Kilraven wondered if she might be talking about the senator's latest flame. But he wasn't about to ask.

"See you," he said, and turned, walking slowly down the beach the way he'd come.

KILRAVEN WALKED IN the back door, hesitating. He really needed Winnie to go to that party with him. He had to convince her without letting her know how important it was. If he had to apologize for what had happened on his knees it would be worth it. He'd never felt closer to solving his daughter's murder.

Winnie was curled up in a chair with a book. She jumped when she heard him come into the room.

"Hi," she said.

"Hi. Guess who I just ran into on the beach?" he asked with pursed lips and twinkling eyes.

"I'll bite. Who?"

"Senator Will Sanders's wife," he told her. He put his hands deep in the pockets of his Bermuda shorts, pulling them tight against the strong muscles of his thighs. "She's invited us to a party Wednesday night."

She was just looking at him, drinking in the impact of that powerful, virile body that hers knew so intimately now. It made her tingle. "I guess you want to go, huh?"

"Why did we come down here, Winnie?" he asked bluntly.

Well, that was blunt enough, she told herself. She flushed a little. "Sorry. Wasn't thinking."

He drew in an angry breath. "Look, I did a stupid thing this afternoon. I didn't mean to, and I'm sorry."

How nice, to reduce a feverish interlude of breathless passion into a traffic citation, she thought wickedly.

She shrugged. "No problem. We all get parking tickets now and again."

He blinked. "Are we having the same conversation?"

She smiled faintly. "Sorry, I don't know where my mind was. Okay, I'll go with you." She put the book down. "She didn't suspect anything?"

"She did until I mentioned that we were recently married," he replied and smiled because the subterfuge had worked as well as he'd thought it would.

"So your hunch paid off."

"You might say that."

"Good for you."

He frowned. She didn't sound pleasant at all. His eyes narrowed as he saw the disappointment in her dark eyes. "Okay, let's get it out in the open. You think because we enjoyed each other that I'm going to want to keep you. That it?"

She went scarlet.

He smiled coolly. "I'm your first man," he said bluntly.

"You're wrapped up in pink daydreams because I know my way around a woman's body without a road map. It was just sex, Winnie. I've abstained for seven years and we're married. Simple as that. I went in over my head because…"

"No need to explain," she interrupted him, standing up, but she didn't meet his eyes. "I'll admit I got off track for a while. Don't worry about it. I may build a few daydreams, but I know exactly where reality begins. I won't try to lock you in a closet and keep you for a sex slave. Honest." She crossed her heart.

He looked as if someone had hit him in the face with a pie.

She moved closer and patted him on the chest. "Now, I know you're disappointed, but I can assure you that there are plenty of women in the world who keep handcuffs and own closets. So you just keep those spirits up until you run into one of them." She yawned deliberately. "Gosh, I'm sleepy. I think I'll have a nap. Watch TV if you like." She waved a hand over her shoulder as she walked toward the bedroom where her things were. "Won't bother me."

She went into the room and closed the door behind her. Then she let the tears roll down her cheeks. But not until then. She was finally learning how to stand up to him. Brute force didn't work, but humor seemed to. If she could just keep her heart from breaking, she might manage to get through the next few days. The trick, she considered, was not to let him see her cry.

KILRAVEN WAS STUNNED. Had he really heard her say that? He went and sat down on the sofa with a hard breath. That was not what he'd expected. He was sure that he had little Winnie Sinclair figured out and pigeonholed. Then she came out with the sex slave quip and he was back to first base. He turned on the news. But then he grinned.

Winnie kept him at a distance with airy smiles and tours of the island, and never let him close enough to touch her. It seemed to irritate him at first. Then, like the quips she came out with, it amused him into relaxing. They spent three days sunning on the beach and walking around Bay Street.

She did very well by pretending that he was her brother. From time to time, she had to hide a fit of the giggles, because he was devastating in swim trunks and when they went in the ocean together and he held her up and grinned at her, she almost lost her poise. But she kept telling herself they were related and they couldn't do more than hold hands.

Amazingly, he did hold hands with her as they walked down the rows of shops. He was more relaxed than she'd ever seen him.

"You're different, here," she said as they paused to look in a shop window at some natty tourist T-shirts.

"No real pressure right now," he said simply, smiling down at her. "I live from adrenaline rush to adrenaline rush. I have for years. It's addictive. In between, I'm just waiting for the next one to come along."

"It's so much stress," she said.

He lifted an eyebrow. "Oh, you wouldn't know about that," he said sarcastically.

She laughed. Her job was one of the most stress-filled ones around. "Yes, but I don't really like pressure. Or stress. Or dangerous things." She sighed as she looked blindly at the T-shirts and realized how dull her life was going to be when all this was over and he was gone again. "I don't think far ahead. I just go day by day."

He turned to her, really interested. "Why?"

She stared down at her sandaled feet. "When I was in my second year of college, I got pneumonia. I had a good friend, Hilda, who lived in the dorm with me." Her eyes were sad. "She was killed in a car wreck. She'd stayed up all night with me when I was running a fever. She was on her way to the pharmacy to get some cough syrup my doctor had called in. And she died. Just like that." She moved restively. "It scared me. I realized how uncertain life was, and how short it could be. I didn't really like economics. It was my major and I'd sort of eased into it without thinking. I realized I didn't like big cities like Dallas, either. So I had Boone and Clark come get me and take me home."

"Tough break," he commented.

"About Hilda, yes. But I was happy after I'd been home a while." She smiled. "My best friend Keely was around to listen to me and go places with me. I didn't have the stress of exams or studying a subject I hated, and I felt I was where I belonged. In the place I loved most." She looked up at him. "Some people go their whole lives moving from city to city, job to job, never belonging to anything or anyone," she said seriously. "And that's fine, for them. But I wasn't like that, and I didn't know it until I had a crisis in my life."

He avoided her eyes. That was how he lived. He was happy with his life. He didn't want to change it. He didn't want ties, stability, a family…

Her hand on his arm brought him out of his thoughts.

"I didn't mean you," she said gently. "I guess it sounded that way."

He searched her dark eyes. "I have nightmares," he said softly. "I see my daughter, screaming for me to help her, and I'm tied down and I can't. I wake up in a cold sweat. It's been that way for seven years."

"And you run from the pain and the memories and the nightmares," she said gently. "But you don't escape anything by running from it." She smiled sadly. "You see, I was running from my father, from his dislike, from his constant criticism. That's why I agreed to go to college in the first place. But in the end, I was more miserable away than I was at home."

"Facing the pain."

She nodded. "He was very sick, the last few weeks of his life. I nursed him. I think we were closer then than we'd ever been. He said," she recalled, "that he'd made some stupid mistakes in his life and it was too late. He said I should never let anger decide which way I stepped in a crossroads." She blinked. "I wonder if he found out about Matt, before he died."

"It's possible." He touched her face tenderly. "You came up on my blind side," he said enigmatically. "I never wanted to get involved with you."

"I know," she said, glowering up at him. "You're an old lobo wolf and I'm just a kid."

He pursed his lips. "I have some looooong red scratches down my back," he said under his breath.

She went scarlet, stepped too quickly and almost fell. He caught her, laughing like a devil.

"You'll never be a kid again, after that," he whispered in her ear.

She flushed, and then laughed when he tugged her close and hugged her. After a minute, he let her go, took her into the shop and bought her a T-shirt with a shark wearing a bib and holding a fork that said "Fight hunger. Send more tourists!"

THEY GOT ALONG very well for a day or two, but then Kilraven's long abstinence and her trim, pert figure in skimpy outfits got the best of him and pricked his hot temper.

"Why the hell can't you cover yourself up?" he asked angrily when she came into the living room in a sundress that left her back bare.

She gasped. "What?"

He got up from the sofa and glared at her. "You can prance around naked for all I care, but I'm not staying married to you when we close this case!"

She raised both eyebrows. "Well, I like that," she said haughtily. "I guess I'll just have to go out and find myself another big, dishy sex slave!"

He wasn't in the mood for humor. He let out a filthy curse, turned on his heel and stormed out the door, down the beach.

Winnie wouldn't have admitted for worlds how much he intimidated her when he had those black moods. She was a little afraid of him, like she was with Boone in the same temper. She knew neither of them would ever hurt her, but they could be scary.

At least she wasn't backing down now. That had to mean she was growing as a person. It did hurt, to hear him say things like that. It hurt so much that it provoked her own temper. When he came back in, she pleaded a headache and went to bed, leaving him to go out to supper alone. He offered to bring her something back, but she swore she couldn't eat. Next morning, she went out early and alone to breakfast, starving. She spent the day in town walking the streets, just so she wouldn't have to fight with him.

But at night it was hard to lie in bed and hear him tossing and turning in the other bedroom, to see him red-eyed from lack of sleep, and know that the memories were tormenting him.

"You don't sleep," she said.

He glared at her. "You could do something about that, if you wanted to."

Her dark eyes were sad. "We've already talked about that."

He laughed coldly. "You think I can't walk away, don't you, Winnie?" he asked in a soft, menacing tone. "You think I liked it so much that I'd even stay married to you to get it again."

"I'm not that stupid," she replied. "What was to like, anyway? I don't even know what to do with a man, I'm so green." She turned away, missing his sudden wince. "I might as well be living in the Victorian age." She ground her teeth together. "The sooner this is all over, the better! I just want to go home!"

She did. It was wearing her nerves thin to be so close to him and not touch him. That day they'd walked around town, he'd been affectionate, relaxed, tender. But ever since, he'd been like a sunburned snake, irritable and disagreeable. It would be painful, but she could hardly wait to go back to her job. Even if it meant having to get over Kilraven all over again.

THE PARTY WEDNESDAY night was attended by a duke's mixture of people, all races and all classes. There were diplomats, a motion picture star, a country-Western singer, a musician, a chef and at least two beachboys.

Patricia Sanders noted Kilraven's surprise at her guest list and grinned. "I don't restrict my list of friends to people with money and influence," she whispered. "See the country star over there?" she indicated a handsome young blond man, and Kilraven nodded. "His mother was a maid at a motel, and his father worked for a sheet metal plant. He could buy and sell my husband with what he pulls down annually."

"Not bad," he commented.

"One of the beachboys was a billionaire import-export business executive," she added, indicating a tall, handsome man with the physique of a wrestler and wavy black hair just a little silvery over the ears. "His family died in a suicide bombing while he was working a deal in the Middle East. He tossed it all and moved down here. He's living on annuities. Not likely to starve, even in this economy."

He was frowning slightly. "You really like people," he said, surprised.

"Yes, I do," she replied. She sipped her drink, noting that Kilraven was nursing a glass of ginger ale. Winnie was talking to a socialite she knew from her childhood, next to the drinks table. "Your wife is still mad at you," she said with twinkling eyes.

He grimaced. "She's not sure she wants a live-in sex slave, but she's debating my future." He realized what he'd said and actually flushed. "Sorry!"

But she was almost bent over double laughing. "That

is not the Winnie Sinclair I know," she told him. "What are you doing to her?"

"Classified. Sorry." He grinned.

Winnie, noting the camaraderie her new husband was sharing with their hostess, excused herself and went to join him.

"You're talking about me, aren't you?" she asked Kilraven. "And just what are you telling Pat?" she added. They'd hardly spoken two words to each other all day, and here he was flirting like crazy with another woman. It infuriated her.

"Nothing compromising," Pat promised her. "Just that you treat him like a live-in sex slave."

Winnie gasped out loud and hit his shoulder as hard as she could.

"Spousal abuse," Kilraven muttered, holding his arm. "Stop that or I'll find a cop."

"There's one right over there, in fact," Pat said gleefully, indicating a very dark Bahamian man in a spotless white uniform with blue-and-red trim and a cap. "I invited him in case anybody got drunk and disorderly."

"I don't drink," Kilraven reminded her.

"I do," Winnie said brightly, sipping her highball. "Let's start a fight."

He took the glass away from her, disapproving. "No more for you."

"Gads!" Winnie exclaimed. "The drinks police!"

"I am not the drinks police," he muttered. "I'm your husband."

"Not for long," she said icily, and her dark eyes punctuated the brag.

"Okay, that's enough," Kilraven said firmly. "You're over your limit."

Winnie gave him a saucy smile. "Am I? And what are you going to do about it?"

He shrugged, glancing toward Pat. "Nice party. Thanks for inviting us. Sorry, but we have to go, now."

"I'm not going anywhere, and you can't make me," Winnie said pertly.

He pursed his lips and his silver eyes twinkled. "You think so?"

He swung her up in his arms with a grin in Pat's direction and carried her right out the door.

"I will never forgive you for this!" Winnie railed at him as he walked up the steps of the beach house and onto the porch. There was thunder and lightning in the distance, and a whipping wind right off the ocean.

"I don't give a damn," he said through his teeth. He put her down and unlocked the door. "You damned near gave away everything!"

"I did not!"

He picked her up again, kicked the door shut and carried her down the hall to her bedroom. He dumped her on the cover and stood over her, smoldering, with his hands on his hips.

She looked up at him through a mental haze. He was very attractive, but her body was telling her graphically that she wasn't ready for any more bedroom gymnastics. She was extremely sore.

His eyes narrowed. "In case you're wondering, I'm not in the mood," he said shortly.

"Good thing," she replied enthusiastically, "because I've misplaced my handcuffs and my whip!"

"You've misplaced…" he began, puzzled. Then he got it. His lips compressed. "You're not handcuffing me!"

"Spoilsport," she muttered. "Okay, then, you can go watch television. I'll just read a book or something."

"What the hell's gotten into you?" he burst out.

She lay back on the bedspread, stretching out her arms and legs. "I'm a sacrificial victim," she said theatrically, "waiting for the volcano to go off."

"Winnie…"

She turned her head and looked at him through a rosy haze. She even smiled. "You are just dynamite in bed," she murmured. Her eyes closed, missing the surprised look on his face. "If we got divorced tomorrow, I could live on that night for the rest of my life. It was…just… incredible…" She was asleep.

Incredible. He smiled in spite of himself. He rummaged through the chest of drawers and pulled out a silky yellow nightgown with lace for cups. He held it up and appraised it with sheer masculine appreciation. His eyes cut around to Winnie. It would serve her right if she woke up in it and didn't know how she'd managed to get it on. And he would enjoy the process.

WINNIE SAT UP in bed with her head throbbing. She couldn't remember how much she'd had to drink, but it must have been excessive. She vaguely recalled having a very public argument with Kilraven, and then being forcibly carried back here. She looked down at herself with surprise. But she certainly didn't recall putting on this nightgown. Well, there was probably a lot she didn't remember. She had no head for alcohol. But she'd just been heartsick at the way Kilraven had been behaving the past few days. Par for the course for him, she thought coldly. Then she recalled what he'd said about abstinence. Maybe he couldn't help himself. But that didn't excuse what he'd done. Damn him, she thought furiously. He never should have touched her in the first place. Now things were complicated.

When she got up and looked for her packet of birth control pills, things got much more complicated. It seemed that in the confusion and haste of their trip, she'd left the pills behind in Kilraven's apartment. That meant that she'd missed two of them. She recalled the instructions vividly. Her hand went to her belly and she swallowed, hard. It was exactly two weeks between periods, the worst and most dangerous time to be intimate, because her periods were regular.

She had to keep her cool. It was unlikely that she'd conceive after just one time. Well, more like three times, she corrected, and blushed. Amazing, that a man could do that. She'd read that they were only good for one time. Maybe Kilraven didn't read books about sex. She recalled some of the things that he'd done to her then, and she decided that he must have read a lot.

Well, it couldn't be helped now. She'd just have to hope that there wouldn't be consequences from her negligence. Kilraven would kill her. He'd have to, at that, because if she turned up pregnant, no way was she having a termination, no matter what.

SHE HAD AN unexpected phone call later in the morning.

"Hi, it's Pat," came the cheery reply when she answered the phone. "Want to go shopping with me down on Bay Street?"

Winnie laughed self-consciously. "Are you sure you want to be seen in public with me after last night?"

"Anybody can get tipsy, dear. I do it all the time. Head hurt?"

"Not so much. I have aspirin."

She laughed. "Come on. I'll pick you up at your front door. What do you say?"

"Okay," Winnie said, trying to sound reluctant. "I guess Kilraven can live without me for a few hours."

"You still call him by his last name?" Pat asked, incredulous.

"He doesn't like people using his first name, and I've heard that he actually threw something at his own brother when he used the nickname for it," Winnie replied. "I'm covering my butt."

There was a pregnant pause. "Really?"

"Oh, stop that." Winnie laughed.

"Come shopping. Girls' morning out."

"I'll be out front in five minutes. I'm not dressing up."

"Neither am I, pet. Come as you are." She hung up.

Winnie threw on a pretty yellow-patterned white sundress and strappy white sandals, ran a comb through her long hair, grabbed her purse and started down the hall. She was wearing the skimpiest thing she'd brought with her, and she hoped it made him howling mad with desire.

Kilraven was standing at the end of the hall, his hands in the pockets of his Bermuda shorts, which he was wearing with an open white shirt that showed off his broad, muscular, hair-roughened chest.

"Where are you going?" he asked coolly.

She moved closer. "Off to meet men!" she exclaimed with big eyes. "Since we're getting divorced soon, I'm in the market for a new sex slave! First I'm going to a bar, then I'm going to sit on the piano with my skirt hiked up…"

"Winnie," he growled.

She made a face. "Pat and I are going shopping."

"Nice work," he said with a lift of his eyebrow.

"Not mine," she replied coolly. "She invited me."

His eyes slid over her with a new sense of possession. He knew that slender young body as no other man ever had. She belonged to him.

She saw that look, and it irritated her. He was never getting near her again.

"Ask her about her brother-in-law, if you can do it without making her suspicious," he said. "We're too close to blow it now."

We. That was almost funny. There was no "we," there was only Kilraven's obsession with finding his family's murderer. She thought about that and calmed down. She was losing her perspective, and that would never do. They weren't a happy couple on honeymoon. They were investigators. She had to keep that in mind. The future was her job and his, not a house with a picket fence.

"I can do what I need to do," she said solemnly. "I won't blow it."

She made him feel guilty. He was throwing her in headfirst, all in an attempt to avenge two murders. He didn't think she could end up on the firing line, but he couldn't guarantee it. "If anything feels wrong, back off," he said curtly. "Don't put yourself in the middle of anything."

"Pat isn't going to get me killed," she said.

His face tautened. "Not intentionally."

"Thanks," she murmured. She started toward the door.

He caught her shoulder as she passed him and looked down into her quiet, solemn young face. He didn't like what he saw. He'd pushed her into this trip against her better judgment. Now he was trying to put the blame for that torrid interlude on her. It wasn't fair.

"No. Thank you," he said gently. "You didn't want to come down here. I browbeat you into it. Now I'm blaming you for things that aren't your fault." He sighed. "I'm sorry for what happened when we got here. I just…lost it."

Well, that was better than nothing, she supposed. "I lost it, too," she replied. "No problem."

"You're sure you're on the Pill?"

Her face flamed. She averted her eyes. "Of course I am!"

The car pulling up out front stopped the conversation.

"I'll be back," she said, moving away.

"If you need me, I'll have my cell with me."

She shrugged. "If there's a crisis about picking out a blouse, I'll be sure to call you."

"Thank you so much," he muttered.

She turned and curtsied. "We aim to please. You can always bake some cookies or tidy up the room if you run out of things to do," she added cheekily.

"My stepmother was right. You are a little blonde chain saw!" he called after her, irritated beyond discretion.

"Sticks and stones…" she sang back.

Muttered curses followed her down the steps.

Patricia had both car windows down and she was laughing when Winnie climbed into the passenger seat of the sleek beige Mercedes. "What was that all about?" she asked.

"He doesn't think it's safe for me to go shopping without him," Winnie muttered. "I suppose he thinks I'll trip over my high heels and fall into the bay and get eaten by seagulls!"

Patricia pursed her lips and turned her attention back to the steering wheel. "Shortest marriage in Comanche Wells's history, huh? I'm just beginning to think that may be right!"

BACK AT THE beach house, Kilraven was brooding. There had been something in the way that Winnie averted her eyes when he'd asked her about being on the Pill. He walked into her bedroom and proceeded to do what he was best at. By the time he finished, he was certain that she hadn't brought anything with her to prevent a child. Not unless she was carrying the pills on her person. And that, as soon as she came back, was his priority. He was going to find out.

CHAPTER FIFTEEN

WINNIE WAS ANIMATED while they walked down Bay Street, through crowds of tourists carrying bags and chattering. Nearby was Prince George Wharf, with cruise ships in port. This was one of the most sophisticated cities in the hemisphere, but at the same time it was like a small fishing village. There were big splashy hotels mingled with little cottages set back off the road in groves of palm trees. Winnie loved everything about it.

"Isn't it amazing that the old British Colonial is still here?" Winnie asked. "Otherwise, Nassau is changing so much that I can't keep up."

"It is amazing," Pat said, smiling. "The grand old lady of the Bahamas. What a history."

"I used to love staying there. Then Daddy decided that we needed our own place."

"I love your house."

"Thanks. Me, too."

Patricia was watching her curiously. She moved through an arcade to a little nook with bougainvillea climbing the walls, where an open-air shop sold conch soup and mixed drinks. "Let's have something to drink," she said.

"Fruit punch for me," Winnie said with a groan. "I'm still not over my headache."

"Poor thing. You really shouldn't drink."

"I know."

Patricia gave in the order and carried the drinks to a little stone table with benches. She handed one to Winnie. "I shouldn't drink, either," she said, and the happy persona fell away. She put her sunglasses aside with a sigh. "But it's the only thing that keeps me from becoming a suicide."

"Pat!"

"Don't worry, I'm not really the type. It's just…" She sipped her drink and sighed. She looked at Winnie. "I'm not an idiot, you know."

"What?"

"First a homicide detective opens that old Kilraven murder file and my husband jumps in to put pressure on the police commissioner to get it closed again. That's after a murder in Jacobsville that raised eyebrows even up in Austin at the state crime bureau. Then a young woman dies who works for Senator Fowler. That's followed by assaults on both detectives working the Kilraven case after Senator Fowler had it reopened again." She looked at Winnie evenly from black eyes. "Then you and Kilraven himself show up next door to my beach house."

Winnie was a good actress. She'd been a leading lady in her sophomore year. She gave Patricia a beaming smile. "Great deduction." She held out her left hand, to display her wedding band and its accompanying diamond. "So I got married to Kilraven just to come down here and ask you questions about a murder…" She frowned. "What has any of that got to do with you?"

Patricia looked stunned.

"Did you kill somebody?" Winnie asked, shocked.

Pat rolled her eyes. "Oh, for God's sake, I must be

getting paranoid." She took a big sip of her drink. "My husband's gallivanting all over Texas with a high-school cheerleader, with carloads of media trying to catch him in the act for their next big political scandal. Will's moldy retainer is threatening a minister. My stepmother... What in the world is the matter with you?"

"Sorry. I just never heard of anybody threatening a minister," she said with a laugh. "Our minister is bald and sixty and wouldn't hurt a fly. He came and sat with my father when he was dying." She was shocked to hear Pat talking about a moldy retainer making threats.

"It does sound strange, doesn't it?" Pat wondered. She took another drink. "He said the man was drawing things he shouldn't. Now I ask you, what in the world does that mean?"

"Beats me," Winnie said carelessly. She grinned. "What are you going to do about the cheerleader?" she asked.

Pat blinked. "Do about her?"

Winnie propped her chin in her hand. "If it were me, I'd go see her folks."

Pat cleared her throat and took another swallow. A big one. "Not if you had a husband with employees like Jay Copper, you wouldn't."

"Oh, what could he do? Threaten you?"

Pat looked down into her drink. She took another swallow. And another. She blinked. "There was a girl, once," she said dully. "Like the cheerleader. She came to one of our parties. I caught Will with her. She was drugged out of her mind. She didn't even know what was happening. I made him send her home. He told Jay to drive her." She took another drink.

"I heard about that from a police officer back home," Winnie said. She frowned. "Her dad got a new Jaguar and all the charges were dropped, right?"

Pat shook her head. "This one never made it back to her house. They found her…" She stopped suddenly. She looked at Winnie with a terrified expression. "You mustn't ever tell anyone I said that, especially your husband. Promise me!"

"Okay, I promise," Winnie said, mentally crossing her fingers. She was so shocked she could hardly manage to put on an act. Jay Copper! Not Hank Sanders, but the old moldy family retainer had gone with the girl who was later found dead. "I don't understand why."

"Just never mind." She put down the drink. "Me and my big mouth! I've been scared to death for years, kept secluded, watched to make sure I never said anything…!"

Winnie put a hand over hers. "I would never do anything to put your life in danger," she said earnestly. "I mean that."

Pat relaxed. "Thanks." She grimaced. "I can't talk to anybody. My husband has me followed everywhere I go. I'm forever looking over my shoulder." She glanced behind her and froze.

Winnie turned. There was a man in a suit wearing dark glasses, standing beside a dark sedan.

"Do you know him?" Winnie asked.

"No."

"He's probably just waiting on a client," Winnie said gently. "You have to loosen up! You're getting paranoid. Honestly. Your husband likes younger women. That makes him a rake, but it doesn't make him a murderer."

Pat looked into her eyes. "Do you think so?" she asked anxiously.

"Of course I do!"

Pat put her face in her hands. "I drink too much. I talk too much. I'll end up in a river somewhere myself one day."

"Now you really sound paranoid. We should get moving. If you sit here, that alcohol is going to do a number on you. Come on. Shops are waiting!"

Pat laughed. "I guess so." She stood up. "You're really nice," she said. "I've only known you from parties, and you always seemed to stand in a corner while Boone and Clark did all the socializing. How are they, by the way?"

"Boone just got married to my best friend. They're very happy."

"And Clark?"

She shook her head. "Clark is mixed up with one wild girl after another. This new one seems to be different, though. She's a librarian."

Patricia smiled. "I'd have liked to have brothers and sisters."

"You can have Clark," Winnie offered.

The other woman swiped at her. "No, thanks. I'm happy as I am."

They walked away from the shop. The man in the suit pulled out a cell phone and started punching in numbers.

WINNIE WAS FRIGHTENED about what she'd learned, but she put on a happy face and wandered all over Nassau with Pat. It was dark when they drove up in front of Winnie's beach house.

"Well, the lights are on," Winnie said. "Maybe he's still there."

"You have to stop fighting with him," Pat advised.

"No. You stop fighting a man like that, and he'll walk all over you," Winnie replied firmly. "I'm not anybody's carpet."

Pat shook her head. "I'm sorry we didn't get to know each other sooner."

Winnie looked back at her. "Me, too." She grinned. "But better late than never."

Pat looked sad. "No. It won't be like that." Suddenly she turned up the car radio and grabbed Winnie's arm, pulling her closer. Her eyes were wild. She spoke into Winnie's ear. "Listen, if I'm not here tomorrow, he'll probably send me to Oklahoma, to his family's old home place," she said quickly. "Jay Copper is there, and I'm scared of what he might do. He'll know I spoke to you... Your husband has a ranch near there. Find an excuse to go there with your husband. Find me. Will you do that?"

"Why...?"

The jangling of Pat's cell phone made her start and cry out. She grabbed it up and opened it, turning down the radio at the same time. "Yes?" Her face paled. She gnawed her lower lip. "Yes. Yes, I will. Right now? Very...very well." She hung up. Her face was tragic. "I have to go." She leaned closer. "Remember what I said!"

Winnie jumped out of the car. Pat drove off without another word.

When she walked in the door, Kilraven was waiting. He was standing in the hall, all business.

"Pack," he said quickly. "I've got a Learjet on the way to pick us up. We're going to Oklahoma."

"You heard us!" she exclaimed.

"Yes, and so did someone else." He turned away. "We'll be lucky if she lives long enough to get there."

"What do you mean?"

He turned. "The car was bugged."

"By you?" she asked hopefully.

"Yes. And probably by her husband's old family retainer. Give me your purse."

She handed it over without a thought. He opened it and turned the contents out onto the coffee table.

"Is it bugged?" she asked, worried.

He stood erect and his eyes were blazing. "Where are your birth control pills?" he asked coldly.

Her heart jumped up into her throat. She'd fallen right into the trap. It didn't take ESP to know that he'd already tossed her room. She sat down with a hard sigh. "They're still in the drawer next to the bed in your guest room. In the rush to the airport, I forgot them."

He didn't say a word.

She looked up at him. "Yes, I know the risk is exponential if you miss one." She glared at him. "But I didn't expect to be tossed onto a bed and ravished after you promised me nothing would happen!"

He stuck his hands in his pockets. "I'm a man," he bit off.

She sighed. "Oh, yes, you are!" she said with such feeling that his pose of indignation was threatened. He turned away.

"We have to beat her to Oklahoma," he said.

"Will they try to kill her, you think?"

He nodded. "Too many people have already died trying to cover up what happened."

"Do you know what happened?"

"I think so," he said. "A lot of it is theory, but I've been adding up what I know. And I spoke with your mother on the phone a few minutes ago. She filled in a few more blank spaces. Pack, and I'll lay it out for you on the way to the airport."

HE DID, SUCCINCTLY. "The senator had a party and invited one of his conquests, a little girl barely in her teens who'd put on plenty of makeup and stuffed her sweater and pretended to be in college. He drugged her and had his way with her, up until his wife caught him. He protested, but by then the girl came to and realized what he'd done, and started yelling about prosecution and told him her true age. He told Jay Copper to take her home. So he did, but with a detour so that he could take advantage of her himself. The senator wasn't the only man who liked young girls in the house. She fought, he subdued her, and somewhere in the struggle she died."

"Oh, brother," she said heavily.

"So then Copper had to cover it up. He faked an automobile accident, destroyed her body so that she wouldn't be recognized and went about his business. The senator was probably horrified when he knew what his right-hand man had done, but he couldn't afford a scandal—he'd just been elected state senator and he had a much higher office in his sights. He saw a whole new world of financial stability opening up for him. The girl would have cost him his career. He wasn't having it ruined by some teen who threatened to go to the news media."

"But, your little girl," she began.

His jaw clenched. "Monica used to go with a boy who

worked for Senator Sanders. He and Hank were friends. Hank told him what happened, and he told Monica. I didn't know it at the time, not until today, when your mother dug it out of a closed file and called me on my cell phone to tell me about it. Monica's ex-boyfriend was killed, but before he died, he spoke with a detective and said he had information about the death of a teenager who'd been disfigured to cover up her identity."

"Oh, no," she said, because she realized where this was going.

"That's right. Hank figured that if Monica knew the truth, she might talk. So he sent a couple of men over, maybe Jay Copper included, to make sure she didn't. My daughter was there with her. She wasn't a target, she was just in the way." He bit his lower lip. "They didn't count on the Jacobsville victim falling in love, getting religion and talking to a minister."

"If Marquez hadn't gone to the media about the minister, he'd be dead, too."

"No doubt about it."

"Pat told me that a moldy old family retainer was threatening a minister who was drawing pictures he shouldn't. Not much guesswork involved in figuring out who, or why," she said.

"Yes. I phoned Jon and told him to get a tail on the minister, just in case."

"Good for you." She shook her head. "All those people, all dead, because of a teenager who woke up too soon and had to be silenced."

"Yes. The worst of it was they didn't find out who the girl really was until three years after she was killed. Her parents were dead by then. They'd thought their daughter was kidnapped. They joined support groups and pestered the police to find her. Then, they died in a horrendous automobile accident in a snowstorm in Colorado, before they could learn the truth."

She closed her eyes. "Dear God. And he got away with it."

"No, he didn't," Kilraven said in the coldest voice she'd ever heard.

"But there are no witnesses left," she argued. "If they can silence the senator's wife..."

"That's why we're going to Oklahoma," he said. "They aren't silencing her."

Her dark eyes glittered with feeling. "They should put the senator and his brother away for a hundred years!"

"I'm all for that. But there's a very real possibility that the senator had no idea what his brother planned to do."

"That's chilling. But he tried to stop the investigation."

"He was protecting his brother," he said. He sighed. "I'd do the same for Jon." He glanced at her. "You'd do it for Boone, or Clark or Matt."

She nodded. "What about my uncle? How is he tied into this, do you know?"

He shook his head. "He probably knew someone in the chain, but he didn't know anything specific enough to make him a target. The only connection we have is the thermos. And that could turn out to be a blind alley. He might have loaned it to the murder victim."

"I like Pat," she said. "I hope we can save her." She glanced at him. "Couldn't you call the FBI?"

"And tell them what? That we have a possible murder? I didn't get tape, Winnie. It's your word against the senator's best attorneys. He'd sue the hell out of the Bu-

reau if I brought Jon in on it." He didn't add that he knew
Garon Grier had been seen with Hank Sanders just recently. That was still a puzzle to him.

She ground her teeth together. "You're a spy! Don't
you know other spies who could help?"

He chuckled. "I'm not a spy. I'm an intelligence operative."

"Semantics!" she argued.

He pursed his lips. "I don't think anyone inside the
law could do us much good. However, I do know a few
people outside it."

"Maybe the senator's evil brother does, too."

"No. These are good guys. I ought to know," he added
as he started punching numbers into his cell phone. "I
trained every damned one of them. Hello? Put Rourke
on the line."

IT WAS A roller-coaster ride for Winnie, who'd never
dreamed that she'd be caught up in a murder investigation that put her own life on the line. It was exciting, just
the same.

They landed at the Lawton–Fort Sill Regional Airport.
Kilraven, too impatient to wait for one of the ranch hands
to drive to town and get them, rented a Lincoln and they
drove to the ranch at what she termed warp speeds, to
Kilraven's amusement.

It was a surprise to Winnie, who was used to their own
large ranch holdings. Now she understood why Kilraven
found it so easy to fit in at society parties. The ranch, Raven's Pride, was built like a Spanish hacienda with many
graceful arches sheltering a long, wide front porch. It was
so big that it filled the horizon as they approached it. The

pastures were fenced and those leading down the half-mile of paved road to the ranch itself were white, spotless. On each side of the road, beautiful purebred Black Angus cattle grazed on fresh bales of hay. Their drinking water was in heated containers.

"It's amazing," Winnie said, staring out the window. "It makes our ranch look like a toy one!"

He chuckled. "It's been here for over a hundred and fifty years," he told her. "I'll tell you the history one day. It has to do with ravens who actually called wolves to sites of carrion, so they could get to the good parts after the wolves did the dirty work. Jon and I can't bear to part with it, although we don't spend much time here. We have a competent manager and submanagers in charge of routine operations."

"It's beautiful."

He smiled. "Cammy keeps the furnishings up-to-date. Oh, boy," he added with a grimace. "That's her car." It was a sleek Mercedes, gold and custom, parked at the front door.

"Not to worry," Winnie said easily. "My blades need sharpening before I attack anyone."

It took him a minute to get it, then he grinned. His wife was full of surprises.

He pulled up to the front porch and helped Winnie out. He threw the keys to a tall, lanky cowboy. "Bring the bags in, then put it in the garage, Rory."

"Yes, sir."

He led Winnie inside, where Cammy was waiting, her arms folded tight across her breasts.

"We're only here for a couple of days," Kilraven said at once.

"No problem, I was just leaving," Cammy said tautly.

"That might be best," he said. He bent and kissed her on the cheek. "We're about to stick our noses into a highly explosive situation with a senator's wife next door. She's the key to solving what happened to Melly."

Cammy dropped her haughty pose immediately. "Oh, no, you mustn't get yourself killed," she said worriedly.

"It's the only chance I have of breaking the case," he said gently.

Cammy looked past him at Winnie. "You're going to risk her life, too?" she asked uneasily. "You just got married!"

"It's not a real marriage," Winnie said quietly. "We had to convince the senator's wife that we had a legitimate reason to be in Nassau."

"But you're married," Cammy argued. She looked up at Kilraven, aghast. "She is a little chain saw," she said surprisingly, "but she's just what you need. You should keep her."

Winnie's jaw had dropped.

Cammy looked at her and shifted uncomfortably. "We're all difficult, in this family," she explained. "Both my sons are hard cases. You can't let them walk on you."

"No problem," Winnie said, recovering her poise. "My father didn't raise me to be a carpet."

Cammy actually smiled. "I've been talking to your mother," she said, surprising her. "A truly amazing woman." She looked up at Kilraven, who was also shocked. "She couldn't get you on your cell phone, so she called here. She says one of her contacts got word that Senator Sanders's brother was on his way to the Sanderses' home place, and he wasn't alone."

"When did she call?" Kilraven asked.

"About ten minutes ago."

He went to the gun case in the living room, unlocked it and started pulling out weapons. At the same time, he pulled out his cell phone, grimacing when he realized that he'd had it cut off, and activated it. He phoned the chief of police at the Lawton Police Department, a friend of his, and briefed him on the problem. He listened, his expression growing colder. He didn't reply to what he'd been advised to do, he simply hung up.

He started loading guns.

Winnie stood next to Cammy, uncertain.

"You're not going to wade in there shooting," Winnie said worriedly.

"Not unless somebody shoots at me first." He cocked the big .45 automatic and slid it into the shoulder holster he'd just put on. He reached for another weapon, which looked like a small automatic rifle.

Winnie stood straighter. "I'm going with you."

Cammy gaped at her. "No!"

"No!" Kilraven said at the same time.

"I can phone Pat and pretend that I'm taking her up on her invitation to visit," she said quickly. "You can hide in the backseat. I'll let you out before I reach the house."

He frowned. This wasn't working out the way he'd planned. The idea of Winnie being in the line of fire was suddenly horrifying to him.

"I'm going alone," he gritted.

"No, you are not!" she returned. She grabbed him by both arms and actually shook him. "You're thinking with your heart, not your mind. You have to be logical. They'll be expecting you to walk in with guns blazing if they overheard Pat talking to me. You'll get yourself killed. What will that accomplish?"

He didn't reply. His eyes were glittering.

"You can let me wear a wire," she said. "I can get tape."

Now he did react, badly. "No. No way in hell."

"If you want a conviction, this is the only way, since all the witnesses are dead!"

He'd wanted nothing more than a conviction. Until right now, when he looked down at the slight figure of his wife. She was so young, so brave. He pictured her the way he'd last seen Monica, face up, mutilated by a shotgun blast...

"I won't let you," he said curtly. "I won't risk your life, not even for a conviction."

Winnie's eyebrows arched. "Well! I thought you didn't want to be handcuffed in a closet and kept as a sex slave!"

Cammy gasped and then burst out laughing at Kilraven's shocked expression.

"Sorry," Winnie told her. "It's a private joke." She let go of Kilraven's arms. "You have to let me do it. Too many people have died. It's time the perpetrators were stopped."

Kilraven hesitated.

"You have the equipment to do a wire, don't you?" she asked.

He nodded.

"Then let's go, before they kill Pat and get away with everything."

Cammy came forward. "She's right," she told him solemnly. "If she has courage enough to do this, you must have it, too."

The two women exchanged quiet glances.

"All right," Kilraven said. "But you'll do exactly as I say," he told Winnie firmly. "I've been doing this a hell of a lot longer than you have."

She saluted him.

He made a rough sound in the back of his throat and went to get the equipment.

"He'll take care of you," Cammy said gently.

Winnie smiled. "I know that. If I didn't trust him, I wouldn't have offered to go."

Cammy touched her blond hair gently. "Nice little chain saw," she cooed.

Winnie grinned. "You're just buttering me up because you know I can make homemade bread."

Cammy laughed.

KILRAVEN HAD HER wired and armed, with a small caliber pistol that fit nicely in her purse. He hoped that nobody at the old home place of Senator Sanders would search her. But if she played her part well, they might get away with it. Winnie had taken basic firearms training when she started working dispatch. She was a natural, Chief Grier had said.

He was going to exit the car within easy reach of the house while she drove up at the door. It was risky. He hated putting her in this position. But she was right. It was the only way they could bring the murderer to justice. Hank Sanders and his politician brother were going to do the time for what had happened to Melly and Monica and all the other victims.

They left Cammy in the house and walked out to the rental car together.

"Gosh, I hope it's insured for gun battles," Winnie thought out loud.

He winced. "Don't say that. The whole idea is not to get in one."

She sighed, turning to him as they reached the driver's seat. She looked up at him with a pert little smile. "Now, do try not to get shot. If you end up in the hospital, we would have to go weeks without sex."

He chuckled. She really was a little doll. As much as he desired her, he also liked her. Right now, he wasn't thinking about her misplaced birth control pills or a future without her or even a return to his stressed and dangerous lifestyle. He was only thinking of today. He sobered. "You sure you want to do this?"

She nodded.

He bent and brushed his mouth very gently over hers. It felt different. He smiled as he did it again. "You drive. I'll shoot," he whispered, recalling an old cop movie they'd both liked and talked about in the past.

She laughed. "That's a deal."

She got in under the wheel and he climbed into the backseat, armed to the teeth.

"You ready?" she asked without looking over her shoulder.

"You bet. Let's go."

WINNIE DIALED PAT's cell number. It rang and rang. She gritted her teeth. Her perfect plan might have just gone over the falls if Hank Sanders was already at the ranch...!

Just when she was about to give up and panic, Pat's voice came on the line. It was flustered and quick. "Hello?"

"Hi! It's Winnie Sinclair!" she said merrily, pretending that she didn't have a care in the world and that nobody was eavesdropping on the call. "You said to come over when you got back from Nassau, and I beat you here!"

"W-Winnie?"

"Yes. What's wrong?" she asked innocently. "You did invite me over to talk about that project of yours? You know, the hurricane fund, to be kept in escrow for Bahamians...?" She was making it up as she went along.

"Oh. Oh! Yes, yes, I did, I'd forgotten."

"Isn't it convenient for me to come over now? I forgot to call. I'm already on the way."

There was a pause, voices murmuring. Pat came back on the line. "Is anybody with you?" she asked.

"With me? Who would be...oh, you mean my husband," she said in a harsh tone. "No, he's not with me. He went back to San Antonio on some case. And we're not speaking."

"I see."

"He can stay in San Antonio for all I care. I may go back down to Nassau. But that's my problem, not yours. I'd love to have coffee or tea or even water with you. Just don't mention my husband to me," she added firmly.

Pat laughed nervously. "No. I won't. Certainly, you can come over. Uh, you'll need to park out front, okay? Do you know how to get here?"

"Of course," Winnie said smartly. "I did a Google search on your ranch and got directions." She laughed.

Pat laughed, too, but not with any humor. "Okay. I'll watch for you."

"See you shortly." Winnie hung up and let out a breath.

"Good job," Kilraven said quietly. "Very good."

"If we get through this, I'm lining up for a job at the FBI as a covert operative," she told him.

"Over my dead body," he muttered. "Okay, slow down when you get to the garage," he said, indicating a long, low building just below the house on the driveway. "I'll jump out. You've got the gun. Can you use it, if you have to?"

"I can do whatever I need to do," she said between clenched teeth.

She felt a big hand on her shoulder. "Good to go."

She nodded. "Good to go."

She slowed down, just out of sight of the house, and he rolled out, closing the door gently behind him. She kept driving, her eyes on the sprawling ranch house ahead. She pulled up at the steps and cut off the engine.

As she picked up her purse and got out of the car, she noticed a big, white-headed man standing at the top of the steps. He was wearing an open-necked white shirt with dark slacks and he looked mean. Very mean.

"Hi," Winnie said with forced cheer. "I'm Winnie Sinclair. I came to see Pat."

"She's inside," the old man said in a surly tone. He jerked his head toward the front door and stepped to one side. But he gave her a look that made her skin crawl.

She nodded and walked ahead. Her knees were knocking, she knew they were. But Kilraven was out there somewhere. He would protect her.

Pat was waiting for her. "Come in," she said with forced brightness. "How nice of you to offer to help with my project! Let's talk in the living room."

Winnie felt herself being led toward a window where potted plants were sitting.

"Are you crazy?" Pat whispered frantically. "Copper made some calls before I got home. Hank's on his way up here right now...!"

"Don't worry," Winnie said softly. "It's all right."

"All right?" Pat ran a hand through her hair. "I overheard Copper tell his nephew that he was going to make sure I never told what I knew about that dead girl. He said he'd killed so many people that one more didn't matter, all because a stupid kid threatened to tell what Will did to her!"

Winnie's heart sank. She knew the wire was going to catch that statement. If she was caught wearing it, her life was over.

"I never thought you'd turn up here. Winnie, they'll kill us both!"

Winnie, who had learned to be calm under pressure from a job on which lives depended, put a soothing hand on her arm and smiled. "It will be all right," she said gently. "You have to trust me."

"What are you going to do?"

Winnie sighed. "You know, I have no idea right now. But I'm sure something will come to me."

There were heavy footsteps and Jay Copper walked into the room with a younger man. They were both heavy-set and unsmiling, and if death had a face, they were wearing it. Winnie clutched her purse. Her heart raced as she wondered if she'd have time to make a grab for the pistol.

Jay Copper smiled. "You think you're so smart," he drawled. "Like I don't know why you came rushing over here, after you'd just been with her in Nassau. You know too much, lady."

"My husband is a Fed," Winnie began, hiding her fear.

"Hell! Your husband is in San Antonio. I was listening when you were talking to Pat," he added, and Winnie pretended to be disturbed.

"We're not going to do both of them here, are we?" the younger man asked coolly. "Hank won't like it. His brother would be right in the middle of the scandal."

"Hank's on his way. He'll help us," Jay said easily.

Winnie felt sick. It was all going wrong. Kilraven was just one man. Even if he was right outside, these men were quick and smart and they were both wearing big automatic pistols. If she tried to shoot it out with them, she'd be killed and so would Pat. The pistol that had made her feel so secure ten minutes ago now felt like just added weight in her purse.

As if Jay knew that, he suddenly reached out and dragged the purse out of her hands, snapping it open. He burst out laughing as he drew it out. "What, did you think you'd hurt somebody with this peashooter?" he asked. "Piece of junk." He handed it to the younger man. "Better go and move her car, so nobody sees it." He tossed him the keys, which had been in the purse.

Before either man could move, there was the sound of another car approaching. Jay looked out the window and tensed until the car was in view, then he relaxed. "It's just Hank," he said. "Go on. Move the car."

"You bet, boss."

He walked out. Winnie and Pat exchanged worried glances.

A car door slammed, then another. There was a pause and an odd sound, and then footsteps coming rapidly up the steps. A tall, striking man walked into the house. He had jet-black hair and black eyes, with a prominent scar on one cheek. He was wearing a designer suit and shoes as polished as a mirror. He hesitated in the doorway and looked at Pat for a long moment. Only then did his eyes cut to Winnie and back to Jay Copper.

"What's going down?" he asked Copper.

"Just another little hiccup in a perfect plan. Nothing to worry you. Why'd you come? I told you I was going to handle this. I always handle problems for the senator." He grinned. "He's my boy. Your dad raised him, but I put him in your mother's belly. She was always keen on me, not that old rich man she married."

Hank hadn't smiled since he walked in. His dark eyes narrowed on the older man's face. "You're making problems for Will, not helping him."

"Oh, sure. Problems." His face darkened. "Where the hell were you when that stupid kid got high and enticed him into the bedroom? Where were you when she woke up naked and screamed and said her daddy's best friend was an anchorman in San Antonio and she was going to tell him everything! Where were you when Will cried his eyes out, scared to death, and begged me to fix it?" He cursed. "I've fixed everything for him since he was a teenager. I've always been around to do that. Nobody hurts my son as long as I'm alive!"

Winnie was standing frozen beside Pat, knowing that everything that horrible man was confessing was going right into a recording device. It would convict him. If she lived to testify about it.

"I was serving my country," Hank said quietly.

"Oh, yeah, serving your country. You're as bad as me," he scoffed. "You run one of the biggest illegal gambling syndicates in the state. How does that serve your country?"

Hank's eyes narrowed. "What are you planning?"

"Why don't you go back to San Antonio and just let me handle this?" Copper asked. "I know what I'm doing."

"You'll have Will hung."

"No, no, these are the last people who know anything about the case." He frowned. "Well, there's those detectives, but they don't have evidence of anything. And that minister has been told that his church will be burned down and his congregation barbequed if he talks to a cop again as long as he lives."

Hank moved closer to the man, smiling. "You've done so much already. I can do this for you. I've got Rourke out in the car. He's good with women."

Winnie felt sick to her stomach, even as she felt there was something familiar about that name, something she should remember...

CHAPTER SIXTEEN

WHILE WINNIE WAS trying to remember why that name sounded so familiar, Hank Sanders was waiting for an answer.

Jay Copper hesitated, but only for a minute. "No, Peppy can help me. He did Dan Jones and that woman who worked for Fowler," he drawled. "We got rid of everybody who could connect Will with the girl's death. I'm teaching Peppy. He's already a chip off the old block."

Hank moved even closer. He smiled. "Yeah. Just as stupid and just as gullible as you are. Uh-uh," he said quickly. His hand was close to the old man's stomach. "You don't want to reach for that automatic. Know why?" His hand moved sharply toward the man. "Because this is a .40 caliber Glock and the clip is full. Besides that, there are two guns aimed right at your head. You make a move and you're as dead as your victims are."

Pat's mouth was open. So was Winnie's. The bad guy was turning against his own people?

The door flew open and Kilraven walked in with a tall, blond man with long hair who wore an eye patch over one eye. They were both carrying pistols.

Winnie almost fell with relief. "I got tape!" she exclaimed joyfully.

"Darling!" Rourke said with passion, approaching her.

"You touch her and you'll be shorter in one place than any man in your whole division," Kilraven gritted.

Rourke made a U-turn and went back toward Hank and Copper.

Hank shoved the old man toward Kilraven. "I hope you brought cuffs," he said. "Where's Peppy?"

"Sleeping soundly on the floor of the backseat of the rental car," Kilraven said, taking a breath of relief that Winnie was still in one piece and unharmed. Listening to her on the wire was the most terrifying few minutes of his life.

"Courtesy of yours truly," Rourke replied with a grin. "Trained him yourself, huh?" he asked Copper. "Very efficient."

"You go to hell," Copper said through his teeth as he was handcuffed. "You traitor!" he yelled at Hank. "You were working with the Feds all along?"

Hank handed the Glock to Rourke. "From the minute they found Dan Jones in the river in Jacobsville," he said shortly. "I never could prove you did the teenager, but I knew you did Dan Jones by the way he was killed and I thought we might just get enough evidence to convict you for that one. That was what you were in prison for, killing a man who cheated the mob in such a way that nobody else was tempted to cheat them. Did you think I'd forgotten?"

"Cop lover!" Copper spat at him. "I'll sell you out, if I have to do it from death row!"

Hank shrugged. "Try it," he said, and he looked every bit as menacing as the older man. "I've got friends on both sides of the law."

"He hasn't got that many on our side. I wouldn't worry too much," Rourke said sotto voce.

"Rourke," Kilraven growled.

Hank laughed. "Let him rail. He and his son can share adjoining cells."

"What do you mean?" Copper asked hesitantly.

"The Feds picked Will up for questioning about two hours ago," Hank said. "Denied him a phone call until I could get up here and save Pat." He glanced over his shoulder at her. "Will's been trying to call, to warn you, but he couldn't get past Copper."

"Nice of him," Pat said through her teeth. "He'll lose his senate seat."

"He'll lose a lot more than that," Hank said. He moved closer. His face tautened. "The girl whose father took a bribe to let Will off the hook for statutory rape, remember her?"

Pat nodded.

"Some San Antonio detective got her to press charges for it, belatedly."

Winnie smiled. She could imagine who that detective was.

"He'll go to prison, won't he, Hank?" Pat asked.

"Most likely." He drew in a long breath. "Going to stand by him, like the long-suffering, faithful little wife, and protect him from the media?" he asked harshly.

Goodness, Winnie thought, that was an odd remark. Then she got a look at his eyes and realized why he'd risked so much to save Pat.

Pat avoided looking at him. "I thought you were up to your neck in the crime syndicate."

"Oh, I am," he said bitterly. "I owed Garon Grier a favor, from another time, and I paid up. But I've never killed anybody, least of all a helpless young girl," he added, sniping at Copper, who glared at him from the next room, where Rourke had parked him temporarily. "Will knew Copper did it, and he kept it to himself until today. He told me, just before I came up here. He confessed the whole thing. My half brother, the accessory to the most horrendous murder I've ever heard about." He stared at Jay Copper with icy eyes. "I hope they hang you both! A man who'd condone doing that to a little girl deserves the same treatment!"

Hank went up in Kilraven's esteem. He'd had a different view of the mobster. Until now.

"Will said she'd asked for it," Jay Copper scoffed. "Those young girls, they're tramps. They just lay in wait for older men who don't have no sense."

Kilraven was seeing his little girl on the floor, covered in blood, imagining if she'd been a few years older and that had happened to her.

Hank moved closer and put a hand on his shoulder. "I should have said something sooner. I had a hunch about the teenager, even your ex-wife's boyfriend. But I never believed my brother could be cold enough to condone the execution of a mother and child."

"Aw, the woman knew what I'd done! Her ex-boyfriend spilled his guts to her," Jay scoffed. "I did him myself."

Kilraven turned. His eyes were terrible. "It was you! You killed my daughter!"

Copper lifted a shoulder. "No. It was Dan Jones. I sent him to do your wife, after her ex-boyfriend spilled his guts to her. Dan was never supposed to hurt the kid, she just got in the way. They said that was why he got religion and started yapping about his evil past. His conscience hurt. He was going to tell that minister all about it." Jay smiled coldly. "But I got to him first."

"What about the thermos?" Winnie asked. "My uncle's thermos was found where the car was in the river."

Copper frowned. "What thermos? Oh, yeah, some guy loaned it to Dan when his got stolen. I had Peppy spike it. Dan was going to talk to a cop in Jacobsville about his past. We heard him say it on the phone talking to that girlfriend of his, so me and Peppy drove down to Jacobsville and ambushed him. He screamed like a little girl."

Little girl. Little girl. Melly, holding out her arms to him. Melly, laughing, saying, "I love you, Daddy! Always remember."

Kilraven took two quick steps toward the man.

Winnie moved right in front of him, very calm and self-assured, and put her hands on his chest. "No," she said softly. "The criminal justice system works. Just give it a chance. Don't give him the easy way out, after all he's done."

Kilraven looked down at her. He hesitated, while the forces inside him went to war. He wanted to kill the man with his bare hands. Melly had died because this fool wanted to protect his son from the law. But so many people had died already.

Winnie was staring up at him with soft, loving brown eyes. He calmed, just looking at her. She gave him comfort. She gave him peace. For the first time in years, he was pulling free of the black melancholy that sat on him from time to time. He drew in a deep breath. "Okay."

She smiled up at him.

"Nice girl," Hank mused, looking at Winnie. "Pity she married you when I'm still available."

"Hey, I'm available, too, and I'm not on the wrong side of the law!" Rourke piped in.

Kilraven shook his head. Rourke was incorrigible. He turned back to Hank. "You might go legit," he suggested. "It worked for Marcus Carrera."

"Who do you think he turned over his San Antonio holdings to in the first place?" he asked, aghast. But then he looked at Pat. "I don't know, though."

Pat looked back. Almost hopefully. Hank smiled. Pat flushed and looked away.

"Whatever I decide, right now I have to get back to San Antonio. Will's staff will be having hysterics, and there's the news media to handle. Thanks," Pat said, including Kilraven, Rourke and Winnie in her gratitude. "And you," she added to Hank. "I thought you were coming up to help him kill me," she said with helpless guilt.

He touched her cheek, very lightly. "I'm no ladykiller," he said with a faint grin.

"Well, I am," Rourke called from the next room. "Or I would be, if I could get past Kilraven there!"

Kilraven whirled, and he wasn't smiling. "She's my wife, damn you! And if you so much as smile at her, I'll make you into the world's first one-eyed soprano!"

Rourke stood up straight. "Yes, sir!"

Winnie was watching Kilraven with a very odd smile. That had sounded like jealousy. Of course, he could have been kidding...

He turned and looked at her. She blushed all the way down her neck. Oh, no. He wasn't kidding!

GARON GRIER TURNED up a few minutes later with a team of U.S. Marshals, whom Winnie found fascinating. She mentioned her great-grandfather to them, and beamed when one of them recognized the name from an honor roll he'd seen. Hank and Grier moved away to speak, after a fuming mad Jay Copper and his nephew had been taken away in handcuffs.

Pat was packing. Rourke was staying well clear of Winnie. Kilraven took her into an adjoining room and removed the wire.

"I'm proud of you," he said quietly, searching her eyes. "Very proud. You could have been killed."

She smiled. "Not likely, with you and your cohorts covering my back. Although I must admit that Hank Sanders came as a shock."

"To me, too, until your mother mentioned seeing him with Grier. Nobody in Texas would ever suspect Garon Grier of being hand in hand with organized crime. He's a real boy scout."

"A nice one," she agreed. She looked up at him. "What now?"

He'd been expecting that question. He drew in a long breath. "We take a breathing space. Just for a few weeks. I need time…"

"Yes." Time to heal, he meant. Time to grieve for his daughter. Maybe even for his wife. She smiled. "What about this?" She held up her wedding ring.

He looked uncomfortable. "I don't have time to see about things right now. We'll talk later."

Nice answer. Smooth. Very smooth. She leaned close. "Should I toss the handcuffs?"

He burst out laughing. The other men glanced at him curiously, but he just threw up a hand and walked out with Winnie.

CAMMY ALMOST HUGGED Winnie to death back at the house. "I was so afraid for you. For both of you," she added, hugging Kilraven, too. She hit him.

"What was that for?" he asked, aggrieved.

"For scaring me! Don't you ever do that again!" she raged. And then she hugged him some more.

WINNIE WENT BACK to work at the 911 center on the early morning to afternoon shift. She excused herself in the middle of a call for a wrecker, motioning to Shirley to fill in for her while she rushed into the restroom and threw up for five minutes. When she came back out, weak and pale and holding a wet paper towel to her face, Shirley turned around from her station and sang, softly, "Rock a bye baby…!"

Everybody around Winnie grinned.

She made a face. "And nobody tell Kilraven," she muttered, "or there will be trouble!"

"Terroristic threats and acts," Shirley whispered.

"That's right. I belong to the Jacobsville Barfing and Terrorism Society," she quipped.

The next day, Shirley presented her with a T-shirt with that logo. She took it home and wore it to supper.

"YOU SHOULD TELL HIM," Boone advised.

"Definitely," Clark added.

Matt gave her a long, sad look. "I miss playing video games with him."

"I miss arguing with him." Gail sighed, still nursing her gunshot wound, and on sick leave from her job in San Antonio.

"You should just tell him," Keely said gently.

"I am not telling him anything," Winnie said firmly. "He'd stay around out of guilt." She sighed. "I haven't heard a word from him in three weeks. He might be talking to a divorce lawyer for all I know. He said he didn't want to get married again and he didn't want another child."

"Oh, sure, that shows," Clark mused, indicating his sister's growing little belly.

Winnie glared at him. "Sometimes things happen."

Everybody laughed except Matt, who looked perplexed.

"Don't worry, in about four years you'll understand a lot more than you do now," his mother said, patting him on the head.

Winnie laughed with them, but she was depressed. It was inevitable that someone was going to see her and tell him. Well, if they could find him. Winnie had no idea where he was. She only hoped that he hadn't gone overseas on some dangerous mission. What Jay Copper had said must have caused him some more pain.

The media was having a field day with Senator Will Sanders. He was in jail awaiting arraignment and there were satellite trucks all over the street where the detention center was located, not to mention all around the senator's home. Pat had escaped back to Nassau. Hank Sanders was also out of touch with his associates. Nobody knew where he was. Just like Kilraven, Winnie thought. She touched her belly and smiled. She loved being pregnant. Maybe she could go and live in Nassau, too, and have the baby and raise it there and Kilraven would never have to know. She pursed her lips. The Jacobsville Baby Hiding and Beachcombing Society. She burst out laughing. When she told them what she'd been thinking, so did they.

KILRAVEN HAD SPENT two weeks in his apartment, out of

touch with the world, even with his brother, while he finally grieved for his little girl. He had videos of her that he'd never had the nerve to watch. Now, he took them out and savored every smile, every little laugh. There she was at her first birthday party, in a frilly dress, looking wide-eyed at the camera, walking and falling and picking up toys and putting them in her mouth. And laughing. Always laughing.

There she was at her second birthday party, with little friends, playing with the birthday cake while Monica fussed and Kilraven chuckled and got odd camera angles while he filmed her. Then it was her third birthday, and she was very pretty and wearing a scarlet dress with white hose. She ran to her daddy, knocking the camera. It lay on the ground, filming feet, while Kilraven picked her up and swung her around, and she was laughing, laughing, kissing his cheek and saying, "I love you, Daddy. Always remember."

"Always remember." He said it aloud, with her, and his eyes filled with tears. Until Winnie, he'd never shed a single one in seven years. He'd held the memory away, pushed it aside, ignored it, used his anger and rage to avoid facing what he faced now: the certainty that his child was dead and that he would never see her again in his lifetime. He would never watch her go on her first date, buy a pretty dress, go through the agony and ecstasy of adolescence, graduate from high school, go to college, have a career, get married and have a family. He'd miss all that. Now he sat in front of his big-screen television, staring at that beautiful little face that was so much like his, as if at a flower that had just blossomed and was cut down in the same instant. Melly was dead. Melly was dead.

He put his head in his hands and let the tears fall. They blinded him. They comforted him. They helped to heal him. After a few minutes, he forced himself to look at the screen. He pushed the start button. And there was Melly, still alive, still laughing, still saying, "I love you, Daddy. Always remember."

"I will, sweetheart," he said huskily. "Always. As long as I live."

Later, he found the framed pictures of her that he'd put away when she died. He took them out, dusted them and put them on the table next to the television.

"We got the man, Melly," he told her smiling face. "We got the man who ended your life. And he'll pay with his own. You can rest easy now, sweetheart. He didn't get away with it."

He touched the framed picture and managed a smile. "I love you. Always remember." His voice broke on the last word.

THREE MONTHS LATER, just back from an assignment to an African nation that he could never admit he'd visited in the line of duty, he walked into the 911 center as casually as if he was taking a tour of it, dressed in an expensive pair of slacks with a black turtleneck sweater and a cashmere jacket over it. Same polished shoes, same arrogant walk. But he wasn't quite as confident as he appeared. Especially when Winnie spotted him as she walked out of the canteen and stopped dead.

He didn't understand why she was so upset until he looked down and saw the evidence that her stomach gave

to her condition. She was wearing the standard uniform
that 911 personnel donned for the job, a navy blue shirt
and dark slacks. But the shirt wasn't tucked in, and it was
pulled fairly tight over that firm little mound. She looked
very sexy, he thought.

She let out a sigh and looked resigned, as she realized
the jig was up. She walked toward him and stopped. He
was so tall. He towered over her. She looked up at him
with resignation in her soft brown eyes and waited for
him to blow up and walk away.

The last thing in the world she expected was for him
to produce a small cloth grocery bag and hand it to her.

She frowned. "What is this?"

"Strawberry ice cream and dill pickles," he said
smartly. He grinned. "I've been reading these books, and
they say that pregnant women can't resist them."

She was still trying to adjust to the smile. The ice
cream was freezing her hand. The pickle jar was heavy.
Kilraven had lost his mind.

He bent and kissed her very gently. "Look deeper,"
he whispered.

Still frowning, she reached deep into the sack and
felt metal. She stopped with her hand buried in the sack,
gaping at him.

"Handcuffs," he whispered. He grinned wider.

She was aware that eyes were darting toward them
from all the busy stations. She felt disquieted. He looked
normal. She glanced into the bag. Handcuffs?

"You can't be a sex slave without handcuffs," he said,
loud enough for people nearby to hear him.

"You animal!" she exclaimed, hitting him and laughing helplessly.

"You can borrow my handcuffs anytime you like, Winnie," one of the female operators who was also a Jacobsville police officer, offered as she rushed by.

"Mine, too," another officer chimed in.

"Nice coworkers." Kilraven beamed. "When can I take you home?" he added.

"I was just going off my shift," she stammered. "I have to get my coat and purse out of my locker."

He took the bag back. "I'll wait for you in the lobby," he whispered.

She just nodded. She walked to the back in a daze. She stayed in the daze past the grinning faces of her friends, all the way out the front door and into the Jaguar, while Kilraven held the door open for her.

She got in and put on her seat belt. She looked at him as he joined her. "Are you all right?"

He smiled. "I'm all right. I've had a rough few weeks, but I think I'm through the worst of it."

She smiled, too. "I guess you noticed that I'm pregnant."

He chuckled. "A lot of people noticed it," he said. "Marquez told me two weeks ago, but I'd just gotten back in from an overseas assignment and I had a lot of loose ends to tie up before I could come down here and start over with you."

"Start over?"

He nodded. He pulled out into the road. "An apartment is no place to raise a child. But we'll have to stay there while we look for a house. That okay with you?"

She was nodding blindly.

"Meanwhile, I've invited your family up for dinner. Jon's cooking. Cammy's going to be there, too." He chuckled. "So you have no excuse not to come with me. Right?"

She was beginning to feel like treasure. "Right."

"That's what I like. Docile agreement."

"Then you'd better divorce me and marry a doormat, Kilraven," she quipped.

He laughed. "No chance of that." He looked at her. "McKuen."

She hesitated. "McKuen," she said, making a caress of it.

He whistled. "Boy, does that do things to my blood pressure when you say it like that."

"Nice to know that I'm not totally unarmed in the war of the sexes."

He smiled and growled softly.

They arrived at his apartment to find her entire family in the lobby.

"We didn't have a key, and your brother Jon has to drive here from Dallas, so he's late getting here," Boone explained with a grin.

Kilraven laughed. "Sorry. I didn't think about the key. Never mind." He walked over to the security guard's station. "I have brought an entire family here for illicit purposes," he began loudly, while Boone's face stretched into utter disbelief.

Winnie laid her hand on Boone's arm. "It's okay," she whispered.

"I am having you drawn and quartered, Kilraven," the guard raged.

"No, no, no, I'm a person of noble birth," Kilraven lectured. "You have to have me beheaded."

The guard frowned. "Beheaded."

Kilraven nodded.

The guard pulled himself erect. "I will have you be-headed, Kilraven!"

"Much better." Kilraven grinned as he rejoined the others. Boone was giving him a cold look.

Kilraven turned back to the guard, pointing at Boone. "I am not taking him upstairs for any sort of illicit purposes," he called out.

"Oh, very good," the guard nodded.

"You married a lunatic," Boone whispered to Winnie.

"I heard that," Kilraven said as he led the way to the elevator. "Keep Trust!" he called to the guard.

The guard grinned. "Hold Fast!"

Kilraven saluted him and motioned the others into the elevator. "It's a Scots thing," he explained. "He's a McLeod. His family motto is 'hold fast.' My mother's people were Hepburns. Ours is 'keep trust.'"

"Another raving mad fan of sixteenth century Scots history," Winnie groaned.

"There, there," Kilraven said with a gentle smile. "You'll adapt."

She looked up at him with so much love in her eyes that he felt blinded by it. He slid an arm around her and pulled her close. "I'll adapt," she promised.

JON ARRIVED, too late to be presented to the security guard in his brother's usual outlandish fashion, with Cammy in tow. She was introduced to the Sinclairs, and she and Gail found a lot in common, including friends. Jon moved into the kitchen and started cooking, with some help from Winnie and Keely. They sat down to a feast fit for an ancient monarch. Then they all had the courtesy to yawn and regret having to leave so soon, because they were so tired. But they ruined it by grinning outrageously as they said good-night at the door. Even Jon and Cammy.

Kilraven closed the door, shaking his head. "What a bunch. But they do blend seamlessly, don't you think? A good omen for the future."

Winnie was looking at the photos on the table beside the television. She turned to him and smiled gently. "She looked just like you."

He nodded. "She was a sweet child. It wasn't right, to hide her away like a guilty secret for so long."

"Yes."

He pulled her against him and touched her belly lightly. "Is it a boy or a girl? You have those skills, like your mother. Guess."

"We can have an ultrasound and know for sure," she said.

He made a face. "Takes all the fun and surprise out of it. Why don't we just wait until the baby comes?"

She smiled from ear to ear. "I was hoping you might say that." She cocked her head up at him. "Are we getting the divorce before or after he's born?"

"He! You said he!"

She glowered. "Figure of speech. Answer the question."

"I suppose we could put it off for a few years. You know, until we're grandparents. Then we can talk about it."

She looked him up and down with soft appreciation. "I was just thinking. The doctor told me I ought to exercise. You know, to keep fit while I'm carrying the baby."

"He did?"

She nodded. She moved closer. She ran her fingers up his chest and over the buttons. His breathing quickened. "And I was thinking that some indoor exercises are every bit as good as walking or jogging and stuff."

"You were." His heart was slamming away.

"Yes. So I thought." She moved even closer and teased around a shirt button. His breathing was very heavy by now. "I thought we might get one of those Wii systems and that program called Wii Fit, so I can exercise indoors."

"Damn!"

She stared up at him. "Damn, what?"

He pulled her hips into his. "I've got a hard-on so bad that I could put it through a wall, and you're talking about a damned exercise machine?"

"Or," she said, breathless, "we could try that thing your buddy did, where he and his wiiifeee…!"

TEN MINUTES LATER, they were sprawled on the carpet, shivering and sweating and gasping for breath.

"Thank God I don't have a sunken living room!" he exclaimed.

She laughed with pure delight. "It would still be worth a broken ankle," she pointed out.

He rolled over and kissed her with enthusiastic delight. "Two," he agreed, and kissed her again.

She tugged him down over her and nuzzled his face with hers. "I love you, McKuen," she whispered softly.

He lifted his head to look into her wide, gentle, dark eyes. She was a fighter, a lover, a mixer, a calm oasis in a storm. She could face down killers, juggle frantic calls and dispatch help with a flair, and in bed she was everything he could ever ask for. Besides all that, she loved him.

He brushed her nose with his, and glittery silver eyes stabbed into hers. "I love you, too."

She was surprised. "You do?" she asked blandly.

"Very much. Of course, I didn't know it until I let you walk into that bear pit wearing a wire." He sobered. "I thought, if she dies in there, they can just put me in the ground beside her. Because there won't be anything left on earth worth living for, if I lose her."

Tears burned her eyes, hot and wet. A sob escaped her throat.

He kissed the tears away. "Why are you crying?" he whispered.

"You were named for a poet," she whispered back. "Now I see why."

He grinned. "I can recite poetry," he told her. "Want to hear some?" He lifted his head. "The boy stood on the burning deck…!"

"Oh, for heaven's sake, not that sort of poetry!"

His eyebrows lifted. "Something more suitable to our current situation, then?" he added, looking down at her pretty nude body with a grin. "There once was a man in Nantucket…"

She kissed him, laughing uproariously.

He kissed her back. "I suppose we should go to bed."

"I suppose."

He cuddled her close in his arms. "On the other hand," he murmured drowsily, "it's warm and cozy here. So what's wrong with the carpet, I always say."

"I always say that, myself," she agreed, and reached up to pull an afghan off the sofa to cover them with.

She closed her eyes and snuggled close to him, warm and loved and happier than she'd ever dreamed of being. He might be dangerous, she thought dreamily, but with courage like that to keep her and the baby safe, she had no more fear of the future. In fact, she could hardly wait to see it. Not that she lacked courage of her own. She was constantly amazed at her own part in their recent brush with death. Only a year ago, she couldn't have imagined herself doing something so bold. Kilraven had influenced her, she thought, and so had her own mother. Perhaps courage was something that only presented itself when it was needed the most.

She glanced toward the photograph of Kilraven's little girl on the table and thought of her own child, lying soft and safe in her belly. This child would never replace Melly. But it would help to heal the old, deep wounds.

As she closed her eyes, far away, she imagined she could hear the sound of a child laughing, a silvery, soft, happy tone; the sound of a lovely little spirit who was, like her father, finally at peace.

* * * * *

A KISS TO REMEMBER

Naima Simone

CHAPTER ONE

"Excuse me. Can I kiss you?"

Remi Donovan blinked at the tall, ridiculously gorgeous man standing at the library's circulation desk.

Impossible. He couldn't have just said what she thought he said. It was Declan Howard in front of her, after all.

"I'm sorry?"

His eyes briefly slid away before landing back on her in their lilac—yes, lilac—glory. "I know this is...unorthodox. And I wouldn't ask if it wasn't an emergency. But can I kiss you? Please?"

An emergency kiss?

Well, *okay.* She'd heard a lot of bullshit in her years—one couldn't have a high school teacher as a best friend, who regularly regaled her with students' excuses about homework and not be well versed in bullshit—but this? It definitely landed in the top ten.

But again. Declan Howard. Recent transplant to Rose Bend, Massachusetts, Declan Howard. Successful businessman Declan Howard.

Secret crush Declan Howard.

She blinked again.

Nope, the face of sharp angles, dramatic slants and masculine beauty didn't still disappear. A proud, clear brow that could rock a Mr. Rochester–worthy scowl. An arrogant blade of a nose that somehow appeared haughty *and* like it'd taken a punch and come out the winner. The slopes of his cheekbones and jaw could've received awards for their melodrama, and that mouth... Well, the less said about that sinful creation the better.

As a matter of fact...

She glanced over her shoulder just to make sure he wasn't talking to someone behind her.

When no one appeared, she turned back to him. Swallowed and forced a nonchalant shrug. He was still standing there wanting to kiss her?

"Um. Sure."

Relief flashed in his eyes. Then they grew hooded, lashes lowering, but not fast enough to hide another flicker of emotion. Something darker, more intense. Something that had her belly clenching in a hard, heavy tug...

His arm stretched across the circulation desk and a big hand curled around the nape of her neck, drawing her forward.

Oh God...

That mouth. She would be a liar if she claimed not to have stared at the wide, sensual curves that were somehow both firm and soft. Both inviting and intimidating. She'd often wondered how the contrast of that slightly thinner top lip would compare to the fuller bottom one.

Now she knew.

In complete, exacting detail.

Perfection.

Giving and demanding. Indulgent and hard. Sharp as the drop in temperature on an October night in the southern Berkshires. And as sweet as the candied apples the middle school PTA sold for their annual fall fundraiser.

His lips molded to hers, sliding, pressing… Parting. First his breath, carrying his earthy cloves-and-cinnamon scent, invaded her. Then his tongue followed, gliding over hers, greeting her before engaging in a sensual dance that teetered on the edge of erotic. And as he sucked on her tongue, then licked the sensitive roof of her mouth, she tipped closer to that edge.

A whimper escaped her, one that she would no doubt be completely mortified over later, and holy hell, he licked that up, too. And gave her a groan in return as if her pleasure tasted good to him.

She released another whimper, this one of disappointment as he withdrew from her. That whimper, too, she'd cringe over later. But now, as the library's recycled air brushed her damp, swollen lips and her lashes lifted, all she cared about was that beautiful mouth making its way back to her and—

Oh God.

She stiffened.

The library. She was in the middle of the library. During lunch hour. Right before the kindergartners from the grade school arrived for Friday Story Circle.

"Um…"

Say something.

You've got your kiss and rocked my proverbial world, now move along unless you'd like to check out a book. Can I suggest Crave *by Tracy Wolff?*

Because of course she'd noticed his preference for YA paranormal fiction. Jesus be a fence, one lip-lock with Declan Howard had rendered her befuddled. She—logical, reasonable, sometimes too plainspoken for her own good Remi—didn't do *befuddled*.

Until now.

"Thank you for that," Declan murmured. His eyes dipped to her mouth, and her breath caught in her throat.

If he tried to kiss her again, she would have to…to… *stop him*. Yes, yes. That's what she was thinking. Stop him.

Didn't matter that heat, smoky and thick, flickered inside her. She pressed her fingertips into the top of the desk, the solidity of the wood grounding her. And if she touched it, she wouldn't lift her hand to her tingling mouth.

"You're welcome. I—" She hadn't been sure what she'd been about to say, but the rest of it evaporated as Tara Merrick appeared behind Declan.

Remi knew the beautiful blonde who worked at The Bath Barn, the shop Tara's mother owned that sold bath products, lotions, perfumes and candles. This was Rose Bend, so of course everyone knew everyone. But Remi had never given the other woman cause to glare at her as she was doing now.

"Declan, I've been looking for you." Tara wrapped a proprietary hand around Declan's forearm, the sugary sweet tone belying the dark fire in her eyes.

"There was no need," Declan said, gently but firmly extricating himself from her grasp.

His purple gaze returned to Remi and, though she resented herself for it, electricity crackled over her skin. She resented it because the pleasure that had fizzed inside her chest like a shaken soda can over *Declan Howard* kissing *her* had fallen flat.

She might've sucked at calculus in college, but she didn't need to know infinitesimals to add one plus one: Declan had only kissed her for Tara's benefit. To make her jealous? To play hard to get? Remi didn't know. What she knew for certain?

It hadn't been because he so desperately needed to get his mouth on her.

It hadn't been because he wanted *her*, Remi Donovan.

And damn if that didn't just slice through her like a fierce winter wind?

"Remi, if you have a moment, I'd—"

She shook her head, cutting off Declan, not allowing her poor heart to flutter over him knowing her name. "I'm sorry but I don't. I really need to get back to work. Do either of you need to check out or return books?"

Her voice didn't waver, and thank God for the smallest of favors. Declan studied her for a long, tense moment. She forced herself to meet his gaze and not back down.

For years, she'd fought the good fight—learning to love herself and to deep-six her people-pleasing tendencies. Right now, she waged an epic inner war against the whisper-soft voice pleading with her to just *Listen to what he has to say.*

Gifting him with an opportunity to apologize for using her? No thanks. She'd had her share of Pride Smackdown XII. The pay-per-view event would air next week.

"No, all good here. Thank you, again." With a nod, he pivoted on his heel and strode toward the exit.

With one last narrow-eyed stare, Tara hurried after him.

Only after the door closed behind both of them, did Remi heave a sigh.

And as a hushed smattering of whispers broke out behind her, she closed her eyes, pinching the bridge of her nose.

Weirdest. Friday. Ever.

CHAPTER TWO

IT WAS OFFICIAL.

Declan had hit rock bottom.

How else could he describe the desperation that had him sitting in his car with an anxious stomach and a numb ass?

Damn, this was humiliating.

Yet, he didn't drive away from his parking space outside the Rose Bend Public Library, where he waited for Remi Donovan to emerge after locking up for the day. Maybe he'd missed his calling. He should've become a private investigator instead of a wealth manager. Uncovering Remi's work schedule had been ridiculously easy. All he'd had to do was sit in one of the library's reading nooks on one of the Thursday and Friday afternoons he visited Rose Bend. Soon enough, he'd overheard Remi, a coworker—a tall, lanky Black man who seemed to own an amazing number of DC shirts and Converse—and their supervisor discuss work schedules.

He shifted in the driver's seat of his Mercedes-Benz S-Class, fingers drumming restlessly on his thigh. If his colleagues in Boston could see him now, their laughter would threaten the buttons on their three-hundred-dollar shirts. After the humor passed, they'd just stare at him, bemused, and offer to escort him to the nearest high-end gentleman's club.

As if staring at another woman's body could possibly

substitute for a certain five-foot-nine frame with gorgeous, natural breasts that would fill his big hands. And a wide flare of hips that never failed to draw his gaze when she strode around the library. And an ass that, by all rights, deserved its own religion.

Fine. He might be a little preoccupied with Rose Bend's beloved librarian.

The librarian whose mouth he claimed for all to see in the middle of the day for his own selfish reasons.

And try as he might—and he did try because he wasn't a prick—he could only rummage up the barest threads of remorse.

Because even though desperation had driven him to that circulation desk with the request of a kiss, desire had chosen her. The need to finally discover if that lush, ripe mouth would taste as good as it promised had won out. And at that first press of lips to lips...

His fingers fisted on his thigh, and he slowly exhaled. Lust tightened inside him... One move and he would snap. As if even now, he dined on that sweet, butterscotch-flavored breath. Licked into the giving depths of her mouth. Twined around that eager tongue. Swallowed that little, needy sound.

"Shit." He shook his head.

Reminiscing about this afternoon wasn't what he'd come here for. Wasn't why he'd set up a stakeout in front of the library. That kiss had been *cataclysmic*, but, in the end, it'd only been the impetus for a plan he needed one Remi Donovan to agree to.

That's all she could be to him—a coconspirator.

He'd learned his lesson the hard way with Tara. If he wanted to do casual friends-with-benefits relationships, he'd have to keep that in Boston, not here in Rose Bend, where the town was too small and everyone knew everyone's business.

Especially when the woman was the daughter of his mother's neighbor and friend.

Yeah, not his brightest moment.

The door to the library opened, spilling a golden slice of light onto the steps before it winked out. He opened his car door, stepping out to watch as Remi appeared, closing the large oak door and locking it.

He stared. Openly. Even though she wore a cream-colored wool coat against the night air, he could easily envision the dark green dress beneath that caressed every wicked curve. Another thing he liked about her. She didn't try to conceal or downplay the gorgeous body God had blessed her with—she worked it. And damn if that confidence wasn't sexy as hell.

Not here for her sexiness, he sternly reminded himself. *Get on with it.*

Firmly closing his car door, he rounded the hood.

Remi's head jerked up, her eyes widening as she spotted him on the curb, near the bottom of the library steps.

She didn't move down the stairs. A tight, almost-tangible tension sprang between them. It vibrated with the memory of that conflagration of a kiss. Of the need for *more* that sang in his veins.

A more he had to deny.

Christ. He tunneled his fingers through his hair. She'd been a beautiful distraction before he'd touched her, before he'd learned the butterscotch-and-sunshine taste of her. But now? Now that he knew? He was finding it difficult to focus on anything else.

He'd graduated from Boston University with a bachelor's degree in business administration and he'd gone on to acquire his dual degree, an Executive MBA in Asset Management. But at this moment, he'd become a student of Remi Donovan. And he wouldn't be satisfied until he earned a PhD.

"I'm sorry for just showing up like this," he said. "But I didn't have your phone number. And showing up during your workday again didn't seem like a good idea."

"No." She finally spoke in a husky tone more appropriate for a sultry siren in an old black-and-white film noir than a small-town librarian. "That definitely wouldn't have been a good idea. As it is, my supervisor is contemplating tacking your picture to the bulletin board with Not Allowed scrawled across the top. I'm not sure if I've successfully convinced her you didn't accost me."

He winced, only half exaggerating. "God, I hope she doesn't resort to that. The library is one of the few places I can actually find some privacy and quiet." He frowned, thinking of Tara hunting him down earlier. "Well, it used to be."

She arched a delicate eyebrow, descending a step. A spiral of gratification whistled through him at that small movement toward him.

"Last I heard, you have a very nice home at the edge of town with plenty of space and, I would imagine, privacy."

The corner of his mouth curled. "Yes, I do have a nice home with a lot of space. But I also have a mother with boundary issues and a key to said nice house, which impedes my privacy." He shook his head, holding out an arm toward his car. "Can I give you a ride home?"

She studied his hand for a moment before lifting her

gaze to him. "No, thank you. I drove to work this morning. Besides, I intended to walk down to Sunnyside Grille for dinner."

"In the dark?"

Declan glanced down the street. It was a little after six and the sun had just settled beyond the horizon in a spectacular display of purple, dark blue and tangerine. If he were a sentimental man, he would remove his cell and capture the beauty of it over the small Berkshires town.

But he wasn't sentimental; he was logical, factual. A man who dealt with numbers, figures and statistics—and data that assured him a woman walking by herself after dark wasn't a good idea.

A rueful smile flirted with her pretty mouth. "This is Rose Bend, not Boston. And the diner is just a few blocks away, not a long walk at all."

"So you're telling me crime doesn't happen in this town?"

"Of course it does. We wouldn't need a police department if it didn't. And if it eases your mind..." She held up her key ring. Showing him the small canister of pepper spray dangling from it. "I'm not an idiot."

"Never thought you were," he murmured, though that coil of concern for her loosened. Silly, when he barely knew her. When today had been the first time he'd really talked to her other than a murmured greeting or nod of acknowledgment. "Would you mind if I joined you?"

She hesitated, and he caught shadows flickering in her hazel gaze. "Why?"

He blinked. "I'm sorry?"

Remi crossed her arms over her chest, but a second later lowered them to her sides. The aborted gesture struck him as curiously vulnerable—and from the trace of irritation that flashed across her face, she obviously regretted that he witnessed it.

Curiosity and protectiveness surged within him. He wanted no part of either. Both were dangerous to him. Curiosity about this woman was a slippery slope into fascination. And from there, captivation, affection. Then... *No.* Been there. Had three years of hell and the divorce papers to prove it.

And this protectiveness. It hinted at a deeper connection, a possession that wasn't possible. A connection he'd avoided in his brief attachments since his ill-fated marriage six years ago. As stunning as Remi was, he wasn't looking for a relationship, a commitment.

At least, not a *real* one.

"Why do you want to join me? And let me help you out. I appreciate the chivalrous offer, but I'm a big girl—" a humorless twist of her lips had an unconscious growl rumbling at the base of his throat "—and I can take care of myself. So what's this really about?"

He parted his lips to... What? Take her to task for that subtle self-directed dig? For cutting him off at the knees by snatching away his excuse for escorting her to the diner? Admiration danced in his chest like a flame, mating with annoyance.

"I do have something to talk about with you. Can I walk you to the diner?"

After another almost-imperceptible hesitation, she nodded. "Okay."

She turned, and he fell into step beside her. Silence reigned between them, and he used the moment to survey the picturesque town that had so completely charmed his mother three years ago that she'd moved here. Elegant, quaint shops, trees heavy with gold, red and orange leaves, lampposts and cute benches lined Main Street. A well-manicured town square, with a colonial-style building housing the Town Hall, and a white, clapboard church with a long steeple soaring toward the sky completed a picture that wouldn't have been out of place on a glossy postcard.

Walking down this sidewalk with people strolling hand in hand or as families, their chatter and laughter floating in the night air, it was easy to forget that heavily populated, traffic-choked Boston lay three hours away.

He tucked his hands in the front pockets of his pants, pushing his coat open. The night air, though cool, felt good on his skin. Inhaling, he held the breath for several seconds, then released it, slowly, deliberately.

"Remi, I apologize if my kissing you earlier today caused you any problems. Sometimes I forget how small towns can be. Especially since I'm only here every other weekend, which isn't the case for you. I'm sorry I didn't take that into account." He paused. "Has anyone…said anything to you?"

"You mean besides my supervisor, who wanted to quarter and draw you, then lectured me on professional decorum? Or do you mean Mrs. Harrison, my hair stylist's grandmother, who'd been standing in the reference section and offered me her advice on how to handle a beast like you? Her words, not mine. Or do you mean Rhonda Hammond, the kindergarten teacher there for Friday Story Circle, who gave me a thumbs-up because she'd heard about it from a friend?"

He grimaced, nodding at a person passing by. "The grapevine is alive and well, I see."

"Thriving."

"Are you in trouble at work?" he gently asked. He'd never forgive himself if his impulsive—and yes, self-ish—actions cost her job. "I know you already spoke to your supervisor, but I can, as well. I'll call first thing Monday—"

"That's not necessary." She stopped next to a bench across from the shadowed windows of a closed clothing boutique. "Declan, could you get to the reason why you showed up at the library?"

He stared down into her upturned face. Dark auburn waves framed her hazel eyes, the graceful slope of her cheekbones, the upturned nose and the wicked sinner's mouth. And that shallow, tempting dent in the center of her chin. It never failed that, whenever his gaze dropped to it, he had to resist the compulsion to dip his finger there. Or his tongue.

Madonna and Delilah. That's what she was. Saint and temptress. An irresistible lure that he had to resist.

"I need your help, Remi," he said, resenting like hell the roughened quality to his voice. Clearing his throat, he continued, "This is going to sound…odd, but… Will you be my woman?"

Her face went blank. "Excuse me?" she whispered.

His words played through his head, and he slashed a hand through the air between them. "Hold on, let me rephrase. Will you *pretend* to be my woman? *Pretend*."

Relief and another, more complicated, murkier emotion wavered in her expression. He peered at her. The need to delve deeper prickled at his scalp.

But that damn curiosity. That protectiveness.

He backpedaled away from her secrets like they had detonators and a steadily ticking clock attached to them.

"Maybe you should start at the beginning." She leveled an inscrutable glance on him, then turned and continued walking down the sidewalk.

Resuming his pace next to her, he huffed out a dry chuckle. "I don't know how to relay this without looking like a dick." Stuffing his hands into the pockets of his coat, he continued, "I don't think it's a secret around here that I...took Tara Merrick out a few times."

"I believe the word you're struggling to find is *date*," she drawled.

He arched an eyebrow. "And I believe *date* is too strong a word," he shot back. "I took her to the movies, dinners—a few of those were at my mom's house so they really don't count, since she and her mother are my mom's neighbors—coffee. Nothing serious."

Remi stopped in the middle of the sidewalk and whipped out her phone. Seconds later, she started tapping on the screen.

"What are you doing?" Frowning, he nudged her to the side, out of the flow of pedestrian traffic.

"I'm pulling up my online dictionary. I mean, I'm just a librarian with a whole reference desk at my disposal, but I'm pretty sure you gave me the very definition of a *date*. But I want to double-check before I call you out. I so hate being wrong."

"Smart-ass," he growled, snatching the cell from her hand and tucking it back in her coat pocket.

His cock perked up at the mere mention of her fantastic ass even as he hungered to press his thumb to the plush bottom curve of her mouth and come away smeared with her deep red lipstick.

"And for your information," he said, voice lower,

heavier, unable to scrub that image of her smeared lips from his mind. "It isn't a date when I'm up-front from the beginning that I'm not looking for any kind of attachment, and I warn her not to expect anything to come out of it. We were just two people enjoying each other's company while I was in town for the weekend. Nothing more. I was very clear about that."

I always am. I always will be.

She tilted her head to the side, her long dark red waves spilling over her shoulder. "Then why bother?"

"Because..." Declan turned, strode off, and the sweet scent of butterscotch and the aroma of almonds assured him she followed. "It made my mother happy. And after years of rarely seeing her smile after my father died, giving her a reason to didn't seem like much of a sacrifice on my part."

Silence beat between them, filled by the chatter of passersby and the low hum of Rose Bend's version of Friday-night traffic.

"That kind of detracts from your dick status," she finally murmured.

He glanced at her, a smile tugging at his mouth. "Thank you... I think."

"That's why you bought a house here, too, isn't it?" She slid him a look, and the too-knowing gleam trickled down his spine like an ice cube. "Mrs. Howard moved to Rose Bend three years ago, but you didn't buy a house here until last year. You're only in town every other weekend—really you could stay with her. There was no need for you to buy a house. But you did it so she would feel like she had family here. So she had her son here."

He shrugged, not liking this feeling of... Vulnerability. Of being so easily read like one of the books at her library.

"It was nothing. Like I said earlier, I need my space. And what little privacy she allows me." He smiled, even if it was wry. "Which brings me back to why I need you." Lust struck a match against the kindling of need in his gut, flaring into flames at his choice of words. He deliberately doused them. "After our...display at the library, Tara seemed to finally back off."

"Not how I saw it," Remi muttered under her breath, but he caught it.

"True, she chased me out of there, but when I told her we were involved, and what she saw was me being dead serious about what I'd been telling her for the past two weeks—which is that there would be no more movies, no more dinners—the truth seemed to sink in. But I'm not fooling myself into believing it will stick. Not if I don't follow it up with reinforced behavior. Otherwise, she'll convince herself kissing you was a fluke, and I didn't mean it when I said she and I were over." He rubbed his hand over his jaw, his five-o'clock scruff scratching his palm. "That we were never a 'we' to begin with."

"So you want me as your beard to run her off?"

He frowned. Her bland tone didn't hint that he'd offended her. Neither did her perfunctory summation. Yet, he still got the sense he had.

"My beard?" he repeated. "No, I wouldn't put it that way—"

"What other way is there to put it?" She waved a hand, dismissing the question. "And what do I get out of this little...bargain? Well, other than the title of the latest woman you dumped when we end the charade."

Oh yes, definitely offense there. And maybe a trace of bitterness.

"Remi." He gently grasped her elbow, drawing her to a halt. "I didn't mean to insult you."

"You didn't," she argued, stepping back and removing herself from his hold. Chin hiked up, she offered him a polite smile that halted just short of her hazel eyes. "I'm sorry, but I have to turn down your proposal."

Fuck the fake girlfriend arrangement. Fuck wanting her agreement. He'd inadvertently hurt her; she didn't need to say it. The evidence drenched those eyes, drowning out the green and gold so only the brown remained, dark and shadowed.

He reached for her.

"Remi—"

"If it's okay with you, I'm going to head back to the library. I'm not hungry anymore."

She sharply pivoted on her ankle boot, but just as she started to head in the opposite direction, the door to the establishment behind them opened and two older couples and a younger one spilled out into the night.

Remi skidded to an abrupt stop, her entire body going as rigid as one of the statues that littered the Boston Public Garden. Concerned, he dragged his gaze from the small group of people to her and shifted closer. Close enough to hear her mutter...

"Shit."

CHAPTER THREE

DECLAN'S CURIOUS STARE damn near burned a hole in the side of Remi's face, but she avoided meeting that sharp lilac scrutiny. Afraid that while she stood there in the middle of the sidewalk in her own version of an O.K. Corral showdown with her parents, her younger sister, Briana, her sister's new fiancé, Darnell Maitland, and his parents, Declan might spy entirely too much.

Too much of what she didn't want him to see.

Like the hated, grimy envy that had no place alongside her happiness for her sister.

Like the uneasy mixture of love and dread for her mother.

Like the anxiety-pocked need to run, run and never stop until her lungs threatened to burst from her chest.

"Remi, honey." Her mother, voice pitched slightly higher, switched rounded eyes from her to Declan and back to her. "What a surprise."

Translation: *What's going on and what're you doing with Declan Howard?*

No. *Nononono.*

Remi smothered a groan. Why was this happening to her? Today must be cursed. First, the hottest, make-her-lady-parts-weep kiss she'd ever experienced. Then the whispers, not-so-subtle high fives and unsolicited comments and advice. Then Declan's surprising appearance after work and his, uh, unconventional proposal.

And now this.

Twenty-six years as her mother's daughter had earned Remi a W-2 and pension in all things Rochelle Donovan. And Remi recognized that particular shrewd gleam in her mother's eyes.

No way in hell could Remi have Rochelle start thinking Remi and Declan were a *thing*.

"Hi, Mom, Dad." She forced herself to move forward and brushed a kiss over her mother's cheek, then gave her big, lovable bear of a father a hug. "Hey, sis. And future in-laws." Her smile for Briana, Darnell and the Maitlands came more naturally to her lips.

After all, it wasn't Briana's fault that she was three years younger than Remi, had fallen in love and was getting married, much to the delight of their mother.

"Hi, sweetie," Sean Donovan greeted. "How's my best girl doing?"

"Hey!" Briana playfully jabbed their father in the side with an elbow. "I'm standing right here."

"Sorry, you weren't supposed to hear that. You know you're my best girl," he teased.

Remi shook her head, grinning at their father and the joke that had been running around their house as long as she'd been alive. All the Donovan girls—her, Briana and Sherri, their oldest sister—knew with 100 percent certainty that Sean loved them equally and completely.

"I was hoping you could join us for dinner tonight," Briana said, then shot her a sly smile. "But now I see why you turned down the invite. You had a better offer. I ain't mad at you," she stage-whispered.

"What?" Remi blinked, heat blasting a path up her chest and into her face. Thank God for the dark. "No, this isn't—" She waved a hand between her and Declan, silently ordering herself not to look at him. "No," she repeated. Firmly. Because that glint hadn't disappeared from either her mother's or sister's gazes. But wait. Hold up a second. "And what invitation? I didn't get..." She glanced at Rochelle.

So did Briana.

"Mom?" Briana frowned. "I asked you to tell Remi about dinner tonight. You didn't call her?"

"I'm sorry, honey. I must've forgot." She winced, lifting a shoulder in an apologetic half shrug. "You were at work anyway, Remi. And besides, you probably would've been uncomfortable as a third wheel."

Anger and hurt coalesced inside her, shimmering bright and hot.

Her mother hadn't forgotten. More like she hadn't wanted to be embarrassed by her middle daughter's perennially single status. And as Briana's gaze narrowed on Rochelle, Remi could tell her sister knew it, as well.

"But," Rochelle continued, smiling at Declan, who'd remained silent since bumping into her family, "since you're here, why don't you join us? We were heading to Mimi's Café for coffee. You, too, Declan. We'd love to have you."

Panic ripped through Remi, and she glanced at Declan. As if he'd been waiting for that moment, his eyes connected with hers, and the clash reverberated like a collision of metal against screeching metal. She *felt* him. In her chest, belly... Lower.

"Declan?" her mother asked again, breaking their

visual connection like cracked glass sprinkling to the ground.

He looked at her mother. Smiled.

"I would be delighted to join you. Thank you for inviting me."

Shit.

Again.

"WHAT THE *HELL*, REMI? I heard Declan Howard kissed you in the middle of the library today, but I thought that was just gossip! But apparently not! You've been holding out on me." Briana hip-checked Remi, her mock scowl promising retribution. "How long has this been going on?"

Remi sighed, sneaking a peek in Declan's direction. He stood with her father and Darnell near the bakery case, talking. Part of her battled the urge to save him from a possible pumping of information by her father. But the other, admittedly petty, half thrilled in leaving him served up to that grilling since he agreed to this craziness.

"Bri, we're just friends," Remi hedged. Were they even that? In the years since his mother had moved to Rose Bend, she'd barely said a handful of words to him.

"Friends who tongue wrestle?" Briana nodded. "Yes, Darnell and I are the best of friends, too."

Remi snickered, then sipped her caramel macchiato. "I have no idea how he puts up with you."

"Right?" Briana beamed. She turned, scanning the café until her gaze landed on her fiancé. And her pretty face softened with such adoration that Remi cleared her throat. As if sensing her attention on him, the handsome IT analyst with dark brown eyes and beautiful almond skin, looked up and sent his fiancée the sweetest smile.

"I'd say, 'Get a room,' but you might take that literally," Remi drawled, those conflicting emotions of envy and happiness warring in her chest again.

Briana chuckled, and Remi rolled her eyes at the lasciviousness of it. *Yech.*

"Bri, I need to borrow your sister for a minute." Rochelle appeared beside Remi, slipping an arm through hers. "You should go entertain your future mother-in-law instead of flirting with your fiancé and making the rest of us blush."

Remi bit back a groan even as she allowed herself to be led away to a corner of the café. She'd been trying to avoid her mother since arriving at Mimi's. Even a cup of her favorite hot beverage couldn't make her forget that her mother had an agenda by inviting her and Declan to join a gathering she'd intentionally excluded Remi from in the first place.

And yeah, best not dwell too long on that.

"Honey, what is that you're drinking?" Rochelle scrunched up her nose.

Dread swished in her stomach like day-old swill. "Caramel macchiato."

"That's nothing but dessert in a cup. Tea is so much better for you." She shook her head, and her disappointment dented the hard-won, forged-in-fire armor of confidence Remi had built around herself—her heart. "Now, tell me about what's going on between you and Declan."

God, if she held in all these sighs, she would end up with gastric issues.

"Mom, don't get ahead of yourself," she warned.

"You know I'm not one to listen to gossip." Remi coughed, earning a narrow-eyed look from her mother. "But I heard about the kiss at the library. Really, Remi, a little more propriety would've been appreciated, but if the story is true…"

Remi didn't confirm or deny, just sipped her drink. But her mother obviously took her silence as confirmation, and a smile that could only be described as cat-ate-the-whole-flock-of-canaries spread across her face.

"If the story is true, then why haven't you brought him by the house for dinner? Do you know how embarrassing it is to hear that my daughter is dating one of the most eligible men in town from someone else? And here I've been so worried about—"

"Mom, please, stop. Declan and I— We're just friends," she interrupted, holding up her free hand, palm out.

Her mother's excited flow of words snapped off like the cracking of a brittle tree limb. She stared at Remi, the delight in her eyes dimming to frustration and… Sadness. It was that sadness that tore through Remi. As if her *mediocrity* actually pained her mother.

Rochelle's gaze dropped down to Remi's body, skimming her dress. Before her mother's scrutiny even lifted back to Remi's face, anxiety and unease churned in her belly. Tension invaded her body, drawing her shoulders back, pouring ice water into her veins.

She knew what was coming.

Braced herself for it.

"Maybe… Maybe if you would try to dress just a bit more appropriately for a woman of your—stature, you could possibly be more than friends. If you wore clothes that…concealed rather than drew attention to problematic areas, perhaps Declan would focus more on your lovely face and ignore everything else."

The gentle tone didn't soften the dagger-sharp thrust or make the wound bleed any less.

That it was her mother who twisted the knife and sought to slice her self-esteem to shreds only worsened the pain.

"I'm only telling you this because I love you, and I want you to be happy like your sisters. You know that, don't you, honey?" Rochelle covered Remi's cold hand, squeezed it, the hazel eyes that Remi had inherited, soft and pleading.

I don't know that! If you cared, if you really loved me like you do Briana and Sherri, then you would see how you're tearing me apart.

The words howled inside her head, shoved at her throat with angry fists. Only the genuine affection in her mother's gaze chained them inside. That and her unwillingness to hurt her mother, even though Rochelle didn't possess the same reluctance.

"If you'll excuse me," Remi murmured, setting her drink down on a nearby table. She couldn't stomach it anymore.

Couldn't stomach... A lot of things anymore.

Without waiting for her mother's reply, she strode over to the small group where Declan stood. He glanced down at her, and that violet gaze sharpened, seeming to bore past the smile she fixed on her face.

Several minutes later, before she had time to fully register being maneuvered, she found herself bundled in her coat on the sidewalk outside the café, Declan at her side.

She didn't speak as they strolled back in the direction of the library, and he didn't try to force her into conversation. The events of the entire day whirled through her mind like a movie reel, pausing on the kiss before speeding on fast-forward to him showing up at the library only to pause on her discussion with her mother.

I want you to be happy like your sisters.

Remi could pinpoint the last time her mother had been proud of her. Because it'd been the time of her last heartbreak, her last failure.

And the whole town had been there to bear witness.

For Rochelle Donovan, happiness meant a husband, marriage, children. And Remi desired that—she did. But if she didn't have them, she wasn't less of a woman, less worthy. Not having the whole fairy-tale wedding and family thing wouldn't be due to the size of her breasts, hips or ass. And she refused to decrease in size—whether in weight, personality or spirit—for someone else to love her.

She'd been willing to do that once. Never again.

And yet... Yet, for a moment, Remi had glimpsed that flicker of pride in her mother's eyes again, and her heart had swelled. It'd been so long.

She was tired of being a failure in her mother's eyes. Of being a disappointment. Was it so wrong to yearn for that light in Rochelle's gaze directed toward her, the one Briana and Sherri took for granted?

Remi knew who she was. Knew her own worth. Owned herself.

But just once...

She slammed to an abrupt halt. And turned to Declan.

To his credit, he didn't appear surprised or alarmed. He just slid his hands into his pants pockets, his coat pushed back to expose that wide chest, flat abdomen and those strong thighs. A swimmer's body—tall, long and lean. And powerful. Staring at him, she combatted the need to step close and closer still, curl against the length of him and just... Rest. She'd come to rely on herself a long time ago, but in the café, she'd uncharacteristically allowed him to take charge. And it'd been a relief. To let someone else carry the burden for a few moments—yes, it'd been a relief.

But that had been an aberration.

She just needed him for one thing.

"I've changed my mind. I'll pretend to be your girl-friend."

Declan cocked his head to the side, studied her for a long moment. "Why have you changed your mind?"

"Does it matter?"

"Yes," he murmured. "I think it does."

A flutter in her belly at his too-soft, too-damn-understanding voice. "No, it doesn't," she said. "Are *you* changing *your* mind?"

Again, he didn't immediately reply. "No, Remi, I'm not. I still need you."

Dammit, he should choose his words more carefully. A greedier woman could read more into that statement.

"Well then, I accept. But I have my own counterpro-posal." When he dipped his chin, indicating she continue, she inhaled a breath, held it, then exhaled, attempting to quell the riot of nerves rebelling behind her navel. "You have to agree to attend Briana's engagement party with me in a month. Four weeks should be more than enough time to convince Tara that we're a legitimate couple." She stuck out her hand. "Deal?"

Declan stared at her palm as if he read all her secrets in the lines and creases. Slowly, he lifted his intense gaze

to hers and, without breaking that connection, engulfed
her hand in his bigger, warmer one.

Then drew her closer.

And closer.

Until his woodsy cloves-and-cinnamon scent surrounded her, warmed her. Seduced her. She sank her teeth
into her bottom lip. Trapping the moan that nudged at her
throat and ached to slip free.

The hand not holding her hand cupped her neck, his
thumb swept the skin under her jaw. She shivered.

And held her breath.

Those beautiful, carnal lips brushed over her forehead.
"Deal."

She exhaled.

These next four weeks were going to be… Killer.

CHAPTER FOUR

Declan: Hey, are you up?

Remi: It's 9:30. I'm not 80.

Declan: Is that a yes?

Remi: *sigh* Yes.

Declan: Is it ok for me to call?

Remi: Sure.

REMI STARED AT her phone screen, heart thudding in her chest, waiting on the black to light up with his name as if she were a teen and the captain of the football team had promised to call. And when the screen lit up with his name, she had to slap her traitorous heart back down with a reality check.

Fake relationship. Get it together. This isn't some chick flick starring Zendaya.

"Hello."

"Why don't I remember you being this snarky before?" he asked in lieu of greeting.

Because we've never had a real conversation past "Hi" and "Excuse me, I need to get to the creamer" at

Mimi's Café. Since saying that would reveal more than she was willing to expose, she went with, "I'm not sure I can answer that. And tell me that's not what you called to ask me."

He snorted. "No. It hit me that we didn't come up with a cover story for how we got together. If our...relationship is going to be believable, we'll have to be of one accord with that."

"Wow." Remi shook her head even though he couldn't see the gesture. "Is even saying the word *relationship* painful?"

"Oh, sweetheart, if you only knew," he drawled.

No, Remi ordered her damn heart again. You will not turn over at that endearment. *Cut the shit!*

She cleared her throat, absently picking at the thread on the couch cushion beneath her. "So do you have any ideas for how we became completely enamored of one another?"

"I'm guessing me trying to stop you from bringing disease and destruction to the earth, but we ended up falling for one another is out?"

A loud bark of laughter escaped her, and she clapped a hand over her mouth even though no one lived with her to hear it. "And what's this disease that I'm so intent on bringing to the earth? Love?"

His mock gasp echoed in her ear. "How did you know?"

She snickered. "Okay, I've read *Pestilence*, too, and Laura Thalassa is brilliant. Oh, which reminds me." She snapped her fingers. "I've been meaning to recommend *Crave* by Tracy Wolff, if you haven't read it already. I think you'll love it."

"Thank you. I'll definitely pick it up." A pause. "How do you know what books I'll love?" he murmured.

Heat surged into her face, and she closed her eyes, lightly banging her head against the back of the couch. Dammit.

"I'm a librarian. It's my job to notice what people are reading." *Nice save*, she assured herself. She hoped. *Please God, let it be a nice save.* "Besides, when a man comes into the library and I catch him unashamedly reading YA paranormal romance, my nerd heart rejoices. And I want to feed his literary addiction."

When he chuckled, she silently breathed a deep sigh of relief. And sent up another prayer of thanksgiving. And maybe a promise to attend service on Sunday. It'd been a while.

"There's our story," Declan said. "We met at the library when you noticed what I was reading and suggested a book you thought I'd like. We struck up a conversation, I asked you out, the rest is history."

"It's like our own book nerd fairy tale."

"Book nerds are the shit."

"Hell yeah we are." Remi grinned, and once more had to order her heart to stop doing dumb things. Like swooning.

"'Night, Remi. And thank you again."

"Good night, Declan."

Remi: I've arranged our first date for Friday night after you get to Rose Bend. Hayride.

Declan: Pass.

Remi: Sorry. Bought the tickets. You wanted to be visible. What's more visible than a hayride?

Declan: Dinner. Coffee. A stroll. Standing in the damn street. All don't involve hay. Or hay.

Remi: We're doing it. Suck it up, city boy.

Declan: Why am I doing this again?

Remi: Hey! You kissed me!

Declan: Oh believe me. I can't forget.

Remi: ...

Declan: Too soon?

Remi: Bundle up. It's going to be cold.

Declan: So the hayride was fun.

Remi: ...

Declan: I can hear you saying I told you so.

Remi: Me? Nooooo.

Remi: But I did.

Declan: No one likes a know-it-all. Even beautiful ones.

Remi: You don't need to do that.

Declan: Do what?

Remi: Do the compliment thing when no one's around to hear it.

Declan: I can be truthful whether I have an audience or not, Remi.

Declan: If it makes you uncomfortable, I won't say or rather type it.

Remi: No it doesn't. Just... It's not necessary.

Declan: Are we having our first argument as a couple?

Remi: I think we are... And just for the record, I win.

Declan: Of course, dear. Yes, dear.

Remi: Such a good fake boyfriend.

Remi: Heads-up. If Tara asks, my nickname for you is baby-cakes.

Declan: WTF??

Remi: She was pushing it. Had to come up with something.

Remi: Ok, kidding. Sorta. But she did corner me today and was her usual petty self.

Remi: Why didn't you tell me you used to be married?

THE PHONE RANG seconds later, and Remi sighed before swiping her thumb across the screen. She should've expected this call, but her stomach still dropped toward her bare feet. All afternoon, since Tara had approached Remi outside Sunnyside Grille after lunch, she'd gone back and forth about whether or not she would ask Declan about his previous marriage.

Over the two weeks they'd been "together," the texts and phone calls had been constant, and when he came to Rose Bend, they'd spent every day together. As couples did. But they weren't real—no matter how her pulse tripped over itself at just the sound of his voice in her ear or the sight of his name in her messages. Or how thick, hot desire twisted inside her when his hand rested on her hip or cupped the back of her neck. A shiver rippled down her spine at just the memory of the possessive touch.

No. Not possessive. She had to remember and remind herself what this was. Fake. A sham. For the benefit of another woman who'd done what Remi could not allow herself to do.

Fall for him.

She could not be that naive or stupid.

Raising the phone to her ear, she said, "Hey."

"Remi," he replied. "What did she say to you?"

"She didn't go into details," she gently reassured him. Because from the tautness of his voice, it seemed as if he needed to be reassured. "It seemed more like she wanted me to know she had information about you that I didn't have." She hesitated but couldn't hold back the question that had been plaguing her for hours. "Why didn't you mention it, Declan?"

"It's not important."

The abrupt, almost-harsh reply echoed in the silence that fell between them, mocking his adamance.

"Your mom might not have moved to town yet during my last relationship, so you may not have heard about it. But it was the topic of conversation three years ago, for months." She inhaled a deep breath, bile pitching in her stomach at the thought of talking about Patrick and the disastrous, public ending of their relationship. But if she wanted Declan to trust her with his story, maybe she had to take that first step.

"Patrick Grey was a resident at the hospital in the next town over but lived here. We met at the annual motorcycle rally, and I fell hard, fast. Handsome, smart, and yeah, he was going to be a doctor. Not bad, right?"

She gave a soft, self-deprecating laugh. Because, yes, bad. If only she hadn't allowed those things to blind her to his other, not-so-favorable traits.

"We were together for a year and a half. And him being a resident, we didn't have a ton of time together. But I loved and enjoyed every minute when we were. So much that when he started criticizing my dinner or breakfast choices, or offering his opinion on what I wore, I didn't see his comments as negative. Just that he was concerned with my health or wanted me to look my very best. But when he started using what he called 'reward systems'— lose five pounds and he would agree to take me to the bar around his work friends—then I couldn't deny what I'd been ignoring."

"Remi," Declan breathed. "You don't have to tell me this."

"I'd like to say that I broke up with him," she continued as if he hadn't spoken, because *yes*, she did need to get this out. She hadn't spoken about it since it happened. It was time to purge herself of this festering wound. "But I can't. One Saturday morning, I walked into Sunnyside Grille to meet my sisters for breakfast since Patrick had to work a double shift. Or so he'd texted me. But that wasn't true. Because when I entered, there he was. Sitting in one of the booths near the door, sharing the Sunnyside Up Special with a slender, gorgeous brunette. Well, that's not true. They weren't sharing it because they were too busy kissing."

She swallowed hard, still seeing Patrick, the man she'd imagined building a life with, giving another woman what he should've only offered her. Three years had dulled that pain to a twinge.

"When he saw me, he didn't even apologize. Instead, he blamed me for sending him to another woman. He wasn't original. The usual. If I'd only taken care of myself, lost the weight, hadn't been so fat and lazy. In front of everyone in that diner. He didn't give a damn about humiliating me in front of my family, the people I'd grown up with. And I was so stunned, so hurt, I stood there and took it. Grace, the owner, came over and ordered him out. Told him to never bring his ass in there. And Cole and Wolf Dennison *escorted* him to the sidewalk." A faint smile curved her lips, and it went to show how she'd healed, because there was a time she'd never believed she could feel any humor with the memory. "But the damage had already been done. People get dumped all the time. But mine had been devastating, humiliating *and* public."

"What happened to the asshole?" he snapped.

She blinked. "Um, I don't know. I don't care. Last I heard, he found a position in a hospital out of state."

"That just means it's going to take me more time to track him down."

"What?" She laughed. "Declan, stop playing."

"Who's playing?" he growled. "And next time I'm in town, I'm treating Cole and Wolf to beers."

"That's…sweet." She smiled, and warmth radiated in her chest. "Thank you."

"You're perfect, Remi. I hope you know that. And fuck him if he was too much of a narcissistic, insecure bastard to realize it. Or I bet he did realize it. But to make himself feel better about himself, he tried to make you smaller. And I'm not talking about the size of your gorgeous ass or hips—which you fucking better not touch. I hope you know any real man would see the beautiful, sexy, brilliant woman you are and not ask you to change a damn thing. Hell, he would have to up his game to be worthy of you."

Her lips popped open. Thank God they were on the phone because she would've hated for him to glimpse the tears stinging her eyes or the heat streaming into her face. If he looked at her now, he would see her feelings for him. She didn't have to cross her bedroom to the mirror over the dresser and know that the need, the hunger, the… No, she backed away from labeling *that* emotion. But she knew those emotions would greet her in her reflection.

"Remi?" he murmured. "Sweetheart?"

Her fingers fluttered to the base of her throat, and she closed her eyes.

"I'm here. And thank you. I… Thank you."

"You're welcome, sweetheart. But I'm only speaking the truth." He sighed. "I get why you shared that with me. Thank you for trusting me. I know it wasn't easy." He paused, and several moments passed where his breath echoed in her ear. "Ava and I started dating in college. People said we were a 'golden couple,' whatever that means. I guess I can see it now. Similar goals—both financial majors, wanted to be entrepreneurs, desired a certain lifestyle, had the same ideals about the family we desired. She was beautiful, driven, ambitious, and I admired all of that about her. So after we graduated, we married."

A hard silence ricocheted down the line, deafening in its heaviness.

"I love my parents, especially my mother. But their marriage… It wasn't healthy. My father wasn't physically abusive, but emotionally, verbally? He cut her down with words, by withholding affection if she didn't have his dinner on the table on time or if she disappointed him in any small way. And my mother's identity was so entangled with his that when he died, she crumbled, didn't know who she was, how to carry on from one day to the next. That's why when she sold the house and moved here, I dropped everything and made it happen. She needed to escape anything that had to do with my father so she could *finally* discover herself apart from him. I think that was one of the things that attracted me to Ava. She had her own identity, her own goals. But I didn't count on that tearing us apart."

Questions pinged against her skull, but she remained quiet, letting him tell his story at his own pace. Yet her whole body ached with the need to wrap around him, hold him.

Protect him.

She shook her head, as if the motion could dislodge the silly idea. Declan didn't need her protection. Didn't need *her*.

"We both entered graduate school and took jobs in our fields. While my career seemed to rise fast, hers didn't go as smoothly. And listen, I'm a white man in a field that is set up for me to succeed. So I understood her frustration. I knew there were certain advantages for me that weren't there for her. But she turned bitter, and she took that bitterness out on the one person who unconditionally loved and supported her—me."

Remi almost asked him to stop because what was coming... It had turned him off relationships all these years later. So it must've scarred him.

"It started with complaining about me not having enough time for her. So no matter how tired I was from work and school, I tried to give her more attention. Then she accused me of being too needy, so I pulled back. I'd arrive at work and discover that my files were missing information, or the numbers had been transposed. Or I had to make a presentation, and the PowerPoint had disappeared from my computer. When we attended my office parties, she either flirted with my colleagues or deliberately insulted them. Or as I later found out, slept with them."

"Shit," she whispered.

"Yes, shit." He chuckled, but it didn't carry any humor.

"She tried to sabotage my career before it could really begin. The betrayal..." He cleared his throat. Paused. "The betrayal when you've done nothing but love a person... It destroys something in you. Your trust. In other people. In yourself. It's not something you forget—or want to repeat."

She got it. God, did she get it.

"She didn't break you, though," she whispered.

"No," he whispered back. "She didn't."

"Declan?"

"Yes."

"I'm glad."

CHAPTER FIVE

LAST HALLOWEEN, DECLAN attended a friend's party, dressed as a pirate, and ended up going home with a sexy as hell cat—or maybe she'd been a mouse.

The Halloween before that, he'd spent the evening at a business dinner. And had his dining partner for dessert.

This Halloween, he stuffed goody bags with candy, toys and small books for the fifty or so excited children that crowded into the Rose Bend Public Library for the Spooks 'n' Books Bash.

Being the town librarian's "boyfriend" definitely had its perks.

He smirked as he tossed a mini pack of M&M's into a plastic bag decorated with goofy ghosts, cats and witches. In the three weeks since he'd started dating Remi, he'd gone to a high school–sponsored haunted house, judged a pumpkin pie contest that she'd volunteered him for when the scheduled judge came down with food poisoning, and gone on his first ever hayride. He'd eaten his first s'more in nineteen years, tasted his first cup of homemade spiced cider ever and snacked on honest-to-God grapenut custard, hauling out and dusting off childhood memories he'd long forgotten.

Yes, these last three weeks had definitely been an experience. As different from his outings with Tara as the Patriots from the Lions. He'd had fun.

Damn.

When had his life stopped being fun?

Not that his life was bad. God, no. It would be the height of white privilege to cry about a challenging career he enjoyed, the luxurious lifestyle it afforded him, the doors to the elite business and social worlds it opened to him. And he indulged in it all.

But did he feel that pure excitement like a child on Christmas morning or a kid soaring down a steep hill on his bike at full speed? Like a teen discovering the bloom of his first crush?

No. That had been missing.

Until now.

Until Remi.

His pulse an uncomfortable throb at his neck, his wrists, he scanned the library, and like a lodestone, his gaze found her. Maybe it was the dark fire of her hair—or the brighter flame of her very essence—but she seemed to gleam like a ruby among the crowd of parents who stood in the outer ring surrounding the children who gathered for story time.

A smile flashed across her face at something, brief but so lovely, and the air in his chest snagged.

Jesus, the power of it.

Like a hard knee to the gut and a gentle brush of fingers across his jaw at the same time.

He blinked, dragging his much-too-fascinated scrutiny away from her and back to the task at hand. Goody bags. Candy. Toys.

"Is this my son over here in the back doing manual labor?" His mother appeared in front of the table, a wide smile stretched across her pretty face. Tiny lines fanned

out from the corners of Janet Howard's blue eyes as she
nabbed a small box of crayons and swung it back and
forth in front of him. "If I didn't see it with my own
eyes…"

He snorted, holding his hand out and curling his fingers, signaling for her to hand over the box. When she
did, with an even-wider grin, he drawled, "Laugh it up
now, woman. But just because I work behind a desk
doesn't mean I don't know the meaning of labor." He
arched an eyebrow. "I mean, who do you think mows
that big yard I have?"

She mimicked the eyebrow gesture. "That reminds
me. James Holland lost your number. But he wanted me
to pass along the message that he would be glad to take
care of your lawn like he does mine."

"Freaking blabbermouth," Declan muttered, dropping
the crayons into the goody bag. No sense of male soli-
darity at all.

"Hi, Declan." Tara strolled up to them, smiling widely.
"This is so cute." She turned, waving a hand in the direction of the larger area set up with game stations, the
story circle and tables of books. "When Janet told me
she was stopping by, I had to tag along. All this time I've
lived here, and I can't believe I've never made it to this
charming little event."

"It's only the second time the library has held it. Remi
started it last year," he said, pride for Remi and the staff's
hard work evident in his voice. He didn't even try to conceal it.

He'd only witnessed the tail end of their labor, helping
set up and put up decorations, but more than one person
had regaled him about all the time and effort she put into

the event. And when his mother's gaze narrowed on him, he met it. There was nothing wrong with being proud of a friend's achievements.

Fuck, he was a terrible liar. Even to himself.

His mother and Tara glanced at one another, then Janet hooked an arm through Tara's, clearly telegraphing where her allegiance lay. "Well, that's nice. I just remembered you mentioning you were spending Halloween here, so I thought we'd come over and see if we can convince you to join us for coffee afterward."

We.

He didn't bother looking at Tara, but kept his attention focused on his mother. "I'm sorry. Remi and I already have plans after this wraps up." Technically, they didn't, and he hated fibbing to his mother, but if he had to take Remi to Sunnyside Grille for a late dinner to make the lie true, he would. "But thanks for supporting the event."

His mother's smile tightened around the edges, and she turned to Tara. "Honey, would you mind giving me a moment with Declan?"

"Not at all," Tara said. He ignored her and the smug note in her voice.

If she expected him to bow to his mother's coercion on her behalf, then neither woman really knew him.

"Son—"

"Mom, I love you, and I would never intentionally disrespect you." He interrupted her before she could get on a roll. He flattened his palms on the table and leaned forward, lowering his voice, not desiring an audience for this long-overdue conversation that he would've preferred to have in private. "But that—" he dipped his head in the direction Tara had disappeared "—is not going to happen.

There has never *been* any chance of it happening. Something I made very clear to Tara even if she decided not to hear me. I only took her out those few times because it made you happy to see me with her. Or with someone."

He stretched an arm out, clasped his mother's hand in his, squeezed. "I love you, Mom. You're the most important person in the world to me. And I would hate to see our relationship damaged in any way by you choosing this hill to die on. Tara's not for me."

"And this new woman is? A woman you haven't brought around and introduced to me, I might add?"

True. And he'd purposefully avoided doing so. His and Remi's relationship was fake; having her meet his mother smacked too much of "real." It crossed a boundary into territory he hadn't been prepared to enter. But Janet arriving here tonight might snatch that choice out of his hands.

Especially since Remi was headed their way.

He straightened, his gaze shifting from his mother and over her shoulder to the sexy, stunning woman walking toward them. How could she make a simple long-sleeved, V-necked shirt, a dark pair of high-waisted skinny jeans and ankle boots so hot?

Lust rippled through him, and he clenched his teeth against the primal pounding of it in his veins... In his cock.

Goddamn.

Kittens batting balls of yarn. Dad's old baseball mitt that smelled like Bengay and sweat. Grandma Eileen's dentures in a glass on the bathroom sink.

Thinking of anything that would prevent him from

springing an erection in front of his mother and all these kids. But most of all his mother.

"Oh." His mother hummed. "That's the way of it."

Declan didn't tear his gaze from Remi. Couldn't. But if by some small miracle he could, yeah, he still wouldn't. Disquiet scurried beneath the throb of need. And he didn't want to glimpse the acknowledgment of that disquiet in his mother's eyes.

"Hey." Remi smiled, glancing down at the table packed with goody bags. "Thank you, Declan. So much. First you saved me with the pie contest and now with this. When my volunteer called out, I thought I was going to have a bunch of screaming kids on my hands." She laughed and turned to his mother. "We've met before, Mrs. Howard, but it's nice to see you again. Thank you for coming tonight."

"Nice to see you, too, Ms. Donovan. Or is it okay to call you Remi, since rumor has it you're dating my son?"

The pointed and faintly accusatory tone wasn't lost on Declan, and apparently not on Remi either, since pink tinged the elegant slant of her cheekbones. But to her credit, she didn't back down.

"Rumors in a small town?" Her lips curled into a rueful twist. "If only we could monetize it, we could single-handedly support our economy. And yes—" she nodded "—I would be honored if you would call me Remi."

Declan smothered a bark of laughter. *Nice side step.* "Remi, my mother's not new to a library. When I was a kid, she used to take me there often and let me pick out any book I wanted, then let me participate in the scavenger hunts or watch afternoon movies. And she even volunteered at our school library sometimes. Or maybe she just wanted to keep an eye on me," he teased.

His mother snorted. "Both."

"Mrs. Howard, I don't know if you'd consider it, but the library can always use volunteers," Remi said.

"Volunteer? Me?" She scoffed, but Declan glimpsed the interest flicker in her eyes, even though her features remained guarded. "What could I possibly do?"

"Whatever you enjoy." Remi half turned, sweeping a hand toward the room. "If you like clerical duties such as helping us entering patron info into our computer system or returning books to the shelves or manning the help desk, that would be wonderful. Or since we are an interactive library, if you love working with the children, you can read to them, help with tutoring, assist us with our events or even man one of those scavenger hunts Declan mentioned."

Declan stared at her. Excitement shone in her hazel eyes, the gold like chips of sunlight, and enthusiasm lit her face so brightly, he blinked at its gleam.

She was beautiful. No—such a paltry, lazy word to describe the purity and loveliness of a spirit enhanced by a stunning face and body.

He'd met gorgeous women, dated them—fucked them.

But they all faded into an obscure corner of his past the longer he looked at Remi. His heart thudded against his sternum, a rhythm that drowned out the chatter of adults, the happy squeals of children. His world narrowed to her, to the fine angle of her cheekbones, the sweet sin of her mouth, the alluring dent in her chin. To the lush, sensual curves of her body.

Panic ripped through him, and out of pure survival, his

mind scrambled back from a treacherous edge his damn heart should've known better than to go anywhere near.

"Declan?" Fingers touched the back of his hand, and just from the delicious burn, he didn't need to glance down and identify its owner. But he did anyway, because *not* looking at Remi Donovan wasn't even an option for him. A small frown creased her brow. "Everything okay?"

"Yes, fine." He flipped her hand over, rubbing his thumb over her palm, catching the small shiver that trembled up her arm. And because that vulnerability still sat on him, he repeated the caress. "I was just thinking how lucky this place is to have someone as loyal, hardworking and beautiful as you."

Her eyes widened, an emotion so tangled, so convoluted flashing in them that he couldn't begin to decipher it. He'd surprised her. Good. Though they were engaged in this arrangement, there was something freeing about being able to touch her, to murmur compliments and neatly, *safely* categorize them under "for the charade."

Like now.

"Thank you," she murmured, giving him one last lingering look before shifting her attention back to his mother. "Do you want to get a cup of hot chocolate, and we can talk more about volunteering?"

"Yes." His mother nodded, and warmth slipped into her expression and voice. "I would like that very much."

"Wonderful. Let's go before the kids beat us to it." She laughed, leading Janet away.

"Is that her plan, then?"

Declan clenched his jaw. Hard. Until the muscles along his jaw ached in protest. Instead of replying to Tara, he walked away from the table, knowing she would follow. Pausing next to a volunteer, he asked her if she would mind watching the goody bags for a moment, and then he continued to a quieter side of the room.

Before he could speak, Tara crossed her arms over her chest, her lips forming a sulky pout that he hoped to God she didn't think was attractive.

"Is that her new plan? To ingratiate herself with your mother?"

"No," Declan said, arching an eyebrow. "That's your strategy. Hers is simply being her. Interested in other people and their needs. Being *nice*. That's who Remi is."

"Please." Tara sneered. "It's an act. No one is that nice. Not without a motive."

"You don't say," he drawled.

Red stained her cheeks, and she huffed out a breath, her chin hiking up.

"That's not what I meant," she said through gritted teeth. "And you know it."

Declan sighed, pinching the bridge of his nose. Briefly closing his eyes, he dropped his arm and met Tara's dark brown eyes, glinting with tears.

"Don't." He didn't bother blunting the sharp edge of his tone.

Maybe if he suspected the tears were authentic, he would've. But he'd witnessed this ploy before; she'd tried to use it on him with no luck, and she regularly employed those tears with his mother with much more success.

"I'm going to say this once again. And this will be the last time, Tara. I've been patient and have tried not to hurt your feelings, but you don't seem to understand kindness. Or you see it as something to take advantage of. There.

Is. No. Us. There never was. There never will be. Hear me. Accept it. Move on. And if you genuinely like my mother and enjoy spending time with her, then fine. But if you're doing it only to get to me, then leave her alone, too. I won't allow you to use her, and more importantly, I won't let you hurt her."

"Where was this concern for a woman's feelings when you led me on?" she scoffed. Tears no longer moistened her eyes, but anger glittered there, and it pulled her mouth taut, turning her beauty as sharp and hard as a diamond. "You shouldn't have slept with me if you *claim* we didn't have anything."

He nodded. "You're right. I shouldn't have allowed my dick to do my thinking. But I've never lied to you, Tara. I was always up-front that we wouldn't have a relationship—that I didn't want that with you. With anyone. I convinced myself that you accepted that, when obviously you had other intentions the entire time. That's on you, not me."

Tara shook her head. "That's not true," she said, quietly, sounding a little lost.

And for a moment, he softened. Thrusting his fingers through his hair, he said, "Tara, I didn't want to hurt you. It's the one thing I actively tried to avoid. And I'm sorry if I did."

"It's just…" Tara turned from him, tightening her arms around herself, her lips rolling in on each other, thinning. When she faced him again, her shoulders lifted, and she fluttered a hand between them. "I know there is affection between us."

"Tara."

"Y'know, whatever you're doing with Remi Donovan isn't fooling me or anyone in this town."

And that quickly, any sympathy for her evaporated. He stiffened, studying her, the frustration pinching her skin tight and adding a jerkiness to her usually fluid movements.

"I don't really give a damn what other people think, including you."

He ignored the voice that pointed out that he'd proposed the bargain with Remi in the first place because of Tara.

"Obviously. Because the thought of you wanting *her*, being with *her*, of all people, is laughable. She's boring, fa—"

"Shut the hell up," he growled. "Say one more word, Tara, and I'll forget that I was raised not to disrespect women."

"Excuse me."

Declan jerked his head up and to the side just as Tara whipped around.

Fuck.

Remi stood there, perfectly composed and calm. And if not for her eyes… His gut twisted, and he fisted his fingers, the blunt tips biting into his palms. The brown nearly swallowed the bright green and gold. If not for that darkness, he would assume she hadn't overheard Tara's ugly words.

Would assume those words hadn't landed direct, agonizing blows.

"Remi." He moved forward, Tara forgotten, his one goal to get to her. To somehow ease that hurt, make it disappear.

But she shifted backward. Away from him. And damn if a spike of pain didn't jab into his chest.

"We're about to give out the goody bags. When you're free, we could use your help passing them out." Dipping her chin, she pivoted and left, shoulders straight and without a glance back at them.

"Tara." His mother stepped forward, and for the first time, Declan noticed her. "I'm going to catch a ride home with a friend. I've known you for three years now, and you've never been anything but kind to me. But hearing you speak so horribly about someone a couple of minutes ago?" Janet shook her head. "It makes me wonder who you are when I'm not around. And if that is a person I want to know."

Janet reached for Declan, squeezed his hand and glanced in the direction Remi had disappeared.

"She's special, and you'd be a fool to let her get away." Brushing a kiss over his cheek, she left.

"She didn't mean…" Tara whispered, her voice catching.

Declan glanced over his shoulder at the other woman, spotting the moisture in her eyes, and for the first time, he believed her tears were real. But they failed to move him.

"She did. You just looked the consequences of your spite and pettiness in the face. I hope you remember them."

He walked away, leaving her alone. Like she deserved.

CHAPTER SIX

WHO KNEW A person could be completely numb inside and still smile, laugh and behave as if humiliation and pain hadn't pummeled her with meaty, bruising fists until she'd become a block of ice?

Seemed every day Remi discovered something new.

Returning to the Halloween event after overhearing Tara and Declan's conversation, then pretending nothing had occurred, had been one of the most difficult things she'd ever done. She'd been grateful for the coldness that had seeped into her veins, her chest.

But the library had emptied of parents, children, staff and volunteers forty-five minutes earlier, and now she sat in the passenger seat of Declan's car as he drove through the quiet streets. She couldn't escape the slow thawing around her heart. Couldn't escape her relentless thoughts. Couldn't escape *her.*

You wanting her, being with her, of all people, is laughable. She's boring, fa—

Remi squeezed her eyes shut, blocking out the scenery passing by her passenger window. Too bad she couldn't block out the memory of Tara's words. The other woman hadn't needed to finish the sentence for Remi to discern how it ended.

Fat.

Boring and fat.

Oh God how that hurt.

The mental door to that vault she tried so hard to keep shut creaked open and more memories crept out. Memories of her mother's and Patrick's voices.

A minute on the lips, a lifetime on the hips, Remi.

I just want you to be healthy, Remi.

Are you sure that choice of dress is wise? It's not very forgiving, is it?

The judgments, backhanded compliments and criticisms framed as concern poured into her mind. It'd taken Remi years, but she'd come to love and accept herself. But there were moments like tonight—like the other night with her mother in the café—when her hard-won confidence took enough of a hit that she wavered.

When she had to remind herself she wasn't lovable *despite* her weight or size.

She was lovable *because* of them.

Smothering a sigh, she silently urged the car to go faster. She longed to get home, drag on her favorite Wonder Woman pajamas, pop open a bottle of wine, put on *Pride and Prejudice*—the version with Keira Knightley and Matthew Macfadyen otherwise known as *the best version*—and lick her wounds.

Tomorrow. Tomorrow she would be okay, but God, she needed tonight.

"Remi, we need to talk about tonight."

The thaw inside her sped up, the red-tinged hurt throbbing. *Home. Just get me home.* It'd been years since she'd last cried in front of someone, and she didn't intend to break that record tonight. Not with him.

"I didn't get a chance to thank you for helping out with setting up and then stepping in when my volunteer didn't show. I really appreciate it. We all did," she said, switching the subject from what she suspected he really wanted to talk about.

"You're welcome. And the deflection isn't going to work," he murmured, voice gentle but firm. Too firm. "Since she would probably never apologize, I'm going to say 'I'm sorry' for Tara. What she sa—"

"Forget it. I have."

"Remi," he tried again.

"Let. It. Go."

Silence permeated the car, weighing down her shoulders, pressing on her chest. She desperately counted the minutes until she arrived home. Rose Bend wasn't that large a town, but right now it felt like the size of Boston.

Finally, he pulled up outside her house. Any other time, she would've taken a moment to admire the cute, quaint cottage that she'd saved for and bought on her own not far from the beautiful Kinsale Inn. But now, the sight of the yellow-and-white home only inspired relief. She reached for the door handle.

"Remi." Declan's hand clasped her wrist. "Wait."

She paused but didn't glance over her shoulder to look at him, instead perched on the passenger seat ready to flee.

"Please don't leave like this. Talk to me, sweetheart."

She trembled at the "sweetheart," her eyes briefly closing.

Whatever you're doing with Remi Donovan isn't fooling me or anyone in this town.

She wasn't his sweetheart, and everyone knew it. Hell, even her own mother found it hard to believe. Because a man like him couldn't desire, couldn't... *Love* a woman like her. A beautiful, charismatic, brilliant, sexy as hell man couldn't want a successful, independent, educated woman just because she happened to wear a size sixteen.

At least, that's what they believed.

Her? Well, before tonight, the last three weeks had offered her hope that Declan was attracted to her. Her mind had warned her that the heated glances, the fleeting caresses to her cheek, the holding of her hand, the jokes and laughter they shared, the phone calls and texts they exchanged—they were all part of the charade. But her heart failed to get the message. Her stupid heart took each gesture as proof that he felt *something* for her.

And she understood now why she grasped that hope so desperately.

Because in these three weeks, each caress, each glance, each compliment had worked toward transforming her longtime crush for him into love.

Yes, she so, so foolishly had fallen in love with Declan Howard.

Her head bowed, forehead pressing against the cold window.

She'd fallen for the most emotionally unavailable man in Rose Bend.

"Talk to you?" she said, leaning back in the seat and turning to him. "What is there to *talk* about? I told you I'm *fine*."

"Actually, you didn't. You just ordered me to let it go. But too many people in your life have done that, and I refuse to be another one who ignores your pain."

She stared at him, forcing her fingers to remain flat on her thighs and not to ball into fists. "Do you want me to admit that what Tara said hurt? Okay, yes. It hurt like hell. Do I want your apology on her behalf? No. I don't want it or need it. It's insulting to both of us. That should sum it up, right? Are we done here? Good."

"Hell no, we're not done. We're friends, dammit."

Oh God, didn't *that* just punch a hole in her chest?

"There. Satisfied? Now, good night."

She reached for the door handle again.

"If you get out of this car, I will follow you to that front door, Remi," he rumbled.

She threw her hands up in the air, loosing a harsh laugh that abraded her throat. "What more do you want from me? A pound of flesh? According to your ex-girlfriend, I can afford to sacrifice a few—"

His arm shot out, and his hand hooked behind her neck, hauling her forward. His mouth crushed down on hers, swallowing the words from her lips. Her moan surged up her throat, offering itself like a sacrifice to him. She was helpless at the erotic onslaught, opening herself wider and wider to this wild thing that masqueraded as a kiss. He took from her over and over, slanting his mouth, diving deep, sucking harder as if starved, as if desperate.

As if afraid she would disappear if he didn't gorge himself in this moment.

Or maybe she was projecting.

Declan lifted his other hand to her chin, swept his hand over the shallow cleft there. Once and twice. Such a simple, small caress, but it echoed in a soft flutter between her legs, and she clenched her thighs against the sweet, erotic sensation.

God, touch me there... Kiss me there.

The plea bounced inside her head, words she longed to

utter aloud. She'd never believed that opportunity would be hers.

Did you want it to be?

The low, insidious whisper slid through her lust-hazed mind. And no matter how hard she pressed her lips to Declan's, how hard she thrust her tongue against his, she couldn't evict the question from her thoughts. Did she? If she took this step with him, there was no coming back. And for her, it wouldn't be just sex. Not with him. Her heart was already involved. Giving him her body, too, would cement an epic fall that would make Icarus's look like a mere stumble.

"Invite me inside."

Declan issued the hoarse plea-wrapped-in-a-demand, and it reverberated loudly in the confines of his car. She stared at him, emotionally on a precipice. One step off could mean joy for her... Or utter heartbreak.

Was she brave enough to find out which?

He brushed his thumb under the curve of her bottom lip, the hand at her nape a gentle weight. But he waited, allowing her to make this decision, even though desire darkened his eyes to indigo and his mouth bore the damp, swollen mark of their raw kiss.

"Come inside."

Inside my house. Inside my body. My heart. My soul.

She issued the invitation, knowing he would only take her up on two of those. And even as he exited the car, rounded the hood and opened her door, she accepted it.

Moments later, she led him into her home, and as soon as they crossed the threshold, Declan closed the door behind them, twisting the lock. All without removing his hooded gaze from her.

Need dug its dark claws into her, and her thighs trembled with the force of it. How was it possible to *want* this much? To feel like if he didn't put his hands on her, his mouth on her, his cock *inside* her, she would crawl out of her skin? Lose her mind?

"Touch me."

Two words. They were all she could push past her constricted throat. They were all that were necessary.

He stalked forward, shrugging out of his coat, peeling his sweater and dark T-shirt over his head, dropping all the clothing to the floor. Her breath expelled from her lungs on a hard, long *whoosh*.

Jesus Christ.

Clothed, he was beautiful.

Bared, with golden skin stretched across taut, flexing muscle, he was magnificent.

She couldn't move, her gaze greedily bingeing on the wide breadth of his shoulders, the wall of his chest, the corded strength of his arms. That ridged ladder of abs with the dark silky line of hair that disappeared beneath the waistband of his pants.

A waistband his hands had dropped to.

"Wait." She popped her palms up in the universal sign of Stop.

"Let me," she whispered. "I want it." She clasped her hands together as if holding her passion for him between them. "I want you."

"I'm yours." He beckoned her closer, and as imperious as it seemed… Damn, it was hot, too. "Come get me."

Oh God, if only that were true, she mused, crossing the few steps toward him. If only he was really hers. To keep. She shook her head. No place for those thoughts here. Stay in the now.

"What're you telling yourself no about?" he murmured, tugging her closer, tunneling his fingers through her hair, his nails scraping over her scalp. Her lashes fluttered closed, and she turned into his big palm, sinking her teeth into the heel, giving him back a little of the pleasure/pain he'd doled out to her. A hiss escaped him, and when he fisted the strands of her hair, pulling, she nipped harder. "This is going to be over before it begins, sweetheart," he warned, dipping his head to take her mouth in a brief but thorough conquering. "Now what're you telling yourself no about?"

No way in hell could she answer that loaded question. So she didn't.

Instead, she tackled his belt and the closure on his pants. Desperation climbed high inside her, neck and neck with lust. She wanted to drown herself in pleasure. In need. In him. Forget about what awaited her tomorrow. Forget the uncertainty.

For the first time, she was taking for herself and damn the consequences.

But he covered her hands with one of his, halting her frantic actions. The other cupped her cheek, tilting her head back.

"So many times I've wondered what goes on behind these lovely hazel eyes. What secrets you're keeping. And it's those moments, I consider switching careers and becoming an archeologist whose main job is unearthing those treasures." He danced his fingertips over her cheekbone, the arch of her nose, the top bow of her lip. "You wouldn't give up those secrets easily, but they would be worth the work. *You* are worth the work."

Her chest squeezed so tight, she locked her teeth around a cry. No one had ever spoken to her like that. She closed her eyes and bowed her head on the pretense of pressing a kiss to the base of his throat. Anything to avoid having him see the love she knew was in her gaze.

Declan gripped the sides of her shirt, balling it in his fists until it untucked from her jeans and bared her stomach. She lifted her arms, stamping down the nerves in her stomach. That dark hot need in his eyes couldn't be faked. He wanted her; he liked her body just as she did. Still… When the top cleared her head and the heat in that indigo gaze flared, the lingering remnants of doubt dissolved like mist.

"Fuck, sweetheart." Lust stamped his features, pulling his skin taut over his cheekbones, his lips appearing fuller, more carnal. "Let me…"

"Please," she damn near whined.

He lifted his hands toward her, but at the last minute, lowered his arms.

"Bedroom," he ground out.

Wordlessly, she turned and led him down the hall and into her shadowed bedroom. Moonlight streamed through the large windows, providing more than enough illumination. But Declan must not have thought so because he crossed to the lamp on her bedside table and switched it on, bathing the room in a warm, golden glow. Then he crossed back to her in that sensual, almost-feline glide of his, and lust wrenched low in her belly, high in her sex. She couldn't contain her whimper. Didn't even try.

When he reached her, Declan slowly lowered to his knees, his pose worshipful, reverent. As were the hands that removed her boots and jeans. As were the lips that pressed a kiss to her hip just above the line of her black panties.

As were the words that ordered her back on the bed, heels to the edge of the mattress.

She shuddered, excitement and vulnerability dueling inside her as she lay exposed to him, evidence of her overwhelming desire for him evident in her soaked flesh, in the damp panel of her underwear.

Teeth nipped at her sensitive inner thigh, and she jerked at the sensation and the taut anticipation of his mouth giving her what she so desperately hungered for.

"Shh," he soothed, brushing a caress over the tender area. "Tell me I can have you, Remi." He grazed his fingertips over her folds, and she gasped at the featherlight touch, arching into it. Her hands fisted the covers at her hips, needing something to anchor her.

"Have me, Declan." She bit her lip, trapping anything else that would've spilled forth without her permission. "Please have me."

Without further prodding, he stripped her panties off and dived into her.

He tongued a path up her folds, swirling and licking. Sucking. No part of her remained a mystery to him. She dived her hands into his hair, clutching the strands and holding on as he lapped at her, his ravenous growl vibrating over her flesh and through her sex.

Two thick fingers pressed against her entrance then inside her, stretching her, filling her. She cried out, grinding against his hand, his mouth. Pleasure struck her, bolt after bolt streaking through her. And as his lips latched on to her clit, and his tongue flicked and circled the pulsing nub, she curled into him, breathless, *aching*.

Declan rubbed a place high inside her, and she exploded, came so hard black crept into the edges of her vision. She tumbled back to the bed, her breath a harsh rasp in her lungs, her bones liquefied. Dimly, she was aware of Declan standing at the foot of the bed and the whisper of clothes sliding over skin.

The mattress dipped, and she focused on the gorgeous sexual beast crouched above her. While she silently watched, he tore open a silver packet, removed a condom and sheathed himself. And *oh God...*

Renewed lust fluttered, then flowed inside her in a molten rush. A cock shouldn't be lovely, but then again, this was Declan. It didn't seem possible that anything about him could be less than perfect. Including his dick. And long, thick, with a flared, plum-shaped head, he was indeed *perfect*. And mouthwatering. Before her mind could send the message to her body, she was reaching for him...

"No, sweetheart." He caught her wrist, bending down to crush an openmouthed kiss to the palm. "I want to make it inside you. Sit up."

He didn't wait for her to comply but tugged on the hand he held. Quickly, he divested her of her bra and dipped his head, sucking a beaded nipple into his mouth. Cradling her, he lifted her breasts, his thumbs circling the tip he hadn't treated himself to yet. Yet.

She clawed at his shoulders, tipping her head back, those pulls of his mouth echoing in her sex. Where she needed him. Now.

"Declan," she whispered. Pleaded.

"Take me in, Remi." He took her hand, wrapped it around him. "You take me."

She did.

Raising her hips, she guided him to her, notched him at her entrance. And cupping his firm ass, welcomed him inside her.

Their twin groans saturated the air.

She'd thought his fingers had filled her. No, they'd just prepared her for this... Possession. This branding.

Never had she felt so *whole*.

Slipping his arms under her shoulders, he gathered her close, and she did the same to him. Clinging to him. He held himself still, allowing her to become accustomed to the size and width of him. And yes, she needed those few moments. But as a fine shiver rippled through his body, she nuzzled the strong line of his jaw, nipping it.

"Move," she urged, flexing her hips against him. "Your turn to take me."

Tangling his fingers in her hair, he tilted her head back and claimed her mouth just as he claimed her body.

Over and over, he tunneled deep, burying his cock inside her, marking her as his. She undulated and arched beneath him, giving even as she accepted. The slap of skin on skin, the musk of sex, the damp release of sex greeting sex punctuated the room, creating music for their bodies' erotic dance. Each thrust, each grind, each growled word of praise shoved her closer to the edge, and she flitted close, then scampered back, not wanting this to end. Needing to be in this moment, in this space with him forever, but the pleasure—the mind-bending, body-aching pleasure—wouldn't permit that.

He reached between them, rubbed a thumb over the rigid bundle of nerves cresting the top of her sex. The scream building inside her was more than a voice; it was physical. And when he pistoned into her once, twice, three times, her body gave it sound.

She flew apart.

Her body. Her mind. Her soul.

Pieces of her scattered, and she doubted she could possibly be whole again.

As he stiffened above her, his hoarse growl of pleasure rumbling against her chest and in her ear, she gave in to the darkness closing in on her.

I love you. I love you.

And as she let go, she whispered the words in her head that she could never permit herself to say aloud.

I LOVE YOU.

Remi's whisper echoed in Declan's mind, crashing against his skull like waves against the shore.

I love you.

She probably hadn't meant to let the admission slip out; she'd been halfway asleep as she uttered those three words that carved fear into his chest.

Maybe she didn't mean them. People said things like that in the heat of passion all the time, and they regretted it later. Let sex—especially such cataclysmic, hot as hell sex—get mixed up and muddled with emotion, and they were temporarily confused. Yes, that was it. Remi didn't—

That wasn't Remi. She might not have meant to say she loved him—might not have intended to let him know—but she'd meant it.

Or else Remi believed she did.

He propped his elbows on his thighs and dropped his head into his hands.

I love you.

A howl churned in his gut, surging up his throat, but at the last second, he trapped it behind clenched teeth. Pain, fear and anger—yes, anger—eddied inside him in a grimy cesspool. He wanted to lash out. To yell that he didn't ask for her love. That love wasn't part of their deal.

He wanted to curl his body behind hers and beg her to take it back, to please take it back. Before *love* crushed them both and he lost the woman he'd come to depend on, to admire, to desire, to need... God, he'd come to need her. Her texts, her calls, her smiles, her...

Everything.

Love would ruin who they were to each other.

Just as it'd diminished his mother, so she'd had to rediscover who she was as a person.

Just as it'd morphed into something ugly and destroyed his marriage.

People used that particular affection as a reason to hurt and damage one another every day, and he wanted no part of it.

Not even from Remi. Especially not from Remi. Because to witness how it would extinguish the light from those beautiful hazel eyes... How it would steal the radiance that shone from her like a beacon piercing darkness...

"I'm surprised you're still here."

Declan slowly straightened, glancing over his shoulder. Remi, with the cover tucked under her arms, sat up, her expression shuttered. Grief careened through him. It'd been weeks since he'd seen that look on her face. Since she'd closed him out.

"Remi..." he murmured, turning to her.

She shook her head. "At first, I thought it was a bad dream, but when I woke up and saw you fully dressed and sitting on the side of the bed as if you couldn't wait to bolt out of here, I knew it wasn't a dream. More of a nightmare."

"Remi, I don't want to hurt you."

She huffed out a low, dry chuckle. "This isn't about hurting me, but just the opposite—you're the one who doesn't want to be hurt."

He couldn't deny that. Hell, if he were brutally honest, he'd been running scared since he'd signed his divorce papers. But he'd been doing it so long, he didn't know how to stop. Didn't know if he had the courage to stop.

Even for her. And if anyone deserved someone to be brave on her behalf, it was Remi.

"You don't want to take the risk of falling in love and being hurt again, of being betrayed. And your greatest fear, Declan? You're afraid of loving someone so much, so deeply, that you lose yourself. That you become your mother. And there's nothing I could say... Not that I would never betray you, never do anything that would demean you rather than support you. Not that I might very well hurt you, but I would hope my love would pave the way for forgiveness, that you would see it wouldn't be intentional. True love only makes you stronger, better. You could never lose yourself in it. Because it would never allow you to become lost."

She spread her hands wide on her crossed legs, staring down at them before lifting her gaze to him. Tears didn't glisten in her eyes, but he almost wished they did. He'd rather have the tears than the bottomless, hard resolve he saw.

"But there wouldn't be any point in trying to make you believe that, because your heart is closed by fear. I'm scared, too, Declan. Scared to trust, to take a leap of faith on love when it's only disappointed me in the past. But I'm willing to take a risk on you. On us." She shook her head. "What I'm not willing to do is fake it any longer or settle."

Her shoulders straightened, and the deep breath she drew in resounded in the room. That, too, held the ring of finality.

"I love you, Declan. And you need to leave."

"Remi, I'm sorry."

"I know you are. And that makes you refusing to fight for yourself, for who we could be, sadder. Now, if you have any feelings for me, any respect at all, please go."

Stay, dammit. Don't you fucking go.

But he stood, exited the bedroom and her house as she requested.

Like the coward he was.

He drove through the dark quiet streets of Rose Bend, images of the evening bombarding him. Of them laughing and working together at the library. Of their kiss in the car. Making love in her bedroom. Of her eyes, dark with pain and pride, ordering him out.

A while later, he pulled his car to a stop and switched it off. But he didn't sit, parked outside his home.

Opening his car door, he numbly climbed out, rounded the vehicle and climbed the steps to the blue-and-white Victorian with the dark blue shutters. Even before he knocked, the front door swung open and his mother stood in the doorway.

"Declan? What on earth? What's wrong?" she asked, tying her robe belt.

"Mom," he rasped. "I messed up."

CHAPTER SEVEN

•

"I LOVE YOUR MOTHER," Briana growled, sailing up to Remi with a smile that appeared more like a feral baring of teeth, "but she is seriously working my last living nerve."

Remi hid her grin behind her glass of wine, sending up a prayer, not for the first time, that she'd found a safe corner out of the path of Hurricane Rochelle. The whole week before the engagement party, their mother had been driving all of them nuts with the preparations. And today, with guests crowded into their home, enjoying the hors d'oeuvres and sipping a variety of beverages and celebrating the happy couple, Rochelle hadn't calmed down yet. After being ordered twice to circle the room with the appetizers, then told she wasn't doing it right, then being barred from the kitchen, Remi had been trying to fly under the radar.

"You know she's in her element. Even if she's acting a little batty. She just wants everything to be perfect for you." Remi slipped an arm around Briana's shoulders, hugging her close. "Besides, you have to give it to her. The place looks ah-mazing. The food is great. The guests are enjoying themselves. And you're engaged to a truly great guy."

"Yeah, you're right," Briana grumbled, then chuckled. As if she couldn't help herself, her sister sought out her fiancé, locating him next to the living room fireplace, surrounded by several of his friends. "He's wonderful. And I can't wait to marry him."

"There you go. Just keep that in mind. And avoid Mom, like I'm doing."

Briana laughed, wrapping an arm around Remi's waist and squeezing. But then she sobered, wincing. "God, Remi, I'm so sorry. I wasn't thinking. Are you okay being here with all—" she twirled her hand in the direction of the party "—this? You know I wouldn't have minded if you begged off. I would've understood."

"*I* would've minded, though. And I'm fine. No way I would've missed my sister's engagement party. But thank you."

God, she loved her sister. Both of them. After Declan left her house a week ago, she'd called her sisters. Sherri and Briana had come right over and stayed with her for most of the weekend, holding her while she cried, bingeing Netflix and snacks with her when she didn't. And they'd been running interference with their mother, whose disappointment at her and Declan breaking up had seared her.

But it didn't make her change her mind or call him. She'd made the right decision for herself.

"What are we doing over here in the corner?" Sherri shoved a sun-dried tomato and basil roll-up in her mouth, following it with a healthy sip of champagne. Her older sister, barely five feet and willow thin, could eat her weight in hors d'oeuvres, run roughshod over her adorable three-year-old twins and rule her husband, who worshipped the ground she walked on. "Talking about people? Ditching Doug so he can't leave me with the kids? Avoiding Mom?"

"C," Remi said, taking her sister's glass and sipping.

"Oh, me, too." Sherri scrunched her nose. "And you know I was just kidding about the kids, right?" When Remi and Briana gave her the blandest of bland looks, she sighed. "*Fine.* Sue me. Doug so owes me for...for sticking his penis in me."

"Wow." Briana slipped the champagne away from their sister with a snicker. "We're going to lay off these until the toast, 'kay?"

"What? No, I—" The doorbell rang, and she clapped her hands, nearly bouncing on the balls of her feet. "That should be the babysitter. She was running late so she offered to pick the twins up from here. Sooo..." She snatched her glass back and took a healthy sip.

"You'd think she didn't get out much," Remi drawled, laughing, but as her mother led the newest guest into the living room, the humor died on her lips. *"Oh God."*

Declan.

Her breath stalled in her lungs, increasing the deafening thud of her heart in her ears, her head. Adrenaline rushed through her, temporarily making her dizzy, and she pressed her palm against the wall, steadying herself.

What was he doing here?

"What is he doing here?" Sherri whispered, echoing the question in Remi's head. "I thought you said he wasn't coming."

Remi had confessed everything to her sisters—the true reason behind The Kiss, the fake relationship, Declan's agreement to be her beard at the engagement party.

"I didn't think he was, either." She couldn't remove her eyes from him. No matter how much her pride begged her to stop making a fool of herself in front of all these people.

She'd been here before, except this scene had taken place in a diner, not at an engagement party. But her romance woes being center stage for the townspeople of Rose Bend again? No. Thank. You.

She straightened, pushing off the wall, and maybe he sensed her movement, because his gaze scanned the room before unerringly landing on her. It was like crashing into a star—hot, consuming and so close to flaming out.

She froze.

Inside, she longed to flee. Away.

Or straight to him.

"Sweet baby Jesus, Remi, that man is in love with you," Briana breathed.

Remi tore her gaze from Declan and frowned at her younger sister.

"What? What're you talking about, Bri?"

"C'mon, Remi—the man showed up at an engagement party. No man shows up at an engagement party all alone, voluntarily, unless, A, he's the groom or one of the parties involved is family, B, he's being blackmailed, or C, he has an agenda. You, big sis, are his agenda. That man is so in love with you." She leaned forward, jabbing a fingertip in her arm. "But I swear to God, if he proposes to you at my engagement party, I'm tackling him to the ground like J. J. Watt. And then I'll show up at your wedding and announce I'm pregnant. And expecting quadruplets."

Remi stared at her sister, caught between laughing hysterically and being horrified. Because she suspected Briana meant it.

"Remi, can you help me in the kitchen for a moment?" Their mother appeared in front of their trio, smiling brightly, but Remi spied the taut edges.

"Sure."

She followed her mom, pausing to smile at a few guests,

putting on a good front, but her belly twisted into knots. Strain rode her shoulders, so by the time they entered the spotless kitchen, where more food platters covered the butcher-block island, her body was rigid with the strain.

"Declan showing up is certainly a surprise," her mother said, leaning back against the edge of the island.

Jumping right into it, are we?

Remi smothered a sigh, wishing she'd stolen Sherri's champagne.

"It is."

Rochelle threw her hands up, huffing out a breath. "Remi, he's here. That means something."

"It could mean a lot of things. The main thing being not wanting to be rude by not showing up." Although, she wondered, too. As of the night she'd kicked him out of her bed, her house, he didn't have an obligation to her anymore. "Mom, don't get your hopes up." She was preaching to the choir. "He's a nice guy, and that's all there is to it. We're done."

"Honey." She shook her head. "Why can't you just put in a little effort? You had a man who actually took an interest in you, and what happened? What did you do?"

Hurt slapped at her, and her head jerked back. "What did *I do*?" she whispered. "Why do you assume it's my fault?"

"Oh stop," Rochelle snapped, slicing a hand through the air. "I'm not assigning blame. I'm just saying I wish you would try harder—"

"And do what?" A calm settled over her. Almost as if she stepped out of her body and gave herself permission to speak, to no longer hold back on every hurt, every wound that she'd paved over with excuses, disregard or laughter. "Talk less, laugh softer. Wear baggier clothes. Lose fifteen pounds. Try harder for Declan or any other man? Or try harder for you, Mom?"

"Remi?" She frowned. "Whatever are you talking about?"

"Maybe at this point you've become so used to criticizing me that you don't notice. And I don't know which is worse—doing it on purpose or being so accustomed to taking my inventory that it has become habit. The problem is, with you, I always come up short. I've never been enough."

"Remi, honey," she whispered, tears glistening in her eyes. "That's not true."

"It is. I don't doubt you love me, Mom. But you have a lousy way of showing it. And if you don't change it, I won't be coming around as much. I can't accept that toxicity in my life anymore. I won't."

She crossed the space separating them, cupped her mother's arms and kissed her cheek.

"I love you, and I love myself. I need you to accept that."

Tears pricked her own eyes and her pulse pounded like a snare drum. She turned and exited the kitchen, moisture blinding her.

"Hey, I got you."

She didn't hesitate. Didn't question. She wrapped her arms around Declan, burying her face against his hard, welcoming chest. And when his arms closed around her, she sighed, relaxed into him. Feeling home.

"Come on, sweetheart," he murmured.

She didn't really pay attention to where he led her, but then the cold air brushed over her face. The backyard. Inhaling a deep breath, she pulled her hand free of his and paced several feet away. His earthy cloves-and-cinnamon scent clung to her nose, and she longed to roll in it, bathe in it. She had to move away, because yes, in a moment of weakness, she'd leaned on him, but she couldn't depend on that. Couldn't depend on him.

"What are you doing here, Declan?"

He studied her for several long moments, his lilac gaze piercing. "You did good, Remi. And I'm damn humbled by you."

She blinked. And blinked again. Stupid tears. Not now. Not in front of him.

"What?"

"I overheard what you said to your mom. That was incredibly brave, and I want to live up to you. Be worthy of that courage." He paused. "I should've never left your house last week. I should've told you no, I wasn't leaving, that I would fight for me, for you. For us."

If she could move, she would've stumbled backward. Or run to him.

But fear, doubt—hope—kept her frozen.

"You called me out, and I was afraid. *Was*, Remi. I knew as soon as I drove away that I made the hugest mistake of my life. Over the last month you have become my friend, my confidante, my lover, my delight, my…freedom. You've helped me free myself from my past simply by being you. By showing me bravery, hope and faith. I want to take that leap with you, Remi. And I'm sorry that I hurt you, that I might've been one more person to make you doubt how beautiful, special and precious you are. If you can trust me with your heart again, I promise never to break it."

He reached into the inside pocket of his suit jacket and withdrew a folded sheet of paper and extended it to her.

As if her arm moved through water, she reached for

that paper, accepted it. Her breath whistled in and out of her parted lips, and she tried to tamp down the hope that seemed determined to rise within her, but it welled too big, too huge.

She unfolded the sheet and scanned it. Once. Twice. After the third time she lifted her gaze to him. That hope she'd tried to stifle soared, and she didn't try to control it. Not when love surged with it.

"You're moving here full-time?" she rasped, the paper trembling in her hand.

"Yes." He moved closer to her, paused, but then eliminated the space between them. His hand rose, hovering next to her cheek, but he didn't touch her. "I'm leasing the building next to Cole Dennison's law firm. Of course, I'll still need to go back to Boston for some meetings, but I can run my business from anywhere. And I choose for it to be here. With you. Because I love you."

She cupped her hand over his, turned her face into it and pressed a kiss to the palm. Then rose on her toes and pressed another to his lips. On a groan, he took her mouth like a man deprived of water, of breath. And she was his oxygen.

God, she knew the feeling.

"Does this mean you're giving me your love again?" he asked, resting his forehead against hers.

She cradled his face between her palms, brushing her thumbs over his cheekbones. Smiling, she brushed a soft kiss to his mouth.

"You never lost it."

* * * * *

Return to the charming town of Rose Bend,
where love always finds a way!

With Love from Rose Bend

Available April 2022
From HQN Books

Don't miss the next book in the Rose Bend series from *USA TODAY* bestselling author

NAIMA SIMONE

He came to Rose Bend to hide.
But she'll help him find everything he's been missing.

"Passion, heat and deep emotion—Naima Simone is a gem!"
—Maisey Yates, *New York Times* bestselling author

Order your copy today!

HQNBooks.com

PHDF5436MAX

Get 4 FREE REWARDS!

We'll send you 2 FREE Books plus 2 FREE Mystery Gifts.

FREE
Value Over
$20

Both the **Romance** and **Suspense** collections feature compelling novels written by many of today's bestselling authors.

YES! Please send me 2 FREE novels from the Essential Romance or Essential Suspense Collection and my 2 FREE gifts (gifts are worth about $10 retail). After receiving them, if I don't wish to receive any more books, I can return the shipping statement marked "cancel." If I don't cancel, I will receive 4 brand-new novels every month and be billed just $7.24 each in the U.S. or $7.49 each in Canada. That's a savings of up to 28% off the cover price. It's quite a bargain! Shipping and handling is just 50¢ per book in the U.S. and $1.25 per book in Canada.* I understand that accepting the 2 free books and gifts places me under no obligation to buy anything. I can always return a shipment and cancel at any time. The free books and gifts are mine to keep no matter what I decide.

Choose one: ☐ **Essential Romance**   ☐ **Essential Suspense**
                  (194/394 MDN GQ6M)   (191/391 MDN GQ6M)

Name (please print)

Address   Apt. #

City   State/Province   Zip/Postal Code

Email: Please check this box ☐ if you would like to receive newsletters and promotional emails from Harlequin Enterprises ULC and its affiliates. You can unsubscribe anytime.

Mail to the **Harlequin Reader Service:**
IN U.S.A.: P.O. Box 1341, Buffalo, NY 14240-8531
IN CANADA: P.O. Box 603, Fort Erie, Ontario L2A 5X3

Want to try 2 free books from another series! Call 1-800-873-8635 or visit www.ReaderService.com.

*Terms and prices subject to change without notice. Prices do not include sales taxes, which will be charged (if applicable) based on your state or country of residence. Canadian residents will be charged applicable taxes. Offer not valid in Quebec. This offer is limited to one order per household. Books received may not be as shown. Not valid for current subscribers to the Essential Romance or Essential Suspense Collection. All orders subject to approval. Credit or debit balances in a customer's account(s) may be offset by any other outstanding balance owed by or to the customer. Please allow 4 to 6 weeks for delivery. Offer available while quantities last.

Your Privacy—Your information is being collected by Harlequin Enterprises ULC, operating as Harlequin Reader Service. For a complete summary of the information we collect, how we use this information and to whom it is disclosed, please visit our privacy notice located at corporate.harlequin.com/privacy-notice. From time to time we may also exchange your personal information with reputable third parties. If you wish to opt out of this sharing of your personal information, please visit readerservice.com/consumerschoice or call 1-800-873-8635. **Notice to California Residents**—Under California law, you have specific rights to control and access your data. For more information on these rights and how to exercise them, visit corporate.harlequin.com/california-privacy.

STRS21MAXR2